S. R.

130°
170°
160°
150°
140°
130°
120°
110°
100°
70°
80°
60°
40°

ALASKA

Kolyma

Indigirka

SEA OF OKHOTSK

SAKHALIN

Yakutsk

Lena

Vitim

Limit of Permafrost

Khabarovsk

Amur

Ussuri

Krasnoyarsk

Lake Baikal

Nerchinsk

Shilka

Irkutsk

Kyakhta

Vladivostok

SEA OF JAPAN

CHINA

Tokio

Yalu

Peking

Port Arthur

Seoul

KOREA

JAPAN

YELLOW SEA

Hwang Ho

THE SOVIET CRUCIBLE

VAN NOSTRAND POLITICAL SCIENCE SERIES

Editor

FRANKLIN L. BURDETTE
University of Maryland

PLISCHKE, E.—*Conduct of American Diplomacy,* 2nd Ed.

DIXON, R. G., JR., and PLISCHKE, ELMER—*American Government: Basic Documents and Materials*

SPROUT, HAROLD and MARGARET—*Foundations of National Power,* 2nd Ed.

LANCASTER, LANE W.—*Government in Rural America,* 2nd Ed.

JORRIN, M.—*Governments of Latin America*

TORPEY, WILLIAM G.—*Public Personnel Management*

PLISCHKE, ELMER—*International Relations: Basic Documents,* 2nd Ed.

GOODMAN, WILLIAM—*The Two-Party System in the United States,* 2nd Ed.

DILLON, CONLEY H., LEIDEN, CARL, and STEWART, PAUL D.—*Introduction to Political Science*

SWARTZ, WILLIS G.—*American Governmental Problems,* 2nd Ed.

BAKER, BENJAMIN—*Urban Government*

ZINK, HAROLD, PENNIMAN, HOWARD R., and HATHORN, GUY B.—*American Government and Politics: National, State, and Local*

ZINK, HAROLD—*Modern Governments,* 2nd Ed.

HENDEL, SAMUEL—*The Soviet Crucible: The Soviet System in Theory and Practice,* 2nd Ed.

LINEBARGER, P. M. A., DJANG, C., and BURKS, A. W.—*Far Eastern Governments and Politics: China and Japan,* 2nd Ed.

HATHORN, GUY B., PENNIMAN, HOWARD R., and ZINK, HAROLD—*Government and Politics in the United States*

MADDOX, RUSSELL W., and FUQUAY, ROBERT F.—*State and Local Government*

SHARABI, H. B.—*Governments and Politics of the Middle East in the Twentieth Century*

ANDREWS, WILLIAM G.—*European Political Institutions*

SPROUT, HAROLD and MARGARET—*Foundations of International Politics*

THE SOVIET CRUCIBLE
The Soviet System
in Theory and Practice

Edited with Introductory Notes by
SAMUEL HENDEL

Professor of Political Science,
The City College of New York

SECOND EDITION

D. VAN NOSTRAND COMPANY, INC.
PRINCETON, NEW JERSEY
TORONTO   LONDON
NEW YORK

TO MY BROTHERS
GEORGE, MORRIS, AND STANLEY

D. VAN NOSTRAND COMPANY, INC.
120 Alexander St., Princeton, New Jersey (*Principal office*)
24 West 40 Street, New York 18, New York

D. VAN NOSTRAND COMPANY, LTD.
358, Kensington High Street, London, W.14, England

D. VAN NOSTRAND COMPANY (Canada), LTD.
25 Hollinger Road, Toronto 16, Canada

Published simultaneously in Canada by
D. VAN NOSTRAND COMPANY (Canada), LTD.

PRINTED IN THE UNITED STATES OF AMERICA

PREFACE

A great American philosopher, Morris Raphael Cohen, wrote in his autobiography that "the highest reverence is due to human reason; the highest duty [is] to search for truth with unbiased mind; and the highest courage [is] to follow the truth always and everywhere regardless of where it may lead us." In the spirit of this apothegm, this book was first compiled; this same spirit, it is hoped, is reflected in this edition.

The Soviet Crucible has been revised and substantially *enlarged*, except for the historical and theoretical sections, which remain virtually intact. Three new chapters have been added: one on nationalities (Chapter 11), another on social welfare and its motivations (Chapter 19), and the third on the New Program adopted at the 22nd Party Congress (Chapter 22). For the rest, in nearly every instance the old material has been retained, supplemented and, it is believed, strengthened by the addition of new and useful commentaries. The new material is specifically identified in both the table of contents and the "Sources of Readings." Only in a few cases was it deemed necessary to excise material.

"Revolutions," wrote Leon Trotsky—who made no small contribution to the art and to the commentary—"are always verbose." This is unquestionably true of the Bolshevik Revolution, about whose philosophical and historical background, and aftermath, probably more has been written than about any other revolution in the history of man. This plethora of material poses some difficulties for an editor of a book of readings. Obviously, anything resembling consensus on what ought to be encompassed in a single volume is precluded. At the same time, it becomes all the more necessary for the editor to state the presuppositions and premises that guided his selections.

No serious and conscientious student of Soviet affairs would deny that wide differences of opinion—often tenably supported—exist among scholars and writers regarding the development, nature, and prospects of the Soviet system. A basic premise on which this book proceeds, accordingly, is that understanding is likely to be enhanced by recognizing and giving considera-

v

tion to variant positions on complex and controversial issues affecting the U.S.S.R.

Another premise is that both the form and substance of Soviet rule in the U.S.S.R. were considerably affected and influenced by *peculiarly Russian* history and circumstances. A selection deals, therefore, with the Tsarist heritage generally, and another treats, in more detailed fashion, the period from about the end of serfdom to the Bolshevik revolution.

This book also reflects the assumption that a knowledge of Marxist and Leninist theory is of great importance for a true understanding of the Soviet order; for, while Leninist theory, in vital respects, departed from Marxist theory—and Marxist-Leninist theory has, in fundamentals, been attenuated or discarded in Soviet practice—theory not only played an important role in organizing the Bolshevik revolution and state, but it is part of the ethos of Soviet society. It has, as Edward Hallett Carr has written, "the status of a creed which purports to inspire every act of state power"; even the emasculation of theory requires appropriate genuflection.

Certainly, Marxist-Leninist theory—however distorted—continues to inspire Communist-led revolutionary movements. As Lenin wrote: "Without a revolutionary theory, there can be no revolutionary movement." Moreover, Marxist-Leninist theory merits evaluation as a body of doctrine claiming scientific validity and universal applicability. (There is an important school of thought which denies that theory has much, if any, relevance to Soviet practice. This position is also represented.)

Selection of readings was further guided by the conviction that the basis for the non-democratic and totalitarian character of Soviet institutions was largely laid—however unwittingly on the part of some who participated in the process—by the end of 1921 with the failure of the World Revolution, and, in the U.S.S.R., the loss by the Bolsheviks of even militant working class support, the destruction of all opposition parties, and the outlawry of factions within the Communist Party. Certainly, this dictatorial basis was fairly definitively established by the end of 1928 when Stalin, after a series of internecine Party struggles, had obtained a position of almost unchallengeable power (although its apogee was probably not reached until some years thereafter). Accordingly, the process by which the Bolshevik Revolution "went wrong," abandoned so-called proletarian democracy and then intra-Party democracy, is closely examined.

Totalitarianism having taken root with the triumph of Stalin, the book shifts to largely contemporary analyses and appraisals of the Soviet political, economic and social systems. Apart from limitations of space which precluded detailed chronological treatment, this is in accord with the intended emphasis on the fundamental character and spirit of Soviet institutions. Similarly, little or no attention is devoted to details of organization and structure of Soviet institutions. These details are of real importance to the specialist, but are not likely to be long remembered by the non-specialist.

On the political side, the Soviet system is examined from several focal points of interest: the provisions of the Constitution (which appears in the appendix); the extent to which constitutional guarantees represent reality and myth in Soviet practice, generally, and in relation to the varied nationalities, specifically; the role of terror as a system of power (including Khrushchev's analyses, in 1956 and in 1961, of the part it played in the Stalin era); the problem of non-violent and orderly succession (with a case study of Khrushchev's own rise to power); the locus of power (considered through the end of the 22nd Party Congress).

In a thoroughly planned economy there is an interrelationship and interdependence between politics and economics beyond anything known under capitalism. The fact is, too, that the belief of Soviet leaders in the ultimate triumph of socialism throughout the world is based, in major part, upon its alleged superiority over capitalism as an economic system. The Soviet economic system—its successes, failures and prospects—is fully and rigorously considered, analyzed, and evaluated.

The last section, "The Impact and Prospects of the Soviet System," which has been substantially enlarged, is concerned with: the nature and motivations of social welfare measures in the U.S.S.R.; the impact of the Soviet system on the beliefs, loyalties, habits, and social behavior of the Soviet people; the durability of Soviet totalitarianism; and, finally, the premises, promises, portents, and prospects of the Communist Party's new program.

The book contains no treatment of Soviet foreign policy or of American foreign policy concerned with the U.S.S.R. In light of the need to make choices, this omission proved unavoidable. Although internal policy was unquestionably affected by Soviet external policy, to do justice to foreign policy—its history, motivations, and limitations—would require another volume.

It is not pretended that the use of diverse sources on many aspects of Soviet theory and practice suggests neutrality. The book reflects a strong personal bias in favor of democracy and against dictatorship. Nevertheless, the attempt has been made to set forth—so far as practical—significant and divergent opinions, including the official Soviet view, on *many* of the great issues discussed. Inevitably, this has meant the inclusion of some of the most distinguished, as well as authoritative, writers in the Soviet field. It is hoped that the varied and conflicting opinions—sometimes among seminal scholars—will make clear the complexities of the subject matter, encourage wider reading, and tend to raise the level of discourse about the U.S.S.R. to a more informed and sophisticated plane.

I am, of course, tremendously indebted to the authors and publishers whose materials are reprinted in this volume. Acknowledgment of permission is specifically made at appropriate points in this book. Separate mention must be made, however, of permission to quote the following:

Ivan Turgenev's "The Threshold," from *A Treasury of Russian Life and Humor,* edited by John Cournos, published by Coward-McCann, Inc., 1943; Alexander Pushkin's "To Chaadayev," from *The Poems, Plays and Prose of Pushkin,* edited by Avrahm Yarmolinsky, published by Random House, Inc., 1936; and Vladimir Kirillov's "We," from *Russian Literature Since the War,* edited by Joshua Kunitz, and published by Boni & Gaer, Inc., 1948. I add a word of appreciation to Mr. R. C. Bentley of Ames, Iowa, for permission to use his Kuban Area photograph.

I am grateful to my students who, over a period of many years, in my courses on the U.S.S.R., have subjected my ideas to critical examination and raised challenging questions. I am also grateful to the many scholars and teachers in the Soviet field who were kind enough to give me their suggestions, advice and, in many instances, the benefit of their experience in the use of *The Soviet Crucible.*

I owe special thanks to Mrs. Theresa Wagner of the Claremont Graduate School, who so willingly and graciously assisted me with many secretarial tasks; to the library staffs at the Honnold Library of Claremont University College, the University of Southern California, the University of California at Los Angeles, Columbia University, and, not least, The City College of New York for their unfailing kindness and cooperation; and to my son, Steven, who returned from the University of Michigan in time to be saddled with some of the final editorial burdens.

My wife, Clara, worked closely with and assisted me in the extensive and intensive search for materials and in their analysis and editing. Of great value, too, were her devotion, encouragement, patience, and sage advice —for all of which I am more grateful than it is possible to put into words.

SAMUEL HENDEL

New York City
November 8, 1962

CONTENTS

(A selection marked * is new to this edition; one marked ** has been substantially enlarged.)

LIST OF ILLUSTRATIONS

Sources of Readings

(A selection marked * is new to this edition; one marked ** has been substantially enlarged. Bracketed numbers refer to pages in *this* volume. Book titles are italicized; all other titles are in quotes.)

ALEKSANDROV, G. F., "The Pattern of Soviet Democracy" (Speech: December 4, 1946) [313]

ARON, RAYMOND, "Soviet Society in Transition" [627]

BAUER, RAYMOND A., INKELES, ALEX, and KLUCKHOHN, CLYDE, *How the Soviet System Works* [576]

BERMAN, HAROLD J., "The Devil and Soviet Russia" [3]

* BOCIURKIW, BOHDAN R., "The Case of Khrushchev" [424]

* BURG, DAVID, "The Voice of a Dissenter: An Interview with a Graduate of Moscow University" [589]

* CAMPBELL, ROBERT W., *Soviet Economic Power* [516, 538]

CARR, E. H., "Who Rules in Soviet Society?" [451]

* CENTRAL ELECTION COMMISSION, "Official Returns on 1962 Election to Supreme Soviet" [330]

* CENTRAL STATISTICAL BOARD OF U.S.S.R., "Progress Under the Plan" [529]

CHAMBERLIN, WILLIAM HENRY, *The Russian Enigma* [12]

COHEN, MORRIS RAPHAEL, "Why I Am Not a Communist" [181]

CURTISS, JOHN C., *The Russian Revolutions of 1917* [194]

DEUTSCHER, ISAAC, *The Prophet Armed* [229]

———, *Russia in Transition* [599]

———, *Stalin: A Political Biography* [264]

DJILAS, MILOVAN, *The New Class* [454]

DOBB, MAURICE, "Comment on Soviet Economic Statistics" [466]

———, *Soviet Economic Development Since 1917* [492]

FAINSOD, MERLE, *How Russia Is Ruled* [114, 361]

FREUD, SIGMUND, *New Introductory Lectures on Psychoanalysis* [111]

* GAFUROV, B. G., "The Solution of the National Question" [334]

HOOK, SIDNEY, *Reason, Social Myths and Democracy* [298]

HUNT, R. N. CAREW, "The Importance of Doctrine" [52]

———, *The Theory and Practice of Communism* [89]

* INKELES, ALEX, "Soviet National Policy in Perspective" [341]

* JASNY, NAUM, "Interpreting Soviet Statistics" [474]

JOUVENEL, BERTRAND DE, "On the Character of the Soviet Economy" [486]

* KENNAN, GEORGE F., "The Confusion of Ends and Means" [635]

I

TOWARD AN UNDERSTANDING OF THE U.S.S.R.

1. A Plea for Objectivity

"Impartiality is a dream; honesty is a duty."

GAETANO SALVEMINI

"Seek simplicity, and distrust it."

A. N. WHITEHEAD

"There is no ill which may not be dissipated, like the dark, if you let in a stronger light upon it. . . . If the light we use is but a paltry and narrow taper, most objects will cast a shadow wider than themselves."

HENRY DAVID THOREAU

"If we begin with certainties, we shall end in doubts; but if we begin with doubts, and are patient in them, we shall end in certainties."

FRANCIS BACON

Chapter 1

A PLEA FOR OBJECTIVITY

Books on Soviet theory and practice are "as the sands of the seashore." Those conforming to official Soviet explanations and rationalizations are uncritically laudatory and often involve distortions of historical fact. At the other extreme are the reports of critics of the U.S.S.R. who picture communism as "a gigantic chamber of intellectual and moral horrors." To be sure, the story abounds in horror. "But this," as Isaac Deutscher writes, "is only one of its elements; and even this, the demonic, has to be translated into terms of human motives and interests." Moreover, consideration should proceed with some understanding and appreciation of the special history, geography, and circumstances which—to an important degree—shaped Soviet policies and institutions. Desirable, too, is avoidance of the oversimplifications often characteristic of extreme cold-war partisanship and pressures.

It must be recognized, however, that even the serious and fair-minded student of Russian affairs confronts many difficulties. For one, pre-revolutionary Russian history is little known in the West except in superficial and imaginative fashion. For another, Marxist-Leninist theory, which purports to be the basis of Soviet practice, is ambiguous and inconsistent in significant segments, and is seldom read except in crudely excerpted form; and the extent of its real influence on Soviet practice is seriously controverted.

Other difficulties derive from the complexity and dynamism of the Soviet system which extends over a vast land mass of more than 8 million square miles and a great variety of peoples who number over 220 millions. In little more than forty years of history the Soviet Union has passed through several more or less clearly differentiated phases of development in its economic, military, religious, minority, educational policies and programs—to name but a few. Then, too, close and detailed knowledge of the background, experience, thinking, and motivations of Soviet leaders is not generally available as it is in respect to their Western counterparts.

Secrecy and censorship (as well as expunging and distortion)—continue to impede the process of gathering reliable information and data about the Soviet system. On the other hand, there has been some noteworthy relaxation and improvement in these areas in recent years. In general, in fields *having little or no military significance, there is little doubt that much official Soviet information is substantially complete and accurate. (A discussion specifically "On the Reliability of Soviet Statistics"—particularly economic statistics—appears in Chapter 15.)*

Notwithstanding formidable difficulties it is, I believe, fair to say that the extent to which Russian policy, and hence Russia itself, is "a riddle wrapped in a mystery inside an enigma," is greatly exaggerated. Even Churchill, who used the phrase with respect to Soviet foreign policy, added "but perhaps there is a key. That key is Russian national interest." Apart from the proceedings at high levels, which are shrouded in great secrecy, there is a considerable body of dependable knowledge and information about many aspects of Soviet life. This is, in no small part, due to the work of devoted scholars, journalists, diplomats, and many others who brought to their writing and comments about the U.S.S.R. a high degree of intellectual integrity and objectivity.

The Berman article is reprinted here as one provocative analysis of the sources and dangers of American misconceptions about the U.S.S.R. It should be added that some Western scholars would take issue with some of his comments—on the viability and durability of the Soviet system, for example. Some of these differences are reflected in various sections of this book.

THE DEVIL AND SOVIET RUSSIA

HAROLD J. BERMAN [*]

An old lady who could never bring herself to speak ill of anyone was asked what she thought of the Devil. "Well," she replied after a pause, "he is very hard-working!"

The old lady understated the Devil's virtues. He is also very intelligent. He knows how to win friends and influence people. In the words of Bishop Emrich of Michigan, writing on *Some Neglected Aspects of Communism,* "the Devil is not a derelict on 'skid row.' He is not a 'bum'; for this type of person is weak, pathetic, disorganized, lacking in will, sick, and not strong enough to stand against a single policeman. . . . The Devil is quite different. . . . He is patient . . . well organized, disciplined, persuasive, and attractive."

[*] Professor of Law at Harvard Law School; research associate and member of the executive committee of the Russian Research Center of Harvard University. He is the author of several books on Soviet law, as well as a book of essays entitled *The Russians in Focus.* The selection originally appeared in *The American Scholar,* Vol. 27 (Spring, 1958), pp. 147-152. By permission.

What makes him the Devil, says Bishop Emrich, is that "with all his virtues he is going in the wrong direction; and since he possesses virtues, he goes in the wrong direction effectively. The Devil, says traditional Christian thought with profound insight, is a fallen angel."

In both Soviet and American thinking there is a strong strain of puritanism which tends to turn opponents into enemies, enemies into devils, and devils into ugly monsters. An American reading what is printed in Soviet literature about life in the United States can only laugh at the fantastic caricatures that are presented to the Russian people as sober realities. It is a bitter truth that Russians who get a chance to read what is written about life in the Soviet Union in American newpapers, magazines and books—and today more and more Russians get that chance—also find, often, not reality but a ridiculous distortion of reality.

In August and September of 1955, I met in Moscow about ten United States senators and representatives who were taking advantage of the new "Geneva spirit" to get a firsthand glimpse of what they previously had known mainly from newspaper accounts and committee reports. Without exception they manifested great surprise, often amounting to amazement, at what they saw. In particular they said they had expected to find the morale of the people and the standard of living much lower than they appeared to be.

In May of 1957 in Moscow, I told this to the head of one of the largest American communications networks, and I added that I thought the American congressmen had expected to find barbed wire in the streets and people walking around with their heads hanging and their bodies bent. He replied, "Well, that's what I had expected to find."

Of the dozens of American tourists whom I met during two visits to Russia, the overwhelming majority said they found conditions of life in Russia much better than they had anticipated. The list includes newspaper editors, businessmen, college professors, college students, agricultural experts, women television broadcasters—and American specialists on Soviet affairs! Many of them said, half in despair and half in jest, "What am I going to say when I get back to the United States?"

It is not for the Russians to complain, of course, if Americans have too black a picture of their country; the Soviet policy of secrecy has been one of the important contributing causes of our misconceptions. But our own press and radio, our own political propaganda and our own scholarship also bear an important share of the responsibility.

Yet the real reason is deeper—deeper than Soviet secrecy, deeper than American one-sidedness in reporting. The fact is that together with a great deal of rubbish there are also excellent accounts of daily life in the Soviet Union by American correspondents in Russia, and there are many American books which analyze Soviet institutions in an objective and scholarly manner. But American readers of these reports and books all too often simply reject, subconsciously, those images which conflict with their pre-conceptions.

Two years ago an American newspaper correspondent in Moscow wrote an account of the May Day parade in which he described people singing and dancing in the streets and enjoying themselves thoroughly. His newspaper published the account, but at the same time it ran an editorial in which it portrayed an embittered Russian people forced by their hated government to demonstrate in favor of a revolution which they did not want.

The correspondent, in recounting this to me, said that he thereupon wrote a letter to his editor in which he said, "I was there—I saw it—they were not bitter, they were happy, they were having a good time." The editorial writer wrote back, in effect, that they may have appeared happy, but that actually they could not have been happy, in view of the evils of the system under which they live.

It is probably fruitless to argue about whether or not Russians are happy. It is of critical importance, however, to recognize that *the notion that because communism is evil the people who live under it must be wretched is based on a false conception of evil.*

It is a false conception of evil which assumes that men who believe in evil doctrines—such as the doctrine of world revolution or the doctrine of the dictatorship of the proletariat—cannot at the same time work to accomplish great humanitarian benefits. It is an elementary fact, for example, that under the leadership of the Communist party of the Soviet Union the number of doctors in Russia increased from about 20,000 in 1917 to about 300,000 in 1957, and that in the same period and under the same leadership illiteracy declined from over 50 per cent to less than 5 per cent.

It is a false conception of evil which assumes that men who ordered the shooting of Hungarian women and children attempting to flee from terror could not at the same time sponsor a series of reforms designed to humanize conditions of detention in Soviet labor camps and to improve the system of criminal trials in the interest of the accused. The assumption sounds so plausible—yet it is contradicted not only in the particular case of the Soviet leadership in 1956 but also countless times in history. Did not Cromwell, the great restorer of English liberties, treat the Irish with barbaric cruelty? Did not Americans who fought for the inalienable rights of "all men" at the same time buy and sell slaves?

A group of prominent American lawyers visited Russia in 1956 in order to observe the Soviet legal system in operation. One of them later published an account of his impressions, the gist of which was that the Soviet legal system, despite some superficial resemblances to the legal systems of civilized countries, is *necessarily* a sham and a farce since the political leaders can and do rely heavily on force and secrecy as instruments of policy, and have absolute power to change the law as they will. Further, he argued, where there is no belief in God there can be no just system for the adjudication of disputes. In view of the satisfaction which all righteous people can derive from this reasoning, it is disconcerting to note that the great system of Roman law was developed under tyrants who employed terror against their enemies, who had absolute power, and who did not believe in God.

Is it really possible that Joseph Stalin, a cruel despot who ordered hundreds of thousands of people suspected of political opposition sent to labor camps in remote regions of Siberia without even the pretense of a fair trial, at the same time established a system of law and justice designed to operate fairly and objectively in nonpolitical cases? It is not only possible: it is a fact. But why should it appear strange?

Our notion that the tyrant can only do wrong is linked, as I have suggested, to our puritan tradition, with its fire-and-brimstone concept of hell. It is linked also to our national immaturity which leads us to see moral issues in terms of black and white, "good guys" versus "bad guys." It is linked, in addition, to an unconscious desire to cover up our own lack of high common purpose by creating an external symbol of evil, a Moby Dick, through which we find a release from our frustrations.

The fire-and-brimstone theory of totalitarianism, popularized in Orwell's *1984* and expounded in learned terms by many of our leading scholars, is comforting to us. Like the Pharisee we can say, "God, I thank thee, that I am not as other men are, extortioners, unjust, adulterers, or even as this publican."

Such self-righteousness blinds us to the true nature of evil. In the Bible the Devil tempts Christ with bread, with power over all the kingdoms of the world, and with miracles. So the totalitarian state offers its followers economic security, political power and sensational technological progress —all in return for one thing: absolute subservience to the high priest of these gods, the party.

But why speak of the positive achievements of the Soviet system, people often ask, when the most important feature of that system is the lack of freedom to defy the party line? And even granting that American writers have exaggerated the violence, injustice, bureaucracy and poverty of life under the Soviet regime, why should we advertise that fact? Don't we thereby weaken ourselves in our fight against communism?

The first answer is that if we have begun to test truth in terms of how useful it is politically, we have already lost the most important battle in the fight against communism. The second answer is that it is only by giving full credit to the positive achievements of the Soviet system that we can prepare ourselves to meet its challenge.

The Soviet system as it exists in popular imagination—with 20 million prisoners in Siberian labor camps, workers ground down by management, every tenth person an informer, people afraid to talk about anything—is no challenge to us at all. Such a system could not survive a single major crisis.

The Soviet system which actually has been created is quite different. It is a working totalitarianism, a viable totalitarian order, capable of surviving the death of its leading personalities, capable, very likely, of surviving even a defeat in war. It is a system which gives promise of achieving the very goals it has set for itself: economic security, political power and technological progress—by the very means it proclaims: absolute subservience to party discipline and the party line.

The challenge of this system is that it meets certain real needs of twentieth-century man—the need for unity and the need for a common social purpose.

It is of no use to fight communism by showing that the materialist aims which it proclaims can be achieved better by democratic means, since the underlying appeal of communism is not only in its aims but also—and primarily—in the process of mobilizing people to achieve those aims. By creating a mobilized social order, the Communist party provides peaceful outlets for service, self-sacrifice, discipline and other virtues usually associated with military life.

If we really want to defeat communism, there is only one way to do it. That way is so obvious one would be embarrassed to speak of it if it were not for the fact that it is the one thing that people who talk about fighting communism generally fail to mention. We must construct a social order in which the goals of justice, mercy and morality take precedence over economic security, political power and technological progress, and we must freely, through voluntary associations, pour into that social order the same spirit of service, self-sacrifice and common purpose that under the Soviet system is induced by party discipline.

Otherwise, Khrushchev's prediction that our grandchildren will be Communists may well come true (though of course they would not call themselves Communists but true democrats), and one of the most cherished American illusions may finally be disproved—that good always triumphs over evil in the end.

II

THE HERITAGE

2. The Tsarist Heritage

TO CHAADAYEV

Not long we basked in the illusion
Of love, of hope, of quiet fame;
Like morning mists, a dream's delusion,
Youth's pastimes vanished as they came.
But still, with strong desires burning,
Beneath oppression's fateful hand,
The summons of the fatherland
We are impatiently discerning;
In hope, in torment, we are turning
Toward freedom, waiting her command. . . .
Thus anguished do young lovers stand
Who wait the promised tryst with yearning.
While freedom kindles us, my friend,
While honor calls us and we hear it,
Come: to our country let us tend
The noble promptings of the spirit. . . .
Comrade, believe: joy's star will leap
Upon our sight, a radiant token;
Russia will rouse from her long sleep;
And where autocracy lies, broken,
Our names shall yet be graven deep.

ALEXANDER PUSHKIN

Chapter 2

THE TSARIST HERITAGE

The form and content of Soviet rule in the U.S.S.R. were considerably affected and influenced by peculiarly Russian history and circumstances —this is undeniable. Can it be doubted, for example, that had a proletarian revolution come to England it would have established institutions and pursued internal policies different in fundamental respects from those which were, in fact, established and pursued in Russia? Early in the twentieth century, England was a country with a powerful industrial base, a large middle class, a mature proletariat, a high degree of literacy, and a developed tradition of democracy. Russia, on the other hand, was then a relatively backward, predominantly agricultural, and largely illiterate country with a long history of despotism and fanaticism—whose Fundamental Laws proclaimed the monarch an "unlimited autocrat" to whom obedience was "ordained by God himself."

This history gave substance to Alexander Herzen's prophetic comment in 1851 that "communism is the Russian autocracy turned upside down," and to the statement of William Henry Chamberlin that "the monarchical absolutism of Nicholas I was the natural parent of the revolutionary absolutism of Lenin." That is not to say that choices made and fortuitous circumstances could not and did not alter the course of Soviet history. It is only to suggest that events must be appraised in the context of the historic background in which they occurred. Some light is shed on that historic background in the broad canvas spread by William Henry Chamberlin and in the detailed story, beginning in 1857, told by George Vernadsky. Historians differ, of course, in their interpretations of Tsarist history but few challenge Mr. Chamberlin's basic thesis. Some of Professor Vernadsky's characterizations of leading figures and policies meet with greater dissent.

THE SOVIET UNION CANNOT ESCAPE
RUSSIAN HISTORY

WILLIAM HENRY CHAMBERLIN*

The Soviet Union cannot escape Russian history. . . . From the moment when the Russians emerge on the historical stage one finds them engaged in grim struggles, first for existence, then for the realization of certain goals of expansion.

Geographically Russia was a bulwark of Europe against Asia and it bore some of the hardest blows inflicted by nomadic invaders from the East. In the early Kiev period of Russian history, in the tenth, eleventh and twelfth centuries, there are records in the old chronicles of constant fighting with the wandering peoples of the steppe, the Polovtsi and Pechenegi.

Russia was submerged in the flood of Tartar conquest in the thirteenth century. The Tartar rule was gradually shaken off during the fourteenth and fifteenth centuries. But Russian history for centuries was an almost continuous series of wars, regular and irregular, declared and undeclared, now with Oriental peoples like the Turks and the Tartars, now with the Western neighbors, Swedes, Poles, Lithuanians, who barred the Russian thrust towards the Baltic Sea.

These wars were an important cause of the wretched poverty of the Russian people. They strained to the limit the human and material resources of the medieval Muscovite state. "The state swelled and the people grew thin." In this brilliant phrase Klyuchevsky summarizes the results of Russia's slow and painful expansion of its frontiers during the seventeenth century. This expansion, like so many episodes in Russian history, was accompanied by a vast sacrifice of human lives. The last available penny was screwed out of the people in taxes, often with the aid of the knout, a peculiarly brutal Russian form of whip. A grotesque situation arose when people voluntarily wished to become serfs, in order to escape tax obligations. This method of tax-evasion became so prevalent that it was made punishable by whipping with the formidable knout. To be compelled to remain free by the threat of being beaten within an inch of your life if you preferred to become a serf: here was a characteristic grim Russian paradox.

With most of its territory a vast plain, Russia lacked natural frontiers.

* Former foreign correspondent in the U.S.S.R., author of many books on the Soviet Union including *Russia's Iron Age* and *The Russian Revolution*. This selection is reprinted from chapters 1 and 2 of *The Russian Enigma* by William Henry Chamberlin, Copyright, 1943, by Charles Scribner's Sons, with permission of the publisher.

It was always vulnerable to land invasion. On four critical occasions its national independent existence hung in the balance as a result of foreign war, sometimes complicated by domestic turmoil. . . . From 1240, when the wild Tartar horsemen of Baty slaughtered the people of Kiev, until 1941 and 1942, when the Germans wrought the same scenes of carnage and destruction with modern weapons, Russia has always lived under the overhanging threat of war.

There were some periods of fairly prolonged external peace, especially in the nineteenth century. But foreign war, actual or threatened, has always been a major force in Russian national development. This constant military pressure was not the only cause that made the Russian Tsar the most complete autocrat in Europe. But it was an important cause. And the organization of the country almost on the basis of an armed camp helped to clamp down the institution of serfdom in Russia. During the early Middle Ages the Russian peasants could move freely, at stated times, from one landlord's estate to another. But during the sixteenth and seventeenth centuries there was increasing pressure to attach the peasant to the service of a single master.

This was the result not only of the greed of the landlord class, but of the military exigencies of the time. The theory was put forward that, as the gentry had to fight in the Tsar's army, the peasants were under an obligation to support, or, in the old Russian phrase, to "feed" the gentry. Peter the Great lent a certain validity to this crude Russian conception of the "social contract" by issuing a series of regulations that added up to a national labor service act. This Tsar of unbounded energy demanded that every young noble should serve the state, either in the armed forces or in the civil administration. . . .

Of course freedom from the threat of foreign invasion was not the only factor that made for the strengthening of American democracy and individualism. The inherited British tradition of political self-government and the sovereignty of law, the absence of any large unassimilable indigenous population, the high standard of literacy, all played their part. But the almost universal American assumption of political democracy and of respect for the constitutional rights of the individual would have been subjected to a much graver strain if our history had been heavily checkered with major wars. . . .

It is difficult for the American, accustomed to the ideas of separation of church and state, of freedom of opinion on religious questions, to understand either the curious mixture of state control and other-wordly mysticism in the Russian Orthodox Church or the doctrinaire atheism of the Communists. There is no parallel in American history for the passionate fanaticism that impelled tens of thousands of dissident Russian Old Believers, in the seventeenth century, to burn themselves alive as a protest against the wickedness of the world, and as a means of escaping from this wickedness and from the persecution of their belief. Both the absolutism of the autocracy and the absolutism of the revolutionary regime are alien to the Western mind, with its traditions of tolerance.

Russia, on its side, scarcely experienced the effect of three great movements which became part of the common heritage of Western Europe and America: the Renaissance, the Reformation and the French Revolution. Each of these movements, in its own way, contributed to the liberation of the human personality, to the strengthening of individualism. . . .

The roots of many Soviet actions and institutions may be sought and found in events and developments that occurred as far back as the days of Ivan the Terrible (1547-1584) and Peter the Great (1689-1725). There is historic justice and appropriateness in the fact that these two strongest figures in the long line of Tsars have been restored to official favor in the Soviet Union and commended to the admiration of the Russian people. Stalin is indebted to both these rulers for many models of policy, especially in such matters as carrying out a thorough liquidation of undesired or suspected individuals and classes.

If one were called on to name a single dominant element in Russian history from the Middle Ages to the present time it would be the unlimited power of the ruler. The Russian Tsar was an autocrat in a measure unparalleled in European countries. He was absolute master of the lives and property of his subjects, like a Turkish Sultan or a Tartar Khan.

Of course democracy, in the modern sense of the term, did not exist in medieval Europe. A network of privileges and distinctions separated the noble from the serf, the knight from the commoner, the wealthy merchant or master craftsman from the poorer classes in the cities. But in this European society there was a system of checks and balances, at least among the higher classes. The Church possessed independent authority and could sometimes bring the haughtiest monarch to his knees in repentance. The nobility often acted as a check on the Crown, the free cities on the nobility. The privileged orders were a counterpoise to each other and to the king. In the absence of any single all-controlling absolutism was the germ of future representative government.

Very different was the situation in Russia. No Tsar went to Canossa to perform public penance. No medieval Russian sovereign found himself obliged to limit his own authority by signing a charter at the demand of rebellious barons. No court would have protected a subject who refused to pay an exorbitant tax or to surrender a piece of property which the Tsar desired. Many Tsars were assassinated in palace conspiracies. But no Russian ruler was judged and sentenced to death by a revolutionary court of his subjects, like Charles I in England and Louis XVI in France.[1]

---

[1] There might have been such a scene in Russian history after the Bolshevik Revolution if it had not been for the exigencies of the Civil War. Nicholas II, his wife, son

The last *zemsky sobor,* the Russian equivalent for a parliament, met in 1649. After that time no national representative assembly was held in Russia until 1906. The upsurge of the revolutionary movement in 1905 induced Nicholas II to promulgate a Constitution, which provided for a Duma, or elected parliament. But this body was quickly reduced to a pale and unrepresentative shadow by arbitrary changes in the election law as soon as the revolutionary tide subsided and the autocracy again felt itself securely in the saddle.

It is not only in the retrospect of modern times that the Russian autocracy seems un-European in its unlimited power. A number of foreigners who visited Russia in the sixteenth and seventeenth centuries reported their impressions of a despotism that went far beyond anything with which they were familiar in their own countries. Ivan the Terrible made a show of his power to a visiting English merchant by ordering one of his courtiers to leap to certain death. When the Tsar asked whether the British sovereign (Queen Elizabeth) possessed similar power the British visitor drily replied that Her Majesty had better use for the necks of her subjects.

There is little trace in Russian thinking of any idea that subjects possessed any rights against the Tsar until the great intellectual awakening and flowering of Russian culture in the nineteenth century.[2] And even then it was deeply significant for the future course of events that the majority of Russian revolutionary theorists were not so much interested in protecting the individual against the state as in using the power of the state to transform society along collectivist lines. Many of these theorists preached what Lenin practised: the remaking of the social order through the dictatorship of a picked revolutionary minority. Had it not been for the autocracy of the Tsars, with its blighting effect on the conception of individual rights and liberties, the dictatorship of the Communist Party might never have come into operation. The one was a natural sequel to the other.

What were the roots of this despotism, unlimited in theory until the Constitution of 1905, although it was moderated in practice by the emergence of a gradually enlarging intelligent public opinion in the latter part of the nineteenth century? At the time when Kiev, the old city on the Dnieper, was the centre of Russian political life, in the tenth and eleventh centuries, Constantinople was the metropolis which the Russians knew best, through trade, through war and through religion. It was through the Greek Orthodox Church that the Russians were converted to Christianity. The

---

and four daughters were simply butchered in the cellar of their place of confinement in Ekaterinburg (now Sverdlovsk) without any formalities of indictment and trial because it was feared that they might be rescued by the advancing anti-Bolshevik forces.

[2] Peter the Great defined his own power in the following expansive terms: "His Majesty is an autocratic monarch, responsible to no one for his policies. He has power and authority to govern his state and lands as a Christian ruler according to his will and understanding."

Byzantine Empire was the state to which they naturally looked as a model.

And this Byzantine influence was entirely in favor of autocracy. The Byzantine Emperor was an absolute ruler, who was sometimes assassinated, but was never subjected to regular control by nobles, parliament or church. The Patriarch of Constantinople never assumed the independence of the Pope of Rome. This spiritual association with Constantinople was emphasized again at a later period. A Russian monk sent a message of greeting to Ivan III, who married a Byzantine Princess, and hailed him as sovereign of "the third Rome" that would never perish. Constantinople, the "second Rome," had just fallen to the Turks.

The Tartar conquest of the thirteenth century also worked in favor of the autocratic principle. Contrary to a general impression abroad, there was not much racial intermingling between Tartars and Russians. After the first orgy of killing and pillaging was over, the Tartar khans were satisfied if the Russian princes rendered tribute and paid occasional visits to the Tartar Court to render homage and seek confirmation of their titles. But the Asiatic despotism of the Tartar conquerors naturally had its effect upon the Russians. Moreover, the Tartar rule isolated Russia from the West and deepened the chasm between Russian and European civilization.

And in the further course of Russian history the forces that made for diversity of political life in Europe were blotted out. Russia became a primitive totalitarian state before the word was used in political terminology.

At one time there was a good deal of lusty, turbulent freedom in the two large trading towns of northwestern Russia, Novgorod and Pskov, which had belonged to the Hanseatic League. But eventually both sank to the level of ordinary provincial towns under the levelling despotism of the Muscovite Tsars. Ivan III took away the great bell that had once called the people of Pskov together for meeting, as a sign that such dangerous liberty was no longer to be permitted. Employing a method that has frequently been applied to undesired classes and groups in the Soviet Union, Ivan deported a considerable number of the Pskov citizens and replaced them with new settlers from Moscow. Ivan the Terrible mercilessly decimated the population of the two cities in reprisal for disloyalty, actual or suspected.

The boyars, as the older Russian nobles were called, also suffered at the hands of this stern Tsar. Ivan, who had been slighted by the boyars as a boy and nourished an implacable hatred for the whole order, built up a terrorist political police devoted to his service. Its members, the *oprichniki*, ranged over the country, clothed in black and displaying their formidable emblem, a dog's head and a broom. This symbolized their mission: to sniff out disloyalty and purge the land of treason.

There was no legal restraint on what the *oprichniki* could do. They were empowered to kill boyars, suspected of treason (the word sabotage was not known in Ivan's day), to violate their wives and seize their estates. The result of this policy was to break the inherited power and prestige of the old nobility and to transfer much of the land, then the principal source of wealth, to a new class, selected by the Tsar for his personal terrorist service and completely dependent on him for favor and advancement. Stalin followed a similar policy, against a different political and social background, when he exterminated many of the surviving Old Bolsheviks and replaced them with henchmen of his own. . . .

Twenty years after Ivan's death Russia was plunged into the crisis of the Troubled Times (1603-1613). The ruthless Ivan, as lustful as he was cruel, had married six times, in defiance of the canons of the Orthodox Church. He was succeeded by his son Fyodor, a weakling in body and mind. When Fyodor died childless, a cunning and ambitious boyar, Boris Godunov, had gained enough influence to insure his election as Tsar by a national assembly. A younger half-brother of the late Tsar Fyodor named Dmitry had died some years earlier. There was a strong suspicion that he had been murdered by order of Boris, in order to pave the way for the latter's accession to the throne.

But the ghost of Dmitry proved fatal to the ambition of Boris to found a dynasty of his own. A young adventurer who gave himself out as the escaped Dmitry found a hospitable reception and political support in Poland. He invaded Russia with a band of followers, accompanied by some Polish troops. This episode touched off the stormy decade of the Troubled Times (1603-1613). This is one of the most obscure and chaotic periods in Russian history. Every disintegrating force in the country was let loose. Cossacks swept up from the South to take part in pillage and devastation. Serfs rebelled and killed their masters. Swedes and Poles intervened. Rival Tsars were chosen and assassinated.

The existence of the Muscovite state seemed to be at stake. But the Russian people displayed their qualities of toughness, resilience, determination not to be ruled by foreigners. Bit by bit order emerged from chaos. A movement to clear the country of the foreigners and restore a strong central government found leaders in Prince Pozharsky, an aristocrat and Kuzma Minin, a man of the common people.

A national assembly, held in 1613, elected a new Tsar, Michael Romanov, first of a dynasty that endured for three centuries. Peace and the opportunity to recover from the ravages of the Troubled Times were purchased by the cession to Poland of some Russian territory in the neighborhood of Smolensk. But from that time on the balance of power, as between Russia and Poland, steadily inclined towards the former. The unlimited despotism of the Tsars was a blighting influence on many aspects of Russian life. But it was more conducive to military success and territorial expansion than the aristocratic anarchy of Poland, where the king was almost powerless and the peasants were held in serfdom. The Polish ruling class, the country gentry, developed a disastrous habit of engaging in factional quarrels which laid the country open to foreign intrigue and intervention, weakened its power of resistance, and was an important cause of the final tragedy, the partition of Poland between Russia, Austria and Prussia towards the end of the eighteenth century.

The Muscovite state gained a valuable ally against Poland in the Cossacks, who had established a wild, free, military republic in the valley of the Dnieper. These Cossacks were in many cases runaway serfs, peasants of the bolder type who preferred frontier fighting to the bondage which prevailed in the settled interior of Russia. They settled along the ill-defined southern fringe of the growing Russian Empire and served both as a spearhead for attack and a screen for defense against Turks and Tartars. The spirit and appearance of these Russian frontiersmen are admirably preserved in a painting by the great artist, Repin, which shows the Cossacks in their camp preparing a defiant reply to the Turkish Sultan.

The Cossacks of the Dnieper had been under Polish rule. But contempt for constituted authority was second nature to the Cossack. The arrogance of the Polish nobility, the uncertain delimitation of Cossack rights and privileges, the difference of religious faith (the Cossacks were Orthodox, the Poles were Roman Catholics) were among the causes of a big Cossack uprising, led by Bogdan Khmelnitsky, in 1648. An extraordinarily spirited equestrian statue of Khmelnitsky in a central square of Kiev still commemorates the anarchical liberty of this medieval Cossack community.

This uprising finally led to the detachment from the Polish state of all land east of the Dnieper and of the city of Kiev, on the western bank. After wavering between Russia, Poland and Turkey, the Cossacks, although with some misgivings and backslidings, accepted Russian rule as the least of the three evils. For some time the Cossacks represented the sole element of turbulent freedom in the despotic Russian state. Stenka Razin and Emilian Pugachev, leaders of the two greatest serf rebellions, were both Cossacks from the Don.

It is worth noting that periods of internal calm in Russian history are broken by terrific explosions of mass revolt. One such explosion began in 1669 under the leadership of Razin, a picturesque Robin Hood type of bandit whose memory is preserved in one of the most haunting of Russian folksongs. His forces rolled up the valley of the Volga, getting reinforcements of fugitive serfs. But he was defeated near Simbirsk, in the Middle Volga region. His motley hordes, with their ill-assorted arms, could not cope with the Government troops, which had received some training from European instructors. His final downfall was hastened by division among the Don Cossacks themselves. The wealthier disliked his primitive levelling tendencies. He was captured and executed in 1671.

Pugachev's revolt ran much the same course as Razin's, although it covered a wider area, including the valley of the Kama, the main tributary of the Volga. His rebellion foreshadowed the Bolshevik Revolution that was to occur a century and a half later inasmuch as it rallied the same forces of discontent that Lenin would mobilize in 1917. Along with discontented serf peasants Pugachev found supporters among the early Russian "proletarians," the laborers in the ironworks of the Urals, and among the Bashkirs, Chuvashes and other non-Russian peoples who live in the valley of the Volga and in the land between the Volga and the Urals. But Pugachev was crushed by the trained soldiers of Catherine II. And after his defeat and execution there were no more big serf revolts. The country was more efficiently policed, communications improved, and the old Cossack *volnost* (an almost untranslatable Russian word meaning uncontrolled liberty) was tamed. As the majority of the Cossacks became well-to-do farmers they lost their rebel spirit and became faithful soldiers of the Tsar, dashing horsemen in war, auxiliary police against strikers and peasant rioters in peace.

When serfdom was abolished, in 1861, it was not under the pressure of a peasant insurrection. It was better, as Tsar Alexander II told a gathering of reluctant landowners, that serfdom should be abolished from above than from below. Perhaps it was because serfdom was abolished in this way, and with a good deal of consideration for the interests of the landowners, that many peasant grievances remained unredressed. Russia, as the experiences of 1905 and 1917 proved, remained ripe for agrarian rebellion.

One very important element in Russia's past heritage is the marked time-lag in the cultural development of the nation. No European country of corresponding population and political importance was so barren in free and questioning minds. During the centuries when religion was the first concern of men's minds in Europe, there was no Russian Thomas Aquinas, Loyola, Pascal, Luther, Calvin or Huss. The most serious schism in the Russian Church took place in the seventeenth century, when the Patriarch Nikon introduced changes in the prayer books and ritual to bring Russian practice into line with that of other churches of the Orthodox rite. These changes were stubbornly and suspiciously resisted by some of the clergy and parishioners, who were known as Old Believers. It is significant of the intellectual sterility of the time in Russia that no important question of theological belief or church organization was involved in this schism, although each side maintained its viewpoint with uncompromising determination and was prepared to give or receive the crown of martyrdom.

There was, to be sure, a certain psychological background for the schism. The Old Believers were averse to all the foreign innovations and administrative changes that took place in the latter part of the seventeenth century and reached their culmination in the reign of Peter the Great. Moussorgsky's magnificent opera, *Khovanstchina,* far too little known outside of Russia, gives an unforgettable imaginative picture of the clash between old and new in Russia on the eve of Peter's reforms and finds its climax in a scene of self-immolation on the part of the Old Believers.

The Russian Church was weakened by the schism. And it lost its last chance to function as even a modest counterpoise to the absolutism of the state when Peter the Great abolished the Patriarchate and placed the Church under the administrative authority of a layman, the Procuror of the Holy Synod.

So Russia did not share the mighty ferment of ideas that coincided in Europe with the struggle between Roman Catholicism and Protestantism. It also missed the humanistic culture of the Renaissance. Until the nineteenth century Russia conveys the impression of a nation asleep, so far as cultural life is concerned. There is no fourteenth-century Russian Dante, no sixteenth-century Russian Shakespeare, no seventeenth-century Russian Newton, no eighteenth-century Russian Voltaire.

Now and then a European would bring into semi-Asiatic Russia some western influence. Scotch and German soldiers of fortune helped to impart the elements of drill and discipline to the raw Russian levies. Italian architects, of whom Rastrelli was the most famous, designed churches and palaces. Skilled artisans were induced to come to Russia, especially in the time of Peter the Great, to teach industrial arts and crafts to the Russians. But there was only a very dim and pale Russian reflection of the humanist movement of the West, of the rediscovery of the Greek and Latin classics, because there were so few Russian scholars. Russia was a force to be reckoned with politically and militarily long before it was able to make a notable contribution to European cuture.

A similar unevenness of development is visible in the Soviet Union in the third decade of its existence. The Soviet accomplishment in building up industrial and military power is out of all proportion to the manifestations of original creative thought under the Communist dictatorship.

Russia was sufficiently part of Europe to be drawn into the wars of the French Revolution and of the Napoleonic period. But the French Revolution aroused no such response in Russia as in the countries of Western and Central Europe. The autocracy, the noble-serf social relation, remained unchanged. The most visible reflection of the influence of the French Revolution in Russia was the unsuccessful revolt of the Decabristi in 1825. They were a group of officers who had imbibed progressive ideas from service abroad in countries which had felt the impact of the French revolutionary changes.

The reign of Peter the Great (1689-1725) marked the transition from the Moscow to the St. Petersburg period in Russian history. That revolutionary autocrat shifted the capital from old, semi-Oriental Moscow to the new capital which he built on the shore of the Gulf of Finland in the style of a European city and gave his own name. A giant of a man, gifted

with enormous mental and physical energy, Peter strove mightily to de-
barbarize Russia, to bring it up to the level of the European civilization of
the time. It was both a personal and perhaps a characteristic national
tragedy that the means which he used to promote this debarbarization
were often extremely cruel and oppressive and won him, in the eyes of some
of his more conservative and superstitious subjects, the reputation of being
the anti-Christ forecast in the Book of Revelations.

From early boyhood Peter broke away from the conventional life of a
Muscovite Tsar, secluded in a palace and surrounded with Oriental
ceremony. He loved to talk and carouse with the adventurous riffraff of
foreigners who lived in the "German Village," a settlement where foreigners
were segregated by order of the Government so that they would not con-
taminate Orthodox Russians with their strange ways and ideas. He learned
to smoke, a heathenish sin in the eyes of the bearded boyars who practised
almost all the other vices. He conceived a very unroyal fondness for working with his hands. Ships, guns, machines, all the material things in which
the West excelled Russia, fascinated the young ruler.

He was the first Tsar who left his own country to travel in Europe.
The story of how he worked incognito in a Dutch shipyard and got into a
fistfight with a fellow-worker is one of the few internationally well-known
anecdotes of Russian history. Peter was far from housebroken and, with
his boon companions, he left behind him a trail of rowdy devastation in
the house which was assigned for his residence in England. The sequel was
a bill for damages and some shocked and disapproving comment.

Peter returned to Russia brimming over with plans for the modernization of the country. He encountered a mutiny of the *streltsi,* which he
promptly quelled, cutting off the heads of the ringleaders with his own
hand. There was nothing gentle about Peter. His son Aleksei, who did not
sympathize with his innovating plans, died as a result of torture which was
inflicted in order to make him disclose the accomplices in a suspected plot.
V. O. Klyuchevsky, most eloquent and philosophical of Russian historians,
sums up the paradox of Peter as reformer in the following sentences:

> His beneficent actions were accomplished with repelling violence. Peter's
> reform was a struggle of despotism with the people, with its sluggishness. He hoped
> through the threat of his authority to evoke initiative in an enslaved society, and
> through a slave-owning nobility to introduce into Russia European science, popular
> education, as the necessary condition of social initiative. He desired that the slave,
> remaining a slave, should act consciously and freely. The inter-action of despotism
> and freedom, of education and slavery—this is the political squaring of the circle,
> the riddle which we have been solving for two centuries from the time of Peter,
> and which is still unsolved. . . .

Although Peter's quick and lively mind seized on many Western discoveries and methods of administration and adapted them for use in Russia,
he made no attempt to introduce into Russia the element of individual

freedom and initiative which contributed much to the scientific and technical progress of the West. The autocracy became stronger than ever. There was no loosening of the chains of serfdom. There was no experimenting with elected representative bodies. The Church was reduced almost to the status of a department of the state.

Throughout the eighteenth century the extension of Russia's frontiers proceeded with the inexorable finality of an expanding glacial ice-cap. The growing weakness of Russia's neighbors, the Poles in the West, the Tartars and Turks in the South and Southwest, favored this extension. Under the reign of Peter's most distinguished successor, Catherine II, Russia reached its natural southern frontier, the Black Sea, and swallowed up the greater part of Poland. It maintained and somewhat improved its western boundary under the shock of the Napoleonic War. During the nineteenth century Russia made no very considerable territorial gain in Europe, but the Empire was rounded out with new conquests in the Caucasus and Central Asia.

More important than any political and military developments was the amazing cultural awakening of Russia in the nineteenth century. There was a flowering of imagination and of creative thought that is all the more impressive because of the previous sterile nature of the Russian intellectual soil. There were a few pioneers of the future Russian culture, like the poet-scientist, M. V. Lomonosov, who helped to establish the Russian literary language in the eighteenth century. But if everything written in Russian before 1800 (old sagas and folksongs excepted) were destroyed by some natural catastrophe, the loss would scarcely be perceptible, except to specialized students. Russia entered the nineteenth century with an intellectual past remarkably blank for a people so numerous and, as the future would show, so gifted artistically. There had been no achievements up to this time in literature or art (the inherited Byzantine ikon-painting excepted), in science and philosophy that could challenge comparison with those of England and France, Germany and Italy. Several causes account for this retarded cultural growth.

There was the long sleep enforced by the Tartar Conquest. There was the chronic exhaustion of national strength and wealth by a long series of wars. The unlimited autocracy was itself no encouragement to free speculation. This might also be said of a state religion that was at once dogmatic and conservative. Cities are the centres of intellectual life, and Russia up to very modern times possessed very few genuine cities, only garrison towns and large trading villages.

The nineteenth century was an era of noteworthy cultural and material progress for all Europe. And Russia was caught up in the wave of this progress. Its two glowing lyric poets, Pushkin and Lermontov, rank with Byron and Shelley among the leading figures in the romantic movement. Both Russian poets found much of their inspiration in the life and legends of the Caucasus, with its magnificent mountain scenery and its medley of picturesque tribes.

In the field of the novel Russia, with its four masters, Tolstoy, Dostoevsky, Turgenev, and Gogol, and its many lesser writers, such as Goncharov, Saltikov-Shchedrin, Chekhov, Gorky, Andreev, easily surpassed the contemporary achievement of any European country, with the possible exception of France. In music it achieved a position second only to Germany, with such composers as Tschaikovsky, Moussorgsky, Rimsky-Korsakov, Rubinstein, Borodin, Glinka and many others. Scientists, such as Metchnikov, Mendeleev and Pavlov, artists like Repin, historians ranging from the old-fashioned courtly Karamzin at the beginning of the century to the brilliant and profoundly thoughtful Klyuchevsky at the end, all made their contribution to this great century of Russian cultural achievement.

This was no mere emergence of individual men of genius and talent. The Russian educated class steadily increased in numbers, although it remained relatively small because of the great masses of illiterate and semiliterate peasants and the still more backward non-Russian Oriental peoples of the Empire. But the quality of this young Russian intelligentsia was out of all proportion to its numbers. In breadth of intellectual interest, in spontaneity and keenness of literary and artistic appreciation, in receptivity to new ideas, the Russian intellectual, the writer, teacher, physician, scientist, artist or student often compared very favorably with men and women of similar educational background in other countries.

To what was, for Russia, a discovery of European art, literature, philosophy, science, social and economic theories the Russian intelligentsia brought an exhilarating sense of new learning, a generous enthusiasm, such as Europe's own humanists felt when they began to decipher the masterpieces of Greece and Rome. Ivan Karamazov, the intellectual among the three brothers of Dostoevsky's mighty novel, apostrophizes Europe in these glowing words:

Precious are the dead that lie there. Every stone over them speaks of such burning life in the past, of such passionate faith in their work, their truth, their struggle and their science that I know I shall fall on the ground and kiss those stones and weep over them.

It is scarcely an exaggeration to say that only in the nineteenth century did Russians begin to come alive as human beings. The personalities of Tsars and Tsarinas, positive or negative, had always been important because of the absolutist character of the government. A few progressive-minded nobles and distinctive generals convey a sense of definite character. But until the nineteenth century the poverty of individual personality in Russia matched the poverty in cultural achievement. Then the ice that seemed to freeze the Russians of earlier generations commenced to crack. Figures of world significance began to emerge.

Perhaps the best known Russian of the last century was Count Leo

Tolstoy. Descendant of an old aristocratic family, author of the two great novels, *War and Peace* and *Anna Karenina,* he attracted international attention by the philosophy of nonviolence, renunciation of wealth, abstinence and simple living which he preached and practised during the later period of his life. He was a successor of Rousseau and a precursor of Gandhi, with whom he had much in common spiritually and intellectually. In his attitude, bordering on anarchism, of rejecting the power of the state, in his repudiation of violence between man and man, Tolstoy expressed the unconscious aspirations of the peasants whom he knew on his estate, and who regarded taxes and military conscription as two of the principal curses of their lives.

Tolstoy escaped exile or imprisonment because of his aristocratic antecedents and because of his international prestige. But he was excommunicated by an officially controlled Church, although he might reasonably have been regarded as a most sincere Christian. Other independent minds were not so fortunate. Alexander Herzen, perhaps the most eloquent Russian publicist of his time, found that he could write freely only in London. N. G. Chernishevsky, a man who might have ranked with Mill and Spencer because of his encyclopedic learning and his fondness for social theory, was broken by a period of long exile in Siberia.

One of the most lovable figures in the revolutionary movement was Prince Peter Kropotkin. He gave up a promising scientific career to take up the hunted, persecuted life of the revolutionary. For a time he was imprisoned in the grim fortress of Peter and Paul, in St. Petersburg. His escape, after he had been transferred to a hospital, was one of the spectacular episodes of the struggle between the revolutionaries and the police. To Darwin's hard law of the survival of the fittest in a world of struggle, Kropotkin opposed a theory of mutual aid, for which he tried to find support in science and in history. Forced to live in exile for many years Kropotkin returned to Russia, an old man, after the Revolution. He found a new form of dictatorial state instead of the voluntary association of free communes of which he had dreamed, and died, sad and disappointed, in 1921.

Another striking figure was Michael Bakunin. Like Kropotkin, he was an Anarchist by conviction. But, unlike the humane and scholarly Prince, he reveled in violent action and was willing to resort to any kind of force and intrigue in order to gain his objective: the total overthrow of existing society and the substitution of anarchist communism. It is psychologically significant that this great Russian Anarchist, who yearned for the destruction of the state, as the source of all evil, who fought on more than one barricade in European insurrections, tried to create secret revolutionary organizations, based on the principle of absolute authority of the leaders. It was this very principle, successfully carried into practice by Lenin, that laid the foundation for the Communist dictatorship.

It was not only dangerous political thinkers like Herzen, Bakunin and Kropotkin who felt the stern hand of the Tsar's police. Authors like Dostoevsky and Turgenev also found themselves in difficulties. Because he had joined a discussion club which was suspected of seditious tendencies, Dostoevsky, under the reactionary rule of Nicholas I, was condemned to death. At the last moment the sentence was commuted to four years of penal servitude in Siberia. Curiously enough, Dostoevsky emerged from this experience not an embittered rebel, but a mystical Christian. His views became more conservative and nationalist in his later years and he satirized the revolutionaries savagely in his novel, *The Possessed.* The Westernized liberal Turgenev was so much harassed by police surveillance that he preferred to spend much of his life abroad.

Yet, although the autocratic system pressed heavily on the individual, especially upon the individual of liberal or radical views, the nineteenth century was still the freest and most progressive period in Russian history. No European country grew so visibly in mental stature between 1800 and 1900. No European land owes so large a part of its heritage of civilization to the effort of a single century. One recalls the enthusiastic words of Gogol, who likened Russia's forward movement to the galloping of a troika, a Russian carriage or sleigh, drawn by three horses:

And, Russia, art thou not also flying onward like a spirited troika that nothing can overtake? The road is smoking beneath thee, the bridges rumble, everything falls back and is left behind. Russia, whither fliest thou? Answer! She gives no answer. The ringing of the bells melts into music. The air, torn to shreds, whirs and rushes like the wind. Everything on earth is flying by. The other states and nations, looking askance, make way for her and stand aside.

The absence of an old cultural tradition lent a quality of reckless boldness to Russia's newly emancipated thinkers. Herzen, the coiner of expressive phrases, described Russia as "the land of outward slavery and inward freedom." Severely curbed by police and censors, the Russian intellectual was free from the invisible West European restraints of custom and convention. From the extremism of autocracy it was an easy step to the opposite pole of extremism: revolutionary dictatorship.

In the heritage of the Russian past one can find many seeds of the great revolution that was to shatter the political and social order, and many foreshadowings of the regime that was to emerge from that revolution. The traditional unlimited power of the government was an excellent preparation for the Communist dictatorship. The Russian folk pattern of bearing great poverty and hardship stoically over long periods of time and then flaring up in an outburst of wild revolt was favorable to the success of a group of determined revolutionaries who would take advantage of one of these moods of all-out rebellion and then lay a heavy yoke of their own on the masses of the people.

The essential newness of Russian conscious thinking on social and economic problems, the exclusion of most educated Russians from positions of practical responsibility, worked in favor of doctrinaire extremism. Russia had missed the individualist aspects of such movements as the Reformation, the Renaissance and the French Revolution. It was less touched than any large European power by the general trend towards parliamentarism and liberalism. Among the obvious causes of the Revolution were the intolerable strain and dislocation imposed by the First World War, the contrasts of wealth and poverty in the country, the hard living conditions of most of the industrial workers and peasants, the discontent of the non-Russian nationalities.

Less obvious, but no less important as a cause was the comparative absence, in Russian historical experience, of anything that would cultivate a strong sense of an individual's right to personal liberty and private property. No Russian was safe against arrest for political reasons. Only a minority of the peasants owned their land on an individual property basis. The number of persons with a conscious personal stake in the avoidance of violent change was smaller than in any other European country. On the very eve of its fall the Tsarist system impressed most observers as a bulwark of conservatism and reaction. But it was also a powder-magazine of violent revolution. . . .

The Bolshevik Revolution made Russia more enigmatical than ever, in the eyes of the outside world. The downfall of Tsarism was generally welcomed in democratic countries. But many of the theories and acts of the victorious revolutionaries seemed harsh and repelling. The denial of political and civil liberties, the "liquidation" of whole classes of the population, the attempt to realize professedly humane ultimate ends by immediate means that were often ruthless and brutal, inspired doubts and questionings, even in the minds of many who were originally sympathetic with the Revolution. . . .

FROM 1857 TO 1914

GEORGE VERNADSKY *

ALEXANDER II

Public opinion had already made itself felt during the life of Emperor Nicholas I, despite all the efforts of censorship and police. Following his death, it could no longer be restrained, the more so because the new emperor, Alexander II, was by nature different from his father. It cannot be

* Formerly at Yale University. Author of *The Expansion of Russia; Lenin, Red Dictator;* and *Political and Diplomatic History of Russia.* The selection is from chapters 10, 11, and 12 of *A History of Russia,* Copyright 1929, 1930, and 1944, by Yale University Press. By permission.

said that his political views differed greatly from those of his father. He had, in fact, the same ideals of enlightened absolutism; but he was of a much gentler and more tolerant disposition. Alexander had been educated in much more humane spirit. His preceptor was the poet Zhukovsky, one of the most noble characters of the first half of the nineteenth century.

The patriotic feelings of Alexander, as of many of his contemporaries, were deeply hurt by the outcome of the Crimean War. Reforms in Russia seemed inevitable, as the old *régime* had proved itself incapable of organizing the defense of Russia. This was admitted prior to his death by Nicholas I, who told Alexander: "I am handing you command of the country in a poor state." The basic defect of the old *régime* was the institution of serfdom. It was consequently natural that the reforms of Alexander II should start with this matter, the more so because the solution of the question had been prepared during the reign of Nicholas I.

In January, 1857, a secret Committee on Peasant Reform was organized. It was composed of several of the highest officials of the Government, but the fear of taking decisive action retarded its work. A decisive step was taken at the initiative of Alexander in the late autumn of 1857, when the emperor authorized the governor-general of Vilna to organize "Provincial Committees" of the nobility in the Lithuanian provinces for the discussion of the terms of the proposed peasant reforms on December 2, 1857. Following this move there was no possibility of retreat; the reforms became inevitable. The nobles of other provinces were forced to request the Government's authorization to form similar committees. Their motives were clearly expressed in the famous speech of Alexander II to the nobility of Moscow: "Better that the reform should come from above than wait until serfdom is abolished from below." . . .

The basic principles of the reform were as follows: Household serfs were to be freed within a period of two years without redemption, but were to receive nothing on gaining their freedom. Peasant serfs were to receive not only their personal freedom, but also certain allotments of land. In determining the dimensions of each peasant's share, the amount of land worked by peasants for their own use under conditions of serfdom was taken into consideration. The serfs had worked both their own lands and the lands of their owner. The area of the allotments granted to the peasants following the reform was equal approximately to the area retained by the landowner. Thus, under the terms of the reform of 1861, the peasants received grants of land which, prior to the reform, had absorbed only half of their labor.

By the terms of the emancipation, the land which the peasants received did not become their private property. It continued to be regarded as the property of the landowner, but was held for the benefit of the peasant. The peasants, though now freedmen, were called upon to pay for the use of this land or to perform certain services for the landowner. The Government, however, was willing to help, if both the landowners and the peasants desired to terminate this relationship. Help was provided in the form of a long-term credit to purchase the land. In those cases where estate-owners agreed to sell the land to their former serfs, the Government paid the landowners the cost of the land with an interest-bearing bond, and this sum was imposed upon the peasant in the form of deferred payments over a period of years. The cost was computed on the basis of the annual payment of the peasant, being worth 6 per cent of the cost of the land. The deferred payments were added to the head tax of the peasant.

The appointed period was forty-nine years. Within twenty years following 1861 about 85 per cent of landowners actually sold to the peasants their part of land in each estate with the above-mentioned assistance of the Government. Even in this case the peasant did not receive the land in complete personal ownership, but each peasant commune or village received the whole area of land in communal ownership under collective responsibility for the redemption payments of all the members of the commune. Special government agents named for the purpose of putting the reform into operation, called mediators, drew up charter deeds for the land in the name of a whole commune. The commune itself divided the land among its members according to the size of families. These subdivisions took place periodically every few years.

Thus, even following the reforms, the peasant did not become an individual property owner or an individual possessing full civil rights, but remained subject to the authority of the commune. Actually the peasants became dependent upon those government bureaucratic agencies which concerned themselves with peasant affairs. It is necessary to add that outside of the commune each peasant could purchase land on the basis of full ownership. This situation is important for the understanding of future events. It explains the continued juridical isolation of the peasants even following the reform. It also preserved in their consciousness the memory of serfdom. The firm bonds of the commune did not permit changes in the manner of owning land. The peasants never forgot that the commune had only half of the former estate. The reform of 1861 seemed incomplete and they dreamed of completing it. Another idea connected with the land commune was that the land was not the property of individuals but was granted in the form of an allotment to serve the uses of the individual. Thus, land within the whole state was regarded by the peasant as a fund which could be drawn upon for further allotments until it was used up. These were the embryonic ideas of the subsequent revolution.

The reform of 1861 was tragically inadequate. There were two ways of really solving the question finally. The first was to leave the possession as well as the ownership of the land with the land-owner. The peasant in this case would have received merely his personal freedom. In the majority of cases, however, under the pressure of necessity, the landowner would have been forced to sell part of his land to his former serfs. The Government could have assisted in this transaction, in the favor of the individual peasants, and not of the communes. The actual result would have been almost the same as it was by the reform of 1861, but the psychological results would have been quite different. Instead of thousands of peasant communes there would have been created millions of peasant landowners. The ideas of a "general fund" and of "allotments" would have been avoided. It was toward this result that the later reforms of Stolypin were directed, but the reforms of Stolypin came forty-five years too late (1906).

The other possibility, in introducing the reform of 1861, was to take all the land away from the estate-owners and to divide it among the peasants. This would have been the simplest solution, which would have prevented all the later upheavals in Russia. If the partition of land had been completed in 1861, there would have been no need for it in 1918 and in that case the Russian revolution would never have been accompanied by such riots as it actually was.

However, in spite of its incompleteness, the reform of 1861 was an ambitious effort which changed the whole old order. After the peasant reform, it seemed easier to start with other reforms which, taken together, completely changed the nature of the Russian state. The other leading "great reforms" of Alexander II were the reforms of the Zemstvo, the towns, the courts, and the military service.

The reform of the Zemstvo in 1864 created for the first time since that of the early Moscow state, real local self-government without regard to class. The basis of the reform consisted in granting to elected representatives of each county (Uyezd) control over the schools, medical affairs, and roads. The elective law provided for the division of electors into three *curias:* the private landowners (nobles and merchants); peasant communes; and townspeople. The representatives elected an "Executive Committee" known as the *Uprava* for a term of three years. The representatives of the Uyezd formed a provincial assembly which elected a provincial Zemstvo Committee (*Uprava*). Following the general spirit of the Zemstvo reforms, similar measures were introduced for town government in 1870. The electors were likewise divided into three *curias,* according to a property census; the amount of taxes paid was totaled and divided into three equal parts, each having an equal number of representatives. Both the Zemstvo and the town authorities succeeded in carrying out work of great cultural importance in Russia prior to the Revolution of 1917.

Of no less significance was the new judicial reform of 1864, of which S. I. Zarudny was the chief promoter. Its basic principles were: the improvement of court procedure; the introduction of the jury and the organization of lawyers into a formal bar. Despite some drawbacks of the Russian courts following 1864, they undoubtedly reached considerable efficiency, and in this respect Russia could be favorably compared with the most progressive European countries. It is necessary, however, to note here the difference between the façade and the foundation of the new Russian state. The peasants in the vast majority of small civil litigations did not use the new courts and had to be content with the "volost" courts, especially organized for them, and from the reign of Alexander III until 1912, they also had to accept the jurisdiction of the "Land Captains."

The last of the major reforms was the introduction of universal military service in 1874. The law of military service was practically the only one of the laws of this time which affected equally all the classes of the Russian people. Here there was no difference between the façade and the structure; it was profoundly democratic in spirit. The recruits were granted privileges only according to their family position. The only son, the only grandson, or only supporter of a family, received full privileges and were registered in the reserve of the second category, that is, in practice, prior to the World War, they were never called into service. With respect to the term of service and promotion, special privileges were recognized in favor of individuals having secondary education. Class differences were not in any way reflected in privileges of military service, with the exception of the selection of the Guards officers from the aristocratic circles of society. The society created by the reforms of Alexander II lasted in its general character until 1905, and in part until 1917. . . .

The internal policy of Alexander II did not bring about political peace in Russia. In spite of his far-reaching social and administrative reforms, he had to face bitter political opposition and direct revolutionary movements. The political opposition to the Government came primarily from the nobility. The idea was current that the nobility, having been deprived of its social and economic privileges, should receive in exchange political privileges, that is, a part of the governing power. This idea appeared during the preparation of the peasant reforms among members of the Provincial Committees who were discontented with the radicalism of the Revising Commission. In addition to the political programs of the nobles, other plans, looking to the reorganization of Russia along constitutional and democratic lines, were advanced, as a continuation of "Decembrist" tradition.

The revolutionary idea was chiefly current among the "Raznochintsi" —that is, individuals of no definite class: the children of peasants and merchants having received secondary or higher education; the children of the clergy who did not desire to enter the church; the children of small civil servants who did not desire to continue the vocation of their fathers; and the children of impoverished nobles. These Raznochintsi rapidly formed a new social class, the so-called "intelligentsia," which included many members of the nobility. The intellectuals grew rapidly with the reforms of Alexander II. The institution of the legal bar, the growth of newspapers and magazines, the increased number of teachers, etc., contributed to the

growth. The intelligentsia consisted of intellectual people in general, but
at first it consisted primarily of people connected with the publication of
papers and magazines or connected with universities. The university students contributed the greatest number of radical and revolutionary leaders.
The majority of the students consisted of men who had no means whatsoever. The average student lived in a state of semi-starvation, earning his
way through the university by giving lessons or by copying. The majority
of the students had no notion of sport and no taste for it. Lack of physical
exercise and consequent ill-health had a crushing effect upon the psychology
of the students.

The leaders of the intelligentsia desired not only radical political
changes but also a social revolution, in spite of the fact that Russian industry was too undeveloped to supply a firm basis for socialism. The Government was criticized for not being radical enough. The more moderate criticism was expressed in the legalized press, while the more bitter criticism
appeared in revolutionary organs published abroad, the best known of
which was *Kolokol* (The Bell), published by Herzen in London. Revolutionary propaganda against the Government immediately took a harsh tone.
In 1862 there appeared a proclamation to the youth of Russia calling for
terrorism and the murder of members of the Government and supporters of
its policy. The appearance of this proclamation was contemporaneous with
a number of cases of incendiarism in St. Petersburg. The Government took
decisive steps; several individuals were arrested and exiled. At the same
time the Polish revolutionary leaders were preparing an uprising in Poland.
The activity of the Russian revolutionary leaders was connected with the
Polish movement. The Polish revolution broke out in 1863. Just prior to
this uprising the Russian Government had started a more liberal policy in
Poland. The introduction of the reform had been put in the hands of a
prominent Polish statesman, Marquis Wielopolski. The radical elements in
Poland decided to *sabotage* the policy of moderate reform. The uprising
was suppressed by military force, after which the last remnants of Polish
independence were abrogated. . . .

A new wave of antigovernment activity arose in the 1870's. Among the
liberal circles of society, the desire grew for elective representation not only
in local self-government (Zemstvos and towns) but also in the central agencies of government. The institution of a parliament was to complete the
unfinished reforms. This movement became particularly strong following
the Turkish War of 1877-78, when the liberated Bulgaria received a constitution. The desire for a constitution in Russia became clearly expressed.
The activity of the revolutionary organizations in Russia during this period
likewise increased. Their activity may be divided into two periods. From
1870 to 1875 the radical intellectuals abstained from direct struggle against
the Government, but undertook preparatory propaganda among the masses
of the people. Many members of the intellectuals of that time went "to the

people," living among the peasants and workmen, teaching schools or becoming agricultural or industrial laborers.

The Government, fearing the results of the propaganda, oppressed the
movement by arresting participants in it. At times the peaceful members
of the movement suffered arrest together with the real propagandists. In
many cases persons were tried and imprisoned or exiled on the mere suspicion and action by the police. The Government's measures aroused the
bitterest feeling among the radical intellectuals. In the middle of the 1870's,
the revolutionaries began to use terrorism and to make attempts against
members of the Government. In 1879, in Lipetsk in central Russia, the
leaders of the revolutionary movement met in secret conference. An Executive Committee was elected at this meeting for the purpose of opposing the
Government. This Executive Committee decided to abandon all attempts
against individual members of the Government and to bend every effort
upon assassinating the head of the Government, Emperor Alexander II.
From that time on, Alexander II was the object of a manhunt by revolutionaries. Attempts were made in rapid succession, one after the other, but
were without success until the attempt made in St. Petersburg in the spring
of 1881, which resulted in the death of Alexander II on March 13, 1881.

The assassination of Alexander II occurred on the very day when the
emperor signed a *ukaz* calling for Representative Committees to advise the
State Council. This was the "constitution" drawn up by Loris Melikov, the
Minister of the Interior. Melikov's idea was that the revolutionary activity
of the intellectuals could not be stopped by police measures alone. In his
opinion the revolutionaries had the moral support of the moderate classes
of society who were discontented with the autocratic policy of the Government. Melikov believed that the Government should placate the moderate
elements of the opposition by means of granting a moderate constitution.
This measure, he believed, would deprive the revolutionaries of the moral
support of these classes. The assassination of Alexander II prevented the
execution of this plan. His son and successor, Alexander III, withdrew the
constitution of Melikov, and the *ukaz* signed by Alexander II was never
published.

ALEXANDER III AND NICHOLAS II

The impression made upon Alexander III by the assassination of his
father lasted during his life. He retained a distrust for all popular movements and influenced by Constantine Pobiedonostsev, expressed a firm belief in the infallibility of the principle of autocracy. The political program
of Alexander III was extremely simple. It consisted in opposing all liberal
and revolutionary movements in Russia and in satisfying, to a certain degree, the urgent economic demands of the Russian people. These principles
of policy were handed down by Alexander to his son Nicholas, who ascended

the throne on the death of his father in 1894. It was only under the pressure of the revolution of 1904-5 that Nicholas agreed to grant a constitution; but up to the second revolution of 1917, and probably to his very death in 1918, Nicholas retained a belief in the principles of policy laid down by his father. . . .

Soon after Nicholas' coronation, intrigues sprang up among his ministers and the grand dukes, whom Nicholas never succeeded in mastering and putting in their proper place. Nicholas did not like to admit that anyone exercised any influence upon him. In fact, however, he was constantly under someone's influence, until he became completely dominated by his wife, Alexandra Feodorovna. An episode illustrating Nicholas' character took place in Moscow during his coronation. Because of the incompetence of the police, a panic occurred at the distribution of gifts in honor of the occasion, in which over one thousand people were crushed to death. This accident took place at the very height of the coronation festivities. There is no doubt that if it had occurred at the coronation of Alexander III, he would have immediately canceled all further celebration. Nicholas, however, had the idea of showing his firmness and made no change of plans. Even the ball at the French Ambassador's the same evening was not canceled. As a matter of fact this was not firmness but tactlessness.

While it is possible to define the internal policy pursued by Alexander III, the same cannot be done for the reign of Nicholas II. His policy consisted simply in continuing by inertia the policy of his father. The internal policy of Alexander III consisted first of all in strengthening governmental control in all directions where free public opinion could be expected to manifest itself. Pursuant to this policy, the laws regarding local self-government were revised. The power of the Government, in the person of the provincial governors, was strengthened as against the power of the Zemstvos. According to the new laws of 1890, the peasants elected only candidates for the Zemstvo, while the governor chose representatives from among these candidates. This law was repealed in 1906. In order to extend governmental supervision over the peasants, the office of "Zemsky Nachalnik" or Land Captain, appointed by the Government from the nobility, was created in 1889. The Zemsky Nachalniks had administrative power in local affairs as well as the function of judge over the peasantry.

Many measures were also taken to repress the intellectuals. The universities were reorganized in 1884. Education became subject to government control. Censorship of the press was strengthened and the majority of newspapers and magazines became subject to the "preliminary censorship" of government agents. The political tendencies of the intellectuals became subject to redoubled watchfulness by the police. Persons who were suspected were subject to police supervision. Attempts at political conspiracies were mercilessly crushed. In 1887 the police discovered a plot to assassinate Alexander III. The guilty parties were executed, among them Alexander

Ulianov, Lenin's eldest brother. In order to grant the police greater freedom, many provinces of Russia were declared in a state of "special protection." This enabled the administration to suspend the normal laws of procedure with respect to political prisoners. Several of the territories of Russia, inhabited by non-Russian peoples, also fell under suspicion. The Government began a policy of forcible "Russianization." This policy was applied particularly to Poland. Measures were also taken against the cultural dominance of the Germans in the Baltic provinces where they formed a minority of the population. Only the landowning class, the Barons, were Germans. The religious life was also subject to restrictions. The Christian dissenters, the evangelical sects, Stundo-Baptists, and Catholics were equally affected. Particular suspicion was leveled against the Jews.

The Jewish question had arisen in Russia in the eighteenth century. A great many Jews had become subjects of the Russian state, following the division of Poland and the annexation of the southwestern Russian territories, which had a large Jewish population. According to the laws of 1804, the Jews were forbidden to settle in the central Russian provinces. The statutes fixed a "pale of settlement" where alone Jews could live. This included the western and southern provinces. Under Alexander III the conditions under which the Jews lived were subjected to further restriction. They were forbidden to settle outside the towns and villages, even within the territories which they might inhabit. The line of demarcation was further restricted in 1887 when the city of Rostov-on-Don was excluded from the pale. In 1891 seventeen thousands Jews were deported from Moscow. Furthermore, a quota of Jews, limited to their proportion of the population, was introduced in government educational institutions. With few exceptions the Jews were not admitted to governmental service.

Seeking to hold the various classes under close observation, the Government searched for a group in society upon which it could itself depend. This group was the Russian nobility. During the reigns of Alexander III and Nicholas II, the Government attempted to secure the support of the nobility by granting it special privileges in respect to local self-government and local justice. In addition a number of financial privileges were granted to the nobility. The dependence of the internal policy upon the nobility was a fatal political error. The Russian nobility was politically dead after the reforms of Alexander II and the beginning of the democratization of Russian life. The attempt to bring it back into political life was an attempt to revive a corpse. Even when the nobility had been a powerful force in Russia, in the eighteenth and the first half of the nineteenth century, the interests of the imperial power seldom agreed with those of the nobility. It was an act of political shortsightedness to seek to establish a close union between the Government and the nobility at a time when the nobility no longer possessed any vitality. This mistaken policy only brought about further discontent with the Government on the part of other classes.

However, it would be unjust to point only to the negative aspects of Russian policy in the last quarter of the nineteenth century for it must be admitted that the Government also carried out reforms improving the social and economic conditions of the majority of the people. Many measures were directed toward the improvement of the condition of the peasantry. First, in the beginning of 1882, a decree was issued ordering compulsory sale to peasants of land on those estates where the sale had not been completed following the emancipation. Furthermore, the instalments to be paid by the peasants for the land were lowered and the head tax was abolished (1886). New regulations were issued making it easy for peasants to rent government lands and aiding them to migrate to the free lands in the eastern part of the Empire. It was partly to further migration that the Siberian railroad was begun in 1892. The reign of Alexander III also marked the beginning of labor legislation in Russia. In 1882 government inspection of factories was instituted and the Government undertook to regulate the conditions of the workers. At the same time the working day of minors and women was limited by law. Labor legislation was continued during the reign of Nicholas II.

The Government also undertook reforms of the finances. The finances of Russia were greatly improved under Nicholas I, but since that time two wars and expensive internal reforms had succeeded in shaking them and the currency had already depreciated. The Government was fortunate in having such a brilliant statesman as Witte. He succeeded in reorganizing Russian finances and in reintroducing gold into circulation in 1897.

All these government measures directed toward improving the economic condition of the country could not, however, outweigh the irritation caused by the police supervision instituted by the Government. The internal policy of Alexander III succeeded in suppressing social discontent and political opposition only for a short time. Actually, in the course of the reign of Alexander III and the first half of the reign of Nicholas II, everything was quiet; but during the second half of the reign of Nicholas II, the accumulated social discontent expressed itself in a violent explosion. . . .

The war with Japan in 1904-1905 resulted in a series of defeats for Russia. The Japanese fleet showed itself to be considerably stronger than the Russian, whose vessels were less well constructed and had weaker armaments. The Japanese fleet soon succeeded in blockading Port Arthur. Soon after the Japanese troops were landed on the mainland.

The Russian army was considerably stronger than the Japanese in numbers. As regards quality, the Russian troops were not inferior to the Japanese. Nevertheless, the war on land was as unfortunate for Russia as the war on the sea. The first failures might be explained by the difficulty of rapidly concentrating Russian troops at the distant battlefield. The whole army depended upon the Siberian railway, which was not even com-

pleted. There was no line around Lake Baikal. But the subsequent defeats
must be explained on psychological grounds. The Russian army went into
battle without enthusiasm. The deep dissatisfaction of the Russian people
with the Government could not fail to be reflected in the army. The war
was unpopular in Russia from the very beginning. Its objects were not understood by the Russian people. It did not seem to them to affect the vital
interests of the country, while every Japanese soldier understood that the
war concerned the vital interests of Japan. . . .

The revolutionary sentiments of the Russian people in 1904-1905 expressed themselves in the most diverse forms. The political activity of the
intellectuals took the form of lectures on politics, the organization of societies of a semipolitical nature, and, in some cases, of riots on the part of
students. The liberal landowners, members of the local (Zemstvo) administration, organized conferences to discuss reforms and a deputation from one
of these congresses was sent to the emperor on June 19, 1905. The workers
took recourse to strikes, the chief aims of which were political, rather than
economic, reforms. The discontent of the peasantry found expression in
agrarian riots, which resulted frequently in the destruction of landowners'
houses or even in the murder of the landowners. Finally, following the ter-
mination of the Japanese war, disorder spread to the army. The soldiers
were affected by socialist propaganda and in many cases revolted against
their officers. Socialist agitators urged the formation of councils composed
of soldiers, an idea which in 1917 proved fatal to the Russian army. Riots
spread from the army to the navy, and on the battleship *Potemkin* the sailors succeeded in temporarily seizing control in June, 1905.

The whole period was characterized by a series of assassinations of
governmental officials by terrorists. The Government first attempted to
deal with the revolutionary sentiments of the people by suppressing disorders with armed force and by disrupting the revolutionary organizations.
The Department of Police introduced secret agents in revolutionary organizations for the purpose of securing evidence against their leaders. The
government agents sometimes became leaders of the revolutionary parties
and took so active a part in the movement that it became impossible for
the Government to determine where revolution began and where provocation ended. It was under circumstances of this kind that the Minister
of the Interior, Plehve, was assassinated. The Department of Police also
attempted to get control over the workers' movement by satisfying their
economic demands and thus drawing them away from political activity.
Zubatov, an agent of the secret police, succeeded in the spring of 1902 in
organizing the workers along purely economic lines in Moscow and was
ordered by Plehve to introduce his system all over Russia.

Following the death of Plehve and the dismissal of Zubatov, the
workers' organization continued to develop of its own momentum. Its new

leader, the priest Gapon, thought of petitioning the Tsar in person to effect the reforms demanded by the workers. On January 22, 1905, a huge crowd of workmen made their way to the Winter Palace in St. Petersburg to appeal to Nicholas II. The day had a tragic end, for, notwithstanding the fact that the workmen were peacefully inclined and unarmed, the crowd was dispersed by gunfire, as a result of which several hundred people were killed or wounded. "Bloody Sunday," as this day came to be called, became a decisive turning point in the history of the opposition of the working classes. It had as its immediate result their alliance with the socialist working class parties. The Government by this time realized that it had no plan to alleviate the situation and no firm support among the people. It consequently decided upon concessions in the matter of political reform. But even in this it moved unwillingly. On August 19, 1905, the order was given to call a national congress, the imperial Duma, which was to have deliberative, but not legislative, functions. This was, however, a half-measure which satisfied no one.

In the autumn of 1905, the situation became critical. A general strike was called throughout Russia. In the cities even the electricity and water supply were cut off; all railroads came to a standstill, with the exception of the Finland Railway. The leadership of the revolutionary group in St. Petersburg was taken by a special council composed of the leaders of the Socialist parties and representatives of the workers. This was the so-called Soviet of Workers' Deputies which was to take a prominent part in the events of 1917. At the first session of the Soviet the number of workers' representatives was only forty. It was increased later to five hundred. The chairman of the Soviet was a lawyer, Khrustalev-Nosar, but the actual leader was the vice-president Bronstein, subsequently known as Trotsky. It should be noted that the pseudonyms employed by many revolutionary leaders were assumed for self-protection against the espionage of the government police. All revolutionary instructions were signed by fictitious names.

The majority of the Soviet was in the hands of the Mensheviks, of whom Trotsky was a prominent member. The Bolsheviks failed to capture control of the first Soviet and regarded it with suspicion. Soviets were formed in some other cities, Moscow, Odessa, and elsewhere; but before they achieved any important results, the Government decided to make far-reaching political concessions. At the initiative of Count Witte, a manifesto, which amounted practically to capitulation by the Government, was issued October 30, 1905.

By this manifesto the imperial Government promised that it would grant to the Russian nation: (1) the fundamental principles of civil liberty —inviolability of person, and liberty of thought, speech, assembly, and organization; (2) democratic franchise; (3) the principle that no law could henceforth be made without the consent of the Duma. A new Prime

Minister, Count Witte, with power to appoint assistants from opposition circles, was named to carry the manifesto into effect. This was the first time in Russia that a united cabinet was formed.

The manifesto was an embodiment of the principal demands of the liberal opposition. The hope was that it would stop the revolutionary activity of this opposition. In this regard the manifesto was an attempt to unite the Government and the Liberal parties against the imminent social revolution. For this reason leaders of the social movement who desired revolution at all costs were opposed to the manifesto. Their arguments were that the Government was not sincere in its promises, that it desired only to stop the revolutionary movement, and that as soon as conditions permitted, it would rescind the manifesto. The Government indeed did hope that the manifesto would stop the revolution; but it was not true that it wished to withdraw the concessions. In fact, it did not do so after its real victory over the revolutionaries. Count Witte, the head of the Government and the author of the manifesto, personally believed in the necessity for reform and had naturally no intentions of retraction. Only the inexperience of the leaders of the Russian liberal movement can explain the decision of the liberal groups to decline all the invitations of Count Witte to enter his ministry. The result was that the manifesto of October 30 did not stop the revolutionary movement at once.

The Socialist parties desired only the triumph of their revolutionary doctrines. The leader of the Bolsheviks, Lenin, who came to Russia following the manifesto of October 30, became the staunchest opponent of the Government's policy. The strikes went on; a second railroad strike lasted from the end of November to the middle of December, and an armed insurrection occurred in Moscow at the end of December, 1905. The irreconcilable policy of the revolutionaries was not supported, however, by the majority of the people, who were fairly well satisfied with the program set forth in the manifesto. The Government was enabled to retake control of the situation. The Soviets were disbanded and the riots were suppressed by force. In several cities *pogroms* against Jews took place, organized by the so-called "Union of the Russian People," a reactionary group whose ideology was of the same pattern as that of German Nazism.

The insurrection at Moscow was not fully suppressed when the Government published a decree on December 24 on the procedure for elections. At the beginning of March, there appeared a manifesto concerning the organization of the new Parliament, which was to be formed of two Houses: the state Duma and the state Council, the first consisting of members elected by the nation, and the second of members half of whom were appointed by the emperor and half elected by the nobility, Zemstvos, and university faculties. The electoral law gave the right of suffrage to the majority of the people, but it was neither equal nor direct. The voters were divided into groups: The workers in several large cities chose their electors to the

Duma separately; the peasants chose electors who formed electoral colleges together with the electors chosen by the large landowners. These councils selected the deputies to the Duma. The electoral law artificially isolated the peasants and the workers and gave them a considerable rôle in the elections. This policy was prompted by the desire on the part of the Government to draw the peasants and the workers away from the opposition parties.

As a further means of appeasing the peasantry, Count Witte had the idea of expropriating the large estates and handing over the lands to the peasants. This project was developed by one of Witte's ministers, Kutler, who subsequently took a prominent part in the financial reorganization of the Soviet Government. The expropriation of large land holdings, however, was bitterly opposed by the estate-owners. Witte did not have enough power to insist upon the measures he proposed, and was forced to cancel his project. This failure reacted upon the operation of the electoral law which was primarily a bid to the peasantry. Just as in the case of the earlier attempts to organize the workers in a manner favorable to the Government, it merely succeeded in stirring up social movements without either satisfying or being able to control them.

The elections to the first Duma took place in March, 1906. On May 10 the state Council and Duma were opened by Nicholas II. The majority of the Duma consisted of opposition deputies; of 490 members, 187 belonged to the Liberal party and 85 to the moderate labor group. The Constitutional Democrats, led by I. Petrunkevich (the other leader, P. Miliukov, being removed under a specious pretext from the list of voters), was the strongest party represented. The Socialist parties boycotted the elections, while the Nationalist and Conservative parties were defeated at the polls and secured only a small number of seats. The results of the elections were disappointing to the Government.

Finding a hostile group in control of the state Duma, Nicholas II immediately dismissed Count Witte and appointed Goremykin in his place. The new Prime Minister was a typical civil servant of the old *régime*. He was chosen, not because he had initiative and political convictions, but, on the contrary, because he lacked these qualities and was ready to execute the orders of the emperor. The appointment of Goremykin was a great political error. The relations between the Government and the Duma rapidly took on an unfriendly character.

The principal point of dispute between the Government and the Duma was the agrarian problem. Its discussion in the Duma aroused the passions of all groups. An agrarian bill, sponsored by the Constitutional Democrats, proposed the expropriation of the large estates and the transfer of land to the ownership of the peasants, granting compensation to the owners. This led to increased agitation against the Duma by the reactionaries. Nicholas II faced the problem of either submitting to the Duma and displeasing the nobility, or of dismissing it and provoking the hostility of the Liberals. On July 21 the Duma was dissolved. As a concession to the Liberals, Goremykin was dismissed and a new man, Stolypin, was appointed Prime Minister.

Stolypin had been Minister of the Interior in the Cabinet of his predecessor in office. He began his service to the Crown as a governor of one of the southern provinces. Before that he had managed his own estates. He had a profound comprehension of the agrarian problem in Russia and possessed the qualities of an outstanding statesman. He was firm, patriotic, and a man of ideas. The opposition parties did not support Stolypin and his program, but they were obliged to reckon with him. Following the dissolution of the Duma, the opposition groups were undecided as to their course. Their psychology was not that of peaceful parliamentary opposition, but that of revolution. They dreaded the possibility of the Government's canceling the whole program of reform and plainly distrusted the emperor. After the dissolution, members of the Duma issued an appeal to the Russian nation to resist the Government by refusing to pay taxes and to refuse conscription into the army. The appeal had no effect upon the people. Its only result was that its authors lost the right of voting in the subsequent elections.

Stolypin first tried to attract some of the leading members of the moderate liberal groups into his Cabinet. They refused to cooperate with him, and he was obliged to draw upon professional bureaucrats. His agrarian policy consisted primarily in destroying the communal ownership of land instituted by the reforms of 1861, and in encouraging peasant ownership of individual farms.

On November 22 the decree abrogating the peasant commune was published. Each peasant was given the right to receive his share of the common land in full ownership. Simultaneously, measures were taken to finance the purchase by the peasantry of Crown lands. Stolypin's measures were an attempt to repair the defects in the reform of 1861 and to create in Russia a new class of small landowners to form the basis for the new state. This program was deemed incompatible with the agrarian bill introduced by the first Duma. The expropriation of nearly all land, the basis of that proposal, was calculated to solve the whole agrarian problem at one stroke. Stolypin's reform required a score of years to produce lasting results.

When the second Duma gathered on March 5, 1907, it proved to be even more hostile to the Government than was the first. The second Duma had a stronger left wing than the first one (180 Socialists); Lenin had abruptly changed his tactics, and the Socialists did not boycott the Duma. The conflict between the Government and the Duma in 1907 was more acute than in 1906. The Government now had a practical program of reform which the Duma did not possess. Fifty-five socialist deputies were charged with organizing a plot against the emperor and the second Duma was dissolved in June, 1907. In order to suppress similar expressions of opposition, the electoral law was changed. The large landowners were given preference over the peasants in selecting representatives to the electoral colleges. The third Duma, elected in November, 1907, had a membership different from that of its predecessors. The majority of deputies now belonged to parties of the right, and the liberal and socialist deputies were in the minority. The result of the two years of political conflict was the victory of Stolypin and the Moderate parties. The new *régime,* it seemed, had succeeded in entrenching itself firmly. However, it was not a true parliamentary government that emerged from the revolutionary period of 1905-1906. . . .

Following the revolutionary period, characterized by the bitter struggle between the Government and the Duma, there began a period of relative quiet. The third Duma sat without interruption through the whole period of its legal existence, from 1907 to 1912, and the elections of 1912 resulted in a triumph of the conservative nationalist groups.

While the political conflict between the Government and the Duma was temporarily solved by the reformed electoral law of 1907, there remained the more troublesome question of dealing with the aftermath of the revolutionary spirit of 1905. The dissatisfaction of that period found continued expression in a number of assassinations of prominent government officials. Premier Stolypin adopted a course of merciless suppression of revolutionary terrorism. Those accused of political crimes were subject to trial by a court-martial, and when found guilty were punished by death. Stolypin's policy in this regard met with severe criticism from the opposition, but was supported by the majority of the conservative members of the Duma. The greatest number of executions during this period occurred in 1908, when the total number reached 782. After this year the number steadily decreased, and in 1911 seventy-three sentences were passed.

Just as political equilibrium seemed to have been reached, Stolypin was assassinated in September, 1911. His place was taken by the Minister of Finance, Kokovtsev. Like his predecessor, he was a Moderate Constitutionalist. He was faced with the constitutional problem of overriding the power of veto vested in the state Council organized at the same time as the Duma, and consisting only partially of elected members. One-half of the members of the Council were appointed by the emperor, and the Prime Minister had little influence in their selection. The Court circles of reactionary aristocrats were irreconcilably opposed to the Duma and succeeded in carrying out their policies without consulting the Prime Minister by direct influence upon the emperor. But notwithstanding irritating incidents of this kind, the Duma proved itself capable of bringing about many favorable changes in the country. Of great importance was the legislation concerning the peasantry, by which the precarious legal status of the peasants was done away with and their civil rights were equalized with those of other citizens.

The reform of local justice was an important measure in this connection. By virtue of the law of June 28, 1912, the general judicial system was to be gradually extended over the peasant population. The Land Captain was displaced in judicial matters by a justice of the peace. The Duma also undertook to organize the educational system and provided for an annual increase of 20,000,000 rubles in the educational budget, which grew steadily from 44,000,000 in 1906 to 214,000,000 in 1917. The number of pupils in the primary schools rose from 3,275,362 in 1894 to 8,000,000 in 1914. Thus on the eve of the war over half of all children of school age in Russia were receiving instruction. It was estimated by the educational committee of the Duma that universal education in Russia would be reached in 1922. The war and the revolution, however, prevented realization of this program. . . .

The creation of the new capitalist structure was accompanied by a rapid economic development of the country. The basic factor of economic development, as in the preceding period, was the rapid growth of population. From the middle of the nineteenth century to the beginning of the twentieth century, the population of Russia doubled. During the first fifteen years of the twentieth century, the population increased 30 per cent. In 1914 it totaled 175,000,000.

Particularly significant was the growth of city population. In 1851 there were less than three and a half million people in the towns or less than 6 per cent of the total population. In 1897 the town population had risen to sixteen and one-third millions or 13 per cent of the whole population, and in 1914 to 17.5 per cent. These figures indicate the growth of the industrial population as compared with the agricultural. According to the census of 1897, 74.2 per cent of the population was agricultural, and 13.3 per cent industrial. Thus, in spite of the growth of the cities and of industry, about three-quarters of Russia's population before the First World War was occupied in agriculture. . . .

The ownership of land in Russia, following the peasant reforms of 1861, underwent great changes. Land rapidly passed into the ownership of the peasants. The peasantry not only retained the lands distributed in 1861, but also acquired new lands by purchase. Thus, simultaneous with the growth of area under cultivation in Russia during the fifty years preceding the First World War, a radical change in the social structure of the agricultural population took place. As a result of the Stolypin reforms of 1906, the peasant communes began to disintegrate, and in 1911 six million households had acquired personal possession of the land. Russia was moving with great strides toward small landownership by citizens possessing equal rights with the rest of the population.

The industrialization of Russia which began in the second half of the nineteenth century increased rapidly until 1914, and in some branches of industry until 1917. We will trace this process briefly. . . .

The Russian cotton industry, prior to the First World War, occupied fourth place in world production. It was exceeded only by Great Britain, the United States, and Germany. In 1905 the Russian cotton industry employed 7,350,683 spindles and 178,506 looms. By 1911 the productive forces of the industry had grown to 8,448,818 spindles and 220,000 looms. The increased production of Russian cotton factories was absorbed partly by the home market and partly by foreign trade. The increase of internal consumption may be illustrated by the fact that in 1890 the per capita consumption of cotton cloth in Russia was 2.31 pounds and in 1910, 4.56 pounds. . . . The metallurgical industries showed a similar development. In 1900, around 1,500,000 tons of pig iron were produced in Russia. By 1914 production had grown to over 3,500,000 tons. . . .

The growth of industrial production was reflected also in mining. Eighty-five per cent of the coal used in Russia was of domestic extraction. The chief center of coal mining was the Donets basin which supplied 55 per cent of Russia's needs for coal. In 1900, 11,000,000 tons were mined in the Donets basin and in 1913 the production rose to 25,000,000 tons.

The exploitation of forests served both domestic needs and foreign trade. In 1904, 13,200,000 rubles worth of lumber was exported. By 1913 exports reached 164,900,000 rubles. Of great importance also was the production of oil, chiefly in the neighborhood of Baku. In 1860 oil production in the Baku area hardly exceeded 160,000 tons. In 1905 production rose to over 7,000,000 tons and in 1913 to around 9,000,000 tons. . . .

Even more rapid than the expansion of industry was the development of railroads in Russia. In the middle of the nineteenth century, the total length of railroads in operation in Russia did not exceed 660 miles. In 1912 the Russian railroad system comprised 40,194 miles and was second only to that of the United States. The greatest achievement was the completion of the great Trans-Siberian Railroad, from 1892 to 1905. Its construction was one of the most daring railroad projects of our time. The length of the line from Moscow to Vladivostok is 5,542 miles. In the construction of this line it was necessary to overcome the greatest natural and technical difficulties—the frozen subsoil and the wildness of the territories penetrated. The cost of the Trans-Siberian Railroad exceeded $200,000,000. It was originally a single-track line, but during the First World War a second line was laid down.

The rapid expansion of Russian industry was accompanied by the creation of a working class on a scale previously unknown in Russia. . . . It was only in 1902 that the Government assented to the legalization of some unions and it was only after the Revolution of 1905 that labor unions were permitted on a large scale by the Law of March 4, 1906.

The Government artificially retarded the development of labor unions and thereby unwittingly fostered the formation of illegal revolutionary organizations. But while restricting the development of labor unions, the Government made efforts to satisfy the principal needs of the workers by means of legislation. Labor legislation in Russia goes back to the 1880's in the reign of Alexander III. In 1897 day work was limited to eleven and a half hours and night work to ten hours. Night work was forbidden for children under seventeen, and children under twelve were not allowed to engage in industrial work of any kind. The legislation of the twentieth century introduced workers' accident compensation in 1903, health insurance in 1912, and accident insurance in 1912. The condition of the working class gradually improved, thanks to increasing wages, particularly in Petrograd and Moscow. At the end of the nineteenth century, the average wage of the Russian worker was only 187 rubles a year. By 1913 it had risen to 300 rubles and in some branches of industry in Petrograd and Moscow to five times this sum. In many factories the low money wages were augmented by free lodgings, hospital services, and factory schools. . . .

In the eighteenth and the first half of the nineteenth century, Russian culture centered chiefly around the large cities and the nobles' estates. From the middle of the nineteenth century, the basic elements of modern civilization, as, for example, education and medical care, spread far and wide, reaching the lowest levels of the city population and the peasant huts. A prominent part in this movement was played by the Zemstvos and city organizations introduced by the reforms of Alexander II. . . .

Over two-thirds of the expenditures of the Zemstvos were for public health and education. The Zemstvo department of Public Health in 1914 expended 82,000,000 rubles. The rural population, prior to 1864 when the Zemstvos were introduced, was almost wholly lacking in medical care. Fifty years later, at the eve of the First World War, the Zemstvos had covered the rural territories with hospitals and dispensaries. The average radius of the medical districts was ten miles. . . .

The expenditure of the Zemstvos on public education in 1914 was 106,000,000 rubles. Most of these sums were expended upon primary schools. In 1914 there were fifty thousand Zemstvo schools with eighty thousand teachers and three million school children. The Zemstvos paid particular attention to the construction of new schools corresponding to modern pedagogical ideas and hygienic requirements. Besides primary education, the Zemstvos also organized their own system of secondary education for the training of teachers and organized courses for the improvement of teaching methods. The Zemstvos likewise organized extension courses and built libraries. In 1914 there were 12,627 rural public libraries in thirty-five of the forty-three Zemstvo governments.

III

THE THEORY

THE THRESHOLD

"To you who desire to cross this threshold, do you know what awaits you here?"

"I know," replied the girl.

"Cold, hunger, abhorrence, derision, contempt, abuse, prison, disease, and death!"

"I know, I am ready. I shall endure all suffering, all blows."

"Not from enemies alone, but also from relatives, from friends."

"Yes, even from them."

"Very well. You are ready for the sacrifice. You shall perish, and nobody will ever know whose memory to honor."

"I need neither gratitude nor compassion. I need no home."

"Are you ready even to commit a crime?"

The girl lowered her head.

"I am ready for crime, too—"

The voice lingered for some time before resuming its questions.

"Do you know," it said at length, "that you may be disillusioned in that which you believe at present, that you may discover that you were mistaken, and that you ruined your young life in vain?"

"I know this, too."

"Enter!"

The girl crossed the threshold, and the heavy curtain fell behind her.

"Fool!" said someone, gnashing his teeth.

"Saint!" someone uttered in reply.

IVAN TURGENEV

Chapter 3

THE ROLE OF THEORY

What is the relation of Marxist theory to Soviet practice? Historic connection apart, has Marxist theory profoundly influenced the policies of the Soviet leaders? There is a school of thought, typified by W. W. Rostow's position in The Dynamics of Soviet Society, *which maintains that Soviet policies and practices have been primarily and essentially a consequence of a singleminded effort by Soviet leaders to maintain their own absolute internal power over Russian society and extend their power vis-à-vis the external world. In this view, "what is left of Marxism is what has been found useful . . . to support the maintenance and enlargement of power by the regime at home and abroad."*

Other Western scholars, while recognizing that Marxist theory, in vital respects, has been subordinated, attenuated, or abandoned in the crucible of Soviet practice, have attributed significant influence to the continuity of theory and its impact on policy. Isaac Deutscher, for example, in his Russia After Stalin, *defines the content of the Stalin era as a "mutual interpenetration of modern technology and* Marxist socialism *with Russian barbarism." (Editor's emphasis.) He argues that before the Soviet regime could embrace certain policies, it "would first have to ban the works of Marx, Engels, and Lenin, that is to say to destroy its own birth certificate and ideological title deeds." And, as R. N. Carew Hunt tells us, the Soviet leaders "have been nurtured" in the Marxist creed since birth, "and it would be strange indeed if they have remained unaffected." It is of some significance, too, that Julian Towster, in the opening words of his* Political Power in the U.S.S.R., *finds it possible to assert: "So great is the stress placed upon the interrelation of theory and practice in the Soviet state that an understanding of its operative constitutional order would lack coherence without due attention to avowed theory."*

But, whatever the merit of either position, Marxist theory is so deeply embedded in the ethos of Soviet society that even attenuation requires obeisance. It has, as Edward Hallett Carr in his Soviet Impact on the West *makes clear, "the status of a creed which purports to inspire every act of*

47

state power and by which every such act can be tested and judged." More-over, it has had "a remarkable capacity to inspire loyalty and self-sacrifice in its adherents; and this success is beyond doubt due in part to its bold claim . . . to be the source of principles binding for every form of human activity including the activity of the state." (On the role of ideology in Soviet society today, see particularly the chapter titled "The Governors and the Governed.") Certainly, theory played a vital role in the making of the Bolshevik and other Communist revolutions and continues to play a part in Communist-led revolutionary movements throughout the world.

In the circumstances, a pertinent and continuing inquiry with which the reader should be concerned throughout is: "What is the relation of Marxist theory to Soviet practice?"

THE PRIORITY OF POWER

W. W. Rostow*

A converging series of influences made Lenin and the hard core of the Bolshevik Party he dominated choose that course which would increase their own direct short-run power, as opposed to any other possible goal open to them, at moments of decision. The means to power early became, in fact, an end in themselves—a result implicit in Lenin's conception and organization of the Bolshevik Party and fully evident in the policy of the Soviet regime by 1921. This fundamental transition appears to have sub-stantial roots in the philosophic bases of Marxism, in Russian history, and in the personalities of the men who dominated the Bolshevik group initially and who subsequently proved best capable of surviving in power.

The concept of the priority of power, which is used throughout the following essay, is a shorthand phrase for a complex phenomenon. It ap-pears important that this conception be distinguished from the notion that, psychologically, the rulers of the Soviet state are motivated, in a personal sense, simply by the desire for power. Indeed, there is an evident enjoy-ment of power present in the lives of Lenin, Stalin, and the others who made the Russian Revolution of November 1917; and they certainly belong with those many figures of history who found it easy to believe that, if power remained concentrated in their hands, larger beneficent purposes would be served. More than that, one of the dynamic, self-reinforcing processes to be discerned in this story is the progressive selection of men

* State Department counsellor and Policy Planning Council chairman. Author of *The Stages of Economic Growth; The Prospects for Communist China;* and *An American Policy in Asia.* This selection is reprinted from pp. 7-11 of *The Dynamics of Soviet Society* by W. W. Rostow. By permission of W. W. Norton & Company, Inc., Copyright 1952, 1953, by Massachusetts Institute of Technology.

who had a respect for power, knew how to use it, and were prepared to take risks in order to achieve it. And there is an equally consistent process of elimination of those unwilling to resolve their conflicts between idealism and their own power position, or less able in the pursuit of the latter. The love of personal power is a legitimate element in the analysis; but we do not attempt to pierce behind it to the deeper psychological roots of the behavior of the chief Bolsheviks; and, more important, this element in the analysis is not taken to be the sole root for the priority of power that has consistently dominated the behavior of the Russian Communists. This essay is not simply a Newtonian elaboration on the theme of personal power maximization.

The priority of power is based, in the first instance, on a combination of Marx's view that there was a determinable form which future history would take and Lenin's conception of the Communist Party as a chosen instrument for the achievement of Marx's prognosis. The Party thus acquired in its own eyes both legitimacy of status and the moral right to force the "correct" historical path—against the will of the majority and against the will, even, of the industrial working men who were designed to be the primary beneficiaries of the whole revolutionary development. In prerevolutionary Russia this essentially conspiratorial conception attracted emotional support due to the frustration of economic, social, and political reform by the tsarist state which led many reformers to concentrate their energy on the task of overthrowing by violence that autocratic regime. The overthrow of a regime by force is, essentially, a problem in the strategy and tactics of power. Further, since the "correct" line is always arguable, in its Russian context this conception had the consequence of moving the Communist Party itself toward a dictatorial form of rule, in which, in the end, one man's judgment would determine the line; and, in the anarchic state of revolutionary and postrevolutionary Russia, the right to lay down the "correct" line was likely to rest with him who knew best how to conduct a struggle for power. The bases for the priority of power lie, then, in converging aspects of the history of Russia and Communism, as well as in the personal characteristics of Soviet leaders. It is inseparably bound up with one aspect of Communist ideology, and gathered its initial emotional force from that fact. The reader should constantly bear in mind that this essay is not based on a simple opposition of ideology and a lust for power. Both conceptions are much more complex than common usage would credit; and, in the Soviet case, they partially converged.

Communist ideology also included, however, a fairly explicit set of economic, social, and political goals, incorporated in the aspirations and programs of various revolutionary groups. Some of these specific goals converged with the effective pursuit of power—for example, the nationalization of industry. Some of them conflicted—for example, the placing of political authority directly in the hands of trade unions and the Soviets, those

Bolshevik-dominated organizations of workers and soldiers on whom the November Revolution was built. The inner core of consistency in the story of the Russian Communists is the priority they were prepared to give to the maintenance and expansion of their own power over other lines of policy, including their willingness to go to any lengths judged to be required to organize and control the Russian peoples in an effort to secure their own continued ascendancy as a regime. In the end, the society they have organized represents a projection out onto an entire state and its peoples of the form and concepts of organization created largely by Lenin for the operation of the Communist Party itself.

Despite the impressive continuity of the priority of power the manner in which it has been exercised has, of course, changed. Lenin, in the immediate postrevolutionary days, may be seen groping among the conflicting leads offered to him by the complex and contradictory heritage of Russian Marxism. There are, in his performance as a political leader, certain unresolved contradictions which, for some historians, justify for Lenin a higher moral status than for Stalin; for example, the relative freedom in which he left Soviet intellectual and cultural life, his unwillingness to use the death penalty against fellow Communists, the bonhomie with which he led the Communist Party (except when seriously challenged), and the relative freedom within the Communist Party for open controversy in his day. There are some real differences between the rule of Lenin and that of Stalin which are of historical interest. On balance, however, in the key decisions he made, the priority of power over other goals, including goals professed by Russian Communists, is evident in Lenin.

Stalin, in this context, appears less hampered than Lenin by the problem of overriding those elements in the Communist heritage which conflicted with the priority of power. His performance has a massive consistency, both in the extensive changes he brought about in the decade after 1928 and in the subsequent stability of the policies and institutions he elaborated. Increasingly, in the years before Stalin's death, one sensed that the Soviet regime was operating less from a conscious and fresh set of decisions, in which alternative possibilities were examined in the light of relatively fixed principles (including the priority of power among them), than from habits and procedures built into heavy inflexible bureaucratic structures. The historical roots of the priority of power and the living experiences which brought it to life seemed far distant from the Soviet Union, enshrined, at best, in such ritualistic documents as the *Short History of the Communist Party of the Soviet Union* and in the youthful memories of the middle-aged and elderly men who now rule Russia. Like almost all else in the Soviet Union, the priority of power as the dominant test for policy appears to have been bureaucratized.

The interaction of the pursuit of power, thus defined, with the problems and resistances it met resulted in decisions which had, in turn, their

consequences; and these consequences created new situations (often in the form of increased resistance) which required further decision. It is essential to this argument that the secondary consequences of given decisions did not lie fully within the control of the Soviet regime and were not, in all cases, either fully predictable or compatible with its primary purposes. The successive application of the priority of power thus yielded an unfolding sequence of decisions which shaped modern Soviet society and, in particular, shaped the institutional form it has assumed since the late 1930's. To understand the present position of that society and the alternatives for it which the future may hold, it is, therefore, necessary to look back to the process by which it has arrived at its present position.

One might have expected that the study of the first professedly Marxist regime in history would constitute an exercise in the analysis of the relations between the economy on the one hand and the social, political, and cultural superstructure on the other. On the contrary, the philosophical implication of the priority of power has been that Hegel, having been allegedly turned on his head by Marx, is set right side up again by Lenin and Stalin. We are examining a peculiarly persistent and single-minded effort to use the maximum powers of a modern state to produce throughout the society it controls the economic, social, political, and cultural changes believed desirable for the maintenance and expansion of power by a small co-optive group. The de facto ideology of the Soviet Union would now more nearly identify the Great Leader and the State as the prime movers of history than the play of economic forces or even the interplay of economic, social, political, and cultural forces. The dilution of executive authority since Stalin's death is unlikely to alter this conception, unless much more drastic changes occur within the Soviet Union. But if our view of the history of society as a fully interacting process is correct, the actual course of the society is not to be determined or understood solely in terms of its political process, even when power is wielded absolutely with the full mechanisms available to a modern state. And, in fact, the evolution of Soviet society consists in large part of a sequence of interactions between the aims of Soviet rulers and the limitations imposed on them not only by Russia's geographical position and natural resources, but also by the stage of Russian history and economic development at which they came to power and by profound cultural forces in Russian society which are capable of only slow change.

Put more precisely, the forms which the efficient pursuit of power has taken have been more heavily determined by certain abiding or slow-changing aspects of the Russian scene than by the ideological or other pre-suppositions which the Soviet rulers brought to their self-designated mission. Those who seek to consolidate and enlarge their power wish their people to work hard and efficiently on the tasks they set. If men are to execute assigned tasks, their motivating interests must be taken into account,

as well as the accretion within them of a long cultural heritage. In fact, men appear to be governed less in their actions by a conscious, rational calculus among alternatives than by habits, customs, and attitudes deeply ingrained in their heritage and personal experience, and tenaciously held. The existence of these forces embedded in cultures does not eliminate the need for men to exercise choice among alternatives; but it limits the range over which those choices are likely to be found acceptable. Lenin said of the Russian peasant: ". . . he is as he is, and will not become different in the near future . . . the transformation of the peasant's psychology and habits is something that requires generations." Although the motivations and cultural outlook of men are certainly subject to change over time, the ruler who wishes prompt as well as efficient performance must take men as he finds them. This, essentially, the Soviet regime has done. Despite varying efforts to shape more profoundly the human beings within Soviet society to its purposes, the regime has generally sought efficiency and conformity from the Russian peoples as it found them and as they have evolved in the past thirty-five years under influences longer lived and more complex than the policy of the Soviet state alone. The consequence of the regime's pragmatic decision, over the years, has helped give a distinct and persistent Russian character to the forms of Communist dictatorship; but it is an important conclusion of this analysis . . . that the Russian mannerisms of the Soviet regime do not imply an identification of the regime's interests with those of the Russian peoples or the Russian nation.

We are thus convinced that the story of Soviet Russia is not only a lesson in the awful potential of totalitarian rule in the context of modern societies; it is also a lesson in the limitations of even the maximum exercise of political power in the face of the nature of cultures and ultimately the resistance, often passive, of men.

THE IMPORTANCE OF DOCTRINE

R. N. Carew Hunt*

MYTHS AND THE MASSES

Virtually all analysts would agree that in the years of struggle before the October Revolution the Bolsheviks took the theory which lay behind their movement in deadly earnest; there is also general agreement that in the 1920's the doctrine acted as a stimulus to the workers, who took pride

* Formerly at St. Antony's College, Oxford University. Author of *The Theory and Practice of Communism; Marxism Past and Present;* and *A Guide to Communist Jargon.* The selection is from *Problems of Communism,* Vol. 7 (March-April 1958), pp. 11-15. By permission.

in building up their country. In the 1930's, however, the situation changed. Stalin assumed absolute power. The machinery of the state and of the secret police was greatly strengthened, and all prospect of establishing a genuine classless society disappeared. With the Stalin-Hitler Pact, if not before, the Soviet Union entered an era which can plausibly be represented as one of naked power politics, perpetuated after World War II in the aggressive and obstructive policies pursued by the regime. Hence it is sometimes argued that Communist ideology has now ceased to possess any importance; that it is simply a top-dressing of sophistries designed to rationalize measures inspired solely by Soviet interests; and that apart from a few fanatics, such as may be found in any society, no one believes in the doctrine any longer, least of all the leaders themselves.

Yet such unqualified assertions are erroneous. Consider, first, the outlook of the ordinary Soviet citizen *vis-à-vis* the ideology. Day in, day out, he is subjected to intensive and skillfully devised propaganda through every known medium, designed to demonstrate that the ideology on which the Soviet Union is based makes it the best of all possible worlds, and that on this account it is encircled with jealous enemies bent on its destruction. The Soviet leadership has always considered it essential that every citizen possess as deep an understanding of Communist principles as his mind is capable of assimilating, and those holding positions of consequence are obliged recurrently to pass through carefully graded schools of political instruction.

It is significant that whenever the leaders feel themselves in a tight corner—as in the recent aftermath of destalinization and the intervention in Hungary—their invariable reaction is to intensify indoctrination in an attempt to refocus public attention on "first principles." As hard-headed men they would certainly not attach such importance to indoctrination if they did not know that it paid dividends—and experience has proved that the persistent repetition of a body of ideas which are never challenged is bound to influence the minds of their recipients. Of course, the present generation does not react to the formal ideology with the same fervor as did its forebears who made the revolution, and there are doubtless those who view official apologetics with a large degree of cynicism. But between total commitment and total disillusionment there are many intermediate positions; it is quite possible for a man to regard much of what he is told as nonsense while still believing that there is something of value behind it, especially if he identifies that "something" with the greatness of his country as "the first socialist state" and believes in its historic mission.

LEADERSHIP CREDENCE—A HOPE OR A HABIT?

More significant, in the present context, than the attitude of the ordinary citizen is that of the ruling elite which is responsible for policy.

What its top-ranking members believe is a question which no one, of course, can answer positively. But before surmising, as do some analysts, that the Soviet leadership cannot possibly believe in the myths it propounds, we should remind ourselves that no class or party ever finds it difficult to persuade itself of the soundness of the principles on which it bases its claim to rule.

The Soviet leaders are fortified in this conviction by the very nature of their creed. They have been nurtured in it from birth, and it would be strange indeed if they had remained unaffected. It has become second nature to these men to regard history as a dialectical process—one of incessant conflict between progressive and reactionary forces which can only be resolved by the victory of the former. The division of the world into antagonistic camps, which is an article of faith, is simply the projection onto the international stage of the struggle within capitalistic society between the bourgeoisie, which history has condemned, and the proletariat, whose ultimate triumph it has decreed. The leaders seem to be confident that history is on their side, that all roads lead to communism, and that the contradictions of capitalism must create the type of situation which they can turn to their advantage.

Democratic governments desirous of recommending a certain policy normally dwell upon its practical advantages. But in the Soviet Union this is not so. Any important change of line will be heralded by an article in *Pravda,* often of many columns, purporting to show that the new policy is ideologically correct because it accords with some recent decision of a party congress, or with Lenin's teaching, or with whatever other criterion may be adopted. How far the policy in question will have been inspired by considerations of ideology as opposed to others of a more mundane nature can never be precisely determined. This, however, is not an exclusive feature of the Communist system; in politics, as for that matter in personal relations, it is seldom possible to disentangle all the motives which determine conduct. The policies of any party or government are likely to reflect its political principles even if they are so framed as to strengthen its position, and there is no reason why the policies adopted by the Soviet leaders should constitute an exception.

Analysts of the "power politics" school of thought hold that the Kremlin leaders are concerned solely with Soviet national interest, and merely use the Communist movement to promote it. Yet here again the difficulty is to disengage factors which are closely associated. The future of the Communist movement cannot be disassociated from the fortunes of the Soviet Union. If the Soviet regime were to collapse, that movement would count for little, and whether it would long survive even in China is doubtful. Recognizing this, non-Russian Communist parties generally have remained subservient to Moscow even when threatened with large-scale defections of rank-and-file members in the face of particularly odious shifts in the Moscow line. . . .

INEFFICIENCY—AN INDEX OF IDEOLOGY

Indeed, . . . the attitude of the Soviet leaders *must* be attributed, at least in part, to the theoretical principles which distinguish Communist regimes from other forms of dictatorship. Certainly the leaders shape and phrase their domestic and foreign policies to fit the general framework established by these principles, and the latter often do not allow much room for maneuver. In fact, their application may sometimes weaken rather than strengthen the country.

To take a simple example, much waste would be avoided if small traders were permitted to operate on a profit basis; the fishmonger, for instance, would have an incentive to put his fish on ice, which he frequently fails to do to the discomfort of the public. Allowance of profits, however, would constitute a return to private enterprise, which cannot be tolerated.

Similarly, in the Communist view it has long been regarded as indefensible to subordinate a higher to a lower form of socialized enterprise. Thus, while it has been apparent for years that Soviet agriculture would be more efficient if the Machine Tractor Stations were handed over to the collective farms, the issue has been consistently dodged, because the MTS are fully state-owned organs and therefore "higher" than the farms, which still belong in part to the peasants. When the economist Venzher advocated this measure some years ago, he was slapped down at once by Stalin, the fact that it had already been adopted in Yugoslavia only making his suggestion the more objectionable. Just two years ago Khrushchev launched an extensive program to strengthen the organization and power of the MTS. Very recently, however, he indicated that the regime was—at long last—prepared to yield to practical necessity on this point; in a speech on farm policy, he advocated the transfer of farm machinery to the collectives, and although his proposals are not yet legalized, it would appear that a number of MTS have already been dissolved.*

The principle of hierarchy has not been repudiated, however, and still governs other aspects of agricultural organization—for example, the relative status of the two forms of agricultural enterprise. From the standpoint of productive efficiency the collective farms are bad, but the state farms are worse. Nonetheless, the latter represent a "higher type" of organization, and thus the present virgin lands campaign has been based upon them.

* Editor's note: The plan was legalized and put into operation in April 1958.

DOGMATISM IN FOREIGN POLICY

. . . The argument can be carried further. By its behavior throughout its history, the Soviet Union has incurred the hostility, or at least the suspicion, of the entire free world. Yet there was no practical reason why it should have done so. After the October Revolution the Bolshevik regime was faced with appalling domestic problems, and it had nothing to gain by courting the animosity of the West. The Soviet leaders might well have built up their country in accordance with the principles to which they were committed without exciting such widespread hostility. What governments do at home is commonly regarded as their own affair. Fundamentally, the regime in Yugoslavia is as Communist as that of the Soviet Union, and was established with an equal ruthlessness. But Tito, having asserted his independence from Moscow, has muffled his attacks on the West, and in turn the Western governments have demonstrated their desire—albeit tempered with caution—to believe in his good faith.

What no country will tolerate is the attempt, deliberately engineered by a foreign power, to overthrow its form of government; this has been the persistent aim and effort of the Soviet regime in defiance of its express diplomatic guarantees of non-interference. It is hard to see how this strategy has assisted the development of Soviet Russia, and that it has never been abandoned cannot be dissociated from those messianic and catastrophic elements in the Communistic creed which influence, perhaps impel, the Soviet drive for world power.

In conclusion, it is frequently stated that communism has created an ideological cleavage between the West and the Soviet bloc. Yet this statement would be meaningless if the issue today were, as some believe, simply one of power politics. An ideology is significant only if it makes those who profess it act in a way they would not otherwise do. The fact that large numbers of persons accept communism would not constitute a danger if it did not lead them to support policies which threaten the existence of those who do not accept it. It is true that many people, especially in backward countries, call themselves Communists without having any clear idea of what it means. Yet the movement would not be the force it has become were there not in every country men and women who sincerely believe in the ideas behind it, which form collectively what we call its ideology.

To represent this ideology as a species of opium with which the Soviet leaders contrive to lull the people while taking care never to indulge in it themselves is to attribute to them an ability to dissociate themselves from the logic of their system—an ability which it is unlikely they possess. For the concepts which make up that system, fantastic as many of them appear to be, will be found on examination to be interrelated, and to be logical extensions of the basic principles to which all Communists subscribe.

To turn it the other way around, Communists claim a theoretical justification for the basic principles in which they believe. But these principles must be translated into appropriate action; and action, if directed by the rulers of a powerful country like the Soviet Union, will take the form of *Realpolitik*. There is no yardstick which permits a measure of the exact relationship between power politics and ideology in the policies which result; but surely neither factor can be ignored.

Chapter 4

MARXISM

Apart from the relevance of Marxist theory to Soviet practice there is, of course, the question of the soundness and acuteness of its analyses and prophecies.

Extreme claims have been made for the validity of Marx's theories. Marx himself stated in 1852:

I cannot claim to have discovered the existence of classes in modern society or their strife against one another. Petty bourgeois historians long ago described the evolution of class struggles, and political economists showed the economic physiology of the classes. I have added as a new contribution the following propositions: 1. That the existence of classes is bound up with certain phases of material production; 2. That the class struggle leads necessarily to the dictatorship of the proletariat; 3. That this dictatorship is but the transition to the abolition of all classes and to the creation of a society of the free and equal.

Marx's co-worker, Engels, insisted that "With the same certainty with which from a given mathematical proposition a new one is deduced, with that same certainty can we deduce the social revolution from the existing social conditions and the principles of political economy."

These broad claims and prophecies are carried to absurd (and probably un-Marxist) lengths in the official (Short) History of the Communist Party of the Soviet Union, *edited by a commission of its Central Committee, in which it is affirmed that mastery of Marxist theory "enables the Party to find the right orientation to any situation" and "to understand the inner connection of current events." Equally fatuous is* Pravda's *assertion that "The Party's decisions, like its entire policy, have always been based upon knowledge of the objective laws of social development, with sober account of all forces, both international and domestic."*

Many modern scholars, although rejecting much of Marx's theory, have nevertheless recognized him as one of the great seminal thinkers in the history of man who greatly enriched our understanding of society and improved our research methodology. Serious students of philosophy, history, economics, and politics, therefore, will examine Marxist theory with a view to its insights and contributions as well as its defects.

MANIFESTO OF THE COMMUNIST PARTY [1]

KARL MARX AND FRIEDRICH ENGELS

In 1847, Marx and Engels were requested to prepare a theoretical and practical party program for the Communist League, a workingmen's association. The Manifesto *was completed in 1848 on the eve of the French Revolution of that year. Written when Marx was 30 and Engels only 28 years of age, the* Manifesto *contains in developed or undeveloped form the fundamentals of Marxist theory. Professor Sidney Hook has called it "undoubtedly the most influential political pamphlet of all time." "What is truly astonishing," he added, "is the extent to which the* Manifesto, *after a century, reads like a contemporary document."*

From the PREFACE by Friedrich Engels (1888):

The Manifesto being our joint production, I consider myself bound to state that the fundamental proposition, which forms its nucleus, belongs to Marx. That proposition is: That in every historical epoch, the prevailing mode of economic production and exchange, and the social organisation necessarily following from it, form the basis upon which is built up, and from which alone can be explained, the political and intellectual history of that epoch; that consequently the whole history of mankind (since the dissolution of primitive tribal society, holding land in common ownership) has been a history of class struggles, contests between exploiting and exploited, ruling and oppressed classes; that the history of these class struggles forms a series of evolutions in which, nowadays, a stage has been reached where the exploited and oppressed class—the proletariat—cannot attain its emancipation from the sway of the exploiting and ruling class—the bourgeoisie —without, at the same time, and once and for all, emancipating society at large from all exploitation, oppression, class distinctions and class struggles. . . .

A spectre is haunting Europe—the spectre of Communism. All the powers of old Europe have entered into a holy alliance to exorcise this spectre: Pope and Czar, Metternich and Guizot, French Radicals and German police-spies.

Where is the party in opposition that has not been decried as communistic by its opponents in power? Where the Opposition that has not hurled back the branding reproach of Communism, against the more advanced opposition parties, as well as against its reactionary adversaries?

Two things result from this fact:

[1] The included footnotes were added by Engels in 1888.

I. Communism is already acknowledged by all European powers to be itself a power.

II. It is high time that Communists should openly, in the face of the whole world, publish their views, their aims, their tendencies, and meet this nursery tale of the spectre of Communism with a manifesto of the party itself. . . .

I. BOURGEOIS AND PROLETARIANS [2]

The history of all hitherto existing society[3] is the history of class struggles.

Freeman and slave, patrician and plebeian, lord and serf, guildmaster and journeyman, in a word, oppressor and oppressed, stood in constant opposition to one another, carried on an uninterrupted, now hidden, now open fight, a fight that each time ended, either in a revolutionary reconstitution of society at large, or in the common ruin of the contending classes.

In the earlier epochs of history, we find almost everywhere a complicated arrangement of society into various orders, a manifold gradation of social rank. In ancient Rome we have patricians, knights, plebeians, slaves; in the Middle Ages, feudal lords, vassals, guild-masters, journeymen, apprentices, serfs; in almost all of these classes, again, subordinate gradations.

The modern bourgeois society that has sprouted from the ruins of feudal society, has not done away with class antagonisms. It has but established new classes, new conditions of oppression, new forms of struggle in place of the old ones.

Our epoch, the epoch of the bourgeoisie, possesses, however, this distinctive feature: It has simplified the class antagonisms. Society as a whole is more and more splitting up into two great hostile camps, into two great classes directly facing each other—bourgeoisie and proletariat.

From the serfs of the Middle Ages sprang the chartered burghers of the earliest towns. From these burgesses the first elements of the bourgeoisie were developed.

---

[2] By bourgeoisie is meant the class of modern capitalists, owners of the means of social production and employers of wage-labour; by proletariat, the class of modern wage-labourers who, having no means of production of their own, are reduced to selling their labour power in order to live.

[3] That is, all *written* history. In 1847, the pre-history of society, the social organisation existing previous to recorded history, was all but unknown. Since then Haxthausen discovered common ownership of land in Russia, Maurer proved it to be the social foundation from which all Teutonic races started in history, and, by and by, village communities were found to be, or to have been, the primitive form of society everywhere from India to Ireland. The inner organisation of this primitive communistic society was laid bare, in its typical form, by Morgan's crowning discovery of the true nature of the *gens* and its relation to the *tribe*. With the dissolution of these primæval communities, society begins to be differentiated into separate and finally antagonistic classes. I have attempted to retrace this process of dissolution in *The Origin of the Family, Private Property and the State*.

The discovery of America, the rounding of the Cape, opened up fresh ground for the rising bourgeoisie. The East-Indian and Chinese markets, the colonisation of America, trade with the colonies, the increase in the means of exchange and in commodities generally, gave to commerce, to navigation, to industry, an impulse never before known, and thereby, to the revolutionary element in the tottering feudal society, a rapid development.

The feudal system of industry, in which industrial production was monopolised by closed guilds, now no longer sufficed for the growing wants of the new markets. The manufacturing system took its place. The guild-masters were pushed aside by the manufacturing middle class; division of labour between the different corporate guilds vanished in the face of division of labour in each single workshop.

Meantime the markets kept ever growing, the demand ever rising. Even manufacture no longer sufficed. Thereupon, steam and machinery revolutionised industrial production. The place of manufacture was taken by the giant, modern industry, the place of the industrial middle class, by industrial millionaires—the leaders of whole industrial armies, the modern bourgeois.

Modern industry has established the world market, for which the discovery of America paved the way. This market has given an immense development to commerce, to navigation, to communication by land. This development has, in its turn, reacted on the extension of industry; and in proportion as industry, commerce, navigation, railways extended, in the same proportion the bourgeoisie developed, increased its capital, and pushed into the background every class handed down from the Middle Ages.

We see, therefore, how the modern bourgeoisie is itself the product of a long course of development, of a series of revolutions in the modes of production and of exchange.

Each step in the development of the bourgeoisie was accompanied by a corresponding political advance of that class. An oppressed class under the sway of the feudal nobility, it became an armed and self-governing association in the mediæval commune; here independent urban republic (as in Italy and Germany), there taxable "third estate" of the monarchy (as in France); afterwards, in the period of manufacture proper, serving either the semi-feudal or the absolute monarchy as a counterpoise against the nobility, and, in fact, corner-stone of the great monarchies in general—the bourgeoisie has at last, since the establishment of modern industry and of the world market, conquered for itself, in the modern representative state, exclusive political sway. The executive of the modern state is but a committee for managing the common affairs of the whole bourgeoisie.

The bourgeoisie has played a most revolutionary rôle in history.

The bourgeoisie, wherever it has got the upper hand, has put an end to all feudal, patriarchal, idyllic relations. It has pitilessly torn asunder the motley feudal ties that bound man to his "natural superiors," and has left no other bond between man and man than naked self-interest, than callous "cash payment." It has drowned the most heavenly ecstasies of religious fervour, of chivalrous enthusiasm, of philistine sentimentalism, in the icy water of egotistical calculation. It has resolved personal worth into exchange value, and in place of the numberless indefeasible chartered freedoms, has set up that single, unconscionable freedom—Free Trade. In one word, for exploitation, veiled by religious and political illusions, it has substituted naked, shameless, direct, brutal exploitation.

The bourgeoisie has stripped of its halo every occupation hitherto honoured and looked up to with reverent awe. It has converted the physician, the lawyer, the priest, the poet, the man of science, into its paid wagelabourers.

The bourgeoisie has torn away from the family its sentimental veil, and has reduced the family relation to a mere money relation.

The bourgeoisie has disclosed how it came to pass that the brutal display of vigour in the Middle Ages, which reactionaries so much admire, found its fitting complement in the most slothful indolence. It has been the first to show what man's activity can bring about. It has accomplished wonders far surpassing Egyptian pyramids, Roman aqueducts, and Gothic cathedrals; it has conducted expeditions that put in the shade all former migrations of nations and crusades.

The bourgeoisie cannot exist without constantly revolutionising the instruments of production, and thereby the relations of production, and with them the whole relations of society. Conservation of the old modes of production in unaltered form, was, on the contrary, the first condition of existence for all earlier industrial classes. Constant revolutionising of production, uninterrupted disturbance of all social conditions, everlasting uncertainty and agitation distinguish the bourgeois epoch from all earlier ones. All fixed, fast-frozen relations, with their train of ancient and venerable prejudices and opinions, are swept away, all new-formed ones become antiquated before they can ossify. All that is solid melts into air, all that is holy is profaned, and man is at last compelled to face with sober senses his real conditions of life and his relations with his kind.

The need of a constantly expanding market for its products chases the bourgeoisie over the whole surface of the globe. It must nestle everywhere, settle everywhere, establish connections everywhere.

The bourgeoisie has through its exploitation of the world market given a cosmopolitan character to production and consumption in every country. To the great chagrin of reactionaries, it has drawn from under the feet of industry the national ground on which it stood. All old-established national industries have been destroyed or are daily being destroyed. They are dislodged by new industries, whose introduction becomes a life and death question for all civilised nations, by industries that no longer work up indigenous raw material, but raw material drawn from the remotest zones; industries whose products are consumed, not only at home, but in every quarter of the globe. In place of the old wants, satisfied by the production of the country, we find new wants, requiring for their satisfaction the products of distant lands and climes. In place of the old local and national seclusion and self-sufficiency, we have intercourse in every direction, universal interdependence of nations. And as in material, so also in intellectual production. The intellectual creations of individual nations become common property. National one-sidedness and narrow-mindedness become more and more impossible, and from the numerous national and local literatures there arises a world literature.

The bourgeoisie, by the rapid improvement of all instruments of production, by the immensely facilitated means of communication, draws all nations, even the most barbarian, into civilisation. The cheap prices of its commodities are the heavy artillery with which it batters down all Chinese walls, with which it forces the barbarians' intensely obstinate hatred of foreigners to capitulate. It compels all nations, on pain of extinction, to adopt the bourgeois mode of production; it compels them to introduce what it calls civilisation into their midst, *i.e.*, to become bourgeois themselves. In a word, it creates a world after its own image.

The bourgeoisie has subjected the country to the rule of the towns. It has created enormous cities, has greatly increased the urban population as compared with the rural, and has thus rescued a considerable part of the population from the idiocy of rural life. Just as it has made the country dependent on the towns, so it has made barbarian and semi-barbarian countries dependent on the civilised ones, nations of peasants on nations of bourgeois, the East on the West.

More and more the bourgeoisie keeps doing away with the scattered state of the population, of the means of production, and of property. It has agglomerated population, centralised means of production, and has concentrated property in a few hands. The necessary consequence of this was political centralisation. Independent, or but loosely connected provinces, with separate interests, laws, governments and systems of taxation, became lumped together into one nation, with one government, one code of laws, one national class interest, one frontier and one customs tariff.

The bourgeoisie, during its rule of scarce one hundred years, has created more massive and more colossal productive forces than have all preceding generations together. Subjection of nature's forces to man, machinery, application of chemistry to industry and agriculture, steam-navigation, railways, electric telegraphs, clearing of whole continents for cultivation, canalisation of rivers, whole populations conjured out of the ground —what earlier century had even a presentiment that such productive forces slumbered in the lap of social labour?

We see then that the means of production and of exchange, which served as the foundation for the growth of the bourgeoisie, were generated

in feudal society. At a certain stage in the development of these means of
production and of exchange, the conditions under which feudal society produced and exchanged, the feudal organisation of agriculture and manufacturing industry, in a word, the feudal relations of property became no
longer compatible with the already developed productive forces; they became so many fetters. They had to be burst asunder; they were burst
asunder.

Into their place stepped free competition, accompanied by a social and
political constitution adapted to it, and by the economic and political sway
of the bourgeois class.

A similar movement is going on before our own eyes. Modern bourgeois society with its relations of production, of exchange and of property,
a society that has conjured up such gigantic means of production and of
exchange, is like the sorcerer who is no longer able to control the powers
of the nether world whom he has called up by his spells. For many a decade
past the history of industry and commerce is but the history of the revolt
of modern productive forces against modern conditions of production,
against the property relations that are the conditions for the existence of
the bourgeoisie and of its rule. It is enough to mention the commercial
crises that by their periodical return put the existence of the entire bourgeois society on trial, each time more threateningly. In these crises a great
part not only of the existing products, but also of the previously created
productive forces, are periodically destroyed. In these crises there breaks
out an epidemic that, in all earlier epochs, would have seemed an absurdity
—the epidemic of over-production. Society suddenly finds itself put back
into a state of momentary barbarism; it appears as if a famine, a universal
war of devastation had cut off the supply of every means of subsistence; industry and commerce seem to be destroyed. And why? Because there is too
much civilisation, too much means of subsistence, too much industry, too
much commerce. The productive forces at the disposal of society no longer
tend to further the development of the conditions of bourgeois property;
on the contrary, they have become too powerful for these conditions, by
which they are fettered, and no sooner do they overcome these fetters than
they bring disorder into the whole of bourgeois society, endanger the existence of bourgeois property. The conditions of bourgeois society are too
narrow to comprise the wealth created by them. And how does the bourgeoisie get over these crises? On the one hand by enforced destruction of a
mass of productive forces; on the other, by the conquest of new markets,
and by the more thorough exploitation of the old ones. That is to say, by
paving the way for more extensive and more destructive crises, and by diminishing the means whereby crises are prevented.

The weapons with which the bourgeoisie felled feudalism to the ground
are now turned against the bourgeoisie itself.

But not only has the bourgeoisie forged the weapons that bring death to itself; it has also called into existence the men who are to wield those weapons—the modern working class—the proletarians.

In proportion as the bourgeoisie, *i.e.*, capital, is developed, in the same proportion is the proletariat, the modern working class, developed—a class of labourers, who live only so long as they find work, and who find work only so long as their labour increases capital. These labourers, who must sell themselves piecemeal, are a commodity, like every other article of commerce, and are consequently exposed to all the vicissitudes of competition, to all the fluctuations of the market.

Owing to the extensive use of machinery and to division of labour, the work of the proletarians has lost all individual character, and, consequently, all charm for the workman. He becomes an appendage of the machine, and it is only the most simple, most monotonous, and most easily acquired knack, that is required of him. Hence, the cost of production of a work-man is restricted, almost entirely, to the means of subsistence that he re-quires for his maintenance, and for the propagation of his race. But the price of a commodity, and therefore also of labour, is equal to its cost of production. In proportion, therefore, as the repulsiveness of the work in-creases, the wage decreases. Nay more, in proportion as the use of machinery and division of labour increases, in the same proportion the burden of toil also increases, whether by prolongation of the working hours, by increase of the work exacted in a given time, or by increased speed of the machin-ery, etc.

Modern industry has converted the little workshop of the patriarchal master into the great factory of the industrial capitalist. Masses of labour-ers, crowded into the factory, are organised like soldiers. As privates of the industrial army they are placed under the command of a perfect hierarchy of officers and sergeants. Not only are they slaves of the bourgeois class, and of the bourgeois state; they are daily and hourly enslaved by the machine, by the over-looker, and, above all, by the individual bourgeois manufac-turer himself. The more openly this despotism proclaims gain to be its end and aim, the more petty, the more hateful and the more embittering it is.

The less the skill and exertion of strength implied in manual labour, in other words, the more modern industry develops, the more is the labour of men superseded by that of women. Differences of age and sex have no longer any distinctive social validity for the working class. All are instru-ments of labour, more or less expensive to use, according to their age and sex.

No sooner has the labourer received his wages in cash, for the moment escaping exploitation by the manufacturer, than he is set upon by the other portions of the bourgeoisie, the landlord, the shopkeeper, the pawnbroker, etc.

The lower strata of the middle class—the small tradespeople, shop-keepers, and retired tradesmen generally, the handicraftsmen and peasants

—all these sink gradually into the proletariat, partly because their diminu-
tive capital does not suffice for the scale on which modern industry is carried on, and is swamped in the competition with the large capitalists, partly
because their specialised skill is rendered worthless by new methods of production. Thus the proletariat is recruited from all classes of the population.

The proletariat goes through various stages of development. With its
birth begins its struggle with the bourgeoisie. At first the contest is carried
on by individual labourers, then by the work people of a factory, then by
the operatives of one trade, in one locality, against the individual bourgeois
who directly exploits them. They direct their attacks not against the bourgeois conditions of production, but against the instruments of production
themselves; they destroy imported wares that compete with their labour,
they smash machinery to pieces, they set factories ablaze, they seek to restore
by force the vanished status of the workman of the Middle Ages.

At this stage the labourers still form an incoherent mass scattered over
the whole country, and broken up by their mutual competition. If anywhere they unite to form more compact bodies, this is not yet the consequence of their own active union, but of the union of the bourgeoisie,
which class, in order to attain its own political ends, is compelled to set the
whole proletariat in motion, and is moreover still able to do so for a time.
At this stage, therefore, the proletarians do not fight their enemies, but
the enemies of their enemies, the remnants of absolute monarchy, the landowners, the non-industrial bourgeois, the petty bourgeoisie. Thus the whole
historical movement is concentrated in the hands of the bourgeoisie; every
victory so obtained is a victory for the bourgeoisie.

But with the development of industry the proletariat not only increases
in number; it becomes concentrated in greater masses, its strength grows,
and it feels that strength more. The various interests and conditions of life
within the ranks of the proletariat are more and more equalised, in proportion as machinery obliterates all distinctions of labour and nearly everywhere reduces wages to the same low level. The growing competition among
the bourgeois, and the resulting commercial crises, make the wages of the
workers ever more fluctuating. The unceasing improvement of machinery,
ever more rapidly developing, makes their livelihood more and more precarious; the collisions between individual workmen and individual bourgeois take more and more the character of collisions between two classes.
Thereupon the workers begin to form combinations (trade unions) against
the bourgeoisie; they club together in order to keep up the rate of wages;
they found permanent associations in order to make provision beforehand
for these occasional revolts. Here and there the contest breaks out into
riots.

Now and then the workers are victorious, but only for a time. The
real fruit of their battles lies, not in the immediate result, but in the ever
expanding union of the workers. This union is furthered by the improved

means of communication which are created by modern industry, and which place the workers of different localities in contact with one another. It was just this contact that was needed to centralise the numerous local struggles, all of the same character, into one national struggle between classes. But every class struggle is a political struggle. And that union, to attain which the burghers of the Middle Ages, with their miserable highways, required centuries, the modern proletarians, thanks to railways, achieve in a few years.

This organisation of the proletarians into a class, and consequently into a political party, is continually being upset again by the competition between the workers themselves. But it ever rises up again, stronger, firmer, mightier. It compels legislative recognition of particular interests of the workers, by taking advantage of the divisions among the bourgeoisie itself. Thus the ten-hour bill in England was carried.

Altogether, collisions between the classes of the old society further the course of development of the proletariat in many ways. The bourgeoisie finds itself involved in a constant battle. At first with the aristocracy; later on, with those portions of the bourgeoisie itself whose interests have become antagonistic to the progress of industry; at all times with the bourgeoisie of foreign countries. In all these battles it sees itself compelled to appeal to the proletariat, to ask for its help, and thus, to drag it into the political arena. The bourgeoisie itself, therefore, supplies the proletariat with its own elements of political and general education, in other words, it furnishes the proletariat with weapons for fighting the bourgeoisie.

Further, as we have already seen, entire sections of the ruling classes are, by the advance of industry, precipitated into the proletariat, or are at least threatened in their conditions of existence. These also supply the proletariat with fresh elements of enlightenment and progress.

Finally, in times when the class struggle nears the decisive hour, the process of dissolution going on within the ruling class, in fact within the whole range of old society, assumes such a violent, glaring character, that a small section of the ruling class cuts itself adrift, and joins the revolutionary class, the class that holds the future in its hands. Just as, therefore, at an earlier period, a section of the nobility went over to the bourgeoisie, so now a portion of the bourgeoisie goes over to the proletariat, and in particular, a portion of the bourgeois ideologists, who have raised themselves to the level of comprehending theoretically the historical movement as a whole.

Of all the classes that stand face to face with the bourgeoisie today, the proletariat alone is a really revolutionary class. The other classes decay and finally disappear in the face of modern industry; the proletariat is its special and essential product.

The lower middle class, the small manufacturer, the shopkeeper, the artisan, the peasant, all these fight against the bourgeoisie, to save from extinction their existence as fractions of the middle class. They are therefore not revolutionary, but conservative. Nay more, they are reactionary, for they try to roll back the wheel of history. If by chance they are revolutionary, they are so only in view of their impending transfer into the proletariat; they thus defend not their present, but their future interests; they desert their own standpoint to adopt that of the proletariat.

The "dangerous class," the social scum (*Lumpenproletariat*), that passively rotting mass thrown off by the lowest layers of old society, may, here and there, be swept into the movement by a proletarian revolution; its conditions of life, however, prepare it far more for the part of a bribed tool of reactionary intrigue.

The social conditions of the old society no longer exist for the proletariat. The proletarian is without property; his relation to his wife and children has no longer anything in common with bourgeois family relations; modern industrial labour, modern subjection to capital, the same in England as in France, in America as in Germany, has stripped him of every trace of national character. Law, morality, religion, are to him so many bourgeois prejudices, behind which lurk in ambush just as many bourgeois interests.

All the preceding classes that got the upper hand, sought to fortify their already acquired status by subjecting society at large to their conditions of appropriation. The proletarians cannot become masters of the productive forces of society, except by abolishing their own previous mode of appropriation, and thereby also every other previous mode of appropriation. They have nothing of their own to secure and to fortify; their mission is to destroy all previous securities for, and insurances of, individual property.

All previous historical movements were movements of minorities, or in the interest of minorities. The proletarian movement is the self-conscious, independent movement of the immense majority, in the interest of the immense majority. The proletariat, the lowest stratum of our present society, cannot stir, cannot raise itself up, without the whole superincumbent strata of official society being sprung into the air.

Though not in substance, yet in form, the struggle of the proletariat with the bourgeoisie is at first a national struggle. The proletariat of each country must, of course, first of all settle matters with its own bourgeoisie.

In depicting the most general phases of the development of the proletariat, we traced the more or less veiled civil war, raging within existing society, up to the point where that war breaks out into open revolution, and where the violent overthrow of the bourgeoisie lays the foundation for the sway of the proletariat.

Hitherto, every form of society has been based, as we have already seen, on the antagonism of oppressing and oppressed classes. But in order to oppress a class, certain conditions must be assured to it under which it can, at least, continue its slavish existence. The serf, in the period of serfdom, raised himself to membership in the commune, just as the petty bourgeois, under the yoke of feudal absolutism, managed to develop into a bourgeois. The modern labourer, on the contrary, instead of rising with the progress of industry, sinks deeper and deeper below the conditions of existence of his own class. He becomes a pauper, and pauperism develops more rapidly than population and wealth. And here it becomes evident, that the bourgeoisie is unfit any longer to be the ruling class in society, and to impose its conditions of existence upon society as an over-riding law. It is unfit to rule because it is incompetent to assure an existence to its slave within his slavery, because it cannot help letting him sink into such a state, that it has to feed him, instead of being fed by him. Society can no longer live under this bourgeoisie, in other words, its existence is no longer compatible with society.

The essential condition for the existence and sway of the bourgeois class, is the formation and augmentation of capital; the condition for capital is wage-labour. Wage-labour rests exclusively on competition between the labourers. The advance of industry, whose involuntary promoter is the bourgeoisie, replaces the isolation of the labourers, due to competition, by their revolutionary combination, due to association. The development of modern industry, therefore, cuts from under its feet the very foundation on which the bourgeoisie produces and appropriates products. What the bourgeoisie therefore produces, above all, are its own grave-diggers. Its fall and the victory of the proletariat are equally inevitable.

II. PROLETARIANS AND COMMUNISTS

In what relation do the Communists stand to the proletarians as a whole?

The Communists do not form a separate party opposed to other working class parties.

They have no interests separate and apart from those of the proletariat as a whole.

They do not set up any sectarian principles of their own, by which to shape and mould the proletarian movement.

The Communists are distinguished from the other working class parties by this only: 1. In the national struggles of the proletarians of the different countries, they point out and bring to the front the common interests of the entire proletariat, independently of all nationality. 2. In the various stages of development which the struggle of the working class against the bourgeoisie has to pass through, they always and everywhere represent the interests of the movement as a whole.

The Communists, therefore, are on the one hand, practically, the most advanced and resolute section of the working class parties of every country, that section which pushes forward all others; on the other hand, theoretically, they have over the great mass of the proletariat the advantage of clearly understanding the line of march, the conditions, and the ultimate general results of the proletarian movement.

The immediate aim of the Communists is the same as that of all the other proletarian parties: Formation of the proletariat into a class, overthrow of bourgeois supremacy, conquest of political power by the proletariat.

The theoretical conclusions of the Communists are in no way based on ideas or principles that have been invented, or discovered, by this or that would-be universal reformer.

They merely express, in general terms, actual relations springing from an existing class struggle, from a historical movement going on under our very eyes. . . .

You are horrified at our intending to do away with private property. But in your existing society, private property is already done away with for nine-tenths of the population; its existence for the few is solely due to its non-existence in the hands of those nine-tenths. You reproach us, therefore, with intending to do away with a form of property, the necessary condition for whose existence is the nonexistence of any property for the immense majority of society. . . .

Just as, to the bourgeois, the disappearance of class property is the disappearance of production itself, so the disappearance of class culture is to him identical with the disappearance of all culture.

That culture, the loss of which he laments, is, for the enormous majority, a mere training to act as a machine.

But don't wrangle with us so long as you apply, to our intended abolition of bourgeois property, the standard of your bourgeois notions of freedom, culture, law, etc. Your very ideas are but the outgrowth of the conditions of your bourgeois production and bourgeois property, just as your jurisprudence is but the will of your class made into a law for all, a will whose essential character and direction are determined by the economic conditions of existence of your class. . . .

Abolition of the family! Even the most radical flare up at this infamous proposal of the Communists.

On what foundation is the present family, the bourgeois family, based? On capital, on private gain. In its completely developed form this family exists only among the bourgeoisie. But this state of things finds its complement in the practical absence of the family among the proletarians, and in public prostitution.

The bourgeois family will vanish as a matter of course when its complement vanishes, and both will vanish with the vanishing of capital.

Do you charge us with wanting to stop the exploitation of children by their parents? To this crime we plead guilty.

But, you will say, we destroy the most hallowed of relations, when we replace home education by social.

And your education! Is not that also social, and determined by the social conditions under which you educate, by the intervention of society, direct or indirect, by means of schools, etc.? The Communists have not invented the intervention of society in education; they do but seek to alter the character of that intervention, and to rescue education from the influence of the ruling class.

The bourgeois claptrap about the family and education, about the hallowed co-relation of parent and child, becomes all the more disgusting, the more, by the action of modern industry, all family ties among the proletarians are torn asunder, and their children transformed into simple articles of commerce and instruments of labour.

But you Communists would introduce community of women, screams the whole bourgeoisie in chorus.

The bourgeois sees in his wife a mere instrument of production. He hears that the instruments of production are to be exploited in common, and, naturally, can come to no other conclusion than that the lot of being common to all will likewise fall to the women.

He has not even a suspicion that the real point aimed at is to do away with the status of women as mere instruments of production.

For the rest, nothing is more ridiculous than the virtuous indignation of our bourgeois at the community of women which, they pretend, is to be openly and officially established by the Communists. The Communists have no need to introduce community of women; it has existed almost from time immemorial.

Our bourgeois, not content with having the wives and daughters of their proletarians at their disposal, not to speak of common prostitutes, take the greatest pleasure in seducing each other's wives.

Bourgeois marriage is in reality a system of wives in common and thus, at the most, what the Communists might possibly be reproached with is that they desire to introduce, in substitution for a hypocritically concealed, an openly legalised community of women. For the rest, it is self-evident, that the abolition of the present system of production must bring with it the abolition of the community of women springing from that system, *i.e.*, of prostitution both public and private.

The Communists are further reproached with desiring to abolish countries and nationality.

The working men have no country. We cannot take from them what they have not got. Since the proletariat must first of all acquire political supremacy, must rise to be the leading class of the nation, must constitute itself *the* nation, it is, so far, itself national, though not in the bourgeois sense of the word.

National differences and antagonisms between peoples are vanishing gradually from day to day, owing to the development of the bourgeoisie, to freedom of commerce, to the world market, to uniformity in the mode of production and in the conditions of life corresponding thereto.

The supremacy of the proletariat will cause them to vanish still faster. United action, of the leading civilised countries at least, is one of the first conditions for the emancipation of the proletariat.

In proportion as the exploitation of one individual by another is put an end to, the exploitation of one nation by another will also be put an end to. In proportion as the antagonism between classes within the nation vanishes, the hostility of one nation to another will come to an end.

The charges against Communism made from a religious, a philosophical, and, generally, from an ideological standpoint, are not deserving of serious examination.

Does it require deep intuition to comprehend that man's ideas, views, and conceptions, in one word, man's consciousness, changes with every change in the conditions of his material existence, in his social relations and in his social life?

What else does the history of ideas prove than that intellectual production changes its character in proportion as material production is changed? The ruling ideas of each age have ever been the ideas of its ruling class.

When people speak of ideas that revolutionise society, they do but express the fact that within the old society the elements of a new one have been created, and that the dissolution of the old ideas keeps even pace with the dissolution of the old conditions of existence.

When the ancient world was in its last throes, the ancient religions were overcome by Christianity. When Christian ideas succumbed in the 18th century to rationalist ideas, feudal society fought its death-battle with the then revolutionary bourgeoisie. The ideas of religious liberty and freedom of conscience merely gave expression to the sway of free competition within the domain of knowledge.

"Undoubtedly," it will be said, "religion, moral, philosophical and juridical ideas have been modified in the course of historical development. But religion, morality, philosophy, political science, and law, constantly survived this change."

"There are, besides, eternal truths, such as Freedom, Justice, etc., that are common to all states of society. But Communism abolishes eternal truths, it abolishes all religion, and all morality, instead of constituting them on a new basis; it therefore acts in contradiction to all past historical experience."

What does this accusation reduce itself to? The history of all past society has consisted in the development of class antagonisms, antagonisms that assumed different forms at different epochs.

But whatever form they may have taken, one fact is common to all past ages, *viz.*, the exploitation of one part of society by the other. No wonder, then, that the social consciousness of past ages, despite all the multiplicity and variety it displays, moves within certain common forms, or general ideas, which cannot completely vanish except with the total disappearance of class antagonisms.

The Communist revolution is the most radical rupture with traditional property relations; no wonder that its development involves the most radical rupture with traditional ideas.

But let us have done with the bourgeois objections to Communism.

We have seen above, that the first step in the revolution by the working class is to raise the proletariat to the position of ruling class, to establish democracy.

The proletariat will use its political supremacy to wrest, by degrees, all capital from the bourgeoisie, to centralise all instruments of production in the hands of the state, *i.e.*, of the proletariat organised as the ruling class; and to increase the total of productive forces as rapidly as possible. . . .

When, in the course of development, class distinctions have disappeared, and all production has been concentrated in the hands of a vast association of the whole nation, the public power will lose its political character. Political power, properly so called, is merely the organised power of one class for oppressing another. If the proletariat during its contest with the bourgeoisie is compelled, by the force of circumstances, to organise itself as a class; if, by means of a revolution, it makes itself the ruling class, and, as such sweeps away by force the old conditions of production, then it will, along with these conditions, have swept away the conditions for the existence of class antagonisms, and of classes generally, and will thereby have abolished its own supremacy as a class.

In place of the old bourgeois society, with its classes and class antagonisms, we shall have an association, in which the free development of each is the condition for the free development of all.

[Section III, "Socialist and Communist Literature," is omitted.]

A CONTRIBUTION TO THE CRITIQUE
OF POLITICAL ECONOMY

KARL MARX*

My investigations led to the conclusion that legal relations as well as forms of State could not be understood from themselves, nor from the

* The excerpt is from the Preface of the work, first published in 1859. In it, according to Lenin, "Marx gives an integral formulation of the fundamental principles of materialism as applied to human society and its history."

so-called general development of the human mind, but, on the contrary, are rooted in the material conditions of life, the aggregate of which Hegel, following the precedent of the English and French of the eighteenth century, grouped under the name of "civil society"; but that the anatomy of civil society is to be found in political economy. . . . The general conclusion I arrived at—and once reached, it served as the guiding thread in my studies —can be briefly formulated as follows: In the social production of their means of existence men enter into definite, necessary relations which are independent of their will, productive relationships which correspond to a definite stage of development of their material productive forces. The aggregate of these productive relationships constitutes the economic structure of society, the real basis on which a juridical and political superstructure arises, and to which definite forms of social consciousness correspond. The mode of production of the material means of existence conditions the whole process of social, political and intellectual life. It is not the consciousness of men that determines their existence, but, on the contrary, it is their social existence that determines their consciousness.

At a certain stage of their development the material productive forces of society come into contradiction with the existing productive relationships, or, what is but a legal expression for these, with the property relationships within which they had moved before. From forms of development of the productive forces these relationships are transformed into their fetters. Then an epoch of social revolution opens. With the change in the economic foundation the whole vast superstructure is more or less rapidly transformed. In considering such revolutions it is necessary always to distinguish between the material revolution in the economic conditions of production, which can be determined with scientific accuracy, and the juridical, political, religious, aesthetic or philosophic—in a word, ideological forms wherein men become conscious of this conflict and fight it out.

Just as we cannot judge an individual on the basis of his own opinion of himself, so such a revolutionary epoch cannot be judged from its own consciousness; but on the contrary this consciousness must be explained from the contradictions of material life, from the existing conflict between social productive forces and productive relationships. A social system never perishes before all the productive forces have developed for which it is wide enough; and new, higher productive relationships never come into being before the material conditions for their existence have been brought to maturity within the womb of the old society itself. Therefore, mankind always sets itself only such problems as it can solve; for when we look closer we will always find that the problem itself only arises when the material conditions for its solution are already present or at least in process of coming into being.

In broad outline, the Asiatic, the ancient, the feudal and the modern bourgeois modes of production can be indicated as progressive epochs in the economic system of society. Bourgeois productive relationships are the last antagonistic form of the social process of production—antagonistic in the sense not of individual antagonism, but of an antagonism arising out of the conditions of the social life of individuals; but the productive forces developing within the womb of bourgeois society at the same time create the material conditions for the solution of this antagonism. With this social system, therefore, the pre-history of human society comes to a close.

THE MATERIALIST CONCEPTION OF HISTORY

George Plekhanov*

Plekhanov, a brilliant polemicist, known as the "father of Russian Marxism," was one of the founders (in 1883) and the intellectual leader of the "Emancipation of Labor," the first Russian Marxist organization. He collaborated closely with Lenin in establishing (in 1900) and in editing "Iskra" (The Spark) but soon broke sharply with him and later denounced the Bolshevik seizure of power. Notwithstanding, Lenin in 1921, said: "It seems to me fitting to remark, for the benefit of the young members of the Party, that one cannot become an intelligent and genuine Communist without having studied—I say advisedly studied—all that Plekhanov has written on philosophy, for it is the best of its kind in international Marxist literature."

The methods by which social man satisfies his needs, and to a large extent these needs themselves, are determined by the nature of the implements with which he subjugates nature in one degree or another; in other words, they are determined by the state of his productive forces. Every considerable change in the state of these forces is reflected in man's social relations, and, therefore, in his economic relations, as part of these social relations. The idealists of all species and varieties held that economic relations were functions of *human nature*; the dialectical materialists hold that these relations are functions of the *social productive forces*. . . .

Man makes history in striving to satisfy his needs. These needs, of course, are originally imposed by nature; but they are later considerably modified quantitatively and qualitatively by the character of the artificial environment. The productive forces at man's disposal determine all his social relations. First of all, the state of the productive forces determines the relations in which men stand towards each other in the social process

* The selection is from George Plekhanov, *The Materialist Conception of History*, International Publishers Co., Inc., 1940, *passim*. By permission. This essay was first published in 1897.

of production, that is, their *economic relations*. These relations naturally give rise to definite interests, which are expressed in *law*. "Every system of law protects a definite interest," Labriola says. The development of productive forces divides society into classes, whose interests are not only different, but in many—and, moreover, essential—aspects are diametrically antagonistic. This antagonism of interests gives rise to conflicts, to a struggle among the social classes. The struggle results in the replacement of the *tribal* organization by the *state* organization, the purpose of which is to protect the dominant interests. Lastly, social relations, determined by the given state of productive forces, give rise to common *morality*, the morality, that is, that guides people in their common, everyday life.

Thus the law, the state system and the morality of any given people are determined *directly* and *immediately* by its characteristic economic relations. These economic relations also determine—but *indirectly* and *mediately*—all the creations of the mind and imagination: art, science, etc.

To understand the history of scientific thought or the history of art in any particular country, it is not enough to be acquainted with its economics. One must know how to proceed from economics to *social psychology*, without a careful study and grasp of which a materialist explanation of the history of ideologies is impossible.

That does not mean, of course, that there is a social soul or a collective national "spirit," developing in accordance with its own special laws and manifesting itself in social life. "That is pure mysticism," Labriola says. All that the materialist can speak of in this case is the prevailing state of sentiment and thought in the particular social class of the particular country at the particular time. This state of sentiment and thought is the result of social relations. Labriola is firmly persuaded that it is not the forms of man's consciousness that determine the forms of his social being, but, on the contrary, the forms of his social being that determine the forms of his consciousness. But once the forms of his consciousness have sprung from the soil of social being, they become a part of history. Historical science cannot limit itself to the mere anatomy of society; it embraces the *totality of phenomena* that are *directly* or *indirectly* determined by social economics, including the work of the imagination. There is no historical fact that did not owe its origin to social economics; but it is no less true to say that there is no historical fact that was not preceded, not accompanied, and not succeeded by a definite state of consciousness. Hence the tremendous importance of social psychology. For if it has to be reckoned with even in the history of law and of political institutions, in the history of literature, art, philosophy, and so forth, not a single step can be taken without it.

When we say that a given work is fully in the spirit of, let us say, the Renaissance, it means that it completely corresponds with the then prevailing sentiments of the classes which set the tone in social life. So long as the social relations do not change, the psychology of society does not change either. People get accustomed to the prevailing beliefs, concepts, modes of thought and means of satisfying given esthetic requirements. But should the development of productive forces lead to any substantial change in the economic structure of society, and, as a consequence, in the reciprocal relations of the social classes, the psychology of these classes will also change, and with it the "spirit of the times" and the "national character." This change is manifested in the appearance of new religious beliefs or new philosophical concepts, of new trends in art or new esthetic requirements. . . .

How does law arise? It may be said that all law represents the supersession or modification of an older law or custom. Why are old customs superseded? Because they cease to conform to the new "conditions," that is, to the new actual relations in which men stand towards each other in the social process of production. Primitive communism disappeared owing to the development of productive forces. However, productive forces develop but gradually. Hence the new actual relations of man to man in the social process of production also develop but gradually. And hence, too, the restrictiveness of the old laws or customs, and, consequently, the need to provide a corresponding *legal* expression for the new *actual* (economic) relations of men also develop but gradually. The instinctive wisdom of the reasoning animal usually follows in the wake of these actual changes. If old laws hamper a section of society in attaining its material aims, in satisfying its urgent wants, it will infallibly, and with the greatest ease, become conscious of their restrictiveness: this requires very little more intelligence than is necessary for the consciousness that tight shoes or heavy weapons are uncomfortable. But, of course, from being conscious of the restrictiveness of an existing law to *consciously striving to abolish it* is a very far cry.

At first, men simply try to get round it in each particular case. Let us recall what used to happen in our country in large peasant families, when, under the influence of nascent capitalism, new sources of earnings arose which were not equal for all members of the family. The customary family code thereupon became restrictive for the lucky ones who earned more than the others. But it was not so easy for these lucky ones to make up their minds to revolt against the old custom, and they did not do so all at once. For a long time they simply resorted to subterfuge, concealing part of their earnings from the elders. But the new economic system grew gradually stronger, and the old family life more and more shaken: those members of the family who were interested in its abolition grew bolder and bolder; sons more and more frequently separated off from the common household, and in the end the old custom disappeared and was replaced by a new custom, arising out of the new conditions, the new *actual* relations, the new *economics* of society.

Man's cognition of his situation more or less lags, as a rule, behind the development of the new actual relations which cause that situation to change. But it does keep in the wake of the actual relations. Where man's conscious striving for the abolition of old institutions and the establishment of a new legal system is weak, there the way for the new system has not yet been properly *paved by the economics of the society*. . . .

All positive law is a defense of some definite interest. How do these interests arise? Are they a product of human will and human consciousness? No, they are created by man's economic relations. Once they have arisen, interests are reflected in one way or another in man's *consciousness*. In order to defend an interest, there must be consciousness of it. Hence every system of positive law may and should be regarded as a product of consciousness. It is not man's consciousness that calls into being the interests that the law protects, and, consequently, it is not man's consciousness that determines the content of law; but the state of social consciousness (social psychology) in the given era does determine *the form which the reflection of the given interest takes in the mind of man*. Unless we take the state of the social consciousness into account we shall be absolutely unable to explain the history of law.

In this history, it is always essential to draw a careful distinction between *form* and *content*. In its *formal* aspect, law, like every ideology, is subject to the influence of all, or, at least of some of, the other ideologies: religious beliefs, philosophical concepts, and so on. This in itself hinders to some extent—and sometimes to a very large extent—the disclosure of the dependence between men's legal concepts and their mutual relations in the social process of production. But that is only half the trouble. The real trouble is that *at different stages of social development a given ideology is subject to the influence of other ideologies in very unequal degrees*. For example, ancient Egyptian, and partly Roman, law was under the sway of religion; in more recent history law has developed (we repeat, and request it to be noted, that we are here speaking of the *formal* aspect) under the strong influence of philosophy. Philosophy had to put up a big fight before it succeeded in eliminating the influence of religion on law and substituting its own influence. This fight was nothing but a reflection in the realm of ideas of the social struggle between the third estate and the clergy, but, nevertheless, it greatly hampered the formation of a correct view of the origin of legal institutions, for, thanks to it, these institutions seemed to be the obvious and indubitable product of a struggle between abstract ideas. . . .

The origin of the symbolical custom by which a woman cuts off her braid on the grave of a brother is to be explained by the history of the family; and the explanation of the history of the family is to be sought in the history of economic development. . . . If the conservatives passionately uphold the old customs, it is because in their minds the idea of an advantageous, precious and customary social system is firmly associated with the idea of these customs. If the innovators detest and scoff at these customs, it is because in their minds the idea of these customs is associated with the idea of restrictive, disadvantageous and objectionable social relations. Consequently, *the whole point lies in an association of ideas.* When we find that a particular tie has survived not only the relations which gave rise to it, but also cognate rites that arose from these same relations, we have to conclude that in the minds of the innovators it was not so strongly associated with the idea of the old, detested order as other customs were. Why so? To answer this question is sometimes easy, but at others it is quite impossible for lack of the necessary psychological data. But even when we are constrained to admit that the question is unanswerable—at least, in the existing state of our knowledge—we must nevertheless remember that the point does not lie in the *force of tradition,* but in definite associations of ideas produced by definite actual relations of men in society.

The history of ideologies is to a large extent to be explained by the rise, modification and breakdown of associations of ideas under the influence of the rise, modification and breakdown of definite combinations of social forces. . . .

From the standpoint of the theory of factors, human society is a heavy load which various "forces"—morality, law, economics, etc., etc.—drag each in its own way along the path of history. From the standpoint of the modern materialist conception of history, the whole thing assumes a different aspect. It turns out that the historical "factors" are mere abstractions, and when the mist surrounding them is dispelled, it becomes clear that men do not make several distinct histories—the history of law, the history of morals, the history of philosophy, etc.—but only one history, the history of their own social relations, which are determined by the state of the productive forces in each particular period. *What is known as ideologies is nothing but a multiform reflection in the minds of men of this single and indivisible history.*

THE ROLE OF THE INDIVIDUAL IN HISTORY

George Plekhanov*

There cannot be the slightest doubt that the materialist conception of the human will is quite compatible with the most vigorous practical activity. . . . *The "disciple" serves as an instrument of this necessity and cannot help doing so,* owing to his social status and to his mentality and temperament, which were created by his status. This, too, is an *aspect of necessity.* Since his social status has imbued him with this character and no other, he

* The selection is from George Plekhanov, *The Role of the Individual in History* (International Publishers Co., Inc., 1940), *passim.* By permission. This essay was first published in 1898.

not only serves as an instrument of necessity and cannot help doing so, but he *passionately desires, and cannot help desiring,* to do so. . . .

While some subjectivists, striving to ascribe the widest possible role to the "individual" in history, refused to recognize the historical progress of mankind as a process expressing laws, some of their later opponents, striving to bring out more sharply the coherent character of this progress, were evidently prepared to forget that *men make history, and, therefore, the activities of individuals cannot help being important in history.* . . .

By virtue of particular traits of their character, individuals can influence the fate of society. Sometimes this influence is very considerable; but the possibility of exercising this influence, and its extent, are determined by the form of organization of society, by the relation of forces within it. The character of an individual is a "factor" in social development only where, when, and to the extent that social relations permit it to be such.

We may be told that the extent of personal influence may also be determined by the talents of the individual. We agree. But the individual can display his talents only when he occupies the position in society necessary for this. Why was the fate of France in the hands of a man who totally lacked the ability and desire to serve society? Because such was the form of organization of that society. It is the form of organization that in any given period determines the role and, consequently, the social significance that may fall to the lot of talented or incompetent individuals.

But if the role of individuals is determined by the form of organization of society, how can their social influence, which is determined by the role they play, contradict the conception of social development as a process expressing laws? It does not contradict it; on the contrary, it serves as one of its most vivid illustrations. . . .

No matter what the qualities of the given individual may be, they cannot eliminate the given economic relations if the latter conform to the given state of productive forces. But the personal qualities of individuals make them more or less fit to satisfy those social needs which arise out of the given economic relations, or to counteract such satisfaction. The urgent social need of France at the end of the eighteenth century was the substitution for the obsolete political institutions of new institutions that would conform more to her economic system. The most prominent and useful public men of that time were those who were more capable than others of helping to satisfy this most urgent need. . . .

Let us assume that Robespierre was an absolutely indispensable force in his party; but even so, he was not the only force. If the accidental fall of a brick had killed him, say, in January, 1793, his place would, of course, have been taken by somebody else, and although this person might have been inferior to him in every respect, nevertheless, events would have taken *the same course* as they did when Robespierre was alive. For example, even under these circumstances the Gironde would probably not have escaped defeat; but it is possible that Robespierre's party would have lost power somewhat earlier. . . . In short, it may have fallen sooner or perhaps later, but it certainly would have fallen, because the section of the people which supported Robespierre's party was totally unprepared to hold power for a prolonged period. At all events, results "opposite" to those which arose from Robespierre's energetic action are out of the question. . . .

Owing to the specific qualities of their minds and characters, influential individuals can change the *individual features of events and some of their particular consequences,* but they cannot change their general *trend,* which is determined by other forces. . . .

In order that a man who possesses a particular kind of talent may, by means of it, greatly influence the course of events, two conditions are needed: First, this talent must make him more conformable to the social needs of the given epoch than anyone else. If Napoleon had possessed the musical gifts of Beethoven instead of his own military genius he would not, of course, have become an emperor. Second, the existing social order must not bar the road to the person possessing the talent which is needed and useful precisely at the given time. This very *Napoleon* would have died as the barely known General, or Colonel, *Bonaparte* had the older order in France existed another seventy-five years.[1] . . .

It has long been observed that great talents appear everywhere, whenever the social conditions favorable to their development exist. This means that every man of talent who *actually appears,* every man of talent who becomes a *social force,* is the product of *social relations.* Since this is the case, it is clear why talented people can, as we have said, change only individual features of events, but not their general trend; *they are themselves the product of this trend; were it not for that trend they would never have crossed the threshold that divides the potential from the real.* . . .

Thus, the personal qualities of leading people determine the individual features of historical events; and the accidental element, in the sense that we have indicated, always plays some role in the course of these events, the trend of which is determined, in the last analysis, by so-called general causes, *i.e.,* actually by the development of productive forces and the mutual relations between men in the social-economic process of production. Casual phenomena and the personal qualities of celebrated people are ever so much more noticeable than deep-lying general causes. The eighteenth century pondered but little over these general causes, and claimed that history was explained by the conscious actions and "passions" of historical personages. . . .

At the present time we must regard the development of productive forces as the final and most general cause of the historical progress of man-

---

[1] Probably Napoleon would have gone to Russia, *where he had intended to go just a few years before the Revolution.* Here, no doubt, he would have distinguished himself in action against the Turks or the Caucasian highlanders, but nobody here would have thought that this poor, but capable, officer could, under favorable circumstances, have become the ruler of the world.

kind, and it is these productive forces that determine the consecutive changes in the social relations of men. Parallel with this *general* cause there are *particular* causes, *i.e., the historical situation* in which the development of the productive forces of a given nation proceeds and which, in the last analysis, is itself created by the development of these forces among other nations, *i.e.,* the same general cause.

Finally, the influence of the *particular* causes is supplemented by the operation of *individual* causes, *i.e.,* the personal qualities of public men and other "accidents," thanks to which events finally assume their *individual features.* Individual causes cannot bring about fundamental changes in the operation of *general and particular* causes which, moreover, determine the trend and limits of the influence of individual causes. Nevertheless, there is no doubt that history would have had different features had the individual causes which had influenced it been replaced by other causes of the same order. . . .

A great man is great not because his personal qualities give individual features to great historical events, but because he possesses qualities which make him most capable of serving the great social needs of his time, needs which arose as a result of general and particular causes. Carlyle, in his well-known book on heroes and hero-worship, calls great men *beginners.* This is a very apt description, A great man is precisely a beginner because he sees *further* than others, and desires things *more strongly* than others. . . .

Bismarck said that we cannot make history and must wait while it is being made. But who makes history? It is made by the *social man,* who is its *sole "factor."* The social man creates his own, social, relationships. But if in a given period he creates given relationships and not others, there must be some cause for it, of course; it is determined by the state of his productive forces. No great man can foist on society relations which *no longer* conform to the state of these forces, or which *do not yet* conform to them.

MARX'S ECONOMIC DOCTRINE

V. I. LENIN*

MARX'S ECONOMIC DOCTRINE

"It is the ultimate aim of this work to reveal the economic law of motion of modern society" (that is to say, capitalist, bourgeois society), writes Marx in the preface to the first volume of *Capital*. The study of the production relationships in a given, historically determinate society, in their genesis, their development, and their decay—such is the content of Marx's economic teaching. In capitalist society the dominant feature is the production of *commodities,* and Marx's analysis therefore begins with an analysis of a commodity.

Value

A commodity is, firstly, something that satisfies a human need; and, secondly, it is something that is exchanged for something else. The utility of a thing gives it *use-value.* Exchange-value (or simply, value) presents itself first of all as the proportion, the ratio, in which a certain number of use-values of one kind are exchanged for a certain number of use-values of another kind. Daily experience shows us that by millions upon millions of such exchanges, all and sundry use-values, in themselves very different and not comparable one with another, are equated to one another. Now, what is common in these various things which are constantly weighed one against another in a definite system of social relationships? That which is common to them is that they are *products of labour.* In exchanging products, people equate to one another most diverse kinds of labour. The production of commodities is a system of social relationships in which different producers produce various products (the social division of labour), and in which all these products are equated to one another in exchange.

Consequently, the element common to all commodities is not concrete labour in a definite branch of production, not labour of one particular kind, but *abstract* human labour—human labour in general. All the labour power of a given society, represented in the sum total of values of all commodities, is one and the same human labour power. Millions upon millions

---

* The selection is from V. I. Lenin, *The Teachings of Karl Marx,* International Publishers Co., Inc., 1930, pp. 18 30. By permission of the publisher. This essay, written by Lenin for a Russian encyclopedia, was completed in November 1914. It presents in summary Marx's doctrines in their most revolutionary—and, from the Bolshevik point of view, most acceptable—form.

of acts of exchange prove this. Consequently, each particular commodity represents only a certain part of *socially necessary* labour time.

The magnitude of the value is determined by the amount of socially necessary labour, or by the labour time that is socially requisite for the production of the given commodity, of the given use-value. ". . . Exchanging labour products of different kinds one for another, they equate the values of the exchanged products; and in doing so they equate the different kinds of labour expended in production, treating them as homogeneous human labour. They do not know that they are doing this, but they do it." As one of the earlier economists said, value is a relationship between two persons, only he should have added that it is a relationship hidden beneath a material wrapping. We can only understand what value is when we consider it from the point of view of a system of social production relationships in one particular historical type of society; and, moreover, of relationships which present themselves in a mass form, the phenomenon of exchange repeating itself millions upon millions of times. "As values, all commodities are only definite quantities of congealed labour time."

Having made a detailed analysis of the twofold character of the labour incorporated in commodities, Marx goes on to analyse the *form of value and of money*. His main task, then, is to study the *origin* of the money form of value, to study the *historical process* of the development of exchange, beginning with isolated and casual acts of exchange ("simple, isolated, or casual value form," in which a given quantity of one commodity is exchanged for a given quantity of another), passing on to the universal form of value, in which a number of different commodities are exchanged for one and the same particular commodity, and ending with the money form of value, when gold becomes this particular commodity, the universal equivalent. Being the highest product of the development of exchange and of commodity production, money masks the social character of individual labour, and hides the social tie between the various producers who come together in the market. Marx analyses in great detail the various functions of money; and it is essential to note that here (as generally in the opening chapters of *Capital*) what appears to be an abstract and at times purely deductive mode of exposition in reality reproduces a gigantic collection of facts concerning the history of the development of exchange and commodity production.

Money . . . presupposes a definite level of commodity exchange. The various forms of money (simple commodity equivalent or means of circulation, or means of payment, treasure, or international money) indicate, according to the different extent to which this or that function is put into application, and according to the comparative predominance of one or other of them, very different grades of the social process of production. [*Capital*, Vol. I.]

Surplus Value

At a particular stage in the development of commodity production, money becomes transformed into capital. The formula of commodity circulation was C-M-C (commodity—money—commodity); the sale of one commodity for the purpose of buying another. But the general formula of capital, on the contrary, is M-C-M (money—commodity—money); purchase for the purpose of selling—at a profit. The designation "surplus value" is given by Marx to the increase over the original value of money that is put into circulation. The fact of this "growth" of money in capitalist society is well known. Indeed, it is this "growth" which transforms money into *capital,* as a special, historically defined, social relationship of production. Surplus value cannot arise out of the circulation of commodities, for this represents nothing more than the exchange of equivalents; it cannot arise out of an advance in prices, for the mutual losses and gains of buyers and sellers would equalise one another; and we are concerned here, not with what happens to individuals, but with a mass or average or social phenomenon.

In order that he may be able to receive surplus value, "Moneybags must . . . find in the market a commodity whose use-value has the peculiar quality of being a source of value"—a commodity, the actual process of whose use is at the same time the process of the creation of value. Such a commodity exists. It is human labour power. Its use is labour, and labour creates value. The owner of money buys labour power at its value, which is determined, like the value of every other commodity, by the socially necessary labour time requisite for its production (that is to say, the cost of maintaining the worker and his family). Having bought labour power, the owner of money is entitled to use it, that is to set it to work for the whole day—twelve hours, let us suppose. Meanwhile, in the course of six hours ("necessary" labour time) the labourer produces sufficient to pay back the cost of his own maintenance; and in the course of the next six hours ("surplus" labour time), he produces a "surplus" product for which the capitalist does not pay him—surplus product or surplus value.

In capital, therefore, from the viewpoint of the process of production, we have to distinguish between two parts: first, constant capital, expended for the means of production (machinery, tools, raw materials, etc.), the value of this being (all at once or part by part) transferred, unchanged, to the finished product; and, secondly, variable capital, expended for labour power. The value of this latter capital is not constant, but grows in the labour process, creating surplus value. To express the degree of exploitation of labour power by capital, we must therefore compare the surplus value, not with the whole capital, but only with the variable capital. Thus, in the example just given, the rate of surplus value, as Marx calls this relationship, will be 6:6, *i.e.,* 100%.

There are two historical prerequisites to the genesis of capital: first, accumulation of a considerable sum of money in the hands of individuals living under conditions in which there is a comparatively high development of commodity production. Second, the existence of workers who are "free" in a double sense of the term: free from any constraint or restriction as regards the sale of their labour power; free from any bondage to the soil or to the means of production in general—*i.e.*, of propertyless workers, of "proletarians" who cannot maintain their existence except by the sale of their labour power.

There are two fundamental ways in which surplus value can be increased: by an increase in the working day ("absolute surplus value"); and by a reduction in the necessary working day ("relative surplus value"). Analysing the former method, Marx gives an impressive picture of the struggle of the working class for shorter hours and of government interference, first (from the fourteenth century to the seventeenth) in order to lengthen the working day, and subsequently (factory legislation of the nineteenth century) to shorten it. Since the appearance of *Capital,* the history of the working-class movement in all lands provides a wealth of new facts to amplify this picture.

Analysing the production of relative surplus value, Marx investigates the three fundamental historical stages of the process whereby capitalism has increased the productivity of labour; (1) simple cooperation; (2) division of labour, and manufacture; (3) machinery and large-scale industry. How profoundly Marx has here revealed the basic and typical features of capitalist development is shown by the fact that investigations of the so-called "kustar" industry* of Russia furnish abundant material for the illustration of the first two of these stages. The revolutionising effect of large-scale machine industry, described by Marx in 1867, has become evident in a number of "new" countries, such as Russia, Japan, etc., in the course of the last fifty years.

But to continue. Of extreme importance and originality is Marx's analysis of the *accumulation of capital,* that is to say, the transformation of a portion of surplus value into capital and the applying of this portion to additional production, instead of using it to supply the personal needs or to gratify the whims of the capitalist. Marx pointed out the mistake made by earlier classical political economy (from Adam Smith on), which assumed that all the surplus value which was transformed into capital became variable capital. In actual fact, it is divided into *means of production* plus variable capital. The more rapid growth of constant capital as compared with variable capital in the sum total of capital is of immense importance in the process of development of capitalism and in that of the transformation of capitalism into Socialism.

The accumulation of capital, accelerating the replacement of workers

---

* Small-scale home industry of a predominantly handicraft nature.

by machinery, creating wealth at the one pole and poverty at the other, gives birth to the so-called "reserve army of labour," to a "relative over-abundance" of workers or to "capitalist overpopulation." This assumes the most diversified forms, and gives capital the possibility of expanding pro-duction at an exceptionally rapid rate. This possibility, in conjunction with enhanced facilities for credit and with the accumulation of capital in the means of production, furnishes, among other things, the key to the under-standing of the *crises* of overproduction that occur periodically in capitalist countries—first about every ten years, on an average, but subsequently in a more continuous form and with a less definite periodicity. From accumu-lation of capital upon a capitalist foundation we must distinguish the so-called "primitive accumulation": the forcible severance of the worker from the means of production, the driving of the peasants off the land, the stealing of the communal lands, the system of colonies and national debts, of protective tariffs, and the like. "Primitive accumulation" creates, at one pole, the "free" proletarian: at the other, the owner of money, the capitalist.

The *"historical tendency of capitalist accumulation"* is described by Marx in the following well-known terms:

The expropriation of the immediate producers is effected with ruthless vandalism, and under the stimulus of the most infamous, the basest, the meanest, and the most odious of passions. Self-earned private property [of the peasant and the handicraftsman], the private property that may be looked upon as grounded on a coalescence of the isolated, individual, and independent worker with his working conditions, is supplemented by capitalist private property, which is maintained by the exploitation of others' labour, but of labour which in a formal sense is free. . . , What has now to be expropriated is no longer the labourer working on his own account, but the capitalist who exploits many labourers. This expropriation is brought about by the operation of the immanent laws of capitalist production, by the centralisation of capital. One capitalist lays a number of his fellow capitalists low.

Hand in hand with this centralisation, concomitantly with the expropriation of many capitalists by a few, the co-operative form of the labour process develops to an ever-increasing degree; therewith we find a growing tendency towards the purposive application of science to the improvement of technique; the land is more methodically cultivated; the instruments of labour tend to assume forms which are only utilisable by combined effort; the means of production are economised through being turned to account only by joint, by social labour; all the peoples of the world are enmeshed in the net of the world market, and therefore the capitalist régime tends more and more to assume an international character. While there is thus a progressive diminution in the number of the capitalist magnates (who usurp and monopolise all the advantages of this transformative process), there occurs a corresponding increase in the mass of poverty, oppression, enslavement, degeneration, and exploitation; but at the same time there is a steady intensifica-tion of the wrath of the working class—a class which grows ever more numerous, and is disciplined, unified, and organised by the very mechanism of the capitalist method of production. Capitalist monopoly becomes a fetter upon the method of production which has flourished with it and under it. The centralisation of the means of production and the socialisation of labour reach a point where they prove incompatible with their capitalist husk. This bursts asunder. The knell of capitalist private property sounds. The expropriators are expropriated. [*Capital,* Vol. I.]

. . . The impoverishment and the ruin of the agricultural population lead, in their turn, to the formation of a reserve army of labour for capital. In every capitalist country, "part of the rural population is continually on the move, in course of transference to join the urban proletariat, the manufacturing proletariat. . . . (In this connection, the term "manufacture" is used to include all non-agricultural industry.) This source of a relative surplus population is, therefore, continually flowing. . . . The agricultural labourer, therefore, has his wages kept down to the minimum, and always has one foot in the swamp of pauperism" (*Capital,* Vol. I). The peasant's private ownership of the land he tills constitutes the basis of small-scale production and causes the latter to flourish and attain its classical form. But such petty production is only compatible with a narrow and primitive type of production, with a narrow and primitive framework of society. Under capitalism, the exploitation of the peasant "differs from the exploitation of the industrial proletariat only in point of form. The exploiter is the same: capital. The individual capitalists exploit the individual peasants through mortgages and usury, and the capitalist class exploits the peasant class through state taxation" (*Class Struggles in France*). "Peasant agriculture, the smallholding system, is merely an expedient whereby the capitalist is enabled to extract profit, interest, and rent from the land, while leaving the peasant proprietor to pay himself his own wages as best he may. . . ."

In agriculture as in industry, capitalism improves the production process only at the price of the "martyrdom of the producers."

The dispersion of the rural workers over large areas breaks down their powers of resistance at the very time when concentration is increasing the powers of the urban operatives in this respect. In modern agriculture, as in urban industry, the increased productivity and the greater mobility of labour are purchased at the cost of devastating labour power and making it a prey to disease. Moreover, every advance in capitalist agriculture is an advance in the art, not only of robbing the worker, but also of robbing the soil. . . . Capitalist production, therefore, is only able to develop the technique and the combination of the social process of production by simultaneously undermining the foundations of all wealth—the land and the workers. [*Capital,* Vol. I.]

SOCIALISM

From the foregoing it is manifest that Marx deduces the inevitability of the transformation of capitalist society into Socialist society wholly and exclusively from the economic law of the movement of contemporary society. The chief material foundation of the inevitability of the coming of Socialism is the socialisation of labour in its myriad forms, advancing ever more rapidly, and conspicuously so, throughout the half century that has elapsed since the death of Marx—being especially plain in the growth of large-scale production, of capitalist cartels, syndicates, and trusts; but also in the gigantic increase in the dimensions and the power of finance capital. The intellectual and moral driving force of this transformation is the proletariat, the physical carrier trained by capitalism itself. The contest of the proletariat with the bourgeoisie, assuming various forms which grow continually richer in content, inevitably becomes a political struggle aiming at the conquest of political power by the proletariat ("the dictatorship of the proletariat"). The socialisation of production cannot fail to lead to the transfer of the means of production into the possession of society, to the "expropriation of the expropriators." An immense increase in the productivity of labour; a reduction in working hours; replacement of the remnants, the ruins of petty, primitive, individual production by collective and perfected labour—such will be the direct consequences of this transformation.

THE PHILOSOPHIC AND ECONOMIC THEORIES OF MARXISM

R. N. CAREW HUNT*

I. THE PHILOSOPHIC THEORY OF MARXISM

Marxism consists of three elements:

1. A dialectical philosophy borrowed from Hegel but transformed into dialectical materialism, from which in turn historical materialism derives.

2. A system of political economy, of which the dynamic part is the labour theory of value, the theory of surplus value and the conclusions drawn from them.

3. A theory of the State and of revolution. . . .

Dialectic and Formal Logic

. . . As a revolutionary, Marx was naturally attracted to the dialectic because it represented everything as being in the state of becoming something else, and to this day Communists are taught that it constitutes a mode of reasoning which is somehow superior to that of formal logic, which is represented as conceiving of everything in fixed and unchangeable terms

* Formerly at St. Antony's College, Oxford University. The selection is from chapters IV and V of R. N. Carew Hunt, *The Theory and Practice of Communism* (New York: The Macmillan Company, fifth revised edition, 1957), copyright by the author, and used with the permission of the publisher.

and as thus providing a convenient intellectual instrument for reactionaries. Thus, Engels says that the dialectic transcends the narrow horizon of formal logic and contains the germ of a more comprehensive view of the world: and that while the latter is all very well "for every-day purposes," it is inadequate to give "an exact representation of the universe"; though the claim of the dialectic to perform this rests on no more secure foundation than that in Marxist hands it can be twisted to explain anything. . . .

Hegel's belief that change is always effected by the fruitful conflict of what he called, indifferently, contradictions or oppositions led him to challenge what he regarded as the barren conflict of affirmation and denial made by formal logic.[1] Unfortunately, he did not at all clearly define what he meant by contradictions, and those to which he refers are of many different kinds. In a given situation, there may be forces that make for peace and others that make for war, and it is doubtless permissible to represent these as contradictions which "exist in unity." [2] But there are other types of contradiction which are by their very nature irreconcilable. If, for example, the statement that "All men are mortal" does not exclude the contrary statement that "Some men are immortal," it is meaningless. But few writers on dialectical materialism distinguish between the various types of contradiction—between what Jules Monnerot, in his able treatment of this problem, calls *contradictions motrices* and *contradictions paralysantes*.[3]

Marxists habitually describe as contradictory any sequences of events that are in some vague sense contrary to one another; and at the same time imply that the contradictions between them are reconcilable, and that it is only outmoded formal logic which asserts the contrary. Yet while it is legimate to regard dialectical logic as a development of formal logic, it contains no new function, and the opposition which Marxists set up between it and formal logic is quite unjustifiable. We may accept it if we like; but its rejection in no way commits us, as Marxists would have it, to regarding everything as fixed and static, and of thus being forever incapable of taking into account the fluidity of the subject matter of thought and of making new judgments as changes in it require them. In fact, Marxists do not hesitate to use such expressions as "Feudalism" and "Capitalism" as fixed terms, as indeed they have to do. They talk continually of the "logic of contradiction," but none of their writings from Marx to Stalin contains any example of reasoning which does not assume that given one thing, another follows from it, which is how we all normally argue.[4] . . .

[1] On Hegel's treatment of the Law of Contradiction see Hans Kelsen, *The Political Theory of Bolshevism* (California University Press, 1949), pp. 14-17.
[2] George H. Sabine, *History of Political Theory* (ed. 1948), pp. 532-535.
[3] Jules Monnerot, *Sociologie du Communisme* (Paris, 1949), pp. 214 f.; see also the German Social Democrat, Edouard Conze, *An Introduction to Dialectical Materialism* (n.d.), p. 57, and for a criticism of Conze, David Guest's *A Textbook of Dialectical Materialism* (1939), pp. 78 f.
[4] Julien Benda, *Trois Idoles Romantiques* (Paris, 1948), p. 162.

All Marxist theoreticians are committed to applying the dialectic to any problem with which they may be dealing, though the result is often totally to obscure it; and the commonest criticism of any scheme that has miscarried is that its authors failed to carry out beforehand a correct dialectical analysis of the situation. For it is on the dialectic that the *Conclusion* of the official *Short History of the Communist Party of the Soviet Union* bases the claim which it makes for the Marxist doctrine, "the power of which," as it declares, lies in the fact that "it enables the Party to find the right orientation to any situation, to understand the inner connection of current events, to foresee their course, and perceive not only how and in what direction they are developing in the present, but how and in what direction they are bound to develop in the future." Without some knowledge of this mode of reasoning it is thus scarcely possible to understand Marxist literature at all. But by reason of its official adoption, it has degenerated into a barren scholasticism such as is taught in all communist centres of learning under the guise of instruction in the art of thinking, of which the best that can be said is that it may perhaps encourage beginners to think historically. Yet we may accept the dialectic as a description of the part played in human affairs by conflicting tendencies and purposes, without necessarily accepting it as a universal law. In the first sense it can be applied with genuine force to the analysis of society, as no one who has read Marx will dispute, and critics like Max Eastman go too far when they condemn it as completely valueless and as a redundant element of Marxist theory.[1]

But although the dialectic may give us valuable insights into the history of human development, the Marxist claim that it constitutes the only scientific approach to reality cannot be allowed. It is not, in fact, scientific at all, and it is only in Russia that scientists are required to set out their ideas in pseudo-dialectical jargon, for which Engel's *Anti-Dühring* provides the model.[2] Marxists argue, indeed, that the processes of nature are governed by the dialectic, though if this be so, it is strange that all the great scientific discoveries should have been made without apparent reference to it. Thus, to take the illustration borrowed from Hegel and used by Engels in Ch. xiii of his *Anti-Dühring*, a grain of barley germinates and dies, and from it there arises a plant which is "the negation of the grain." This plant grows, and finally produces a stalk at the end of which are further grains of barley. "As soon as these are ripened the stalk dies and is in turn negated"; and as a result of this "negation of the negation," the original grain of barley is multiplied tenfold. But such changes cannot justly be represented as contradictions, nor does the emergence of ten grains of barley from a single grain constitute a "qualitative" change (since the

[1] Cp. Karl Mannheim, *Ideology and Utopia* (1936), pp. 115-116.
[2] See Monnerot, p. 215: but cp. J. B. S. Haldane, *Dialectical Materialism and Modern Science* (n.d.), and J. D. Bernal, *The Foundations of Necessity* (1949), pp. 370 f., 410 f., 423 f.

grains remain barley), or issue in a "higher reformulation," such as the dialectic is understood to effect. In fact, the seed-flower-fruit cycle simply brings us back to where we started.[1]

Again, the world of the scientist is not one in which everything is in a state of becoming, for if it were, most scientific investigation would have to be abandoned. As it is, the scientist is aware that the phenomena with which he is dealing change so imperceptibly as to justify him in regarding them as static, and his work becomes possible only because he can, for all practical purposes, isolate them into closed systems. He will, of course, consider his particular group of phenomena in their relation to others; but the idea that they can be comprehended only as a part of the Whole is one which belongs to metaphysics rather than to science. And, finally, there is, as Röpke points out, a profound gulf between the attempt to comprehend the world through the critical intelligence, as the scientist seeks to do within his own field, and the attempt to identify that intelligence with the world. For the process of becoming and our idea of that process are different things, and science lends no warrant to the notion that it is possible to establish a mystical union between the two.[2]

Marx's Materialism and His Theory of Knowledge

Marx rejected, or at least believed he had rejected, the whole of Hegel's idealist philosophy while retaining his dialectic method. He had many faults to find with Hegel's system, but his fundamental criticism of it is contained in a famous passage in the Introduction to the first volume of *Capital:*

> My own dialectic method is not only different from the Hegelian, but is its direct opposite. For Hegel . . . the thinking process is the demiurge (creator) of the real world, and the real world is only the outward manifestation of "the Idea." With me, on the other hand, the ideal is nothing else than the material world reflected by the human mind and translated into terms of thought.

. . . But what Marx does is to take over the essential property of that Absolute upon which, in Hegel's system, both mind and nature depend, and apply it to a material world of which he had declared mind to be simply a by-product. The Marxist version of the dialectic is indeed open to serious objection. The dialectic can properly be applied to the development of ideas through the conflict of contradictions, and Hegel provides a rational explanation of that development. Yet, although dialectical materialism can point to something analogous to contradictions in the material world, not only are these analogies altogether arbitrary, but even if they were not, it would still remain a complete mystery why the material world should exhibit them. Dialectical materialism in fact asserts that matter is

---

[1] Sidney Hook, The *"Laws" of the Dialectic* (*Polemic,* November-December, 1946), pp. 9 f.

[2] Wilhelm Röpke, *Le Crise de Nôtre Temps* (Neuchâtel, 1947), p. 68; Benda, pp. 166 f.

matter, but that it develops as ideas do. Only while we can see why ideas develop as they do, as for example in discussion, there is no conceivable reason why material things should develop in the same way. Eastman maintains, however, that Marx was by no means as successful in getting rid of Hegel as he had supposed, and that having declared the world to be made up of unconscious matter, he then found himself obliged to read into matter the very essence of Hegel's Absolute, so that his system is in fact a return to the animism of primitive man which attributes human values to trees and other material objects.[1]

This criticism is perhaps less applicable to Marx than it is to Engels, who both in his *Anti-Dühring* and in his *Dialectics of Nature* maintained that natural processes are dialectical, as modern dialectical materialists continue to do. There are indeed passages in *Capital* which suggest that Marx held the same view, and indeed if the dialectic is a universal principle, it is hard to see upon what grounds the order of nature is to be excluded from its operation. Marx's real interest, however, was in the process of social development, and this he certainly believed to be dialectical. Unfortunately, for a writer who claimed that his work was scientific, he took altogether insufficient pains to make himself understood, and was often obscure and careless in expression. Thus it is not always clear whether his dialectic is one of material economic forces or of the class struggle to which their development gives rise; and his anxiety to stress the importance of the former led him frequently to use language which suggests that they somehow possess the property of developing dialectically, so that by throwing the emphasis upon them rather than upon the human framework within which they can alone operate, he exposed himself to the charge of endowing his material universe with qualities which transcend its physical nature and belong to the order of metaphysics. . . .

Historical Materialism

Historical materialism, or the materialist interpretation of history, is simply dialectical materialism applied to the particular field of human relations within society. The dialectic supplies the clue to the whole process. In the preface to his *Critique of Political Economy* Marx starts by asking what is the principle that governs all human relations, and his answer is that it is the common end which all men pursue, that is, the production of the means to support life, and next to production, the exchange of things produced. Man has to live before he can start to think. Hence the ultimate determinant of social change is not to be found in his ideas of eternal truth and social justice, but in changes in the mode of production and exchange. . . .

Marx distinguishes five economic forms, or modes, of production— primitive communal, slave, feudal, capitalist and socialist. Under the first,

[1] Max Eastman, *Marxism. Is it a Science?*, p. 23.

the means of production are socially owned. Under the second, the slave-owner owns them. Under the third, the feudal lord partially owns them, as his men have some property. Under the fourth, the capitalist owns the means of production, but not his men, whom he can no longer dispose of as he pleases, though they are compelled to work for him. Under the fifth, which has not yet come into existence, the workers themselves will own the means of production and, with the abolition of the contradictions inherent in Capitalism, production will reach its fullest development. Both from the point of view of production and of freedom, each of these stages represents an advance upon its predecessor, this being in accordance with the dialectic principle that every new stage takes up whatever was of value in that which it has "negated"—the principle that had led Hegel to declare in the Introduction to his *Philosophy of History* that, "The Oriental World knows only *one* that is free, the Greeks and Romans recognize that *some* are free, the German nations have attained to the knowledge that *all* are free." Thus, Marx commends the early capitalists because they had broken down the barriers imposed by Feudalism, but argues that the system has outlived its usefulness and has become an obstacle to the further development of the productive forces.

To understand social revolutions we have therefore to distinguish between changes in the productive forces and the various ideological forms in which men become conscious of the conflict and fight it out. The real cause is always the former; but men are seldom aware of this, and will believe that they are fighting for religion, political liberty or any other ideological motive. Marxists contend that it is, indeed, on the basis of this illusion that most history has been written, the true cause of revolutions having been thus concealed until Marx revealed it. They have to adopt this position because it is an article of their faith that every great movement in history—the rise of Islam, the Renaissance or any other—was ultimately due to an economic cause.

This, then, was the theory which Engels claimed, at Marx's graveside, to have made as great a contribution to the science of social relations as had Darwin's theory to natural science.

Just as Darwin discovered the law of evolution in organic nature, so Marx discovered the law of evolution in human history; he discovered the simple fact, hitherto concealed by an overgrowth of ideology, that mankind must first of all eat and drink, have shelter and clothing, before it can pursue politics, religion, science, art, etc.; and that therefore the production of the immediate material means of subsistence, and consequently the degree of economic development attained by a given people or during a given epoch, form the foundation upon which State institutions, the legal conceptions, the art and even the religious ideas of the people concerned have been evolved, and in the light of which these things must be explained, instead of vice versa as had hitherto been the case.[1]

[1] *Selected Works,* II, p. 153; see also Engels' preface to the 1885 German edition of Marx's *Eighteenth Brumaire,* in which he makes a somewhat similar claim, *ibid.,* pp. 223-224.

The Class Struggle

We have seen that the productive forces at any given period always develop appropriate forms of productive relations, and that, except among the most primitive communities, these are always relations of exploitation which divide society into classes. It is, however, characteristic of Marx that having devoted the greater part of his life to writing about the class struggle he should never have defined what he meant by a class, a question that he raised in the last chapter of the third volume of *Capital,* but without answering it. He recognizes, however, that classes are not homogeneous, and that there will be as many of them as there are well-marked degrees of social status. But he is not much concerned with their functional differences, because, for the purpose of the class struggle, he holds that all classes are ultimately divisible into two, one of which controls the means of production, while the other does not, and that the antagonism to which this gives rise creates a profound contradiction. Yet it is through this very contradiction that progress is effected, since, as we have seen, it is through the conflict of thesis and antithesis that we reach the synthesis which brings us one step nearer to our goal.[1]

The force which lies behind the dialectic of history and moves the world is not therefore the clash of nations, as Hegel and the majority of historians had supposed, but the clash of classes or the class struggle. Class interest thus takes the place of national interest, which is always found upon examination to be no more than the interest of the ruling class. Marx did not pretend to have discovered the class struggle; but he claimed to have proved that the existence of classes is bound up with a "particular historic phase in the history of production," that it must inevitably lead to the dictatorship of the proletariat, and that the dictatorship will be a transitional stage which will end with the abolition of all classes and the establishment of a classless society.[2]

The class struggle is thus held to offer an explanation of phenomena for which traditional history cannot account, and in particular of the trend towards increasing productivity. Men work blindly within a social system which forces them to act in accordance with what they believe to be their class interest, and it is vain to blame them for so doing. As all are caught in the network, they can do nothing to change its nature. This is one of the reasons why Marx does not believe in social technology, and incidentally why Marxism is no guide to the practice of government, as Lenin was later to discover. Yet all the time the class struggle is inevitably leading to the transformation of society. As the productive forces change, the class which

---

[1] On the class struggle see K. R. Popper, *The Open Society and its Enemies* (1945), II, pp. 103 f.; Venable, *Human Nature,* pp. 98 f.; J. L. Gray, *Karl Marx and Social Philosophy in Social and Political Ideas of the Victorian Age* (ed. F. J. C. Hearnshaw, 1933), pp. 141 f.

[2] Letter to Weydemeyer of March 5th, 1852, *Correspondence,* p. 57.

has hitherto controlled them is confronted by a new class, which claims to be able to administer them more efficiently; and just as the merchants and craftsmen were able to challenge the feudal lord of the later Middle Ages, so will the wage-earner challenge the capitalist and wrest economic power from him. Thus there will be brought about the final emancipation of mankind, seeing that there is no class below the proletariat, which is at the bottom of the social scale. But to accelerate this process, the class-consciousness of the worker must first be developed, that is, he must be made to realize his class interest and become conscious of that same power with which Hegel had endowed the nation. The class-conscious proletarian is thus the worker who is not only aware of his class situation, but is also proud of his class and assured of its historic mission.

Yet Marx nowhere seeks to prove that the worker *is,* in fact, fitted for the role assigned to him; nor does it occur to him that the negation of Capitalism may lead to the emergence of a wholly new class which is strictly speaking neither capitalist nor proletarian. The belief in human perfectibility that he had inherited from the eighteenth century led him to believe that a classless society, inherently desirable on ethical grounds, must be the next stage in social evolution; while as a revolutionary and agitator he saw in the working-class movement the only available instrument for the achievement of this aim in the immediate future, and was thus induced to regard it as the final "negation of the negation."

The belief in the class struggle as the "inner essence" of history vitiates the thinking of Marxists by leading them to attribute to the proletariat attitudes and judgments which are, in fact, confined to little groups of revolutionaries.[1] The classical economists were in the habit of generalizing widely about a class of factors of production which they called "labour," and to which they opposed an equally chimerical general monopoly of employers. But this classification breaks down upon analysis. So also does the Marxist version of the class struggle. It is, in fact, a myth, and the very exhortation of the workers to unite is an admission that there is no natural proletarian solidarity, as is attested by the relations in any particular country between male and female labour, skilled and unskilled, white and coloured. Still less is there an identity of interests between workers in different countries. Measures which perpetuate the poverty of the workers in one country are beneficial to those in another; while in no advanced country will the workers accept cheap foreign labour. And, again, all experience has hitherto proved that whenever the existence of any country appears to be threatened from without, its preservation is regarded as the dominant interest by all classes.[2]

---

[1] Max Eastman, *Stalin's Russia and the Crisis of Socialism* (1940), p. 217.
[2] L. H. Robbins, *The Economic Basis of the Class Struggle* (1939), pp. 17 f.; Franz Borkenau, *Socialism, National or International* (1942), pp. 14 f.

Finally, Marx's thesis that all conflict among men arises from the class struggle, albeit of undoubted tactical value as calculated to convince the masses that their misfortunes are attributable to the capitalist system and will disappear with the victory of the proletariat, is none the less fallacious. For the supreme source of conflict in life is the inevitable opposition between the claims of the individual and those of society—a conflict which is not reducible to the class struggle and cannot be dialectically resolved (even were it desirable that it should be) because it is a part of the unchanging human situation.

Criticism of Historical Materialism

Marx's philosophy of history is regarded, even by his critics, with a greater respect than any other part of his doctrine, though it did not exert much influence until after his death. It rests on two theses. The first is that economic causes are fundamental, and the second that they operate in accordance with the dialectic principle. The latter is nowadays accepted only by Marxists, but the former commands a much wider allegiance.

The claim that the dialectic furnishes the clue to history cannot, indeed, be seriously defended, even if we are prepared to accept it as an explanation of the processes of thought. Any proposition, such as that "All property is theft," can be developed dialectically because it supplies a starting point. But as Karl Federn points out in his most valuable study, history proceeds as an unending stream of which no one knows the beginning or the end. It provides no *terminus a quo,* and thus makes it impossible to determine which of its stages are thesis, antithesis or synthesis.[1] Any historical event can be shown with equal plausibility to be a synthesis of two contradictory elements in the past, or as a thesis for which some other event will then be chosen to provide the antithesis. Thus, the Norman Conquest can be represented as a synthesis of Roman and Anglo-Saxon cultures, or as a thesis of which the age of the Plantagenets and that of the Tudors are respectively the antithesis and the synthesis. Such irresponsible treatment simply reduces history to a game for which the only qualifications are a lively imagination and much ignorance.

Further, we have seen that the dialectic, as used by Hegel, is essentially an optimistic doctrine, since every synthesis is an advance towards the Absolute; while Marx similarly contends that every successive stage of society which arises on account of the internal contradictions of the preceding stage constitutes a "higher" form. If history were a continuous record

[1] Karl Federn, *The Materialistic Conception of History* (1939), pp. 209 f.; for a recent statement of the Marxist thesis see Jean Bruhat, *Destin de l'Histoire* (Paris, 1948); see also M. M. Bober, *Karl Marx's Interpretation of History* (Harvard University Press, 1927), pp. 297-315; for a well-reasoned statement of the Marxist case see R. Mondolfo, *Il materialismo storico in Federico Engels* (1912, ed. Florence, 1952); H. B. Acton, *The Illusion of the Epoch* (1955), pp. 107 f.

of progress, this would be well enough. But it is as much a tale of dissolution and decay; and to this part of it the dialectic cannot be applied.[1]

Again, the dialectical approach to history becomes extremely dangerous when it is accepted *de fide,* as it offers no objective standard as to the sense and rationality of action; and the fanatical devotion to it of the Russian leaders is certainly a hindrance to them rather than a help. The inter-war years abound in examples of policies, allegedly based on dialectical analyses, which served neither Russian nor communist interests. A notable instance was the discovery that the pre-condition of a communist victory in Germany was that Hitler should enjoy what it was assumed would be only a brief spell of authority. The Communists were therefore instructed to attack the Social Democrats instead of combining with them against the common enemy, with the result that he came into power and crushed them both.[2] Similarly, the line which Stalin imposed upon the Chinese Communists, in support of which a whole literature of theoretical justification was forthcoming, proved singularly unfortunate. They were ordered to adopt a policy which lay beyond their power to carry out, or at least to do so as Stalin desired, and thus played into the hands of the Kuomintang which wellnigh exterminated them. The party was driven into the remoter districts, to emerge many years later under conditions which had never been foreseen, and are unlikely to have been viewed by Moscow with entire satisfaction.[3]

But Marx's first thesis, that the economic factor is fundamental for all social institutions and particularly for their historical development, is of much greater importance. It has exercised a profound influence, and all modern writers are indebted to him even if they do not know it. Any return to pre-Marxist social theory is inconceivable. Indeed, as K. R. Popper points out, his thesis is sound enough so long as we use the term "fundamental" loosely and do not lay too much stress upon it; and practically all social studies will profit if they are conducted against the background of the "economic conditions" of society. In this qualified sense his "economism" represents a valuable advance in the methods of social science, and has suggested many lines of enquiry that have greatly extended our knowledge.[4]

None the less, it is open to serious criticism in the extreme form in which Marx presented it. He asserts in the *Critique of Political Economy* that there are two factors in production, the productive forces and the pro-

---

[1] John Plamenatz, *What is Communism?* (1946), pp. 39-40.

[2] A. L. Rowse, *The Use of History* (1946), pp. 136-137.

[3] Stalin defended his policy in his speech to the Central Committee of August 1st, 1927, printed in *Marxism and the National and Colonial Question,* pp. 232 f. For a criticism of it see Harold R. Isaacs, *The Tragedy of the Chinese Revolution* (1938, revised edition, Stanford, 1951) and Robert C. North, *Moscow and the Chinese Communists* (Stanford, 1953), pp. 66-121.

[4] Popper, II, p. 99.

ductive relations which derive from them. Conceived in purely economic terms, they constitute the substructure, which is primary; while all the manifestations of the mind of Man as reflected in his religion, laws, institutions and the like, constitute the superstructure, which is secondary. In other words, the mind and all that it creates is a part of the superstructure which is determined by the economic substructure. We are therefore left to suppose, as was pointed out above, that the productive forces somehow develop automatically, though in fact they *are developed*, e.g., by new discoveries, the responsible agency being the intelligence of Man and the use which he makes of it.[1] As Koestler put it, "Marxist society has a basement-production and an attic-intellectual-production; only the stairs and lifts are missing."[2]

That Marx was aware of this difficulty is shown by the many passages in which he treats the political and social institutions of the superstructure as a part of the substructure, as indeed he is obliged to do if he is to make sense of his theory, since it is obvious that it is only in proportion as men reach a certain level of political and social development that they are likely to make discoveries or possess the resources to exploit them. His disciples do likewise, and, as John Plamenatz says, no good Marxist will ever hesitate to include elements of the superstructure in the substructure whenever he finds it convenient to do so.[3] The truth is that while Marx was ultimately led to admit an interconnection between the two, he never clearly worked out what it was, and that if he had attempted to do so he would have had to abandon his theory.

Now it is quite certain that the forms of production have far-reaching consequences and are of the greatest importance in history. But, as Federn observes, the question is whether it is true that the intellectual, cultural and political forms of any community not only depend for their existence upon economic production, but are in all their modifications also determined by it. When Marx said that "men must be able to live in order to be able to make history," he did not simply mean that society depends on production for its existence, as this would have been a view that no one would have contested. Air is an essential condition of life. But if a scientist should succeed in proving that institutions and opinions depend upon the particular composition of the atmosphere, he would have made a very important discovery indeed. What Marx meant was that the way in which men produce determines the entire complex of ideas and institutions which make up the social order.[4]

The proofs which Marxists adduce to substantiate this are taken either from pre-history or from history; the method is to show that an economic

---

[1] Federn, pp. 15 f.; but cp. Bober, pp. 11-27.
[2] *The Yogi and the Commissar* (1945), p. 70.
[3] Plamenatz, p. 35.
[4] Federn, pp. 30 f.

change occurred at a certain time, that some decades or centuries later a change took place in the ideas or institutions of the same people, and then to attribute the second change to the first. Thus, Karl Kautsky accounts for Puritanism in England by saying that "the transition from a natural to a monetary system of economy caused the lower classes to fall a prey to a sombre Puritanism." Why this should be so is not explained; in fact, the transition to a monetary economy had been completed by the fourteenth century, whereas Puritanism did not appear until towards the end of the sixteenth century. Again, Antonio Labriola explains why the aborigines of North America did not attain a high degree of civilization on the ground that it was the Europeans who introduced wheat and domestic animals which had previously been lacking. But not only were there other forms of food, but vast herds of bison roamed the North American plains which the Red Indians might have tamed, just as did the Negroes the buffalo and the Mongols the yak. That they did not do so was simply because it was not among their gifts.[1]

Marxist writers thus forever repeat the truism that men must eat and clothe themselves before they can undertake political activity and the like. But this is to confuse the condition of such activity with its cause. It is significant that it is to primitive society that they turn whenever possible for their illustrations, since the more primitive a community, the greater will be the part which physical necessity plays in its life—as is equally true of the individual. As civilization advances, men become possessed of more complex desires which cannot be so easily related to elemental needs, such as the love of power which has led to so many conflicts. But having decided that every movement must have an economic cause, Marxists do not study the movement in order to find out what really lies behind it, but look round for any economic cause that may possibly explain it.[2]

In finding such a cause they are assisted by the equivocal use that they make of the concept of "historical necessity" which Marx and Engels borrowed from Hegel. "Necessity" means something—whether good or bad is immaterial—which is bound to occur because it is the inevitable result of a cause. Yet Marxists commonly apply it in the quite different sense of "desirable." Thus, we are told that England had a liberal constitution because she needed strong personalities to develop her commercial empire; whereas it would be far nearer the truth to say that because she had a free constitution, and other countries had not, the strong personalities had full scope and were in a position to found it. Again, the emergence of a great man at a critical period in a nation's history is attributed to "necessity," so that Engels points out that Napoleon "did not come by chance, and that if he had not come another man would have taken his place." Yet

[1] *Ibid.*, pp. 36-38, 40-41.
[2] Federn, p. 73.

no great man emerged to save the civilization of Greece and Rome.[1] But then Marxists invariably belittle the role of "so-called great men," arguing that they do no more than identify themselves with conditions which are independent of them. As Croce puts it, "Homer had sung, Plato had philosophized, Jesus and Paul had transformed moral consciousness quite unaware that they were simply the instruments of an economic process to which all their work was ultimately reducible."[2] For to concede that such men shape history would be inconsistent with the principle that it is determined by economic forces, and these last have, therefore, to be made responsible for their emergence. Thus, Hessen maintains that Newton was not inspired to discover the law of gravitation by being hit on the head by an apple as the discovery was demanded by the economic needs of his time.[3]

Nor do Marxists make any allowance for the contingent element that enters into history. Bertrand Russell gives some brilliant examples of seemingly fortuitous events which have had a decisive influence. It was, as he points out, touch and go whether the German Government would allow Lenin to return to Russia in 1917, and if the particular minister had said "No" when in fact he said "Yes," it is difficult to believe that the Russian revolution would have taken the course it did. Again, if Genoa had not ceded Corsica to France in 1768, Napoleon, born there in the year following, would have been an Italian and would have had no career in France. Yet it can scarcely be seriously maintained that without him the history of France would have been the same.[4]

The social relations which form the subject-matter of history are, in fact, far too complex to be determined by any single cause. Historical materialism does not explain why peoples living under similar conditions of production have developed widely divergent civilizations.[5] It does not explain why the Christian religion was independently accepted by races as different as the civilized Romans and the semi-barbarous Slavs and Irish. Nor, incidentally, does it explain why totally different ideologies should be held by men who share the same cultural background, so that the founders of Socialism, including Marx and Engels themselves and most of the leaders of the nineteenth-century labour movement, should have belonged to the bourgeoisie. As Federn puts it, the relation between the economic substructure and the superstructure resembles that between the soil of a field

[1] Op. cit., pp. 220-222.

[2] Sul Problema Morale dei nostri Tempi in Pensiero Politico e Politica Attuale (Bari, 1946, pp. 7-8).

[3] B. Hessen, The Economic Roots of Newton's Principia (1931). On the general Marxist thesis all manifestations of intellectual and artistic activity are determined by the state of the productive forces in any given age; see Plekhanov, In Defence of Materialism (ed. 1947), pp. 200 f.

[4] Freedom and Organization (1935), pp. 228-229.

[5] Bober, pp. 278 f.

and the plants growing in it. We know that the plants sprang from the soil, and that if there were no soil there would be no plants; but we do not know who sowed the seeds, or where they come from, or why those plants grow there and not others.[1]

Finally, Marx had no right to appeal to economics in support of his theory. As L. H. Robbins points out, economics is not, as was once held, the study of the causes of material welfare, but of those aspects of behaviour which arise from the scarcity of means to achieve given ends. As to whether the ends in themselves are good or bad, it is strictly neutral; but if the attainment of one set of ends involves the sacrifice of others, it has an economic aspect.[2] The notion, entertained by men like Carlyle and Ruskin, that economics is concerned with purely material ends is false, though they may perhaps be excused for having held it, as it was generally accepted by the economists of their day. Nor can it be argued, save on the basis of the crudest Benthamite psychology, that the economic motive always prevails.

Again, economics is not to be confused with technology. It is not interested in technique as such, but only in so far as it is one of the influences that determine scarcity. The manner in which men will apply the various skills of which they become masters will largely depend upon considerations which are psychological and have nothing to do with economics. But Marx's economic interpretation of history explains all major events by changes in the *technique of production,* thus implying that ultimate valuations are merely its by-products, and without taking into account the very different ways in which men may use it. His doctrine, as Robbins puts it, "is a general statement about the causation of human motive which, from the point of view of economic science, is sheer metaphysics. The label 'materialist' fits the doctrine. The label 'economic' is misplaced. Economics may well provide an important instrument for the elucidation of history. But there is nothing in economic analysis which entitles us to assert that all history is to be explained in 'economic' terms, if 'economic' is to be used as equivalent to the technically material. The materialist interpretation of history came to be called the economic interpretation of history, because it was thought that the subject-matter of economics was the cause of material welfare. Once it is realized that this is not the case, the materialist conception must stand or fall on its own merits. Economic science lends no support to its doctrines." [3]

.   .   .   .   .

The claim that historical materialism rests upon scientific laws contained the implication that history was an exact science, and that it was thus possible to foretell its future development. Yet neither Marx nor

---

[1] Federn, p. 100.
[2] *The Nature and Significance of Economic Science* (1932), pp. 7 f., 24-25.
[3] *Ibid.,* pp. 43-44.

Engels was a historian, and the value of their work lies solely in their penetrating observation of a certain number of contemporary facts. In his *Capital* Marx does indeed make considerable use of history to support conclusions at which he had arrived independently, but the book in no way proves historical materialism to be true, and in fact, assumes that as it is self-evident no proof is required. His anxiety to represent history as an exact science, and his "historicism" which made him believe that the main function of science was to predict the future, led him, however, constantly to maintain that society was governed by "inexorable laws" operating independently of the will of man, and thus beyond his power to change. "When a society," he says in the Introduction to *Capital*, "has discovered the natural law that determines its own movement . . . it can neither overleap the natural phases of its evolution nor shuffle out of them by a stroke of the pen." All it can do "is to shorten and lessen the birth pangs." But this committed him to a view of history not altogether consistent with that implied by his theory of knowledge as *Praxis,* of which the function is to "change the world," so that, as he and Engels both declare, "History does nothing" seeing that "man makes his own history, even though he does not do so on conditions chosen by himself." [1] Doubtless what they both wished to convey was that man was able to become the master of his destiny; but in their desire to stress the scientific character of their doctrine they succeeded in making a great many people think that they meant the exact opposite, and that the course of history was wholly predetermined.[2]

By the nineties Engels had become aware of this, and in a letter to Joseph Bloch he admits that many contemporary Marxists were turning out "a rare kind of balderdash":

According to the materialist conception of history, [he says], the determining element . . . is *ultimately* the production and reproduction in real life. More than this neither Marx nor I have ever asserted. If, therefore, somebody twists this into the statement that the economic element is the *only* determining one, he transforms it into a meaningless, abstract and absurd phrase. The economic situation is the basis, but the various elements of the superstructure . . . also exercise their influence upon the historical struggle, and in many cases preponderate in determining their form. There is an interaction of all those elements in which, amid all the endless *hosts* of accidents . . . the economic movement finally asserts itself as necessary . . . Marx and I are ourselves partly to blame for the fact that younger writers sometimes lay more stress on the economic factor than is due to it. We had to emphasize this main principle in opposition to our adversaries, who denied it, and we had not always the time, the place or the opportunity to allow the other elements involved in the interaction to come into their rights.[3]

Marxist writers hold that the above puts the whole matter in a just perspective. Yet, in fact, Engels has to admit an interaction between the superstructure and the substructure, which is, indeed, assumed by the ap

---

[1] Hook, *From Hegel to Marx*, pp. 38 f.
[2] Edmund Wilson, *To the Finland Station* (1940), pp. 180 f.
[3] September 21st, 1890, *Correspondence*, pp. 475-476.

peal, "Workers of the World Unite!"; for if there were none, it was useless
to preach revolution, and there would be nothing for the proletariat to do
save passively to await the working out of the dialectical process, of which
it was the ultimate beneficiary. But he does not seek to explain its nature,
and repeats that the "economic situation" is the basis which always "ultimately" asserts itself. His concession, as T. D. Weldon puts it, is "an elaborate attempt to have it both ways, to accept the incompleteness of the Marxist hypothesis and to pass this off as a matter of no great moment." [1] In
practice, Marxists habitually write as if economic factors were the sole determinants, and rarely if ever make allowances for any others.

As, however, Marx and Engels are concerned with the origin of the
superstructure rather than with its influence upon the development of
society, they tend to assign to it a purely passive role. In his *Dialectical and
Historical Materialism* (1938) Stalin goes further, and insists that once a
superstructure has arisen, it becomes "a most potent force which facilitates
. . . the progress of society." Indeed "new social ideas and theories arise
precisely because they are necessary to society, because it is impossible to
carry out the urgent tasks of the development of the material life of society
without their organizing, mobilizing and transforming action." [2] He returned to this theme in his *Concerning Marxism in Linguistics* (1950):
"The superstructure is a product of the basis, but this does not mean that
it merely reflects it, that it is passive, neutral, indifferent to the fate of its
basis, to the fate of classes, to the character of the system. On the contrary,
having come into being, it becomes an exceedingly active force, actively
assisting its basis to take shape and consolidate itself, and doing everything
it can to help the new system finish off and eliminate the old basis and the
old classes." [3]

This would seem to be a more positive view than that of Marx and
Engels. Yet two points should be noted. First, Stalin is only able to represent the superstructure as a "potent force" because, as all Marxists do, he
attributes to the substructure or base the property of being able to produce
"new ideas and theories" whenever the material needs of society require
them, though no explanation is given as to why this should be so. Secondly,
as he was himself largely responsible for the form the superstructure had
assumed in Russia, he could very well represent it as playing an "active"
role, and indeed could scarcely do otherwise. [4]

While therefore Marx and Engels have much to say about the power
of men to transform nature and, in so doing, to transform themselves and
the society in which they live, and while both maintain that it is in the
knowledge of external reality and the power to use that knowledge for

[1] *States and Morals* (1946), p. 158.
[2] *History of the Communist Party of the Soviet Union* (Moscow, 1943), pp. 116-117.
[3] P. 4.
[4] For a full discussion of Stalin's views see Henri Chambre, *Marxism en Union
Soviétique* (Paris, 1955), pp 457-483.

definite ends that human freedom consists, they never resolve the central problem. If man is to be in any real sense the master of his destiny, it can be only through his ideas and opinions. But these belong to the super-structure, and the form they take is determined by the substructure. All they will admit is that an interaction takes place between the two, though upon what principle they do not tell us. But once an interaction has been conceded, the whole thesis is undermined, since we are no longer dealing with a purely economic factor, but with one which has been itself in part determined by non-economic factors. To say after this that the economic factor must always be decisive is meaningless.

The common-sense view is surely this. Man is a being endowed with intelligence, and this develops as he rises in the scale of civilization. Through it he provides himself with the means of subsistence, and at the same time with the laws, art forms and the like that he regards as necessary for his security and well-being. The two are part of the same process, and there is no occasion to bring them into opposition and to make the one dependent upon the other. If it be true that the way in which men think and the various institutional and other forms to which their ideas give rise are influenced by the manner in which they make their living, the converse is equally true. Marx is a good servant but a bad master. He was quite right in drawing attention to the importance of the economic factor, which had been seriously neglected, but he gave it an undue prominence and thus over-simplified the complexity of the social situation, as his followers have continued to do to this day. . . .

II. MARXIST ECONOMICS

. . . We have already seen that it is the Marxist contention that at some remote and unspecified period of history society became divided into two classes, one of which obtained control over the means of production, while the other possessed nothing but its labour power. This labour power, which Marx calls "variable capital," the capitalist (the contemporary rep-resentative of the possessing class) buys and sets to work on the various means of production—raw materials, machinery and the like—that consti-tute what he calls "constant capital." Now, labour possesses the unique property of being able to produce more than is required for its subsistence and replacement. The worker receives as wages only what is sufficient to maintain him; and if it took a whole day's work to produce this, the ques-tion of surplus value would not arise, nor incidentally would it be to any-one's advantage to employ him. What, in fact, happens is that a man works for ten hours, and in the first, say, five of these (which constitute what Marx calls "socially necessary labour") he produces all the value he is to receive as wages. Of the value produced during the second five hours he gets nothing, and it is stolen from him by his employer. The difference between the value created during the period of socially necessary labour and that created during the period in excess of it is what Marx calls "surplus value," and is the measure of the worker's "exploitation." Thus the value produced by the worker far exceeds the value of his means of subsistence, that is, the value of his labour power which he receives from the capitalist as wages. But by remunerating labour in the form of wages, the division between paid and unpaid labour time is concealed.

Variable capital, *i.e.*, labour, alone produces value, and constant capital produces none. Machinery is simply "stored up labour," that is, something upon which labour has already been expended. Sources of wealth, such as unworked mineral deposits, have, indeed, an exchange value, because people are prepared to give money for them, but this is only on account of their potential value, that is, the value they will have when labour is applied to them. Orthodox economic theory teaches that the production of anything that has value calls for the cooperation of four agents—land (raw materials), labour, capital and organization (management)—and that each agent receives its share of the product: land as rent, labour as wages, capital as interest and management (or more strictly the element of uncertainty which enters into production) as profits. Marx rejects this view and isolates labour from the other agents of production. It alone is the source of value, and is alone entitled to the value it is alleged to create.

In the first volume of *Capital* Marx argues that as profit is created solely by surplus value, and as labour is the sole value-producing agency, the rate of profit will depend upon what he calls the "organic composition of capitals," that is, the proportion of labour (variable capital) to machinery (constant capital) employed in a given undertaking; and that it will thus tend to fall in proportion as technological improvements lead to the employment of less labour. Yet although this conclusion logically followed from his premises, it was demonstrably false in practice. Marx was aware of the difficulty, to which he refers in a letter to Engels of August 1862.[1] But he did not face it at the time, and set it aside for further treatment. There the matter rested until 1883, when he died.

Engels had seriously miscalculated the time that would be needed to put in order the unpublished portion of *Capital,* and the second and third volumes did not appear until 1885 and 1894 respectively. Meanwhile, as E. H. Carr has pointed out, certain followers of the German economist Rodbertus had accused Marx of plagiarizing from the works of their master, and Engels had retorted by challenging them to produce the solution to the above problem, thus drawing increased attention to it.[2] It was, indeed, eagerly awaited, but when it appeared in the third volume it caused widespread disillusionment. For it was now contended that although the rate of profit did depend on the relation of variable to constant capital if the

[1] *Briefwechsel*, III, p. 77.
[2] Carr, *Karl Marx*, pp. 270-271.

whole capital of the world was taken into account (and of this no proof was given), this did not apply to the profits of particular businesses, which tended to equalize themselves according to the state of trade. As Joan Robinson points out, Marx's demonstration simply amounts to the tautology that if wages are constant (and elsewhere he denies that they are) the rate of profit will fall as capital per man increases.[1]

What, after all this, is left of the labour theory of value? We are asked to believe that there is an abstract property called "value" which belongs to any labour-produced commodity, and which, while purporting to be its exchange value, does not, in fact, correspond to its price or even to its average price. And we are further asked to believe that there is a second abstraction, called "surplus value," which determines profits in general but not profits in particular, and bears no relation to the standard of wages of the workers whose exploitation it is supposed to measure. Marx first says that the value of a commodity corresponds to the amount of labour put into it, and if he had stuck to this, he would, as Plamenatz points out, at least have made clear in what sense he was using the term. But he then goes on to call this value "exchange value," and to spend many pages describing just how the value of one commodity is expressed in terms of another, thus inevitably suggesting that they do actually tend to exchange in accordance with the relative amounts of labour required to produce them. He then has to confess that they do not, in fact, exchange in this manner, and would only do so if the same proportions of capital and labour were employed in their production; and thus, he ends by confusing both himself and his readers.[2] Actually, he is ultimately driven to admit that exchange value is governed by the market, that is, by the law of supply and demand, which makes nonsense of his theory that it is derived from labour only. . . .

Marx's economic doctrine may be summarized as follows. Labour alone creates value. All profits are derived from unpaid labour time. Capitalists are driven by competition to accumulate capital, which becomes concentrated in fewer and fewer hands, with the result that the smaller businesses disappear and their owners are driven back into the working-class. The accumulation of capital in the form of labour-saving devices reduces the use of human labour and at the same time the profits of the capitalists, who are therefore compelled to offset their losses by intensifying the exploitation of their workers, over whom the increase of unemployment has given them an even stronger hold and who are now prepared to work on any terms. Hence the misery of the workers, eventually almost the entire population, will progressively become more and more unendurable. This will lead them to combine for their own protection, and so create a force which will eventually destroy the whole system.

It has been necessary to dwell upon Marx's theory of value at some

[1] *An Essay on Marxian Economics* (1949), p. 36.
[2] Plamenatz, pp. 33-34.

length because he regarded it, as do all Marxists, as the cornerstone of his system, though it only introduces an element of confusion, and he has nothing of importance to say which could not have been expressed equally well without it. We have seen that it is not a theory of value at all, and that his value and surplus value are pure abstractions. It is in fact a theory of exploitation, designed to show that the propertied class has always lived on the labour of the non-propertied class. It is therefore on the assumption that labour—by which is meant wage-labour—is the only value-producing agency, that the theory stands or falls. But it is a false assumption because, as is characteristic of Marxist dogmas, it concentrates upon one single factor in a highly complex situation to the exclusion of all others. Thus capital is itself a product of labour. Someone has laboured to produce it, and has then decided to forego the immediate consumption of the value created in order to create further value, as it is clearly in the interests of society that he should do. As, however, not everyone is willing to do this, the owner of capital finds himself in possession of something that has a scarcity value and thus commands its market price. The Marxist argument that capital produces value only when labour is applied to it is simply that of the medieval Schoolmen. Labour without capital is equally unproductive. The capitalist system is open to abuses like any other. Yet those who desire to abolish it would do well to reflect that the only alternative to the profit-and-loss motive that has so far shown any indication of being equally effective is the fear of punishment imposed by a totalitarian State.

Moreover, as Popper points out, the whole of Marx's theory of value is redundant. For if we assume, as is fundamental to his case, a free market in which there is always a greater supply of labour than there is a demand for it, the law of supply and demand becomes sufficient to explain all the phenomena of "increasing misery" without bringing value into it.[1] Marx was on strong grounds so long as he restricted himself to the conditions prevailing under *laissez-faire* Capitalism at the time when he was writing, and his analysis of these conditions was an important contribution to the study of social relations. He was quite right in pointing out that labour was not receiving its fair share; but he failed to see that there might be other ways of dealing with the problem than by revolution, and that he himself had provided one of the most effective of these by calling upon the workers to unite. The organization of labour, collective bargaining and State intervention in its various forms were to revolutionize the situation and to make nonsense of the law of increasing misery, save in so far as it applies to Russia, where the promise of the millennium remains unfulfilled and all verbs, it has been said, are conjugated in the future tense.

Nor did Marx discern that the middle-class, so far from being crushed out of existence, would greatly increase in strength. The capitalist to whom

[1] *Op. cit.*, II, pp. 165.

Engels had first called his attention was commonly the owner of his business. But the great extension of jointstock companies in the second half of the century—following in this country upon the Companies Act of 1862, which extended the principle of limited liability—had the effect of creating a new type of capitalist in the person of the shareholder, who had no part in the management of the concern, which he delegated to paid officials. The result was at least temporarily to broaden the basis of the capitalist system by creating a new middle-class which had an interest in retaining it either as investors concerned with their dividends, or as members of the managerial salariat, whose lower ranks felt themselves superior to the proletariat from which they had been largely recruited.

Keynes has described *Capital* as "an obsolete economic text book . . . not only scientifically erroneous, but without interest or application for the modern world." [1] Yet the modern world continues to take an interest in it, for, like every great revolutionary treatise, its power lies rather in its central idea than in the arguments used to support it, which may often enough be found untenable. To the Victorians the capitalist system appeared the embodiment of permanence and stability, and, in general, this belief persisted up to 1914. From that conflict many held that it had emerged even stronger than ever. Yet, as Carr has shown, its character had changed. The old-fashioned Capitalism—what Marx called "bourgeois Capitalism"—had broken down, partly because it had evolved away from a free competitive system of individuals and small units into a highly organized system of large-scale enterprises; and partly because of the increasing strength and organization of the workers, who were bound to resent the old privileged order, and to insist that the new order should contain increasing elements of Socialist-planned economy which made for a more equal distribution of goods. This transformation had taken place over most of Western Europe by the First World War; after that war Capitalism in the older sense never came back, and there was an uneasy interregnum during which the two rival systems jostled one another without finding any working compromise.[2] These years were marked by violent economic crises, accompanied by greater mass unemployment than had been known since the Industrial Revolution started. The concentration of capital proceeded; while labour continued to organize itself, though it is claimed that the workers did not thereby become revolutionary-minded. Then came the Second World War, and few will contend that the capitalist system is the stronger for it. Many of Marx's prophecies have, indeed, been falsified. Yet, looked at objectively, it is too early to say that his central thesis has been disproved; and we should do well to recall Jung's observation upon Columbus, who "by using

---

[1] *Essays in Persuasion* (New York, 1932), p. 300.
[2] *Problems of Writing Modern Russian History* (*The Listener*, October 7th, 1948, pp. 548 f.).

subjective assumptions, a false hypothesis, and a route abandoned by modern navigation, nevertheless discovered America."

For, when every criticism has been made, *Capital* remains a very great book, and if the greatness of a book is to be measured by its influence, one of the most important ever written. Marx presents a view of the world which cannot be disregarded—a world in which, as Edmund Wilson puts it, "commodities bear rule and make men their playthings." His highly abstract reasoning provides the clue to this economic labyrinth. "It is," Wilson says, "his great trick to hypnotize us by the shuttling of the syllogisms which he produces with so scientific an air, and then suddenly to remind us that these principles derive solely from the laws of human selfishness which are as unfailing as the force of gravitation." The exposition of his theory is always followed by a documented picture of the capitalist laws at work, until "we feel that we have been taken for the first time through the real structure of our civilization, and that it is the ugliest that ever existed—a state of things where there is very little to choose between the physical degradation of the workers and the moral degradation of the masters." [1]

But this account of the matter is not altogether satisfactory. Marx does indeed hold that the capitalist system is morally objectionable, though he fails to show how its evils will be removed by getting rid of the capitalists, as they certainly have not been in the Soviet Union. Yet he is careful not to ascribe these evils to the capitalists themselves, nor to impute to such persons a larger share of original sin than other members of the community possess. For they are, like the workers they exploit, the prisoners of a system. They have to operate in accordance with its laws, and these are not "laws of human selfishness," but the laws which govern the development of the productive forces, and which demand that it must inevitably take the particular historical form it has done, though they will equally inevitably end by destroying it. It is true that Communist propaganda is designed to convince the workers that capitalism is simply the expression of the selfish interests of a minority which deliberately exploits the majority for its own advantage. But this was not Marx's teaching—at least when he was writing seriously.

[1] *Op. cit.*, pp. 271-272.

A BRIEF PSYCHOLOGICAL CRITIQUE

SIGMUND FREUD*

The strength of Marxism obviously does not lie in its view of history or in the prophecies about the future which it bases upon that view, but in its clear insight into the determining influence which is exerted by the economic conditions of man upon his intellectual, ethical and artistic reactions. A whole collection of correlations and causal sequences were thus discovered, which had hitherto been almost completely disregarded. But it cannot be assumed that economic motives are the only ones which determine the behaviour of men in society. The unquestionable fact that different individuals, races and nations behave differently under the same economic conditions, in itself proves that the economic factor cannot be the sole determinant. It is quite impossible to understand how psychological factors can be overlooked where the reactions of living human beings are involved; for not only were such factors already concerned in the establishment of these economic conditions, but, even in obeying these conditions, men can do no more than set their original instinctual impulses in motion —their self-preservative instinct, their love of aggression, their need for love, and their impulse to attain pleasure and avoid pain. In an earlier lecture we have emphasised the importance of the part played by the super-ego, which represents tradition and ideals of the past, and which will resist for some time the pressure exerted by new economic situations. . . .

It is probable that the so-called materialistic conceptions of history err in that they underestimate this factor. They brush it aside with the remark that the "ideologies" of mankind are nothing more than resultants of their economic situation at any given moment or superstructures built upon it. That is the truth, but very probably it is not the whole truth. Mankind never lives completely in the present; the ideologies of the super-ego perpetuate the past, the traditions of the race and the people, which yield but slowly to the influence of the present and to new developments, and, so long as they work through the super-ego, play an important part in man's life, quite independently of economic conditions. . . .

And, finally, we must not forget that the mass of mankind, subjected

* Reprinted from pp. 243-244, 95-96, 244-245 of *New Introductory Lectures on Psychoanalysis* by Sigmund Freud, Copyright, 1933, by Sigmund Freud. By permission of W. W. Norton & Company, Inc.

though they are to economic necessities, are borne on by a process of cultural development—some call it civilisation—which is no doubt influenced by all the other factors, but is equally certainly independent of them in its origin; it is comparable to an organic process, and is quite capable of itself having an effect upon the other factors.

Chapter 5

MARXISM INTO LENINISM

Although Lenin did assert that "in no sense do we regard the Marxist theory as something complete and unassailable," he generally severely castigated socialists who, in his view, departed from Marx, once writing: "You cannot eliminate even one basic assumption, one substantial part of this philosophy of Marxism (it is as if it were a solid block of steel) without abandoning objective truth, without falling into the arms of the bourgeois-reactionary falsehood."

Lenin's insistence upon his own rigid orthodoxy did not, in the judgment of Professor Sabine, prevent him from being "responsible for the most considerable changes that any follower of Marx ever made in the master's teaching."

Bolshevism before 1917, and the nature and significance of Lenin's contributions to theory and to preparation for revolution—as well as his divergencies from Marx—are examined in the pages that follow.

This material has more than just an historic importance. It was Lenin, above any other single individual, whose conceptions shaped the Bolshevik Party, who "made" the Bolshevik revolution and supplied its theoretical justification, and it was his ideas and policies which often decisively shaped the Soviet system in a formative period with consequences that persist to this day. Soviet Russia is more in the image of Lenin than of Marx. The "downgrading" of Stalin has served only to enhance Lenin's importance within the U.S.S.R. and to Communist movements throughout the world. Lenin's ideas and practices merit, therefore, the most careful study.

113

BOLSHEVISM BEFORE 1917

MERLE FAINSOD*

An acute observer of Russian society in the late nineteenth and early twentieth centuries might have found the potential of revolution in every corner of the realm. Had he predicted that it would be the Bolsheviks who would ultimately inherit the Tsar's diadem, most of his contemporaries would probably have dismissed him as mad. Until 1917, the tiny handful of revolutionaries who followed the Bolshevik banner appeared to be swallowed in the vastness of Russia. Lenin, in a speech before a socialist youth meeting in Zurich on January 22, 1917, expressed strong doubts that he would "live to see the decisive battles of this coming revolution." The sudden rise of Bolshevism from insignificance to total power was as great a shock to the Bolshevik leaders as it was to those whom Bolshevism displaced.

Yet it would be the height of superficiality to treat the triumph of Bolshevism as a mere accident. The great crises of history are rarely accidents. They have their points of origin as well as their points of no return. The doctrine, the organizational practices, and the tactics which Bolshevism developed in its period of incubation enabled it to harness the surge of revolutionary energy released by deeper forces of social unrest and war. If in the process Bolshevism also succeeded in replacing the lumbering, inefficient police absolutism of Tsardom and the short-lived democratic experiment of the Provisional Government by the first full-scale venture in modern totalitarianism, that result too was implicit in the doctrinal, organizational, and tactical premises on which the structure of Bolshevism was built.

THE DEVELOPMENT OF DOCTRINE

Until the 1880's the Russian revolutionary movement, as was natural in a country so predominantly agricultural, revolved around the peasant and his fate. Whatever may have been the tactical divergences among Narodnik intellectuals—whether they dedicated themselves to agitation or terror—their whole orientation was toward Ilya of Murom, the peasant hero of the folk poems (byliny), who, as Masaryk puts it, "when the country is in straits

* Professor of Government at Harvard University. Author of Smolensk Under Soviet Rule; International Socialism and the World War; and of many articles on the U.S.S.R. Reprinted by permission of the publishers from chapter 2 of Merle Fainsod's How Russia Is Ruled (Cambridge, Mass.: Harvard University Press, Copyright, 1953, by The President and Fellows of Harvard College). For footnote references, see original source.

. . . awakens from his apathy, displays his super-human energy, and saves the situation." Even the industrial awakening of the seventies did little to disturb this fundamental preoccupation with the peasant and his destiny.

Narodnik philosophers from Herzen to Lavrov and Mikhailovsky were not unaware of Marx and Engels; indeed, the Narodniks were largely responsible for translating Marx and Engels into Russian and introducing them to a wide audience of the intelligentsia. For the Narodniks, however, the stages of industrialization and proletarianization which Marx and Engels described were dangers to be avoided rather than paths to be traversed. Nor were Marx and Engels themselves at first certain that the course of economic development in Russia would have to recapitulate that of the West. In a letter which Marx wrote in 1877 to a Russian publication, *Notes on the Fatherland,* he referred to his theory of capitalist development as not necessarily everywhere applicable and spoke of Russia as having "the best opportunity that history has ever offered to a people to escape all the catastrophes of capitalism." By 1882 Marx and Engels began to qualify their views on the possibility of Russian exceptionalism. In an introduction to a new Russian translation of the *Communist Manifesto,* they saw the capitalist system in Russia "growing up with feverish speed." They still thought, however, that the mir might "serve as a starting-point for a communist course of development" but only "if the Russian revolution sounds the signal for a workers' revolution in the West, so that each becomes the complement of the other."

By 1892 Engels had in effect written off the mir as a Narodnik illusion. In a letter to Danielson, the Narodnik translator of *Capital,* Engels commented, "I am afraid that we shall soon have to look upon your mir as no more than a memory of the irrecoverable past, and that in the future we shall have to do with a capitalistic Russia." In a brief reference to earlier hopes, he continued, "If this be so, a splendid chance will unquestionably have been lost." To the end of their lives, Marx and Engels remained warm admirers of the Narodnaya Volya and its courageous revolutionary Narodnik successors. Terror, for Marx and Engels, had a special justification in the struggle against Russian absolutism, and they deplored the efforts of their own Russian Marxist followers to discredit the Narodnik revolutionaries. Indeed, one of the last interventions of Engels in Russian affairs was his attempt in 1892 to arrange a merger of Narodniks and Marxists into a single party. The effort, needless to say, failed.

THE BEGINNINGS OF RUSSIAN MARXISM

Russian Marxism as an independent political movement originated in the split in 1879 of the Narodnik organization *Zemlya i Volya* (Land and Freedom). The seceders, who stood for propaganda and agitation as opposed to terrorism, established a rival organization, the *Chërnyi Peredel*

(Black Repartition), to propagate their doctrines. One of their leaders was Plekhanov, soon to be known as the father of Russian Marxism, but then still clinging to the Narodnik belief in the peasant as the driving force of revolution. The roundup of revolutionaries which followed the assassination of Alexander II in 1881 caused Plekhanov to flee abroad. His break with Zemlya i Volya on the issue of terror, the apparent bankruptcy of Narodnik policies in the reaction which followed 1881, and the manifest failure of the peasantry to respond either to agitation or terror impelled Plekhanov to reëxamine his views. The search for a new faith led him to Marxism. In 1883 Plekhanov, Paul Axelrod, Leo Deutsch, and Vera Zasulich, all of whom had been members of the Chërnyi Peredel, joined in establishing the first Russian Marxist organization, the group known as *Osvobozhdenie Trudc* (Emancipation of Labor). Plekhanov from the beginning was the intellectual leader of the group. In a series of brilliantly written polemical works, he laid the doctrinal foundations for Russian Marxism.

Russian Marxism thus emerged out of disillusionment with the Narodnik infatuation with the peasantry. As a result, it quickly took on a strong anti-peasant orientation. "The main bulwark of absolutism," argued the 1887 program of the Emancipation of Labor group, "lies in the political indifference and the intellectual backwardness of the peasantry." In a later pamphlet by Plekhanov, *The Duty of the Socialists in the Famine,* the point was put even more strongly:

The proletarian and the muzhik are political antipodes. The historic role of the proletariat is as revolutionary as the historic role of the muzhik is conservative. The muzhiks have been the support of oriental despotism for thousands of years. The proletariat in a comparatively short space of time has shaken the "foundations" of West European society.

Since peasant worship still exercised a powerful hold on the minds of the Russian revolutionary intelligentsia, the task of Plekhanov, and later of Lenin, was to undermine this faith and to turn the attention of the intellectuals from the village to the city, where capitalism was taking root and a new industrial proletariat was in process of creation. There, argued Plekhanov, was the coming revolutionary force. The challenge to the Narodniks was summed up in his famous dictum: "The revolutionary movement in Russia can triumph only as a revolutionary movement of the working class. There is not, nor can there be, any other way!"

The sharp antithesis which Plekhanov made between revolutionary worker and backward peasant had great polemical value in combating the influence of Narodnik ideology. But it also meant that the Social-Democratic movement turned its back on the countryside. Its long-term legacy was an attitude of suspicious distrust toward the peasantry which affected both the Bolshevik and Menshevik wings of Russian Social-Democracy and was never altogether extirpated. Even so perceptive and skillful a revolutionary engineer as Lenin did not really sense the revolutionary potential of the peasantry until the peasant risings of the 1905 revolution forced him to reëxamine the tenets of his faith.

The first problem of the early Russian Marxists was to win acceptance for their proposition that Russia was launched on an irreversible course of capitalist development and that the Narodnik dream of skipping the stage of capitalism and leaping directly from the mir to socialism was nothing but a mirage. The struggle in its inception was a battle of books and pamphlets. The polemic of the Marxists against the Narodniks was even welcomed by the government, since in its eyes the Narodniks were still dangerous revolutionaries and the Marxists were viewed as essentially a rather harmless literary group.

The diffusion of Marxism among the intellectuals of the nineties was also attended by confusion about its content and significance. For many of the "fellow-travelers" of the Legal Marxist period, "Marxist" was hardly more than a generic name for the protagonists of the industrial development which appeared to be in full triumph in the early nineties. Even Peter Struve, who counted himself a Marxist in that period and drafted the manifesto of the First Congress of the Russian Social-Democratic Labor Party, held in Minsk in 1898, could end his "Critical Remarks on the Problem of the Economic Development of Russia" (1894) with the appeal: "Let us recognize our backwardness in culture and let us take our lessons from capitalism." For still others, the so-called Economists of the late nineties, Marxism meant little more than "bread and butter" trade unionism, bargaining with employers for that extra kopeck on the ruble for which Lenin had such fierce contempt. Other professed Marxists—and by 1899 Struve had become one of them—responded to Bernstein's challenge to orthodox Marxism by establishing a Russian branch of Critical Revisionism, a movement which was to lead them from Marxism to idealism and to an eventual break with the Social-Democratic Party.

In the face of these divergent trends (later to be described as deviations), the doctrinal problem which Plekhanov and Lenin faced in the nineties was to buttress the orthodox Marxian analysis and to reassert its revolutionary content. In the international socialist controversies of the period, Plekhanov and Lenin took their stand with Kautsky, the guardian of the true faith, against the heterodoxies of Bernstein. In Russia they denounced the objectivism of the Legal Marxists and the reformist tendencies of Economism and Critical Revisionism. For both Plekhanov and Lenin, Marxism was a revolutionary creed not to be diluted by opportunistic waverings.

During this period, Plekhanov was still the master and Lenin the pupil. Both considered themselves orthodox Marxists. Marx's panorama of capitalist development seemed to imply that the socialist revolution stood its greatest chance of success in those countries in which the processes of in-

dustrialization were most highly advanced and in which the working class
formed a substantial part of the population. How apply such a recipe for
a successful socialist revolution to Russia with its nascent industrialism,
its weakly developed proletariat, and its overwhelmingly peasant population? Confronted with Russia's industrial backwardness, both Plekhanov
and Lenin agreed that the first order of business was to achieve a bourgeois-
democratic revolution in Russia. With the further development of Russian
capitalism, Russia would become ripe for a successful proletarian revolt.
In this analysis they merely followed the familiar two-stage sequence laid
down in the *Communist Manifesto*. Plekhanov, the theorist, was to remain
loyal to this formulation for the rest of his life. Lenin, the activist, was to
find it increasingly uncongenial, and though he continued for many years
to pay it verbal tribute, his whole revolutionary career was essentially an
escape from its confines.

THE PROBLEM OF INDUSTRIAL BACKWARDNESS

The question of the shape and pace of the Russian revolution was
to produce furious controversies among Social-Democrats of all shades.
The heart of the problem was Russia's industrial backwardness and the
political consequences to be drawn from it. The Social-Democratic Labor
Party based itself on a weak and still-undeveloped industrial proletariat.
What was the role of the party to be? Should it attempt to seize power at
the first promising opportunity or would it have to wait patiently until
Russia's industrialization matched that of the most advanced Western nations? If it limited its immediate activities to organizing the proletariat
and helping the bourgeoisie to overthrow the autocracy, would the party
not be strengthening its most dangerous enemy by surrendering to it the
power of the state? If, on the other hand, the party emphasized its hostility
to the bourgeoisie and its role as capitalism's gravedigger, would the
bourgeoisie not be driven to unite its fortunes with those of the autocracy?
Questions such as these might be argued in terms of Marxian exegesis, but
the answers that were evolved depended more on temperament than on
theory.

The Menshevik wing of Russian Social-Democracy, with which Plekhanov was finally to ally himself, saw the arrival of socialism in Russia as
the climax of a long process of development. The Menshevik response to
the challenge of industrial backwardness was to preach the postponement of
the socialist revolution until industrial backwardness had been overcome.
Strongly influenced by orthodox Western Marxism and impressed by the
weakness of the Russian industrial proletariat, the Mensheviks concluded
that a socialist Russia was a matter of the distant future and that the immediate task was to clear the way for a bourgeois, middleclass revolution.
Their first charge as good Marxists was to help the bourgeoisie to carry out

its own historical responsibilities. They were therefore prepared to conclude alliances with liberal bourgeois forces who opposed the autocracy and to join them in fighting for such limited objectives as universal suffrage, constitutional liberties, and enlightened social legislation. Meanwhile, they awaited the further growth of capitalism in Russia to establish the conditions for a successful socialist revolution. Essentially, the Mensheviks had their eye on Western European models; they expected to march to power through legality and to be the beneficiaries of the spontaneous mass energy which the creation of a large industrial proletariat would release.

At the opposite extreme from the Menshevik conception was the theory of "permanent revolution" developed by Parvus and adopted by Trotsky during and after the 1905 revolution. For Parvus and Trotsky, the industrial backwardness of Russia was a political asset rather than a liability. As a result of backwardness and the large role played by state capitalism, the Russian middle class was weak and incapable of doing the job of its analogues in Western Europe. Thus, according to Parvus' and Trotsky's dialectic of backwardness, the bourgeois revolution in Russia could be made only by the proletariat. Once the proletariat was in power, its responsibility was to hold on to power and keep the revolution going "in permanence" until socialism was established both at home and abroad. The Russian revolution, Trotsky thought, would ignite a series of socialist revolutions in the West. This "permanent revolution" would offset the resistance which developed. Thus Trotsky's prescription for Russia's retarded economy was a new law of combined development. The two revolutions—bourgeois-democratic and proletarian-socialist—would be combined, or telescoped, into one. The working class would assert its hegemony from the outset and leap directly from industrial backwardness into socialism. Implicit in the Trotsky-Parvus formula was a clear commitment to the theory of minority dictatorship for Russia. An industrial proletariat which was still relatively infinitesimal in numbers was called upon to impose its will and direction on the vast majority of the population. Out of such theoretical brick and straw, the edifice of Soviet totalitarianism was to be constructed.

The position of Lenin and the Bolshevik wing of the Russian Social-Democratic Party was much closer in spirit to Trotsky than to the Mensheviks, though the verbal premises from which Lenin started seemed indistinguishable from the Menshevik tenets. Like the Mensheviks, Lenin proclaimed that Russia was ripe for only a bourgeois-democratic revolution. His *Two Tactics of Social-Democracy in the Democratic Revolution* (1905) contained at least one formulation which Mensheviks would wholeheartedly have endorsed:

The degree of economic development of Russia (an objective condition) and the degree of class consciousness and organization of the broad masses of the proletariat (a subjective condition inseparably connected with the objective condition) make the immediate complete emancipation of the working class impossible. Only the most ignorant people can ignore the bourgeois nature of the democratic revolution which is now taking place. . . . Whoever wants to arrive at socialism by a different road, other than that of political democracy, will inevitably arrive at absurd and reactionary conclusions, both in the economic and the political sense. If any workers ask us at the given moment why not go ahead and carry out our maximum program we shall answer by pointing out how far the masses of the democratically disposed people still are from socialism, how undeveloped class antagonisms still are, how unorganized the proletarians still are.

Again, in the same pamphlet, Lenin reiterated: "We Marxists should know that there is not, nor can there be, any other path to real freedom for the proletariat and the peasantry, than the path of bourgeois freedom and bourgeois progress."

While dicta such as these can be and have been cited to establish a basic area of agreement between Mensheviks and Bolsheviks on the two-stage perspective of the Russian revolution, the kinship was more illusory than real. Plekhanov summed up one of the important differences when he observed to Lenin, "You turn your behind to the liberals, but we our face." For Lenin, as for Trotsky, the bourgeois liberals were a weak and unreliable reed. Like Trotsky, Lenin came to believe that the proletariat would have to take leadership in completing the bourgeois revolution; but unlike both Trotsky and the Mensheviks, Lenin looked to an alliance with the peasantry to provide the proletariat with a mass base.

In this rediscovery of the strategic significance of the peasantry, Lenin reclaimed the Narodnik heritage which both he and Plekhanov had done so much to repudiate in the nineties. In the essay on *Two Tactics,* Lenin declared:

Those who really understand the role of the peasantry in a victorious Russian revolution would not dream of saying that the sweep of the revolution would be diminished if the bourgeoisie recoiled from it. For, as a matter of fact, the Russian revolution will begin to assume its real sweep . . . only when the bourgeoisie recoils from it and when the masses of the peasantry come out as active revolutionaries side-by-side with the proletariat.

The first task was to consolidate "the revolutionary-democratic dictatorship of the proletariat and the peasantry." After this was achieved, the socialist revolution would become the order of the day. Lenin's formula thus envisaged two tactical stages: first, the alliance of proletariat and peasantry to complete the democratic revolution, and second, an alliance of the proletariat and village poor to initiate the socialist revolution.

Given Lenin's activist temperament, it was inevitable that he should feel greater affinity for Trotsky's revolutionary dynamism than for the Mensheviks' passive fatalism. As the excitement of the 1905 revolution mounted, we find him speaking the language of Trotsky: "From the democratic revolution we shall at once, and just in accordance with the measure of our

strength, the strength of the class-conscious and organized proletariat, begin
to pass to the socialist revolution. We stand for uninterrupted revolution.
We shall not stop half way." Despite many intervening conflicts, the bond
with Trotsky was to be sealed by the experiences of 1917. The dialectic
of backwardness was "resolved" by the Bolshevik seizure of power.

Out of that adventure a new theory of revolution was to be developed
with world-wide applications. Stalin has given it authoritative exposition:

> Where will the revolution begin? . . .
> Where industry is more developed, where the proletariat constitutes the
> majority, where there is more culture, where there is more democracy—that was
> the reply usually given formerly.
> No, objects the Leninist theory of revolution; *not necessarily where industry is
> more developed*, and so forth. The front of capitalism will be pierced where the
> chain of imperialism is weakest, for the proletarian revolution is the result of the
> breaking of the chain of the world imperialist front at its weakest link; and it may
> turn out that the country which has started the revolution, which has made a
> breach in the front of capital, is less developed in a capitalist sense than other, more
> developed, countries, which have, however, remained within the framework of
> capitalism.

Thus Marx, who turned Hegel on his head, was himself turned on his
head. Industrial backwardness was transformed from obstacle to opportunity. The concept of the dictatorship of the proletariat shifted from a
weapon of the majority into a tool of minorities. Consciousness triumphed
over spontaneity, and the way was cleared for the organized and disciplined
revolutionary elite capable of transmuting the grievances of a nation into
a new formula of absolute power.

ORGANIZATION: THE ELITE PARTY

The organizational conception embodied in Bolshevism was essentially
an incarnation of this elitist ideal. "Give us an organization of revolution
aries," said Lenin, "and we shall overturn the whole of Russia!" It was
Lenin who forged the instrument, but the seeds of his conspiratorial conceptions were planted deep in Russian history and were nurtured by the
conditions of the revolutionary struggle against the autocracy. Pestel among
the Decembrists, Bakunin, Nechayev, Tkachev, and the Narodnik conspirators of the seventies and early eighties, all provided organizational proto-
types of the professional revolutionary as the strategic lever of political
upheaval. It was a tradition from which Lenin drew deep inspiration even
when he found himself in profound disagreement with the particular programs which earlier professional revolutionaries espoused. His works are
filled with tributes to the famous revolutionaries of the seventies (figures
like Alekseyev, Myshkin, Khalturin, and Zhelyabov). In developing his
own conceptions of party organization in *What Is to Be Done?* he refers to
"the magnificent organization" of the revolutionaries of the seventies as

one "which should serve us all as a model." Lenin's conviction that Russian Marxism could triumph only if led by a disciplined elite of professional revolutionaries was reënforced by his own early amateur experiences as a member of the Petersburg League of Struggle for the Emancipation of the Working Class. This organization was easily penetrated by the police, and the first effort of Lenin and his collaborators in 1895 to publish an underground paper—"The Workers' Cause"—resulted in the arrest of Lenin and his chief associates and a quick transfer of domicile to Siberia.

It is against this background that the organizational conceptions of Lenin took shape. By 1902, with the publication of *What Is to Be Done?* they were fully developed. In this essay, the seminal source of the organizational philosophy of Bolshevism, Lenin set himself two main tasks: (1) to destroy the influence of Economism with its repudiation of revolutionary political organization and its insistence on trade unionism as the basic method of improving the welfare of the working class, and (2) to build an organized and disciplined revolutionary Marxist party which would insure the triumph of socialism in Russia.

The polemic against the Economists clearly revealed Lenin's elitist preconceptions. More than a quarter of a century earlier Tkachev had written: "Neither in the present nor in the future can the people, left to their own resources, bring into existence the social revolution. Only we revolutionists can accomplish this . . . Social ideals are alien to the people; they belong to the social philosophy of the revolutionary minority." Now Lenin was to repeat:

The history of all countries shows that the working class, exclusively by its own effort, is able to develop only trade union consciousness. . . . This [Social-Democratic] consciousness could only be brought to them from without. . . . The theory of socialism . . . grew out of the philosophic, historical, and economic theories that were elaborated by the educated representatives of the propertied classes, the intellectuals . . . quite independently of the spontaneous-growth of the labor movement. . . .

Our task, the task of Social-Democracy, is to *combat spontaneity,* to *divert* the labor movement from its spontaneous, trade unionist striving to go under the wing of the bourgeoisie, and to bring it under the wing of revolutionary Social-Democracy.

To accomplish this objective, Lenin sought to weld together a disciplined party of devoted adherents, "a small, compact core, consisting of the most reliable, experienced and hardened workers, with responsible agents in the principal districts and connected by all the rules of strict secrecy with the organization of revolutionaries." . . . [Editor's note: The article next ensuing is a substantial excerpt from Lenin's *What Is to Be Done?*]

Democratic management, Lenin held, was simply inapplicable to a revolutionary organization. *What Is to Be Done?* disclosed the profoundly elitist and anti-democratic strain in Lenin's approach to problems of organization. It also made clear that in Lenin's new model party, leadership would be highly centralized, the central committee would appoint local committees, and every committee would have the right to coöpt new members. But it still left a precise blueprint to be worked out. This was the task which Lenin undertook to perform at the Second Party Congress of the Russian Social Democratic Labor Party, which met in Brussels and then in London in the summer of 1903. Lenin prepared for this Congress with a meticulous attention to detail of which he alone among his revolutionary contemporaries was capable. His one desire was to construct a compact majority which would dominate the Congress and build a party willing "to devote to the revolution not only their spare evenings, but the whole of their lives."

The foundations seemed to be well laid. The rallying point of the "compact majority" was *Iskra* (The Spark), a journal which had been established abroad in 1900 largely on Lenin's initiative. Wisely, Lenin and his young associates, Martov and Potresov, enlisted the coöperation of Plekhanov and other members of the Emancipation of Labor group as co-editors. The association generated its own sparks; Lenin has provided a vivid record of the conflict in his "How the Spark Was Nearly Extinguished." But the quarrels for supremacy were composed; Lenin still needed the prestige of the older generation of revolutionaries in mobilizing adherents to the *Iskra* platform. Meanwhile, Lenin retained control of the secret agents who smuggled *Iskra* into Russia and maintained the closest connections with the underground organizations which distributed the journal. This organization of *Iskra* men was to provide the core of Lenin's majority at the Second Congress.

When the Second Congress assembled in Brussels in 1903, thirty-three votes, a clear majority of the fifty-one official votes, belonged to the *Iskra* faction. The remaining eighteen delegates represented a collection of Bundists (members of the All-Jewish Workers' Union of Russia and Poland), Economists, and miscellaneous uncommitted representatives, whom the Iskraites described contemptuously as "the Marsh" because they wallowed in a quagmire of uncertainty. The Iskraites appeared to be in full control. They named the presidium and easily pushed through their draft program and various resolutions on tactics.

The next order of business was the adoption of the party rules, and here trouble developed. The Iskraites were no longer united; Lenin and Martov offered rival drafts. The initial issue was posed by the definition of party membership. Lenin's draft of Paragraph One read: "A Party member is one who accepts its program and who supports the Party both financially and *by personal participation in one of the Party organizations.*" Martov's formulation defined a party member as "one who accepts its program, supports the Party financially and renders it regular personal assistance under the direction of one of its organizations." To many of the delegates, the difference in shading between the two drafts appeared slight, but as the discussion gathered momentum, the differences were magnified until a basic, and ultimately irreconcilable, question of principle emerged.

The issue was the nature of the party. Lenin wanted a narrow, closed party of dedicated revolutionaries operating in strict subordination to the center and serving as a vanguard of leadership for the masses of workers who would surround the party without belonging to it. Martov desired a broad party open to anyone who believed in its program and was willing to work under its direction. Martov conceded the necessity of central leadership, but he also insisted that party members were entitled to have a voice in its affairs and could not abdicate their right to think and influence party policy.

As the debate raged, the *Iskra* group fell apart. Plekhanov rallied to Lenin's defense; the Leninist formula seemed to him admirably adapted to protect the party against the infiltration of bourgeois individualists. Axelrod and Trotsky supported Martov. To Axelrod it seemed that Lenin was dreaming "of the administrative subordination of an entire party to a few guardians of doctrine." And after the Congress had adjourned, Trotsky, in a sharp attack on Lenin, provided the classic formulation of the opposition. In Lenin's view, he pointed out, "the organization of the Party takes the place of the Party itself; the Central Committee takes the place of the organization; and finally the dictator takes the place of the Central Committee." It was to turn out a more somber and tragic vision of things to come than Trotsky realized at the time.

At the Congress, Martov's draft triumphed by a vote of twenty-eight to twenty-two. But Lenin had not yet shot his last bolt. He still retained the leadership of a majority of the Iskraites, though his group was now a minority in the Congress. This minority was soon transformed into a majority by a series of "accidents" to which Lenin's parliamentary maneuvering and planning contributed. When the Congress rejected the Bundist claim to be the sole representative of the Jewish proletariat, the five delegates of the Bund withdrew from the Congress. Their departure was followed by the withdrawal of the delegates from the League of Russian Social-Democrats, an Economist-dominated organization, which the Congress voted to dissolve on Lenin's motion. With the exit of these two groups, the *Iskra* majority became the Congress majority and proceeded to elect its representatives to the central party organs. It was this triumph which gave Lenin's caucus the title of Bolsheviks (the majority men), while his defeated opponents became known as Mensheviks (the minority men).

But the triumph was short-lived. The central party institutions elected by the Second Congress consisted of the editors of *Iskra*, the Central Committee in Russia, and a Party Council of five members (two representing *Iskra*, two the Central Committee, and a fifth elected by the Congress). The Board of Editors of *Iskra* was given power equal to and indeed above that of the Central Committee. Disputes between *Iskra* and the Central

Committee were to be settled by the Party Council. Lenin, Plekhanov, and Martov were elected as editors of *Iskra*. Martov refused to serve unless the original editorial board, which included Axelrod, Zasulich, and Potresov, was restored. Lenin and Plekhanov were thus left in exclusive control. The Central Committee in Russia was composed entirely of Bolsheviks, and they were given power to coöpt other members. The party apparatus appeared to be safely in Bolshevik hands when Plekhanov, out of a desire to heal the breach with his old associates, acceded to Martov's conditions and insisted on the restoration of the original *Iskra* board. Lenin promptly withdrew, and at one stroke *Iskra* was transformed into an organ of Menshevism.

Differences now began to develop in the Bolshevik Central Committee in Russia; a majority group emerged which advocated a policy of conciliation toward the Mensheviks. Three Mensheviks were coöpted into the Central Committee, and in the summer of 1904 this strategic power position, which Lenin had regarded as impregnable, passed over to the opposition. After all his careful planning and apparent triumph, Lenin was left isolated and alone, betrayed by his own nominees in Russia, alienated from the leading figures of the emigration, and the chief target of abuse in the party organ which he had been primarily instrumental in establishing.

After a temporary fit of utter discouragement, Lenin rallied and began once more to gather his forces. The remnants of the faithful in the emigration were welded into a fighting organization. Connections were re-established with the lower party committees in Russia, and a new body, the Bureau of the Committee of the Majority, was established to coordinate the work of Lenin's supporters. Toward the end of 1904 a new paper, *Vperëd* (Forward), was founded as the organ of the bureau. A second effort to capture control of the party organization was now in the full tide of preparation. But this time the Mensheviks were wary and refused to attend the so-called Third Congress of the Social-Democratic Labor Party, which assembled on Lenin's initiative in London in May 1905. The Mensheviks met separately in Geneva.

The 1905 revolution brought Bolsheviks and Mensheviks closer together. Responding to the *élan* of the uprising, Mensheviks became more militant and Bolsheviks seemed to abandon their distrust of uncontrolled mass organization. As Lenin put it, "The rising tide of revolution drove . . . differences into the background. . . . In place of the old differences there arose unity of views." Joint committees were formed in many cities, and finally a Joint Central Committee was created on a basis of equal representation to summon a "Unity" Congress. Both parties were flooded with new members for whom the old quarrels were ancient history and the practical tasks of the moment were paramount. The misgivings of the leaders were swept aside in a widespread yearning for unity.

The Fourth so-called "Unity" Congress, which took place at Stockholm in 1906, reflected this surge from below. Thirty-six thousand workers took part in the election of delegates. Menshevism flourished on legality, and of the one hundred eleven voting delegates selected, sixty-two were Mensheviks and forty-nine Bolsheviks. As a result, the Mensheviks dominated the proceedings. They wrote the program and resolutions and controlled the leading party organs. The Central Committee elected by the Congress was composed of seven Mensheviks and three Bolsheviks; the editorial board for the central party newspaper (which never appeared) was composed exclusively of Mensheviks. Perhaps the most important organizational action taken at the Congress was the admission of the Bund and the Polish and Latvian Social-Democratic parties as constituent units in the united party. The Polish and Latvian parties joined as autonomous organizations operating in their respective territorial areas; the Bund renounced its claim to be the sole representative of the Jewish proletariat on the understanding that it would be permitted to retain its program of national cultural autonomy and to organize Jewish workers without respect to territorial boundaries. The admission of these groups introduced an additional complication into the power structure of the party. Given the relatively even distribution of strength between Mensheviks and Bolsheviks in this period, the balance of power now shifted to the Bund and the Polish and Latvian Social-Democrats, and their votes became of crucial significance in shaping the party's future course.

Although Lenin suffered defeat at the Stockholm Congress, he continued to maneuver for ascendancy. The Bolshevik factional apparatus was maintained, and funds to finance the apparatus were partly obtained through "expropriations" (robberies and holdups). The effort to capture local organizations was continued, and Menshevik policies were attacked with relentless ferocity. As a result of this activity, the Bolsheviks registered marked gains at the Fifth Congress, held in London in 1907. While the precise strength of the Bolshevik and Menshevik blocs is still in dispute, all accounts agree that the Bolsheviks achieved a slight preponderance over the Mensheviks at the Congress.

This did not mean, however, that the Bolsheviks controlled the Congress. The real power of decision rested with the Bund and the Polish and Latvian Social-Democrats, who exercised a role of balance between the conflicting Russian factions. On the whole, the Mensheviks attracted Bundist support, while the Bolsheviks were dependent on the Poles and Latvians for such majorities as they obtained. While the Bolsheviks failed to secure the support of the national delegates in their efforts to condemn the work of the Menshevik Central Committee and of the Duma fraction of the party and were themselves condemned for their sponsorship of "expropriations," they were able to defeat the Mensheviks on a number of important resolutions. The Menshevik policy of cooperating with the Kadets was repudiated. The proposal of Axelrod and other leading Mensheviks to call a non-party labor congress and to transform the Social-Democratic Party into a broad, open labor party was denounced by Lenin as "Liquidationism" and decisively rejected by the Congress. But the Bolsheviks were unable to achieve a dependable, monolithic majority, and the elections to the Central Committee yielded five Bolsheviks, four Mensheviks, two Bundists, two Polish Social-Democrats, and one Latvian Social-Democrat.

During the period of reaction and repression which accumulated momentum after the London Congress, both Menshevik and Bolshevik segments of the party underwent a serious crisis. Party membership crumbled away, and police spies penetrated such remnants of the organizational apparatus as remained. The crisis was particularly acute for the Mensheviks. Potresov, in a letter to Axelrod toward the end of 1907, reflected an almost hopeless despondency:

> Complete disintegration and demoralisation prevail in our ranks. Probably this is a phenomenon common to all parties and fractions and reflects the spirit of the times; but I do not think that this disintegration, this demoralisation have anywhere manifested themselves so vividly as with us Mensheviks. Not only is there no organisation, there are not even the elements of one.

The situation within Bolshevik ranks was not much better. "In 1908," notes the Bolshevik historian Popov, "the Party membership numbered not tens and hundreds of thousands, as formerly, but a few hundreds, or, at best, thousands." The plight of the Moscow organization was not atypical. From the end of 1908 to the end of 1909, membership declined from five hundred to one hundred fifty; in the next year the organization was completely destroyed when it fell under the control of a police spy. The Bolsheviks, by virtue of their conspiratorial traditions and tight discipline, made a better adjustment than the Mensheviks to the rigors of illegal existence, but even Bolshevik vigilance could not prevent the secret agents of the police from penetrating the underground hierarchy and rising to high places in the party apparatus. Meanwhile, the leaders of both the Bolshevik and Menshevik factions fled abroad once more where they were soon engaged in resurrecting old quarrels and giving birth to new differences.

Both factions fell victim to internal dissension. The Mensheviks divided between the "Liquidators" (as Lenin dubbed them), who counseled the abandonment of the underground party and concentration on legal work in the trade unions and the Duma, and the "Party" Mensheviks, who continued to insist on the necessity of an illegal organization. Bolshevism spawned in rapid succession a bewildering series of controversies. First, there were the "Duma Boycotters," led by Bogdanov, at that time one of Lenin's closest associates. On this issue Lenin joined with the Mensheviks and supported party participation in the election of the Third Duma. Then there were the "Otzovists" and "Ultimatumists," the former demanding the immediate recall or withdrawal of the Duma party delegation and the latter insisting that an ultimatum be dispatched to the delegation with the proviso that its members should immediately be recalled if the instructions contained in the ultimatum were rejected. Lenin again opposed both tendencies. Next came the philosophical heresies, the Neo-Kantian "Machism" of Bogdanov and the "God-Creator" religionism of Lunacharsky and Gorky. These were heresies that Lenin endured as long as the heretics were enrolled in his political camp; they became intolerable only when Bogdanov and the rest challenged his control of the party faction. Finally, there were the Bolshevik "Conciliators" who insisted that peace be made with the Mensheviks after Lenin had determined that a final split was essential.

In the parlance of latter-day Bolshevism, each of these "deviations" had to be "liquidated" if Lenin was to build the party in his own image. He was determined to accomplish precisely that task. The first act took place in the summer of 1909 at an enlarged editorial conference of *Proletarii*, the organ of the Bolshevik caucus. Again Lenin made careful advance preparations, and equipped with the necessary votes, he carried a resolution declaring that Boycottism, Otzovism, Ultimatumism, God-Construction, and Machism were all incompatible with membership in the Bolshevik faction. Over bitter protest, Bogdanov was ousted from the Bolshevik central leadership where he had been second only to Lenin, and he and his associates were declared "to have placed themselves outside the faction." Expelled from the fold, the dissidents proceeded to declare themselves "true Bolsheviks," established a new journal utilizing an old name, *Vperëd,* and became known during the next years as Vperëdist Bolsheviks.

Having disposed of the Vperëdists, Lenin confronted the new opposition of the so-called Conciliators, or Party Bolsheviks, who called for reconciliation with the expelled faction and unity with the Mensheviks. At a plenary session, held in January 1910, of the Central Committee elected by the London Congress, Lenin received a sharp rebuff when the Conciliators turned against him. The conference voted to discontinue the Bolshevik paper *Proletarii* as well as the Menshevik *Golos Sotsial-Demokrata* (Voice of the Social-Democrat) and to replace both with a general party organ, *Sotsial-Demokrat,* which would have two Menshevik editors, Martov and Dan, two Bolshevik editors, Lenin and Zinoviev, and one representative of the Polish Social-Democrats, Warski, to break any deadlocks that might develop.

Again the attempt at "unity" miscarried. With the support of Warski, Lenin won control of the new party journal and denied the Menshevik editors the right to publish signed articles in what was supposed to be the organ of the united party. Martov replied by attempting to discredit Lenin through an exposure of the seamy side of Bolshevism—the holdups, the counterfeiting, and "expropriations" which Lenin had allegedly sanctioned and defended.

Lenin now moved toward an open and irrevocable break. Despite the protest of the Bolshevik Conciliators, he summoned an All-Russian Party

Conference which met in Prague in January 1912 to ratify the split. Although the conference was dominated by a carefully selected group of Lenin's most reliable supporters, the uneasiness of the delegates in the face of Lenin's ruthless determination to move toward schism manifested itself in a belated decision to invite Plekhanov, Trotsky, and others to attend. To Lenin's great relief, both Plekhanov and Trotsky refused on the ground that the conference was too one-sided and imperiled party unity. Martov and the Menshevik Liquidators were not invited. The Bund and the Polish and Latvian Social-Democrats also stayed away.

The "Rump Parliament" proceeded to assume all the rights and functions of a party congress (indeed, Lenin called it The Sixth Congress of the Russian Social-Democratic Labor Party). The old Central Committee created by the London Congress was declared dissolved, and a new "pure" Bolshevik Central Committee was elected from which all Bolshevik Conciliators were excluded. The Prague Conference marked the decisive break with Menshevism and the turning point in the history of Bolshevism as an independent movement. There were to be many subsequent attempts to bring the Bolsheviks back into the fold of a united party, but all were doomed to failure. The last effort, sponsored by the International Socialist Bureau of the Second International, was slated to take place at the Vienna Congress of the Second International in August 1914. War intervened, and the congress was never held. By an ironical turn of events, the International which attempted to close the breach in the Russian party was itself split by the Bolsheviks whom it tried to bring to heel.

The early organizational history of Bolshevism, which has been briefly summarized here, holds more than historical interest. The experience of the formative years left an ineradicable stamp on the character and future development of the party. It implanted the germinating conception of the monolithic and totalitarian party. The elitism which was so deeply ingrained in Lenin, the theory of the party as a dedicated revolutionary order, the tradition of highly centralized leadership, the tightening regimen of party discipline, the absolutism of the party line, the intolerance of disagreement and compromise, the manipulatory attitude toward mass organization, the subordination of means to ends, and the drive for total power —all these patterns of behavior which crystallized in the early years were destined to exercise a continuing influence on the code by which the party lived and the course of action which it pursued.

WHAT IS TO BE DONE?
BURNING QUESTIONS OF OUR MOVEMENT

V. I. Lenin*

This document, completed and published in 1902, is one of the most important in all Marxist-Leninist literature. Lenin's theoretical and practical conceptions of the nature, structure, and role of the Party had a most profound influence in shaping the Bolshevik movement. Although Lenin's elitist conception of the Party was then intended to apply only to the period before the seizure of power and only in the conditions of Russian autocracy, it remains an attribute of the Party organization to this day.

Without a revolutionary theory there can be no revolutionary movement. This cannot be insisted upon too strongly at a time when the fashionable preaching of opportunism is combined with absorption in the narrowest forms of practical activity. . . .

The Russian workers will have to undergo trials immeasurably severe; they will have to take up the fight against a monster, compared with which anti-Socialist laws in a constitutional country are but pigmies. History has now confronted us with an immediate task which is *more revolutionary than all the immediate tasks* that confront the proletariat of any other country. The fulfilment of this task, the destruction of the most powerful bulwark, not only of European, but also (it may now be said) of Asiatic reaction, places the Russian proletariat in the vanguard of the international revolutionary proletariat. We shall have the right to count upon acquiring the honourable title already earned by our predecessors, the revolutionaries of the seventies, if we succeed in inspiring our movement—which is a thousand times wider and deeper—with the same devoted determination and vigour.

I. THE SPONTANEITY OF THE MASSES AND THE CLASS-CONSCIOUSNESS OF SOCIAL-DEMOCRACY

The Beginning of the Spontaneous Movement

. . . Strikes occurred in Russia in the seventies, and in the sixties (and also in the first half of the nineteenth century), and these strikes were ac-

---

* The selection is from the pamphlet by the same title (International Publishers Co., Inc., 1929), *passim.* By permission of the publisher.

companied by the "spontaneous" destruction of machinery, etc. Compared with these "revolts" the strikes of the nineties might even be described as "conscious," to such an extent do they mark the progress which the labour movement had made since that period. This shows that the "spontaneous element," in essence, represents nothing more nor less than consciousness in an *embryonic form*. Even the primitive rebellions expressed the awakening of consciousness to a certain extent: The workers abandoned their age-long faith in the permanence of the system which oppressed them. They began . . . I shall not say to understand, but to sense the necessity for collective resistance, and emphatically abandoned their slavish submission to their superiors. But all this was more in the nature of outbursts of desperation and vengeance than *struggle*. The strikes of the nineties revealed far greater flashes of consciousness: Definite demands were put forward, the time to strike was carefully chosen, known cases and examples in other places were discussed, etc. While the revolts were simply uprisings of the oppressed, the systematic strikes represented the class struggle in embryo, but only in embryo. Taken by themselves, these strikes were simple trade union struggles, but not yet Social-Democratic struggles. They testified to the awakening antagonisms between workers and employers, but the workers were not and could not be conscious of the irreconcilable antagonism of their interests to the whole of the modern political and social system, *i.e.*, it was not yet Social-Democratic consciousness. In this sense, the strikes of the nineties, in spite of the enormous progress they represented as compared with the "revolts," represented a purely spontaneous movement.

We said that *there could not yet be* Social-Democratic consciousness among the workers. This consciousness could only be brought to them from without. The history of all countries shows that the working class, exclusively by its own effort, is able to develop only trade-union consciousness, *i.e.*, it may itself realise the necessity for combining in unions, to fight against the employers and to strive to compel the government to pass necessary labour legislation, etc.

The theory of Socialism, however, grew out of the philosophic, historical and economic theories that were elaborated by the educated representatives of the propertied classes, the intellectuals. The founders of modern scientific Socialism, Marx and Engels, themselves belonged to the bourgeois intelligentsia. Similarly, in Russia, the theoretical doctrine of Social-Democracy arose quite independently of the spontaneous growth of the labour movement; it arose as a natural and inevitable outcome of the development of ideas among the revolutionary Socialist intelligentsia. At the time of which we are speaking, *i.e.*, the middle of the nineties, this doctrine not only represented the completely formulated programme of the Emancipation of Labour group but had already won the adhesion of the majority of the revolutionary youth in Russia.

Hence, simultaneously we had both the spontaneous awakening of the masses of the workers—the awakening to conscious life and struggle, and the striving of the revolutionary youth, armed with the Social-Democratic theories, to reach the workers. In this connection it is particularly important to state the oft-forgotten (and comparatively little-known) fact that the early Social-Democrats of that period, *zealously carried on economic agitation* (being guided in this by the really useful instructions contained in the pamphlet *Agitation* that was still in manuscript) but they did not regard this as their sole task. On the contrary, *right from the very beginning* they brought up the general historical tasks of Russian Social-Democracy, and particularly the task of overthrowing the autocracy. . . .

Bowing to Spontaneity

. . . Since there can be no talk of an independent ideology being developed by the masses of the workers in the process of their movement* then *the only choice is:* Either bourgeois, or Socialist ideology. There is no middle course (for humanity has not created a "third" ideology, and, moreover, in a society torn by class antagonisms there can never be a non-class or above-class ideology). Hence, to belittle Socialist ideology *in any way,* to *deviate from it in the slightest degree* means strengthening bourgeois ideology. There is a lot of talk about spontaneity, but the *spontaneous* development of the labour movement leads to its becoming subordinated to bourgeois ideology, it means developing *according to the programme* of the *Credo,* for the spontaneous labour movement is pure and simple trade unionism, is *Nur-Gewerkschaftlerei,* and trade unionism means the ideological subordination of the workers to the bourgeoisie. Hence, our task, the task of Social-Democracy, is to *combat spontaneity,* to *divert* the labour movement, with its spontaneous trade-unionist striving, from under the wing of the bourgeoisie, and to bring it under the wing of revolutionary Social-Democracy. . . .

But why, the reader will ask, does the spontaneous movement, the movement along the line of least resistance, lead to the domination of bourgeois ideology? For the simple reason that bourgeois ideology is far older in origin than Social-Democratic ideology; because it is more fully developed and because it possesses *immeasurably* more opportunities for becoming widespread. And the younger the Socialist movement is in any given country, the more vigorously must it fight against all attempts to entrench non-Socialist ideology, and the more strongly must it warn the workers against those bad counsellors who shout against "exaggerating the conscious elements," etc. . . .

* This does not mean, of course, that the workers have no part in creating such an ideology. But they take part not as workers, but as Socialist theoreticians, like Proudhon and Weitling; in other words, they take part only to the extent that they are able, more or less, to acquire the knowledge of their age and advance that knowledge. . . .

II. TRADE-UNION POLITICS AND SOCIAL-DEMOCRATIC POLITICS

Political Agitation and Its Restriction by the Economists

. . . Social-Democrats lead the struggle of the working class not only for better terms for the sale of labour power, but also for the abolition of the social system which compels the propertyless class to sell itself to the rich. Social-Democracy represents the working class, not in its relation to a given group of employers, but in its relation to all classes in modern society, to the state as an organised political force. Hence, it not only follows that Social-Democrats must not confine themselves entirely to the economic struggle; they must not even allow the organisation of economic exposures to become the predominant part of their activities. We must actively take up the political education of the working class, and the development of its political consciousness. . . .

All and sundry manifestations of police tyranny and autocratic outrage, in addition to the evils connected with the economic struggle, are equally "widely applicable" as a means of "drawing in" the masses. The tyranny of the Zemstvo chiefs, the flogging of the peasantry, the corruption of the officials, the conduct of the police towards the "common people" in the cities, the fight against the famine-stricken and the suppression of the popular striving towards enlightenment and knowledge, the extortion of taxes, the persecution of the religious sects, the severe discipline in the army, the militarist conduct towards the students and the liberal intelligentsia—all these and a thousand other similar manifestations of tyranny, though not directly connected with the "economic" struggle, do they, in general, represent a *less* "widely applicable" method and subject for political agitation and for drawing the masses into the political struggle? The very opposite is the case. Of all the innumerable cases in which the workers suffer (either personally or those closely associated with them) from tyranny, violence, and lack of rights, undoubtedly only a relatively few represent cases of police tyranny in the economic struggle as such. Why then should we beforehand *restrict* the scope of political agitation by declaring *only one* of the methods to be "the most widely applicable," when Social-Democrats have other, generally speaking, not less "widely applicable" means? . . .

Revolutionary Social-Democracy always included, and now includes, the fight for reforms in its activities. But it utilises "economic" agitation for the purpose of presenting to the government, not only demands for all sorts of measures, but also (and primarily) the demand that it cease to be an autocratic government. Moreover, it considers it to be its duty to present this demand to the government, not on the basis of the economic struggle *alone,* but on the basis of all manifestations of public and political life. In a word, it subordinates the struggle for reforms to the revolutionary struggle for liberty and for Socialism, in the same way as the part is subordinate to the whole. . . .

III. THE PRIMITIVENESS OF THE ECONOMISTS
AND THE ORGANISATION OF REVOLUTIONISTS

Primitive Methods and Economism

. . . These people, who cannot pronounce the word "theoretician" without a contemptuous grimace, who describe their genuflections to common lack of training and ignorance as "sensitiveness to life," reveal in practice a failure to understand our most imperative *practical* task. To laggards they shout: Keep in step! don't run ahead! To people suffering from a lack of energy and initiative in organisational work, from lack of "plans" for wide and bold organisational work, they shout about the "tactics-process"! The most serious sin we commit is that we *degrade* our political and *our organisational* tasks to the level of immediate, "palpable," "concrete" interests of the every-day economic struggle; and yet they keep singing to us the old song: Give the economic struggle itself a political character. We say again: This kind of thing displays as much "sensitiveness to life" as was displayed by the hero in the popular fable who shouted to a passing funeral procession: May you never get to your destination. . . .

Workers, average people of the masses, are capable of displaying enormous energy and self-sacrifice in strikes and in street battles, with the police and troops, and are capable (in fact, are alone capable) of *determining* the whole outcome of our movement—but the struggle against the *political* police requires special qualities; it can be conducted only by *professional* revolutionists. And we must not only see to it that the masses "advance" concrete demands, but also that the masses of the workers "advance" an increasing number of such professional revolutionists from their own ranks. Thus we have reached the question of the relation between an organisation of professional revolutionists and the pure and simple labour movement. . . .

Organisation of Workers, and Organisation of Revolutionists

It is only natural that a Social-Democrat who conceives the political struggle as being identical with the "economic struggle against the employers and the government," should conceive "organisation of revolutionists" as being more or less identical with "organisation of workers." . . .

It is the fact that on questions of organisation and politics the Economists are forever lapsing from Social-Democracy into trade unionism. The political struggle carried on by the Social-Democrats is far more extensive and complex than the economic struggle the workers carry on against the employers and the government. Similarly (and indeed for that reason), the organisation of revolutionary Social-Democrats must inevitably *differ* from the organisations of the workers designed for the latter struggle. The workers' organisations must in the first place be trade organisations; secondly,

they must be as wide as possible; and thirdly, they must be as public as conditions will allow (here, of course, I have only autocratic Russia in mind).
On the other hand, the organisations of revolutionists must be comprised
first and foremost of people whose profession is that of revolutionists (that
is why I speak of organisations of *revolutionists,* meaning revolutionary
Social-Democrats). . . .

In countries where political liberty exists the distinction between a
labour union and a political organisation is clear, as is the distinction between trade unions and Social-Democracy. The relation of the latter to the
former will naturally vary in each country according to historical, legal and
other conditions—it may be more or less close or more or less complex (in
our opinion it should be as close and simple as possible); but trade-union
organisations are certainly not in the least identical with the Social-
Democratic party organisations in those countries. In Russia, however, the
yoke of autocracy appears at first glance to obliterate all distinctions between
a Social-Democratic organisation and trade unions, because *all* trade unions
and *all* circles are prohibited, and because the principal manifestation and
weapon of the workers' economic struggle—the strike—is regarded as a
crime (and sometimes even as a political crime!). Conditions in our country, therefore, strongly "impel" the workers who are conducting the economic struggle to concern themselves with political questions. They also
"impel" the Social-Democrats to confuse trade unionism with Social-
Democracy. . . .

The workers' organisations for carrying on the economic struggle should
be trade-union organisations; every Social-Democratic worker should, as far
as possible, support and actively work inside these organisations. That is
true. But it would be far from being to our interest to demand that only
Social-Democrats be eligible for membership in the trade unions. The only
effect of this, if it were attempted, would be to restrict our influence over
the masses. Let every worker who understands the necessity for organisation,
in order to carry on the struggle against the employers and the government,
join the trade unions. The very objects of the trade unions would be unattainable unless they united all who have attained at least this elementary
level of understanding, and unless they were extremely wide organisations.
The wider these organisations are, the wider our influence over them will
be. They will then be influenced not only by the "spontaneous" development of the economic struggle, but also by the direct and conscious action of
the Socialists on their comrades in the unions. But a wide organisation cannot be a strictly secret organisation (since the latter demands far greater
training than is required for the economic struggle). How is the contradiction between the necessity for a large membership and the necessity for
strictly secret methods to be reconciled? . . .

In order to achieve this purpose, and in order to guide the nascent
trade-union movement in the direction the Social-Democrats desire, we must

first fully understand the foolishness of the plan of organisation with which the St. Petersburg Economists have been occupying themselves for nearly five years. That plan is described in the Rules of a Workers' Fund, of July, 1897 and also in the Rules for a Trade Union Workers' Organisation, of October, 1900. The fundamental error contained in both these sets of rules is that they give a detailed formulation of a wide workers' organisation and confuse the latter with the organisation of revolutionists. . . .

A small, compact core, consisting of reliable, experienced and hardened workers, with responsible agents in the principal districts and connected by all the rules of strict secrecy with the organisations of revolutionists, can, with the wide support of the masses and without an elaborate set of rules, perform *all* the functions of a trade-union organisation, and perform them, moreover, in the manner Social-Democrats desire. Only in this way can we secure the *consolidation* and development of a *Social-Democratic* trade-union movement, in spite of the gendarmes.

It may be objected that an organisation which is so loose that it is not even formulated, and which even has no enrolled and registered members, cannot be called an organisation at all. That may very well be. I am not out for names. But this "organisation without members" can do everything that is required, and will, from the very outset, guarantee the closest contact between our future trade unionists and Socialism. Only an incorrigible utopian would want a *wide* organisation of workers, with elections, reports, universal suffrage, etc., under autocracy.

The moral to be drawn from this is a simple one. If we begin with the solid foundation of a strong organisation of revolutionists, we can guarantee the stability of the movement as a whole, and carry out the aims of both Social-Democracy and of trade unionism. If, however, we begin with a wide workers' organisation, supposed to be most "accessible" to the masses, when as a matter of fact it will be most accessible to the gendarmes, and will make the revolutionists most accessible to the police, we shall neither achieve the aims of Social-Democracy nor of trade unionism; . . .

It is far more difficult to catch ten wise men than it is to catch a hundred fools. And this premise I shall defend no matter how much you instigate the crowd against me for my "anti-democratic" views, etc. As I have already said, by "wise men," in connection with organisation, I mean *professional revolutionists,* irrespective of whether they are students or workingmen. I assert: 1. That no movement can be durable without a stable organisation of leaders to maintain continuity; 2. that the more widely the masses are drawn into the struggle and form the basis of the movement, the more necessary is it to have such an organisation and the more stable must it be (for it is much easier then for demagogues to side-track the more backward sections of the masses); 3. that the organisation must consist chiefly of persons engaged in revolution as a profession; 4. that in a country with a despotic government, the more we *restrict* the membership of this organisation to persons who are engaged in revolution as a profession and who have been professionally trained in the art of combating the political police, the more difficult will it be to catch the organisation; and 5. the *wider* will be the circle of men and women of the working class or of other classes of society able to join the movement and perform active work in it. . . .

We can never give a mass organisation that degree of secrecy which is essential for the persistent and continuous struggle against the government. But to concentrate all secret functions in the hands of as small a number of professional revolutionists as possible, does not mean that the latter will "do the thinking for all" and that the crowd will not take an active part in the movement. On the contrary, the crowd will advance from its ranks increasing numbers of professional revolutionists, for it will know that it is not enough for a few students and workingmen waging economic war to gather together and form a "committee," but that professional revolutionists must be trained for years; the crowd will "think" not of primitive ways but of training professional revolutionists. The centralisation of the secret functions of the *organisation* does not mean the concentration of all the functions of the *movement*. The active participation of the greatest masses in the dissemination of illegal literature will not diminish because a dozen professional revolutionists concentrate in their hands the secret part of the work; on the contrary, it will *increase tenfold.*

Only in this way will the reading of illegal literature, the contribution to illegal literature, and to some extent even the distribution of illegal literature *almost cease to be secret work,* for the police will soon come to realise the folly and futility of setting the whole judicial and administrative machine into motion to intercept every copy of a publication that is being broadcast in thousands. This applies not only to the press, but to every function of the movement, even to demonstrations. The active and widespread participation of the masses will not suffer; on the contrary, it will benefit by the fact that a "dozen" experienced revolutionists, no less professionally trained than the police, will concentrate all the secret side of the work in their hands—prepare leaflets, work out approximate plans and appoint bodies of leaders for each town district, for each factory district, and for each educational institution (I know that exception will be taken to my "undemocratic" views, but I shall reply to this altogether unintelligent objection later on).

The centralisation of the more secret functions in an organisation of revolutionists will not diminish, but rather increase the extent and the quality of the activity of a large number of other organisations intended for wide membership and which, therefore, can be as loose and as public as possible, for example, trade unions, workers' circles for self-education, and the reading of illegal literature, and Socialist, and also democratic, circles for *all other sections of the population,* etc., etc. We must have *as large a number as possible* of such organisations having the widest possible variety of functions, but it is absurd and dangerous to *confuse these with organisa-tions of revolutionists,* to erase the line of demarcation between them, to dim still more the already incredibly hazy appreciation by the masses that to "serve" the mass movement we must have people who will devote them-selves exclusively to Social-Democratic activities, and that such people must *train* themselves patiently and steadfastly to be professional revolutionists.

Aye, this consciousness has become incredibly dim. The most grievous sin we have committed in regard to organisation is that *by our primitive-ness we have lowered the prestige of revolutionists in Russia.* A man who is weak and vacillating on theoretical questions, who has a narrow outlook, who makes excuses for his own slackness on the ground that the masses are awakening spontaneously, who resembles a trade-union secretary more than a people's tribune, who is unable to conceive a broad and bold plan, who is incapable of inspiring even his enemies with respect for himself, and who is inexperienced and clumsy in his own professional art—the art of com-bating the political police—such a man is not a revolutionist but a hopeless amateur!

Let no active worker take offence at these frank remarks, for as far as insufficient training is concerned, I apply them first and foremost to myself. I used to work in a circle that set itself a great and all-embracing task: and every member of that circle suffered to the point of torture from the realisa-tion that we were proving ourselves to be amateurs at a moment in history when we might have been able to say—paraphrasing a well-known epigram: "Give us an organisation of revolutionists, and we shall overturn the whole of Russia!" And the more I recall the burning sense of shame I then expe-rienced, the more bitter are my feelings towards those pseudo-Social-Demo-crats whose teachings bring disgrace on the calling of a revolutionist, who fail to understand that our task is not to degrade the revolutionist to the level of an amateur, but to *exalt* the amateur to the level of a revolutionist.

The Scope of Organisational Work

. . . If we had such an organisation, the more secret it would be, the stronger and more widespread would be the confidence of the masses in the party, and, as we know, in time of war, it is not only of great importance to imbue one's own adherents with confidence in the strength of one's army, but also the enemy and all *neutral* elements; friendly neutrality may some-times decide the outcome of the battle. If such an organisation existed on a firm theoretical basis, and possessed a Social-Democratic journal, we would have no reason to fear that the movement will be diverted from its path by the numerous "outside" elements that will be attracted to it. . . .

Our very first and most imperative duty is to help to train working-class revolutionists who will be on the same level *in regard to party activity* as intellectual revolutionists (we emphasise the words "in regard to party ac-tivity," because although it is necessary, it is not so easy and not so imperative to bring the workers up to the level of intellectuals in other respects). Therefore, attention must be devoted *principally* to the task of *raising* the workers to the level of revolutionists, but without, in doing so, necessarily *degrading* ourselves to the level of the "labour masses." . . .

A workingman who is at all talented and "promising," *must not be left* to work eleven hours a day in a factory. We must arrange that he be maintained by the party, that he may in due time go underground, that he change the place of his activity, otherwise he will not enlarge his experience, he will not widen his outlook, and will not be able to stay in the fight against the gendarmes for several years. As the spontaneous rise of the labouring masses becomes wider and deeper, it not only promotes from its ranks an increasing number of talented agitators, but also of talented organisers, propagandists, and "practical workers" in the best sense of the term (of whom there are so few among our intelligentsia). In the majority of cases, the latter are somewhat careless and sluggish in their habits (so characteristic of Russians).

When we shall have detachments of specially trained working class revolutionists who have gone through long years of preparation (and, of course, revolutionists "of all arms") no political police in the world will be able to contend against them, for these detachments will consist of men absolutely devoted and loyal to the revolution, and will themselves enjoy the absolute confidence and devotion of the broad masses of the workers. The *sin* we commit is that we do not sufficiently "stimulate" the workers to take this path, "common" to them and to the "intellectuals," of professional revolutionary training, and that we too frequently drag them back by our silly speeches about what "can be understood" by the masses of the workers, by the "average workers," etc. . . .

"Conspirative" Organisation and "Democracy"

. . . Against us it is argued: Such a powerful and strictly secret organisation, which concentrates in its hands all the threads of secret activities, an organisation which of necessity must be a centralised organisation, may too easily throw itself into a premature attack, may thoughtlessly intensify the movement before political discontent, the ferment and anger of the working class, etc., are sufficiently ripe for it. . . .

It is precisely at the present time, when no such organisation exists yet, and when the revolutionary movement is rapidly and spontaneously growing, that we *already observe* two opposite extremes (which, as is to be expected, "meet") *i.e.*, absolutely unsound Economism and the preaching of moderation, and equally unsound "excitative terror," which strives artificially to "call forth symptoms of its end in a movement that is developing and becoming strong, but which is as yet nearer to its beginning than to its end" [V. Zasulich, in *Zarya*, Nos. 2-3, p. 353]. And the example of *Rabocheye Dyelo* shows that *there are already* Social-Democrats who give way to both these extremes. This is not surprising because, apart from other reasons, the "economic struggle against the employers and the government" *can never* satisfy revolutionists, and because opposite extremes will always arise here and there. Only a centralised, militant organisation, that consistently carries out a Social-Democratic policy, that satisfies, so to speak, all revolutionary instincts and strivings, can safeguard the movement against making thoughtless attacks and prepare it for attacks that hold out the promise of success.

It is further argued against us that the views on organisation here expounded contradict the "principles of democracy." Now while the first mentioned accusation was of purely Russian origin, this one is of *purely foreign* origin. And only an organisation abroad (the League of Russian Social-Democrats) would be capable of giving its editorial board instructions like the following:

Principles of Organisation. In order to secure the successful development and unification of Social-Democracy, broad democratic principles of party organisation must be emphasised, developed and fought for; and this is particularly necessary in view of the anti-democratic tendencies that have become revealed in the ranks of our party. [*Two Congresses*, p. 18.]

. . . Every one will probably agree that "broad principles of democracy" presupposes the two following conditions: first, full publicity and second, election to all functions. It would be absurd to speak about democracy without publicity, that is a publicity that extends beyond the circle of the membership of the organisation. We call the German Socialist Party a democratic organisation because all it does is done publicly; even its party congresses are held in public. But no one would call an organisation that is hidden from every one but its members by a veil of secrecy, a democratic organisation. What is the use of advancing *"broad* principles of democracy" when the fundamental condition for this principle *cannot be fulfilled* by a secret organisation. "Broad principles" turns out to be a resonant, but hollow phrase. . . .

Nor is the situation with regard to the second attribute of democracy, namely, the principle of election, any better. In politically free countries, this condition is taken for granted. "Membership of the party is open to those who accept the principles of the party programme, and render all the support they can to the party"—says paragraph 1 of the rules of the German Social-Democratic Party. And as the political arena is as open to the public view as is the stage in a theatre, this acceptance or non-acceptance, support or opposition, is announced to all in the press and at public meetings. Every one knows that a certain political worker commenced in a certain way, passed through a certain evolution, behaved in difficult periods in a certain way; every one knows all his qualities, and consequently, knowing all the facts of the case, *every party member can decide for himself whether or not to elect this person for a certain party office.* The general control (in the literal sense of the term) that the party exercises over every act this person commits on the political field brings into being an automatically operating mechanism which brings about what in biology is called "survival of the fittest." "Natural selection," full publicity, the principle of election and general control provide the guarantee that, in the last analysis, every political worker will be "in his proper place," will do the work for which he is best fitted, will feel the effects of his mistakes on himself, and prove before all the world his ability to recognise mistakes and to avoid them.

Try to put this picture in the frame of our autocracy! Is it possible in Russia for all those "who accept the principles of the party programme and render it all the support they can," to control every action of the revolutionist working in secret? Is it possible for all the revolutionists to elect one of their number to any particular office when, in the very interests of the work, he *must conceal his identity* from nine out of ten of these "all"? Ponder a little over the real meaning of the high-sounding phrases that *Rabocheye Dyelo* gives utterance to, and you will realise that "broad democracy" in party organisation, amidst the gloom of autocracy and the domination of the gendarmes, is nothing more than a *useless and harmful toy*. It is a useless toy, because as a matter of fact, no revolutionary organisation has ever practiced *broad* democracy, nor could it, however much it desired to do so. It is a harmful toy, because any attempt to practice the "broad principles of democracy" will simply facilitate the work of the police in making big raids, it will perpetuate the prevailing primitiveness, divert the thoughts of the practical workers from the serious and imperative task of training themselves to become professional revolutionists to that of drawing up detailed "paper" rules for election systems. . . .

The only serious organisational principle the active workers of our movement can accept is: Strict secrecy, strict selection of members, and the training of professional revolutionists. If we possessed these qualities, "democracy" and something even more would be guaranteed to us, namely: Complete, comradely, mutual confidence among revolutionists. And this something more is absolutely essential for us because, in Russia, it is useless to think that democratic control can serve as a substitute for it. It would be a great mistake to believe that because it is impossible to establish real "democratic" control, the members of the revolutionary organisation will remain altogether uncontrolled. They have not the time to think about the toy forms of democracy (democracy within a close and compact body enjoying the complete mutual confidence of the comrades), but they have a lively sense of their *responsibility*, because they know from experience that an organisation of real revolutionists will stop at nothing to rid itself of an undesirable member. Moreover, there is a very well-developed public opinion in Russian (and international) revolutionary circles which has a long history behind it, and which sternly and ruthlessly punishes every departure from the duties of comradeship (and does not "democracy," real and not toy democracy, represent a part of the conception of comradeship?). Take all this into consideration and you will realise that all the talk and resolutions that come from abroad about "anti-democratic tendencies" has a nasty odour of the playing at generals that goes on there.

STATE AND REVOLUTION

V. I. LENIN

This pamphlet, written during World War I and completed while Lenin was in exile following the March revolution, is presented here in abridged and rearranged form.

In his Preface, dated August 1917, Lenin wrote: "The unheard-of horrors and miseries of the protracted war are making the position of the masses unbearable and increasing their indignation. An international proletarian revolution is clearly rising. The question of its relation to the state is acquiring a practical importance."

So far as the impact on the Russian revolution was concerned, with some ambiguity, he commented that "The Revolution is evidently completing the first stage of its development" and added, "but, generally speaking, this revolution can be understood in its totality only as a link in the chain of Socialist proletarian revolutions called forth by the imperialist war."

Marx's doctrines are now undergoing the same fate which, more than once in the course of history, has befallen the doctrines of other revolutionary thinkers and leaders of oppressed classes struggling for emancipation. During the lifetime of great revolutionaries, the oppressing classes have invariably meted out to them relentless persecution, and received their teaching with the most savage hostility, most furious hatred, and a ruthless campaign of lies and slanders. After their death, however, attempts are usually made to turn them into harmless saints, canonizing them, as it were, and investing their name with a certain halo by way of "consolation" to the oppressed classes, and with the object of duping them; while at the same time emasculating and vulgarizing the real essence of their revolutionary theories and blunting their revolutionary edge. At the present time the bourgeoisie and the opportunists within the Labor Movement are co-operating in this work of adulterating Marxism. They omit, obliterate, and distort the revolutionary side of its teaching, its revolutionary soul, and push to the foreground and extol what is, or seems, acceptable to the bourgeoisie. . . .

THE STATE AS THE PRODUCT OF THE IRRECONCILABILITY OF CLASS ANTAGONISMS

Let us begin with the most popular of Engels' works, *The Origin of the Family, Private Property, and the State.* Summarizing his historical analysis Engels says:

> The State in no way constitutes a force imposed on Society from outside. Nor is the State "the reality of the Moral Idea," "the image and reality of Reason," as Hegel asserted. The State is the product of Society at a certain stage of its development. The State is tantamount to an acknowledgment that the given society has become entangled in an insoluble contradiction with itself, that it has broken up into irreconcilable antagonisms, of which it is powerless to rid itself. And in order that these antagonisms, these classes with their opposing economic interests, may not devour one another and Society itself in their sterile struggle, some force standing, seemingly, above Society, becomes necessary so as to moderate the force of their collisions and to keep them within the bounds of "order." And this force arising from Society, but placing itself above it, which gradually separates itself from it—this force is the State.

Here, we have, expressed in all its clearness, the basic idea of Marxism on the question of the historical role and meaning of the State. The State is the product and the manifestation of the irreconcilability of class antagonisms. When, where and to what extent the State arises, depends directly on when, where and to what extent the class antagonisms of a given society cannot be objectively reconciled. And, conversely, the existence of the State proves that the class antagonisms *are* irreconcilable. . . .

According to Marx, the State is the organ of class *domination,* the organ of oppression of one class by another. Its aim is the creation of order which legalizes and perpetuates this oppression by moderating the collisions between the classes. But in the opinion of the petty-bourgeois politicians, the establishment of order is equivalent to the reconciliation of classes, and not to the oppression of one class by another. To moderate their collisions does not mean, according to them, to deprive the oppressed class of certain definite means and methods in its struggle for throwing off the yoke of the oppressors, but to conciliate it. . . .

But what is forgotten or overlooked is this:—If the State is the product of the irreconcilable character of class antagonisms, if it is a force standing above society and "separating itself gradually from it," then it is clear that the liberation of the oppressed class is impossible without a violent revolution, and without the destruction of the machinery of State power, which has been created by the governing class and in which this "separation" is embodied. . . .

BOURGEOIS DEMOCRACY

In capitalist society, under the conditions most favorable to its development, we have a more or less complete democracy in the form of a democratic republic. But this democracy is always bound by the narrow framework of capitalist exploitation, and consequently always remains, in reality, a democracy only for the minority, only for the possessing classes, only for the rich. Freedom in capitalist society always remains more or less the same as it was in the ancient Greek republics, that is, freedom for the slave owners. The modern wage-slaves, in virtue of the conditions of capitalist exploitation, remain to such an extent crushed by want and poverty that they "cannot be bothered with democracy," have "no time for politics"; so that, in the ordinary peaceful course of events, the majority of the population is debarred from participating in public political life. . . .

Democracy for an insignificant minority, democracy for the rich—that is the democracy of capitalist society. If we look more closely into the mechanism of capitalist democracy, everywhere—in the so-called "petty" details of the suffrage (the residential qualification, the exclusion of women, etc.), in the technique of the representative institutions, in the actual obstacles to the right of meeting (public buildings are not for the "poor"), in the purely capitalist organization of the daily press, etc., etc.—on all sides we shall see restrictions upon restrictions of democracy. These restrictions, exceptions, exclusions, obstacles for the poor, seem slight—especially in the eyes of one who has himself never known want, and has never lived in close contact with the oppressed classes in their hard life, and nine-tenths, if not ninety-nine hundredths, of the bourgeois publicists and politicians are of this class! But in their sum these restrictions exclude and thrust out the poor from politics and from an active share in democracy. Marx splendidly grasped the *essence* of capitalist democracy, when, in his analysis of the experience of the Commune, he said that the oppressed are allowed, once every few years to decide which particular representatives of the oppressing class are to represent and repress them in Parliament! . . .

In a democratic Republic, Engels wrote, "wealth wields its power indirectly, but all the more effectively," first, by means of "direct corruption of the officials" (America); second, by means of "the alliance of the government with the stock exchange" (France and America). At the present time, imperialism and the domination of the banks have reduced to a fine art both these methods of defending and practically asserting the omnipotence of wealth in democratic Republics of all descriptions. . . .

We must also note that Engels quite definitely regards universal suffrage as a means of capitalist domination. Universal suffrage, he says (summing up obviously the long experience of German Social-Democracy), is "an index of the maturity of the working class; it cannot, and never will, give anything more in the present state." The petty-bourgeois democrats such as our Socialist-Revolutionaries and Mensheviks and also their twin brothers, the Social-Chauvinists and opportunists of Western Europe, all expect a "great deal" from this universal suffrage. They themselves think and instil into the minds of the people the wrong idea that universal suffrage in the "present state" is really capable of expressing the will of the majority of the laboring masses and of securing its realization. . . .

Take any parliamentary country, from America to Switzerland, from France to England, Norway and so forth; the actual work of the State is done behind the scenes and is carried out by the departments, the chancelleries and the staffs. Parliament itself is given up to talk for the special purpose of fooling the "common people." . . .

Two more points. First: when Engels says that in a democratic republic, "not a whit less" than in a monarchy, the State remains an "apparatus for the oppression of one class by another," this by no means signifies that the *form* of oppression is a matter of indifference to the proletariat, as some anarchists "teach." A wider, more free and open form of the class struggle and class oppression enormously assists the proletariat in its struggle for the annihilation of all classes.

Second: only a new generation will be able completely to scrap the ancient lumber of the State—this question is bound up with the question of overcoming democracy, to which we now turn.

DICTATORSHIP OF THE PROLETARIAT

The forms of bourgeois States are exceedingly various, but their substance is the same and in the last analysis inevitably the *Dictatorship of the Bourgeoisie*. The transition from capitalism to Communism will certainly bring a great variety and abundance of political forms, but the substance will inevitably be: the *Dictatorship of the Proletariat*. . . .

The State is a particular form of organization of force; it is the organization of violence for the purpose of holding down some class. What is the class which the proletariat must hold down? It can only be, naturally, the exploiting class, i.e., the bourgeoisie. The toilers need the State only to overcome the resistance of the exploiters, and only the proletariat can guide this suppression and bring it to fulfillment, for the proletariat is the only class that is thoroughly revolutionary, the only class that can unite all the toilers and the exploited in the struggle against the bourgeoisie, for its complete displacement from power. . . .

But the dictatorship of the proletariat—that is, the organization of the advance-guard of the oppressed as the ruling class, for the purpose of crushing the oppressors—cannot produce merely an expansion of democracy. *Together* with an immense expansion of democracy—for the first time becoming democracy for the poor, democracy for the people, and not democracy for the rich—the dictatorship of the proletariat will produce a series of restrictions of liberty in the case of the oppressors, exploiters and capitalists. We must crush them in order to free humanity from wage-slavery; their resistance must be broken by force. It is clear that where there is suppression there must also be violence, and there cannot be liberty or democracy. . . .

The replacement of the bourgeois by the proletarian State is impossible without a violent revolution. . . . There is [in *Anti-Dühring*] a disquisition on the nature of a violent revolution; and the historical appreciation of its role becomes, with Engels, a veritable panegyric on violent revolution. . . . Here is Engels' argument:

> That force also plays another part in history (other than that of a perpetuation of evil), namely a *revolutionary* part; that, as Marx says, it is the midwife of every old society when it is pregnant with a new one; that force is the instrument and the means by which social movements hack their way through and break up the dead and fossilized political forms—of all this not a word by Herr Dühring. Duly, with sighs and groans, does he admit the possibility that for the overthrow of the system of exploitation force may, perhaps, be necessary, but most unfortunate if you please, because all use of force, forsooth, demoralizes its user! And this is said in face of the great moral and intellectual advance which has been the result of every victorious revolution! . . . And this turbid, flabby, impotent, parson's mode of thinking dares offer itself for acceptance to the most revolutionary party which history has known!

In the *Communist Manifesto* are summed up the general lessons of history, which force us to see in the State the organ of class domination, and lead us to the inevitable conclusion that the proletariat cannot overthrow the bourgeoisie without first conquering political power, without obtaining political rule, without transforming the State into the "proletariat organized as the ruling class"; and that this proletarian State must begin to wither away immediately after its victory because in a community without class antagonisms, the State is unnecessary and impossible.

WHAT IS TO REPLACE THE SHATTERED STATE MACHINERY?

In 1847, in the *Communist Manifesto,* Marx was as yet only able to answer this question entirely in an abstract manner, stating the problem rather than its solution. To replace this machinery by "the proletariat organized as the ruling class," "by the conquest of democracy"—such was the answer of the *Communist Manifesto.* . . .

Refusing to plunge into Utopia, Marx waited for the experience of a mass movement to produce the answer to the problem as to the exact forms which this organization of the proletariat as the dominant class will assume and exactly in what manner this organization will embody the most complete, most consistent "conquest of democracy." Marx subjected the ex-

periment of the [Paris] Commune, although it was so meagre, to a most
minute analysis in his *Civil War in France*. . . .

> The Commune was the direct antithesis of the Empire. It was a definite
> form . . . of a Republic which was to abolish, not only the monarchical form of
> class rule, but also class rule itself.

What was this "definite" form of the proletarian Socialist Republic?
What was the State it was beginning to create? "The first decree of the
[Paris] Commune was the suppression of the standing army, and the substitution for it of the armed people," says Marx. . . . But let us see how,
twenty years after the Commune, Engels summed up its lessons for the fighting proletariat. . . .

> Against this inevitable feature of all systems of government that have existed
> hitherto, viz., the transformation of the State and its organs from servants into the
> lords of society, the Commune used two unfailing remedies. First, it appointed to
> all posts, administrative, legal, educational, persons elected by universal suffrage;
> introducing at the same time the right of recalling those elected at any time by the
> decision of their electors. Secondly, it paid all officials, both high and low, only
> such pay as was received by any other worker. The highest salary paid by the
> Commune was 6,000 francs (about £240).
> Thus was created an effective barrier to place-hunting and career-making, even
> apart from the imperative mandates of the deputies in representative institutions
> introduced by the Commune over and above this. . . .

The lowering of the pay of the highest State officials seems simply a
naive, primitive demand of democracy. One of the "founders" of the new-
est opportunism, the former Social-Democrat, E. Bernstein, has more than
once exercised his talents in the repetition of the vulgar capitalist jeers at
"primitive" democracy. Like all opportunists, like the present followers of
Kautsky, he quite failed to understand that, first of all, the transition from
capitalism to Socialism is impossible without "return," in a measure, to
"primitive" democracy. How can we otherwise pass on to the discharge of
all the functions of government by the majority of the population and by
every individual of the population. And, secondly, he forgot that "primitive democracy" on the basis of capitalism and capitalist culture is not the
same primitive democracy as in pre-historic or pre-capitalist times. Capitalist culture has created industry on a large scale in the shape of factories,
railways, posts, telephones, and so forth: and *on this basis* the great majority of functions of "the old State" have become enormously simplified
and reduced, in practice, to very simple operations such as registration,
filing and checking. Hence they will be quite within the reach of every
literate person, and it will be possible to perform them for the usual "working man's wage." This circumstance ought to and will strip them of all
their former glamour as "government," and, therefore, privileged service.

The control of all officials, without exception, by the unreserved application of the principle of election and, *at any time,* re-call; and the approximation of their salaries to the "ordinary pay of the workers"—these are simple and "self-evident" democratic measures, which harmonize completely the interests of the workers and the majority of peasants; and, at the same time, serve as a bridge leading from capitalism to Socialism. . . .

To organize our whole national economy like the postal system, but in such a way that the technical experts, inspectors, clerks and, indeed, all persons employed, should receive no higher wage than the working man, and the whole under the management of the armed proletariat—this is our immediate aim. This is the kind of State and the economic basis we need. This is what will produce the destruction of parliamentarism, while retaining representative institutions. This is what will free the laboring classes from the prostitution of these institutions by the capitalist class. . . .

For the mercenary and corrupt parliamentarism of capitalist society, the Commune substitutes institutions in which freedom of opinion and discussion does not become a mere delusion, for the representatives must themselves work, must themselves execute their own laws, must themselves verify their results in actual practice, must themselves be directly responsible to their electorate. Representative institutions remain, but parliamentarism as a special system, as a division of labor between the legislative and the executive functions, as creating a privileged position for its deputies, *no longer exists.* Without representative institutions we cannot imagine a democracy, even a proletarian democracy; but we can and *must* think of democracy without parliamentarism, if our criticism of capitalist society is not mere empty words, if to overthrow the supremacy of the capitalists is for us a serious and sincere aim, and not a mere "election cry" for catching working men's votes. . . .

The dictatorship of the proletariat, the period of transition to Communism, will, for the first time, produce a democracy for the people, for the majority, side by side with the necessary suppression of the minority constituted by the exploiters. Communism alone is capable of giving a really complete democracy, and the fuller it is the more quickly will it become unnecessary and wither away of itself. In other words, under capitalism we have a State in the proper sense of the word: that is, a special instrument for the suppression of one class by another, and of the majority by the minority at that. Naturally, for the successful discharge of such a task as the systematic suppression by the minority of exploiters of the majority of exploited, the greatest ferocity and savagery of suppression is required, and seas of blood are needed, through which humanity has to direct its path, in a condition of slavery, serfdom and wage labor.

Again, during the *transition* from capitalism to Communism, suppression is *still* necessary; but in this case it is suppression of the minority of exploiters by the majority of exploited. A special instrument, a special machine for suppression—that is, the "State"—is necessary, but this is now a transitional State, no longer a State in the ordinary sense of the term. For the suppression of the minority of exploiters, by the majority of those who were *but yesterday* wage slaves, is a matter comparatively so easy, simple and natural that it will cost far less bloodshed than the suppression of the risings of the slaves, serfs or wage laborers, and will cost the human race far less. And it is compatible with the diffusion of democracy over such an overwhelming majority of the nation that the need for any *special machinery* for *suppression* will gradually cease to exist. The exploiters are unable, of course, to suppress the people without a most complex machine for performing this duty; but *the people* can suppress the exploiters even with a very simple "machine"—almost without any "machine" at all, without any special apparatus—by the simple *organization of the armed masses* (such as the Councils of Workers' and Soldiers' Deputies, we may remark, anticipating a little).

Finally, only under Communism will the State become quite unnecessary, for there will be *no one* to suppress—"no one" in the sense of a *class,* in the sense of a systematic struggle with a definite section of the population. We are not utopians, and we do not in the least deny the possibility and inevitability of excesses by *individual persons,* and equally the need to suppress such excesses. But, in the first place, for this no special machine, no special instrument of repression is needed. This will be done by the armed nation itself, as simply and as readily as any crowd of civilized people, even in modern society, parts a pair of combatants or does not allow a woman to be outraged. And, secondly, we know that the fundamental social cause of excesses which violate the rules of social life is the exploitation of the masses, their want and their poverty. With the removal of this chief cause, excesses will inevitably begin to "wither away." We do not know how quickly and in what stages, but we know that they will be withering away. With their withering away, the State will also wither away.

THE "WITHERING AWAY" OF THE STATE

Engels' words regarding the "withering away" of the State enjoy such a popularity, are so often quoted, and reveal so clearly the essence of the common adulteration of Marxism in an opportunist sense that we must examine them in detail. Let us give the passage from which they are taken.

The proletariat takes control of the State authority and, first of all, converts the means of production into State property. But by this very act it destroys itself, as a proletariat, destroying at the same time all class differences and class antagonisms, and with this, also, the State.

Engels speaks here of the *destruction* of the capitalist State by the proletarian revolution, while the words about its withering away refer to the remains of a *proletarian* State *after* the Socialist revolution. The capitalist State does not wither away, according to Engels, but is *destroyed* by the proletariat in the course of the revolution. Only the proletarian State or semi-State withers away after the revolution. . . .

A general summary of his views is given by Engels in the following words:—

Thus, the State has not always existed. There were societies which did without it, which had no idea of the State or of State power. At a given stage of economic development which was necessarily bound up with the break up of society into classes, the State became a necessity, as a result of this division. We are now rapidly approaching a stage in the development of production, in which the existence of these classes is not only no longer necessary, but is becoming a direct impediment to production. Classes will vanish as inevitably as they inevitably arose in the past. With the disappearance of classes the State, too, will inevitably disappear. When organizing production anew on the basis of a free and equal association of the producers, Society will banish the whole State machine to a place which will then be the most proper one for it—to the museum of antiquities side by side with the spinning-wheel and the bronze axe.

FIRST PHASE OF COMMUNIST SOCIETY: SOCIALISM

It is this Communist society—a society which has just come into the world out of the womb of capitalism, and which, in all respects, bears the stamp of the old society—that Marx terms the first, or lower, phase of Communist society.

The means of production are now no longer the private property of individuals. The means of production belong to the whole of society. Every member of society, performing a certain part of socially-necessary labor, receives a certificate from society that he has done such and such a quantity of work. According to this certificate, he receives from the public stores of articles of consumption, a corresponding quantity of products. After the deduction of that proportion of labor which goes to the public fund, every worker, therefore, receives from society as much as he has given it.

"Equality" seems to reign supreme. . . . But different people are not equal to one another. One is strong, another is weak; one is married, the other is not. One has more children, another has less, and so on.

With equal labor [Marx concludes] and, therefore, with an equal share in the public stock of articles of consumption, one will, in reality, receive more than another, will find himself richer, and so on. To avoid all this, "rights," instead of being equal, should be unequal.

The first phase of Communism, therefore, still cannot produce justice and equality; differences and unjust differences in wealth will still exist, but the *exploitation* of man by man will have become impossible, because it will be impossible to seize as private property the *means of production,* the factories, machines, land, and so on. . . .

"He who does not work neither shall he eat"—this Socialist principle is *already* realized. "For an equal quantity of labor an equal quantity of products"—this Socialist principle is also already realized. Nevertheless, this is not yet Communism, and this does not abolish "bourgeois law," which gives to unequal individuals, in return for an unequal (in reality) amount of work, an equal quantity of products.

This is a "defect," says Marx, but it is unavoidable during the first phase of Communism; for, if we are not to land in Utopia, we cannot imagine that, having overthrown capitalism, people will at once learn to work for society *without any regulations by law;* indeed, the abolition of capitalism does not *immediately* lay the economic foundations for such a change. . . .

The State is withering away in so far as there are no longer any capitalists, any classes, and, consequently, any *class* whatever to suppress. But the State is not yet dead altogether, since there still remains the protection of "bourgeois law," which sanctifies actual inequality. For the complete extinction of the State complete Communism is necessary.

THE HIGHER PHASE OF COMMUNIST SOCIETY: COMMUNISM

Marx continues:

In the higher phase of Communist society, after the disappearance of the enslavement of man caused by his subjection to the principle of division of labor; when, together with this, the opposition between brain and manual work will have disappeared; when labor will have ceased to be a mere means of supporting life and will itself have become one of the first necessities of life; when with the all-round development of the individual, the productive forces, too, will have grown to maturity, and all the forces of social wealth will be pouring an uninterrupted torrent—only then will it be possible wholly to pass beyond the narrow horizon of bourgeois laws, and only then will society be able to inscribe on its banner: "From each according to his ability; to each according to his needs."

Only now can we appreciate the full justice of Engels' observations when he mercilessly ridiculed all the absurdity of combining the words "freedom" and "State." While the State exists there can be no freedom. When there is freedom there will be no State.

The economic basis for the complete withering away of the State is that high stage of development of Communism when the distinction between brain and manual work disappears; consequently, when one of the principal sources of modern *social* inequalities will have vanished—a source, moreover, which it is impossible to remove immediately by the mere conversion of the means of production into public property, by the mere expropriation of the capitalists.

This expropriation will make it possible gigantically to develop the forces of production. And seeing how incredibly, even now, capitalism *retards* this development, how much progress could be made even on the basis of modern technique at the level it has reached, we have a right to say, with the fullest confidence, that the expropriation of the capitalists will result inevitably in a gigantic development of the productice forces of human society. But how rapidly this development will go forward, how soon it will reach the point of breaking away from the division of labor, of the destruction of the antagonism between brain and manual work, of the transformation of work into a "first necessity of life"—this we do not and *cannot* know.

Consequently, we are right in speaking solely of the inevitable withering away of the State, emphasizing the protracted nature of this process, and its dependence upon the rapidity of development of the *higher phase* of Communism; leaving quite open the question of lengths of time, or the concrete forms of this withering away, since material for the solution of such questions is not available.

The State will be able to wither away completely when society has realized the formula: "From each according to his ability; to each according to his needs"; that is when people have become accustomed to observe the fundamental principles of social life, and their labor is so productive, that they will voluntarily work *according to their abilities.* "The narrow horizon of bourgeois law," which compels one to calculate, with the pitilessness of a Shylock, whether one has not worked half-an-hour more than another, whether one is not getting less pay than another—this narrow horizon will then be left behind. There will then be no need for any exact calculation by society of the quantity of products to be distributed to each of its members; each will take freely "according to his needs." . . .

The scientific difference between Socialism and Communism is clear. That which is generally called Socialism is termed by Marx the first or lower phase of Communist society. In so far as the means of production become public property, the word Communism is also applicable here, providing that we do not forget that it is not full Communism. . . .

By what stages, by means of what practical measures humanity will proceed to this higher aim—this we do not and cannot know. But it is important that one should realize how infinitely mendacious is the usual capitalist representation of Socialism as something lifeless, petrified, fixed once for all. In reality, it is only with Socialism that there will commence a rapid, genuine, real mass advance, in which first the majority and then the *whole* of the population will take part—an advance in all domains of social and individual life.

LENIN AND COMMUNISM

GEORGE H. SABINE*

LENIN'S RELATION TO MARXISM

Lenin's Marxism was in the last degree dogmatic and orthodox, supported by the *ipsissima verba* of the master and designed in large part to provide a creed for a fighting organization of professional revolutionists. Yet it was responsible for the most considerable changes that any follower of Marx ever made in the master's teaching. Lenin professed a regard, almost a reverence, for theory as an indispensable part of the equipment of a revolutionary movement. He conceived of theory as a guide to action, not as a body of statically true doctrine, but as a mass of suggestive ideas, to be recognized and picked out in a concrete situation, to be used in assessing its possibilities, and to be modified in the application. There is no doubt that Lenin was a genius in adapting both his thought and his action to circumstances, while at the same time he continued to pursue what he believed to be the essentials of his program.

It was this remarkable combination of suppleness and rigidity that made him an incomparable leader. He could follow a policy almost to the breaking-point but not quite; he could change before either his followers or his opponents knew that a crisis had occurred; he could give way when he must and come back when he could; and always he could make a change of front appear as the logical next step in a prearranged program of advance. Often it is difficult to tell what was a valid application of principles, what was legitimate recognition of new facts, and what was sheer opportunism. Opportunism in respect to the philosophy of Marx was the theme of Lenin's bitterest and most constant condemnation. Yet the changes that he made even in Marxian theory were certainly very considerable, and it is doubtful whether Lenin himself always appreciated their extent.

Stalin[1] has said that there are three interpretations of Lenin's relation to Marx, all at least partially correct. The first is that he reverted from the final form of Marx's philosophy, stated mainly in *Capital,* to its more revolutionary form contained in the early pamphlets. It is true that one of Lenin's chief purposes was to save Marxism from the opportunists and

---

* Formerly Professor of Philosophy at Cornell University. The selection is from pp. 719-738, 741-742 of *A History of Political Theory,* First Edition, by George H. Sabine. By permission of Henry Holt & Co., Inc., Copyright 1937.

[1] *Leninism,* Eng. trans. by E. and C. Paul (London, 1928), p. 13.

make it again a revolutionary creed, and references to *Capital* were comparatively few in his works. But in itself this says nothing about Lenin; he was certainly not interested in substituting one literary tradition for another. The second interpretation is that he adapted Marxism to the state of affairs in Russia, and this also is true, since his life was spent as a leader of one branch of the Russian socialist party and most of what he wrote had to do with that party or with the Russian Revolution. But this interpretation, if taken as a sufficient account of his work, is equivalent to saying that, from his own point of view, Lenin's work was a failure. For he certainly believed that Marxism was a general social philosophy having more than merely a national application. The third interpretation of Lenin's work is that it brought Marx down to date, taking account of the further evolution of capitalist society and reformulating the theory and the tactics of Marxism in the light of developments of which Marx saw only the beginning. From this point of view Lenin's philosophy is regarded as Marxism in the latest or imperialist stage of the capitalist system, and the modifications which he made are merely the perfecting of the system. This is certainly the light in which Lenin himself would wish his ideas to be viewed.

It is true that some of Lenin's most important and characteristic doctrines had to do with the organization and tactics proper to the Russian socialist party and that the part which he was finally able to play in Russia in 1917 depended upon his leadership, during the preceding fifteen years, of one wing of that party. Organized in 1898 as the organ of the urban proletariat and largely with the purpose of substituting revolutionary mass-tactics for sporadic acts of violence, the party at once divided into two factions which, by the accident of their relative strength in the party convention of 1903, came to be known as Bolshevik and Menshevik (majority and minority, respectively). The differences between the two factions turned upon the nature of the organization most suitable to the new party, and Lenin led the group that stood for a tight organization under rigid discipline, not too large for secrecy, and providing leadership for the less class-conscious but potentially revolutionary masses in the trade-unions and among the workers. This question of party organization formed the subject of Lenin's first important work, the pamphlet entitled *What Is To Be Done?* The conclusion reached is suggested in the following passage:

A small, compact core, consisting of reliable, experienced and hardened workers, with responsible agents in the principal districts and connected by all the rules of strict secrecy with the organizations of revolutionists, can, with the wide support of the masses and without an elaborate set of rules, perform all the functions of a trade-union organization, and perform them, moreover, in the manner Social Democrats desire.

TRADE-UNIONIST AND SOCIALIST IDEOLOGY

Though *What Is To Be Done?* has to do chiefly with the question of organization, it touches, and very characteristically, upon important points of Marxian theory. Lenin's opponents objected that his limited, rigidly disciplined party was a virtual denial of the Marxian principle that the relations of production in capitalism form the proletarian class and its characteristic revolutionary ideology. Hence, they argued, a revolutionary movement must arise spontaneously; it cannot be "made," since neither force nor exhortation can run ahead of the underlying industrial conditions upon which the proletarian state of mind depends. Lenin met this argument, which had certainly the color of sound Marxism, with a flat denial. The argument, he asserted, confuses the mentality of trade-unionism with that of socialism. Spontaneously the workers do not become socialists but trade-unionists; socialism has to be brought to them from the outside by middle-class intellectuals.

We said that *there could not yet be* Social-Democratic consciousness among the workers [in the Russian strikes in the 1890's]. This consciousness could only be brought to them from without. The history of all countries shows that the working class, exclusively by its own effort, is able to develop only trade-union consciousness, *i.e.*, it may itself realize the necessity for combining in unions, to fight against the employers and to strive to compel the government to pass necessary labor legislation, etc.

The socialist theory of Marx and Engels, he continued, was created by educated representatives of the bourgeois intelligentsia and it was introduced into Russia by the same group. A trade-union movement is incapable of developing an ideology for itself and in consequence the choice must lie between allowing it to fall a prey to the ideology of the middle class or indoctrinating it with the ideology of socialist intellectuals.

It is true that this contrast between socialism and the spontaneously developed mentality of the working class was not altogether of Lenin's making and that he was able to quote a passage from Kautsky to support it. It referred to a deep-seated uncertainty in Marx's philosophy: the relation between the nonvoluntary effects of economic conditions in producing a mentality characteristic of social classes and the voluntary efforts of individuals to modify or direct the ideological results of those conditions. Many critics had asked, If socialism is inevitable, why work for it? The vigor of socialist parties had sometimes been sapped by too much dependence on natural growth. Though Lenin was touching an old question, he was raising it in a peculiarly provocative form. For if the growth of capitalist production creates in the proletariat only the mentality that makes trade-union tactics possible, the Marxian principle that all ideology is a superstructure built upon the foundation of production-relations apparently ought to imply that trade-unionism is the final answer of the proletariat to capitalism.

Nothing could be farther from Marx's meaning. On the other hand, if socialism and a socialist ideology must be produced by a bourgeois intelligentsia and introduced into the proletariat "from the outside," what can it mean to say that material conditions of production and not "ideas" are the effective causes of social revolution? And still more difficult to understand, why should capitalist production, which creates the opposed bourgeois and proletarian classes and their ideologies, bring into existence a middle-class intelligentsia devoted to the task of making an ideology for the proletariat? Either the class-struggle does not wholly determine the mentality of the class or else it produces in the middle class a perverted form of class-consciousness that devotes itself to the destruction of the class.

Lenin's conception of the party and its relation to a proletarian movement was intelligible in the light of the situation in Russia, but it was doubtfully Marxian. Marx's emphasis had always been upon the evolution of class-consciousness under the influence of the relations of production, and apparently he always assumed that his own philosophy represented the ideology that capitalist production tended to create in the working-class. This philosophy can only "shorten and lessen the birth-pangs"; it cannot help a society to "overleap the natural phases of evolution." Lenin's conception was in principle quite different. Not only in Russia—a country in which, as he repeatedly said, Marxism is peculiarly in danger of being perverted by the ideas of the petty bourgeoisie—but everywhere the working class is unable to work out an ideology of its own. It is hung between two ideologies, that of the bourgeoisie and that of the middle-class socialist intelligentsia. Its fate is to be captured by one or the other and the essential tactical problem of the party is to capture it.

The argument ran parallel to one that Marx had used in another connection, that the peasantry and petty bourgeoisie, having no future in a developing capitalist society, must fall under the control either of capitalists or proletarians and ultimately of the latter. Lenin used this argument of the proletariat itself. The result is that for him the rôle of the party became enormously more important, since it became responsible for a spread of socialist ideology that Marx regarded as largely a normal result of the class-struggle itself, and that the rôle of intellectuals in the party was correspondingly magnified, since they had to bring this ideology to the working class "from the outside." This explains the great importance that Lenin always attached to theory as the guide of tactics. The party became a picked body of the intellectual and moral élite, in the midst of all working-class movements, to be sure, and providing leadership, but always distinguishable from the body of workers. It seems clear that, even as early as 1902, and quite without reference to imperialist capitalism, Lenin had evolved a theory of the party which does not follow from anything in Marx and is even incompatible with what most socialists thought that Marx meant.

THE SOLIDARITY OF THE PARTY

The communist party thus becomes a staff-organization in the struggle of the proletarian class for power, and Marxism is the creed that holds it together, the guide of its action, and the subject-matter by which it extends the circle of class-consciousness. Ideal union through the principles of Marxism and material union through rigid organization and discipline were the two foundationstones upon which, from the beginning of his career, Lenin proposed to build a revolutionary movement. Two passages may be placed side by side to show how constantly this purpose was maintained. The first is from his pamphlet, *One Step Forward, Two Steps Backward,* published in 1904:

> The proletariat has no weapon in the struggle for power except organization. . . . Constantly pushed down to the depths of complete poverty the proletariat can and will inevitably become an unconquerable force only as a result of this: that its ideological union by means of the principles of Marxism is strengthened by the material union of an organization, holding together millions of toilers in the army of the working class.

The second is from a resolution adopted at a congress of the Communist International in 1920:

> The Communist Party is part of the working class: its most progressive, most class-conscious and therefore most revolutionary part. The Communist Party is created by means of selection of the best, most class-conscious, most self-sacrificing, and far-sighted workers. . . . The Communist Party is the lever of political organization, with the help of which the more progressive part of the working class directs on the right path the whole mass of the proletariat and the semi-proletariat.[2]

Obviously within the party individual freedom, not only of action but of opinion, must be strictly subordinated to discipline and unity of command. For ideology is itself part of the class-struggle, an ideal agency of discipline and organization. Nothing can surpass the dogmatism with which at all times, from 1902 on, Lenin asserted the integrity of the Marxian philosophy and its revolutionary value.

> To belittle socialist ideology *in any way,* to *deviate from it in the slightest degree,* means strengthening bourgeois ideology.[3]

Freedom of criticism is opportunism, eclecticism, and absence of principle, a kind of "Bernstein revisionism."

[2] These two passages are quoted by W. H. Chamberlin, *The Russian Revolution, 1917-1921,* Vol. II (New York, 1935), p. 361.

[3] *What Is To Be Done?* The italics are Lenin's.

We are marching in a compact group along a precipitious and difficult path, firmly holding each other by the hand. We are surrounded on all sides by enemies, and are under their almost constant fire. We have combined voluntarily; especially for the purpose of fighting the enemy and not to retreat into the adjacent marsh. . . . And now several in our crowd begin to cry out—let us go into this marsh! [4]

In part, then, "theory" meant for Lenin a creed, a dogma to be held integrally and unswervingly as part of the tactics of battle. Yet it would be easy to quote an equal number of passages in which he asserted that theory is the guide of action, subject to the vicissitudes of life and circumstance and to be changed remorselessly as occasion demands. In the pamphlet *One Step Forward, Two Steps Backward,* he tells of his delight in the seemingly discouraging wrangling of party-conferences:

Opportunity for open fighting. Opinions expressed. Tendencies revealed. Groups defined. Hands raised. A decision taken. A stage passed through. Forward! That's what I like! That's life! It is something different from the endless, wearying intellectual discussions, which finish, not because people have solved the problem, but simply because they have got tired of talking.[5]

This fixed faith in the constancy of principles, coupled with freedom of controversy within the bounds fixed, is almost like scholasticism. . . .

IMPERIALIST CAPITALISM

The outbreak of the World War turned Lenin's attention more definitely toward international affairs and led to the formulation of his theory of the imperialist war and of communism in the imperialist stage of capitalism, which must be regarded as his chief contribution to Marxist theory.[6] The war brought to a head all the smoldering differences that had divided socialists for years, such as the support of national interests, the voting of war-credits, and participation in bourgeois governments. After a little hesitation nearly all socialists fell in behind their national governments. Lenin, an exile in Switzerland, stood out and belabored the opportunism and chauvinism of the Second International for its betrayal of socialism. In this he continued the attacks which he had been making for years upon every form of revisionism, only now he included in his condemnation nearly all socialists everywhere, except his own wing of the Russian party and a few other dissenters like Karl Liebknecht and Rosa Luxemburg in Germany. From the beginning Lenin argued that the attempt to apportion guilt among the belligerent nations was nonsense, that all were dominated

[4] *Ibid.*
[5] Quoted by Lenin's wife, N. K. Krupskaya, *Memories of Lenin,* Eng. trans. by E. Verney (New York, 1930), pp. 102 f.
[6] See the *Collected Works,* Vols. XVIII and XIX, especially *Under a Stolen Flag, Socialism and War* (with G. Zinoviev), *Imperialism: The Highest Stage of Capitalism;* also Bukharin's *Imperialism and World Economy* (New York, 1929). These were written in 1915 and first published after the March Revolution in 1917.

by the same kind of economic motives, and that the war was essentially a capitalist quarrel about the division of booty. In this quarrel the working class of no nation has any vital concern; certainly, he said, the Russian workers have no interest in taking away the spoils of one young robber (Germany) in order to give it to two old ones (England and France). But Lenin was at no time a pacifist. His object from the first was to "turn the imperialist war into a civil war."

The "betrayal of socialism" by the socialists was obviously an anomaly from the point of view of Marx's philosophy as it was commonly understood. For the class-struggle ought to have been growing sharper and society more clearly divided into bourgeoisie and proletariat as capitalism developed. Hence Lenin, as the most rigid of Marxians and the enemy of all revisionism, must supplement the theory to account for what appeared like a gross exception. He began with an unquestionable historical fact: the period after 1871 was mainly one in which socialist parties had grown by peaceful means to a size where they could hope to succeed by parliamentary tactics. Inevitably there was an infiltration of petty bourgeois membership and ideology, and the substitution of trade-union for revolutionary tactics. But since ideology must follow the relations of production, this fact itself needs to be traced back to the inherent development of the capitalist system. This Lenin accomplished by supposing that in the successful imperialist countries the expansion of markets and the increase of production had enabled a small part of the workers, especially in the skilled trades, to profit. This produced between 1871 and 1914 a kind of backwash in the class-struggle. A small but influential part of the workers joined with the capitalists to exploit the great mass of unskilled workers, especially workers in backward countries and colonies. The ideology of this movement was petty bourgeois. It fell a victim to the illusion of peaceful evolution and the harmony of class-interests. This theory may well have been suggested to Lenin by Engels' observations on the British labor-movement and the effect of foreign trade upon it.

This secondary movement in the class-struggle was thus due to the peculiar qualities of capitalism in the period, and these in turn corresponded definitely to a certain stage in the development of the capitalist system as a whole. In his description of this imperialist stage of capitalism Lenin assembled a number of characteristics that had been described by many authors before him, both socialist and non-socialist, expanding Marx's account of capitalist accumulation. The units in which industry is organized steadily tend to grow larger until they become monopolies, either of a whole industry or of a vertical string of related industries. The market becomes world-wide and prices both of commodities and of labor tend to be fixed in the world-market. Competition practically ceases within the nation and so loses the power to keep down prices, while more and more it assumes the form of rivalry between national monopolies. At the same time tariffs cease to nourish infant industries and become weapons in national trade-wars. With the formation of industrial combinations banking capital is fused with industrial capital, and industry comes more and more under bankers' control. Capital itself becomes a significant item of export. The steady pressure for larger markets and the demand for raw materials, both inherent in the expansion of capitalist production, result in an international scramble for undeveloped territory and the control of backward peoples. In international politics the vital question becomes the partition of exploitable territory and population; in internal politics capitalist control becomes more direct, with the result that parliamentary institutions become more and more a sham. Reduced to its essentials an imperialist war, such as that begun in 1914, is a struggle between syndicates of German capitalists with their subsidiaries and syndicates of allied French and English capitalists with their subsidiaries for the control of Africa. To be sure, eddies and backwashes occur, as in the hope of Russian capitalists to get Constantinople or of the Japanese to exploit China; in the backward nations there are even *bona fide* nationalist movements, as in Serbia or India.

THE IMPERIALIST WAR

Now the purpose of Marxian theory is to provide a guide to proletarian tactics, and tactics must be fitted to the nature of the epoch in which they are used. The theory of imperialist capitalism enabled Lenin to advance a new theory of the significant periods in the evolution of European society. The turning-points he took to be 1871—fixed apparently by the Paris Commune, the last important revolutionary outbreak—and 1914, the beginning of the first imperialist war. Between the French Revolution and 1871 capitalism was on an ascending curve and the bourgeoisie was a progressive class, compared with the remnants of feudalism which it displaced. In this period it produced its characteristic—and, in their time and place, its valuable—social and political consequences, notably the democratization of government and the liberation of nationalities. The proletariat was in a process of formation and was therefore obliged to adjust itself to the expanding power of the bourgeoisie. Consequently it was sound socialist tactics to inquire, as Marx did in 1859, whether the international interests of the proletariat would be best served by the success of Austria or France. War in this period was, by and large, an agency in the forming and freeing of nationalities, and socialists could logically cooperate with this process. The period from 1871 to 1914 was, so to speak, the flat top of the curve, the age of capitalist domination and incipient decay, in which the class-struggle was confused by a false appearance of conciliation and the capitalist organization of society took on the monopolist and imperialist characteristics just described.

In 1914 the World War signalized the end of this period, the beginning of the precipitate fall of the curve of capitalism. The bourgeoisie has now become a decaying and reactionary class, interested not in production but in consumption, with the typical psychology of the *rentier*,[7] and following a policy imposed on it by finance capitalism. In this period there must occur a series of imperialist convulsions, of which the war is the first but not necessarily the last, and in it the situation has again become definitely revolutionary from the point of view of a proletarian party. In 1914 a progressive bourgeoisie is ridiculous; there can be no question of an alliance between the proletariat and any group of national imperialist capitalists; the purpose of the working class must be the overthrow—almost certainly by violence[8]—of international finance capitalism.

By this very able supplementation and extension of Marx's analysis of capitalism, Lenin could interpret the existing national and international situation by means of the categories provided in the Marxian system. The opposing interests of imperialist national groupings could be presented as the outgrowth of "contradictions" between the productive forces of industry and the restraints imposed on it by an outworn ideology, and the imminence of a proletarian revolution could be deduced as Marx had already deduced it in the 1840's. According to Lenin, the contradiction in 1914 lies substantially between the international nature of industry and the restraints imposed by national political divisions. The ruling class which controls production, and labor as well, is divided into national groups with competing interests that have no counterpart in the system of production itself. National states, under the control of these artifical groupings, have become a clog upon the normal development of production. The new ideology of national solidarity and self-sufficiency, with the corresponding policies of tariff-exclusion and national monopoly, stands square across the path of expansion appropriate to the economic system, and this expansion appears in the perverted form of imperialist annexation. Inevitably, according to the theory, the underlying forces of production must assert their mastery. The war will centralize political power, destroy small states, and expand monopoly. But it will also bring the class-struggle, as one of the permanent forces of capitalist society, back to its normal proportions, temporarily distorted by imperialism.

The war severs the last chain that binds the workers to the masters, their slavish submission to the imperialist state. The last limitation of the proletariat's philosophy is being overcome: its clinging to the narrowness of the national state, its patriotism. The interests of the moment, the temporary advantage accruing to it from the imperialist robberies and from its connections with the imperialist state,

[7] Cf. Bukharin's analysis of Böhm-Bawerk's theory of value as representing the ideology of a consuming class, *The Economic Theory of the Leisure Class*, New York, 1927. The book was written in 1914 before the War and first published in 1919.

[8] Kautsky was arguing that the peaceful development of a world-economy within the capitalist system was possible.

become of secondary importance compared with the lasting and general interests of the class as a whole, with the idea of a social revolution of the international proletariat which overthrows the dictatorship of finance capital with an armed hand, destroys its state apparatus and builds up a new power, a power of the workers against the bourgeoisie.[9]

The plan of Lenin's revision, it should be noted, was that already followed by Engels in 1895 when he acknowledged, in editing Marx's pamphlet on the French Revolution of 1848, that capitalism "still had great capacity for expansion" beyond what he and Marx supposed at the earlier date. But the theory also has a remarkable capacity for expansion. What is foretold by means of it is always the end, and the revision consists in putting in new intermediate stages between the present and the end. This is hardly scientific prediction, as dialectical materialists like to believe. A predetermined end that arrives by an unknown path and after an interval of time that cannot be specified belongs rather to the realm of vitalist evolution than to that of scientific prediction. There are, of course, probabilities that make a proletarian revolution more or less likely and that give it more or less chance of success if it occurs. Such probabilities depend in no way upon dialectic, and conversely the supposed necessity of the proletarian revolution seems to have nothing to do with probability. It is envisaged as a tendency, or drive, or force directed toward a result, and capable of persisting against setbacks and counter currents. This is the sort of quality that vitalists have always attributed to the vital force and that Hegel attributed to the Idea, but there is little about it that is empirical or scientific.

BOURGEOIS AND PROLETARIAN REVOLUTION

Lenin's theory of capitalist imperialism supplied additional justification for the revolutionary tactics which he had always advocated. In 1917 the March Revolution, and his return to Russia in April, turned his attention toward the question of revolution in Russia. It led at once to an even more daring departure from what had been thought to be the implications of Marxism. The revolution which had created the Kerensky government was, by Marxian standards, a bourgeois revolution; it took power from the old nobility and gave it to the middle class. It was a settled principle of Marxism that any revolution, bourgeois or proletarian, occurs not through a sporadic application of force but must be prepared by the proper political and economic development. It followed that the bourgeois revolution must be "completed" before the proletarian revolution could properly be begun. It was this settled interpretation of Marxism that, to the astonishment of his followers and finally of Marxists everywhere, Lenin proceded to set aside as antiquated. He at once perceived that

---

[9] Bukharin, *Imperialism and World Economy*, Eng. trans., p. 167.

the essence of the situation in Russia was what he called "dual power," the existence side by side of the bourgeois Provisional Government and the soviets.[10] With the insight of a tactical genius he saw in this situation the possibility of an immediate revolution by the combined workers and peasants, if only these two forces could be held together. The soviets he chose to interpret as the embryo of a revolutionary dictatorship following a type set by the Paris Commune of 1871, thus spreading over them the aegis of Marxian theory, though Marxists had been, and still were, a small minority among their members.

The conception that a time of preparation must elapse between the bourgeois and the proletarian revolutions Lenin boldly relegated to "the archive of 'Bolshevik' pre-revolutionary antiques," and in the name of "living Marxism."

It is necessary to acquire that incontestable truth that a Marxist must take cognizance of living life, of the true facts of reality, that he must not continue clinging to the theory of yesterday, which, like every theory, at best only outlines the main and the general, only approximately embracing the complexity of life. . . . Whoever questions the "completeness" of the bourgeois revolution from the old viewpoint, sacrifices living Marxism to a dead letter. According to the old conception, the rule of the proletariat and peasantry, their dictatorship, can and must follow the rule of the bourgeoisie. In real life, however, things have already turned out otherwise; an extremely original, new, unprecedented interlocking of one and the other has taken place.[11]

That Lenin grasped "living life" was perhaps proved by the success of the new revolution a few months later, but it was also true that he had made a great departure from what Marx's philosophy had always been thought to mean. Nothing in the whole system was better settled than the proposition that a revolutionary ideology can be created only by the training of the proletariat in capitalist industry. The theory that politics depends upon the relations of production implies this. Marx had said that the final purpose of *Capital* was to show that no nation could "overleap the natural phases of evolution." Engels in the *Anti-Dühring* had used three chapters to show that force can do no more than supplement a revolutionary situation prepared by economic development. In 1915 Lenin had believed that a socialist revolution in Russia was impossible, though he hoped for a democratic republic there and for socialist revolutions in more advanced countries.[12] Even in 1917, before coming to Russia, he thought of a Russian revolution as a temporary expedient which might indeed fail, but which might succeed until the situation could be saved by its becoming "a prologue to the world socialist revolution." [13] His change of position, as he frankly

[10] *On Dual Power* and *Letters on Tactics, Collected Works,* Vol. XX, Bk. I, pp. 115 ff. Lenin had been in Petrograd less than a week.

[11] *Ibid.,* p. 121.

[12] *Collected Works,* Vol. XVIII, pp. 81 f.; 198.

[13] *Ibid.,* Vol. XX, Book I, pp. 85 f.

admitted, was an inspiration of the moment. On the other hand, it was merely an extension of the changes in Marxian theory that he had made years before. He had always considered socialist ideology as the creation of the intelligentsia rather than as a spontaneous product of industrial relations, and he had always contemplated a situation in which this ideology was actually possessed by a very small proportion of workers.

Lenin's rather abrupt reversal of an important part of traditional Marxism was helped also by his theory of capitalist imperialism. For from this point of view it was possible to argue that the chances of a revolution in any single country depended upon the international situation as well as upon its internal condition. The strain of war might well break capitalism "at its weakest point," and this need not be in those countries where capitalism itself is most highly developed. Probably, however, what carried conviction among Lenin's Russian followers in 1917 was their belief that proletarian revolution was imminent throughout Europe and that the revolution in Russia was merely a "prologue." In 1924 Trotsky and his followers still held that a proletarian revolution could not permanently succeed or be carried through completely in a single country, though by that time the continued existence of the revolutionary government had made this view a "deviation." In 1925 Stalin argued that the limitation on communism in one country was merely the risk of interference from the outside. In effect this leaves little or nothing of the older idea that societies pass through a normal series of industrial stages and that their political history and ideology follow their economic development. Thus Stalin has argued that a proletarian revolution differs from a bourgeois revolution partly by the fact that the former brings a socialist economy into existence, while a capitalist economy precedes the latter, and Bukharin has argued that in periods of revolution the course of development goes from ideology to technology, thus reversing the normal order.[14] The older theory remains, if at all, only as applied to the whole international development of capitalism and the revolutionary ideology.

The relation of socialism to political democracy forms a special phase of this general question about the preparation of the proletarian revolution, and here, too, there was a substantial difference between Lenin and Marx, or at least what other Marxists supposed that Marx meant. When Lenin returned to Russia he was the leader of a minority even among the socialists, who were themselves a minority in the bourgeois government. In Russia at large the industrial proletariat was of course a tiny minority in the whole population, and Lenin never doubted that success would fall to the party that could gain the support, or at least the acquiescence, of the peasants. He made no secret of his opposition to the Provisional Government, but until July he did not favor armed resistance to it. He repeatedly

[14] Stalin, *Leninism*, Eng. trans. by E. and C. Paul (London, 1928), p. 20; Bukharin, *Historical Materialism* (New York, 1925), p. 262.

denied that his group was for seizure of power by a minority or for economic reforms not ripe "in the consciousness of an overwhelming majority."
But such phrases have to be taken in the light of his theory of the party,
held since 1903, which contained no implication of majority-rule as a political institution. In August he came out flatly with the assertion that in
politics majority-rule is a "constitutional illusion." The permanent force
is the domination of a class; majority-rule is impossible unless the interests
of the ruling class happen to coincide with the interests of the majority,
and history is full of cases where the more organized, more class-conscious,
better armed minority has forced its will upon a majority.

At the decisive moment and in the decisive place you *must prove the stronger
one*, you must *be victorious*.[15]

Even in the evolution that leads up to decisive moments, majority-rule had
for Lenin no virtue as a political right. It was rather a scheme of skillful
compromise by which the leading minority keeps in touch with its followers.

The task of a truly revolutionary party is not to declare the impossible
renunciation of all compromises, but to be able *through all compromises,* as far
as they are unavoidable, to remain true to its principles, to its class, to its revolutionary task.[16]

This was in fact Lenin's most astonishing and most valuable quality as
a leader, and he referred to his compromises on occasion as "democracy,"
but obviously they had no relation to democracy as an institution.[17] The
truth is that democracy had no significant place in Lenin's conception of
political evolution. On the other hand, most Marxists would have agreed
that Kautsky accurately represented Marx's opinion when he said, in
criticism of the Russian Revolution, that "the education of the masses, as
well as of their leaders, in democracy is a necessary condition of socialism. . . ."

Lenin's Marxism presents the anomaly of being at once the most
dogmatic assertion of orthodox adherence to the principles of the master
and at the same time the freest rendering of it on points where circumstances required its modification. For him Marxism was at once the creed
of a party, having the function of all creeds that give unity to a militant
organization, and also a guide to action, to be shaped at need to new occasions. Yet the creed itself stood in the way of frankly empirical revision
or the abandonment of parts in the light of new facts; if it were revised it

---

[15] *Collected Works,* Vol. XXI, Bk. I, p. 68. Lenin's italics.

[16] *Collected Works, ibid.,* p. 152.

[17] A striking example was Lenin's adoption in November, 1917, of a land-policy which
he took whole from his opponents and which he fully expected to fail. For the time
being he was powerless to do anything else so he made a virtue of "democracy." The
later coercion of the peasants was perfectly logical from his point of view. See W. H.
Chamberlin, *The Russian Revolution,* Vol. 1, p. 326.

must develop its own changes dialectically. The revisions which Lenin made were sometimes perilously close to abandonment. Retaining the strictest letter of economic determinism, according to which politics and every form of ideology must be explained ultimately by the economic system, he magnified both the rôle of the party and of the middle-class intellectual in the party, while he minimized the spontaneous creation of a socialist ideology in the proletariat by the relations of production. He abandoned the belief that capitalist development in any single country, with its attendant political manifestations, runs through a normal or standard series of stages, so that, as Marx had said, "A country in which industrial development is more advanced than in others, simply presents those others with a picture of their own future." Much of the plausibility of the contention that this was merely an extension of Marxism depended on the expectation that the proletarian revolution was about to become general, and this proved to be a mistake. In the future the theory can again be made to square with any state of the facts by adding more stages to the development of capitalism. What Lenin's career illustrated most obviously was not precision of theory but the enormous power in a crisis of a leader with character and insight, aided by even a small group of self-confident and disciplined men who are willing relentlessly to follow their convictions. This surely is a result which no logic can deduce from dialectical materialism, unless indeed it be the logic of faith.

GERMAN MARXISM AND RUSSIAN COMMUNISM

JOHN PLAMENATZ*

There is a side of Lenin's teaching which, though it adds nothing important to Marxism and no longer inspires the behavior of the Communist Party, is yet well worth studying for the insight it gives us into the character of the greatest revolutionary of our age. Lenin has been called a realist, and indeed was one, and yet was also a Utopian simpler and more credulous than most. If we look at *The State and the Revolution,* perhaps the most often read of all his pamphlets, we can see how narrow the understanding and how little the foresight of the man who, more than any other, has changed our modern world.

The State and the Revolution consists of quotations from Marx and Engels so put together and explained as to justify the revolutionary Marx-

* Fellow of Nuffield College, Oxford. Author of *The Revolutionary Movement in France, 1815-71.* The selection is from pp. 240-247 of the book by the same title, published by Longmans, Green & Co., Inc., 1954. By permission of the publisher.

ism of the Bolsheviks and confound all their critics. The too ample commentary on the quotations is a rude[1] defence of the "pure doctrine" against the Majority socialists in Germany and the Mensheviks in Russia. Lenin's pamphlet seeks to prove, against the German Social-Democrats, that Marx and Engels never ceased to be revolutionary socialists, but does not offer us a coherent theory of the state. On the contrary, it draws attention to what might otherwise have escaped notice—to the absence of any such theory in the writings of Marx and Engels; it also draws attention to other faults invisible to Lenin, to the reckless assertions and bad logic of the two men who seemed to him the most profound of thinkers.

We can find in Lenin's pamphlet arguments—as if by anticipation—against much that happened in Russia after 1920 and that Trotsky later condemned. The pamphlet is, of course, still printed in Russia and approved by the authorities, who do not think it dangerous to themselves. It is an authorized text subject to official interpretation, and therefore not to be taken literally. It has proved easy enough to teach the youth of Russia to admire it without drawing from it any inconvenient practical consequences. They are made familiar with it, and the familiarity breeds a kind of careless reverence not far removed from contempt.[2] But the fact remains that the pamphlet can be taken literally, and that those who so take it, if they happen to be Marxists, will soon find themselves looking at the Russia of Stalin through the eyes of Trotsky.

Marx produced two doctrines of the state, and would neither explain how they are connected nor abandon one of them. He said that the state is an instrument of class oppression, and also that it is often a parasitic growth on society, making class oppression possible even when the government is not the agent of any class. Lenin accepted both these doctrines without noticing that they are incompatible or attempting to adjust them to one another. He also accepted the theory of Engels that the state emerges as soon as there arise in society classes with irreconcilable interests, its function being to keep the peace between them. Lenin, like Engels, never thought it necessary to explain how it is that the peace cannot be kept except by sacrificing the interests of all classes but one to that one class. Nor did he explain how the keeping of peace within society differs from

[1] Marx was a most rude and scornful controversialist, and his disciples have mostly imitated his manners, whose freedom from "bourgeois hypocrisy" they have greatly admired. It seems not to have occurred to them that discourtesy, by causing men from motives of vanity to defend the indefensible and to waste time on irrelevancies, is a serious obstacle in the search for truth. Or if it has occurred to them, they have disregarded it in practice.

[2] We, too, are brought up in the same way. When we are young we are taught to admire the saying: "Sell all that thou hast and give to the poor." When we first hear it, it can do us no harm, for we are children with nothing to sell and nothing to give. And when we grow up, we quickly discover that the advice is impracticable. This process of inoculation against the impossible virtues, which we ought to admire but not to practise, is a usual part of nearly all education. Whether it is necessary, the psychologist must decide.

the conciliation of interests; he merely said, repeating Engels, that the function of the state is to keep the peace between "irreconcilable" classes, and to keep it in the interest of only one class among them. Lenin had fewer doubts than either of his masters and was never tempted to question their assumptions; he therefore never pondered their curious doctrine that, though the social classes have *irreconcilable* (and not merely different) interests, it is somehow possible to keep the peace between them. He quietly accepted in the way of doctrine whatever they offered him, including this far from self-evident assumption that to maintain social peace and order is not to conciliate interests. For the difference between these two functions he had never a thought to spare.[3]

In *The State and the Revolution,* Lenin repeats, again following Engels, that the existence of armies and police forces is proof enough that class interests cannot be reconciled. Special instruments must, he thinks, be created to maintain the supremacy of the ruling class. The alternative hypothesis, which is perhaps more plausible, that these instruments were first created in the common interest and then enabled those who controlled them to become a ruling class, never occurs to him, though he also repeats the argument of Engels that the state arises out of the need to hold class antagonisms in check, a need presumably felt by all the classes and whose satisfaction is therefore a common interest.

On the basis of this theory of the state—or, rather, of this collection of

---

[3] Interests are not solid things of determinate shapes, which, like the parts of a jig-saw puzzle, either can or cannot be fitted into each other. How is one man's interest reconciled with another's? There are two words of uncertain meaning in this question—"interest" and reconciled." A man's interests can surely be no more than the objects of his more persistent desires, the things for whose sake he works and makes sacrifices; and the interests of a class merely the objects of the most persistent desires common to persons having more or less the same status in society. The interests, whether of individuals or classes, very frequently conflict; if one man gets all he wants another must often get less, and so it must also be with classes. How are interests "reconciled"? They are "reconciled," presumably, whenever the men or classes that pursue them observe the rules whose general observance is social peace. How then, if the rules are observed, can interests be irreconcilable? We can perhaps say, as many philosophers have done, that the more rules are observed because they are felt to be just, the greater the harmony between men's interests; and that, conversely, the more they are observed from fear of punishment, the less that harmony. This, at least, is a distinction which makes sense; but, in that case, what becomes of the "irreconcilable" interests of different classes in a society where, say, bourgeois morality prevails? Let us suppose for a moment that some travellers' tales are true, and that American workers really do not mind their employers being ten or a hundred or even a thousand times richer than themselves, that they would rather keep their one chance in ten thousand of becoming rich than have governments, however democratically elected, take over the factories they work in; let us also suppose that they require no more of governments than that they should tax the rich to give everyone modest provision against ill-health, unemployment, and old age. Are their interests and those of their employers "irreconcilable" still? What could be meant by calling them so? When classes are at peace and little force is required to keep that peace, surely the man who calls their interests "irreconcilable" merely betrays his desire that there should be disputes where there are none, or that what disputes there are should be more bitter.

ideas about the state—Lenin seeks to establish as orthodox Marxism two propositions neglected or denied by the German Majority Socialists: 1. that the bourgeois state and all its instruments must be destroyed by the proletariat, and 2. that it is the "dictatorship of the proletariat" (that is, the proletarian and not the bourgeois state) which is destined to "wither away." There are interesting corollaries of these propositions, but they are the two major theses of the pamphlet. . . .

The bourgeois state must be destroyed because it cannot be used for proletarian purposes. Lenin's assumption is that every ruling class dominates society in its own peculiar way, and therefore requires its own political institutions, its peculiar instruments of government. The bourgeois state has a natural tendency to grow stronger and more elaborate, to become an always fatter parasite feeding on the body of society. It maintains an army, a police force and a bureaucratic machine, whose interests cannot be those of society as a whole. The bourgeois find it easy to tolerate this parasite, because, while it exists, it maintains the conditions of their economic and social supremacy.

The dictatorship of the proletariat, the workers' state or "half-state" (as Lenin sometimes called it), is not a growing parasite whose function is to maintain the social conditions of class exploitation; it is the instrument of the workers and peasants, of the great majority, who use it to destroy the last traces of class exploitation.

It is therefore the dictatorship of the proletariat and not the bourgeois state that will wither away. The workers' state is strongest at the moment of its birth, and must from that moment weaken until it dies. Lenin called it a "half-state" because its function is not to perpetuate the conditions of its own life but to destroy them. It is repressive and therefore a state; but it is also the instrument of the great majority. In the words of Lenin: "Since the majority of the people themselves suppress their oppressors, a 'special force' for suppression is no longer necessary! In this sense the state begins to wither away." In the bourgeois state, the minority exploit the majority, and the condition of this exploitation is the growing strength of certain instruments of government, of organizations that perpetuate themselves because their members have corporate interests of their own. In the proletarian state the majority suppress the minority, and, being the majority, have no need to use for instruments organizations that are self-perpetuating and parasitic. On the contrary, the organizations they use are democratically controlled, and they gradually disappear as the work of suppression is completed.

Lenin, when he wrote *The State and the Revolution,* had never had even a day's administrative experience. He had been for years a member of the Russian Social-Democratic Party, an undisciplined and quarrelsome body, and had later created his own Bolshevik organization; but he had never taken even a subordinate part in government. That is why he could write,[4] only a few months before the Bolshevik revolution, that "the great majority of the functions of the old state power have been so simplified and can be reduced to such simple operations of registration, filing and checking, that they can be easily performed by every literate person." Lenin believed that capitalism makes the tasks of government easier. Why, then, has the bourgeois state become so massive? Lenin's answer is that successive revolutions have made it so; that the parasite has fed on its host and is swollen with its blood. This was the simple answer that satisfied Lenin in 1917, when he still refused to believe that the spread of industry makes society so complex that only a large, varied and highly trained administration can control it. "We ourselves," he said, "the workers, shall organize large-scale production on the basis of what capitalism has already created . . . we shall reduce the role of state officials to a simple carrying out of our instructions as responsible, revocable, and modestly paid 'managers.' . . . Overthrow the capitalists . . . smash the bureaucratic machine of the modern state—and you will have a mechanism of the highest technical equipment, free from the parasite, capable of being operated by the workers themselves, who will hire their own technicians, managers and bookkeepers, and pay them all—as, indeed, all state officials in general— ordinary workmen's wages." Only a Bolshevik could have been so innocent in the summer of 1917.

The German Social-Democrats, of course, knew better. They had outgrown Marxism, though not the vanity that made them cling to their reputations as leading Marxists. They had hitherto not needed to reject the more irresponsible utterances of Marx and Engels; it had been enough to take little notice of them. But with the Bolsheviks in the ascendant, and their own extremists restive, they had learnt to dislike what they had previously ignored. Above all, they had come to dislike the phrase "the dictatorship of the proletariat," and now wanted to minimize its importance. Experience had taught them that the bourgeois state is not merely an instrument of class oppression, that it is not a mere parasite feeding on the social body, that the departments of the state established by the old society would be necessary to the new one; they knew, in short, what we all know when we have no special motive for refusing to admit the obvious; they knew that the government of modern industrial society is altogether too difficult to be entrusted to persons not specially trained for it. They knew that direct rule by the workers is impossible, and that the most to be hoped for is as much responsibility to them as the devices of democracy will allow. The administrative machine must not be smashed; it must be preserved and adapted to new uses. For without it socialism is impossible—socialism

---

[4] The explanation falls short of the truth. In matters so simple common sense can enlighten us even when we have no experience. Such blindness as Lenin's is the effect not of inexperience but of devotion to false doctrines.

which requires so great an intervention of public authority in the daily business of our lives. . . .

It is odd that Marx's description of the Commune, his disingenuous account of a government inspired by the doctrines of his great rival Proudhon, should have been the stone that broke in two the great international socialist movement most of whose leaders called themselves Marxists. What is less odd—for nothing is more usual than that men's actions should give the lie to their doctrines—is that, within a year or two of writing *The State and the Revolution,* Lenin should have proved that Kautsky was right after all. Lenin soon found himself obliged to establish a highly centralized administrative machine in Russia, finding that he could not govern without it. The constitution of the new Bolshevik state was federal, but that federalism was a mere pretence; all real power belonged to the closely disciplined Communist Party. Most of the old departments of state were brought to life again, albeit under new names; and the political police were soon more active than they had been under the Tsars.

Chapter 6

ENDS AND MEANS

━━

The ultimate end envisaged by Marx of a stateless, classless society, "when, along with the all-round development of individuals, the productive forces too have grown, and all the springs of social wealth are flowing more freely," from which there will have vanished all need for organized force, and in which men will be content to contribute to society in accordance with their abilities and be rewarded according to need—however Utopian and visionary, and, in the minds of some, undesirable—is of undoubted nobility. It is an end which revolutionary anarchists and evolutionary socialists, as well as Communists, accept.

Even the more immediate theoretical end of the Communist philosophy, that is, socialism—ownership in common of the basic means of production and distribution and a planned economy—finds support among many reformists, Christian socialists, and others.

A major distinguishing characteristic of the Communist Party lies in the means it was prepared to and did in fact use and justify to seize and hold power. In State and Revolution, *Lenin, it will be recalled, insisted upon "the necessity of fostering among the masses" the belief that "the replacement of the bourgeois by the proletarian state is impossible without a violent revolution." (In this, he explicitly rejected Marx's "exceptionalism." Marx had said in 1872—a position later echoed by Engels—that "we do not deny that there are certain countries, such as the United States and England . . . in which the workers may hope to secure their ends by peaceful means.")*

Apart from Lenin's belief that capitalist power made violent proletarian revolution necessary, he insisted, in general, "that morality is wholly subordinated to the interests of the class struggle of the proletariat"—a position that was more fully developed and theoretically justified by Trotsky in Their Morals and Ours. *The far-reaching implications and consequences of the Leninist view of the relation of ends and means are discussed by Morris Raphael Cohen and Harold J. Laski.*

172

Parenthetically, reference must be made to the contemporary views of the Soviet leadership on the necessity for violent revolution to overturn capitalism and achieve socialism—although obviously these had no bearing on the tactics pursued in the Bolshevik revolution or on the theoretical position for years thereafter. The New Program of the Communist Party, adopted October 31, 1961, reads in part as follows:

The working class and its vanguard—the Marxist Leninist parties—seek to accomplish the socialist revolution *by peaceful means*. . . . In the conditions prevailing at present, in some capitalist countries the working class, headed by its forward detachment, has an opportunity to unite the bulk of the nation, win state power without a civil war and achieve the transfer of the basic means of production to the people upon the basis of a working-class and popular front and other possible forms of agreement and political cooperation between different parties and democratic organizations. The working class, supported by the majority of the people and firmly repelling opportunist elements incapable of renouncing the policy of compromise with the capitalists and landlords, can defeat the reactionary, anti-popular forces, win a solid majority in parliament, transform it from a tool serving the class interests of the bourgeoisie into an instrument serving the working people, launch a broad mass struggle outside parliament, smash the resistance of the reactionary forces and provide the necessary conditions for a peaceful socialist revolution. . . .

Where the exploiting classes resort to violence against the people, the possibility of a *non-peaceful transition to socialism* should be borne in mind. Leninism maintains, and historical experience confirms, that the ruling classes do not yield power of their own free will. Hence, the degree of bitterness of the class struggle and the forms it takes will depend not so much on the proletariat as on the strength of the reactionary groups' resistance to the will of the overwhelming majority of the people, and on the use of force by these groups at a particular stage of the struggle for socialism. In each particular country the actual applicability of one method of transition to socialism or the other depends on concrete historical conditions.

It may well be that as the forces of socialism grow, the working-class movement gains strength and the positions of capitalism are weakened, there will arise in certain countries a situation in which it will be preferable for the bourgeoisie, as Marx and Lenin foresaw, to agree to the basic means of production being purchased from it and for the proletariat to "pay off" the bourgeoisie.

The success of the struggle which the working class wages for the victory of the revolution will depend on how well the working class and its party master the use of *all forms* of struggle—peaceful and non-peaceful, parliamentary and extra-parliamentary—and how well they are prepared for any swift and sudden replacement of one form of struggle by another form of struggle. . . . But whatever the form in which the transition from capitalism to socialism is effected, that transition can come about only through revolution.

Whether the present position of the Central Committee of the Communist Party of the Soviet Union represents a decisive break with Lenin on the necessity for violent overthrow of capitalism has been controverted. There are those who believe that the Communists are convinced of the superiority of socialism and of its ultimate appeal, that they appreciate the dangers of war, and therefore are prepared to eschew revolutionary methods.

On the other hand, typical of an opposing view is that of Stefan T. Possony who wrote:

The Communists did not forswear violence at all, provided you go to the trouble of reading the fine print. . . . The need for the application of violence against bourgeois nations with strong military and police force was reaffirmed. On the assumption that the Communists will not succeed in talking the United States into dismantling its security forces, this country will remain a strong power. Hence it will have to be subjected to violence—or else the world revolution will have to be called off. The Communists continue to proclaim that the revolution will occur. Hence if logic means anything, nonviolent methods of revolution, while perhaps feasible in some countries without military and police forces, are not applicable to the United States.

COMMUNIST ETHICS

V. I. LENIN*

First of all, I shall deal here with the question of Communist ethics.

You must train yourselves to be Communists. The task of the Young Communist League is to organise its practical activity in such a manner that in studying, in organising and consolidating itself, and in fighting on, it will be training itself and all those who regard it as their leader. It will thus be training Communists. The whole work of training, educating, and instructing the present-day youth must be directed towards imbuing them with Communist ethics.

But is there such a thing as Communist ethics? Is there such a thing as Communist morality? Of course there is. It is frequently asserted that we have no ethics, and very frequently the bourgeoisie makes the charge that we Communists deny all morality. That is one of their methods of confusing the issue, of throwing dust into the eyes of the workers and peasants.

In what sense do we deny ethics, morals?

In the sense in which they are preached by the bourgeoisie, which deduces these morals from god's commandments. Of course, we say that we do not believe in god. We know perfectly well that the clergy, the landlords, and the bourgeoisie all claimed to speak in the name of god, in order to protect their own interests as exploiters. Or, instead of deducing their ethics from the commandments of morality, from the commandments of god, they deduced them from idealistic or semi-idealistic phrases which in substance were always very similar to divine commandments.

We deny all morality taken from superhuman or non-class conceptions.

* From a speech delivered at the Third All-Russian Congress of the Young Communist League of the Soviet Union on October 2, 1920.

We say that this is a deception, a swindle, a befogging of the minds of the workers and peasants in the interests of the landlords and capitalists.

We say that our morality is wholly subordinated to the interests of the class-struggle of the proletariat. We deduce our morality from the facts and needs of the class-struggle of the proletariat.

The old society was based on the oppression of all the workers and peasants by the landlords and capitalists. We had to destroy this society. We had to overthrow these landowners and capitalists. But to do this, organisation was necessary. God could not create such organisation.

Such organisation could only be created by the factories and workshops, only by the trained proletariat, awakened from its former slumber. Only when this class had come into existence did the mass movement commence which led to what we have to-day—to the victory of the proletarian revolution in one of the weakest countries in the world—a country which for three years has resisted the attacks of the bourgeoisie of the whole world. We see how the proletarian revolution is growing all over the whole world. And we can say now, on the basis of experience, that only the proletariat could have created that compact force which is carrying along with it the once disunited and disorganised peasantry—a force which has withstood all the attacks of all the exploiters. Only this class can help the toiling masses to unite their forces, to close their ranks, to establish and build up a definitely Communist society and finally to complete it.

That is why we say that a morality taken from outside of human society does not exist for us; it is a fraud. For us morality is subordinated to the interests of the proletarian class-struggle.

THEIR MORALS AND OURS

LEON TROTSKY*

This essay was Trotsky's reply to the charge that Stalin, Lenin, and Trotsky were equally amoral. It was published in 1938 in America. "Written as a polemic at a particular time," according to its editor, "Trotsky's pamphlet is unquestionably one of his enduring contributions to Marxism. It is the first systematic exposition of the Marxist conception of the relation between means and ends as a dialectical interrelation." It is probably true that although Trotsky was then in exile from the U.S.S.R.—his attack on Stalin and Stalinism apart—his justification of Bolshevik "amorality" would be found unexceptional by the Communist leaders.

* The selection is from *Their Morals and Ours* (Mexico: Pioneer Publishers Co.), *passim*. By permission of the publisher.

This pamphlet was written many years after the Revolution. But during the civil and international war that followed, Trotsky wrote The Defence of Terrorism *(completed May, 1920). There he gave expression to some of the ideas he was later to develop more fully and systematically, inter alia, "The revolution does require of the revolutionary class that it should attain its end by all methods at its disposal—if necessary, by an armed rising: if required, by terrorism," and "Terror can be very efficient against a reactionary class which does not want to leave the scene of operations."*

Bourgeois evolutionism halts impotently at the threshold of historical society because it does not wish to acknowledge the driving force in the evolution of social forms: *the class struggle.* Morality is one of the ideological functions in this struggle. The ruling class forces *its* ends upon society and habituates it into considering all those means which contradict its ends as immoral. That is the chief function of official morality. It pursues the idea of the "greatest possible happiness" not for the majority but for a small and ever diminishing minority. Such a regime could not have endured for even a week through force alone. It needs the cement of morality. The production of this cement constitutes the profession of the petty-bourgeois theoreticians and moralists. They radiate all the colors of the rainbow but in the final analysis remain apostles of slavery and submission.

"MORAL PRECEPTS OBLIGATORY UPON ALL"

Whoever does not care to return to Moses, Christ or Mohammed; whoever is not satisfied with eclectic *hodge-podges* must acknowledge that morality is a product of social development; that there is nothing immutable about it; that it serves social interests; that these interests are contradictory; that morality more than any other form of ideology has a class character.

But do not elementary moral precepts exist, worked out in the development of mankind as a whole and indispensable for the existence of every collective body? Undoubtedly such precepts exist but the extent of their action is extremely limited and unstable. Norms "obligatory upon all" become the less forceful the sharper the character assumed by the class struggle. The highest form of the class struggle is civil war which explodes into mid-air all moral ties between the hostile classes.

Under "normal" conditions a "normal" man observes the commandment: "Thou shalt not kill!" But if he kills under exceptional conditions for self-defense, the jury acquits him. If he falls victim to a murderer, the court will kill the murderer. The necessity of courts as well as that of self-defense, flows from antagonistic interests. In so far as the state is concerned, in peaceful times it limits itself to legalized killings of individuals so that in time of war it may transform the "obligatory" commandment, "Thou shalt not kill!" into its opposite. The most "humane" governments, which in peaceful times "detest" war, proclaim during war that the highest duty of their armies is the extermination of the greatest possible number of people. . . .

This vacuity in the norms obligatory upon all arises from the fact that in all decisive questions people feel their class membership considerably more profoundly and more directly than their membership in "society." The norms of "obligatory" morality are in reality filled with class, that is, antagonistic content. The moral norm becomes the more categoric the less it is "obligatory upon all." The solidarity of workers, especially of strikers or barricade fighters, is incomparably more "categoric" than human solidarity in general.

The bourgeoisie, which far surpasses the proletariat in the completeness and irreconcilability of its class consciousness, is vitally interested in imposing *its* moral philosophy upon the exploited masses. It is exactly for this purpose that the concrete norms of the bourgeois catechism are concealed under moral abstractions patronized by religion, philosophy, or that hybrid which is called "common sense." The appeal to abstract norms is not a disinterested philosophic mistake but a necessary element in the mechanics of class deception. The exposure of this deceit which retains the tradition of thousands of years is the first duty of a proletarian revolutionist. . . .

THE CRISIS IN DEMOCRATIC MORALITY

. . . At the extreme left wing of the "left" fraternity stands a small and politically completely insignificant grouping of German émigrés who publish the paper *Neuer Weg* (The New Road). Let us bend down lower and listen to these "revolutionary" indicters of Bolshevik amoralism. In a tone of ambiguous pseudo praise the *Neuer Weg* proclaims that the Bolsheviks are distinguished advantageously from other parties by their absence of hypocrisy—they openly declare what others quietly apply in fact, that is, the principle: "the end justifies the means." But according to the convictions of *Neuer Weg* such a "bourgeois" precept is incompatible with a "healthy socialist movement." "Lying and worse are not permissible means of struggle, as Lenin still considered." The word "still" evidently signifies that Lenin did not succeed in overcoming his delusions only because he failed to live until the discovery of *The New Road*.

In the formula, "lying and worse," "worse" evidently signifies—violence, murder, and so on, since under equal conditions violence is worse than lying; and murder—the most extreme form of violence. We thus come to the conclusion that lying, violence, murder are incompatible with a "healthy socialist movement." What, however, is our relation to revolution? Civil war is the most severe of all forms of war. It is unthinkable not only without violence against tertiary figures but, under contemporary technique, without killing old men, old women and children. Must one be reminded of Spain? The only possible answer of the "friends" of republican Spain sounds like this: Civil war is better than fascist slavery. But this completely correct answer merely signifies that the *end* (democracy or socialism) justifies, under certain conditions, such *means* as violence and murder. Not to speak about lies! Without lies war would be as unimaginable as a machine without oil. In order to safeguard even the session of the Cortes (February 1, 1938) from fascist bombs the Barcelona government several times deliberately deceived journalists and their own population. Could it have acted in any other way? Whoever accepts the end: victory over Franco, must accept the means: civil war with its wake of horrors and crimes.

But, after all, do not lying and violence "in themselves" warrant condemnation? Of course, even as does the class society which generates them. A society without social contradictions will naturally be a society without lies and violence. However there is no way of building a bridge to that society save by revolutionary, that is, violent means. The revolution itself is a product of class society and of necessity bears its traits. From the point of view of "eternal truths" revolution is of course "anti-moral." But this merely means that idealist morality is counter-revolutionary, that is, in the service of the exploiters.

"Civil war," will perhaps respond the philosopher caught unawares, "is however a sad exception. But in peaceful times a healthy socialist movement should manage without violence and lying." Such an answer however represents nothing less than a pathetic evasion. There is no impervious demarcation between "peaceful" class struggle and revolution. Every strike embodies in an unexpanded form all the elements of civil war. Each side strives to impress the opponent with an exaggerated picture of its resoluteness to struggle and its material resources. Through their press, agents, and spies the capitalists labor to frighten and demoralize the strikers. From their side, the workers' pickets, where persuasion does not avail, are compelled to resort to force. Thus "lying and worse" are an inseparable part of the class struggle even in its most elementary form. It remains to be added that the very conception of *truth* and *lie* was born of social contradictions. . . .

THE "AMORALISM" OF LENIN

The Russian "Social Revolutionaries" were always the most moral individuals: essentially they were composed of ethics alone. This did not prevent them, however, at the time of revolution from deceiving the Russian

peasants. In the Parisian organ of Kerensky, that very ethical socialist who
was the forerunner of Stalin in manufacturing spurious accusations against
the Bolsheviks, another old "Social Revolutionary" Zenzinov writes: "Lenin,
as is known, taught that for the sake of gaining the desired ends communists can, and sometimes must 'resort to all sorts of devices, manœuvres and
subterfuge' . . ." (New Russia, February 17, 1938, p. 3). From this they
draw the ritualistic conclusion: Stalinism is the natural offspring of Leninism.

Unfortunately, the ethical indicter is not even capable of quoting honestly. Lenin said: "It is necessary to be able . . . to resort to all sorts of
devices, manœuvres, and illegal methods, to evasion and subterfuge, in order to penetrate into the trade unions, to remain in them, and to carry on
communist work in them at all costs." The necessity for evasion and
manœuvres, according to Lenin's explanation, is called forth by the fact
that the reformist bureaucracy, betraying the workers to capital, baits revolutionists, persecutes them, and even resorts to turning the bourgeois police
upon them. "Manœuvres" and "subterfuge" are in this case only methods
of valid self-defense against the perfidious reformist bureaucracy. . . .

Norman Thomas speaks about "that strange communist amorality in
which nothing matters but the party and its power" (Socialist Call, March
12, 1938, p. 5). . . . In the eyes of Thomas and his kind the party is only
a secondary instrument for electoral combinations and other similar uses,
not more. His personal life, interests, ties, moral criteria exist outside the
party. With hostile astonishment he looks down upon the Bolshevik to
whom the party is a weapon for the revolutionary reconstruction of society,
including also its morality. To a revolutionary Marxist there can be no
contradiction between personal morality and the interests of the party, since
the party embodies in his consciousness the very highest tasks and aims of
mankind. It is naive to imagine that Thomas has a higher understanding
of morality than the Marxists. He merely has a basic conception of the
party. . . .

The clerks of the ruling classes call the organizers of this party "amoral-
ists." In the eyes of conscious workers this accusation carries a complimen-
tary character. It signifies: Lenin refused to recognize moral norms established by slave-owners for their slaves and never observed by the slave-
owners themselves; he called upon the proletariat to extend the class
struggle into the moral sphere too. Whoever fawns before precepts established by the enemy will never vanquish that enemy!

The "amoralism" of Lenin, that is, his rejection of supra-class morals,
did not hinder him from remaining faithful to one and the same ideal
throughout his whole life; from devoting his whole being to the cause of
the oppressed; from displaying the highest conscientiousness in the sphere
of ideas and the highest fearlessness in the sphere of action; from maintain-

ing an attitude untainted by the least superiority to an "ordinary" worker, to a defenseless woman, to a child. Does it not seem that "amoralism" in the given case is only a pseudonym for higher human morality? . . .

DIALECTICAL INTERDEPENDENCE OF END AND MEANS

A means can be justified only by its end. But the end in its turn needs to be justified. From the Marxist point of view, which expresses the historical interests of the proletariat, the end is justified if it leads to increasing the power of man over nature and to the abolition of the power of man over man.

"We are to understand then that in achieving this end anything is permissible?" sarcastically demands the Philistine, demonstrating that he understood nothing. That is permissible, we answer, which *really* leads to the liberation of mankind. Since this end can be achieved only through revolution, the liberating morality of the proletariat of necessity is endowed with a revolutionary character. It irreconcilably counteracts not only religious dogma but all kinds of idealistic fetishes, these philosophic gendarmes of the ruling class. It deduces a rule for conduct from the laws of the development of society, thus primarily from the class struggle, this law of all laws.

"Just the same," the moralist continues to insist, "does it mean that in the class struggle against capitalists all means are permissible: lying, frame-up, betrayal, murder, and so on?" Permissible and obligatory are those and only those means, we answer, which unite the revolutionary proletariat, fill their hearts with irreconcilable hostility to oppression, teach them contempt for official morality and its democratic echoers, imbue them with consciousness of their own historic mission, raise their courage and spirit of self-sacrifice in the struggle. Precisely from this it flows that *not* all means are permissible. When we say that the end justifies the means, then for us the conclusion follows that the great revolutionary end spurns those base means and ways which set one part of the working class against other parts, or attempt to make the masses happy without their participation; or lower the faith of the masses in themselves and their organization, replacing it by worship for the "leaders." Primarily and irreconcilably, revolutionary morality rejects servility in relation to the bourgeoisie and haughtiness in relation to the toilers, that is, those characteristics in which petty-bourgeois pedants and moralists are thoroughly steeped.

These criteria do not, of course, give a ready answer to the question as to what is permissible and what is not permissible in each separate case. There can be no such automatic answers. Problems of revolutionary morality are fused with the problems of revolutionary strategy and tactics. The living experience of the movement under the clarification of theory provides the correct answer to these problems. . . .

Two classes decide the fate of modern society: the imperialist bourgeoisie and the proletariat. The last resource of the bourgeoisie is fascism, which replaces social and historical criteria with biological and zoological standards so as thus to free itself from any and all restrictions in the struggle for capitalist property. Civilization can be saved only by the socialist revolution. To accomplish the overturn, the proletariat needs all its strength, all its resolution, all its audacity, passion and ruthlessness. Above all it must be completely free from the fictions of religion, "democracy" and transcendental morality—the spiritual chains forged by the enemy to tame and enslave it. Only that which prepares the complete and final overthrow of imperialist bestiality is moral, and nothing else. The welfare of the revolution—that is the supreme law! . . .

WHY I AM NOT A COMMUNIST

MORRIS RAPHAEL COHEN*

What distinguishes present-day Communists is not . . . their professed ultimate goal or their analysis of our economic ills, but their political remedy or program—to wit, the seizure of power by armed rebellion and the setting up of a dictatorship by the leaders of the Communist Party. To be sure, this dictatorship is to be in the name of the *proletariat*, just as the fascist dictatorship was in the name of *the whole nation*. But such verbal tricks cannot hide the brute facts of tyrannical suppression necessarily involved in all dictatorship. For the wielders of dictatorial power are few, they are seldom if ever themselves toilers, and they can maintain their power only by ruthlessly suppressing all expression of popular dissatisfaction with their rule. And where there is no freedom of discussion, there is no freedom of thought.

This program of civil war, dictatorship, and the illiberal or fanatically intolerant spirit which war psychology always engenders may bring more miseries than those that the Communists seek to remove; and the arguments to prove that such war is desirable or inevitable seem to me patently inadequate.

Communists ignore the historic truth that civil wars are much more destructive of all that men hold dearest than are wars between nations; and all the arguments that they use against the latter, including the "war to end war," are much more cogent against civil wars. Wars between nations are

* Late Professor of Philosophy, The City College of New York. President of the American Philosophical Association, 1929. Author of *Reason and Nature; Law and the Social Order; Faith of a Liberal;* and other works. The selection is from Morris Raphael Cohen, "Why I Am Not a Communist," *Modern Monthly* (April, 1934), Vol. 8, No. 3. Reprinted with permission of the administrators of the estate of Morris Raphael Cohen.

necessarily restricted in scope and do not prevent—to a limited extent they even stimulate—co-operation within a community. But civil wars necessarily dislocate all existing social organs and leave us with little social capital or machinery to rebuild a better society. The hatreds which fratricidal wars develop are more persistent and destructive than those developed by wars that terminate in treaties or agreements.

Having lived under the tyranny of the Czar, I cannot and do not condemn all revolutions. But the success and benefits of any revolution depend on the extent to which—like the American Revolution of 1776, the French Revolution of 1789, and the anti-Czarist Revolution of March 1917—it approximates national unanimity in the co-operation of diverse classes. When armed uprisings have been undertaken by single oppressed classes, as in the revolt of the gladiators in Rome, the various peasant revolts in England, Germany, and Russia, the French Commune of 1871, or the Moscow uprising of 1905, they have left a deplorably monotonous record of bloody massacres and oppressive reaction. The idea that armed rebellion is the only or the always effective cure for social ills seems to me no better than the old superstition of medieval medicine that blood-letting is the only and the sovereign remedy for all bodily ills.

Communists may feel that the benefits of the Revolution of 1917 outweigh all the terrific hardships which the Russian people have suffered since then. But reasonable people in America will do well to demand better evidence than has yet been offered that they can improve their lot by blindly imitating Russia. Russian breadlines, and famine without breadlines, are certainly not *prima facie* improvements over American conditions. [Editor's note: The article was written in 1934.] At best a revolution is a regrettable means to bring about greater human welfare. It always unleashes the forces that thrive in disorder, the brutal executions, imprisonments, and, what is even worse, the sordid spying that undermines all feeling of personal security. These forces, once let loose, are difficult to control and they tend to perpetuate themselves. If, therefore, human well-being, rather than mere destruction, is our aim, we must be as critically-minded in considering the consequences of armed revolution as in considering the evils of the existing regime.

One of the reasons that lead Communists to ignore the terrific destruction which armed rebellion must bring about is the conviction that "the revolution" is inevitable. In this they follow Marx, who, dominated by the Hegelian dialectic, regarded the victory of the proletariat over the bourgeoisie as inevitable, so that all that human effort can hope to achieve is "to shorten and lessen the birth pangs" of the new order. There is, however, very little scientific value in this dialectic argument, and many Communists are quite ready to soft-pedal it and admit that some human mistake or misstep might lead to the triumph of fascism. The truth is that the dialectic method which Marx inherited from Hegel and Schelling is an outgrowth of speculations carried on in theologic seminaries. The "system" of production takes the place of the councils or the mills of the gods. Such Oriental fatalism has little support in the spirit and method of modern science. Let us therefore leave the pretended dialectic proof and examine the contention on an historical basis.

Historically, the argument is put thus: When did any class give up its power without a bloody struggle? As in most rhetorical questions, the questioner does not stop for an answer, assuming that his ignorance is conclusive as to the facts. Now, it is not difficult to give instances of ruling classes giving up their sovereignty without armed resistance. The English landed aristocracy did it in the Reform Bill of 1832; and the Russian nobility did it in 1863 when they freed their serfs, though history showed clearly that in this way not only their political power but their very existence was doomed (for money income has never been so secure as direct revenue from the land, and life in cities reduced the absolute number of noble families). In our own country, the old seaboard aristocracy, which put over the United States Constitution and controlled the government up to the Jacksonian era, offered no armed resistance when the backwoods farmers outvoted them and removed church and property qualifications for office and for the franchise.

But it is not necessary to multiply such instances. It is more important to observe that history does not show that any *class* ever gained its enfranchisement through a bloody rebellion carried out by its own unaided efforts. When ruling classes are overthrown it is generally by a combination of groups that have risen to power only after a long process. For the parties to a rebellion cannot succeed unless they have more resources than the established regime. Thus the ascendancy of the French bourgeoisie was aided by the royal power which Richelieu and Colbert used in the seventeenth century to transform the landed barons into dependent courtiers. Even so, the French Revolution of 1789 would have been impossible without the co-operation of the peasantry, whose opposition to their ancient seigneurs was strengthened as the latter ceased to be independent rulers of the land. This is in a measure also true of the supposedly purely Communist Revolution in Russia. For in that revolution, too, the peasantry had a much greater share than is ordinarily assumed. After all, the amount of landed communal property (that of the crown, the church, etc.) which was changed by the peasants into individual ownership may have been greater than the amount of private property made communal by the Soviet regime. Even the system of collective farms is, after all, a return to the old *mir* system, using modern machinery. The success of the Russian Revolution was largely due to the landlords' agents who, in their endeavor to restore the rule of the landlords threw the peasantry into the arms of the Bolshevists.

Indeed, the strictly Marxian economics, with its ideology of surplus-value due to the ownership of the means of production, is inherently inapplicable to the case of the peasant who cultivates his own piece of ground.

Even more important, however, is it to note that no amount of repetition can make a truth of the dogma that the capitalist class alone rules this country and like the Almighty can do what it pleases. It would be folly to deny that, as individuals or as a class, capitalists have more than their proportionate share of influence in the government, and that they have exercised it unintelligently and with dire results. But it is equally absurd to maintain that they have governed or can govern without the co-operation of the farmers and the influential middle classes. None of our recent constitutional amendments—not the income-tax amendment, not the popular election of the United States Senators, not woman suffrage, neither prohibition nor its repeal—nor any other major bit of legislation can be said to have been imposed on our country in the interests of the capitalist class. The farmers, who despite mortgages still cling to the private ownership of their land, are actually the dominant political group even in industrial states like New York, Pennsylvania, and Illinois.

The Communist division of mankind into workingmen and capitalists suffers from the fallacy of simplism. Our social structure and effective class divisions are much more complicated. As the productivity of machinery increases, the middle classes increase rather than decrease. Hence a program based entirely on the supposed exclusive interests of the proletariat has no reasonable prospect. Any real threat of an armed uprising will only strengthen the reactionaries, who are not less intelligent than the Communist leaders, understand just as well how to reach and influence our people, and have more ample means for organization. If our working classes find it difficult to learn what their true interests are and do not know how to control their representatives in the government and in the trade unions, there is little prospect that they will be able to control things better during a rebellion or during the ensuing dictatorship.

If the history of the past is any guide at all, it indicates that real improvements in the future will come like the improvements of the past—namely, through co-operation among different groups, each of which is wise enough to see the necessity of compromising with those with whom we have to live together and whom we cannot or do not wish to exterminate.

I know that this notion of compromise or of taking counsel as the least wasteful way of adjusting differences is regarded as hopelessly antiquated and bourgeois, but I do not believe that the ideas of so-called Utopian socialists have really been refuted by those who arrogate the epithet "scientific" to themselves. The Communists seem to me to be much more Utopian and quite unscientific in their claims that the working class alone can by its own efforts completely transform our social order.

I do not have very high expectations from the efforts of sentimental benevolence. Yet I cannot help noticing that the leaders of the Communists and of other revolutionary labor movements—Engels, Marx, Lassalle, Luxemburg, Liebknecht, Lenin, and Trotsky—have not been drawn to it by economic solidarity. They were not workingmen nor even all of workingmen's families. They were driven to their role by human sympathy. Sympathy with the sufferings of our fellow men is a human motive that cannot be read out of history. It has exerted tremendous social pressure. Without it you cannot explain the course of nineteenth-century factory legislation, the freeing of serfs and slaves, or the elimination of the grosser forms of human exploitation. Though some who regard themselves as followers of Karl Marx are constantly denouncing reformers who believe in piecemeal improvement and hope rather that things will get worse so as to drive people into a revolution, Marx himself did not always take that view. Very wisely he attached great importance to English factory legislation which restricted the number of hours per working day, for he realized that every little bit that strengthens the workers strengthens their resistance to exploitation. Those who are most oppressed and depressed, the inhabitants of the slums, do not revolt—they have not energy enough to think of it. When, therefore, Mr. Strachey and others criticize the socialists for not bringing about the millennium when they get into power, I am not at all impressed. I do not believe that the socialists or the Labor Party in England have been free from shameful error. But neither have the Communists, nor any other human group, been free from it. Trite though it sounds, it is nevertheless true that no human arrangement can bring about perfection on earth. And while the illusion of omniscience may offer great consolation, it brings endless inhumanity when it leads us to shut the gates of mercy. Real as are our human conflicts, our fundamental identity of interest in the face of hostile nature seems to me worthy of more serious attention than the Communists have been willing to accord it.

If liberalism were dead, I should still maintain that it deserved to live, that it had not been condemned in the court of human reason, but lynched outside of it by the passionate and uncompromisingly ruthless war spirit, common to Communists and Fascists. But I do not believe that liberalism is dead, even though it is under eclipse. There still seems to me enough reason left to which to appeal against reckless fanaticism.

It is pure fanaticism to belittle the gains that have come to mankind from the spirit of free inquiry, free discussion, and accommodation. No human individual or group of individuals can claim omniscience. Hence society can only suffer serious loss when one group suppresses the opinions and criticisms of all others. In purely abstract questions compromise may often be a sign of confusion. One cannot really believe inconsistent principles at the same time. But in the absence of perfect or even adequate knowledge in regard to human affairs and their future, we must adopt an experimental attitude and treat principles not as eternal dogmas, but as hy-

potheses, to be tried to the extent that they indicate the general direction of
solution to specific issues. But as the scientist must be ever ready to modify
his own hypothesis or to recognize wherein a contrary hypothesis has merits
or deserves preference, so in practical affairs we must be prepared to learn
from those who differ with us, and to recognize that however contradictory
diverse views may appear in discourse they may not be so in their practical
applications.

Thus, the principles of Communism and individualism may be held
like theologic dogmas, eternally true and on no occasion ever to be contaminated one by the other. But in fact, when Communists get into power
they do not differ so much from others. No one ever wished to make everything communal property. Nor does anyone in his senses believe that any
individual will ever with impunity be permitted to use his "property" in
an antisocial way when the rest of the community is aroused thereby. In
actual life, the question how far Communism shall be pushed depends more
upon specific analyses of actual situations—that is, upon factual knowledge.
There can be no doubt that individualism à la Herbert Hoover has led millions to destruction. Nevertheless, we must not forget that a Communist
regime will, after all, be run by individuals who will exercise a tremendous
amount of power, no less than do our captains of industry or finance today.
There is no real advantage in assuming that under Communism the laboring classes will be omniscient. We know perfectly well how labor leaders
like John Lewis keep their power by bureaucratic rather than democratic
methods. May it not be that the Stalins also keep their power by bureaucratic rather than democratic methods?

Indeed the ruthless suppression of dissent within the Communist Party
in Russia and the systematic glorification of the national heroes and military
objectives of Czarist days suggest that the Bolshevik Revolution was not so
complete a break with the Russian past as most of its friends and enemies
assumed in earlier days. In any event we have witnessed in the history of
the Communist movement since 1917 a dramatic demonstration of the way
in which the glorification of power—first as a means of destroying a ruling
class, then as a means of defending a beleaguered state from surrounding
enemies, and finally as a means of extending Communism to neighboring
lands—comes imperceptibly to displace the ends or objectives which once
formed the core of Communist thought. Thus, one by one, the worst features of capitalist society and imperialism, against which Communism cut
its eye teeth in protest—extreme inequality in wages, speed-up of workers,
secret diplomacy, and armed intervention as a technique of international
intercourse—have been taken over by the Soviet Union, with only a set of
thin verbal distinctions to distinguish the "good" techniques of Communism from the corresponding "bad" techniques used by capitalism. As is
always the case, the glorification of power dulls the sense of righteousness

to which any movement for bettering the basic conditions of human living must appeal.

The Communist criticism of liberalism seems to me altogether baseless and worthless. One would suppose from it that liberalism is a peculiar excrescence of capitalism. This is, however, not true. The essence of liberalism—freedom of thought and inquiry, freedom of discussion and criticism —is not the invention of the capitalist system. It is rather the mother of Greek and modern science, without which our present industrial order and the labor movement would be impossible. The plea that the denial of freedom is a temporary necessity is advanced by all militarists. It ignores the fact that, when suppression becomes a habit, it is not readily abandoned. Thus, when the Christian Church after its alliance with the Roman Empire began the policy of "compelling them to enter," it kept up the habit of intolerant persecution for many centuries. Those who believe that many of the finer fruits of civilization were thereby choked should be careful about strengthening the forces of intolerance.

When the Communists tell me that I must choose between their dictatorship and Fascism, I feel that I am offered the choice between being shot and being hanged. It would be suicide for liberal civilization to accept this as exhausting the field of human possibility. I prefer to hope that the present wave of irrationalism and of fanatical intolerance will recede and that the great human energy which manifests itself in free thought will not perish. Often before, it has emerged after being swamped by passionate superstitions. There is no reason to feel that it may not do so again.

"POWER TENDS TO CORRUPT. . . ."

Harold J. Laski*

The Marxian view of a secretly armed minority assuming power at a single stroke is unthinkable in the modern state. It would have to imply either the existence of a government so weak that it had practically ceased to be a government at all, or, what is perhaps an equivalent, a population actively sympathetic to the revolutionary minority. The resources of publicity in modern civilization make impossible the private preparation of the gigantic effort assumed by the Marxian hypothesis.

* Late Professor of Political Science at the London School of Economics. Author of *Communism; Reflections on the Revolution of Our Time, Faith, Reason and Civilization;* and many other books. The selection is from pp. 42-45 of *Karl Marx: An Essay,* first published in America by the League for Industrial Democracy in 1933. By permission of the publisher.

But this is only the beginning of the difficulty. Marx assumed throughout his analysis a system of compact states the life of which was mainly determined by economic considerations, and each relatively independent of its neighbors. Each of these assumptions is only partially true of the modern world. A State like England, which is wholly dependent on foreign trade, could not undergo a successful revolution except upon the assumption that her neighbors viewed its results with benevolence. Such an attitude on the part, for instance, of America is very unlikely, and the rupture of Anglo-American trade would be fatal to any revolution in this country. Nor is that all. It is quite clear that the division a revolution would imply must, in its workings, be very partially determined by economic considerations.

In a country like America, for example, there would be at least three other factors of vital importance. An American communist revolution would have to cope with problems of distance which would probably render it abortive at a very early stage. It would not, as in France, be a matter of the immense impact of the capital on the life of the nation; Washington is relatively insignificant in the perspective of America. To control the whole continent would involve controlling the most complicated railway system in the world. And even if that difficulty could be surmounted, a complex of nationalist differences would have to be assuaged. German, French, English, Irish, Polish, these have their special characteristics which the American capitalist has been able to exploit to their common disadvantage; it is difficult to see how an appeal to a communist minority of each would result in the transcendence of these differences. Even then, the religious problem remains; and the hold of the churches upon the mind, particularly, of the Latin peoples would not be easy to loosen. For Marx, insisting only upon the economic motive, it is easy to ignore these difficulties, but it is far too narrow an outlook not to realize at the outset that appeal can be made to other incentives every whit as strong. And even if it were argued that Marx could in our own time assume that the day of such prejudice as nationality and religion engender is passing (which is doubtful), and that the barriers built by economic difference are now alone important, his conclusions would not follow. For in a period of universal suffrage, it ought then to be possible to capture the seat of power at the polls, and throw upon the capitalist the onus of revolting against a socialist democracy.

There are, however, other approaches to the problem which Marx did not adequately consider. There is, in the first place, the general result upon society of the practice of violence, particularly when the destructive nature of modern warfare is borne in mind; and, in the second, there is the special psychological result upon the agents of the opposing forces in such a regime. Marx did not consider these possibilities, in part because he judged that, in any case, the conflict was inevitable, and also because he was convinced that whatever sacrifices had to be made would be ultimately justified by the result. Such an attitude is, of course, simply an instance of his general failure to weigh sufficiently the substance of a political psychology. In part, also, it is the corollary of a determinism which the facts in issue at no point justify. For it is obvious that if revolution, with its attendant violence, is justified for any cause in which you happen to believe profoundly, no modern state can hope for either security or order.

The war has shown clearly that the impulses of savagery which are checked by peace are, when loosed, utterly destructive of the foundations of a decent existence. If life became an organized and continuous jacquerie, civilization could quite easily be reduced to the state where, as in Mr. Wells's imaginary but far from impossible picture, some aged survivor may tell of an organized Europe as a legend which his grandchildren cannot hope to understand. Violence, on the grand scale, in fact, so far from proving an avenue to communism, would be the one kind of existence in which the impulses demanded by a communist state had no hope of emergence. For the condition of communism is the restraint of exactly those appetites which violence releases; and Marx has nowhere indicated how this difficulty could be met.

Even beyond this issue, a further point must be raised. Marx has assumed the seizure of power, and a period of rigorous control until the people are prepared for communism. But he has not shown what approximate length that period is to be, nor what certainty we have that those who act as controllers of the dictatorship will be willing to surrender their power at the proper time. It is a commonplace of history that power is poisonous to those who exercise it; there is no reason to assume that the Marxian dictator will in this respect be different from other men. And, *ex hypothesi*, it will be more difficult to defeat his malevolence since his regime will have excluded the possibility of opposition. No group of men who exercise the powers of a despot ever retain the habit of democratic responsibility. That is obvious, for instance, in the case of men like Sir Henry Maine and Fitzjames Stephen, who, having learned in India the habit of autocratic government, become impatient on their return to England of the slow process of persuasion which democracy implies.

To sit continuously in the seat of office is inevitably to become separated from the mind and wants of those over whom you govern. For the governing class acquires an interest of its own, a desire for permanence, a wish, perhaps, to retain the dignity and importance which belong to their function; and they will make an effort to secure them. That, after all, is only to insist that every system of government breeds a system of habits; and to argue as a corollary therefrom that the Marxian dictatorship would breed habits fatal to the emergence of the regime Marx had ultimately in view. The special vice of every historic system of government has been its inevitable tendency to identify its own private good with the public welfare.

To suggest that communists might do the same is no more than to postulate their humanity. And it may be added that if they surrender power at a reasonable time, the grounds for so doing, being obviously in their nature noneconomic, would thereby vitiate the truth of the materialistic interpretation of history.

IV

TOWARD THE BOLSHEVIK TRIUMPH

We, the countless, redoubtable legions of Toil,
We've conquered vast spaces of oceans and lands,
Illumined great cities with suns of our making,
Fired our souls with proud flames of revolt.
Gone are our tears, our softness forgotten,
We banished the perfume of lilac and grass,
We exalt electricity, steam and explosives,
Motors and sirens and iron and brass. . . .
Our arms, our muscles cry out for vast labors,
The pain of creation glows hot in our breast
United, we sweeten all life with our honey,
Earth takes a new course at our mighty behest.
We love life, and the turbulent joys that intoxicate,
We are hard, and no anguish our spirit can thaw.
We—all, We—in all, We—hot flames that regenerate,
We ourselves, to ourselves, are God, Judge, and Law.

VLADIMIR KIRILLOV

"I am compelled to reject Bolshevism for two reasons: First, because the price mankind must pay to achieve Communism by Bolshevik methods is too terrible; and secondly because, even after paying the price, I do not believe the result would be what the Bolsheviks profess to desire."

BERTRAND RUSSELL

"Instead of being a destructive force, it seems to me that the Bolsheviki were the only party in Russia with a constructive program and the power to impose it on the country."

JOHN REED in *Ten Days That Shook the World*

Chapter 7

WAR AND REVOLUTIONS

═══

*The First World War which linked Russia with the French and British
democracies against imperial Germany at the outset aroused considerable
support among the Russian people for their government in its war effort.
The detailed process by which enthusiasm turned to bitter discontent and
then disaffection is traced by John S. Curtiss in the pages that follow.*

*The fundamental and historic backwardness and inequities of Russia's
political, economic, and social structures and, more immediately, the privations of war, the inequalities of burdens, the incompetency and corruption
of the imperial court, military inefficiency, and widespread agitation, cul-
minated in March 1917 in the collapse of Tsardom in what has been called
"one of the most leaderless, spontaneous, anonymous revolutions of all
time"; "elemental, and for that reason all the more conclusive."*

*The Bolshevik revolution, on the other hand, was carefully premedi-
tated and planned. It is interesting to speculate on which of the decisions
made during the War, and particularly after the March revolution, strengthened the Bolshevik position. (It is probably true that while the Bolsheviks
never commanded majority support, at the time of the November revolution, "the active masses of workers and soldiers were, in the main, on the
side of the coup, or at least regarded it with friendly neutrality"—as William Henry Chamberlin wrote.) Such speculation may provide some insight
on Bolshevik success in Russia and have importance in relation to revolutionary movements and ferment elsewhere in the world.*

*The "indifference" with which the arbitrary dissolution of the Con-
stituent Assembly was received by the nation after the freest and most equal
election in all its history was further evidence of the people's lack of deep
understanding of or commitment to democracy. The critical decision on
land having apparently already been made, the majority of peasants were
not prepared to fight to preserve democracy, for, to them, as Michael T.
Florinsky wrote, "freedom did not mean the introduction of parliamentary
institutions about which they knew nothing, but the immediate division*

. . . of the landed estates in which they saw the real reason for their poverty and misery." That this "indifference" was to turn into "sullen discontent" with the program of collectivization did not alter the immediate situation.

THE RUSSIAN REVOLUTIONS OF 1917

JOHN S. CURTISS*

THE RUSSIAN EMPIRE IN THE FIRST WORLD WAR

Background of the War. . . . In June, 1914, when the Austrian Archduke Francis Ferdinand was assassinated with the complicity of Serbian terrorists, the Russian government at first warned the Serbs to make amends. But when Austria-Hungary presented an ultimatum apparently designed to lead to war against Serbia, and when Vienna quickly declared war, Russia sought to protect her small ally against the Austrians. The Russians began partial mobilization against Austria, but then, under pressure from his generals, the Tsar reluctantly agreed to full mobilization, knowing that this might well lead Germany to declare war. Germany did so on July 19/ August 1, 1914.[1] From a Balkan quarrel the war had become a general one.

The First Months of the War. When war came, Russia was stronger than ever before. There was considerable popular support for the government, and political conflict almost vanished. The Duma, in an outburst of patriotism, voted full support and gave the government a free hand. The people responded well to the call for mobilization. Even most of the socialists gave their support. As for the Bolshevik group in the Duma, who sharply opposed the war, it was quickly arrested and exiled to Siberia.

The Russian army, thoroughly reorganized after the Japanese war, had more artillery and machine guns than before, and an excellent spirit. But, in spite of belief in victory in a few months, the army was poorly prepared to fight the best military power in the world. The Russians had far fewer guns per division than the Germans, and no heavy field guns. Even worse, the Russians, with feeble facilities for making ammunition, had only 1,000 shells per gun, while the Germans had 3,000 per gun and ample capacity to make more. The Russians were also woefully lacking in machine guns, with only 4,100 in the whole army. Their supply and medical system were primitive, their communications weak, and their aviation was far inferior to the

* Professor of History, Duke University. The selection is from pp. 21-87 of *The Russian Revolutions of 1917* (Princeton, N. J.: D. Van Nostrand Co., Inc., 1957). By permission of the publisher.
    [1] The first date is that of the old Russian calendar, the other is the same date corresponding to the new Soviet calendar (identical with that of the West).

Germans. Against the Austrians the Russians could more than hold their own, but from the beginning the Germans far outclassed them.

Even more disastrous, the Russian high command was poorly organized. It was only on the second day that the Grand Duke Nicholas, uncle of the Tsar, was named commander-in-chief, much to his surprise. He himself stated that at first he wept copiously because he did not know how to perform his new duties. Although he had some success, his appointment was unfortunate. His chief-of-staff, General Ianushkevich, had had no field experience, and other high commanders were also poorly trained. V. A. Sukhomlinov, the Minister of War, was either extremely incompetent or a traitor. . . .

The Russian Disasters of 1915. By the spring of 1915 the Russians, in spite of heavy losses, had pushed to the crest of the Carpathians and even through some of the passes to the Hungarian plain. The Russians depended chiefly upon the bayonet, as their ammunition was almost gone. With their extended lines and almost silent cannon the Russians invited a German counter-stroke, which came suddenly in April, 1915. With massed guns and heavy air attacks the Teutons cut the Russian army to pieces, whole units surrendering in confusion. The Germans pursued relentlessly, striking along the whole front, and threatened to entrap the Russians in Poland. The Russian cannon were limited at best to one shell per gun per day. Even the infantry lacked rifle ammunition, and reserve troops often had no rifles, but were forced to lie unarmed under fire until the rifles of the killed and wounded could be made available. Yet the Russian army held together under these demoralizing conditions, and late in the fall the Germans halted their offensive on a line running from just west of Riga to the corner of Galicia.

Naturally, the Russian losses during this period were immense. At the height of the German drive, the killed and wounded numbered 235,000 per month, and 200,000 prisoners were lost each month. During 1915 alone, the Russians lost some 2,000,000 men killed and wounded, and 1,300,000 prisoners, bringing the total losses since the outbreak of the war to 4,360,000. It is no wonder that the British General Knox, who was with the Russian forces, stated that the army had come through a trial that "would have been fatal to most armies." The remnants of the army, although replenished in numbers, were inferior in quality, as the great quantities of regular officers and noncoms put out of action could never be replaced. Moreover, the morale of the Russians never could be restored.

Political Results of the Defeats. Inevitably, news of the difficulties of the army filtered back to the Duma as early as January, 1915. At that time the members sharply questioned Sukhomlinov, the Minister of War, only to be told that the supply situation was satisfactory. The Duma could do nothing, even though it was sure that this answer was untrue. The leading political figures of the country met and repeatedly urged basic reforms in the government, only to be snubbed by the Tsar. The movement for reform grew, however, and early in the summer of 1915 two-thirds of the Duma organized the Progressive Bloc, headed by P. N. Miliukov, to ask necessary reforms and the "Ministry of Confidence" that was so widely demanded. When the Duma reconvened on June 19, 1915, there was a fierce attack upon the reactionary and incompetent ministers, who had opposed the mobilization of the public forces to support the war. As a result, the Tsar replaced three of the worst with able and respected conservatives. . . . The hopes of the Progressive Bloc were high.

The Sway of Rasputin. The Empress Alexandra, a fanatical believer in the autocratic power of the Emperor, had long been under the influence of Rasputin, who urged her to combat the progressive tendencies. She had already expressed her hatred of Guchkov. In August, she and Rasputin persuaded the Tsar to dismiss the Grand Duke Nicholas, the commander-in-chief, and go to the front and take command himself. When the news leaked out, there was general consternation in the Duma, as the Tsar had no military training. Moreover, his absence from Petrograd would leave the government without a head. The feeling grew so strong that the ministers, under strong pressure from the Duma and the general public, on August 21 sent the Tsar a joint letter urging him to reconsider his decision. Only the aged Goremykin, the submissive Premier, opposed the protest. The letter, however, failed to deter the Tsar, who left for Headquarters on August 23. The ministers did not learn of his departure until two days later. By this act Nicholas cut himself off from the ministers. In reality, he turned over his political powers to the Empress, whom he encouraged to dabble in matters of state. The Empress, in turn, was firmly under the influence of Rasputin. And, thus, the great empire was dominated by a debauched and ignorant peasant, with whom no decent man could cooperate. The Empress, trusting firmly in him, threw herself into the work of running the state with dire results. The doom of the Empire was sealed.

The Brusilov Offensive in 1916. In spite of the fatal turn in political life, the Russian army made a remarkable recovery over the winter of 1915-1916. The troops were rested and re-equipped, and heavy contingents of new men were added to the ranks. . . . In fact, as the German army also had improved greatly since 1914, the improved Russian army was even more inferior to the Germans than before. None the less, it was decided to take the offensive in 1916, to relieve the Allies, hard pressed in France, and especially to succor the Italians after the rout at Caporetto.

The Russian commanders facing the Germans had little hope of success, but Brusilov, commander in Galicia, was sure of success against the Austrians and was given command of the offensive. Thanks to effective artillery fire and numerical superiority, the Russians quickly overwhelmed the Austrians on a wide front and captured 400,000 prisoners. But with German aid the Austrians again halted the Russians with heavy losses. The Russians had diverted large German forces from France and had saved Italy. Moreover, Brusilov's success had finally lured Rumania into the war on the allied side— although Rumania soon experienced disaster. But in spite of these successes, the offensive was unwise. In 1916 the Russians lost more than 2,000,000 men killed and wounded, and 350,000 prisoners. Even more important, the morale of the Russian army was ruined beyond repair, and its collapse seemed certain. The army was ripe for revolution.

Ministerial Leapfrog. After the Tsar had gone to the front, the internal situation worsened rapidly. The country's economy began to display alarming signs of weakness. Inflation, slow at first, soon gained momentum, and prices soared. For the swollen populations of the cities this brought great hardship, as wages, pitifully low at best, lost their purchasing power. The misery of the working people was intensified by a growing shortage of food. The peasants found it unprofitable to sell their grain for inflated money, especially as there were few manufactured goods to buy with it. In addition, the railroads proved unable to cope with the enormous problem of supplying the huge army as well as the civilian population, and often available food supplies could not be transported. Food riots and strikes became more frequent, although the government dealt severely with the participants. A fuel shortage added to the woes of the urban inhabitants. As for the peasants, they were fairly docile, but they were more and more disgusted with the war, which had taken so many of their men and was constantly taking more.

Under these circumstances, able administration was imperative. It was not, however, supplied. Instead, the Empress, egged on by Rasputin, campaigned for the removal of the able men appointed by the Tsar in the summer of 1915. Two of them were dismissed in September, and a few months later two others went. Polivanov, the capable Minister of War, was especially hated by the Empress, who wrote to her husband: "A greater traitor than Sukhomlinov." When Nicholas finally gave in and removed him, she wrote: "Oh, the relief! Now I can sleep well." More and more the reputable men of Russia found it impossible to work under the influence of Rasputin, who, steeped in debauchery, was surrounded by a crowd of unprincipled adventurers. During the last eighteen months of the empire, the public was regaled with the spectacle of the "ministerial leap-frog," as one corrupt politician succeeded another in the positions of power, while Rasputin pulled the strings. In December, 1915, Nicholas removed old Goremykin because of his inability to cope with the strong opposition to him. His successor, however, was Stürmer, a shady and disreputable politician for whom nobody had a good word. This appointment caused consternation at home and abroad, as he was incorrectly believed to be pro-German. He kept his post for almost a year. At first he posed as a friend of the Duma, to the great delight of the public.

But as the governmental scandals grew ever more noisome, and as the inability of the administration to deal with the food situation became more obvious, public opinion grew more and more vehement against Stürmer's government. Finally, the naming of A. D. Protopopov as Minister of Interior outraged Duma and public alike. Even the Tsar protested against him, but the urging of the Empress and Rasputin won out. It was not long before Protopopov's proven connections with Rasputin infuriated the citizenry, while his unbalanced mental state made him obviously unfit for the key post of Minister of Interior. Feeling ran so high that he did not dare appear before the Duma, over which he had once presided. In November, 1916, the Tsar decided to dismiss him, but the Empress in despair fought for him, and Protopopov remained in power until the end.

   The Rising Tide of Unrest. Protopopov failed signally in his efforts to control the situation. In October, 1916, he sought to smash a city-wide strike in Petrograd by using two regiments of the garrison to reinforce the police. The troops, however, fired, not on the strikers, but on the police—an ominous note. Reports from the front frequently stressed that the soldiers wanted only peace and bread. Opposition to the war was so great that some officers feared to lead their troops in action lest they be shot by their own men. Protests demanding basic reforms were adopted by the *zemstvos* and the town governments, by the financial interests, by the nobility, and countless other organized groups. The situation grew so menacing that members of the Tsar's family met in secret to consider deposing the Tsar and the Empress as a means of avoiding the coming revolution. Generals and members of the Duma conferred concerning similar action, but nobody dared to take the lead.

   On November 1, 1916, the Duma met for the first time in five months. Miliukov, leader of the Progressive Bloc, delivered a scathing attack on "the dark forces" around the throne, ending each part of his indictment with the question: "Is this stupidity or is it treason?" He was followed by several of the conservatives, who furiously denounced Rasputin and Stürmer. The latter, terrified, dared not challenge the Duma, in spite of the great wrath of the Empress. For once the Tsar acted independently by dismissing Stürmer and replacing him with a decent man, who insisted on removing Protopopov. The frantic Empress went to Headquarters, however, and secured the Tsar's promise to keep him, so that the dismissal of Stürmer brought little improvement. Fresh speeches in the Duma condemning Rasputin and his henchmen showed the enormous dissatisfaction of the Russian educated public, but produced no change in the government. The only result was further to infuriate the Empress, who demanded that the Tsar dismiss the Duma. "Russia loves to feel the whip."

   One consequence of the speeches in the Duma was that several of the highest nobility of Russia decided to assassinate Rasputin in order to save the regime. Prince Yusupov, related to the Tsar by marriage, and the Grand Duke Dimitry, nephew of the Tsar, plied Rasputin with poisoned wine, and when that failed to take effect, he was shot and his body dumped into the river. When the corpse was recovered, the Tsar and the Empress attended his funeral upon the palace grounds. Rasputin's removal had no effect upon the political life of the land, which continued to drift toward revolution.

THE FIRST REVOLUTIONARY MONTHS

The Mounting Crisis. In the first two months of 1917, dissatisfaction in Russia grew rapidly. The inflation advanced at a fast pace, with severe effects upon the working population, which showed its exasperation by an increasing number of strikes. The food shortages angered all, especially the women who had to wait in line for hours in the bitter cold, sometimes to find that there was no food to be had. In the rising popular fury the radical parties played little part, as the Mensheviks were still supporting the war and the Bolsheviks, with their chief figures in exile abroad or in Siberia, could accomplish little. The revolutionary movement was thus largely spontaneous and unexpected, even though it had long been foreseen. . . .

The Uprising. The insurrection began almost unnoticed. Early in March, 1917, a strike of workers of Petrograd's great Putilov Works turned thousands of men onto the streets, to demonstrate against the government and to appeal to the workers of other plants. March 8, International Woman's Day, regularly celebrated by the workers, brought thousands of women from the breadlines to swell the crowds. Red flags and banners with the slogan "Down with the Autocracy!" made their appearance. The police, however, had no great trouble in dispersing the crowds, and the unrest seemed no greater than on previous occasions. By the 9th there were nearly 200,000 strikers in the streets, demonstrating in the center of the city. Cossacks called out to disperse the crowds refused to charge them, and on one occasion they bowed to the crowd which applauded their inactivity. But the unrest apparently still was not threatening; the British ambassador cabled London: "Some disorders occurred today, but nothing serious."

On March 10 the movement grew in intensity, and the Tsar wired General Khabalov, commander of the garrison, to disperse the crowds with rifle fire. The next day preparations were made to subdue the demonstrations. Police with machine guns were placed in the upper stories of buildings overlooking main thoroughfares, and regiments of the garrison fired with considerable effect on crowds in several parts of the city. The government seemed to have won. But that night the troops in their barracks decided not to shoot down the crowds in the future. When ordered to march on the morning of the 12th, one of the regiments refused, shot the commander, and poured into the streets to join the crowds. Other regiments were quickly won over to the revolution. Together with the workers they hunted down the police and broke into the arsenals, where 40,000 rifles were captured and distributed to the workers. While these events were occurring, M. V.

Rodzianko, President of the Duma, wired the Tsar, warning him of the seriousness of the situation and urging immediate reforms to avert a catastrophe. Nicholas said impatiently to his Court Chamberlain: "That fat Rodzianko has written me some nonsense, to which I shall not even reply."

Victory of the Revolution. By nightfall of March 12 it was all over. As the revolution surged ahead, General Khabalov sought to bring into play his special reserve of troops, but found himself able to collect no more than six companies. This force was sent to drive back the victorious crowds, but on contact with the insurrectionists they melted away, the men going over to the crowds, and the officers into hiding. Finally, late in the day, Khabalov, with less than two thousand men, took refuge in the Winter Palace, only to be asked to leave by the Grand Duke Michael. They went to the nearby Admiralty building, to disperse completely on the following day. The revolution was in full control of Petrograd. The overturn was marked by few excesses and by light casualties. Aside from burning the police stations and hunting down the police, the crowds shed little blood. In all, 1,315 persons, chiefly soldiers and citizens, were killed or wounded. In the rest of the vast Russian Empire, the revolution spread rapidly, with little fighting. . . .

The Revolutionary Government. The Duma was in session when the disorders began, but on March 12 they were prorogued by order of the Tsar, prepared well in advance. The deputies hesitated whether to obey the order of dismissal, but after some thought they accepted it, lest they give aid and comfort to the revolutionaries. They moved from their official meeting place to a room across the hall, where they organized as an unofficial committee with the purpose "of restoring order and to deal with institutions and individuals." In the meantime, as early as March 9, some of the revolutionary leaders, with memories of 1905, suggested the election of a Soviet of Workers' Deputies, and several factories did hold elections. It was only on March 12, however, that the Soviet assembled in the Tavrida Palace, across the hall from the meeting of the Duma committee. After it had been joined by delegates from the garrison regiments, it changed its name to Soviet of Workers' and Soldiers' Deputies. Both the Soviet and the Duma were visited by hordes of workers and soldiers, who looked to them for leadership. The Soviet busied itself with the practical matters of the moment —patrolling the streets, feeding the soldiers who had joined the revolution, and similar matters, while the Duma leaders sought to preserve an effective government for the country.

Most of the Duma leaders were convinced monarchists, who felt that a Tsar was essential, even though the abdication of Nicholas II could not be avoided. So it was decided to send a delegation to the Tsar to ask him to abdicate, naming his brother Michael as regent. With some difficulty two of them made their way to the Tsar, who had come part way back to the capital. Before they arrived, Nicholas had heard from all the leading generals that his abdication was essential, so when the delegates appeared he surprised them by readily abdicating in favor of Michael. Back in Petrograd, however, the Duma leaders found it impossible to persuade the masses to accept *any* Tsar and barely escaped violence when they came out for Michael. Nevertheless, on March 16 a group of the Duma leaders, headed by Miliukov, visited Michael to urge him to take the throne. The Grand Duke, however, realizing the public hostility to a monarchy, refused to take the crown except from a Constituent Assembly. Hence, Russia became a republic *de facto,* although the formal declaration of the republic came much later.

Formation of the Provisional Government. The members of the Duma committee felt that they had no right to form a government, but as they realized that if they did not, the leaders of the Soviet, more radical in their outlook, would do so, they decided to take power, "otherwise others will take it, those who have already elected some scoundrels in the factories." Miliukov, especially, sought to establish the authority of the new government by negotiating with the leaders of the Soviet. The latter, however, did not desire to rule, as they were men inexperienced in governmental affairs. Moreover, they were moderate socialists, who believed that at this moment the revolution was bourgeois in character, as the workers were too weak to set up the dictatorship of the proletariat. Hence, the Soviet chiefs felt that power should be entrusted to the leaders of the bourgeoisie, drawn from the ranks of the Duma.

Consequently, on March 14, the leaders of the Duma and the Soviet conferred about the powers and program of the new government, which took office on March 16. The Premier of the Provisional Government was Prince G. E. Lvov, a noted liberal; Guchkov was Minister of War, and Miliukov was Foreign Minister. Alexander Kerensky took the post of Minister of Justice. He was nominally a right-wing Socialist Revolutionary, although he was basically conservative. But his enthusiasm for the revolutionary overturn and his inspiring speeches had made him a popular hero and had won him election to the Soviet. He joined the Provisional Government while retaining his membership in the Soviet for the purpose of serving as a link between the two bodies.

The program of the new regime, approved by the Soviet, provided for a full amnesty, broad civil liberties, and complete legal equality of all. Trade unions and strikes were declared legal. The manifesto promised immediate preparation for a constituent assembly, to be elected by universal, direct, equal, and secret voting. Local government was also to be elected. Finally, the soldiers were promised full civil rights, upon condition that firm discipline was observed. This program, which was necessarily a compromise between the Duma and the Soviet, said nothing about the vital issues: the war, and the distribution of land to the peasants. On these points no agreement was possible.

Like its program, the government itself was an uneasy compromise between the Soviet and the leaders of the former Duma. The latter, drawn from the middle-class parties, were quite conservative and instinctively distrusted the masses and the Soviet which represented them. For its part, the Soviet had no great confidence in the Provisional Government. Backed as it was by the vast majority of the workers and the soldiers of the Petrograd garrison, the Soviet undertook to support the Provisional Government only as long as the latter remained true to the cause of the revolution. It compelled the government to arrest the Tsar.

Order No. 1. One of the first acts of the Soviet was to issue its famous Order No. 1 to the troops, to ensure that they would not be used for counter-revolutionary purposes. It was drawn up on March 14 at the suggestion of some of the soldiers. It provided for the election of committees of soldiers in all army units, which were to obey the Soviet and were to keep control of the arms, which were not to be turned over to the officers. The troops were to obey their officers and the Provisional Government, but only insofar as their orders were not in conflict with those of the Soviet. Saluting off duty and elaborate honors to officers were abolished, and the officers were forbidden to be harsh toward their men. These instructions were in part a symptom of the distrust of the officers felt by the rank and file, who had seen that their officers had given no support to the revolution. Discipline in the army had begun to crumble well before the fall of the Tsar. Nevertheless, Order No. 1 doubtless contributed much to the further collapse of the authority of the commanders and of the discipline essential to any effective body of troops. Thus, the Provisional Government lacked effective military support and was dependent for its authority upon the backing of the Soviet.

An Era of Good Feeling. Although in the first weeks after the fall of the monarchy the dualism or divided control of the state held latent the seeds of conflict, matters for a time went fairly smoothly. The Soviet, which grew to over three thousand members, was dominated largely by the soldier delegates, who were usually noncommissioned officers, company clerks, or other partly educated persons, who were not especially radical in their views. Most of them were under the influence of the Socialist Revolutionaries, who supported the war and were not eager for further radicalism. For the most part the workers were led by the Mensheviks, who also supported the war. The latter were convinced that Russia was by no means ready for a proletarian dictatorship, so they were quite ready to let the upper classes represented by the Provisional Government run the country. Even the Bolsheviks did not take an extreme stand at this time.

Kamenev and Stalin, who returned from Siberia during these early days, in their *Pravda* editorials held that, while the war was imperialist in nature, until a general peace became possible there should be no attempt to make a separate peace, and the Russian army should continue to defend the country. And, indeed, even if the Bolsheviks *had* been inspired by the radical views of Lenin, who was fretting in exile in Switzerland, they were too few in numbers and too weak in influence to disturb the relative calm . . .

The Moderate Attitude of the Masses. In general, the army, although it had long since lost any enthusiasm for the war, still thought along traditional lines of its duty to defend the country. . . .

As early as March, 1917, the peasants began to call for peasant Soviets to consider the land question. Nevertheless, they still remembered their punishment in 1906 and 1907 too well to act rashly, and for a time they were willing to wait. The workers, who had immediately gained the eight hour day as a result of the revolution, also were not yet ready for further insurrection. In March, 1917, factory committees, elected by the workers, were set up, to represent the workers in negotiating with the employers. Although there was much friction between committees and employers, in the early spring the committees were seeking higher wages for the employees rather than confiscation of the factories. As yet the moderate socialists had not been replaced by the militant Bolsheviks who later dominated the committees, and the workers were not in a revolutionary frame of mind.

The Rising Conflict Over Foreign Policy. At first the Provisional Government took the position that the revolution had changed nothing in Russia's foreign policy. Miliukov, the Foreign Minister, hastened to assure the Allies that Russia stood by her treaty obligations and warmed their hearts by stating that the Tsar had been overthrown because his government had not been able to wage war with sufficient energy—a far from correct statement. Miliukov was especially interested in obtaining Constantinople and the Dardanelles for Russia, which had been promised by the secret treaties of 1915. The moderate socialists who dominated the Soviet, however, felt that the war was essentially imperialistic in character and hoped that the peoples of the other warring states would also overturn their governments and demand peace.

With this end in view, on March 27 the Soviet issued a "Manifesto to the Peoples of the World," calling on them to oppose actively the annexationist policies of their governments. The Russian democracy, the manifesto promised, would resist to the death all efforts of its ruling classes to pursue such a policy. The peoples of the West, especially in Germany, should rise in revolution against kings, landowners, and bankers, and thus bring about a revolutionary peace. But until this should happen, the Soviet declared, the Russian revolution would not retreat before conquering bayonets nor allow itself to be crushed by outside force. This manifesto was widely hailed by the socialist press, which strongly demanded a peace "without annexations and indemnities."

Miliukov, however, did not share this attitude. Early in April he issued a press interview stating that Russia was fighting to unite the Ukrainian parts of the Austro-Hungarian Empire with Russia and to gain Constantinople and the Straits. These objectives, he declared, could not be regarded as annexation. This utterance aroused a storm of protest. Conflict was averted, however, when the Provisional Government published a "Declaration on War Aims" renouncing annexations and upholding self-determination. It added, however, that Russia should not "emerge from the great struggle humiliated, undermined in her vital strength." The Provisional Government stated its determination "to protect national rights while strictly fulfilling the obligations assumed toward the Allies." In these vague phrases Miliukov saw support for his design to win Constantinople.

Lenin's Return. The news of the fall of the monarchy and the forming of the Provisional Government found Lenin in Switzerland, where he had spent much of the war years. During this period he had formulated his attitude toward the war. Capitalism, he held, must inevitably lead to imperialism, and imperialism is bound to produce war for the interests of the capitalists. In such a conflict the working class had no interest, but should strive to transform the war into a civil war. The socialists of Europe who had supported their nation's cause after Serajevo were thus traitors to the proletariat. Only a true Marxist party could be trusted to end the war in the interests of the working class. . . .

Swiss socialist leaders arranged with the German government to let him and a number of other Russian exiles travel across Germany in a sealed car to Denmark; from there he made his way to Sweden and Finland, and on April 16 he reached Petrograd. Although he had expected to be arrested by the Provisional Government, to his surprise he was met by a deputation from the Soviet and a guard of honor at the Finland Station. He impatiently turned from his official welcome to address the throngs of people in a fiery speech ending with the words: "Long live the socialist revolution!"

The April Theses. On April 17, the day after his arrival, Lenin presented his revolutionary program to two gatherings: one of Bolsheviks, and the second of Bolsheviks and Mensheviks together. The program, known as the April Theses, contained ten points. It declared that the war was still an imperialistic one, to be ended by the overthrow of capitalism and fraternization of the soldiers with the enemy. The revolution, he held, should immediately take the power from the hands of the bourgeoisie and give it to the proletariat and poorer peasants. No support should be given to the Provisional Government, which should be replaced by the Soviet of Workers' Deputies. All large estates were to be nationalized and turned over to the Soviets of Farmhands' Deputies.

This program, in particular as it concerned the war, horrified even the Bolshevik leaders, who felt that it was utterly unrealistic. The Mensheviks regarded Lenin as so visionary as to be ludicrous and felt joy at his impracticability. His program was promptly rejected by the Bolsheviks, 12 to 2, and *Pravda* wrote that his proposals were based upon an incorrect analysis of the revolution. But Lenin was not dismayed by this reception. He pushed his program in incessant speeches to streams of men and women who came to hear him, and so simple and so logical did his points of "End the war" and "All land to the peasants" seem that he won their complete support. His propaganda enjoyed such success among the masses that his party swung over to his side, and at an All-Russian Conference of Bolsheviks in May it strongly approved the program that it had rejected three weeks before. Thus, the lines began to form for a struggle between the Provisional Government and the masses, urged on by Lenin.

THE MOUNTING CRISIS

The Fall of Miliukov. Miliukov's trickery in attempting to cover his annexationist aims with vague words soon came out into the open. When it was discovered that the Allies had not heard of the "Declaration of War Aims," there was a strong demand that he communicate it officially to them. He did so on May 1, but accompanied the Declaration with a covering note, in which he affirmed that Russia was determined to carry the war "to a decisive conclusion," in order to obtain "sanctions and guarantees" which would make new wars impossible. ("Sanctions and guarantees" sounded ominously like annexations.) Finally, he again promised to "fulfill Russia's obligations to her Allies." When, on May 3, this note became public, it was taken as a deliberate challenge to the wishes of the public. The people felt that their strivings for peace had been nullified by the obstinate Foreign Minister.

A crisis of extreme seriousness resulted, with mass demonstrations in front of the seat of the Provisional Government. Although some of the demonstrators supported Miliukov, most of them, including fully armed regiments, carried banners demanding peace without annexations and indemnities, the end of the war, and the dismissal of Miliukov. On the next day, there were even stronger demonstrations, in which there were demands for the end of the Provisional Government. General L. G. Kornilov, commander of the Petrograd garrison, wanted to use his troops to smash the demonstration, but severe bloodshed was averted by the Petrograd Soviet, which ordered that no regiment should come out into the streets without an order signed by the Soviet. Kornilov, angered by this check upon his authority, resigned his command and went to the front.

The demonstration was quickly checked by the orders of the Soviet. The Provisional Government hastened to calm the public by issuing its explanation of Miliukov's note, which it sent to the Allied ambassadors. It practically disavowed Miliukov's interpretation and repeated the pacifist phrases of the earlier declarations. As Miliukov held to his views, he now had to give up the Foreign Ministry, and he refused a lesser post. Likewise Guchkov, Minister of War, also resigned, in part because of poor health, and partly from despair with the trend of events. These resignations led to a reorganization of the Provisional Government, which reformed with nine ministers from the former Duma (chiefly Cadets), and six moderate socialists from the Soviet. It was hoped that this coalition would end the friction between the Soviet and the Provisional Government. The result, however, was to transfer the disharmony into the midst of the government itself. Probably the chief figure in the new regime was Kerensky, the Minister of War. . . .

The Lull Before the Storm. The Provisional Government, and especially the Cadet party, which was rapidly absorbing the other conservative parties, seemed little concerned over the rise of the Bolsheviks. . . . The Bolsheviks, while growing, remained a considerable minority, while the moderate socialists remained in control of the Soviet. But here, too, the reality was not reassuring to the moderates. While the masses out of habit voted for socialists, at the same time they often would vote for Bolshevik resolutions. Nevertheless, when the First Congress of Soviets met on June 16, 1917, the Bolsheviks and allied groups had only 137 out of the 1,090 members. Tseretelli, a moderate leader of the Petrograd Soviet, was sufficiently encouraged by the lack of Bolshevik strength to declare in his speech that the government was secure, "as there is no political party in Russia which at the present time would say: 'Give us power.'" But at this point Lenin spoke from his seat: "Yes, there is!" . . .

The Military Debacle. On July 1, 1917, the Russian offensive began in Galicia. The Russians, with great superiority in numbers and thanks to an unprecedented artillery preparation, penetrated the Austrian lines at several points near Lvov and took several thousand prisoners. Soon, however, they encountered unexpected resistance. The attack, which on other fronts had had no success, bogged down after twelve days. On July 19, the Germans and Austrians began a counter-drive which met almost no opposition as the Russians fled headlong. All discipline vanished and the rout intensified, accompanied by terrible outrages inflicted on the civilians as the troops fled. Finally the line stabilized after all Galicia had been given up; but it was the decision of the enemy rather than Russian resistance that ended the retreat. General Kornilov, who was appointed to command the Southwest Front on July 20, demanded the death penalty in the front areas, and immediately used machine guns and artillery on masses of deserters and mutineers. On July 25, the Provisional Government restored the death penalty and set up special military tribunals to deal with major offenses. But not even these measures accomplished much, for the morale of the army was ruined beyond repair.

The July Insurrection. While the Russian offensive was continuing, violence erupted in Petrograd. The masses of workers, already very hostile toward the Provisional Government, and the soldiers of the garrison, fearful that they might be sent to the front, grew impatient with the apparent timidity of the Bolshevik leadership. On July 16 the First Machine Gun Regiment, an especially radical unit, marched forth, although both the Soviets and the Bolsheviks sought to restrain them. The revolutionary call of the soldiers was eagerly obeyed by other troop units and by hundreds of thousands of workers, whom the Bolsheviks reluctantly led, in order to keep them from getting completely out of hand. On July 17, perhaps 500,000 in huge columns poured through the streets with banners demanding "All Power to the Soviets!" and "Down with the Provisional Government!" They converged on the Tavrida Palace, seat of the Central Executive Committee of the Soviets, to demand that this body assume power in place of the Provisional Government. Feelings ran extremely high, as the demonstrators, augmented by a large force of fierce sailors from Kronstadt, armed to the teeth, streamed through the streets. Occasional shots were fired, at which the demonstrators, believing themselves under attack from neighboring buildings, broke into the houses to hunt for snipers. Several score of persons were killed, and over one hundred wounded. Some of the ministers had narrow escapes. Kerensky was almost captured on the first day, and Victor Chernov, the socialist Minister of Agriculture, escaped death at the hands of sailors only through the intervention of Trotsky.

In the meantime, in the palace, the Central Executive Committee, composed chiefly of Mensheviks and Socialist Revolutionaries, was beset by masses of furious armed men who demanded that they take power—something they refused to do. A stalemate developed as frustrated soldiers and workers threatened the frightened but stubborn leaders of the Soviet to induce them to take power. But the long discussions proved fruitless, and the Bolsheviks, who could easily have seized all Petrograd by giving the order, failed to do so, so that eventually the demonstrators grew weary and went home. The sailors boarded their ships and went back to Kronstadt, and the Central Executive Committee could breathe more freely.

Reaction Against Lenin and the Bolsheviks. The tide of revolt receded as quickly as it had risen. Several of the Guards regiments, which had not taken part in the demonstration, were informed on July 17 that the Minister of Justice had documentary proof that Lenin was a German agent. The Guards, convinced by this, at once put themselves at the orders of the government and the Central Executive Committee. The danger was now over, and on the following day government forces raided and wrecked the offices and plant of *Pravda* and occupied without a struggle the Fortress of Peter and Paul and the Bolshevik headquarters. On July 19 a Bolshevik leaflet announced that the demonstration was at an end.

The documents charging Lenin and other Bolshevik leaders with treason were published in the newspapers, much to the annoyance of Kerensky, who claimed that this had prevented Lenin's capture and punishment.

Other ministers were very dubious about the documents and their source. The middle classes, however, were easily convinced of the correctness of the charges, as they remembered that Lenin had left Switzerland in a German train. Warrants were issued for his arrest, and also for Zinoviev and Kamenev. But Lenin and Zinoviev hid, although they protested their innocence. Lenin at first wanted to stand trial, but as he was persuaded by his associates that he might be murdered in prison, he escaped to Finland, where the Russian police could not follow. He stayed in Helsingfors until autumn. Trotsky and several other Bolsheviks were arrested, but were soon released.

It is perhaps worth stating that most historians of repute do not believe that Lenin was a German agent, even though the Germans had enabled him to return to Russia. . . .

Government Policy After the July Days. The Provisional Government took advantage of its improved position to take further action. Legislation was adopted against incitement to mutiny. Regiments that had taken the lead in the uprising were disbanded and the men sent to the front, in some cases with the use of force. Several of the Bolshevik newspapers were closed and circulation of such publications among the troops was forbidden. . . .

The moderate and the conservative elements of Russia had been granted a new lease of life by the unexpected outcome of the July Days. Neither group, however, took advantage of the opportunity to satisfy the enormous popular demand for peace and land, which was the basis of the strength of the Bolsheviks. The moderate Left continued to advocate prosecution of the war to victory and urged that the land and other problems be deferred until the Constituent Assembly, which, it must be said, they did little to hasten. Thus, they did nothing of significance to win the masses from the Bolsheviks and, hence, remained without any real popular following. As for the Right—landowners, capitalists, army officers, and other upper-class elements—they had never accepted the revolutionary regime in their hearts, and now that the rabble had been subdued, they felt that they discerned the delightful possibility of a strong man—a military dictatorship—to sweep aside all this rubbish of socialists and soviets and to establish sound law and order again, as before the revolution.

THE KORNILOV MOVEMENT

The Illusion of Calm. Although the collapse of the July demonstration had apparently ended all danger from the Bolsheviks, the improvement in the government's position was largely on the surface, while underneath the situation grew worse. On instructions from Lenin, the Bolsheviks concentrated their efforts on the factory committees, which were becoming more and more aggressive. The factory workers found that the rapid inflation raised prices far more than they could raise their wages, and the poorer paid were especially hard hit. The declaration of the textile workers that their children were dying like flies as a result of hunger was not entirely rhetoric. Hence, the lot of the workers became unbearable and they turned to the factory committees for redress and to the Bolsheviks for leadership. . . .

To add to the woes of the government, the national minorities became increasingly self-assertive. As Poland and most of the Baltic states were held by the Germans, they were not an active problem; but both Finland and the Ukraine were becoming restless. . . .

The Kerensky Government. The coalition formed after the July Days failed to endure, for on July 21 Prince Lvov resigned his post as Premier in disapproval of the socialist policy of Chernov, Minister of Agriculture, and others. Kerensky thereupon took office as Premier. After much negotiating and scheming a new government was installed in early August, with eleven socialists and seven nonsocialists. In spite of the preponderance of socialists, however, the new government was more conservative than its predecessor, as the socialists, frightened by the events of July, had lost all trace of revolutionary zeal. More and more, Kerensky dominated the scene. . . .

The Rise of General Kornilov. . . . General L. G. Kornilov, the new commander-in-chief, was a dashing soldier who had won great fame by his exploits in the war as well as by his spectacular personality. A Siberian, with somewhat Mongolian features, he was followed with devotion by a bodyguard of wild Caucasian cavalrymen, whose language he knew. In May, as commander of the Petrograd garrison, he had wished to smash the demonstration against Miliukov, and when the Soviet had prevented this he had resigned to go to the front. Kornilov's reputation as a Napoleonic figure had been further enhanced by his ruthless measures in dealing with the routed troops after the disastrous July offensive. He was greatly admired by Boris Savinkov, the former Socialist Revolutionary who had become head of the Ministry of War under Kerensky, and as Kerensky felt that Kornilov would be successful in reviving the fighting spirit of the army, the general had been named commander-in-chief on July 31. Kornilov's conditions for taking over this post, amounting to a virtual free hand with the army, as well as the extension of full military control to the rear military areas, indicated that he would be a difficult person to handle. The friction caused by this stand was soon eliminated when Kornilov agreed to a compromise, but the incident gave a hint of trouble to come.

Kornilov's Dictatorial Tendencies. Kornilov, who had little knowledge of politics, soon became a storm center. He was instinctively hostile to all socialists, whether extreme or mild, and he disliked Kerensky, although he promised to work with him. The Leftist press, which saw in him a danger to the revolution, attacked him strongly, asking that he be replaced by a general more in sympathy with the revolutionary cause. Conservatives and reactionaries became his enthusiastic allies. The Union of Cossack Troops warned that the consequences for the army would be disastrous if he were removed—an opinion voiced by other military organizations. . . .

The Moscow State Conference. Kornilov's *coup d'état* was already taking shape by August 25. It gained even greater momentum as a result of the Moscow State Conference, which took place on August 25-28. Ironically enough, this meeting, whose purpose was to demonstrate the unity of all behind the government, met in a Moscow without streetcars and without lights; even the restaurants were not functioning, thanks to a one-day general strike called by the Bolsheviks. The Conference, far from supporting Kerensky's government, turned into an overt demonstration of the Right, whose hostility toward Kerensky was plain to see. . . .

The Preliminaries to the Uprising. The outcome of the Moscow State Conference was to confirm Kornilov and his supporters in the belief that Kerensky could never restore order in Russia, for which Kornilov was the essential man. Rodzianko, Miliukov, and other leaders of the Duma period, energetically enrolled landowners and financial magnates in well financed organizations to further the cause, while generals and officers built up organizations of officers and military cadets to support the march on Petrograd by uprisings at the right moment. Kornilov's chief-of-staff later claimed that there were thousands in Petrograd waiting to strike in support of the movement. On September 6, Savinkov, head of the War Ministry under Kerensky, with the latter's approval, visited Kornilov at Headquarters and approved the commander's demands for introducing the death penalty in the rear, Savinkov also told him that as a Bolshevik uprising was expected within a few days, he should send a cavalry corps to the capital to protect the Provisional Government.

This request, which Kornilov had already anticipated by sending troops, was part of the political scheme to which Savinkov was a party. Kerensky was to be invited to dismiss the government and form a new one in which he, Kornilov, and Savinkov would be the dominant figures. If Kerensky refused, the troops were to be brought into play. Unfortunately for the success of the scheme, V. N. Lvov, a lesser political figure, undertook to persuade Kerensky to cooperate, and thereby gave the Premier warning. Kerensky, realizing that if the scheme went through his freedom, if not his life, would be in danger, at once took steps against the conspiracy. After arresting Lvov, on September 9 he ordered Kornilov to resign and asked for support from the Soviet and from the ministers. The Soviet at once gave him full support, but the Cadet ministers resigned from the government, apparently hoping to cause its collapse. . . .

The Collapse of the Movement. Undismayed by Kerensky's opposition, Kornilov persisted in his undertaking, issuing a blast against the Provisional Government, charging it with collaborating with the Germans and ruin-

Peter the Great.

Tsar Nicholas II and his family.

The Zaporozhye Cossacks. The Cossacks are composing a provocative letter to Sultan Mahomet IV of Turkey. The painting is by the Russian artist Ilya Repin.

The Bolshevik attack on the Winter Palace. The artist V. Kuznetsov shows the Bolsheviks storming the headquarters of the Provisional Government in November 1917.

The first Russian Revolution of 1905, "Barricades in Moscow," from a painting by I. Vladimirov.

Lenin addressing armed workers and peasants in 1919.

ing the army and the country. He appealed to the populace in a manifesto full of nationalist and religious phrases, which, however, had already lost their potency. With almost complete support from the Allies, and even aided by a British unit of armored cars, whose men had donned Russian uniforms, he was certain of success. Most of the army leaders were with him, he was sure of the Wild Division and the Cossacks, and he counted on the aid of other disciplined troops. The garrison of Petrograd seemed to have no great enthusiasm for fighting for Kerensky. As for the Petrograd populace, he felt that they, unorganized and leaderless, would remain in sullen apathy, "an indifference that submits to the whip." General Krymov and the other field commanders were ordered to advance on Petrograd.

As soon as the Soviet in Petrograd realized the approaching danger, it hastened to act. Despairing of Kerensky's leadership, the Soviet leaders threw themselves into the work of defending the capital. On September 9, moderate socialists and Bolsheviks combined in a "Committee for Struggle against Counter-Revolution" to defeat Kornilov. The garrison was put in a state of readiness, neighboring troops were called to their aid, and large numbers of eager sailors from Kronstadt arrived, with more coming from other parts of the fleet. Under Bolshevik leadership the Petrograd workers were mobilized. Trenches were dug, barbed wire was strung, barricades were built in the city streets. The Red Guards from the factories, who had been disarmed after the July Days, were again given weapons, and turned out, full of fight. Strong detachments were sent to break up the officers' organizations that had planned to rise as Krymov's forces approached. The conspiratorial center in the Hotel Astoria was taken without difficulty, and a sweeping series of arrests and searches eliminated other groups of plotters. A colonel sent by Kornilov to direct the movement fled to Finland. In all, some 7,000 arrests were made by the Soviet, thus ending all danger of an officers' uprising in Petrograd.

The Failure of the Troop Movements. Not content to await the arrival of the attacking forces, the Soviet had sent word to the railway workers to impede the movement of the hostile troops. At the orders of their union the men cut telegraph wires, put locomotives out of commission, blocked tracks by tipping over freight cars, tore up rails. As the troop trains progressed, they were switched off in the wrong direction and finally halted, isolated and helpless. . . .

The Aftermath of the Kornilov Coup. Kerensky, who had been saved by the spontaneous action of the Soviet and the Bolsheviks, was far from happy about his position after the episode. He now realized that, with the power of the Right destroyed, the Left had gained greatly in strength. Hence, he sought to use the remaining conservatives as a counterweight to the now rising popular forces. To replace Kornilov as commander-in-chief Kerensky named, not one of the generals in sympathy with the revolution, but General Alexeev, who had been hand-in-glove with Kornilov. Moreover, Kerensky ordered that, until Alexeev arrived at Headquarters, the army should continue to obey Kornilov's orders. Alexeev promptly cancelled the movement of strong revolutionary forces to subdue Kornilov's Headquarters garrison. It was only with the greatest reluctance that he had the insurgent general arrested on September 14, along with his most obvious supporters. The arrested men were transferred to a town in the Ukraine, where they were nominally imprisoned. The jailers were none other than Kornilov's devoted Caucasian bodyguard.

An extraordinary investigating committee was sent out to gather evidence against the conspirators, but they showed no willingness to take action and soon released all but the five chief participants. It was obvious that Kerensky's government was not willing to deal harshly with the insurgents. To the masses of soldiers and workers, who had been willing to risk their lives to suppress the Kornilov insurrection, this tenderness toward the defeated generals seemed as treasonable as the uprising itself.

THE AFTERMATH OF THE KORNILOV AFFAIR

Another Chance for Kerensky. After the threat from Kornilov had been removed, Kerensky, although his prestige was badly shaken by his unwillingness to punish the rebels, still had an opportunity to bring the government into line with the aspirations of the people. It is conceivable that if he had accepted reality and had decided to support the demand for peace and had approved a land program satisfactory to the peasants, a more violent revolutionary outbreak could still have been avoided. A moderate democratic regime was perhaps still possible. Instead of making a sharp change in direction, however, the government remained much as before. It still depended on the old Central Executive Committee of the Soviet which had been elected in the earlier, conservative period and which did not represent the feelings of the masses. The Socialist Revolutionaries and the Mensheviks who composed it had been left behind by the rapid march of events. Beneath the surface the Soviets were beginning to swing to the Bolsheviks, while peasants and soldiers were no longer willing to support the war and to wait for a much-postponed Constituent Assembly to deal with the land problem. The appeal of the Right to counter-revolutionary force had made the masses far more impatient with the inaction of the government and more ready to decide the issue by a new resort to the enormous revolutionary force that still remained.

More than ever the government of Russia centered in Kerensky. After the crisis was over, the ministers, who had tendered their resignations, remained in office for a time on a day-to-day basis. In September 14, a Directory or inner cabinet of five men, headed by Kerensky, was set up to determine policy. On the same day, Russia was proclaimed a republic. This step, which merely recognized what had long been obvious, met with strong opposition on the part of the conservatives, who asserted that it exceeded the powers of the Provisional Government. Many felt that beneath the legalistic basis for the protest there lingered a strong hope on the part of the conservatives that somehow the monarchy could be restored. . . .

The Failure of the Socialist Revolutionaries. Kerensky's failure to take advantage of the collapse of the Right was paralleled by the failure of his party—the Socialist Revolutionaries. This party, the largest political organization in Russia before the revolution, expanded enormously after the fall of the Tsar. It had long enjoyed the support of the teeming peasant millions, and now that many of these millions were in uniform and had rifles in their hands their political activity had greatly increased. They joined the Socialist Revolutionary party in such numbers that the party was not able to digest the huge mass. Several of its most effective leaders had died shortly before the revolution, leaving Victor Chernov, a theorist and writer rather than a practical politician, to deal with the vital problems of the times. Other Socialist Revolutionary leaders, especially those like Kerensky, who had represented the party in the Duma, became more and more conservative and lost touch with the masses. . . .

The Split in the Ranks of the SR's. While the Socialist Revolutionary leaders for the most part were becoming more conservative, the rank and file were becoming more and more radical. In May, 1917, the SR's held their Third All-Russian Congress, at which, in spite of a strong tendency of the Right faction to secede, Chernov's program was adopted, calling for a just and speedy peace and for a positive socialist policy of labor and agrarian legislation. This evidence that the bulk of the party wanted to follow a progressive policy was lost on the leaders, except Chernov, who before long was forced from power. . . .

The Breakdown of the Army and Navy. To the millions of Russian soldiers, suffering from hunger and cold in the trenches, the Kornilov insurrection added a new and more infuriating grievance. The soldiers had been distrustful of their officers, most of whom had taken no part in the struggle for the overthrow of the Tsar. The men were convinced that the war was an imperialistic struggle for Constantinople and Galicia, and when the July offensive was attempted, it confirmed these beliefs. Now they had seen their highest commanders, who had insistently demanded the death penalty as punishment for desertion and mutiny, rise in rebellion against the revolution. Many of the other officers had sought to aid the Kornilov mutiny and few had taken a stand against it. Moreover, after the rank and file of the army, together with the populace of Petrograd, had suppressed this revolt, it became clear that none of the guilty leaders—to say nothing of the lesser culprits—would pay with his life. . . .

Fraternization with the enemy became common—in part induced by Bolshevik or German propaganda, but often a spontaneous expression of distaste for the business of killing. Any active measures against the enemy were bitterly opposed: when artillerymen, less infected with the mutinous spirit, opened fire on the enemy lines, thus inviting retaliation against the Russian trenches, the Russian infantry cut the telephone wires to the batteries and even beat the gunners if they persisted in firing. Violence against officers increased after the Kornilov affair. Numerous officers were arrested by their men or were forced to resign. In some cases, privates or corporals were elected to replace them. Riots occasionally occurred, in which officers were beaten or killed. Sometimes enlisted men fired into the quarters of their officers at night or threw hand-grenades into the officers' mess. Even the soldiers' committees and the commissars with the troops were not immune from attack if they tried to uphold the authority of the officers.

The Russian navy was an especially radical part of the armed forces. Kronstadt had become a hotbed of revolt early in the revolution and remained so, in spite of all that Kerensky could do. The naval bases at Helsingfors and Sveaborg were also radical. The crews of all the ships of the Baltic fleet were strongly behind the Bolsheviks and would have played a big role in the Kornilov affair if stubborn fighting had developed. The Black Sea fleet, on the other hand, for some time maintained its discipline under Admiral Kolchak, and in the spring of 1917 it even supported the war. But eventually it, too, succumbed to the revolutionary virus. By the middle of June the sailors began disarming their officers. Kolchak threw his sword into the sea rather than give it up and resigned his command in disgust. By October, 1917, the Black Sea fleet was as radical as the Baltic fleet.

The Rising Peasant Movement. In the early days of the revolution the peasants had not taken the law into their own hands, but had apparently decided to wait for the Constituent Assembly to deal with the land problem. In the meantime, Chernov, Minister of Agriculture, took steps to prepare the basis for a future transfer of the land of the landowners to the peasants. But Chernov was forced from office with little to show for his efforts, and the Constituent Assembly was repeatedly postponed. The peasants, whose conviction remained firm that the land should go to him who tilled it, grew weary of waiting. . . .

In the autumn months of 1917 the climax was reached. More and more frequently the peasants marched in a body to the estates of the landowners, broke into the manor houses, and pillaged without mercy. If the gentry submitted without resistance, they were usually permitted to go in peace. The livestock, implements, furniture, and other useful articles, as well as the land, were divided up by the peasants, who then usually burned the manors and other buildings, to make sure that the owners would not return. Often much wanton damage was done: the leaves of fine library books were torn out for cigarette paper, and paintings by famous artists were cut from their frames to make canvas trousers. . . .

The Upsurge of the Workers. The factory workers had been, from the beginning of the revolution, the most radical element in Russia. Repeatedly, in Petrograd, the proletarians had given proof of their readiness to seek an extreme solution of their difficulties. After the frustration of the masses in the July Days, the workers had been somewhat subdued, and their units of Red Guards had been largely disarmed by the government. But their grievances had not been remedied, but rather had become more burdensome as the galloping inflation cut sharply into the buying power of their wages. Food riots grew increasingly frequent.

To make matters worse, after midsummer there were increasingly frequent closings of factories, which threw harassed men out of work. Probably, in most cases, these shutdowns were caused by such unavoidable factors as shortages of fuel or raw materials like steel, rubber, and cotton. But the desperate workers were always prone to think that the closings were lockouts intended to compel the workers to reduce their wage demands, especially as the employers were known to have expressed wrath on this score. The remark allegedly made by Riabushinsky, a great industrialist, rang from one end of Russia to the other: "Perhaps . . . we need the bony hand of hunger, the poverty of the people, which would seize by the throat all these false friends of the people, all those democratic Soviets and committees." Whether it was said or not, it was widely believed, and it infuriated the workers, who needed little to anger them. . . .

The Rising Power of the Bolsheviks. With soldiers, peasants, and workers in a militant frame of mind, the Bolsheviks found themselves in a steadily improving position. They could gain little support among the peasants, but the soldiers, both at the front and in the garrisons in the rear, were turning to them and rejecting less radical advisers. Likewise the workers, who had never believed the charges against Lenin, in the fall of 1917 almost completely gave their allegiance to the Bolsheviks. . . .

Control of the workers and the garrison troops led inevitably to control of the Soviets through their frequent elections. On September 12 the Bolsheviks obtained a majority in the Petrograd Soviet, and on October 8 it elected Trotsky as its president. The Moscow Soviet was won by the Bolsheviks on September 18, and many of the provincial Soviets were coming under their control.

The party of Lenin was strong not only in the two capitals, but also in the Volga towns, the industrial centers of the Urals, the Donets Basin, and in other industrial towns of the Ukraine. Moreover, the Bolsheviks had as allies the Left Socialist Revolutionaries, who had a considerable following in the army and among the peasants. Thus, the Bolsheviks had effective support in many important areas of Russia and need no longer fear that a Red Petrograd would be opposed by the rest of the country.

Lenin's Insistence on an Uprising. Lenin, still in Finland, was immensely cheered by the results of the Kornilov insurrection. In the latter part of September, he wrote a letter to the Central Committee of the Bolshevik party demanding the seizure of power and reviving the slogan "All Power to the Soviets." This letter, however, was promptly rejected by the Central Committee as unrealistic. He followed this with two secret letters to the Central Committee saying that the time was ripe for seizure. His arguments, however, failed to sway the committee. . . .

Another letter, "The Crisis Is Ripe," repeated his earlier arguments that the Bolsheviks now had strong support from the masses and added a new argument: the revolution in Germany, he declared, was fast approaching and would back up the revolt in Russia. To show his sincerity and determination, Lenin offered his resignation to the Central Committee in order that he might have freedom of action. The offer was refused, but Lenin continued to oppose the decision of his party by writing to various local organizations of the Bolsheviks and to the populace to urge support for his program.

One of Lenin's most effective strokes was a pamphlet, *Can the Bolsheviks Hold State Power?* In it he strove to refute the arguments of some of the more moderate Bolsheviks, who held that, even if an insurrection should prove successful, it would not be supported by the rest of the country and in the end would be drowned in a sea of blood. Lenin, however, argued that if a few hundred thousand landowners and Tsarist officials could rule Russia for centuries, the Bolsheviks, who already enjoyed the support of great masses of the people, could hold power. Especially, he stated, when the lowly and the poor began to see that the new Soviet government would suppress the rich and strip them of their wealth, which would be given to the needy poor, then "no power of the capitalists and kulaks . . . can conquer the people's revolution."

Gradually, Lenin's persistent urging won out over the doubts of his fellow Bolsheviks. On October 22, he returned to Petrograd in disguise and on the following day he spoke at a crucial meeting of the Central Committee. His passionate emphasis on the need for an uprising and his reproaches of "indifference" to this question turned the tide in his favor, albeit with difficulty. The vote was ten to two in favor of an insurrection, with Zinoviev and Kamenev opposed. The Central Committee also named a Political Bureau to carry out the preparations for the revolt. . . .

On October 29, Lenin again presented his arguments to an enlarged meeting of the Central Committee. He told the Bolsheviks that there would be either a dictatorship of the Right or the Left, and that the party should not be guided solely by the feelings of the masses, who were inclined to waver from one side to the other. He also expressed faith in the coming German revolution. Once more he won, but again Zinoviev and Kamenev voiced their doubts, which may have been shared by others present. Kamenev then resigned from the Central Committee. Two days later a letter from Zinoviev and Kamenev appeared in Maxim Gorky's *Novaia Zhizn,* announcing that the Bolsheviks were preparing an armed uprising, which the signers felt was a dangerous mistake. Lenin, infuriated, condemned their action as "strike-breaking" and "a crime." He followed this up with a letter to the Central Committee, which met without him on November 2, asking that the two be expelled from the party.

Nevertheless, an effort was made to patch the matter up. Kamenev resigned from the Central Committee, which enjoined the two members to refrain from further public opposition to the policy of the party. Lenin's demand for their expulsion from the party was not dealt with. Lenin seems to have been satisfied with the action taken, for on November 6, when the Central Committee met to prepare for the revolutionary action on the morrow, Kamenev resumed his seat as though he had never resigned. Lenin's policy was about to be applied.

THE OVERTHROW OF THE PROVISIONAL GOVERNMENT

Bolshevik Preparations. The Bolshevik leaders, who, on October 23, had decided to undertake an armed insurrection, at first did little to prepare for it. On October 22, a proposal of the Mensheviks for the formation of a Military Revolutionary Committee to coordinate the defense of Petrograd, chiefly against the advancing Germans, offered a convenient way to organize the uprising. The Military Revolutionary Committee, as it was finally set up by the Petrograd Soviet, became a sort of general staff for the insurrection. Thanks to a boycott of the committee by the moderate socialists, the Bolsheviks completely controlled it. The Left Socialist Revolutionaries and Anarchists in the committee deferred to the Bolsheviks. Thus, the latter, headed by Trotsky, were able freely to prepare the troops of the garrison of Petrograd and of the surrounding towns, to expand and equip the Red Guards, and in other ways to get ready. . . .

The Fortress of Peter and Paul, which sprawled on the river bank across from the Winter Palace, appeared to be an obstacle to Bolshevik success. After many discussions as to how to win control of its neutral garrison, Trotsky, on November 5, casually went to the fortress and, finding a soldiers' meeting in progress, promptly addressed it. The soldiers, who were probably wavering already, needed little urging to join the insurrectionary forces. Thus, one of the government's main strongholds fell without a shot being fired. Moreover, the arsenal of Peter and Paul contained large stocks of rifles, which were promptly turned over to the Red Guards, who were among the most active forces at the disposal of the Military Revolutionary Committee. . . .

The Government Acts. Finally, in a meeting on November 5, the government decided to strike against the Bolshevik menace. The forces of junkers (military cadets) in Petrograd were to be called out to close the Bolshevik newspapers, to arrest the leading Bolsheviks, and to subdue the Military Revolutionary Committee. Reliable troops were to be brought to the capital, including junkers from the school at Oranienbaum, shock troops, and artillery. On November 6, the government forces moved. The junkers seized the printing shop where *Pravda* was published, scattered the type, and confiscated some 8,000 copies. The cruiser *Aurora*, anchored in the Neva near the Winter Palace, was ordered to put to sea for a training cruise. A Woman's Battalion of Death moved into the Winter Palace, the seat of the government, along with some junkers and a few Cossacks. Junkers seized and raised several of the main bridges and occupied important government buildings, including the main telephone and postal building. This show of force, like many of the actions of the Provisional Government, was both ineffectual and late. The reaction was immediate and strong.

The Attack on the Provisional Government. The Military Revolutionary Committee at once counter-attacked. Troops were ordered to retake and guard the printing establishments, which by 11 o'clock were again in Red hands. The orders to the *Aurora* were countermanded, and it again dropped anchor. Sailors from its crew landed and helped the Red Guards seize and lower the bridges. . . .

At night the Red forces moved to attack, quickly overrunning the main railway stations and the remaining bridges. Torpedo boats from the Baltic fleet moved into the Neva to aid in the assault. On the morning of November 7, the State Bank and the main telephone station were taken, with very little bloodshed. The government now held little of the city but the Winter Palace. The vastly superior forces of the attackers and their high discipline had overwhelmed the weak and dispirited defenders. It must be said, however, that the Red forces were poorly led, as for hours they failed to make use of their opportunity to crush the defenders at once. But not even the gift of much precious time could save the government.

Kerensky's Flight. In the interim Kerensky was in the Winter Palace trying to obtain reinforcements. Several regiments of Don Cossacks promised their support, but failed to appear. When Kerensky telephoned them over a secret wire that was still functioning, they repeatedly assured him that they "were getting ready to saddle the horses." But the horses were never saddled. Likewise, Kerensky's own party, the Socialist Revolutionaries, could provide him with no armed forces.

Eventually, therefore, the Premier realized that the government's position was hopeless and decided to flee Petrograd, hoping to bring back troops to retake the capital. One of his aides requisitioned a car belonging to a Secretary of the American Embassy, and thus, flying the American flag, Kerensky escaped through the Bolshevik patrols to go for help.

The Fall of the Winter Palace. . . . The insurgents moved slowly toward the Winter Palace and, early in the evening, summoned it to surrender. Most of the military men there, realizing the hopelessness of the situation, urged acceptance, but the ministers refused to submit. They shut themselves up in the palace, defended by a small force of junkers and the Woman's Battalion of Death. Barricades of firewood were thrown up in the palace square, and the tiny force settled down for a siege. Part of the garrison had already slipped away, and the morale of those that remained was not high. . . .

For the most part the fighting consisted of rather aimless firing, while groups of men filtered in through the innumerable entrances to the palace. At first, the defenders were able to disarm the attackers, but as the latter increased in numbers they succeeded in disarming the garrison.

Finally, the last remnants of junkers sought to stand outside the inner room where the ministers were sitting, but they were quickly ordered to surrender. Antonov, the Red leader, promptly arrested the ministers and sent them off under guard to the Fortress of Peter and Paul. Passing through the infuriated crowd, they were almost lynched, but their guards succeeded in delivering them unharmed. A few days later they were put under house arrest in their homes, and before long they were given their freedom. The revolution was still relatively humane.

There was still opposition to the Bolshevik revolution in Petrograd. The moderate socialists—Mensheviks and Socialist Revolutionaries—resigned from the Congress of Soviets in protest against the overthrow of the government. After vainly trying a protest march, they withdrew to the city Duma, where, with delegates from the Council of the Republic and the old Central Executive Committee, they formed a Committee for the Salvation of the Fatherland and the Revolution. But it could do little but issue angry protests and appeal for support against the lawless action of the Bolsheviks. The new revolutionary regime held Petrograd. . . .

The Revolution in the Rest of Russia. In Moscow, in contrast to Petrograd, there was long and stubborn fighting. . . . In the rest of the country, especially in the main Russian areas, the change in power occurred more easily. Although in some places it took weeks, it was almost bloodless, as there were few to fight for the fallen government. In some of the minority areas, however, more enduring opposition regimes were set up. . . .

The attempt to use the army as a center of opposition failed. The Soviet government proceeded to establish complete control over all the command posts, so that a threat from that direction was no longer possible. Indeed, the army as an organized force was rapidly going out of existence, as a vast flood of deserters moved homeward. Only the Cossacks, the Georgians, and the [Ukrainian] *Rada* remained in defiance of the Soviet authorities. They, indeed, were too weak to be a threat, as they were menaced by attack from the sketchy Soviet military forces. The Soviet government was accepted throughout the rest of the vast territory of Russia, and no effective challenge to its power was visible anywhere in this expanse.

THE FIRST MEASURES OF THE SOVIET GOVERNMENT

First Steps of the New Regime. On November 7, while the fighting
for Petrograd was still going on, Lenin made his first public appearance
before the Petrograd Soviet. To it he proclaimed in triumph the coming
of "the workers' and peasants' revolution" which he had long predicted.
He then sketched the immediate program of the victors: the destruction of
the old governing machine and the creation of a new one, the immediate
ending of the war, and the satisfying of the peasants by a decree wiping
out the property rights of the nobility. Then, turning to the international
scene, he hailed the movement of the workers "which is already beginning
to develop in Italy, England, and Germany," and closed with the cry:
"Long live the world socialist revolution!"

Secession of the Moderates. Lenin did not appear before the Second
Congress of Soviets when it met that evening. As had been expected, it
was predominantly Bolshevik: some 390 out of the total membership of
850 were followers of Lenin, with more than 100 of the Left Socialist Revolutionaries, who were allied with the Bolsheviks. There were not more
than 80 Mensheviks, including members of the Jewish *Bund,* while the pro-
Kerensky Socialist Revolutionaries had a mere 60 delegates. From the
beginning, the moderates refused to accept the revolutionary overturn and
bitterly denounced the insurrection as treason to the revolution. Representatives of the army joined the attack by terming the uprising a betrayal
of the army and a crime against the people. The Mensheviks, the Socialist
Revolutionaries, and the Bund followed these utterances by walking out
of the Congress in protest against the revolt, whose cannon could be heard
in the distance. . . .

Lenin's Proposals. Lenin, who had spent the night resting beside Trotsky, appeared before the Congress of Soviets on November 8. After several
preliminary speeches, Lenin rose, to receive a loud ovation. He then read
a "proclamation to the peoples and the governments of all the fighting
nations." It contained a pledge to abolish secret diplomacy and to publish
immediately the secret treaties with the Allies, as well as a renunciation of
the special privileges granted to Russia. The proclamation went on to
propose an armistice lasting three months, and appealed to the working
people of England, France, and Germany to take "decisive, energetic, and
persistent action" to bring about a successful peace and at the same time to
achieve the liberation of the masses of exploited working people "from
all slavery and exploitation." After a brief discussion the proposal was
adopted with vast enthusiasm: one delegate who ventured to vote against
it felt it safer to drop his opposition. The Congress then sang the *"Inter-
nationale,"* the anthem of international revolutionary socialism.

The next point on the agenda was land for the peasants. A short decree proposed by Lenin abolished private landholding at once and without compensation. Private, state, crown, and church lands were to be turned over to land committees and Soviets of Peasants' Deputies for distribution to the peasants. The rules for the distribution of the land were set forth in an Instruction appended to the decree. The Instruction, which Lenin had obtained from a compilation of peasant resolutions prepared by the Soviet of Peasants' Deputies, provided for a complete ban on private ownership of land, prohibition of the buying and selling of land, and for the use of the land solely by persons who would work it with their own and their families' labor. This measure, which would promote a mass of small peasant farms, was contrary to accepted Marxist views. Hence, there was some objection to it from Bolshevik members of the Congress. Lenin, however, frankly stated that this was a Socialist Revolutionary proposal which he felt it necessary to adopt in order to win the support of the peasant masses. On this basis, the Congress approved it.

The Formation of the Soviet Government. While the above measures were readily approved, it proved more difficult to form the revolutionary government. In spite of the secession of the moderate socialists and their opposition to the revolutionary overturn, the Left Socialist Revolutionaries and the Menshevik Internationalists were extremely eager to have a coalition of all socialist parties instead of a purely Leftist government. Likewise *Vikzhel,* the railway workers' union, insisted on a coalition, threatening to stop all rail traffic unless agreement were reached. The demand for an all socialist government was also warmly endorsed by many of the Bolsheviks. Consequently, in spite of the scorn of Lenin and Trotsky for the moderates, it was necessary to try to form a coalition. But while this was being attempted a government was needed, and so an all-Bolshevik cabinet was set up. Several posts were offered to the Left Socialist Revolutionaries, but they refused to enter the government. So the Council of People's Commissars was approved, with Lenin as President, Trotsky as Commissar for Foreign Affairs, and Rykov as Commissar for Internal Affairs. Most of the other appointees were men who were not well known; among them was Joseph Stalin, Commissar for Nationalities.

A Coalition Government? The possibilities of a coalition regime were explored at length at a conference that met on November 11, 1917. The negotiations lasted for some time, but because of the stiff demands of the moderate socialists they produced no result. At first the socialists insisted that the Military Revolutionary Committee be dissolved and that Lenin and Trotsky be excluded from the government. Later, after the Bolsheviks had consolidated their power in both Moscow and Petrograd, there was less pressure for a coalition and Lenin was able to overcome the moderate Bolsheviks. Nevertheless, on November 17, five of the Bolsheviks of the Central Committee—among them Zinoviev, Kamenev, and Rykov—resigned in protest against the rejection of a coalition. There were also resignations from the cabinet over the same issue.

Lenin was not dismayed by this revolt within his party. He answered it with a furious manifesto from the Central Committee upholding his course and terming the dissenters "waverers and doubters." Such men counted for little, he said, when the Soviet government was supported by "millions of workers in the towns, soldiers in the trenches, peasants in the villages, ready to achieve at any cost the victory of peace and the victory of socialism." This ended the revolt.

None the less, in November the Bolsheviks reached an understanding with the Left Socialist Revolutionaries, and 108 delegates from the Peasant Congress were added to the Soviet Executive Committee. On December 22, the Left Socialist Revolutionaries accepted three posts in the Council of People's Commissars. Thus, a coalition of a sort was finally established, although not so broad in its makeup as the one that had been demanded.

Miscellaneous Actions of the Soviet Government. From the first days of its existence, the new government wrestled with a whole series of problems and wrote a remarkable record of achievements—many of which, it must be said, existed only on paper. Almost immediately there was a sweeping strike of government workers, who refused to recognize the new order. For a regime without a shred of experience in governing this proved most difficult, especially as the State Bank was among the striking institutions. For days the government could obtain no funds, and only the use of force and the opening of the vaults made money available to the Bolshevik rulers of Russia. On December 27, all banks were nationalized and occupied by forces of troops, while the vaults and safe deposit boxes were opened by a commissar. Eventually, the funds of the striking civil servants ran out and they returned to duty in January, 1918.

Economic Measures. During the first few months, decrees flowed forth in a rapid stream. One of the first was a decree directed to the working people, informing them that economic power had been transferred to them. The nationalization of banks was next, followed by a ban on dividends and securities. On February 10, 1918, a decree annulled all debts of the Russian government, including foreign debts. Contrary to Bolshevik doctrine, Lenin was in no hurry to nationalize industry and even wanted the managerial personnel to continue to work on fairly generous terms. Nevertheless, "workers' control" meant supervision and much outright interference by the workers, so that the conditions in the factories became chaotic. When this led to the shutting down of enterprises, the Supreme Economic Council, created on December 15, had the power to nationalize them.

There was a general levelling down of the standard of living—in part by the ever rising inflation, and in part by decree: members of the Council of Commissars were restricted to 500 rubles per month, with allowances for dependents, and to one room for each member of the family. The ending of private ownership of multiple dwellings was another levelling measure: the city Soviets took them over and sought to equalize the housing facilities, often moving families from the slums into the half-empty apartments of wealthy citizens. The food situation proved to be the most insoluble problem. Try as they would, the Soviet authorities could not obtain more bread for the cities, and the amounts issued on rations fell drastically. To the hungry workers there was left only the consolation that the hated "bourgeois" were faring even worse than they.

Political and Social Legislation. Important political and social decrees were also issued during the first months. To cope with secret enemies of the regime, drunken mobs that invaded mansions in search of liquor, and food speculators, on December 20 Felix Dzerzhinsky, a fanatical Polish Communist, became head of the All-Russian Extraordinary Commission, whose name, abbreviated to *Cheka,* became dreaded throughout Russia. A system of revolutionary tribunals was set up to deal with political cases, while new, informal "people's courts" dispensed ordinary justice by common sense rather than law books. The Soviet legislators also found time to reform the Russian alphabet and the calendar. Sweeping new laws made marriage and divorce equally easy to obtain and legalized all children, whether born of registered or informal unions. The full legal equality of men and women was also proclaimed.

The Church and the Revolution. . . . Many of the measures of the new regime angered the churchmen, who hoped ardently for its overthrow, and on February 1, 1918, the Patriarch issued a pastoral letter to the people. It strongly indicted the Soviet leaders for having caused violence and outrages. "Your acts are not merely cruel, they are the works of Satan, for which you will burn in hell fire in the life hereafter. . . ." To this he added his anathema. To the believers, he issued a call to organize in defense of the church, for "the gates of Hell shall not prevail against it."

This, however, did not deter the Soviet authorities, who on February 5, 1918, published a law by which "the church was separated from the state, and the school from the church." Religion was made a private matter for the citizens, and no religious functions or ceremonies were permitted in any institution of government, whether national or local. Religious teaching was barred from all schools, public and private alike. Even the theological schools were ordered closed. The property of churches and religious societies was nationalized, although church buildings might be turned over to congregations of believers for free use for public worship.

This measure was strongly opposed by the leaders of the Orthodox church, but, in spite of their angry protests, the government put it into effect. There were some demonstrations in opposition to it, and occasional riots, at times accompanied by bloodshed. But the government persisted in its purpose. Perhaps the fact that the churches remained open and no attempt was made to prevent divine worship explains why this legislation, which was unfavorable to the Russian church, did not produce any effective explosions of popular wrath.

The Problem of the Constituent Assembly. One of the worst dilemmas for the Bolsheviks was caused by the Constituent Assembly. The Provisional Government had promised to convene this body speedily, but nothing was done about it for months. Finally, the government set November 25 as the date for the elections. Thus, when the Bolsheviks took power they were in a quandary. Before they had seized power, one of their effective slogans had been for "Speedy Convocation of the Constituent Assembly!" But, while they were on record as wanting it to meet soon, Lenin and the other Bolsheviks had reason to believe that vast numbers of peasants as usual would vote for the Socialist Revolutionaries. It seemed likely that the new Soviet government would be challenged by a body in which the Bolsheviks would be only a minority. Lenin firmly held that the Soviets, which excluded the propertied classes, were a higher form of democracy than a body elected by universal suffrage. His solution was to postpone the elections, but it was decided to hold them and to convene the Assembly, which should, however, be dissolved if it proved troublesome.

The Result of the Elections. Although the Bolsheviks made no effort to dominate the elections, which began on November 25, the Cadet party was especially handicapped by the fact that many of their leaders were in hiding or in prison, and their newspapers were largely suppressed. The voting gave the Bolsheviks only 175 of the 707 elected members of the Constituent Assembly. The SR's (Socialist Revolutionaries) had 410—a substantial majority—and most of the other delegates were anti-Bolshevik. Yet the figures do not tell the whole story. The Bolsheviks were now in alliance with the Left SR's, who had had a majority of the Peasant Congress. Although the Left SR's had only 40 out of the 410 SR delegates, it seems probable that their following in the country was far stronger than their representation in the Constituent Assembly.

Above all, the realities of power favored the Bolsheviks. They had full majorities in Petrograd and Moscow and their strength was great in other industrial centers. Their government had the positions of power in the cities and in the army, while the opposition's strength lay chiefly in the unorganized millions of peasants. Moreover, the Bolsheviks were united and determined, with a clearcut program which seemed to meet the needs of the people. The opposition was unorganized and lacked driving force. Also, it was unable to offer an alternative to the program that the Bolsheviks were already carrying out.

The Attitude of the Bolsheviks. The Bolsheviks, realizing that the Constituent Assembly would become the focal center for all anti-Bolshevik elements, whether socialist or upper class, were determined not to permit it to play the counter-revolutionary role that the French National Assembly had played in 1848. On December 11, 1917, the Soviet government forcibly prevented an attempt of former ministers of the Provisional Government to convene the Assembly ahead of time. Shortly thereafter, Lenin wrote his "Theses on the Constituent Assembly," published in *Pravda* on December 26, 1917. Here he stated that a Constituent Assembly had been highly desirable after the fall of the Tsar, when the revolution was still in its moderate or "bourgeois" stage. Now, however, the revolution was in its socialist stage, with the Bolsheviks establishing the dictatorship of the proletariat and its allies, the poorer peasantry. As for the bourgeoisie, they were in open counter-revolution. Hence, any attempt to treat the Constituent Assembly from a purely theoretical, legalistic point of view was treason to the proletariat. Either the Assembly would declare its acceptance of the Soviet government and its program, or else the crisis that would result "can be solved only by revolutionary means."

In order to cut the ground from beneath the feet of the Constituent Assembly, it was decided to have the Third Congress of Soviets meet three days after the opening of the Assembly, and the Congress of Peasant Deputies a few days later. On January 16, the Central Executive Committee drafted a Declaration of Rights of the Toiling and Exploited People, for adoption by the Assembly. It opened with a declaration that Russia was a republic of Soviets, to which all power belonged, and a statement that it was a "free union of free nations, as a federation of national Soviet republics." There followed a long pronouncement for the Constituent Assembly to make, upholding Soviet policy and legislation. Finally, two paragraphs stated that, as the Constituent Assembly had been elected on the basis of party lists compiled before the changed situation after the fall of the Provisional Government, "it would be basically incorrect to set itself up against the Soviet power. . . ." Furthermore, the Assembly, supporting the Soviet regime, would recognize that its role was merely to be "the general working out of the fundamental principles of the socialist reconstruction of society."

The Dissolution of the Constituent Assembly. Lenin and his followers, then, had already made up their minds to deal rigorously with the Constituent Assembly unless it proved to be tame and toothless. Nevertheless, realizing that this body, advocated for decades by Russian liberals and revolutionaries, might enjoy immense prestige in the eyes of the populace, they did not want to shock public opinion by unnecessarily brutal treatment of it. It was permitted to meet, but the vicinity of the Tavrida Palace was surrounded by heavily armed troops, and the galleries were crowded with soldiers and sailors with rifles, pistols, and cartridge belts. For their part, the SR's had sought the support of some regiments, but as they refused to let them come out under arms, even those soldiers who sympathized with the moderates refused their appeal. A demonstration of civilian sympa-

thizers with the Assembly—largely intellectuals and other white-collar workers—occurred, but it met the well-armed troops and was dispersed by gunfire, with some loss of life.

When the meeting opened, Sverdlov, a veteran Bolshevik, seized temporary control in order to read the Declaration of the Rights of the Toiling
and Exploited People. After briefly urging the Assembly to adopt it, he
withdrew to his seat. The big bloc of SR's now took over, electing Chernov
as permanent chairman, in spite of Bolshevik warnings that they should
support the program of active socialism. The session dragged on for almost twelve hours. At midnight the crucial vote was taken on the Bolshevik
declaration, which lost, 237 to 138. Later, the Bolsheviks withdrew from
the meeting, because of its "counter-revolutionary majority." The Left SR's
withdrew an hour later. Not long before daybreak the sailor in command
of the guard, apparently under orders from Lenin, asked that the meeting
adjourn "because the guard is tired." There was a brief flurry of activity,
during which a resolution on land and an appeal to the Allies for peace
were read and declared approved. Neither of these differed greatly from
the measures taken by the Second Congress of Soviets after the fall of the
Kerensky government. Then, a little before five in the morning, the meeting adjourned until late afternoon.

The Constituent Assembly never met again. The Central Executive
Committee, after a strong speech by Lenin, declared that it was dissolved,
and an armed guard at the doors prevented it from reconvening. There
was scarcely any protest against the dissolution: The Constituent Assembly
had given no heroic leadership to the people and had failed to gain effective
support. Probably if it had been convened six months before, the result
would have been far different.

Chapter 8

THE CRUSHING OF OPPOSITION

---

*In the months following the Bolshevik revolution, its leaders antici-
pated that the revolt in Russia would unleash a socialist revolution in the
West. Pending this anticipated revolution, Lenin insisted that the government come to terms with the Germans. After some serious indecision and
wrangling in the Party—which touched off a German military attack—
Lenin finally won out and the Treaty of Brest-Litovsk was signed on March
3, 1918. Under this treaty, Russia lost more than 1¼ million square miles
of territory containing a population of 62 millions, half of her industrial
plants, and a third of her best farm area. Three days later, Lenin stated:*

The revolution will not come as quickly as we expected. History has proved
this, and we must be able to take this as a fact, we must be able to reckon with
the fact that the world Socialist revolution cannot begin so easily in the advanced
countries as the revolution began in Russia—the land of Nicholas and Rasputin,
the land in which the overwhelming majority of the population was quite indifferent to the conditions of life of the people in the outlying regions. In such
a country it was quite easy to start a revolution, as easy as lifting a feather.

*Thereafter, however, Lenin alternated between optimism and pessimism on
the prospects of revolution in the West.*

*The "peace" of Brest-Litovsk set off a chain of developments that al-
most encompassed the destruction of Bolshevik power. During the next
few years the Soviets were engaged in civil war with forces ranging from
the monarchist-restorationists at the extreme right to the left Social Revolutionaries. Many of these forces had the support—financial and otherwise
—of Allied powers. And some of these powers, including Japan, Great
Britain, France, and the United States sent military forces into Russia. The
justification was the necessity of re-establishing an Eastern front in the
desperate war against Germany, but the record is clear that other considerations—territorial spoils, fear of revolution, or detestation of the Bolsheviks—also played a part.*

*Of course, the effort to destroy the Bolshevik régime was never massive
and coordinated, and the Americans, particularly, did much to balk annex-*

227

ationist ambitions. The consequences, however, were to leave a residue of great bitterness in the U.S.S.R. against the interventionist powers and create an encirclement psychosis which, whatever its uses for propaganda purposes, also was grounded in history.

During the period of civil war and intervention—which endured into 1922—the Bolsheviks outlawed all opposition parties (socialist as well as nonsocialist) and imposed a ban on factions within the Communist Party itself. Why? Marxian theory had not suggested that the dictatorship of the proletariat might be equated with the rule of one socialist party. And, according to Lenin, the dictatorship of the proletariat was to bring with it "a widening of the practical utilization of democracy by those oppressed by capitalism, by the laboring classes, as has never yet been seen in the whole world."

Many explanations have been offered for the failure of proletarian "democracy." One explanation placed responsibility on the internal and external foes of Bolshevism: ". . . Soviet 'totalitarianism' was not inevitable nor necessarily implicit in the Bolshevism of 1917-18 but was forced upon it, with death as the alternative, by the decisions of Russian democrats and the Western Democracies." Another, proffered by W. W. Rostow, suggested that "the maintenance of the internal power machine has had a clear priority over any other goal of Soviet policy." Another may be inferred from Merle Fainsod's Bolshevism Before 1917, in which he holds that "the early organizational history of Bolshevism . . . implanted the germinating conception of the monolithic and totalitarian party."

The democratic failure has been explained, additionally, for example, by the weakness and backwardness of the Russian economy and proletariat, and the basic incompatibility between large-scale economic planning and any form of democracy. Recently, in this latter vein, R. N. Carew Hunt wrote: "What Lenin early came to see was that a nation-wide planned economy was incompatible with the parliamentary democracy of the West. If production is to be planned, some body of persons must do the planning, and this becomes impossible if the plan is liable to be reversed at any moment by a vote in a popular assembly." And, finally, there are the distinctive contributions made to this discussion in the excerpts from the writings of Isaac Deutscher and Leonard Schapiro in these pages.

Varied explanations of the disparity between Marxist theory and Soviet practice have been alluded to in the hope that they will induce an appreciation of the complexities of judgment involved and encourage the reader to explore the problem further. It may be suggested, too, that important implications extending beyond the U.S.S.R. may ensue from the acceptance of one or another explanation.

DEFEAT IN VICTORY

ISAAC DEUTSCHER*

The years of world war, revolution, civil war, and intervention had resulted in the utter ruin of Russia's economy and the disintegration of her social fabric. From a ruined economy the Bolsheviks had had to wrest the means of civil war. In 1919, the Red Army had already used up all stocks of munitions and other supplies. The industries under Soviet control could not replace them by more than a fraction. Normally southern Russia supplied fuel, iron, steel, and raw materials to the industries of central and northern Russia. But southern Russia, occupied first by the Germans and then by Denikin, was only intermittently and during brief spells under Soviet control. When at last, at the end of 1919, the Bolsheviks returned there for good, they found that the coal-mines of the Donets valley were flooded and the other industries destroyed. Deprived of fuel and raw materials, the industrial centres of the rest of the country were paralysed. Even towards the end of 1920, the coal-mines produced less than one-tenth and the iron- and steel-works less than one-twentieth of their pre-war output. The production of consumer goods was about one-quarter of normal. The disaster was made even worse by the destruction of transport. All over the country railway tracks and bridges had been blown up. Rolling stock had not been renewed, and it had only rarely been kept in proper repair, since 1914. Inexorably transport was coming to a standstill. (This, incidentally, was one of the contributory causes of the Red Army's defeat in Poland. The Soviets had enlisted five million men, but of these less than 300,000 were actually engaged in the last stages of the Polish campaign. As the armies rolled onward, the railways were less and less capable of carrying reinforcements and supplies over the lengthening distances.) Farming, too, was ruined. For six years the peasants had not been able to renew their equipment. Retreating and advancing armies trampled their fields and requisitioned their horses. However, because of its technically primitive character, farming was more resilient than industry. The muzhik worked with the wooden *sokha,* which he was able to make or repair by himself.

The Bolsheviks strove to exercise the strictest control over scarce resources; and out of this striving grew their War Communism. They nationalized all industry. They prohibited private trade. They dispatched

---

* Author of *Stalin: A Political Biography; Soviet Trade Unions;* and *Russia in Transition.* This selection is from chapter XIV of *The Prophet Armed* (New York: Oxford University Press, Inc., 1954). Reprinted by permission of the publisher.

workers' detachments to the countryside to requisition food for the army and the town-dwellers. The government was incapable of collecting normal taxes; it possessed no machinery for doing so. To cover government expenses, the printing-presses produced banknotes day and night. Money became so worthless that wages and salaries had to be paid in kind. The meagre food ration formed the basic wage. The worker was also paid with part of his own produce, a pair of shoes or a few pieces of clothing, which he usually bartered away for food.

This set of desperate shifts and expedients looked to the party like an unexpectedly rapid realization of its own programme. Socialization of industry would have been carried out more slowly and cautiously if there had been no civil war; but it was, in any case, one of the major purposes of the revolution. The requisitioning of food, the prohibition of private trade, the payment of wages in kind, the insignificance of money, the government's aspiration to control the economic resources of the nation, all this looked, superficially, like the abolition of that market economy which was the breeding-ground of capitalism. The fully grown Communist economy about which Marxist text-books had speculated, was to have been a natural economy, in which socially planned production and distribution should take the place of production for the market and of distribution through the medium of money. The Bolshevik was therefore inclined to see the essential features of fully fledged communism embodied in the war economy of 1919-20. He was confirmed in this inclination by the stern egalitarianism which his party preached and practised and which gave to war communism a romantic and heroic aspect.

In truth, war communism was a tragic travesty of the Marxist vision of the society of the future. That society was to have as its background highly developed and organized productive resources and a superabundance of goods and services. It was to organize and develop the social wealth which capitalism at its best produced only fitfully and could not rationally control, distribute, and promote. Communism was to abolish economic inequality once for all by levelling up the standards of living. War communism had, on the contrary, resulted from social disintegration, from the destruction and disorganization of productive resources, from an unparalleled scarcity of goods and services. It did indeed try to abolish inequality; but of necessity it did so by levelling down the standards of living and making poverty universal.[1]

The system could not work for long. The requisitioning of food and the prohibition of private trade for the time being helped the government to tide over the direst emergencies. But in the longer run these policies aggravated and accelerated the shrinkage and disintegration of the economy. The peasant began to till only as much of his land as was necessary to keep

---

[1] The reader will find a detailed and instructive account of war communism in E. H. Carr, *The Bolshevik Revolution*, vol. ii.

his family alive. He refused to produce the surplus for which the requisitioning squads were on the look-out. When the countryside refuses to produce food for the town, even the rudiments of urban civilization go to pieces. The cities of Russia became depopulated. Workers went to the countryside to escape famine. Those who stayed behind fainted at the factory benches, produced very little, and often stole what they produced to barter it for food. The old, normal market had indeed been abolished. But its bastard, the black market, despoiled the country, revengefully perverting and degrading human relations. This could go on for another year or so; but, inevitably the end would be the breakdown of all government and the dissolution of society. . . .

Matters came to a head on 12 January 1920, when Lenin and Trotsky appeared before the Bolshevik leaders of the trade unions and urged them to accept militarization. Trotsky defended his own record. If his Commissariat, he said, had "pillaged" the country and exacted severe discipline. it had done so to win the war. It was a disgrace and a "sin against the spirit of the revolution" that this should now be held against him, and that the working class should be incited against the army. His opponents were complacent about the country's economic condition. The newspapers concealed the real state of affairs. "It is necessary to state openly and frankly in the hearing of the whole country, that our economic condition is a hundred times worse than our military situation ever was. . . . Just as we once issued the order 'Proletarians, to horse!', so now we must raise the cry 'Proletarians, back to the factory bench! Proletarians, back to production!' " [2] The nation's labour force continued to shrink and degenerate. It could not be saved, reconstituted, and rehabilitated without the application of coercive measures. Lenin spoke in the same vein. Yet the conference almost unanimously rejected the resolution which he and Trotsky jointly submitted. Of more than three score Bolshevik leaders only two men voted for it. Never before had Trotsky or Lenin met with so striking a rebuff.

Trotsky's strictures on the complacency of his critics were not unjustified. The critics did not and could not propose any practical alternative. They, too, clung to war communism and disavowed only the conclusion Trotsky had drawn from it. He had little difficulty therefore in exposing their inconsistency. Yet there was a certain realism and valuable scruple in their very lack of consistency. Trotsky's opponents refused to believe that the wheels of the economy could be set in motion by word of military command, and they were convinced that it was wrong for a workers' state to act as a press gang towards its own working class.[3] . . . They argued that compulsory labour was inefficient. "You cannot build a planned economy,"

[2] Trotsky, *Sochinenya*, vol. XV, pp. 27-52.
[3] This controversy filled the pages of *Ekonomicheskaya Zhizn* and *Pravda* throughout January 1920.

exclaimed Abramovich, the Menshevik, "in the way the Pharaohs built their pyramids." [4] Abramovich thus coined the phrase, which years later Trotsky was to repeat against Stalin. . . .

For a time the Polish war blunted the edge of this controversy. Peril from without once again induced people to accept without murmur policies which, before, had aroused their intense resentment. At the height of the war, Trotsky, surrounded by a team of technicians, made a determined effort to set the railways in motion. By this time the stock of locomotives had been almost entirely wasted. Engineers forecast the exact date—only a few months ahead—when not a single railway in Russia would be working. Trotsky placed the railway men and the personnel of the repair workshops under martial law; and he organized systematic and rapid rehabilitation of the rolling stock. He went into the repair workshops to tell the workers that the country was paying for their slackness in blood: the paralysis of transport had encouraged the Poles to attack. "The situation of the worker," he declared, "is grievous in every respect . . . it is worse than ever. I would deceive you if I were to say that it will be better to-morrow. No, ahead of us are months of heavy struggle until we can lift our country out of this terrible misery and utter exhaustion, until we can stop weighing our bread ration on the chemist's scales." [5] When the railwaymen's trade union raised objections to his action, he dismissed its leaders and appointed others who were willing to do his bidding. He repeated this procedure in unions of other transport workers. Early in September he formed the *Tsektran*, the Central Transport Commission, through which he brought the whole field of transport under his control. The Politbureau backed him to the hilt as it had promised. To observe electoral rights and voting procedures in the unions seemed at that moment as irrelevant as it might seem in a city stricken with pestilence. He produced results and surpassed expectations: the railways were rehabilitated well ahead of schedule—"the blood circulation of the economic organism was revived"—and he was acclaimed for the feat.[6]

But no sooner had the Polish war been concluded than the grievances and dissensions exploded anew and with greater force than before. He himself provoked the explosion. Flushed with success, he threatened to "shake up" various trade unions as he had "shaken up" those of the transport workers. He threatened, that is, to dismiss the elected leaders of the unions and to replace them by nominees who would place the nation's economic interest above the sectional interests of the workers. He grossly overstepped the mark. Lenin now bluntly dissociated himself from Trotsky and per-

---

[4] *Tretii Vserossiskii Syezd Profsoyuzov*, p. 97.

[5] See his speech at the Muromsk workshops of 21 June 1920 in *Sochinenya*, vol. xv, p. 368.

[6] For the famous Order no. 1042 concerning the railways see op. cit., pp. 345-7. Later in the year Trotsky was placed at the head of special commissions which took emergency action to rehabilitate the industries of the Donets valley and of the Urals.

suaded the Central Committee to do likewise. The Committee openly called the party to resist energetically "militarized and bureaucratic forms of work": and it castigated that "degenerated centralism" which rode roughshod over the workers' elected representatives. It called on the party to re-establish proletarian democracy in the trade unions and to subordinate all other considerations to this task.[7] A special commission was formed to watch that these decisions were carried out. Zinoviev presided over it, and, although Trotsky sat on it, nearly all its members were his opponents.[7] . . .

The deeper ill which afflicted the whole system of government, and of which this tug-of-war was merely a symptom, lay in the frustration of the popular hopes aroused by the revolution. For the first time since 1917 the bulk of the working class, not to speak of the peasantry, unmistakably turned against the Bolsheviks. A sense of isolation began to haunt the ruling group. To be sure, the working class had not come to regret the revolution. It went on to identify itself with it; and it received with intense hostility any openly counter-revolutionary agitation. "October" had so deeply sunk into the popular mind that Mensheviks and Social Revolutionaries now had to preface their criticisms of the government with an explicit acceptance of the "achievements of October." Yet the opposition to current Bolshevik policies was just as intense and widespread. The Mensheviks and Social Revolutionaries, who in the course of three years had been completely eclipsed and had hardly dared to raise their heads, were now regaining some popular favour. People listened even more sympathetically to anarchist agitators violently denouncing the Bolshevik régime. If the Bolsheviks had now permitted free elections to the Soviets, they would almost certainly have been swept from power.[8]

The Bolsheviks were firmly resolved not to let things come to that pass. It would be wrong to maintain that they clung to power for its own sake. The party as a whole was still animated by that revolutionary idealism of which it had given such abundant proof in its underground struggle and in the civil war. It clung to power because it identified the fate of the republic with its own fate and saw in itself the only force capable of safeguarding the revolution. It was lucky for the revolution—and it was also its misfortune—that in this belief the Bolsheviks were profoundly justified. The revolution would hardly have survived without a party as fanatically devoted to it as the Bolsheviks were. But had there existed another party equally devoted and equally vigorous in action, that party might, in con-

---

[7] See the report of the Central Committee in *Izvestya Tsentralnovo Komiteta RKP*, no. 26, 1920, and G. Zinoviev, *Sochinenya*, vol. vi, pp. 600 ff.

[8] Many Bolshevik leaders explicitly or implicitly admitted this. See Lenin, *Sochinenya*, vol. xxxii, pp. 160, 176, 230 and *passim;* Zinoviev in *Desyatyi Syezd RKP*, p. 190. In a private letter to Lunacharsky (of 14 April 1926) Trotsky describes the "menacing discontent" of the working class as the background to the controversy of 1920-1. *The Trotsky Archives.*

sequence of an election, have displaced Lenin's government without con-
vulsing the young state. No such party existed. The return of Mensheviks
and Social Revolutionaries would have entailed the undoing of the October
Revolution. At the very least it would have encouraged the White Guards
to try their luck once again and rise in arms. From sheer self-preservation
as well as from broader motives the Bolsheviks could not even contemplate
such a prospect. They could not accept it as a requirement of democracy
that they should, by retreating, plunge the country into a new series of civil
wars just after one series had been concluded.

Nor was it by any means likely that a free election to the Soviets would
return any clear-cut majority. Those who had supported Kerensky in 1917
had not really recovered from their eclipse. Anarchists and anarcho-
syndicalists, preaching a "Third Revolution," seemed far more popular
among the working class. But they gave no effective focus to the opposition;
and they were in no sense pretenders to office. Strong in criticism, they
possessed no positive political programme, no serious organization, national
or even local, no real desire to rule a vast country. In their ranks honest
revolutionaries, cranks, and plain bandits rubbed shoulders. The Bolshevik
régime could be succeeded only by utter confusion followed by open counter-
revolution. Lenin's party refused to allow the famished and emotionally
unhinged country to vote their party out of power and itself into a bloody
chaos.

For this strange sequel to their victory the Bolsheviks were mentally
quite unprepared. They had always tacitly assumed that the majority of
the working class, having backed them in the revolution, would go on to
support them unswervingly until they had carried out the full programme
of socialism. Naïve as the assumption was, it sprang from the notion that
socialism was the proletarian idea *par excellence* and that the proletariat,
having once adhered to it, would not abandon it. That notion had under-
lain the reasoning of all European schools of Socialist thought. In the vast
political literature produced by those schools the question of what Socialists
in office should do if they lost the confidence of the workers had hardly ever
been pondered. It had never occurred to Marxists to reflect whether it was
possible or admissible to try to establish socialism regardless of the will of
the working class. They simply took that will for granted. For the same
reason it had seemed to the Bolsheviks as clear as daylight that the proletarian dictatorship and proletarian (or Soviet) democracy were only two
complementary and inseparable aspects of the same thing: the dictatorship
was there to suppress the resistance of the propertied classes; and it derived
its strength and historic legitimacy from the freely and democratically expressed opinion of the working classes. Now a conflict arose between the
two aspects of the Soviet system. If the working classes were to be allowed
to speak and vote freely they would destroy the dictatorship. If the dictatorship, on the other hand, frankly abolished proletarian democracy it

would deprive itself of historic legitimacy, even in its own eyes. It would cease to be a proletarian dictatorship in the strict sense. Its use of that title would henceforth be based on the claim that it pursued a policy with which the working class, in its own interest, ought and eventually must identify itself, but with which it did not as yet identify itself. The dictatorship would then at best represent the idea of the class, not the class itself.

The revolution had now reached that cross-roads, well known to Machiavelli, at which it found it difficult or impossible to fix the people in their revolutionary persuasion and was driven "to take such measures that, when they believed no longer, it might be possible to make them believe by force." For the Bolshevik party this involved a conflict of loyalties, which was in some respects deeper than any it had known so far, a conflict bearing the seeds of all the turbulent controversies and sombre purges of the next decades.

At this cross-roads Bolshevism suffered a moral agony the like of which is hardly to be found in the history of less intense and impassioned movements. Later Lenin recalled the "fever" and "mortal illness" which consumed the party in the winter of 1920-1, during the tumultuous debate over the place of the trade unions in the state. This was an important yet only a secondary matter. It could not be settled before an answer had been given to the fundamental question concerning the very nature of the state. The party was wholly absorbed in the controversy over the secondary issue, because it was not altogether clearly aware of the primary question and was afraid to formulate it frankly in its own mind. But as the protagonists went on arguing they struck the great underlying issue again and again and were compelled to define their attitudes.

It is not necessary here to go into the involved and somewhat technical differences over the trade unions, although the fact that the drama of the revolution revealed itself in a seemingly dry economic argument significantly corresponded to the spirit of the age.[9] Suffice it to say that, broadly speaking, three attitudes crystallized. The faction led by Trotsky (and later by Trotsky and Bukharin) wanted the trade unions to be deprived of their autonomy and absorbed into the machinery of government. This was the final conclusion which Trotsky drew from his conflicts with the trade unions. Under the new dispensation, the leaders of the unions would, as servants of the state, speak for the state to the workers rather than for the workers to the state. They would raise the productivity and maintain the discipline of labour; they would train workers for industrial management; and they would participate in the direction of the country's economy.

At the other extreme the Workers' Opposition, led by Shlyapnikov and Kollontai, protested against the government's and the party's tutelage over the unions. They denounced Trotsky and Lenin as militarizers of

[9] A detailed account of the debate can be found in Deutscher, *Soviet Trade Unions* (*Their place in Soviet labour policy*), pp. 42-59.

labour and promoters of inequality. In quasi-syndicalist fashion they demanded that trade unions, factory committees, and a National Producers' Congress should assume control over the entire economy. While Trotsky argued that the trade unions could not in logic defend the workers against the workers' state, Shlyapnikov and Kollontai already branded the Soviet state as the rampart of a new privileged bureaucracy.

Between these two extremes, Lenin, Zinoviev, and Kamenev spoke for the main body of Bolshevik opinion and tried to strike a balance. They, too, insisted that it was the duty of the trade unions to restrain the workers and to cultivate in them a sense of responsibility for the state and the nationalized economy. They emphasized the party's right to control the unions. But they also wished to preserve them as autonomous mass organizations, capable of exerting pressure on government and industrial management.

Implied in these attitudes were different conceptions of state and society. The Workers' Opposition and the so-called *Decemists* (the Group of Democratic Centralism) were the stalwart defenders of "proletarian democracy" *vis-à-vis* the dictatorship. They were the first Bolshevik dissenters to protest against the method of government designed "to make the people believe by force." They implored the party to "trust its fate" to the working class which had raised it to power. They spoke the language which the whole party had spoken in 1917. They were the real Levellers of this revolution, its high-minded, Utopian dreamers. The party could not listen to them if it was not prepared to commit noble yet unpardonable suicide. It could not trust its own and the republic's fate to a working class whittled down, exhausted, and demoralized by civil war, famine, and the black market. The quixotic spirit of the Workers' Opposition was apparent in its economic demands. The Opposition clamoured for the immediate satisfaction of the workers' needs, for equal wages and rewards for all, for the supply, without payment, of food, clothing, and lodging to workers, for free medical attention, free travelling facilities, and free education.[10] They wanted to see fulfilled nothing less than the programme of full communism, which was theoretically designed for an economy of great plenty. They did not even try to say how the government of the day could meet their demands. They urged the party to place industry, or what was left of it, once again under the control of those factory committees which had shown soon after the October Revolution that they could merely dissipate and squander the nation's wealth. It was a sad omen that the people enveloped in such fumes of fancy were almost the only ones to advocate a full revival of proletarian democracy.

Against them, Trotsky prompted the party to cease for the time being the advocacy and practice of proletarian democracy and instead to con-

[10] *Desyatyi Syezd RKP*, p. 363; A. M. Kollontai, *The Workers' Opposition in Russia.*

centrate on building up a Producers' Democracy. The party, to put it more plainly, was to deny the workers their political rights and compensate them by giving them scope and managerial responsibility in economic reconstruction. At the tenth congress (March 1921), when this controversy reached its culmination, Trotsky argued:

> The Workers' Opposition has come out with dangerous slogans. They have made a fetish of democratic principles. They have placed the workers' right to elect representatives above the party, as it were, as if the party were not entitled to assert its dictatorship even if that dictatorship temporarily clashed with the passing moods of the workers' democracy. . . . It is necessary to create among us the awareness of the revolutionary historical birthright of the party. The party is obliged to maintain its dictatorship, regardless of temporary wavering in the spontaneous moods of the masses, regardless of the temporary vacillations even in the working class. This awareness is for us the indispensable unifying element. The dictatorship does not base itself at every given moment on the formal principle of a workers' democracy, although the workers' democracy is, of course, the only method by which the masses can be drawn more and more into political life.[11]

The days had long passed when Trotsky argued that the Soviet system of government was superior to bourgeois parliamentarianism because under it the electors enjoyed, among other things, the right to re-elect their representatives at any time and not merely at regular intervals; and that this enabled the Soviets to reflect any change in the popular mood closely and instantaneously, as no parliament was able to do. His general professions of faith in proletarian democracy now sounded like mere saving clauses. What was essential was "the historical birthright of the party" and the party's awareness of it as the "indispensable unifying element." Euphemistically yet eloquently enough he now extolled the collective solidarity of the ruling group in the face of a hostile or apathetic nation.

Lenin refused to proclaim the divorce between the dictatorship and proletarian democracy. He, too, was aware that government and party were in conflict with the people; but he was afraid that Trotsky's policy would perpetuate the conflict. The party had had to override trade unions, to dismiss their recalcitrant leaders, to break or obviate popular resistance, and to prevent the free formation of opinion inside the Soviets. Only thus, Lenin held, could the revolution be saved. But he hoped that these practices would give his government a breathing space—his whole policy had become a single struggle for breathing spaces—during which it might modify its policies, make headway with the rehabilitation of the country, ease the plight of the working people, and win them back for Bolshevism. The dictatorship could then gradually revert to proletarian democracy. If this was the aim, as Trotsky agreed, then the party must reassert the idea of that democracy at once and initiate no sweeping measures suggesting its abandonment. Even though the régime had so often had recourse to co-

[11] *Desyatyi Syezd RKP*, p. 192. See also p. 215.

ercion, Lenin pleaded, coercion must be its last and persuasion its first resort.[12] The trade unions ought therefore not to be turned into appendages of the state. They must retain a measure of autonomy; they must speak for the workers, if need be against the government; and they ought to become the schools, not the drill-halls, of communism. The administrator —and it was from his angle that Trotsky viewed the problem—might be annoyed and inconvenienced by the demands of the unions; he might be right against them in specific instances; but on balance it was sound that' he should be so inconvenienced and exposed to genuine social pressures and influences. It was no use telling the workers that they must not oppose the workers' state. That state was an abstraction. In reality, Lenin pointed out, his own administration had to consider the interests of the peasants as well as of the workers; and its work was marred by muddle, by grave "bureaucratic distortions," and by arbitrary exercise of power. The working class ought therefore to defend itself, albeit with self-restraint, and to press its claims on the administration. The state, as Lenin saw it, had to give scope to a plurality of interests and influences. Trotsky's state was implicitly monolithic.

The tenth congress voted by an overwhelming majority for Lenin's resolutions. Bolshevism had already departed from proletarian democracy; but it was not yet prepared to embrace its alternative, the monolithic state.

.   .   .   .   .

While the congress was in session the strangest of all Russian insurrections flared up at the naval fortress of Kronstadt, an insurrection which, in Lenin's words, like a lightning flash illumined reality.

The insurgents, sailors of the Red Navy, were led by anarchists. Since the end of February they had been extremely restless. There had been strikes in nearby Petrograd; a general strike was expected; and Kronstadt was astir with rumours of alleged clashes between Petrograd workers and troops. The crews of the warships were seized by a political fever reminiscent of the excitement of 1917. At meetings they passed resolutions demanding freedom for the workers, a new deal for the peasants, and free elections to the Soviets. The call for the Third Revolution began to dominate the meetings, the revolution which was to overthrow the Bolsheviks and establish Soviet democracy. Kalinin, President of the Soviet Republic, made a flat-footed appearance at the naval base; he denounced the sailors as "disloyal and irresponsible" and demanded obedience. A delegation of the sailors sent to Petrograd was arrested there.

Soon the cry "Down with Bolshevik tyranny!" resounded throughout Kronstadt. The Bolshevik commissars on the spot were demoted and imprisoned. An anarchist committee assumed command; and amid the sailors' enthusiasm the flag of revolt was hoisted. "The heroic and generous Kron-

[12] *Desyatyi Syezd RKP.*, pp. 208 ff.

stadt," writes the anarchist historian of the insurrection, "dreamt of the liberation of Russia. . . . No clear-cut programme was formulated. Freedom
and the brotherhood of the peoples of the world were the watchwords. The
Third Revolution was seen as a gradual transition towards final emancipation; and free elections to independent Soviets as the first step in this
direction. The Soviets were, of course, to be independent of any political
party—a free expression of the will and the interests of the people." [13]

The Bolsheviks denounced the men of Kronstadt as counterrevolutionary mutineers led by a White general. The denunciation appears to
have been groundless. Having for so long fought against mutiny after
mutiny, each sponsored or encouraged by the White Guards, the Bolsheviks could not bring themselves to believe that the White Guards had no
hand in this revolt. Some time before the event, the White émigré press
had indeed darkly hinted at trouble brewing in Kronstadt; and this lent
colour to the suspicion. The Politbureau, at first inclined to open negotiations, finally resolved to quell the revolt. It could not tolerate the challenge from the Navy; and it was afraid that the revolt, although it had
no chance of growing into a revolution, would aggravate the prevailing
chaos. Even after the defeat of the White Guards, numerous bands of
rebels and marauders roamed the land from the northern coasts down to
the Caspian Sea, raiding and pillaging towns and slaughtering the agents
of the government. With the call for a new revolution bands of famished
Volga peasants had overrun the *gubernia* of Saratov, and later in the year
Tukhachevsky had to employ twenty-seven rifle divisions to subdue them.[14]
Such was the turmoil that leniency towards the insurgents of Kronstadt was
certain to be taken as a sign of weakness and to make matters worse.

On 5 March Trotsky arrived in Petrograd and ordered the rebels to
surrender unconditionally. "Only those who do so," he stated, "can count
on the mercy of the Soviet Republic. Simultaneously with this warning I
am issuing instructions that everything be prepared for the suppression of
the mutiny by armed force. . . . This is the last warning." [15] That it
should have fallen to Trotsky to address such words to the sailors was another of history's ironies. This had been his Kronstadt, the Kronstadt he
had called "the pride and the glory of the revolution." How many times
had he not stumped the naval base during the hot days of 1917! How many
times had not the sailors lifted him on their shoulders and wildly acclaimed

[13] Alexander Berkman, *Der Aufstand von Kronstadt*, pp. 10-11.
[14] See the correspondence between S. Kamenev, Shaposhnikov, and Smidovich with
the commander of the Saratov area, and Tukhachevsky's report to Lenin of 16 July 1921.
The Trotsky Archives. And here is a characteristic message sent to Lenin from Communists in the sub-Polar region on 25 March 1921: "The Communists of the Tobolsk
region in the North are bleeding white and sending their fiery farewell greetings to the
invincible Russian Communist Party, to our dear comrades and our leader Lenin. Perish-
ing here, we carry out our duty towards the party and the Republic in the firm belief
in our eventual triumph." Ibid.
[15] Trotsky, *Sochinenya,* vol. xvii, book 2, p. 518.

him as their friend and leader! How devotedly they had followed him to
the Tauride Palace, to his prison cell at Kresty, to the walls of Kazan on
the Volga, always taking his advice, always almost blindly following his
orders! How many anxieties they had shared, how many dangers they had
braved together! True, of the veterans few had survived; and even fewer
were still at Kronstadt. The crews of the *Aurora,* the *Petropavlovsk,* and
other famous warships now consisted of fresh recruits drafted from Ukrainian peasants. They lacked—so Trotsky told himself—the selfless revolutionary spirit of the older classes. Yet even this was in a way symbolic of
the situation in which the revolution found itself. The ordinary men and
women who had made it were no longer what they had been or where
they had been. The best of them had perished; others had become absorbed
in the administration; still others had dispersed and become disheartened
and embittered. And what the rebels of Kronstadt demanded was only what
Trotsky had promised their elder brothers and what he and the party had
been unable to give. Once again, as after Brest, a bitter and hostile echo
of his own voice came back to him from the lips of other people; and once
again he had to suppress it.

The rebels ignored his warning and hoped to gain time. This was the
middle of March. The Bay of Finland was still icebound. In a few days,
however, a thaw might set in; and then the fortress, bristling with guns,
defended by the whole Red Navy of the Baltic, assured of supplies from
Finland or other Baltic countries, would become inaccessible, almost
invincible. In the meantime even Communists joined in the revolt, announcing that they had left "the party of the hangman Trotsky." The
fortress, so Trotsky (or was it Tukhachevsky?) resolved, must be seized
before ice floes barred the approach. In feverish haste picked regiments and
shock troops were dispatched to reinforce the garrison of Petrograd. When
the news of the mutiny reached the tenth congress, it aroused so much
alarm and anger that most of the able-bodied delegates rushed straight
from the conference hall in the Kremlin to place themselves at the head of
the shock troops which were to storm the fortress across the Bay of Finland.
Even leaders of the Workers' Opposition and *Decemists* who, at the congress, had just raised demands not very different from those the rebels
voiced, went into battle. They, too, held that the sailors had no right to
dictate, hands on triggers, even the justest of demands.

White sheets over their uniforms, the Bolshevik troops, under Tukhachevsky's command, advanced across the Bay. They were met by hurricane
fire from Kronstadt's bastions. The ice broke under their feet; and wave
after wave of white-shrouded attackers collapsed into the glacial Valhalla.
The death march went on. From three directions fresh columns stumped
and fumbled and slipped and crawled over the glassy surface until they too
vanished in fire, ice, and water. As the successive swarms and lines of at-

tackers drowned, it seemed to the men of Kronstadt that the perverted
Bolshevik revolution drowned with them and that the triumph of their
own pure, unadulterated revolution was approaching. Such was the lot of
these rebels, who had denounced the Bolsheviks for their harshness and
whose only aim it was to allow the revolution to imbibe the milk of human
kindness, that for their survival they fought a battle which in cruelty was
unequalled throughout the civil war. The bitterness and the rage of the
attackers mounted accordingly. On 17 March, after a night-long advance
in a snowstorm, the Bolsheviks at last succeeded in climbing the walls.
When they broke into the fortress, they fell upon its defenders like revenge-
ful furies.

On 3 April Trotsky took a parade of the victors. "We waited as long
as possible," he said, "for our blinded sailor-comrades to see with their own
eyes where the mutiny led. But we were confronted by the danger that
the ice would melt away and we were compelled to carry out . . . the attack." [16] Describing the crushed rebels as "comrades," he unwittingly inti-
mated that what he celebrated was morally a Pyrrhic victory. Foreign Communists who visited Moscow some months later and believed that Kronstadt
had been one of the ordinary incidents of the civil war, were "astonished
and troubled" to find that the leading Bolsheviks spoke of the rebels without any of the anger and hatred which they felt for the White Guards and
interventionists. Their talk was full of "sympathetic reticences" and sad,
enigmatic allusions, which to the outsider betrayed the party's troubled
conscience.[17]

·   ·   ·   ·   ·

The rising had not yet been defeated when, on 15 March, Lenin introduced the New Economic Policy to the tenth congress. Almost without
debate the congress accepted it. Silently, with a heavy heart, Bolshevism
parted with its dream of war communism. It retreated, as Lenin said, in
order to be in a better position to advance. The controversy over the
trade unions and the underlying issue at once died down. The cannonade
in the Bay of Finland and the strikes in Petrograd and elsewhere had
demonstrated beyond doubt the unreality of Trotsky's ideas: and in the
milder policies based on the mixed economy of subsequent years there was,
anyhow, no room for the militarization of labour.

The controversy had not been mere sound and fury, however. Its
significance for the future was greater than the protagonists themselves
could suppose. A decade later Stalin, who in 1920-1 had supported Lenin's

[16] Trotsky, *Sochinenya*, vol. xvii, book 2, p. 523.

[17] André Morizet, *Chez Lénine et Trotski*, pp. 78-84 and V. Serge, *Mémoires d'un
Révolutionnaire*, chapter iv, describe the Kronstadt period from the standpoint of foreign
Communists in Russia. Both writers accepted the party's case, although both sympathized
with the rebels.

"liberal" policy, was to adopt Trotsky's ideas in all but name. Neither Stalin nor Trotsky, nor the adherents of either, then admitted the fact: Stalin—because he could not acknowledge that he was abandoning Lenin's attitude for Trotsky's; Trotsky—because he shrank in horror from his own ideas when he saw them remorselessly carried into execution by his enemy. There was hardly a single plank in Trotsky's programme of 1920-1 which Stalin did not use during the industrial revolution of the thirties. He introduced conscription and direction of labour; he insisted that the trade unions should adopt a "productionist" policy instead of defending the consumer interests of the workers; he deprived the trade unions of the last vestige of autonomy and transformed them into tools of the state. He set himself up as the protector of the managerial groups, on whom he bestowed privileges of which Trotsky had not even dreamt. He ordered "Socialist emulation" in the factories and mines; and he did so in words unceremoniously and literally taken from Trotsky.[18] He put into effect his own ruthless version of that "Soviet Taylorism" which Trotsky had advocated. And, finally, he passed from Trotsky's intellectual and historical arguments ambiguously justifying forced labour to its mass application. . . .

The Bolshevik party still defended the principle of proletarian democracy against Trotsky; but it continued to depart from it in practice.

It was only in 1921 that Lenin's government proceeded to ban all organized opposition within the Soviets. Throughout the civil war the Bolsheviks had harassed the Mensheviks and Social Revolutionaries, now outlawing them, now allowing them to come into the open, and then again suppressing them. The harsher and the milder courses were dictated by circumstances and by the vacillations of those parties in which some groups leaned towards the Bolsheviks and others towards the White Guards. The idea, however, that those parties should be suppressed on principle had not taken root before the end of the civil war. Even during the spells of repression, those opposition groups which did not plainly call for armed resistance to the Bolsheviks still carried on all sorts of activities, open and clandestine. The Bolsheviks often eliminated them from the Soviets or reduced their representation by force or guile. It was through the machinery of the Soviets that Lenin's government organized the civil war; and in that machinery it was not prepared to countenance hostile or neutral elements. But the government still looked forward to the end of hostilities when it would be able to respect the rules of Soviet constitutionalism and to readmit regular opposition. This the Bolsheviks now thought themselves unable to do. All opposition parties had hailed the Kronstadt rising; and so the Bolshe-

---

[18] At the beginning of 1929, a few weeks after Trotsky's expulsion from Russia, the sixteenth party conference proclaimed "Socialist emulation," quoting *in extenso* the resolution written by Trotsky and adopted by the party in 1920. The author's name was not mentioned, of course.

viks knew what they could expect from them. The more isolated they themselves were in the nation the more terrified were they of their opponents. They had half-suppressed them in order to win the civil war; having won the civil war they went on to suppress them for good.

Paradoxically, the Bolsheviks were driven to establish their own political monopoly by the very fact that they had liberalized their economic policy. The New Economic Policy gave free scope to the interests of the individualistic peasantry and of the urban bourgeoisie. It was to be expected that as those interests came into play they would seek to create their own means of political expression or try to use such anti-Bolshevik organizations as existed. The Bolsheviks were determined that none should exist. "We might have a two-party system, but one of the two parties would be in office and the other in prison"—this dictum, attributed to Bukharin, expressed a view widespread in the party. Some Bolsheviks felt uneasy about their own political monopoly; but they were even more afraid of the alternative. Trotsky later wrote that he and Lenin had intended to lift the ban on the opposition parties as soon as the economic and social condition of the country had become more stable. This may have been so. In the meantime, however, the Bolsheviks hardened in the conviction, which was to play so important a part in the struggles of the Stalinist era, that any opposition must inevitably become the vehicle of counter-revolution. They were haunted by the fear that the new urban bourgeoise (which soon flourished under the N.E.P.), the intelligentsia, and the peasantry might join hands against them in a coalition of overwhelming strength; and they shrank from no measure that could prevent such a coalition. Thus, after its victory in the civil war, the revolution was beginning to escape from its weakness into totalitarianism.

Almost at once it became necessary to suppress opposition in Bolshevik ranks as well. The Workers' Opposition (and up to a point the *Decemists* too) expressed much of the frustration and discontent which had led to the Kronstadt rising. The cleavages tended to become fixed; and the contending groups were inclined to behave like so many parties within the party. It would have been preposterous to establish the rule of a single party and then to allow that party to split into fragments. If Bolshevism were to break up into two or more hostile movements, as the old Social Democratic party had done, would not one of them—it was asked—become the vehicle of counter-revolution?

In the temper of the party congress of 1921 there was indeed something of that seemingly irrational tension which had characterized the congress of 1903. A split similarly cast its shadow ahead—only the real divisions were even more inchoate and confused than in 1903. Now as then Trotsky was not on the side of the controversy to which he would eventually belong. And now as then he was anxious to prevent the split. He therefore raised no objection when Lenin proposed that the congress should prohibit organized groups or factions within the party; and he himself disbanded the faction he had formed during the recent controversy.[19] This was not yet strictly a ban on inner party opposition. Lenin encouraged dissenters to express dissent. He liberally invited them to state their views in the Bolshevik newspapers, in special discussion pages and discussion sheets. He asked the congress to elect the leaders of all shades of opposition to the new Central Committee. But he insisted that opposition should remain diffuse and that the dissenters should not form themselves into solid leagues. He submitted a resolution, one clause of which (kept secret) empowered the Central Committee to expel offenders, no matter how high their standing in the party. Trotsky supported the clause, or, at any rate, raised no objection to it; and the congress passed it. It was against Shlyapnikov, Trotsky's most immitigable opponent, that the punitive clause was immediately directed; and against him it was presently invoked. It did not occur to Trotsky that one day it would be invoked against himself.

The arrangement under which opposition was permitted provided it remained dispersed could work as long as members of the party disagreed over secondary or transient issues. But when the differences were serious and prolonged it was inevitable that members of the same mind should band together. Those who, like the Workers' Opposition, charged the ruling group with being animated by "bureaucratic and bourgeois hostility towards the masses" could hardly refrain from concerting their efforts against what they considered to be a sinister and formidably organized influence within the party. The ban on factions could thus at first delay a split only to accelerate it later. . . .

When he was still at the threshold of his career, Trotsky wrote: "A working class capable of exercising its dictatorship over society will tolerate no dictator over itself." By 1921 the Russian working class had proved itself incapable of exercising its own dictatorship. It could not even exercise control over those who ruled in its name. Having exhausted itself in the revolution and the civil war, it had almost ceased to exist as a political factor. Trotsky then proclaimed the party's "historical birthright," its right to establish a stern trusteeship over the proletariat as well as the rest of society. This was the old "Jacobin" idea that a small, virtuous and enlightened minority was justified in "substituting" itself for an immature people and bringing reason and happiness to it, the idea which Trotsky had abjured as the hereditary obsession of the *Decembrists,* the *Narodniks,* and the Bolsheviks. This "obsession," he himself had argued, had reflected the atrophy or the apathy of all social classes in Russia. He had been convinced that with the appearance of a modern, Socialist working class that atrophy had been overcome. The revolution proved him right. Yet after their paroxysms of energy and their titanic struggles of 1917-21 all classes

---

[19] Among the leaders of the faction were, apart from Trotsky and Bukharin, Dzerzhinsky, Andreev, Krestinsky, Preobrazhensky, Rakovsky, Serebriakov, Pyatakov and Sokolnikov.

of Russian society seemed to relapse into a deep coma. The political stage, so crowded in recent years, became deserted and only a single group was left on it to speak boisterously on behalf of the people. And even its circle was to grow more and more narrow.

When Trotsky now urged the Bolshevik party to "substitute" itself for the working classes, he did not, in the rush of work and controversy, think of the next phases of the process, although he himself had long since predicted them with uncanny clear-sightedness. "The party organization would then substitute itself for the party as a whole; then the Central Committee would substitute itself for the organization; and finally a single dictator would substitute himself for the Central Committee."

The dictator was already waiting in the wings.

THE ORIGIN OF THE COMMUNIST AUTOCRACY

LEONARD SCHAPIRO*

LENINISM TRIUMPHANT

Lenin had first formulated his doctrine on the organization of the social democratic party in 1902. This is what he wrote in September of that year to a party worker in a letter which was reproduced and widely circulated:

While in the matter of ideology and of practical *control* of the movement and of the revolutionary struggle we need the *maximum possible centralization* for the proletariat, so far as concerns *information* on the movement the centre needs the *maximum possible decentralization*. . . . We must centralize control over the movement. We must likewise . . . *decentralize* as much as possible the *responsibility before the party* of each individual member. . . . We must particularly bear in mind . . . the *centre will be powerless* if we do not at the same time put into effect the *maximum decentralization* both as regards responsibility to the centre, and as regards information at the centre on all the wheels and little cogs of the party machine. . . . In order that the centre should be able not only to advise, to persuade, and to argue (as we have been doing up till now) but really to direct the orchestra, it is essential for it to know in detail who plays what fiddle and where, what instrument he has studied and is studying, and where, who is playing out of tune, and where, and why (when the music begins to grate on the ear), and who should be transferred, and how and whither he should be transferred in order to get rid of the discord, and so forth.[1]

* Reprinted by permission of the publishers from chapter XVIII of Leonard Schapiro's *The Origin of the Communist Autocracy* (Cambridge, Mass.: Harvard University Press, 1955); and also by permission of the London School of Economics and Political Science.
[1] *Lenin*, Vol. V, pp. 179-92. Cf. his "Chto delat?," *Lenin*, Vol. IV, pp. 359-508. The first edition of this work carried as its epigraph a quotation from Lassalle: "The party strengthens itself by purging itself."

This plan, though designed for the purposes of revolution, was not substantially altered after the revolution had been accomplished. It was not,
however, until 1921, with the development of the party Secretariat and
Orgbureau, that it began to be put into practice. Nor was it until 1921
that Lenin was able to achieve the other fundamental principle of his
scheme of party organization, the monopoly of control over proletariat and
peasantry. The latter was only accomplished with the elimination from
the political scene of socialist opponents, and especially of the Mensheviks,
whose influence in the trade unions presented the most serious competition
to the Communists.

Before the revolution the conflict between the two wings of Russian social democracy had centred much more on questions of organization and method than on questions of theory. With the
coming of the February Revolution, Bolsheviks and Mensheviks alike
did not scruple to jettison theoretical principles to which each had previously adhered. The same process can be observed after the October Revolution, during the years of the civil war. Once again, it was much less
dispute over the theory of marxism which divided Bolsheviks and Mensheviks than questions of organization and method. The Mensheviks, in
particular, had in practice abandoned, within a year of the revolution, the
most cherished tenet of orthodox Russian marxists, that a socialist revolution should only take place after a long period of "bourgeois" democracy,
by conceding the "historical necessity" of the October Revolution. In
introducing his New Economic Policy Lenin did little more than take
over and put into practice a doctrine evolved by the Mensheviks—after
first removing the Mensheviks from the political scene.

Even in the case of relations between the Bolsheviks and the Socialist
Revolutionaries, it was to some extent true that what divided the two
parties was more often disagreement over methods of government than
widely divergent theoretical beliefs. The left wing of the Socialist Revolutionaries immediately accepted the Bolshevik revolution, and only broke
with the Bolsheviks on the question of the tactics to be adopted in preserving the revolutionary government in power. But even the rest of the party,
who at first repudiated the Bolshevik revolution, accepted it in the end
when they found that their struggle against the revolutionary government
was helping a counter-revolutionary government to power. The capitulation of many of their number to the Communists, and the hesitations of
those who did not capitulate, proved this beyond doubt. Lenin had in
turn accepted, at any rate temporarily, the socialist revolutionary theory of
land distribution to the peasantry, and had abandoned the bolshevik programme of immediate nationalization. Once again, as before the revolution,
the main source of conflict between Lenin and Russian socialism proved to
be questions of organization and method—such as the *Vecheka*, the uncontrolled bureaucracy, or the subordination of the trade unions to central-

ized party control. Above all, the great majority of socialists were not prepared to tolerate the suppression of democratic liberties. The victory of the Bolsheviks over the socialists can of course in large measure be explained by the constant use of force. But there were other causes at work which were also of importance in helping to assure this victory.

The first reason was the war with Germany. The efforts of the Second International had not yet by the summer of 1914 produced unity in the ranks of the great majority of Russian social democrats who rejected Lenin's authoritarian tactics. But on the eve of the war it seemed as if Lenin's tactics were at last going to bring about in Russian social democracy the cohesion which it had hitherto lacked. The war put an end to this movement, which, had it succeeded, might well have left Lenin and his followers by the wayside as an offshoot of the main trend of Russian politics, of little more historical importance than Tkachev before him. For the division caused by the war brought the internationalist wings of both Mensheviks and Socialist Revolutionaries much nearer to Lenin's group of extremists in the Second International than to their own "defensist" colleagues, who appeared to them to be betrayers of socialist principles. In Russia, during the critical and chaotic months between March and November 1917, large sections of both the Socialist Revolutionaries and of the Mensheviks, namely, the Left Socialist Revolutionaries and Martov's Internationalists, occupied positions much closer to the Bolsheviks than to the "defensists" in their respective parties. When they realized that Lenin's policy had led not to the promised revolutionary war, but to Brest-Litovsk, they broke with the Bolsheviks, but it was by then too late. Moreover, even among the "defensist" socialists, if one excepts a few realists like Plekhanov, or romantic patriots like Savinkov, there were many whose outward support of national defence was nevertheless qualified by demands for such action as made effective defence impossible. Their attitude only served to strengthen the hands of the Bolsheviks.

Equally important for the victory of bolshevism was the advantage which the Bolsheviks derived from the moral scruples of their socialist opponents. It is now a commonplace to argue that the Provisional Government, headed by the socialist Kerensky, could easily have prevented the bolshevik revolution by taking effective and timely action against a mere handful of men and their skeleton organization. But, to argue thus is to look at the Bolsheviks through the eyes of 1921, or 1951, and not of 1917. In August or September 1917 the Provisional Government, largely composed of socialists and headed by a socialist prime minister, was understandably reluctant to use the methods of the overthrown autocracy against ostensibly socialist opponents, however extremist their views or actions. When it was goaded into taking some steps against the Bolsheviks after the abortive rising of July 1917, its measures were half-hearted and quite ineffective. It was not for nothing that the bolshevik leaders subsequently maintained that their coup d'état in November 1917 had proved easy beyond expectation.

The hesitation of their political opponents to take up arms against the Bolsheviks played as great a part in their retention of power after 1917. The Mensheviks rejected armed opposition from the first, though a minority of the party was for a short time in favour of it, and a few individuals broke with their party and joined one or other of the anti-bolshevik forces or conspiracies. As regards the party as a whole, such a course was foreign to their tradition, their temperament, and be it said their capabilities. The case of the Socialist Revolutionaries was different. They were neither a marxist nor a proletarian party and the peasants whom they represented had given them an ostensible mandate in the elections to the Constituent Assembly against the bolshevik usurpation of power. Unlike the Mensheviks, many of their number were in November 1917 anxious to fight to victory against Germany and the Central Powers, and the bolshevik surrender outraged their patriotic sentiments. Even the internationalist Left Socialist Revolutionaries were not devoid of such sentiment. Their indignation at the treaty of Brest-Litovsk, though primarily due to what they regarded as the betrayal of the cause of world revolution, was not untinged with the romantic notions harboured by their intelligentsia of the enraged Slav masses rising against the invading West. Moreover, violence had always been an influential factor in socialist revolutionary tradition. Yet, the story of the Socialist Revolutionaries' struggle against the Bolsheviks is one of indecision, hesitation, disunity, and divided loyalty. The refusal of the Central Committee of the main party to take up arms in defence of the Constituent Assembly, at a time when there were still armed forces available to support the attempt, lost them an opportunity which never recurred, and dealt a great blow to their prestige.

The treaty of Brest-Litovsk goaded them at last into co-operation with the forces of the Western Allies and into an armed struggle against the Bolsheviks. But the weak governments which the Socialist Revolutionaries set up fell, and were replaced by military dictatorships. By November 1918 the ill-assorted partnership of inexperienced and doctrinaire socialists on the one hand, and politically illiterate and reactionary army officers on the other, had come to an end. The Socialist Revolutionaries' insistence on the adoption of a full socialist policy in the midst of a civil war had contributed not a little to the debâcle. Moreover, in November 1918 the defeat of Germany removed the circumstance which in the eyes of many Socialist Revolutionaries had alone justified armed struggle against the Bolsheviks. The fight against Lenin's government could now no longer be viewed as a means of restoring the Eastern front against Germany, but became open civil war. A number of the party capitulated to the Bolsheviks, preferring political extinction to a struggle which, though it might defeat the Bolsheviks, would do so at the cost of putting reactionary monarchists into power.

Within Russia the remnants of the party organization renounced recourse to arms for the duration of the civil war. From the end of 1918 onwards the armed activity against the Communists by Socialist Revolutionaries inside Russia was limited to the participation of individuals in the fighting in the civil war and in a few conspiratorial organizations, while abroad groups of émigrés endeavoured to enlist the support of the Western Allies for more effective intervention. The party organization waited to lead a popular rising on a national scale, which never came. Thus, of the opponents of the Bolsheviks during the years of the civil war, those who had moral authority to justify their resistance, the socialists, hesitated to use the method of the coup d'état. The reactionary White Armies, which remained in the field against the Bolsheviks, had no such scruples. But they, in turn, lacked the moral authority which could have won them popular support, and might have ensured their success.

These were the negative reasons for the Bolsheviks' success. There were positive reasons as well. In contrast to their socialist opponents, the Bolsheviks were resolute, and bold in decision. Under Lenin's leadership, and because of it, they were not afraid to jettison their doctrine where the all-important question of power was involved—not afraid, in fact, of that "opportunism" for which Lenin so frequently reviled his socialist opponents. Besides this, the personality of Lenin, his political skill as well as his clarity of thought and incisiveness in the analysis of a situation, were without rival anywhere on the Russian political scene. Among social democrats, certainly Plekhanov, perhaps Martov, were his equals as theorists. Neither of them even approximated to Lenin as a political leader. Among the Socialist Revolutionaries there is no single name that even invites comparison with Lenin, whether as a theorist or as a political leader. But perhaps Lenin's greatest achievement for bolshevism was his success in harnessing to marxism the smouldering passions of the Russian people, which centuries of autocracy had engendered. It is true that in the last few years before the war it was marxism in its moderate, Western form of trade unionism and parliamentary democracy that seemed at long last to be taking some root in Russia. But this was only the beginning of a new process in a country in which habits of constitutionalism and legality still remained to be formed. The more traditional instinctive form of Russian socialism was not menshevik marxism, but the *Narodnik* mystique of the Socialist Revolutionaries, with its belief that it was Russia's destiny to follow a path quite distinct from that of capitalist Europe, and its faith in the natural socialism of the Russian peasant; and with its sense of the dark forces of anarchy which could so easily be conjured up.

In Russia [wrote Bakunin] the robber is the only true revolutionary. . . . The robbers in the woods, in the cities and in the villages, robbers all over Russia, and robbers imprisoned in the innumerable jails throughout the country make up one, indivisible, closely linked world,—the world of the Russian revolution. . . . He who wishes to plot revolution in earnest in Russia, he who desires a popular revolution, must enter this world.

There was not a Russian socialist, Bolshevik, Menshevik, or *Narodnik*, who did not know the significance of this world. But whereas all Mensheviks and the majority of Socialist Revolutionaries recoiled from it in horror, hoping to exorcise it in the end from Russian society, Lenin was not afraid of alliance with it.

The victory of the Bolsheviks in November 1917 did not, however, mean the victory of a united party. The struggles which reached their culmination at the Tenth Party Congress in March 1921 need have caused no surprise. Lenin's rapid and sudden switches of doctrine in response to the exigencies of policy placed considerable strain on the loyalty of his bewildered followers. One need only recall as instances the sudden abandonment and discard of the two orthodox phases of revolution: the repeated promise of revolutionary war jettisoned in favour of an immediate peace on any terms in March 1918; the rapid ending of workers' control, and the sudden and unheralded switch from war communism to the New Economic Policy. To anyone who based his conduct on a political theory it was no easy matter to follow Lenin through the many mutations of his policy. Yet for all this, it was not solely or primarily from the failure of Lenin's followers to realize as rapidly as Lenin the practical reasons for his switches of theory, that the most serious opposition arose inside the Russian communist party.

There was nothing peculiar to Russia in the fact that a revolutionary theory should have undergone a change when once the attempt had been made to put it into practice. Nor is the difference between political programmes before and after the coming into office of the party which sponsors them confined to revolutionary parties. Lenin's departures from his promises, or from marxist doctrine, could not by themselves have engendered the feverish excitement which characterized the Russian communist party during 1921. Indeed, some of the most fundamental departures both from orthodox theory and from party promises took place without arousing any serious opposition within the communist party at all. Perhaps this ready acceptance by the Russian Communists of the need to subordinate theory to keeping in power is best illustrated by their attitude to that all important question, the state in a socialist society.

It will be recalled that the Russian social democrats, alone of all European marxists, had accepted as an item of their programme the "dictatorship of the proletariat." Marx had used this phrase almost casually, on isolated occasions, to designate the temporary form which the struggle of the proletariat with its opponents would take immediately after its seizure of power. He had never defined or elaborated the shape which he thought a revolutionary government would assume in practice. But, since in Marx's conception the proletarian revolution was to take place at a moment when the vast exploited majority finally rose against a small minority of exploiters, it was plain that this dictatorship would be temporary and short-lived. Moreover, since the seizure of power by the proletariat would inaugurate the advent of the classless society, and since the state existed only as a device for preventing class conflict from erupting into violence, it followed, in marxist analysis, that the state must begin to wither away progressively from the moment that the proletariat had seized and consolidated its power.

On the very eve of the bolshevik revolution Lenin still fully accepted this analysis. In his *State and Revolution,* written in August and September 1917 while he was in hiding—a work written with care and much thought, and a statement of principles to which he attached the utmost importance —Lenin fully accepted the classical marxist analysis. "The proletarian state," he wrote, "will begin to wither away immediately after its victory, since in a society without class contradictions, the state is unnecessary and impossible." True, it would not, as the anarchists demanded, simply be abolished overnight. But neither, according to Lenin, would it resemble, while it lasted, the state which it had overthrown, with its police and other machinery of repression. Supported as it would be by the overwhelming mass of the population, it would enforce its will "almost without any special machinery." [2]

These words, it should be emphasized, were not part of the demagogy with which the Bolsheviks captured the support of the masses between March and November 1917, since *State and Revolution* was not published until the spring of 1918. By the time Lenin's words were published, the *Vecheka* had been active for several months, and not even the most sanguine marxist could have discerned any signs of the state beginning to wither away. When the question of "withering away" came up in March 1918, at the Seventh Party Congress, Lenin now impatiently brushed it aside. "One may well wonder when the state will begin to wither away. . . . To proclaim this withering away in advance is to violate historical perspective." It was Bukharin, the Left Communist, who had raised the question. Many years passed before the question was raised again. The Left Communists, the Democratic Centralists, the Workers' Opposition,—all accepted the need for the terror, the *Vecheka,* the unbridled powers of the executive. The reason was not, perhaps, far to seek. The Bolsheviks, so far from winning over the great majority of the country after they had seized power, as doctrine demanded, remained a small, unpopular minority, ruling by force. Their survival in sole power depended upon the state and the apparatus which they had created, and few Communists were prepared to question the necessity for this survival.

Thus, so far as one of the most fundamental departures from marxist theory was concerned, the realities of power operated to dictate its ac-

[2] *Lenin,* Vol. XXI, pp. 388, 431-2.

ceptance, and without much discussion at that. The same proved to be
the case with some other crucial questions of marxist theory which did
cause some division within the communist party during the civil war. The
Left Communists were opposed to Lenin not only on the question of peace,
but also on fundamental questions of economics and politics. But, when
once Lenin's peace policy appeared to be justified in practice, their opposition on questions of theory faded away. The Democratic Centralists,
who opposed a fairly reasoned alternative to Lenin's doctrine of party
organization, capitulated at the Tenth Party Congress in March 1921 without firing a shot. Yet both these groups included some of the best intellectuals in the party. The main struggles on questions of theory—on the
New Economic Policy, on socialism in one country, on the nature and meaning of the October Revolution, on the withering away of the state, on
dialectical materialism—all lay ahead. But by the time these debates began
to develop, in 1923 and in the succeeding years, questions of theory had
largely become a screen or an instrument for a struggle to capture, or
resist, the party apparatus among the men who had in 1921 helped to
create it.

Indeed, so little did questions of doctrine animate the Russian Communists for some time after the October Revolution, that the biggest departure from marxism of all passed unnoticed. The main opposition within
the communist party, the Workers' Opposition and the general discontent
loosely linked with it, only came to a head at the end of 1920, with the
virtual end of the civil war. This was not surprising. Until then the
Soviet régime had been engaged in a life and death struggle for survival,
of which the issue was at no time certain. The common danger created
unity, and discontent with such matters as over-centralization, or interference in trade union affairs was assuaged by the faith that these were
temporary, if necessary evils, which would be put right when the danger
had been averted. The failure to analyse the theoretical implications of
policy was understandable during the civil war, while the existence of the
new state was in danger. But the blindness to questions of theory continued
after the civil war, when the Soviet state was no longer in peril from outside attack, but the communist monopoly of power was threatened from
the inside. When in March 1921 the foundation of the future state structure was laid, it became apparent that no one within the communist party
had grasped the theoretical issues which were at stake, perhaps not even
Lenin. For what now took place was no less than a reversal in practice of
the very basis of marxist teaching, that the political machine is the mere
reflection or superstructure of the economic structure. Henceforward, political power was to control the economic form of society.

The coup d'état of November 1917 had been accepted as a proletarian
revolution, cutting short the democratic phase—that is, accepted as such by
the Communists; the Mensheviks, who continued to believe that the October

Revolution, in spite of appearances, remained in essence a bourgeois, democratic revolution, nonetheless accepted its "historical necessity." The first impact of Lenin's unorthodox decision to seize power had thrown his followers into confusion. But the confusion did not last long. The unexpected failure of their opponents to rally and overthrow the new communist government was probably as powerful an advocate for the correctness of Lenin's decision as any theoretical doctrine. So long as war communism remained the official policy, the virtual one party state which existed in the country after the peace of Brest-Litovsk might have appeared to many to be justified as the correct political superstructure for the putting into effect of extreme socialist policies.

But by the spring of 1921 war communism had failed. It was now to be replaced by an economic system in which there would be room for private capitalist enterprise and interests. Marxist logic therefore demanded that the political machine corresponding to such an economic system should be composed of parties representing the interests of the various classes which were now to be tolerated, in a state which was no longer regarded even in theory as a one class state. Lenin himself had conceded this theoretical necessity in 1905, when he had argued that so long as the revolution had not emerged from the democratic, and therefore multi-class stage, government should take the form of a coalition dictatorship of the peasantry and the proletariat. Yet, in 1921 no serious opinion within the communist party was prepared to challenge the monopoly of all political power by their own proletarian party, though many Communists were ready to criticize the abuses which proceeded from the monopoly. In this respect the simple mutineers at Kronstadt, who at all events demanded political freedom for all workers' and peasants' parties, may be said to have proved themselves better marxists than the Communists.

The question can be looked at from another aspect in which marxist theory plays no part. The Bolsheviks had never proclaimed the one party state as their avowed policy before the revolution. The seizure of power had been ostensibly accomplished in the name of the soviets in which several parties were represented. When Lenin's decision to govern alone became apparent immediately after the October Revolution it even provoked a short-lived crisis inside the bolshevik ranks. For some years to come the fiction that the Communists were but one party among many was maintained. The suppression of the socialists was, with the exception of the short period between June and November 1918, invariably bolstered by charges such as "counter-revolution," or speculation: it was not action openly taken against political opponents. The communist policy of defaming the political integrity of all socialists dates from this time. Up to 1921 it was not difficult for the Communists to justify to themselves their decision to take, and keep, power alone. The socialists had after all failed to achieve between March and November 1917 a solid and efficient government, and had then repudiated the Bolsheviks, who were at any rate prepared to take the responsibility for decisive action. The peace with Germany had been bitterly opposed by Mensheviks and Socialist Revolutionaries alike. Was it not logical that the Communists should take upon themselves the burden of government alone? The Socialist Revolutionaries had for a time even sided with the anti-bolshevik forces in the civil war.

But all these factors had ceased to exist in 1921. The socialist parties inside Russia, or those of them who still had an opportunity of voicing their views, were vying with one another in their loyalty to the ideals of the revolution as such, while condemning the excess of the Communists. There was not the remotest threat of any right wing or counter-revolutionary restoration. Long after 1921, though deprived of all political power and though many of their number were in prison or exiled, the intelligentsia and the middle-class continued to serve the Soviet state. The emigré socialists and *Kadety* even developed a whole philosophy of collaboration with the Communists in order to build up Russia, and many of them returned to implement what they considered to be their duty. There was opposition inside Russia, to be sure. But as the programme of the Kronstadt insurgents, which was typical of this opposition, shows, it was opposition not to Soviet government but to the Communists' monopoly of power, and to their party's illegal methods of preserving it.

Those, and there are many,[3] who justify the Communists' elimination of their socialist opponents in 1921 by the necessity of safeguarding the "revolution" from its enemies ignore two essential facts: first, that enmity against the Communists was not enmity against the revolution, i.e., the Soviet form of government, but against the methods of communist rule in the name of that revolution. It was therefore not only an enmity of the Communists' own creation, but one which it was in their power to remove without danger to the revolution, though with undoubted risk to their own monopoly of power. To be sure, Lenin and the Communists identified "the revolution" with themselves. But it was an identification made by them alone, which did not correspond to facts. Secondly, that a large number,

---

[3] See e.g. *Deutscher*, [Stalin], p. 226, "It was true enough that concern for the revolution compelled Bolshevism to take the road chosen by the tenth congress . . ."; *Carr*, [The Bolshevik Revolution], *I*, p. 183. The latter concludes that the demise of the legal opposition "cannot fairly be laid at the door of one party. If it was true that the Bolshevik régime was not prepared after the first few months to tolerate an organized opposition, it was equally true that no opposition party was prepared to remain within legal limits. The premise of dictatorship was common to both sides of the argument." This judgment ignores not only the Mensheviks, but most of the Socialist Revolutionaries as well. The premise of dictatorship was certainly common to both sides in Lenin's "argument" with Denikin. But what relation to fact does such an assertion bear in the case of Martov and the Mensheviks, whose policy was founded upon the need to "remain within legal limits"? Or in the case of the Samara Socialist Revolutionaries, who gave up the fight for fear it might assist the victory of a right wing dictatorship? The charge that the Mensheviks were not prepared to remain within legal limits is part of the Bolsheviks' case; it does not survive an examination of the facts.

perhaps even the majority, of the conscious proletariat, were in early 1921 menshevik or menshevik sympathizers. The revolutionary nature of this party's policy, which accorded political freedom to workers and peasants alone, and advocated large scale nationalization of industry and state control of foreign trade, cannot be conjured away, as is normally done by apologists of Lenin's policy, by describing it as "bourgeois." The socialists were not eliminated in 1921 because they were counter-revolutionary. They were described as counter-revolutionary in order to justify their elimination.

The fate of the socialists was sealed when it became apparent that in their criticism of communist methods they were speaking much the same language as the many malcontents inside the communist party. The realization of the extent of the support which the Kronstadt mutineers could muster, even inside the communist party within the naval garrison, had come as a grave shock. But different considerations applied to the Workers' Opposition. There was no vestige in their programme of any quarrel with the communist leaders for their treatment of socialist opponents, or of the peasantry. It was a mixture of the early syndicalism which the Communists had abandoned, utopianism, and nostalgia for the lost enthusiasm of the first months. They combined with it some well-founded criticism of the abuses of bureaucracy and of excessive party discipline and control. The communist leaders may have been right in seeing in the existence of this critical group a potential party split. The moral case for the Workers' Opposition was perhaps not very strong. They demanded freedom for themselves, but had no thought of conceding it to others. When they complained of control by the centre over the communist committees in the trade-unions, they did not pause to think that those same communist committees for which they demanded more freedom of action did not hesitate to impose their will on a trade union membership, some fourteen times their number, which was bitterly opposed to them. They accepted the state of affairs in which a party of a few hundred thousand could impose its will by force on millions of workers who did not support them. But they did not realize that if a minority party is to survive in sole power against the will of the great majority, it can only do so if it maintains the strictest discipline and control by its leaders over its own members. Once again the Kronstadt mutineers proved themselves more mature politicians than the Workers' Opposition.

But if the communist leaders were right in sensing in the Workers' Opposition a danger of a party split, they were wrong in attempting to identify the views of this opposition with menshevism. It is true that one of the fundamental differences between bolshevism and menshevism, which had even preceded the formal split in 1903, had been disagreement on the value of the spontaneous effort of the masses. The Mensheviks, following Plekhanov, and Lavrov before him, believed that the revolution must be the work of the masses themselves. Lenin had replaced this view by the doctrine that, left to themselves, the masses will be content with palliative reforms, and must therefore be led on to revolution by a party of professional revolutionaries. This difference of view was reflected in the rival formulas put forward for incorporation in the party statute by Lenin and Martov at the Second Congress in 1903—Lenin's, confining membership to those who "personally participate in one of the party organizations," i.e. put themselves under party discipline; and Martov's, extending it much more widely to all who "co-operate" with the party "under the direction of one of its organizations." The Mensheviks were concerned with the relations between the social democratic party and the proletariat as a whole, or, in other words, with the nature of and, more important, the degree of leadership which the party of the proletariat should exercise over that proletariat. It was in this context that, in opposition to Lenin, they claimed that a greater degree of initiative should be left to the workers themselves as distinct from the party which claimed to speak in their name.

But the Workers' Opposition were concerned with an entirely different question, the relation of the party at a low level to the party at a higher level. They were not concerned with the workers outside that party, who formed the majority. It is true that in their demands for less restriction on the freedom of local party and trade union committees, for example, the Workers' Opposition may have appeared at times to be speaking the same language as the Mensheviks. But the Mensheviks wanted free elections in the trade unions, which would have put socialist, but not communist majorities into power. The Workers' Opposition did not seek to alter the rigged elections which ensured communist majorities, but merely sought to safeguard the local trade union committee or cell from being replaced by central nominees. It was also true that Mensheviks and Workers' Opposition shared in common a somewhat romantic faith in the superiority of the proletariat actually engaged in manual labour over the professional party bureaucrat, or the intellectual. But in basic political aims the two were poles apart.

The balance sheet of political support was not an encouraging one for the communist party in March 1921. Among the peasantry it had lost most, if not all, the support or at least neutrality which had once played an important part in achieving victory both in November 1917 and in the civil war. Even among the proletariat dislike of the Communists had grown. With it grew the popularity of the socialist parties, notably of the Mensheviks. No communist leader could have had any doubt, and some, such as Zinoviev, openly admitted, that in any free election to any soviet, or trade union committee, in March 1921 the number of communist candidates elected would have been small. It was true that much of this unpopularity was due to privations brought about by the civil war. But it was also true that much of it was due to the revolt of the Russian people against the unfairness, the violence, and the illegality with which the Communists suppressed all who did not accept their rule without question. The Kronstadt revolt proved this beyond any doubt.

In these circumstances there were only two policies open to Lenin. Either to resign himself to his failure to win over the majority, to moderate the policy by which his monopoly of power had been secured and to accept the consequent loss of that monopoly. Or, to preserve his monopoly of political power at all costs, and at the same time make the task of preserving it easier by removing, at the price of sacrificing communist doctrine, some of the economic causes of discontent. He chose the second course. But it was plain that this policy could only be successfully achieved by a disciplined party, united, if necessary by force, for the difficult task which now confronted it. There could be no room for party democracy. The trade union discussion, which had revealed the personal rivalries dividing the party as well as the wide divergence of view on fundamental questions of policy, had proved that. The views of the Democratic Centralists, of Preobrazhensky or Krestinsky, of Shlyapnikov or Kollontai, suffered from the contradiction that they stood for two incompatible aims: *both* a democratic communist party, *and* the exclusion of all other parties from power. It was this circumstance more than any other which determined their quick collapse at the Tenth Party Congress.

Lenin easily steered his policy to victory at this congress. He was still the outstanding figure in the party, much as he had been in 1917. There was no rival leader within sight who could have succeeded in rallying the discontented inside the party around himself and in raising a revolt against Lenin; even if there had been anyone, which there was not, who had the courage to assume such a rôle. The only possible candidate would have been Trotsky. But Trotsky was much too close in outlook to Lenin on the vital question of communist monopoly of power to have thought of such a course. Moreover, his personal popularity was already seriously impaired in 1921 by policies associated with his name. Nor is there the slightest reason to suppose that he ever contemplated such a move for a moment. The Workers' Opposition lacked any leaders of note, the intellectual Democratic Centralists had no thought of struggle, and certainly no stomach for it. It was therefore easy for Lenin to carry the leaders of his party with him, in spite of the misgivings which some of them uttered, and perhaps many more felt.

It is plain that in 1921, as in 1917, many followed Lenin without completely realizing where he was leading them. The full significance of his policy then may have been no more apparent than had been the full significance of the seizure of power. In November 1917 a number of bolshevik leaders cavilled when they discovered that what they had believed to be seizure of power by the soviets was in reality seizure of power by the bolshevik party. In 1921 those who followed Lenin believed that what was being achieved was the consolidation of the power of the communist party.

Many of them were to rebel once again, in 1923, when they discovered that what had really taken place was the consolidation in power of the central party apparatus. But it was then too late.

Thus once again, in 1921 as in 1917, the personal qualities and influence of Lenin proved the decisive factor. In 1917 the political immaturity and inexperience of the Russian parties had played into the hands of anyone both resolute enough to seize power, and untroubled by the doubts and hesitancies which beset the more scrupulous. After 1918 Lenin's democratic opponents had no armed forces at their disposal. Their sole hope of overthrowing the Communists might have been in alliance with the White Armies. The overwhelming majority of them had not been prepared to accept such an alliance for fear that the only outcome would be the downfall of the revolution, and the restoration of the monarchy. The population, distracted by hardships of every kind, was able to achieve no more than a peasant guerrilla war and the Kronstadt revolt.

In 1921 the fate of the country lay in the hands of Lenin. He had a chance of burying past enmities and of carrying the vast majority of the country with him in an attempt to build up ruined Russia on the basis of co-operation and legal order, and not of the dictatorship of an unpopular minority. It is difficult to escape the conclusion that a greater man than Lenin would have seized this chance. But Lenin's genius lay in the technique of grasping and holding power. He was a great revolutionary, but not a statesman. His conviction that he and his followers alone held the secret of successful rule in their hands was, to a large extent, the product of the struggle by which he had achieved his position. But from his fateful decision in the spring of 1921 flowed all the consequences of the one party dictatorship which became apparent in the subsequent years of Soviet history.

Two main consequences derived from Lenin's political policy of 1921, both of enormous importance for the future history of Soviet Russia. The first was the emergence of what Engels has so well described as the "conventional hypocrisy." During the civil war there was at any rate some justification for the view that "he who is not with us is against us." In the heat of battle it was possible for the Communists to see in those socialists who were fighting against them enemies of the revolution, without seeming to do undue violence to truth. After 1921, the lumping together of Mensheviks, Workers' Opposition, serious theoretical critics, and malcontents inside the communist party as counter-revolutionaries was a falsification, and everyone knew it.

The acceptance of this official lie by almost the entire leadership of the communist party inevitably led to the result that whoever among them was strong enough to exploit it in his own interest had the rest of them at his mercy. What is the difference between the attempt by Lenin to expel Shlyapnikov, in 1921, and the expulsion of Trotsky six years later, if both

can be justified by the same argument—that the stability of the dictatorship is the supreme law? But this, in turn, leads to the second main consequence of Lenin's policy. For, who has the power to decide by what faction
the stability of the régime is to be best served? Clearly, he who manipulates
the apparatus of the party, and can thereby ensure both the necessary majorities at the centre and implicit obedience to central orders throughout
the country. The malignant figure of the General Secretary, Stalin, has become only too familiar in its portrayal by disappointed oppositionists,
defeated by the apparatus which he controlled. But it was Lenin, with
their support, who equipped him with the weapons, and started him upon
his path.

V

TOWARD THE DICTATORSHIP OF STALIN

9. The Triumph of Stalin

O great Stalin, O leader of the peoples,
Thou who broughtest man to birth,
Thou who fructifiest the earth,
Thou who restorest the centuries,
Thou who makest bloom the spring,
Thou who makest vibrate the musical chords.
Thou, splendor of my spring, O thou,
Sun reflected by millions of hearts. . . .
                    Translation of Uzbek poem in *Pravda,* August 28, 1936

"Comrades! The cult of the individual acquired such monstrous size chiefly because Stalin himself, using all conceivable methods, supported the glorification of his own person. This is supported by numerous facts. One of the most characteristic examples of Stalin's self-glorification and of his lack of even elementary modesty is the edition of his *Short Biography,* which was published in 1948.

"This book is an expression of the most dissolute flattery, an example of making a man into a godhead, of transforming him into an infallible sage, 'the greatest leader,' 'sublime strategist of all times and nations.' Finally no other words could be found with which to lift Stalin up to the heavens.

"We need not give here examples of the loathsome adulation filling this book. All we need to add is that they all were approved and edited by Stalin personally and some of them were added in his own handwriting to the draft text of the book."

NIKITA S. KHRUSHCHEV, *February 25, 1956*

Chapter 9

THE TRIUMPH OF STALIN

One of the more interesting and important questions is why and how Stalin was able to emerge from a position of relative obscurity to one of unexcelled power in the history of the modern world. (While it is probably true that Stalin was far abler than some critics have suggested, he was, when compared with certain other of the Bolshevik leaders, a gray mediocrity, hardworking, pedestrian, and uninspired.) A more serious, and related, question is how did it happen that, under the aegis of a theory which was designed to liberate man from exploitation, so crass and pervasive a dictatorship could arise and develop.

Relevant, of course, to these questions are the explanations considered or suggested in the previous section. But there are additional and variant explanations offered by Isaac Deutscher, Leon Trotsky, John Plamenatz, and Sidney Hook which merit consideration.

A few words should be added in regard to the historic circumstances under which Stalin consolidated his power—apart from those dealt with in the pages that follow. By 1928, under the New Economic Policy (NEP) —which had abolished requisitioning from the peasantry, encouraged private trade and small-scale enterprise while the "commanding heights" of industry remained under state administration—productivity had been restored to prewar levels. However, the grain surplus available for urban consumption or export was only at one-third prewar level. In the minds of Stalin and other Soviet leaders, NEP did not provide an adequate basis for large-scale investment in, and subsidization of, a massive industrialization. Moreover, a large class of peasant proprietors and business entrepreneurs presented at least a potential threat to the regime. Stalin decided to embark, therefore, upon wholesale collectivization of agriculture to support industrialization.

The first five-year plan, which went into effect on October 1, 1928, engendered tremendous enthusiasm and a spirit of sacrifice, particularly among the youth. On the other hand, it resulted in massive and sullen resistance by the kulaks who slaughtered cattle and refused to sow or reap. The immediate consequences were the deportation of hundreds of thousands of kulaks to the far reaches of Siberia and a famine in the Ukraine in 1932-33—which took at least a million and a half lives. In this situation, as difficulties developed, as suspicions, fears, and bitterness intensified, as arrests and executions of obstructionists, saboteurs, and scapegoats became commonplace, the dependence upon and power of Stalin grew mightily.

STALIN

Isaac Deutscher*

Few important developments in history are so inconspicuous and seem so inconsequential to their contemporaries as did the amazing accumulation of power in the hands of Stalin, which took place while Lenin was still alive. Two years after the end of the civil war Russian society already lived under Stalin's virtual rule, without being aware of the ruler's name. More strangely still, he was voted and moved into all his positions of power by his rivals. There was to be an abundance of sombre drama in his later fight against these rivals. But the fight began only after he had firmly gripped all the levers of power and after his opponents, awakening to his role, had tried to move him from his dominant position. But then they found him immovable.

Three of the offices he held immediately after the civil war were of decisive importance: he was the Commissar of Nationalities, the Commissar of the Workers' and Peasants' Inspectorate, and a member of the Politbureau.

As Commissar of Nationalities he dealt with the affairs of nearly half the population of the Russian Soviet Federative Socialist Republic, as the state that had replaced old Russia was now called. Sixty-five millions of its 140 million inhabitants belonged to non-Russian nationalities. They represented every possible level of civilization, from the quasi-European way of life of the Ukrainians to the primitive, tribal existence of 25 million Turkmen-shepherds. Byelorussians, Kirghizians, Uzbeks, Azerbaidjans, Tartars, Armenians, Georgians, Tadzhiks, Buriats, and Yakuts, and a host of others for which there seem to be no names in the English tongue, found themselves in various intermediate phases of development between tribal community and modern society. Bolshevism, eager to attract all these nationalities and to wipe away their memories of Tsarist oppression, offered

* The selection is from chapter VII of *Stalin: A Political Biography* (New York: Oxford University Press, 1949). Reprinted by permission of the publisher.

autonomy and self-government to all of them. Few such groups had any
degree of "national" consciousness. Fewer still had acquired the minimum
of education indispensable for self-government. For the management of
their affairs they were dependent on help from outside: that is, from the
Commissariat of Nationalities. To most of them the doctrinal problems of
communism were as remote as the theories of Einstein were to the Khans of
Bokhara. In their lands the revolution meant the freeing of the primitive
communities from the dominance of Emirs, Khans, and Mullahs, and a
degree of Europeanization.

Apart from the Ukraine, ruled by an independent-minded government
under Christian Rakovsky, the Commissariat of Nationalities faced primarily Russia's vast, inert, oriental fringe. None of the leaders who had
spent most of their adult life in western Europe was as fit to head that Commissariat as Stalin. His first-hand knowledge of the customs and habits of
his clients was unsurpassed. So was his capacity to deal with the intricacies
of their "politics," in which blood feuds and oriental intrigue mixed with
a genuine urge towards modern civilization. His attitude was just that mixture of patience, patriarchal firmness, and slyness that was needed. The
Politbureau relied on this and refrained from interfering.

The Asiatic and semi-Asiatic periphery thus became his first undisputed domain. Immediately after the revolution, when the leadership of the
nation belonged to the turbulent and radical cities of European Russia, in
the first place to Petersburg and Moscow, the weight of that periphery was
not much felt. With the ebb of revolution, the primitive provinces took
their revenge. They reasserted themselves in a thousand ways, economic,
political, and cultural. Their spiritual climate became, in a sense, decisive
for the country's outlook. The fact that so much of that climate was oriental
was of great significance. Stalin, who was so well suited to speak on behalf
of Russian communism to the peoples of the oriental fringe, was also well
suited to orientalize his party. During his years at the Commissariat he
made and widened his contacts with the Bolshevik leaders of the border-
lands, on whose devoted support he could count, and of whom so many were
to be found in his entourage at the Kremlin later on.

He was appointed Commissar of the Workers' and Peasants' Inspectorate in 1919, on Zinoviev's proposal. The Rabkrin, as the Commissariat was
called, was set up to control every branch of the administration, from top
to bottom, with a view to eliminating the two major faults, inefficiency
and corruption, which the Soviet civil service had inherited from its Tsarist
predecessor. It was to act as the stern and enlightened auditor for the whole
rickety and creaking governmental machine; to expose abuses of power and
red tape; and to train an *élite* of reliable civil servants for every branch of
the government. The Commissariat acted through teams of workers and
peasants who were free at any time to enter the offices of any Commissariat
and watch the work done there. In the end, teams of the Rabkrin regularly

attended private departmental conferences and even the meetings of the Council of Commissars. This system was devised as a method of training an *élite* for the civil service; but as a result of it the Rabkrin was able to keep its eye on every wheel of the governmental machine.[1]

The whole bizarre scheme of inspection was one of Lenin's pet ideas. Exasperated by the inefficiency and dishonesty of the civil service, he sought to remedy them by extreme and ruthless "control from below," and the Commissariat was to be the means. The choice of Stalin for the job gives a measure of Lenin's high confidence in him, for the Inspectorate was to be a sort of a super-government, itself free from every taint and blemish of officialdom.

Lenin's cure proved as bad as the disease. The faults of the civil service, as Lenin himself frequently pointed out, reflected the country's appalling lack of education, its material and spiritual misery, which could be cured only gradually, over the lifetime of at least a generation. The Rabkrin would have had to be a commissariat of angels in order to rise, let alone raise others, above the dark valley of Russian bureaucracy. With his characteristic belief in the inherent virtues of the working classes, Lenin appealed to the workers against his own bureaucracy. The mill of officialdom, however, turned the workers themselves into bureaucrats. The Commissariat of the Inspectorate, as Lenin was to discover later on, became an additional source of muddle, corruption, and bureaucratic intrigue. In the end it became an unofficial but meddlesome police in charge of the civil service. But let us not run ahead of our story. Suffice it to say here that, as the head of the Inspectorate, Stalin came to control the whole machinery of government, its working and personnel, more closely than any other commissar.

His next position of vantage was in the Politbureau. Throughout the civil war, the Politbureau consisted of five men only: Lenin, Trotsky, Stalin, Kamenev, and Bukharin. Ever since the break between Bolsheviks and Social Revolutionaries, this had been the real government of the country. Lenin was the recognized leader of both government and party. Trotsky was responsible for the conduct of the civil war. Kamenev acted as Lenin's deputy in various capacities. Bukharin was in charge of press and propaganda. The day-to-day management of the party belonged to Stalin. The Politbureau discussed high policy. Another body, which was, like the Politbureau, elected by the Central Committee, the Organization Bureau (Orgbureau), was in charge of the party's personnel, which it was free to call up, direct to work, and distribute throughout the army and the civil service according to the demands of the civil war. From the beginning of 1919 Stalin was the only permanent liaison officer between the Politbureau and

---

[1] See Lenin, *Sochinenya*, vol. xxvii, pp. 14-20; *Letters of Lenin*, pp. 455-6, 474-5. Zinoviev's speeches in *8 Syezd RKP* (*b*), pp. 162-3, 501, 225-6, and 290-1; and *Kratkii Otchet Narkom. R.K.I.*

the Orgbureau. He ensured the unity of policy and organization; that is, he marshalled the forces of the party according to the Politbureau's directives. Like none of his colleagues, he was immersed in the party's daily drudgery and in all its kitchen cabals.

At this stage his power was already formidable. Still more was to accrue to him from his appointment, on 3 April 1922, to the post of General Secretary of the Central Committee. The eleventh congress of the party had just elected a new and enlarged Central Committe and again modified the statutes. The leading bodies of the party were now top-heavy; and a new office, that of the General Secretary, was created, which was to co-ordinate the work of their many growing and overlapping branches. It was on that occasion, Trotsky alleges, that Lenin aired, in the inner circle of his associates, his misgivings about Stalin's candidature: "This cook can only serve peppery dishes." [1] But his doubts were, at any rate, not grave; and he himself in the end sponsored the candidature of the "cook." Molotov and Kuibyshev were appointed Stalin's assistants, the former having already been one of the secretaries of the party. The appointment was reported in the Russian press without any ado, as a minor event in the inner life of the party.

Soon afterwards a latent dualism of authority began to develop at the very top of the party. The seven men who now formed the Politbureau (in addition to the previous five, Zinoviev and Tomsky had recently been elected) represented, as it were, the brain and the spirit of Bolshevism. In the offices of the General Secretariat resided the more material power of management and direction. In name the General Secretariat was subordinate to the illustrious and exalted Politbureau. But the dependence of the Politbureau on the Secretariat became so great that without that prop the Politbureau looked more and more like a body awkwardly suspended in a void. The Secretariat prepared the agenda for each session of the Politbureau. It supplied the documentation on every point under debate. It transmitted the Politbureau's decisions to the lower grades. It was in daily contact with the many thousands of party functionaries in the capital and the provinces. It was responsible for their appointments, promotions, and demotions. It could, up to a point, prejudice the views of the Politbureau on any issue before it came up for debate. It could twist the practical execution of the Politbureau's decisions, according to the tastes of the General Secretary. Similar bodies exist in any governmental machinery but rarely acquire independent authority. What usually prevents them from transgressing their terms of reference is some diffusion of power through the whole system of government, effective control over them, and, sometimes, the integrity of officials. The over-centralization of power in the Bolshevik leadership, the lack of effective control, and, last but not least, the personal

[1] L. Trotsky, *Mein Leben*, p. 450.

ambitions of the General Secretary, all made for the extraordinary weight that the General Secretariat began to carry barely a few months after it had been set up.

The picture would be incomplete without mention of another institution, the Central Control Commission, that came to loom large in Bolshevik affairs. Its role *vis-à-vis* the party was analogous to that of the Commissariat of the Inspectorate *vis-à-vis* the governmental machine: it audited party morals. It was formed at the tenth congress, in 1921, on the demand of the Workers' Opposition, with which the congress had otherwise dealt so harshly. It was in charge of the so-called purges. These, too, were initiated by the tenth congress, on the demand of the Opposition. They were intended to cleanse the party periodically of careerists, who had climbed the band-wagon in great numbers, of Communists who had acquired a taste for bourgeois life, and commissars whose heads had been turned by power. Lenin adopted the idea and intended to use it in order to stop his followers departing from the party's puritanic standards. But he also turned one edge of the purges against "anarcho-syndicalists," waverers, doubters, and dissidents, against the real initiators of the new practice.

The procedure of the purges was at first very different from what it became in later years. The purges were no concern of the judiciary. They were conducted by the party's local control commissions before an open citizens' forum, to which Bolsheviks and non-Bolsheviks had free access. The conduct of every member of the party, from the most influential to the humblest, was submitted to stern public scrutiny. Any man or woman from the audience could come forward as a witness. The Bolshevik whose record was found to be unsatisfactory was rebuked or, in extreme cases, expelled from the party. The Control Commission could impose no other penalties than these.

The original motive behind the purges was almost quixotic. It was to enable the people to crack periodically a whip over their rulers. But, since the ruling party was convinced that in all essentials of policy it could not really submit to popular control, these new devices for reviving popular control were *a priori* irrelevant and could not but prove ineffective. They illustrated the party's already familiar dilemma: its growing divorce from the people and its anxiety to preserve its popular character; the dilemma that underlay Lenin's pathetic experiments with his party in the last two years of his political activity. The purges were to serve as a substitute for real elections; they were to remove corrupted members, without removing the party, from power.[1]

---

[1] The purges provided a good cover for all sorts of private vendettas. In May 1922, Lenin wrote in a letter to Stalin: ". . . the purging of the party revealed the prevalence, in the majority of local investigation committees, of personal spite and malice. . . . This fact is incontrovertible and rather significant." In the same letter Lenin complained about the lack of partymen with "an adequate legal education . . . capable of resisting all purely local influences." See *The Essentials of Lenin*, vol. ii, p. 809.

The Central Control Commission in Moscow soon became the supreme court of appeal for the victims of the purges all over the country. Originally, it was to be independent from the Central Committee and the Politbureau. Later it was put on an almost equal footing with the Central Committee; and the two bodies regularly held joint sessions. The General Secretariat was the co-ordinating link between them. Thus, unofficially, Stalin became the chief conductor of the purges.

Lenin, Kamenev, Zinoviev, and, to a lesser extent, Trotsky, were Stalin's sponsors to all the offices he held. His jobs were of the kind which could scarcely attract the bright intellectuals of the Politbureau. All their brilliance in matters of doctrine, all their powers of political analysis would have found little application either at the Workers' and Peasants' Inspectorate or at the General Secretariat. What was needed there was an enormous capacity for hard and uninspiring toil and a patient and sustained interest in every detail of organization. None of his colleagues grudged Stalin his assignments. As long as Lenin kept the reins of government they looked upon him merely as Lenin's assistant; and all of them readily accepted Lenin's leadership. Neither they nor Lenin noticed in time the subtle change by which Stalin was gradually passing from the role of assistant to that of coadjutor.

·   ·   ·   ·   ·

Less than two months after Stalin's appointment to the post of General Secretary, the reins of government slipped from Lenin's hands. By the end of May 1922, he suffered his first stroke of arteriosclerotic paralysis. Almost speechless, he was taken out of the Kremlin to the country-side, near Moscow. Not until the middle of the autumn did he recover sufficiently to return to office; and then his activity was very short. At the end of the autumn a second stroke put him out of action; and at the end of the winter, in March 1923, a third stroke removed him finally from the political scene, though his body still wrestled with death until 21 January 1924.

The impact of Lenin's illness on the Bolshevik leadership can hardly be exaggerated. The whole constellation ceased, almost at once, to shine with the reflected light of its master mind or to move in the familiar orbits. Lenin's disciples and satellites (only Trotsky belonged to neither of these categories) began to feel for their own, independent ways. Gradually they were shedding those characteristics of theirs that were merely imitative, their second, and better, nature. The negative side of Lenin's overwhelming and constant influence on his followers now became strikingly apparent. Just how overwhelming it had been can be seen from the circumstance, attested by Trotsky, that during the years of their apprenticeship with their leader, Zinoviev and Kamenev had acquired even Lenin's handwriting. They were now to go on using his handwriting without the inspiration of his ideas.

Stalin was in a sense less dependent on Lenin than were his colleagues;

his intellectual needs were more limited than theirs. He was interested in
the practical use of the Leninist gadgets, not in the Leninist laboratory of
thought. His own behaviour was now dictated by the moods, needs, and
pressures of the vast political machine that he had come to control. His political philosophy boiled down to securing the dominance of that machine
by the handiest and most convenient means. In an avowedly dictatorial
régime, repression often is the handiest and most convenient method of
action. The Politbureau may have been thrown into disarray by Lenin's
disappearance; the General Secretariat was not. On the contrary, since it
had no longer to account for what it did to the vigilant and astute super-
visor, it acted with greater firmness and self-confidence. The same was
true of the Workers' and Peasants' Inspectorate. . . .

.   .   .   .   .

It was about this time that a triumvirate, composed of Stalin, Zinoviev,
and Kamenev, formed itself within the Politbureau. What made for the
solidarity of the three men was their determination to prevent Trotsky
from succeeding to the leadership of the party. Separately, neither could
measure up to Trotsky. Jointly, they represented a powerful combination
of talent and influence. Zinoviev was the politician, the orator, the dema-
gogue with popular appeal. Kamenev was the strategist of the group, its
solid brain, trained in matters of doctrine, which were to play a paramount
part in the contest for power. Stalin was the tactician of the triumvirate and
its organizing force. Between them, the three men virtually controlled the
whole party and, through it, the Government. Kamenev had acted as
Lenin's deputy and presided over the Moscow Soviet. Zinoviev was the
chairman of the Soviet of Petersburg, soon to be renamed Leningrad. Stalin
controlled most of the provinces. Zinoviev was, in addition, the President
of the Communist International, whose moral authority in Russia was then
great enough to make any pretender strive for its support.

Finally, the three men represented, as it were, the party's tradition.
Their uninterrupted association with Bolshevism dated back to the split of
1903; and they held seniority in leadership. Of the other members of the
Politbureau, apart from Trotsky, Bukharin was considerably younger, and
Tomsky, the leader of the trade unions, had only recently become a member
of it. Seniority carried with it the halo of a heroic past, distinguished by
unflagging devotion to Bolshevism. The three men refused now to follow
that "ex-Menshevik," Trotsky, who, after an association with the party
which had lasted only five years, had come to be commonly regarded as
Lenin's successor. This motive, the only one that made for their solidarity,
impelled them to act in concert. As the other members of the Politbureau
walked each his own way, the triumvirs automatically commanded a majority. Their motions and proposals, on which they usually agreed before

every session of the Politbureau, were invariably carried. The other members were bound hand and foot by the discipline of the Politbureau—any attempt by one of them to discuss their inner controversies in public would have appeared as an act of disloyalty . . .

.   .   .   .   .

Since the promulgation of the N.E.P. in 1921, Russia's economy was beginning to recover. But the process was slow and painful. Industry was still unable to meet the country's most essential needs. It failed to supply the countryside with the goods that would induce peasants to sell food. Low wages, unemployment, and starvation were driving the working class to despair. Since trade unions refused to take up the workers' demands, discontent exploded in "unofficial" strikes. The restive mood penetrated into the ruling party. Clandestine opposition groups were discovered within its ranks. Some of these groups were half Menshevik; others were wholly Bolshevik and consisted of remnants of the oppositions that had been banned in 1921 as well as of new elements. Their main plank was the demand for freedom of criticism inside the party. Some of the dissenters were expelled, others imprisoned. These were the first instances of clandestine opposition among Communists. So far, the secret groups had acted without concert and lacked leadership. The triumvirs feared a link-up between their rivals and the discontented rank and file.[1]

They reacted to the crisis in a self-contradictory manner. They put before the Central Committee a motion about the need to restore democracy and freedom of discussion for the members of the party. On the other hand, they mobilized the political police against the secret oppositions. The police found that ordinary Bolsheviks often refused to co-operate in tracing the opposition groups. Dzerzhinsky asked the Politbureau to authorize the police to take action against uncooperative Bolsheviks, too. At this point the fight between Trotsky and the triumvirs entered a new phase. Without making it quite clear whether he thought that Dzerzhinsky's demand should be granted, Trotsky attacked the triumvirate. What had happened, he stated, was symptomatic of the party's state of mind, its sense of frustration, and its distrust of the leaders. Even during the civil war "the system of appointment [from above] did not have one-tenth of the extent that it has now. Appointment of the secretaries of provincial committees is now the rule." He granted that there was a grain of demagogy in the demands for a workers' democracy, "in view of the incompatibility of a fully developed workers' democracy with the régime of the dictatorship." But the discipline of the civil war ought to have given place to "a more lively and broader party responsibility." Instead, "the bureaucratization of the party machine had developed to unheard of proportions; and criticism and dis-

[1] J. Stalin, *Sochinenya*, pp. 354-61; N. Popov, *Outline History*, vol. ii, pp. 194-204.

content, the open expression of which was stifled, were driven underground, assuming uncontrollable and dangerous forms." [1]

The triumvirs evaded the issues raised by Trotsky and charged him with malevolence, personal ambition, neglect of his duties in the Government, and so on. They accused him of trying to establish himself as Lenin's successor. [2] This last charge was, in a sense, true, for the fight over the succession was inherent in the situation. Yet this as well as the other charges were beside the point, for the crisis in the party, as Trotsky diagnosed it, was a fact.

In the middle of this exchange forty-six prominent Communists issued a declaration the gist of which was identical with Trotsky's criticisms. [3] . . . It is not certain whether Trotsky directly instigated their demonstration. So far he conducted his dispute with the triumvirs behind the closed doors of the Politbureau. The party at large was under the impression that he had all the time been whole-heartedly behind the official policy. He thus had the worst of both worlds: he had been burdened with responsibility for a policy to which he had been opposed; and he had done nothing to rally in time those who might have supported him.

In November the alarm caused by the crisis led the triumvirs to table a motion in favour of democratic reform in the party. As in the Georgian affair, so now Stalin agreed to make any verbal concession to Trotsky. The motion was carried by the Politbureau unanimously. Trotsky had no choice but to vote for it. On 7 November, the sixth anniversary of the revolution, Zinoviev officially announced the opening of a public discussion on all issues that troubled the Bolshevik mind. The state of siege in the party, so it might have seemed, was at last being lifted.

This was not the case. The state of affairs against which the opposition rose was not merely the result of Stalin's or the other triumvirs' ambition and ill will. It had deeper roots. The revolution had saved itself by building up a massive political machine. The apathy, if not the hostility, of the masses drove it to rely increasingly on rule by coercion rather than by persuasion. Who could say with any certainty that the time had now come to reverse all this, to scrap or even curb the political machine, and to rely on the soundness of popular opinion? Who could be sure that this would not have impaired the safety of the revolution? If a workers' democracy was needed, did that mean that the Mensheviks and the Social Revolutionaries were to be allowed to come back? Most of Stalin's critics, including Trotsky, agreed that the Mensheviks should remain outlawed. In their view, the time had not yet come to lift the state of siege in the republic—they wanted it to be lifted in the party only. But was it at all possible that the party should be an island of freedom in a society doomed, for good or evil, to

---

[1] M. Eastman, *Since Lenin Died*, Appendix IV, pp. 142-3.
[2] N. Popov, *Outline History*, vol. ii, pp. 144-96.
[3] N. Popov, *Outline History*, vol. ii, pp. 144-96.

dictatorial rule? Apart from all this, the massive dictatorial machine had now a vested interest in self-perpetuation, which it was able to identify with the broader interest of the revolution. Both sides in the dispute were aware of the dilemma; but while to one of them, the opposition, that awareness was a source of weakness, to the other it was a source of strength.

Trotsky consequently demanded not more than a limited reform, to be promulgated from above, a degree of administrative liberalism. He had been careful so far to refrain from any appeal to public opinion, even Communist opinion, against the rulers. Yet he felt the need for bringing the dispute into the open. The official inauguration of a public discussion gave him the opportunity to do so, the opportunity, that is, to appeal to public opinion against the rulers and to do so with the rulers' own formal permission. His inconsistency, real or apparent, was dictated by deeper considerations. He believed that it should be possible to strike a balance between dictatorship and freedom, that it should be possible to restrict or broaden the one or the other, according to circumstances. He hoped that with Russia's economic recovery and the progress of socialism, the régime would be able to rely less and less upon coercion and more and more upon willing support. The revolution should be able to recapture its own youth. The divorce between the revolution and the people, he thought, was of a temporary character. The triumvirs, and especially Stalin, were far less hopeful.

Here we touch the root of most of the differences between Trotskyism and Stalinism. Both insisted on their basic loyalty to the Marxist outlook; and there is no reason to doubt the sincerity of their professions. For both factions to claim allegiance to Marxism and Leninism was as natural as it is for Protestants and Catholics to swear by Christianity. In the one case as in the other the professions of faith, common to both sides, offer almost no clue to their antagonism. What underlay Trotsky's attitude was a cautious and yet very real revolutionary optimism, a belief that, if only the rulers pursued the right Socialist policy, the working classes would support them. This belief had indeed been implicit in the Marxist philosophy; and Stalin never openly contradicted it. But between the lines of his policies there is always present a deep disbelief in the popularity of socialism, and even more than that: an essentially pessimistic approach to man and society. . . .

Meanwhile the one text of Lenin that might have removed the earth from under Stalin's feet, his will, was still unknown to the party and to himself. Only in May, four months after Lenin's death, was it read out at a plenary session of the Central Committee, which was to decide whether the document should be made public at the forthcoming congress of the party. "Terrible embarrassment paralysed all those present," so an eyewitness describes the scene.[1] "Stalin sitting on the steps of the rostrum looked small and miserable. I studied him closely; in spite of his self-control

[1] B. Bazhanov, *Stalin, der Rote Diktator*, pp. 32-4.

and show of calm, it was clearly evident that his fate was at stake." In the
atmosphere of the Leninist cult, it seemed almost sacrilegious to disregard
Lenin's will. At this, for him, fateful moment he was saved by Zinoviev.
"Comrades," so Zinoviev addressed the meeting, "every word of Ilyich
[Lenin] is law to us. . . . We have sworn to fulfil anything the dying Ilyich
ordered us to do. You know perfectly well that we shall keep that vow."
(Many among the audience drop their eyes—they cannot look the old actor
in the face.) "But we are happy to say that in one point Lenin's fears have
proved baseless. I have in mind the point about our General Secretary.
You have all witnessed our harmonious co-operation in the last few months;
and, like myself, you will be happy to say that Lenin's fears have proved
baseless." Kamenev followed with an appeal to the Central Committee that
Stalin be left in office. But if this was to happen it was not advisable to publish Lenin's will at the congress. Krupskaya protested against the suppression of her husband's testament, but in vain. Trotsky, present at the meeting, was too proud to intervene in a situation which affected his own standing too. He kept silent, expressing only through his mien and grimaces
his disgust at the scene. Zinoviev's motion that the testament should not be
published, but only confidentially communicated to picked delegates, was
then passed by forty votes against ten. Stalin could now wipe the cold sweat
from his brow. He was back in the saddle, firmly and for good.

The solidarity of the triumvirs stood this extraordinary test because
both Zinoviev and Kamenev were as convinced that they had nothing to
fear from Stalin as they were afraid of Trotsky. Zinoviev, the President of
the Communist International, was still the senior and the most popular
triumvir. Kamenev was conscious of his intellectual superiority over his
partners. Both looked upon Stalin as upon their auxiliary; and, though
they were sometimes uneasy about a streak of perversity in him, neither suspected him of the ambition to become Lenin's sole successor. Nor, for that
matter, did any such suspicion enter the mind of the party as a whole. It
was not, on the other hand, very difficult to arouse in the party distrust of
Trotsky. The agents of the triumvirate whispered that Trotsky was the
potential Danton or, alternatively, the Bonaparte of the Russian revolution.
The whispering campaign was effective, because the party had, from its
beginnings, been accustomed to consult the great French precedent. It had
always been admitted that history might repeat itself; and that a Directory
or a single usurper might once again climb to power on the back of the
revolution. It was taken for granted that the Russian usurper would, like
his French prototype, be a personality possessed of brilliance and legendary
fame won in battles. The mask of Bonaparte seemed to fit Trotsky only too
well. Indeed, it might have fitted any personality with the exception of
Stalin. In this lay part of his strength.

The very thing which under different circumstances would have been
a liability in a man aspiring to power, his obscurity, was his important asset.

The party had been brought up to distrust "bourgeois individualism" and to strive for collectivism. None of its leaders looked as immune from the former and as expressive of the latter as Stalin. What was striking in the General Secretary was that there was nothing striking about him. His almost impersonal personality seemed to be the ideal vehicle for the anonymous forces of class and party. His bearing seemed of the utmost modesty. He was more accessible to the average official or party man than the other leaders. He studiously cultivated his contacts with the people who in one way or another made and unmade reputations, provincial secretaries, popular satirical writers, and foreign visitors. Himself taciturn, he was unsurpassed at the art of patiently listening to others. . . .

Nor did Stalin at that time impress people as being more intolerant than befitted a Bolshevik leader. He was, as we have seen, less vicious in his attacks on the opposition than the other triumvirs. In his speeches there was usually the tone of a good-natured and soothing, if facile, optimism, which harmonized well with the party's growing complacency. In the Politbureau, when matters of high policy were under debate, he never seemed to impose his views on his colleagues. He carefully followed the course of the debate to see which way the wind was blowing and invariably voted with the majority, unless he had assured his majority beforehand. He was therefore always agreeable to the majority. To party audiences he appeared as a man without personal grudge and rancour, as a detached Leninist, a guardian of the doctrine who criticized others only for the sake of the cause. He gave this impression even when he spoke behind the closed doors of the Politbureau. In the middle of the struggle Trotsky still described Stalin to a trusted foreign visitor as "a brave and sincere revolutionary." [1] A few descriptions of scenes in the Politbureau give a vivid glimpse of Stalin, the good soul:

When I attended a session of the Politbureau for the first time [writes Bazhanov] the struggle between the triumvirs and Trotsky was in full swing. Trotsky was the first to arrive for the session. The others were late, they were still plotting. . . . Next entered Zinoviev. He passed by Trotsky; and both behaved as if they had not noticed one another. When Kamenev entered, he greeted Trotsky with a slight nod. At last Stalin came in. He approached the table at which Trotsky was seated, greeted him in a most friendly manner and vigorously shook hands with him across the table.[2]

During another session, in the autumn of 1923, one of the triumvirs proposed that Stalin be brought in as a controller into the Commissariat of War, of which Trotsky was still the head. Trotsky, irritated by the proposal, declared that he was resigning from office and asked to be relieved from all posts and honours in Russia and allowed to go to Germany, which then seemed to be on the brink of a Communist upheaval, to take part in

[1] M. Eastman, *Since Lenin Died*, p. 55.
[2] B. Bazhanov, *Stalin, der Rote Diktator*, p. 21.

the revolution there. Zinoviev countered the move by asking the same for himself. Stalin put an end to the scene, declaring that "the party could not possibly dispense with the services of two such important and beloved leaders." [1]

He was slowly stacking his cards and waiting. The opposition, though again condemned by the thirteenth congress in May 1924, was still a factor to be reckoned with. The attitude of the Communist International had also to be considered. The leaders of European communism, Germans, Poles, and Frenchmen, had either protested against the discrediting of Trotsky or attempted to persuade the antagonists to make peace. It took Zinoviev a lot of wire-pulling to silence those "noises off." He had behind him the prestige of the only victorious Communist party, the international myth, so to say, of the October revolution, from which only very few Communists dared to break away. He also had at his disposal the treasure of the International, to which the Russian party was the greatest single contributor and on which some European parties were, up to a point, dependent. Enough that by using all means of pressure, after the expulsion or demotion of many Communist leaders, the triumvirate succeeded in extracting a pronouncement against the Russian opposition from the fifth congress of the International, which sat in Moscow in June and July 1924. Stalin, who had so far kept aloof from the Comintern, addressed in private its Polish commission and castigated the Poles for their bias in favour of Trotsky.[2]

Dissension among the triumvirs was yet another reason for Stalin's caution. Not until a year later, in 1925, did they fall out; but even now personal jealousies troubled their relations. Zinoviev and Kamenev began to feel that Stalin was tightening his grip on the party machine and excluding them from control. Stalin was envious of their authority in matters of doctrine. Shortly after the condemnation of Trotsky, he made his first public attack, irrelevant in content, on Kamenev's doctrinal unreliability.[3] Each of the triumvirs had enough ground to think that a split between them might drive one of them to join hands with Trotsky against the others. This motive did not impel Zinoviev and Kamenev, who eventually were to coalesce with Trotsky, to soften their attacks on him; but it did enter into Stalin's tactical calculations. As a tactician he proved himself superior to his partners.

Finally, he was still waiting for the adversary to make the blunders that were inherent in his attitude. Trotsky had accepted the Leninist cult, even though his rational mind and European tastes were outraged by it. The uniform of Lenin's disciple was, anyhow, too tight for him. The Leninist *mystique,* however, had already grown too powerful for anybody who wanted to get the hearing of a Communist audience to ignore it, let

[1] *Ibid.,* p. 52.
[2] J. Stalin, *Sochinenya,* vol. vi, pp. 264-72.
[3] *Ibid.,* p. 257.

alone challenge it. Trotsky thus involved himself in fighting on ground
where he was weak. The triumvirs hurled at him old anti-Trotskyist quotations from Lenin and, what was even more embarrassing to him, his own
strictures on Lenin which he had uttered twelve or fifteen years ago. In
the mind of the young Communist, the selection of such quotations added
up to a picture of Trotsky malevolently opposing Lenin at every turn of
events, from the split in 1903 to the debates over Brest Litovsk and the trade
unions. In the light of the Leninist dogma, Trotsky stood condemned.

For Trotsky to reject the dogma would have meant to appeal against
the party to non-communist opinion. This was the one thing that Stalin
could be quite sure Trotsky would not do. Outside the party, formless revolutionary frustration mingled with distinctly counter-revolutionary trends.
Since the ruling group had singled out Trotsky as a target for attack, he
automatically attracted the spurious sympathy of many who had hitherto
hated him. As he made his appearance in the streets of Moscow, he was
spontaneously applauded by crowds in which idealistic Communists rubbed
shoulders with Mensheviks, Social Revolutionaries, and the new *bourgeoisie*
of the N.E.P., by all those indeed who, for diverse reasons, hoped for a
change.[1] Precisely because he refused to rally in his support such mixed
elements, he showed timidity and hesitancy in almost every move he made.
He could not stop opposing the triumvirs who had identified themselves
with the party; and yet even in his rebellion he still remained on his knees
before the party. Every move he made was thus a demonstration of weakness. Stalin could afford to wait until his rival defeated himself through a
series of such demonstrations.

It is here that the knot was tied which was to be cut only in the tragic
purge trials twelve and thirteen years later. It is here, too, that the most
important clue to the understanding of those trials is to be found. At the
congress in May 1924, Trotsky, facing the implacably hostile phalanx of
party secretaries, was on the point of surrendering to his critics and abjur-
ing the opposition. Krupskaya, Radek, and others exhorted the antagonists
to make peace. Zinoviev, however, was not to be persuaded. He demanded
that Trotsky should surrender in his thoughts as well as in his deeds, that
he should admit that he had been wrong in his criticisms. In the history
of Bolshevism this was the first instance where a member of the party was
vaguely charged with a "crime of conscience," a purely theological accusation. Its motive was tactical, not theological: Trotsky, submitting to party
discipline but not recanting, still seemed to the triumvirs a formidable foe.
Zinoviev therefore added to the terms of his submission an obviously un-
acceptable point, which would compel Trotsky to go on waging the unequal
struggle. Thus, the first suggestion of a "crime of conscience" against the
party was made by the man who, twelve years later, was to go to his death
with appalling recantations of his own "crimes of conscience." Stalin, at

[1] M. Eastman, *Since Lenin Died*, p. 128, and B. Bazhanov, *Stalin, der Rote Diktator*.

least in appearance, had nothing to do with that. He repeatedly stated that the only condition for peace was that Trotsky should stop his attacks. He repeatedly made the gesture that looked like the stretching out of his hand to his opponent.

Trotsky's reply to Zinoviev was pregnant with the tragedy that was to overwhelm Zinoviev and Kamenev even more cruelly than himself:

> The party [Trotsky said] in the last analysis is always right, because the party is the single historic instrument given to the proletariat for the solution of its fundamental problems. I have already said that in front of one's own party nothing could be easier than to acknowledge a mistake, nothing easier than to say: all my criticisms, my statements, my warnings, my protests—the whole thing was a mere mistake. I, however, comrades, cannot say that, because I do not think it. I know that one must not be right *against* the party. One can be right only with the party, and through the party, for history has created no other road for the realization of what is right. The English have a saying: "Right or wrong—my country." With far greater historic justification we may say: right or wrong, on separate particular issues, it is my party. . . .[1]

These words of the leader of the opposition resembled less the words a patriotic Englishman might use than those of a medieval heretic, confessing his heresy, rueful and yet stubborn in his conviction, able to see no salvation beyond the Church and yet none in the Church either. Stalin sarcastically dismissed Trotsky's statement, saying that the party made no claim to infallibility. . . .

·   ·   ·   ·   ·

Stalin first formulated his ideas on socialism in one country in the autumn of 1924. Belief in socialism in one country was soon to become the supreme test of loyalty to party and state. In the next ten or fifteen years nobody who failed that test was to escape condemnation and punishment. Yet, if one studies the "prolegomena" to this article of Stalinist faith, one is struck by the fact that it was first put forward by Stalin almost casually, like a mere debating point, in the "literary discussion." For many months, until the summer of the next year, none of Stalin's rivals, neither the other triumvirs nor Trotsky, thought the point worth arguing. Nor was Stalin's own mind fixed. In his pamphlet *The Foundations of Leninism,* published early in 1924, he stated with great emphasis that, though the proletariat of one country could seize power, it could not establish a Socialist economy in one country. . . .

He now stated [later in 1924] that the efforts of Russia alone would suffice for the *complete* organization of a Socialist economy. A Socialist economy—this had so far been taken for granted—was conceivable only as an economy of plenty. This presupposed a highly developed industry

---

[1] *13 Syezd Vsesoyuznoi Komunisticheskoi Partii,* pp. 166 and 245. See also M. Eastman, *Since Lenin Died,* pp. 88-9.

capable of ensuring a high standard of living for the whole people. How then, the question arose, could a country like Russia, whose meagre industry had been reduced to rack and ruin, achieve socialism? Stalin pointed to Russia's great assets: her vast spaces and enormous riches in raw materials. A proletarian government could, in his view, through its control of industry and credit, develop those resources and carry the building of socialism to a successful conclusion, because in this endeavour it would be supported by a vast majority of the people, including the peasants.

This, the most essential, part of Stalin's formula was very simple. It proclaimed in terms clear to everybody the self-sufficiency of the Russian revolution. It was true that Stalin begged many a question. He did not even try to meet the objections to his thesis that were raised later by his critics. One objection that most peasants, attached as they were to private property, were certain to put up the strongest resistance to collectivism, he simply dismissed as a heretical slander on the peasantry. Nor did he seriously consider the other argument that socialism was possible only on the basis of the intensive industrialization already achieved by the most advanced western countries; and that Russia by herself would not be able to catch up with those countries. According to his critics, socialism could beat capitalism only if it represented a higher productivity of labour and higher standards of living than had been attained under capitalism. The critics deduced that if productivity of labour and standards of living were to remain lower in Russia than in the capitalist countries then socialism would, in the long run, fail even in Russia. Nor did Stalin ever try to refute their forecast that in an economy of scarcity, such as an isolated Russian economy would be, a new and glaring material inequality between various social groups was certain to arise.

But, whatever the flaws in Stalin's reasoning, flaws that were obvious only to the most educated men in the party, his formula was politically very effective. It contained, at any rate, one clear and positive proposition: we are able to stand on our own feet, to build and to complete the building of socialism. This was what made the formula useful for polemical and practical purposes. It offered a plain alternative to Trotsky's conception. For a variety of reasons, however, Stalin did not present his thesis in that plain and clear-cut form. He hedged it round with all sorts of reservations and qualifications. One reservation was that the victory of socialism in Russia could not be considered secure so long as her capitalist environment threatened Russia with armed intervention. Socialism in a single state could not be beaten by the "cheap goods" produced in capitalist countries of which his critics spoke; but it might be defeated by force of arms. In the next few years Stalin himself constantly held that danger before Russia's eyes and thereby seemed to weaken his own case. Moreover, he went on to express, though with ever decreasing confidence, a belief in the proximity of international revolution. He proclaimed the absolute self-sufficiency of

Russian socialism in one half of his thesis and disclaimed it in the other.

The strangeness of that passionate ideological dispute does not end here. As the controversy developed, Stalin ascribed to his critics the view that it was not possible to build socialism in Russia. He then presented the issue as one between those who believed in the "creative force" of the revolution and the "panic mongers" and "pessimists." Now the issue was not as simple as that. His critics were beyond question not guilty of the things imputed to them. They, too, asserted that it was possible and necessary to organize the country's economy on Socialist lines. Trotsky in particular had, since the end of the civil war, urged the Politbureau to begin gearing up the administration for planned economy; and in those early days he first sketched most of the ideas that were later to be embodied in the five-year plans.[1]

The student of the controversy may thus often have the uncanny feeling that its very object is indefinable; that, having aroused unbounded passion and bitterness, it simply vanishes into thin air. Stripped of polemical distortions and insinuations, the debate seems in the end, to the student's astonishment, to centre on a bizarre irrelevancy. The point was not whether socialism could or should be built but whether the building could be *completed* in a single isolated state.

"TESTAMENT"

V. I. LENIN

In mid-December 1922, Lenin suffered a stroke and felt the nearness of death. On December 25, he dictated a memorandum to his secretary to be made known to the Party in the event of his death. On December 30, he turned his attention to a conflict in Georgia (U.S.S.R.) and in his notes spoke of "the hastiness and administrative impulsiveness" of Stalin and added that "it behooves us to hold Stalin . . . politically responsible for this genuine Great Russian nationalistic campaign." On January 4, 1923, he dictated a postscript to his "Testament."

Subsequently, in the early months of 1923, when Lenin had recovered

---

[1] N. Bukharin in his *Kritika Ekonomicheskoi Platformy Oppozitsii*, entirely devoted to a criticism of Trotsky's, Piatakov's, and Preobrazhensky's economic ideas, quotes Trotsky's letter to the Central Committee (8 October 1923), in which Trotsky summed up his policy as follows: "Planned economy; severe concentration of industry; severe reduction of costs" (p. 54). In his *Novyi Kurs,* published later in the year, Trotsky urged the subordination of financial and monetary policy to the needs of industrialization (ibid., pp. 71-2). This brought upon him the charge that he advocated the "dictatorship of industry" and "super-industrialization." See N. Bukharin, op. cit., pp. 3, 53-4.

somewhat from his illness, he launched a devastating attack on Stalin. His March 4 article in Pravda, *without direct mention of Stalin, bitterly assailed the Workers' and Peasants' Inspectorate, which Stalin headed. The next day, Lenin "broke off" all personal relations with Stalin and prepared for his denunciation. But soon, thereafter, Lenin became incapacitated again. He died on January 21, 1924.*

The "Testament," although known to the Soviet leaders, was not published in the Soviet press until May 18, 1956, when a part of it first appeared in Komsomolskaya Pravda, *the Young Communist newspaper, to explain what was behind the attack on the "cult of the individual."*

By the stability of the Central Committee, of which I spoke before, I mean measures to prevent a split, so far as such measures can be taken. For, of course, the White Guard in *Russkaya Mysl* (I think it was S. E. Oldenburg) was right when, in the first place, in his play against Soviet Russia he banked on the hope of a split in our party, and when, in the second place, he banked for that split on serious disagreements in our party.

Our party rests upon two classes, and for that reason its instability is possible, and if there cannot exist an agreement between those classes its fall is inevitable. In such an event it would be useless to take any measures or in general to discuss the stability of our Central Committee. In such an event no measures would prove capable of preventing a split. But I trust that is too remote a future, and too improbable an event, to talk about.

I have in mind stability as a guarantee against a split in the near future, and I intended to examine here a series of considerations of a purely personal character.

I think that the fundamental factor in the matter of stability—from this point of view—is such members of the Central Committee as Stalin and Trotsky. The relation between them constitutes, in my opinion, a big half of the danger of that split, which might be avoided, and the avoidance of which might be promoted, in my opinion, by raising the number of members of the Central Committee to fifty or one hundred.

Comrade Stalin, having become General Secretary, has concentrated an enormous power in his hands; and I am not sure that he always knows how to use that power with sufficient caution. On the other hand, Comrade Trotsky, as was proved by his struggle against the Central Committee in connection with the question of the People's Commissariat of Ways and Communications, is distinguished not only by his exceptional abilities—personally he is, to be sure, the most able man in the present Central Committee—but also by his too far-reaching self-confidence and a disposition to be too much attracted by the purely administrative side of affairs.

These two qualities of the two most able leaders of the present Central Committee might, quite innocently, lead to a split; if our party does not take measures to prevent it, a split might arise unexpectedly.

I will not further characterize the other members of the Central Committee as to their personal qualities. I will only remind you that the October episode of Zinoviev and Kamenev was not, of course, accidental, but that it ought as little to be used against them personally as the non-Bolshevism of Trotsky.

Of the younger members of the Central Committee, I want to say a few words about Bukharin and Pyatakov. They are in my opinion, the most able forces (among the youngest) and in regard to them it is necessary to bear in mind the following: Bukharin is not only the most valuable and biggest theoretician of the party, but also may legitimately be considered the favorite of the whole party; but his theoretical views can only with the very greatest doubt be regarded as fully Marxist, for there is something scholastic in him (he never has learned, and I think never has fully understood, the dialectic).

And then Pyatakov—a man undoubtedly distinguished in will and ability, but too much given over to administration and the administrative side of things to be relied on in a serious political question.

Of course, both these remarks are made by me merely with a view to the present time, or supposing that these two able and loyal workers may not find an occasion to supplement their knowledge and correct their one-sidedness.

December 25, 1922

Postscript: Stalin is too rude, and this fault, entirely supportable in relations among us Communists, becomes insupportable in the office of General Secretary. Therefore, I propose to the comrades to find a way to remove Stalin from that position and appoint to it another man who in all respects differs from Stalin only in superiority—namely, more patient, more loyal, more polite and more attentive to comrades, less capricious, etc. This circumstance may seem an insignificant trifle, but I think that from the point of view of preventing a split and from the point of view of the relation between Stalin and Trotsky which I discussed above, it is not a trifle, or it is such a trifle as may acquire a decisive significance.

January 4, 1923

THE REVOLUTION BETRAYED

LEON TROTSKY*

THE SOVIET THERMIDOR

1. Why Stalin Triumphed . . . A political struggle is in its essence a struggle of interests and forces, not of arguments. The quality of the leadership is, of course, far from a matter of indifference for the outcome of the conflict, but it is not the only factor, and in the last analysis is not decisive. Each of the struggling camps moreover demands leaders in its own image.

The February revolution raised Kerensky and Tseretelli to power, not because they were "cleverer" or "more astute" than the ruling tsarist clique, but because they represented, at least temporarily, the revolutionary masses of the people in their revolt against the old regime. Kerensky was able to drive Lenin underground and imprison other Bolshevik leaders, not because he excelled them in personal qualifications, but because the majority of the workers and soldiers in those days were still following the patriotic petty bourgeoisie. The personal "superiority" of Kerensky, if it is suitable to employ such a word in this connection, consisted in the fact that he did not see farther than the overwhelming majority. The Bolsheviks in their turn conquered the petty bourgeois democrats, not through the personal superiority of their leaders, but through a new correlation of social forces. The proletariat had succeeded at last in leading the discontented peasantry against the bourgeoisie.

The consecutive stages of the great French Revolution, during its rise and fall alike, demonstrate no less convincingly that the strength of the "leaders" and "heroes" that replaced each other consisted primarily in their correspondence to the character of those classes and strata which supported them. Only this correspondence, and not any irrelevant superiorities whatever, permitted each of them to place the impress of his personality upon a certain historic period. . . .

It is sufficiently well known that every revolution up to this time has been followed by a reaction, or even a counter-revolution. This, to be sure, has never thrown the nation all the way back to its starting point, but it has always taken from the people the lion's share of their conquests. The victims of the first reactionary wave have been, as a general rule, those pioneers, initiators, and instigators who stood at the head of the masses in

* The selection is from Chapter 5 and the Appendix of the book by the same title, written by Trotsky in 1936 (New York: Pioneer Publishers, 1945). By permission of the publisher.

the period of the revolutionary offensive. In their stead people of the second line, in league with the former enemies of the revolution, have been advanced to the front. Beneath this dramatic duel of "coryphées" on the open political scene, shifts have taken place in the relations between classes, and, no less important, profound changes in the psychology of the recently revolutionary masses. . . .

A revolution is a mighty devourer of human energy, both individual and collective. The nerves give way. Consciousness is shaken and characters are worn out. Events unfold too swiftly for the flow of fresh forces to replace the loss. Hunger, unemployment, the death of the revolutionary cadres, the removal of the masses from administration, all this led to such a physical and moral impoverishment of the Parisian suburbs that they required three decades before they were ready for a new insurrection.

The axiomlike assertions of the Soviet literature, to the effect that the laws of bourgeois revolutions are "inapplicable" to a proletarian revolution, have no scientific content whatever. The proletarian character of the October revolution was determined by the world situation and by a special correlation of internal forces. But the classes themselves were formed in the barbarous circumstances of tsarism and backward capitalism, and were anything but made to order for the demands of a socialist revolution. The exact opposite is true. It is for the very reason that a proletariat still backward in many respects achieved in the space of a few months the unprecedented leap from a semifeudal monarchy to a socialist dictatorship, that the reaction in its ranks was inevitable. This reaction has developed in a series of consecutive waves. External conditions and events have vied with each other in nourishing it. Intervention followed intervention. The revolution got no direct help from the west. Instead of the expected prosperity of the country an ominous destitution reigned for long. Moreover, the outstanding representatives of the working class either died in the civil war, or rose a few steps higher and broke away from the masses. And thus after an unexampled tension of forces, hopes and illusions, there came a long period of weariness, decline and sheer disappointment in the results of the revolution. The ebb of the "plebeian pride" made room for a flood of pusillanimity and careerism. The new commanding caste rose to its place upon this wave.

The demobilization of the Red Army of five million played no small role in the formation of the bureaucracy. The victorious commanders assumed leading posts in the local Soviets, in economy, in education, and they persistently introduced everywhere that regime which had ensured success in the civil war. Thus on all sides the masses were pushed away gradually from actual participation in the leadership of the country.

The reaction within the proletariat caused an extraordinary flush of hope and confidence in the petty bourgeois strata of town and country, aroused as they were to new life by the NEP, and growing bolder and bolder.

The young bureaucracy, which had arisen at first as an agent of the proletariat, began now to feel itself a court of arbitration between the classes.
Its independence increased from month to month.

The international situation was pushing with mighty forces in the
same direction. The Soviet bureaucracy became more self-confident, the
heavier the blows dealt to the world working class. Between these two facts
there was not only a chronological, but a causal connection, and one which
worked in two directions. The leaders of the bureaucracy promoted the
proletarian defeats; the defeats promoted the rise of the bureaucracy. The
crushing of the Bulgarian insurrection and the inglorious retreat of the
German workers' party in 1923, the collapse of the Esthonian attempt at
insurrection in 1924, the treacherous liquidation of the General Strike in
England and the unworthy conduct of the Polish workers' party at the installation of Pilsudski in 1926, the terrible massacre of the Chinese revolution in 1927, and, finally, the still more ominous recent defeats in Germany and Austria—these are the historic catastrophes which killed the faith
of the Soviet masses in world revolution, and permitted the bureaucracy to
rise higher and higher as the sole light of salvation. . . .

Two dates are especially significant in this historic series. In the second
half of 1923, the attention of the Soviet workers was passionately fixed upon
Germany, where the proletariat, it seemed, had stretched out its hand to
power. The panicky retreat of the German Communist Party was the
heaviest possible disappointment to the working masses of the Soviet Union.
The Soviet bureaucracy straightway opened a campaign against the theory
of "permanent revolution," and dealt the Left Opposition its first cruel
blow. During the years 1926 and 1927 the population of the Soviet Union
experienced a new tide of hope. All eyes were now directed to the East
where the drama of the Chinese revolution was unfolding. The Left Opposition had recovered from the previous blows and was recruiting a phalanx of new adherents. At the end of 1927 the Chinese revolution was
massacred by the hangman, Chiang-kai-shek, into whose hands the Communist International had literally betrayed the Chinese workers and peasants. A cold wave of disappointment swept over the masses of the Soviet
Union. After an unbridled baiting in the press and at meetings, the
bureaucracy finally, in 1928, ventured upon mass arrests among the Left
Opposition.

To be sure, tens of thousands of revolutionary fighters gathered around
the banner of the Bolshevik-Leninists. The advanced workers were indubitably sympathetic to the Opposition, but that sympathy remained passive. The masses lacked faith that the situation could be seriously changed
by a new struggle. Meantime the bureaucracy asserted: "For the sake of an
international revolution, the Opposition proposes to drag us into a revolutionary war. Enough of shake-ups! We have earned the right to rest.
We will build the socialist society at home. Rely upon us, your leaders!"

This gospel of repose firmly consolidated the *apparatchiki* and the military and state officials and indubitably found an echo among the weary workers, and still more the peasant masses. Can it be, they asked themselves, that the Opposition is actually ready to sacrifice the interests of the Soviet Union for the idea of "permanent revolution?" In reality, the struggle had been about the life interests of the Soviet state. The false policy of the International in Germany resulted ten years later in the victory of Hitler —that is, in a threatening war danger from the West. And the no less false policy in China reinforced Japanese imperialism and brought very much nearer the danger in the East. But periods of reaction are characterized above all by a lack of courageous thinking.

The Opposition was isolated. The bureaucracy struck while the iron was hot, exploiting the bewilderment and passivity of the workers, setting their more backward strata against the advanced, and relying more and more boldly upon the kulak and the petty bourgeois ally in general. In the course of a few years, the bureaucracy thus shattered the revolutionary vanguard of the proletariat.

It would be naïve to imagine that Stalin, previously unknown to the masses, suddenly issued from the wings fully armed with a complete strategical plan. No indeed. Before he felt out his own course, the bureaucracy felt out Stalin himself. He brought it all the necessary guarantees: the prestige of an old Bolshevik, a strong character, narrow vision, and close bonds with the political machine as the sole source of his influence. The success which fell upon him was a surprise at first to Stalin himself. It was the friendly welcome of the new ruling group, trying to free itself from the old principles and from the control of the masses, and having need of a reliable arbiter in its inner affairs. A secondary figure before the masses and in the events of the revolution, Stalin revealed himself as the indubitable leader of the Thermidorian bureaucracy, as first in its midst. . . .

Personal incidents in the interval between these two historic chapters were not, of course, without influence. Thus the sickness and death of Lenin undoubtedly hastened the denouement. Had Lenin lived longer, the pressure of the bureaucratic power would have developed, at least during the first years, more slowly. But as early as 1926 Krupskaya said, in a circle of Left Oppositionists: "If Ilych were alive, he would probably already be in prison." The fears and alarming prophecies of Lenin himself were then still fresh in her memory, and she cherished no illusions as to his personal omnipotence against opposing historic winds and currents.

The bureaucracy conquered something more than the Left Opposition. It conquered the Bolshevik party. It defeated the program of Lenin, who had seen the chief danger in the conversion of the organs of the state "from servants of society to lords over society." It defeated all these enemies, the Opposition, the party and Lenin, not with ideas and arguments, but with its own social weight. The leaden rump of the bureaucracy outweighed the head of the revolution. That is the secret of the Soviet's Thermidor.

2. The Degeneration of the Bolshevik Party. The Bolshevik party prepared and insured the October victory. It also created the Soviet state, supplying it with a sturdy skeleton. The degeneration of the party became both cause and consequence of the bureaucratization of the state. It is necessary to show at least briefly how this happened.

The inner regime of the Bolshevik party was characterized by the method of *democratic centralism*. The combination of these two concepts, democracy and centralism, is not in the least contradictory. The party took watchful care not only that its boundaries should always be strictly defined, but also that all those who entered these boundaries should enjoy the actual right to define the direction of the party policy. Freedom of criticism and intellectual struggle was an irrevocable content of the party democracy. The present doctrine that Bolshevism does not tolerate factions is a myth of the epoch of decline. In reality the history of Bolshevism is a history of the struggle of factions. And, indeed, how could a genuinely revolutionary organization, setting itself the task of overthrowing the world and uniting under its banner the most audacious iconoclasts, fighters and insurgents, live and develop without intellectual conflicts, without groupings and temporary factional formations? The farsightedness of the Bolshevik leadership often made it possible to soften conflicts and shorten the duration of factional struggle, but no more than that. The Central Committee relied upon this seething democratic support. From this it derived the audacity to make decisions and give orders. The obvious correctness of the leadership at all critical stages gave it that high authority which is the priceless moral capital of centralism.

The regime of the Bolshevik party, especially before it came to power, stood thus in complete contradiction to the regime of the present sections of the Communist International, with their "leaders" appointed from above, making complete changes of policy at a word of command, with their uncontrolled apparatus, haughty in its attitude to the rank and file, servile in its attitude to the Kremlin. But in the first years after the conquest of power also, even when the administrative rust was already visible on the party, every Bolshevik, not excluding Stalin, would have denounced as a malicious slanderer anyone who should have shown him on a screen the image of the party ten or fifteen years later.

The very center of Lenin's attention and that of his colleagues was occupied by a continual concern to protect the Bolshevik ranks from the vices of those in power. However, the extraordinary closeness and at times actual merging of the party with the state apparatus had already in those first years done indubitable harm to the freedom and elasticity of the party regime. Democracy had been narrowed in proportion as difficulties increased. In the beginning, the party had wished and hoped to preserve freedom of political struggle within the framework of the Soviets. The civil war introduced stern amendments into this calculation. The opposition parties were forbidden one after the other. This measure, obviously in conflict with the spirit of Soviet democracy, the leaders of Bolshevism regarded not as a principle, but as an episodic act of self-defense.

The swift growth of the ruling party, with the novelty and immensity of its tasks, inevitably gave rise to inner disagreements. The underground oppositional currents in the country exerted a pressure through various channels upon the sole legal political organization, increasing the acuteness of the factional struggle. At the moment of completion of the civil war, this struggle took such sharp forms as to threaten to unsettle the state power. In March 1921, in the days of the Kronstadt revolt, which attracted into its ranks no small number of Bolsheviks, the tenth congress of the party thought it necessary to resort to a prohibition of factions—that is, to transfer the political regime prevailing in the state to the inner life of the ruling party. This forbidding of factions was again regarded as an exceptional measure to be abandoned at the first serious improvement in the situation. At the same time, the Central Committee was extremely cautious in applying the new law, concerning itself most of all lest it lead to a strangling of the inner life of the party.

However, what was in its original design merely a necessary concession to a difficult situation, proved perfectly suited to the taste of the bureaucracy, which had then begun to approach the inner life of the party exclusively from the viewpoint of convenience in administration. Already in 1922, during a brief improvement in his health, Lenin, horrified at the threatening growth of bureaucratism, was preparing a struggle against the faction of Stalin, which had made itself the axis of the party machine as a first step toward capturing the machinery of state. A second stroke and then death prevented him from measuring forces with this internal reaction.

The entire effort of Stalin, with whom at that time Zinoviev and Kamenev were working hand in hand, was thenceforth directed to freeing the party machine from the control of the rank-and-file members of the party. In this struggle for "stability" of the Central Committee, Stalin proved the most consistent and reliable among his colleagues. He had no need to tear himself away from international problems; he had never been concerned with them. The petty bourgeois outlook of the new ruling stratum was his own outlook. He profoundly believed that the task of creating socialism was national and administrative in its nature. He looked upon the Communist International as a necessary evil which should be used so far as possible for the purposes of foreign policy. His own party kept a value in his eyes merely as a submissive support for the machine

Together with the theory of socialism in one country, there was put into circulation by the bureaucracy a theory that in Bolshevism the Central

Committee is everything and the party nothing. This second theory was in any case realized with more success than the first. Availing itself of the death of Lenin, the ruling group announced a "Leninist levy." The gates of the party, always carefully guarded, were now thrown wide open. Workers, clerks, petty officials, flocked through in crowds. The political aim of this maneuver was to dissolve the revolutionary vanguard in raw human material, without experience, without independence, and yet with the old habit of submitting to the authorities. The scheme was successful. By freeing the bureaucracy from the control of the proletarian vanguard, the "Leninist levy" dealt a death blow to the party of Lenin. The machine had won the necessary independence. Democratic centralism gave place to bureaucratic centralism. In the party apparatus itself there now took place a radical reshuffling of personnel from top to bottom. The chief merit of a Bolshevik was declared to be obedience. Under the guise of a struggle with the Opposition, there occurred a sweeping replacement of revolutionists with *chinovniks*.[1] The history of the Bolshevik party became a history of its rapid degeneration. . . .

Of the Politburo of Lenin's epoch there now remains only Stalin. Two of its members, Zinoviev and Kamenev, collaborators of Lenin throughout many years as émigrés, are enduring ten-year prison terms for a crime which they did not commit. Three other members, Rykov, Bukharin and Tomsky, are completely removed from the leadership, but as a reward for submission occupy secondary posts. And, finally, the author of these lines is in exile. The widow of Lenin, Krupskaya, is also under the ban, having proved unable with all her efforts to adjust herself completely to the Thermidor.

[Editor's note: Zinoviev and Kamenev were executed in August 1936. Tomsky committed suicide on August 23, 1936, when "implicated" in the same case, and Rykov and Bukharin were executed in March 1938. Trotsky died on August 21, 1940, in Mexico City, from wounds inflicted by an assassin.]

The members of the present Politburo occupied secondary posts throughout the history of the Bolshevik party. If anybody in the first years of the revolution had predicted their future elevation, they would have been the first in surprise, and there would have been no false modesty in their surprise. For this very reason, the rule is more stern at present that the Politburo is always right, and in any case that no man can be right against the Politburo. But, moreover, the Politburo cannot be right against Stalin, who is unable to make mistakes and consequently cannot be right against himself.

Demands for party democracy were through all this time the slogans of all the oppositional groups, as insistent as they were hopeless. The above-

---

[1] Professional governmental functionaries.

mentioned platform of the Left Opposition demanded in 1927 that a special law be written into the Criminal Code "punishing as a serious state crime every direct or indirect persecution of a worker for criticism." Instead of this, there was introduced into the Criminal Code an article against the Left Opposition itself.

Of party democracy there remained only recollections in the memory of the older generation. And together with it had disappeared the democracy of the soviets, the trade unions, the co-operatives, the cultural and athletic organizations. Above each and every one of them there reigns an unlimited hierarchy of party secretaries. The regime had become "totalitarian" in character several years before this word arrived from Germany. "By means of demoralizing methods, which convert thinking communists into machines, destroying will, character and human dignity," wrote Rakovsky in 1928, "the ruling circles have succeeded in converting themselves into an unremovable and inviolate oligarchy, which replaces the class and the party." Since those indignant lines were written, the degeneration of the regime has gone immeasurably farther. The G.P.U. has become the decisive factor in the inner life of the party. If Molotov in March 1936 was able to boast to a French journalist that the ruling party no longer contains any factional struggle, it is only because disagreements are now settled by the automatic intervention of the political police. The old Bolshevik party is dead, and no force will resurrect it. . . .

In spite of the October revolution, the nationalization of the means of production, collectivization, and "the liquidation of the kulaks as a class," the relations among men, and that at the very heights of the Soviet pyramid, have not only not yet risen to socialism, but in many respects are still lagging behind a cultured capitalism. In recent years enormous backward steps have been taken in this very important sphere. And the source of this revival of genuine Russian barbarism is indubitably the Soviet Thermidor, which has given complete independence and freedom from control to a bureaucracy possessing little culture, and has given to the masses the well-known gospel of obedience and silence.

We are far from intending to contrast the abstraction of dictatorship with the abstraction of democracy, and weigh their merits on the scales of pure reason. Everything is relative in this world, where change alone endures. The dictatorship of the Bolshevik party proved one of the most powerful instruments of progress in history. But here too, in the words of the poet, "Reason becomes unreason, kindness a pest." The prohibition of oppositional parties brought after it the prohibition of factions. The prohibition of factions ended in a prohibition to think otherwise than the infallible leaders. The police-manufactured monolithism of the party resulted in a bureaucratic impunity which has become the source of all kinds of wantonness and corruption.

3. **The Social Roots of Thermidor.** We have defined the Soviet Thermidor as a triumph of the bureaucracy over the masses. We have tried to disclose the historic conditions of this triumph. The revolutionary vanguard of the proletariat was in part devoured by the administrative apparatus and gradually demoralized, in part annihilated in the civil war, and in part thrown out and crushed. The tired and disappointed masses were indifferent to what was happening on the summits. These conditions, however, important as they may have been in themselves, are inadequate to explain why the bureaucracy succeeded in raising itself above society and getting its fate firmly into its own hands. Its own will to this would in any case be inadequate; the arising of a new ruling stratum must have deep social causes. . . .

We must now prolong our analysis of the conditions of the transition from capitalism to socialism, and the role of the state in this process. Let us again compare theoretic prophecy with reality. "It is still necessary to suppress the bourgeoisie and its resistance," wrote Lenin in 1917, speaking of the period which should begin immediately after the conquest of power, "but the organ of suppression here is now the majority of the population, and not the minority as has heretofore always been the case. . . . In that sense the state *is beginning to die away*." In what does this dying away express itself? Primarily in the fact that "in place of special institutions of a privileged minority (privileged officials, commanders of a standing army), the majority itself can directly carry out" the functions of suppression. Lenin follows this with a statement axiomatic and unanswerable: "The more universal becomes the very fulfillment of the functions of the state power, the less need is there of this power." The annulment of private property in the means of production removes the principal task of the historic state—defense of the proprietary privileges of the minority against the overwhelming majority.

The dying away of the state begins, then, according to Lenin, on the very day after the expropriation of the expropriators—that is, before the new regime has had time to take up its economic and cultural problems. Every success in the solution of these problems means a further step in the liquidation of the state, its dissolution in the socialist society. The degree of this dissolution is the best index of the depth and efficacy of the socialist structure. We may lay down approximately this sociological theorem: The strength of the compulsion exercised by the masses in a worker's state is directly proportional to the strength of the exploitive tendencies, or the danger of a restoration of capitalism, and inversely proportional to the strength of the social solidarity and the general loyalty of the new regime. Thus the bureaucracy—that is, the "privileged officials and commanders of a standing army"—represents a special kind of compulsion which the masses cannot or do not wish to exercise, and which, one way or another, is directed against the masses themselves.

If the democratic soviets had preserved to this day their original strength and independence, and yet were compelled to resort to repressions and compulsions on the scale of the first years, this circumstance might of itself give rise to serious anxiety. How much greater must be the alarm in view of the fact that the mass soviets have entirely disappeared from the scene, having turned over the function of compulsion to Stalin, Yagoda and company. And what forms of compulsion! First of all we must ask ourselves: What social cause stands behind this stubborn virility of the state and especially behind its policification? The importance of this question is obvious. In dependence upon the answer, we must either radically revise our traditional views of the socialist society in general, or as radically reject the official estimates of the Soviet Union.

Let us now take from the latest number of a Moscow newspaper a stereotyped characterization of the present Soviet regime, one of those which are repeated throughout the country from day to day and which school children learn by heart: "In the Soviet Union the parasitical classes of capitalists, landlords and kulaks are completely liquidated, and thus is forever ended the exploitation of man by man. The whole national economy has become socialistic, and the growing Stakhanov movement is preparing the conditions for a transition from socialism to communism." (*Pravda,* April 4, 1936.) The world press of the Communist International, it goes without saying, has no other thing to say on this subject. But if exploitation is "ended forever," if the country is really now on the road from socialism, that is, the lowest stage of communism, to its higher stage, then there remains nothing for society to do but to throw off at last the straitjacket of the state. In place of this—it is hard even to grasp this contrast with the mind!—the Soviet state has acquired a totalitarian-bureaucratic character.

The same fatal contradiction finds illustration in the fate of the party. Here the problem may be formulated approximately thus: Why, from 1917 to 1921, when the old ruling classes were still fighting with weapons in their hands, when they were actively supported by the imperialists of the whole world, when the kulaks in arms were sabotaging the army and food supplies of the country,—why was it possible to dispute openly and fearlessly in the party about the most critical questions of policy? Why now, after the cessation of intervention, after the shattering of the exploiting classes, after the indubitable successes of industrialization, after the collectivization of the overwhelming majority of the peasants, is it impossible to permit the slightest word of criticism of the unremovable leaders? Why is it that any Bolshevik who should demand a calling of the congress of the party in accordance with its constitution would be immediately expelled, any citizen who expressed out loud a doubt of the infallibility of Stalin would be tried and convicted almost as though a participant in a terrorist plot? Whence this terrible, monstrous and unbearable intensity of repression and of the police apparatus? . . .

A raising of the material and cultural level ought, at first glance, to lessen the necessity of privileges, narrow the sphere of application of "bourgeois law," and thereby undermine the standing ground of its defenders, the bureaucracy. In reality the opposite thing has happened: the growth of the productive forces has been so far accompanied by an extreme development of all forms of inequality, privilege and advantage, and therewith of bureaucratism. That too is not accidental.

In its first period, the Soviet regime was undoubtedly far more equalitarian and less bureaucratic than now. But that was an equality of general poverty. The resources of the country were so scant that there was no opportunity to separate out from the masses of the population any broad privileged strata. At the same time the "equalizing" character of wages, destroying personal interestedness, became a brake upon the development of the productive forces. Soviet economy had to lift itself from its poverty to a somewhat higher level before fat deposits of privilege became possible. The present state of production is still far from guaranteeing all necessities to everybody. But it is already adequate to give significant privileges to a minority, and convert inequality into a whip for the spurring on of the majority. That is the first reason why the growth of production has so far strengthened not the socialist, but the bourgeois features of the state.

But that is not the sole reason. Alongside the economic factor dictating capitalistic methods of payment at the present stage, there operates a parallel political factor in the person of the bureaucracy itself. In its very essence it is the planter and protector of inequality. It arose in the beginning as the bourgeois organ of a workers' state. In establishing and defending the advantages of a minority, it of course draws off the cream for its own use. Nobody who has wealth to distribute ever omits himself. Thus out of a social necessity there has developed an organ which has far outgrown its socially necessary function, and become an independent factor and therewith the source of great danger for the whole social organism.

The social meaning of the Soviet Thermidor now begins to take form before us. The poverty and cultural backwardness of the masses has again become incarnate in the malignant figure of the ruler with a great club in his hand. The deposed and abused bureaucracy, from being a servant of society, has again become its lord. On this road it has attained such a degree of social and moral alienation from the popular masses, that it cannot now permit any control over either its activities or its income. . . .

"SOCIALISM, IN ONE COUNTRY"

. . . In Lenin's "Declaration of the Rights of the Toiling and Exploited People"—presented by the Soviet of People's Commissars for the approval of the Constituent Assembly during its brief hours of life—the "fundamental task" of the new regime was thus defined: "The establishment of a socialist organization of society and the victory of socialism in all countries." The international character of the revolution was thus written into the basic document of the new regime. No one at that time would have dared present the problem otherwise! In April 1924, three months after the death of Lenin, Stalin wrote, in his brochure of compilations called *The Foundations of Leninism:* "For the overthrow of the bourgeoisie, the efforts of one country are enough—to this the history of our own revolution testifies. For the final victory of socialism, for the organization of socialist production, the efforts of one country, especially a peasant country like ours, are not enough—for this we must have the efforts of the proletarians of several advanced countries." These lines need no comment. The edition in which they were printed, however, has been withdrawn from circulation.

The large-scale defeats of the European proletariat, and the first very modest economic successes of the Soviet Union, suggested to Stalin, in the autumn of 1924, the idea that the historic mission of the Soviet bureaucracy was to build socialism in a single country. . . .

The "theory" of socialism in one country—a "theory" never expounded, by the way, or given any foundation, by Stalin himself—comes down to the sufficiently sterile and unhistoric notion that, thanks to the natural riches of the country, a socialist society can be built within the geographic confines of the Soviet Union. With the same success you might affirm that socialism could triumph if the population of the earth were a twelfth of what it is. In reality, however, the purpose of this new theory was to introduce into the social consciousness a far more concrete system of ideas, namely: the revolution is wholly completed; social contradictions will steadily soften; the kulak will gradually grow into socialism; the development as a whole, regardless of events in the external world, will preserve a peaceful and planned character. Bukharin, in attempting to give some foundation to the theory, declared it unshakably proven that "we shall not perish owing to class differences within our country and our technical backwardness, that we can build socialism even on this pauper technical basis, that this growth of socialism will be many times slower, that we will crawl with a tortoise tempo, and that nevertheless we are building this socialism, and we will build it." We remark the formula: "Build socialism even on a pauper technical basis," and we recall once more the genial intuition of the young Marx: with a low technical basis "only want will be generalized, and with want the struggle for necessities begins again, and all the old crap must revive. . . ."

Socialism must inevitably "surpass" capitalism in all spheres—wrote the Left Opposition in a document illegally distributed in March 1927— "but at present the question is not of the relation of socialism to capitalism in general, but of the economic development of the Soviet Union in relation to Germany, England and the United States. What is to be understood by the phrase 'minimal historic period'? A whole series of future five-year plans will leave us far from the level of the advanced countries of the West. What will be happening in the capitalist world during this time? . . . If you admit the possibility of its flourishing anew for a period of decades, then the talk of socialism in our backward country is pitiable tripe. Then it will be necessary to say that we were mistaken in our appraisal of the whole epoch as an epoch of capitalist decay. Then the Soviet Republic will prove to have been the second experiment in proletarian dictatorship since the Paris Commune, broader and more fruitful, but only an experiment. . . . Is there, however, any serious ground for such a decisive reconsideration of our whole epoch, and of the meaning of the October revolution as a link in an international revolution? No! . . . In finishing to a more or less complete extent their period of reconstruction [after the war] . . . the capitalist countries are reviving, and reviving in an incomparably sharper form, all the old pre-war contradictions, domestic and international. This is the basis of the proletarian revolution. It is a fact that we are building socialism. A greater fact, however, and not a less—since the whole in general is greater than the part—is the preparation of a European and world revolution. The part can conquer only together with the whole. . . . The European proletariat needs a far shorter period for its take-off to the seizure of power than we need to catch up technically with Europe and America. . . . We must, meanwhile, systematically narrow the distance separating our productivity of labor from that of the rest of the world. The more we advance, the less danger there is of possible intervention by low prices, and consequently by armies. . . . The higher we raise the standard of living of the workers and peasants, the more truly shall we hasten the proletarian revolution in Europe, the sooner will that revolution enrich us with world technique, and the more truly and genuinely will our socialist construction advance as a part of European and world construction." This document, like the others, remained without answer—unless you consider expulsions from the party and arrests an answer to it. . . .

To be sure, the isolation of the Soviet Union did not have those immediate dangerous consequences which might have been feared. The capitalist world was too disorganized and paralyzed to unfold to the full extent its potential power. The "breathing spell" proved longer than a critical optimism had dared to hope. However, isolation and the impossibility of using the resources of world economy even upon capitalistic bases (the amount of foreign trade has decreased from 1913 four to five times) entailed, along with enormous expenditures upon military defense, an extremely disadvantageous allocation of productive forces, and a slow raising of the standard of living of the masses. But a more malign product of isolation and backwardness has been the octopus of bureaucratism.

The juridical and political standards set up by the revolution exercised a progressive action upon the backward economy, but upon the other hand they themselves felt the lowering influence of that backwardness. The longer the Soviet Union remains in a capitalist environment, the deeper runs the degeneration of the social fabric. A prolonged isolation would inevitably end not in national communism, but in a restoration of capitalism.

If a bourgeoisie cannot peacefully grow into a socialist democracy, it is likewise true that a socialist state cannot peacefully merge with a world capitalist system. On the historic order of the day stands not the peaceful socialist development of "one country," but a long series of world disturbances: wars and revolutions. Disturbances are inevitable also in the domestic life of the Soviet Union. If the bureaucracy was compelled in its struggle for a planned economy to dekulakize the kulak, the working class will be compelled in its struggle for socialism to debureaucratize the bureaucracy. On the tomb of the latter will be inscribed the epitaph: "Here lies the theory of socialism in one country."

TROTSKYISM

JOHN PLAMENATZ*

As an indictment of Stalinism, Trotsky's account of Soviet Russia is formidable. So much so, indeed, that some version or other of it has been adopted by nearly all Stalin's more plausible critics. But the account is not only an attack on Stalinism; it is also an apology for Trotsky and Lenin. For it was their revolution that Stalin betrayed, misunderstood and corrupted.

As an apology for the Bolshevik revolution, Trotsky's account is not impressive. It makes the assumptions that Lenin made about the condition of western capitalism and the prospect of immediate world revolution. Trotsky, no more than Lenin, understood how it was that the German Social-Democrats, nourished on Marxism and enjoying in their own country incomparably greater working-class support than the Bolsheviks had ever done in Russia, could not make a proletarian revolution. He, too, spoke of treachery and corruption in a bourgeois environment. It never occurred to him that the German workers, knowing the 'sham democracy' of the bourgeois better than he did, might have learnt to like it and to prize the benefits it brought them. Every sign of disorder in Germany seemed to him

* Fellow of Nuffield College, Oxford. The selection is from pp. 303-305 of *German Marxism and Russian Communism*, Longmans, Green & Co., Inc., 1954. By permission of the publisher.

to announce the coming proletarian revolution in the West—the revolution so much needed by the Bolsheviks to justify their desperate hazard of 1917 but which the German workers felt they could do without. Blinded by Marxism, Trotsky even mistook the great and rapid increase in the number of civil servants in western countries for evidence that bourgeois repression was increasing as bourgeois predominance grew less secure. Though he survived Lenin by many years, he would not—perhaps because he dared not—recognize the emergence of the democratic welfare state. That state has, no doubt, inefficiencies and injustices peculiar to itself, but they are not faults that lead to proletarian revolution. The welfare state is no more bourgeois than the Communist state is proletarian. These old-fashioned categories no longer apply, but the Communist still believes that they do, and therefore systematically misdescribes the world he lives in.[1]

The Bolshevik revolution was never betrayed, for both Lenin and Trotsky miscalculated when they made it. They quite misread the situation in the West; for there never was reasonable hope of proletarian revolution in Germany, or in any other major industrial country during or after the First World War. The Bolshevik revolution was premature and the coming of Stalinism, whose causes Trotsky described so well, was therefore (on Marxian premises) inevitable. If Marxism is true, not all the valiant efforts of Lenin and Trotsky could have prevented the emergence of some such system as Stalin later stood for. The 'objective conditions' of his success were created by the Bolshevik revolution—which was itself a betrayal of Marxism but which no Marxist could betray.

Nor were these efforts as valiant as Trotsky, after his quarrel with Stalin, tried to make them out. In *Two Tactics,* the long and elaborate pamphlet in which Lenin first put forward the doctrine of 'uninterrupted revolution,' there is nothing said about the Russian workers and Social-Democrats slightly anticipating in their country a movement soon to sweep the whole capitalist world. That argument was lightly touched upon in 1905, but was not made much of until many years later, when it seemed to Lenin that war was exhausting all the Great Powers and that Tsardom had not long to live. The doctrine of 'uninterrupted revolution' was revived, and this argument used to defend it against the Mensheviks. Trotsky himself, who was a more lucid and consistent advocate of 'uninterrupted revolution' than Lenin, long thought it inevitable in Russia whatever happened elsewhere.

Moreover, most of the evil consequences of premature revolution were

---

[1] Not only the Communist but the westerner also. We still commonly speak of England and France as capitalist countries, though they are no longer capitalist in the sense understood by Marx and his contemporaries. The political and social theorist cannot avoid using words with several or changing meanings, but he can take care not to treat an argument which is valid when a word is used in one sense as if it were valid when it is used in another. Communists, whether followers of Trotsky or Stalin, usually neglect this simple precaution.

already apparent before Lenin died. They were, indeed, consequences of courses that the Bolsheviks had felt themselves driven to in their 'valiant efforts' to retain power. They had had to fight hard to defeat numerous enemies, and most of the institutions that Trotsky afterwards considered preclusive of socialism had been created to give victory to the Bolsheviks. After the civil war they had somewhat relaxed their hold on an almost stifled economy but had kept all their instruments of coercion; and Trotsky for one had never suggested that they could do without them. His strong dislike for these instruments was not evident until there was no longer a hope of his using them.

There can be no doubt that Stalin was right and Trotsky wrong in the dispute between them about the imminence of proletarian revolution outside Russia. There was not, after 1920, even the glimmer of a hope of it in any great industrial country. Had the Bolsheviks exerted themselves to stimulate it, they would have failed miserably and have united all the Powers against them. Western governments were willing enough to let the Bolsheviks play the masters in exhausted Russia, provided they kept their hands off the rest of Europe. It did not greatly concern them who killed whom, or how many millions starved, in so remote, impoverished and barbarous a country. They were too much occupied with their own quarrels and too little recovered from the effects of war to embark on new adventures in Russia. They had, for a time, while they thought the Whites might beat the Reds, thrust their little fingers just a short way into the Russian mess, but had got nothing for themselves or their friends by doing so. Russia, they now thought, was best left alone. She was the victim of a dreadful and catching disease, and should be kept away from other nations and allowed to cure herself as best she might. The western governments wanted to have as little to do with her as possible, and she was therefore safe from them. Only the reckless policy advocated by Trotsky could have caused them to change their minds, and drive the Bolsheviks out of Russia before they had time to make her and themselves formidable.

REFLECTIONS ON THE RUSSIAN REVOLUTION

Sidney Hook*

DEMOCRACY AND THE DICTATORSHIP OF THE PARTY

The key to the Russian economy, to the evolution of Russian culture since the early years of the revolution, to its ghastly purges and juridical

* Professor of Philosophy, New York University. Author of *From Hegel to Marx* and *Marx and the Marxists*. The selection is from pp. 165-168 of *Reason, Social Myths and Democracy* (New York: The Humanities Press). By permission of the publisher.

frame ups, is to be found in the character of the Russian state power. The Russian state is marked by the concentration of all political and economic power in the hands of the Communist Party. Other political parties of the working class are forbidden, even in the "democratic" Stalin Constitution. The organization of factions within the Communist Party is punishable by exile to concentration camps or by death. The Soviets and Parliament have the same function in Russia as the Reichstag [under Hitler] in Germany —emphatic rubber stamps for policies decided by the Political Committee of the Party. Begun as a dictatorship of a class, the Russian Revolution developed through the dictatorship of the Communist Party into the dictatorship of the Secretariat. Questions of causation are always tangled knots, but I think it can be established that, given the conditions in which the Russian Revolution was begun, the only *controllable* factor that led to the degeneration of the Russian Revolution and its Thermidorian regime was the abrogation of working-class and peasant democracy, signalized by the suppression of all other political parties and the concentration of all power in the hands of the Communist Party.

Let us cast a glance in this light at the various reasons given by Trotsky for the Soviet Thermidor. The immaturity of the productive forces, the belatedness of the world revolution, the decimation of the best fighters and the idealists, the weakening of morale, the death of Lenin—none of them was in the control of the Bolshevik party. And if together they constitute a sufficient explanation of the Thermidor, then degeneration and betrayal were unavoidable no matter who was at the helm or what political forms prevailed. Trotsky, however, is far from establishing a direct and relevant connection between any or all of these factors and the corruption of socialist program and ideals in the Soviet Union. But there is one factor which he does mention as having a direct bearing upon the emergence of Stalinism from Bolshevism, whose importance, however, he immediately proceeds to deny by subordinating it to those mentioned above. "It is absolutely indisputable that the domination of a single party served as the juridical point of departure for the Stalinist totalitarian system. But the reason for this development lies neither in Bolshevism nor in the prohibition of other parties as a temporary war measure, but the number of defeats of the proletariat in Europe and Asia" (*Stalinism and Bolshevism,* 1938).

Domination here is a weak word. A political party can *dominate* even in a democracy which offers it a mandate after the give and take of free discussion. What Trotsky means is the exclusive *dictatorship* of the party, and on other occasions he has not hesitated to say so. The more forcibly the Communist Party exercised its dictatorship over other working-class parties, the more pervasive became the dictatorship of the Secretariat within the Communist Party itself. Times without number Trotsky has maintained that had genuine democratic processes prevailed in the Soviet and in the Party, Stalin's policies would not have prevailed. That is to say, were there Soviet, or even Party, democracy, Stalin's policies would not have prevailed *even though* the revolution was delayed, Lenin dead, and the productive forces undeveloped. Trotsky's policies were quite different from those of Stalin's and they were based every whit as much upon recognition of the objective situation in Russia and in the world generally. But on Trotsky's own analysis, the failure to adopt them was due *not* to the common objective situation but to the absence of workers' and party democracy. Were Trotsky to deny this, he would be admitting that the defeat of his policies was necessary, inevitable, and justifiable, and the denial would make nonsense of his eloquent criticisms of the strangulation of the Soviets and Party under Stalin.

Despite his cosmic optimism, even Trotsky acknowledges that there will always be some periods in which the objective situation is unfavorable, as was true in 1924. Where contrary policies are advocated to meet the situation, absence of workers' and party democracy means that the policy of those who have the dictatorial power in their hands will be adopted, irrespective of whether it is an intelligent one or whether it leads to a *cul de sac*. Even if we assume identity of interests between the dictators and the rank and file, we cannot assume infallibility on the part of the dictating bureaucracy in adopting appropriate measures to realize the common interests.

On every concrete question on which Trotsky has been defeated in Russia, the proximate cause has been, not the level of the productive forces at home or the political situation abroad, but the denial of equal rights of assembly, agitation, and publication to him and to his followers, and the persecution, imprisonment, and often the execution of those of his followers who have tried to exercise these rights. Had Trotsky's policies been turned down in a genuinely functioning workers' and party democracy, the factors he mentions might be relevant in explaining why the electorate refused to give him its confidence. But as it was, Stalin's policies, which led directly to the Thermidor, prevailed because the dictatorship *of* the party was transformed into a dictatorship *over* the party.

It does not require much perspicacity to realize that the dictatorship of a political party cannot for long be effective without its own internal organization becoming dictatorial. The necessity of *controlling* the mass of the population over whom the party wields a dictatorship, of effectively combating enemies, real and alleged, of imposing a uniform ideology, compels the party to assume a military, sometimes called monolithic, structure. The interests of the non-party masses which cannot be openly expressed because of the absence of free political institutions, naturally tend to express themselves in differences within the party itself, in factional groupings of various sorts.

But the dictatorship of the party cannot be effectively wielded unless the facts and appearance of division in its own ranks are concealed from the non-party masses. To conceal this division and to parade the maximum amount of unity, the ruling group in the party must regulate and control the expression of opinion among the rank and file. It must exercise an even stricter supervision of the party press than it does of the non-party press. Now in order to exercise the proper supervision the leading group must itself be unified. Dissidents are isolated, gagged into silence, exiled, deported, and shot. The rule of the leading group must be fortified by a mythology which glorifies "the leader," "the beloved disciple," "the man of iron" who tops the pyramidal structure and whose word on any subject is law. Opposition of any kind is equated with treason. Decisions are "unanimously" approved; failure, no matter for what reason, becomes sabotage; silence today, a sign of betrayal tomorrow; the instruments of one purge become the victims of another. Historical variations may appear at some points in this evolution from the dictatorship *of* a political party to the dictatorship *over* the party. The general pattern of Russian development, however, fits the facts: from the outlawing of other working-class political parties, to the prohibition of factions in the Communist Party . . . to ruthless police terror against *all* dissidents under Stalin.

VI

THE SOVIET POLITICAL SYSTEM

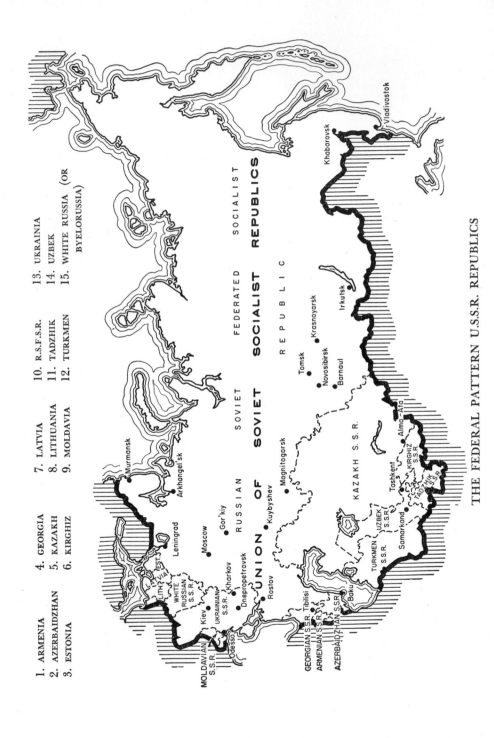

THE FEDERAL PATTERN U.S.S.R. REPUBLICS

1. ARMENIA
2. AZERBAIDZHAN
3. ESTONIA

4. GEORGIA
5. KAZAKH
6. KIRGHIZ

7. LATVIA
8. LITHUANIA
9. MOLDAVIA

10. R.S.F.S.R.
11. TADZHIK
12. TURKMEN

13. UKRAINIA
14. UZBEK
15. WHITE RUSSIA (OR BYELORUSSIA)

Chapter 10

MYTH AND REALITY: CONSTITUTIONAL GUARANTEES

The first Soviet Constitution, which went into effect on July 19, 1918, on the eve of civil war and intervention, was limited in its application to the Russian Socialist Federated Soviet Republic. By its terms,

The principal object of the Constitution of the RSFSR . . . consists in the establishment of the dictatorship of the urban and rural proletariat and the poorest peasantry, in the form of the strong All-Russian Soviet power, with the aim of securing the complete suppression of the bourgeoisie, the abolition of the exploitation of man by man, and the establishment of socialism, under which there shall be neither class divisions nor State authority.

Although it provided disproportionate representation for the proletariat, it made no mention of the Communist Party, which did not then enjoy a legal monopoly of power.

The first All-Union Constitution, which was approved by the Second Congress of Soviets on January 31, 1924, was closely patterned after the 1918 Constitution. The U.S.S.R. was declared "a trustworthy bulwark against world capitalism, and a new decisive step along the path of the union of the workers of all countries in a World Socialist Soviet Republic." The Constitution stated that each Republic "retains the right of free withdrawal from the Union."

The 1924 Constitution was replaced by the "Stalin" Constitution, in effect December 5, 1936, which eliminated all disproportionate representation (see Articles 134, 135, and 136) and, on the other hand, accorded to the Communist Party a special position (see Article 126). Speaking generally, the Soviet Constitution (which is set forth in an appendix and merits careful reading)—in form, structure, and definition of fundamental rights and duties of citizens—would appear to be one of the most advanced and forward-looking in the world. To what extent this is reality and to what extent myth are the subjects of the discussions next ensuing.

*In the extraordinary speech that Stalin delivered on November 25, 1936
—set forth herein—after extolling the virtues of the Soviet economic and
social systems, he declared that "the Constitution of the U.S.S.R. is the
only thoroughly democratic constitution in the world"—a viewpoint echoed
by Andrei Vyshinsky, who affirmed that "Soviet democracy and the Soviet
state are a million times more democratic than the most democratic bourgeois republic."*

*The whole question could perhaps be dismissed with the statement that
these affirmations must rest on a particular definition of democracy and
that the Russians are free to define democracy any way they please. But,
in light of the great attraction and appeal of the democratic concept
throughout the world—attested to by the use of the term "People's Democracy"—it may be well to consider whether the Russian claim can be
supported by any meaningful, rational, and consistent definition of democracy.*

*To begin with, no honest observer could seriously claim that Soviet
practice conforms to the criteria suggested, for example, by Robert M.
MacIver:*

It was a necessary condition of democracy everywhere that opposing doctrines
remained free to express themselves, to seek converts, to form organizations, and so
compete for success before the tribunal of public opinion. Any major trend of
opinion could thus register itself in the character and in the policies of government.

*The "ritualistic exercises in unanimity" of the kind described by
Frederick L. Schuman, and reflected in the statistics of the elections to the
Supreme Soviet (in the pages hereafter), cannot be said to meet these tests.
It is revealing that, although in the course of World War II seven nationalities were deported en masse for either dubious loyalty or disloyalty, their
votes in favor of the official list, in the elections to the Supreme Soviet in
1937, were stated to have been well in excess of 90 per cent. And, it must be
noted, in this connection, that Stalin did concede that the 1936 Constitution
"leaves unchanged the present leading position of the Communist Party of
the U.S.S.R.,"—that is to say, its monopoly of power concentrated in few
hands.*

*What is more, the very constitutional "guarantees" of freedom of speech
and related freedoms (see Article 125) are qualified by the clearly implied
limitation that they are not being granted generally but "in conformity with
the interests of the working people, and in order to strengthen the socialist
system," a judgment resting, of course, with the Party leadership. Even
before these "guarantees" were adopted,* Pravda *warned that:*

He who makes it his task to unsettle the socialist structure, to undermine socialist
ownership, . . . is an enemy of the people. He gets not a scrap of paper, he does
not set foot over the threshold of the printing press, to realize his base designs. He
gets no hall, no room, no cover to inject poison by word of mouth.

What then are the bases upon which the claim of the Soviet regime to democracy may be urged? It is believed that a careful reading of the Stalin and Aleksandrov speeches will indicate that the claim rests upon two propositions. The first of these is that the Communist Party (through its leadership) has served the interests of the Soviet people by strengthening the power of the nation and bringing to the people great economic and social benefits.

It must be conceded that, under the domination of the Communist Party, the U.S.S.R. has made great advances in industrialization and education, in some cultural areas, and in the eradication of many forms of discrimination and inequality characteristic of the Tsarist period. But, the price paid in suffering and hardship has also been of tremendous magnitude. Whether the benefits conferred outweighed the suffering imposed is a matter of some importance—which is discussed at various points in this volume—but surely has no relevance to the existence or nonexistence of political democracy in the Soviet Union. The essence of political democracy, in any meaningful sense, must certainly lie in self-government *rather than in service to the interests of the people (although it is of course probably true that in the long run self-government alone will provide good government). If democracy does not involve self-government, but only good government, then the term not only loses all connection with its historic connotations but may be reduced to a manifest absurdity to describe the most thorough-going dictatorship provided only that it is benevolent or enlightened (or, perhaps, only claims to be so).*

The second proposition upon which the Communist claim to democracy may be said to rest is that, because of the "great concord" of the Soviet peoples and in the absence of hostile or antagonistic classes, "there are no grounds for the existence of several parties, and therefore for the existence of freedom of such parties in the U.S.S.R." This position of Stalin's was recently reaffirmed when Khrushchev, speaking in Kiev, said: "The Party and the people in our country are as one. So why do the Soviet people need other parties? Or are they to be created especially for the people in capitalist countries who are not satisfied with the socialist system?"

Whether it is true in fact that Russia has a classless society in any sense is certainly questionable. (See the chapter entitled Who Rules in Russia?*) But, conceding the absence of antagonistic classes in the U.S.S.R. and a "great concord" of the Soviet people on the* ends *defined by Marxism—a large concession for the sake of argument—can it serve to equate the power of a small group of leaders within one Party with "democracy"? Is it really possible to argue in light of the known facts of Soviet history that at all times during the Party's (or Stalin's) monopoly of power, all of the Soviet people were agreed on the* means *to be used to achieve the agreed ends? Were all "as one" on the tempo of industrialization, or on "socialism in one country"; or on aid to World Revolution; or on the dissolution of*

the Comintern; or on the official attitude toward religion, art, and literature? Did (and do) good socialists disagree among themselves about these
and myriad other questions—especially in light of occasional drastic shifts
in policy—without finding any legal means to express dissent from official
policy? The answer to these questions is in part given by Khrushchev's
own denunciation of the wanton purges of the 30's based, concededly, in
large part on nothing more than honest disagreement with Stalin.

In expressing the viewpoint that in no meaningful sense is it possible
to speak of political democracy in the U.S.S.R., it is not suggested that the
Soviet Constitution as a whole is devoid of significance beyond clothing
"the realities of arbitrary power in the protective garb of tradition and
legitimacy." It does establish the economic basis of the Soviet state and
mark the aspiration for a free and equal society. Whether this will remain
no more than aspiration depends upon many complex factors with which,
in one way or another, various sections of this book are concerned.

ON THE NEW SOVIET CONSTITUTION

JOSEPH V. STALIN*

THE NEW SOCIETY

The complete victory of the socialist system in all spheres of the national economy is now a fact. This means that exploitation of man by
man is abolished—liquidated—while the socialist ownership of the implements and means of production is established as the unshakable basis of
our Soviet society. (*Loud applause.*)

As a result of all these changes in the national economy of the U.S.S.R.,
we have now a new socialist economy, knowing neither crises nor unemployment, neither poverty nor ruin, and giving to the citizens every possibility to live prosperous and cultured lives.

Such, in the main, are the changes which took place in our economy
during the period from 1924 to 1936. Corresponding to these changes in
the sphere of the economy of the U.S.S.R., the class structure of our society
has also changed. As is known, the landlord class had already been liquidated as a result of the victorious conclusion of the Civil War.

As for the other exploiting classes, they shared the fate of the landlord
class. The capitalist class has ceased to exist in the sphere of industry. The
kulak class has ceased to exist in the sphere of agriculture. The merchants

* From a speech delivered to the Extraordinary Eighth Congress of Soviets on November 25, 1936.

and speculators have ceased to exist in the sphere of distribution. In this way, all exploiting classes are proved to have been liquidated. . . .

What do these changes signify? They signify, first, that the dividing line between the working class and the peasantry, as well as that between these classes and the intelligentsia, is becoming obliterated and that the old class exclusiveness is disappearing. This means that the distance between these social groups is more and more diminishing. They signify, secondly, that the economic contradictions between these social groups is subsiding, is becoming obliterated. They signify, finally, that the political contradictions between them are also subsiding, becoming obliterated. Such is the position concerning the changes in the sphere of class structure in the U.S.S.R.

The picture of the changes in social life in the U.S.S.R. would be incomplete without a few words regarding the changes in another sphere. I have in mind the sphere of national interrelations within the U.S.S.R. As is well known, the Soviet Union comprises about sixty nations, national groups and nationalities. The Soviet state is a multi-national state. . . .

The very absence of the exploiting classes which are the principal organizers of strife among the nationalities, the absence of exploitation, breeding mutual distrust and fanning nationalist passions, the fact that the power is held by the working class, which is the enemy of all enslavement and the faithful bearer of ideas of internationalism, the materialization in reality of mutual aid of the peoples in all fields of economic and social life, and finally the high development of the national culture of the peoples of the U.S.S.R., culture that is national in form and socialist in content—as a result of all these and similar factors, the peoples of the U.S.S.R. have radically changed their characteristics. Their feeling of mutual distrust has disappeared. The feeling of mutual friendship has developed, and thus fraternal cooperation of the peoples has been established in the system of a single union state. As a result, we now have a fully formed multi-national socialist state, which has passed all tests and which has a stability which any national state in any part of the world may well envy. (*Loud applause.*) . . .

THE NEW CONSTITUTION

How are these changes in the life of the U.S.S.R. reflected in the draft of the new Constitution? In other words, what are the main specific features of the draft Constitution submitted for consideration at the present congress? . . .

The draft of the new Constitution of the U.S.S.R. proceeds from the fact of the abolition of the capitalist system, from the fact of the victory of the socialist system in the U.S.S.R.

The main foundation of the draft of the new Constitution of the

U.S.S.R. is formed of the principles of socialism and its chief mainstays, already won and put into practice, namely, the socialist ownership of land, forests, factories, shops and other implements and means of production; abolition of exploitation and exploiting classes; abolition of poverty for the majority and luxury for the minority; abolition of unemployment; work as an obligation and duty and the honor of every able-bodied citizen according to the formula: "He who does not work, neither shall he eat," *i.e.,* the right of every citizen to receive guaranteed work; the right to rest and leisure; the right to education, etc. The draft of the new Constitution rests on these. . . .

The draft of the new Constitution of the U.S.S.R. proceeds from the fact that antagonistic classes no longer exist in our society, that our society consists of two friendly classes: the workers and peasants, that precisely these toiling classes are in power, that the state guidance of society (dictatorship) belongs to the working class as the advanced class of society, that the Constitution is needed to consolidate the social order desired by and of advantage to the toilers. Such is the third specific feature of the draft of the new Constitution. . . .

The draft of the new Constitution of the U.S.S.R. is profoundly international. It proceeds from the premise that all nations and races have equal rights. It proceeds from the premise that color or language differences, differences in cultural level or the level of state development as well as any other difference among nations and races, cannot serve as grounds for justifying national inequality of rights.

It proceeds from the premise that all nations and races irrespective of their past or present position, irrespective of their strength or weakness, must enjoy equal rights in all spheres, economic, social, state and the cultural life of society. Such is the fourth feature of the draft of the new Constitution. The fifth specific feature of the draft of the new Constitution is its consistent and fully sustained democracy. From the viewpoint of democracy, the bourgeois constitutions may be divided into two groups. One group of constitutions openly denies or virtually negates equality of the rights of citizens and democratic liberties. The other group of constitutions willingly accepts and even advertises democratic principles, but in doing so makes such reservations and restrictions that democratic rights and liberties prove to be utterly mutilated.

They talk about equal suffrage for all citizens but immediately limit it by residential, educational and even by property qualifications. They talk about equal rights of citizens, but immediately make the reservation that this does not apply to women, or only partly applies to them, etc. A specific feature of the draft of the new Constitution of the U.S.S.R. is that it is free from such reservations and restrictions.

Active and passive citizens do not exist for it; for it all citizens are active. It recognizes no difference in the rights of men and women, "of fixed abode" and "without fixed abode," with property or without property, educated or uneducated. For it all citizens are equal in their rights. Neither property status nor national origin, nor sex, nor official standing, but only the personal capabilities and personal labor of every citizen determine his position in society.

Finally, there is one other specific feature in the draft of the new Constitution. Bourgeois constitutions usually limit themselves to recording the formal rights of citizens without concerning themselves about the conditions for exercising these rights, about the possibility of exercising them, the means of exercising them. They speak about equality of citizens but forget that real equality between master and workman, between landlord and peasants, is impossible if the former enjoy wealth and political weight in society, while the latter are deprived of both; if the former are exploiters and the latter are exploited.

Or again: they speak of free speech, freedom of assemblage and of the press, but forget that all these liberties may become empty sound for the working class if the latter is deprived of the possibility of having at its command suitable premises for meetings, good printshops, sufficient quantity of paper, etc.

A specific feature of the draft of the new Constitution is that it does not limit itself to recording formal rights of citizens, but transfers the center of gravity to questions of the guarantee of these rights, to the question of the means of exercising them. It does not merely proclaim the equality of the rights of citizens but ensures them by legislative enactment of the fact of liquidation of the regime of exploitation, by the fact of liberation of citizens from any exploitation.

It not only proclaims the right to work, but ensures it by legislative enactment of the fact of non-existence of crises in Soviet society, and the fact of abolition of unemployment. It not merely proclaims democratic liberties but guarantees them in legislative enactments by providing definite material facilities. It is clear, therefore, that the democracy of the new Constitution is not the "usual" and "generally recognized" democracy in general, but socialist democracy. . . .

BOURGEOIS CRITICS OF THE CONSTITUTION

A few words about bourgeois criticism of the draft Constitution. . . . As for the allegation that the Constitution of the U.S.S.R. is an empty promise, a Potemkin village, I would like to refer to a number of established facts which speak for themselves. . . .

After organizing industry and agriculture on new, socialist lines, with a new technical basis, Soviet power brought about such a state of affairs that now agriculture in the U.S.S.R. produces one and a half times more than in pre-war times, industry produces seven times more than pre-war, and the national income has increased fourfold compared to pre-war. All of these are facts and not promises. (*Prolonged applause.*)

The Soviet power abolished unemployment, carried into life the right to work, the right to rest and leisure, and the right to education, ensured better material and cultural conditions for workers, peasants and intellectuals, ensured the introduction of universal, direct and equal suffrage with secret ballot for citizens. All of these are facts and not promises. (*Prolonged applause.*)

Finally, the U.S.S.R. produced a draft of the new Constitution which is not a promise but is a record and legislative enactment of these universally known facts, a record and legislative enactment of what has already been achieved and won. . . .

There is [another] group of critics. . . . This group charges that the draft makes no change in the existing position of the U.S.S.R.; that it leaves the dictatorship of the working class intact, does not provide for freedom of political parties, and preserves the present leading position of the Communist Party of the U.S.S.R. And, at the same time, this group of critics believes that the absence of freedom for parties in the U.S.S.R. is an indication of the violation of the fundamental principles of democracy.

I must admit the draft of the new Constitution really does leave in force the regime of the dictatorship of the working class, and also leaves unchanged the present leading position of the Communist Party of the U.S.S.R. (*Loud applause.*)

If our venerable critics regard this as a shortcoming of the draft Constitution, this can only be regretted. We Bolsheviks, however, consider this as a merit of the draft Constitution. (*Loud applause.*) As for freedom for various political parties, we here adhere to somewhat different views.

The party is part of the class, its vanguard section. Several parties and consequently freedom of parties can only exist in a society where antagonistic classes exist whose interests are hostile and irreconcilable, where there are capitalists and workers, landlords and peasants, kulaks and poor peasants.

But in the U.S.S.R. there are no longer such classes as capitalists, landlords, kulaks, etc. In the U.S.S.R. there are only two classes, workers and peasants, whose interests not only are not antagonistic but, on the contrary, amicable. Consequently there are no grounds for the existence of several parties, and therefore for the existence of freedom of such parties in the U.S.S.R. There are grounds for only one party, the Communist Party, in the U.S.S.R. Only one party can exist, the Communist Party, which boldly defends the interests of the workers and peasants to the very end. And there can hardly be any doubt about the fact that it defends the interests of these classes. (*Loud applause.*)

They talk about democracy. But what is democracy? Democracy in capitalist countries where there are antagonistic classes is in the last analy-

sis democracy for the strong, democracy for the propertied minority.
Democracy in the U.S.S.R., on the contrary, is democracy for all. But from
this it follows that the principles of democracy are violated not by the draft
of the new Constitution of the U.S.S.R. but by the bourgeois constitutions.

That is why I think that the Constitution of the U.S.S.R. is the only
thoroughly democratic constitution in the world.

THE PATTERN OF SOVIET DEMOCRACY

G. F. ALEKSANDROV*

All the critics of Soviet democracy are united in one requirement that
these people wish to set for so-called "pure," "genuine" democracy. The
foreign press—not only newspapers and magazines, but a large number of
the books issued in recent years—tiresomely poses one and the same question: if the Bolsheviks are right and they are indeed carrying out democratic principles, why is there only one political party in the Soviet Union?
Is not the constant struggle of several parties the sign of "true" democracy?
Is not freedom of speech, of assembly, of thought concerning the social
system and government policy, not better assured if several political parties
compete; if the government policy is carefully considered from the point
of view of the interests of various social groups, various political principles
and various parties?

This question, as is self-evident, presents several aspects: does the presence of two or more parties bespeak the democratic structure of society?
Is the view, widely held today among bourgeois politicians, true that the
more parties there are fighting for power, the more perfect and broader
the democracy? And finally, do the arrows of the modern critics of Soviet
democracy hit the mark when they consider it undemocratic for the people
to have a single party?

As is known, the very concept of "democracy" means popular sovereignty in general. The majority of those discussing the question of democracy agree that by democracy is meant a system of political relations within
society which assures the development of society and its institutions in the
interests of the people and with the participation of the people itself.
Glimmers of this thought shine through even the haziest reasoning of the
most mystically inclined modern bourgeois philosophers. Consequently,

* Member of the Academy of Sciences of the U.S.S.R. Author of *The History of
Western Philosophy*. The selection is from pp. 21-26 of the translation by Leo Gruilow
of a speech delivered at a session of the Academy of Sciences on December 4, 1946, and
widely distributed in the U.S.S.R. Reprinted with the permission of the publisher, Public
Affairs Press, Washington, D. C.

from the historical and social points of view, the character of democracy is revealed not by whether the form of government and the state system are connected with the existence of one, two, or more parties, but by the content of political institutions, the nature of the state and the nature of the internal and foreign policies followed by the state and its governments. For example, who does not know of the abundance of political organizations and the existence of a sharp struggle among social classes and groups in Athens of the fifth and fourth centuries, B.C.? Or of the struggle of various social classes and cliques in ancient Rome? Yet who dares term those cities and the countries they represented, with their slaveholding system of life, examples of democratic organization of society, on the basis of the abundance of competing political groupings?

But is it worth while turning to such ancient examples to prove the falsity, the contrived nature and the artificiality of this "argument" of critics of Soviet democracy? To expose this "argument," constantly cited, lo, these more than twenty years, by all sorts of political sharpers, one can turn to modern history and even to the present situation in those very United States of America or in Great Britain, where in recent years one could gather a whole harvest of all sorts of newly-come "critics," "investigators" and just plain political rowdies—specialists in "democracy."

English and American politicians and social scientists often cite their countries as examples for others, as countries of basically two parties and thereby presumably completely democratic. But in politics one cannot take reasoning of this sort on faith. Why, many labor members of Parliament themselves consider that the Labor and Conservative parties of England *do not differ in principle* on many quite important contemporary questions. Some call themselves Conservative and carry out a frankly imperialistic, expansionist policy; others call themselves Labor, socialists, the workers' party, but often, particularly in the field of foreign relations, carry out the very same policy.

The same can be said concerning the U.S.A. More than thirty years ago Lenin pointed out that the two bourgeois parties in America were distinguished by particular stability and vigor after the civil war over slavery in 1860-65. The party of former slaveholders is the so-called "Democratic Party." The party of the capitalists, standing for emancipation of the Negroes, developed into the "Republican Party."

After the emancipation of the Negroes, the difference between the two parties grew less and less. The struggle of these parties was conducted primarily over the question of higher or lower tariffs. This struggle did *not possess serious* significance for the masses of the people. The people were deceived and deflected from their vital interests by means of the effective and empty *duels* of the two bourgeois parties. This so-called 'two-party system' prevailing in America and England, was one of the most powerful means of hindering the rise of an independent workers', i.e., a truly socialistic, party.[1]

[1] Lenin, *Collected Works* (Russian Edition), Vol. XVI, p. 190.

However, if the modern supporters of "two-party democracy" do not hesitate to put to us any—in their opinion—"tricky" questions, then, on the basis of mutual politeness and those same democratic principles, we Soviet people, in turn, would like to put a few questions to the variegated "specialists" in democracy, to those who love to pose questions: if the existence of two, three or more parties corresponds to a truly democratic way of life, then why, for instance, do the Laborites fight the Conservatives on questions, yet fly into a fury at the mere mention of the English Communists? If the existence of several parties is the real sign of genuine democracy, it would seem sensible and logical to encourage and support any opposition movement in England, and to afford an opportunity for free expression of the views of parties which have not obtained a majority in Parliament. Yet everybody knows that as a matter of fact the Laborites are not guided by this principle; as a matter of fact they strive to dislodge the Conservative Party and, if they could, apparently they would be happy to obtain all the seats in Parliament now held by Conservatives, without particular concern that the existence of one party in Parliament would be a "violation" of democratic principles. No, apparently when the democratic or undemocratic character of the state is discussed, the question is not whether there is one or several parties. Who will believe that certain Laski-type theoreticians of the Labor Party and the other various lovers of "defending" democracy are interested in the existence of their political foes and extension of their foes activity? Yet only thus must one interpret the passionate argument for the necessity of preserving a system of two or more parties in order to preserve democracy! No, the point is merely that today the Laborites still lack the strength to finish off their political foes in the electoral struggle and to win over the whole of society to their side.

That is why it seems entirely probable that the thesis of identity between democracy and the struggle of two or more parties within society is the thesis of those who today are in no position to win over to their side the majority of society; the thesis of those who know that in the conditions of bourgeois society, that is, in the conditions in which society lives and develops on the basis of a struggle of diverse social classes, there can be no place for a single party which would express with equal success the interests of opposed social classes. As long as antagonistic class society exists, the struggle among various political parties, expressing the struggle of classes, is inevitable. In this and only in this lies the essence of the question so often asked in foreign literature: is democracy compatible with a one-party system? Is not the existence of several parties in society the sign of true, genuine democracy?

We Soviet people give a clear and unequivocal answer: no, it is not. The democratic or anti-democratic nature of public life, of a state, of a government's policy, is determined not by the number of parties but by the substance of the policy of this state, of these parties—by whether this or that policy is carried out in the interests of the people, in the interests of its overwhelming majority, or in the interests of its minority. That is how matters stand with regard to the first question—whether democracy coincides with the existence of one or several parties in society.

It is natural that all the arguments of the foreign "specialists" in democracy revolve around the question of one party in the Soviet Union. For what relationship does the realization of the truly democratic principles of socialist society bear to the position of leadership held in this society by the one and only party, namely, the Communist Party? . . .

Soviet democracy expresses the principles of a socialist society. As is known, socialist society begins where and when the exploiting classes—landowners, manufacturers, financial magnates, bankers, kulaks, speculators and other social groups living on unearned income—cease to exist, and society begins to develop on the basis of a friendly alliance of the workers, peasants and intelligentsia. As long as exploiting classes exist, they strive to protect their political interests in society, to create their political organizations and to have their own parties for the protection of their private interests and the subordination of the interests of society to the interests of the given clique or social group. But after the new social order, namely, the socialist order, triumphs in all fields, no place remains in society for the classes oppressing other classes: the time comes of a great concord of the people and the creation of the deepest unity of all society. In this period the former need and the former necessity for the existence of divergent political parties disappears.

That party which is best able to express the deepest fundamental interests of the whole of society and can point the way to the quickest practical plan for establishing the foundations of a new life—a life without exploiters and parasites; that party which, by its organizational work, is able to rally around it all of society, and lead it along the new paths of building communism; that party, finally, which by its devoted, self-sacrificing service to the people has won unquestionable and undisputed authority throughout the whole of society—that particular party can express historically the deepest desires, life aims and ideals of the tremendous majority of the population of the country. It is precisely in this historical situation that the necessity and any possibility for the existence of divergent parties in society disappears completely. In the Soviet Union such a single party really exists and works for the welfare of the people—the party of the Communists, the Leninist party, guided by its leader, Comrade Stalin. The Soviet people have linked themselves with the party of the Bolsheviks and have adopted its program and ideas for their own.

Any other party that might arise in Soviet society could have only one program: a program of return to the past, to the old, to the life liquidated by our people: a program of struggle against socialism.

THE POLITY OF OLIGARCHY

Frederick L. Schuman*

1. UNION OF SOVIETS

In the Soviet system of power, elected law-makers have long been dominated by executive policy-makers named by the Party, with the shadow of terror never remote. In turn, the Party—and State and nation as well— have been dominated during most of four decades by the Leader, even though the great and good Lenin and the great and bad Stalin are now both dead and the "cult of the individual" has given way to *Kollectivnost:* collective or collegial leadership. Here, as elsewhere among men, the naked and ugly realities of power have been suitably garbed in seemly raiment to persuade those from whom obedience is expected that the regime is not a mere aggregation of arbitrary and self-chosen despots but is a dedicated group of guardians of a Supreme Law, devoted to Political Truth, Civic Virtue, and the Common Good. The devices of bourgeois "constitutionalism" have often fulfilled this function in the West. They were borrowed early by the Marxist rulers of Muscovy to serve this need and were elaborated into "the most democratic constitution in the world" precisely during the bloodiest years of the terror. . . .

Between 1929 and 1935 the economic and social order of the U.S.S.R. underwent the most drastic transformation that has ever occurred in a similar period in any major community. In the Soviet Union, as elsewhere, political practices deeply imbedded in the habits of rulers and ruled change less rapidly than the texture of social living and the activities by which men and women earn their daily bread. Political vocabularies, with their sacred stereotypes and highly emotionalized symbols and slogans, are modified even more slowly. Political man, even when a citizen of a revolutionary State, is a conservative animal. Communists, however, pride themselves on their energy as innovators and swear by the Marxist dictum that political institutions are but the superstructure of class relations flowing out of prevailing modes of production. The collectivization of agriculture and the tremendous upsurge of industrialization, accompanied by crises and convulsions, transformed Soviet society and economy almost beyond

* Woodrow Wilson Professor of Government, Williams College. Author of *The Commonwealth of Man; Night Over Europe;* and *Europe on the Eve.* The selection is reprinted from chapter 7 of *Russia Since 1917* by Frederick L. Schuman, by permission of Alfred A. Knopf, Inc. Copyright 1957 by the author.

recognition. The Party leadership therefore concluded in the course of the Second Five Year Plan that the constitutional structure dating from the early period of the NEP was no longer appropriate to the needs of a new epoch.

The Seventh All-Union Congress of Soviets voted on February 6, 1935, to appoint a Constitution Commission to draw up an amended text embodying equal suffrage, direct election, secret ballot, and recognition of "the present relation of class forces" in the light of the growth of socialist industry, the end of the kulaks, and the triumph of collectivization. On the next day the CEC named a Commission of 31 to draft a new document. Stalin became its president. In June 1936 the completed draft was published in hundreds of thousands of copies and in all languages of the U.S.S.R. General discussion was encouraged and almost demanded by the Party leaders. Over half a million meetings were held, attended by no less than 36,000,000 people. After many thousands of proposed changes were sifted out, 150 were given serious consideration and 43 were adopted.

At the Extraordinary Eighth Congress of Soviets on November 25, 1936, Stalin delivered a lengthy address on the revised draft. He dwelt first on the changes of recent years which had "eliminated all the exploiting classes"; "transformed the proletariat into the working class of the U.S.S.R., which has abolished the capitalist economic system, has established the socialist ownership of the instruments and means of production, and is directing Soviet society along the road to communism"; converted the peasants into collective farmers, "emancipated from exploitation"; and established a new Soviet Intelligentsia, serving the masses. The new Constitution, continued Stalin, must not be a program of the future—e.g., the achievement of communism—but a "summary of the gains already achieved"—e.g., socialism. . . .

On December 1, 1936, the deputies unanimously adopted a Resolution (*Izvestia,* December 2, 1936) approving the draft and appointing an Editorial Commission of 220 members to put it in final form. . . .

For these gains, declared Y. A. Yakovlev, "we are obliged to the best Leninist, the creator of the new Constitution, the great son of the Soviet people of whom our nation is proud, who in the family of every worker and peasant is called the father of toilers—our leader, Comrade Stalin!" (Ovation.)

In addressing the Congress on the same day, Nikita S. Khrushchev, a member of the Politburo, declared (*Izvestia,* December 2, 1936):

The Fascists, especially the German, are now shouting about their triumph over Marxism, but this "triumph" is one of jesters and clowns of the Middle Ages. And here we are accepting our Constitution and celebrating the victory of Marxism-Leninism-Stalinism, a victory which is not only ours but is also that of toilers the world over. . . . The German Fascists have illusions about the breakdown of our Socialist State and they rave about seizing lands to the East. . . . If the Fascists

attack us, we, our Red Army, together with the German working class, will drown
Fascism not in glory but in their own blood. . . . All the toilers of our country know
that the brains of the Revolution and the cement strengthening the forces of the
Revolution is our Bolshevik Party, the Party of Lenin-Stalin. . . . In the Stalin
epoch, the epoch of victorious socialism, the working class under the leadership of
our great leader [*Vozhd*] will conduct a far-reaching battle for the final victory of
communism and for its triumph the world over.

Headlines in the Soviet press spoke of "Unforgettable Days," "Great
Charter for Liberated Humanity," "The Stalinist Constitution Lights Our
Way," "For Strengthening the Peace and Security of the U.S.S.R." On
December 5, 1936, which was made a national holiday, the Eighth Congress
unanimously adopted the Constitution as finally revised by the Editorial
Commission.

The new charter abolished class discriminations in voting, indirect
elections, and balloting for candidates by a public show of hands. Provision was made (§§134-42) for "universal, direct, and equal suffrage by secret
ballot." All persons over 18, save lunatics and criminals deprived of electoral rights by a court sentence, were granted the right to vote and to be
elected, "irrespective of race or nationality, religion, educational and
residential qualifications, social origin, property status, or past activities."
All deputies in all Soviets—Union, Republican, and local—were to be
chosen by direct election in single-member constituencies. All voting was
henceforth to be confidential and by ballot. All deputies were subject to
recall by a majority of their electors. The right to nominate candidates
(141) was secured to "public organizations and societies of the working
people: Communist Party organizations, trade unions, cooperatives, youth
organizations, and cultural societies." These provisions were made applicable to all elections throughout the territory of the Union. In contrast
to the United States, where citizenship is defined by the federal Constitution
and suffrage by the States within the limits of federal constitutional restrictions, both citizenship and suffrage in the U.S.S.R. are defined in the Union
Constitution.

Major changes in the structure of federal government were also introduced. The old Congress of Soviets, with its CEC of two houses, was
replaced by a bicameral national legislature, the Supreme Soviet of the
U.S.S.R., elected for four years. The Soviet of the Union, corresponding
to the U. S. House of Representatives, consists of deputies chosen from
districts of 300,000 population each. It had 569 members at the outset, and
647 by 1941 as a result of the annexations of 1939-40. [Its membership was
791 in 1962.] The Soviet of Nationalities in the original draft was to have
been appointive, like the U. S. Senate prior to the 17th Amendment. In
response to popular proposals, which Stalin expressly approved, this upper
chamber was made elective on the basis of 25 deputies for each Union Republic, 11 for each Autonomous Republic, 5 for each Autonomous Region,

and 1 for each National Region. Its membership was 574 at the outset and 713 by 1941. [Its membership was 652 in 1962.] All federal legislation requires a majority vote in each house. The two chambers, meeting jointly, choose a Presidium of 42 members, headed by a President (Brezhnev). The Presidium has 15 (originally 11) Vice-Presidents, one for each Union Republic. The Supreme Soviet is normally convened by its Presidium twice a year, with special sessions meeting on the call of the Presidium or of any one of the Republics. The Supreme Soviet appoints the Union Sovnarkom, consisting at the outset of 25 Union Commissariats and 15 Union-Republican Commissariats.

The Soviet Constitution, unlike that of the United States, does not purport to establish what is generally termed a "presidential" system of government. Its scheme (on paper) comes closer to a "parliamentary" system, comparable to that of the United Kingdom, the French Republic, the Weimar Republic, and other Continental democracies. . . .

On paper this design for power establishes a completely democratic system of government by all modern definitions of democracy. It was currently hailed in the U.S.S.R. as "the most democratic constitution in the world." To what extent and in what sense, if any, it has been a vehicle of democracy in its actual operation will be considered below. . . .

2. THE SOCIALIST STATE

. . . Here the fiction of the "dictatorship of the proletariat" confronted the fact of rulership by a managerial elite. Here the juridical theory of a government by Soviets, local, regional, and national, faced the practice of the monolithic and monopolistic oligarchy of the Party. Within the Party, Lenin's concept of "democratic centralism," postulating the responsibility of the leaders to the led, gave way to Stalin's totalitarian machine, ruthlessly exacting obedience from the led to the leaders. Within the leadership, collective deliberations and decisions often gave way, prior to Stalin's demise, to a species of Cæsarism.

Any account of government in the U.S.S.R. must, if it is to do justice to reality, simultaneously take account of the paradoxes and avoid their exaggeration into the totality of Soviet political experience. Whether the comments to follow will achieve this goal is doubtful, but they will at least be directed toward its attainment.

As regards the "federal" character of the Soviet Union and of its largest unit, the Russian Socialist Federated Soviet Republics, Communist publicists claimed from the outset that Soviet federalism represented the final resolution of the "nationality problem" of the Tsarist Empire, with its scores of ethnic groups and its pogroms, oppressions, and efforts at "Russification." [Editor's note: see Chapter 11.] A new day allegedly dawned, suffused with the light of tolerance, equality, and brotherhood among equals—reflected, as of 1941, in the formal existence within the RSFSR of 15 "Autonomous Soviet Socialist Republics" (ASSR), of 6 "autonomous regions" (AR), and 9 "National Districts," plus 2 ASSR's (Adzhar and Abkhazian) and 1 AR (South Ossetian) in Georgia, 1 ASSR (Nakhichevan) and 1 AR (Nagorno-Karabakh) in Azerbaijan, 1 ASSR (Kara-Kalpak) in Uzbekistan, and 1 AR (Gorno-Badakhan) in Tadjikistan.

Within these far-flung Eurasian areas of mixed populations and many national minorities, peace and harmony were officially declared to be assured by autonomy and "self-determination" for all, each enjoying its own language and culture "national in form, but proletarian in content," and all united in a federation of "Union Republics"—ultimately 16 in number, including Estonia, Latvia, Lithuania, and Moldavia, annexed in 1940, and reduced to 15 in July 1956 with the absorption of the Karelo-Finnish SSR, the smallest in population, into the RSFSR. . . .

To what degree has "Soviet federalism" been a reality and to what degree a fiction among the national groups of the U.S.S.R.? The letter of the law is clear. Art. 123 of the Constitution of 1936 asserts:

Equality of rights of citizens of the U.S.S.R., irrespective of their nationality or race, in all spheres of economic, State, cultural, social, and political life, is an indefeasible law. Any direct or indirect restriction of the rights of, or, conversely, any establishment of direct or indirect privileges for, citizens on account of their race or nationality, as well as any advocacy of racial or national exclusiveness or hatred and contempt, is punishable by law.

In pursuit of this aspiration, Soviet policy-makers brought literacy to the "backward peoples" of the Caucasus and Central Asia, often in Latin alphabets to begin with and later in Cyrillic alphabets. The forgotten men of Transcaucasia, Turkestan, and remote Siberia not only learned how to read and write their own tongues but came into possession of schools, libraries, hospitals, and factories, with resulting living standards far above those of other Asian peoples beyond the Soviet frontier. In all the ordinary social and civic relationships among human beings, Soviet society—in this respect, at least, conforming to the highest ideals of Christianity and liberalism—achieved at times an approximation to complete freedom from racial and national prejudice and discrimination.

But if the question be posed as to whether "federalism" in the Western sense—i.e., a formula for uniting separate sovereignties into a union in which each yields certain powers to a common authority and retains all others in local autonomy—is a reality of political life in the U.S.S.R., the only possible verdict must be a negative one. . . .

The Soviet scheme of government embodies on paper many of the attributes of federalism. The 1936 Constitution describes the U.S.S.R. as "a federal State formed on the basis of the voluntary association of Soviet Socialist Republics, having equal rights" (§13). Twenty-three federal powers are enumerated, with all others left to the Republics (§§14-15). The

Soviet equivalent of Article VI of the American Constitution is found (cf. Appendix) in §§19, 20, 105, and 130, by which the primacy of federal law is assured. Amendments to the Union Constitution (§146) require a two-thirds vote of each chamber of the Supreme Soviet but do not, as in the United States, require ratification by state legislatures—i.e., the Supreme Soviets of the Union Republics. These, however, are equally represented in the Soviet of Nationalities and in theory (§17) could secede if dissatisfied with a constitutional amendment. In a semantic *tour de force,* Stalin and his collaborators, in framing the Union Constitution of 1936, provided for an unqualified right of secession. "Of course," commented Stalin (November 25, 1936) in a masterpiece of understatement, "none of our Republics would actually raise the question of seceding from the U.S.S.R."

In practice Soviet "federalism" has been, from beginning to end, a pretense. Repeatedly over the years boundaries have been changed (e.g., the transfer of the Crimea from the RSFSR to the Ukraine in February 1954, and the absorption of the Karelo-Finnish SSR into the RSFSR in July 1956), the division of powers has been altered, and whole populations have been uprooted not through any "federal" procedure of decision-making but by joint decrees of the Union Sovnarkom or Council of Ministers and the Central Committee of the Party. In his indictment of Stalin (February 24-5, 1956), Khrushchev noted indignantly that in 1943-4, on the order of the *Vozhd,* all the people of the Karachai AR, and of the Kalmyk, Chechen-Ingush, and Kabardino-Balkar ASSR's were deported to Asia, along with the inhabitants of the Crimean Tartar and Volga German ASSR's, both unmentioned by Khrushchev.

The Ukrainians avoided meeting this fate only because there were too many of them and there was no place to which to deport them. . . . Not only a Marxist-Leninist but also no man of common sense can grasp how it is possible to make whole nations responsible for inimical activity, including women, children, old people, Communists, and Komsomols, to use mass repression against them, and to expose them to misery and suffering for the hostile acts of individual persons or groups of persons.

In Stalin's last years, moreover, anti-Semitism and other forms of discrimination against minority peoples became a marked feature, despite semantic disguises, of the official conduct of Soviet policy-makers. In happier days to come, federalism may be given practical meaning in the public law and political life of the U.S.S.R. During most of the unhappy past it has been a fiction or a fraud.*

* Joshua Kunitz, in his otherwise perceptive and illuminating essay "The Jewish Problem in the USSR" (*Monthly Review,* March and April 1953), argues that *popular* anti-Semitism was widespread after 1945 but that no *official* anti-Semitism existed. It is doubtless true that no individuals were persecuted or discriminated against because of Jewish origin *per se,* provided that they were willing to renounce their Jewish religious and cultural heritage. But Party and Government alike, prior to Stalin's demise, savagely attacked not only political Zionism, or even the slightest supicion thereof, but suppressed

A like judgment is warranted by the record on many other aspects of the theory of Soviet governance in contrast to the practice of the arts of power by the oligarchs. On paper the Soviet Constitution establishes a "parliamentary" system on the British and Continental model. Cabinets in both the U.S.S.R. and the Union Republics are chosen by, and from, the freely elected members of legislative bodies and may, in principle, be altered or displaced by the deputies who appoint them. In fact any such relationship is wholly contrary to reality. The persisting pattern of Soviet public life, still unaltered in 1957 despite hopes and prospects of change, was formerly established by the oligarchs in 1937. Its genesis therefore merits review.

The first election held under the 1936 Constitution took place on December 12, 1937, for the new Supreme Soviet. In preparation for the event the old federal CEC appointed a Central Electoral Commission, which directed a hierarchy of local commissions in registering voters and candidates, conducting propaganda, supervising the preparation of ballots, envelopes, and ballot boxes, counting the ballots, and announcing the results. Electoral districts, established at least 45 days before the election, were to be fixed by the CEC and subsequently by the Supreme Soviet itself. For purposes of registering voters and casting and counting ballots (but not for purposes of representation) the RSFSR was divided into 93,927 precincts, of which 2,047 were on boats. The population of some of the urban precincts was as large as 150,000, while districts in the lesser Republics varied between 5,000 and 20,000 inhabitants.

Candidates were proposed in the constituencies by trade unions, cooperatives, Komsomol units, cultural societies, army regiments, collective farms, and the primary organizations of the Party, with the latter in most instances advising other groups in areas where it was decided not to nominate a Party member. No candidate could be nominated by an individual, but all voters were entitled to attend meetings where nominees were proposed. Efforts of church congregations to propose candidates were disallowed by the Electoral Commission. Procedure conformed closely to the Election Regulations later issued by the Supreme Soviet. Voting lists were compiled by agents of city and rural Soviets on the basis of house rolls, membership lists of collective farms, and personal canvassing. In the absence of any residence requirement, all temporary and permanent inhabitants were listed alphabetically in each precinct. Those moving before election day or engaged in travel were granted certificates by local Soviets, entitling them to vote wherever they might be. The lists thus compiled were posted in local Soviet HQ 30 days before the election. All citizens were entitled to complain of omissions or errors, with each complaint to be

---

all manifestations of Hebrew or Yiddish culture, even to the extent of executing, on trumped-up charges, numerous Yiddish writers and artists. Amends have since been made. The realities of 1948-53, however, suggest that Kunitz's dichotomy is a distinction without a difference. Cf. Solomon M. Schwarz: *The Jews in the Soviet Union* (Syracuse University Press, 1953).

dealt with inside of 3 days by the Soviet Executive Committee, with appeal to the People's Courts, which were required to reach a decision in open hearings within 3 days in the presence of the complainant and a representative of the Soviet.

Qualifications for candidates were the same as those for voters, except that no candidate could be a member of an Electoral Commission and each was required to consent in writing to be a nominee. The names of proposed candidates were to be published in the local press 25 days before the election. Ballots were to be printed 15 days before the election. In most districts several candidates were proposed, usually by acclamation in the various nominating groups. But in all districts only one candidate for each seat in the Soviet of the Union and the Soviet of Nationalities (1,143 in all) appeared on the ballot. Of the total thus nominated, 37 were dropped and replaced by others, on the order of the Central Electoral Commission. This elimination of all but one candidate normally took place within the 10 days between the publishing of names and the printing of ballots. The procedure was nowhere set forth by law or decree. It amounted to a highly informal "primary," inevitably guided by the local Party members. The choice of deputies was thus made not at the election but during the campaign in the name of a "bloc of Party and non-Party people." Of the 569 candidates for the Soviet of the Union, 81% (and of the 574 candidates for the Soviet of Nationalities, 71%) were members or candidates of the Party. Others were designated as "non-Party Bolshevists."

Soviet theory continued to anticipate multiple nominations for membership in the Supreme Soviet. The statutes provided for "run-off" elections two weeks after the original polling if less than half of the registered voters cast ballots or if no candidate received an absolute majority. While it does not appear that this familiar democratic device, or the constitutional right of popular recall, has ever been applied to federal offices, the possibility of at least 3 candidates for a single seat was clearly contemplated. Mayors of cities were at this period elected by popular choice through secret ballot from among four or five candidates. The same was true for members of village and urban Soviets, in which non-Party members usually constitute two-thirds or three-quarters of the deputies.

If the first federal election day was a gala occasion, the preceding nation-wide campaign to get out the vote had all the earmarks of an educational crusade. . . . The goals were unanimity now and solidarity forever. Polls were open from 6 A.M. until midnight. Moscow and other cities were aglow with bunting, garlands, and flags. Stalin, Molotov, and Voroshilov voted in precinct 58 of the Lenin election district of the capital. Others voted by millions in town and countryside, in lonely villages and remote valleys, in Arctic outposts and desert oases, on ships at sea, and even at railway stations, where booths were set up for passengers in transit.

Of the 93,639,458 enfranchised Soviet citizens, 90,319,436, or 96%, cast ballots. Of the ballots for deputies to the Soviet of the Union, 636,808 were invalid and 632,074 had names crossed out. In electing the members of the Soviet of Nationalities, the voters cast 1,487,582 invalid ballots and crossed out names in 562,402 instances. . . .

The pattern thus established was followed undeviatingly up to the 40th anniversary of the October Revolution. To Western liberals, it is a travesty of representative democracy, since there can plainly be no effective freedom or representation or democracy in ritualistic exercises in unanimity. To many Russians, unfamiliar with Western ways or disposed to regard them as "bourgeois frauds," the ceremonials perhaps recall with nostalgia and gratitude the age-long search of the Slavs for unity in the face of schisms within and hostility from without—reflected paradoxically in the *liberum veto* in the Diet of the old Kingdom of Poland and in the requirement of unanimity for major decisions in the ancient Russian *Veche* or Assembly. As recently as 1956, when portents of a new dispensation were numerous, only one name for each office appeared on Soviet ballots, even in neighborhood "elections" of judges of the local People's Courts and of their two lay assistants, all chosen for two-year terms and most of them, incidentally, women.

On March 14, 1954, the ritual was repeated, with 120,727,826 voters (out of 120,750,816) choosing 708 and 639 deputies, respectively, for the two chambers of the Supreme Soviet, of whom 1,050 were Party members, 297 were non-Party, and 348 were women, with the proportions of non-Party deputies and women deputies almost identical in the two houses. [Editor s note: For the results of the recent election see the following article.]

Soviet legislative procedure has, thus far, followed a comparable pattern. Soviet "law-makers" are not salaried officials but part-time deputies with other jobs, paid travel expenses and *per-diem* allowances out of public revenue. On the federal, Republican, and local levels, they hear and consider legislative proposals presented by the Ministers, listen to reports and speeches, rarely advance proposals of their own, discuss bills in committees, but in their final "decisions" always vote unanimously in favor of whatever projects the Party leadership has resolved to adopt as public policy. Their function, not unlike that of Western parliamentarians in this respect, is to reflect local expectations, demands, grievances, and hopes, and to act as *liaison* agents between the Party leadership and administrative bureaucracy, on the one hand, and their constituents on the other. But they have possessed, thus far, no powers of decision, save insofar as their advice may influence the judgment of the top-level oligarchs whose ultimate conclusions have long been sacrosanct on the premise (long unquestioned but vaguely acknowledged to be dubious and dangerous since Stalin's demise) that the Party is infallible and therefore above criticism or challenge. . . .

3. THE RIGHTS OF MAN

Within the limits of oligarchy, what are the realities and what are the fictions of the "constitutional rights" of Soviet citizens as elaborately set forth in Chapters X and XI of the Charter of 1936? The answer is less simple than many Western commentators have assumed. "Real liberty," declared Stalin to Roy Howard (cf. *Izvestia,* December 8, 1936), "can be had only where exploitation is destroyed, where there is no oppression of one people by another, where there is no unemployment and pauperism, where a person does not shiver in fear of losing tomorrow his job, home, bread. Only in such a society is it possible to have real, and not paper, liberty, personal and otherwise."

This "reality" proved meaningless over many years to the millions of Soviet citizens arrested by agents of the OGPU, NKVD, or MVD and consigned to forced-labor camps in Siberia and the Far North, where only the hardiest survived the rigors of arduous work, meager diet, miserable living conditions, and systematic terrorization and exploitation—pending the amnesties, relaxations, and "mellowing" of the police-state regime since Stalin's death.

Many other rights solemnly guaranteed by the Supreme Law of Soviet-land remained "dead letters" during most of the two decades after 1936. Freedom of speech, press, assembly, and association (§§125, 126) and inviolability of persons, homes, and correspondence (§§127, 128) were often honored more in the breach than in the observance, as was acknowledged at Party Congress XX and thereafter. The same was true of intellectual, scientific, and academic freedom, particularly in the black years of Stalin's posturing as the infallible source of all truth and taste—when the *Vozhd* and his agents felt in duty bound to impose "Socialist Realism" on writers, artists, and musicians, Lysenko's fantasies on biologists, "Marxist physics" on other scientists, etc. Political privileges (§§134-42) have been less rights than duties, and have, in any case, only a tangential relationship to public policy-making and the selection of representatives. The independence of the courts (§112) and the protection of the individual against arbitrary arrest, imprisonment, or execution (§§111, 127, 128) remained fictitious so long as the MVD possessed the right to punish alleged political offenders without public trial, so long as the criminal code permitted penalization "by analogy" of acts not defined as crimes but held dangerous to the State, so long as the death penalty was prescribed (as in the act of August 7, 1932) for theft of public property, and so long as the full rigors of the criminal code were made applicable (as in the act of April 7, 1935) to juvenile delinquents.

Freedom of conscience and worship (§124), or the lack thereof, have undergone many vicissitudes during the four decades of Soviet power. The sequence began with open persecution by a regime of atheists of many churchmen and believers during the years when the established Orthodox Church, smarting from Soviet disestablishment and dispossession of most of its wealth, championed Autocracy and the cause of the White Armies. The charter of 1936 re-enfranchised the clergy. The "League of the Militant Godless," founded in 1925 and directed by Emilian Yaroslavsky, claimed 10,000,000 members by 1932 but had declined to 3,000,000 by 1940. When Communist efforts to extirpate religion had clearly failed and the new Church patriotically rallied to the defense of the State against the Nazi invaders, the League was dissolved and its publishing facilities were transferred to the Orthodox priesthood. On September 12, 1943, an officially sponsored *Sobor* elected Metropolitan Sergei of Moscow Patriarch of all Russia. Upon his death a new *Sobor* in January 1945 elected Metropolitan Alexei as Patriarch. Meanwhile, in October of 1943 a State Council on Church Affairs, headed by Georgi Karpov, was set up to promote "genuine religious freedom."

Any congregation willing to pay the salary of a cleric and the costs of building maintenance may conduct services in church, mosque, or synagogue. But religious instruction of the young outside of home is still (1957) forbidden. No church receives any financial aid from the State save for the restoration and upkeep of ecclesiastical structures of historic or artistic importance—most of which, however, are without congregations and have been converted into museums. Under these circumstances religious life languishes despite formal freedom of worship.

Soviet citizens enjoy certain other "constitutional rights" that are more substance than shadow. Individual and collective property rights, along with rights of ownership and inheritance of income, personal property, savings, and private houses (§§7-10), appear to be well respected within the limits already indicated. The major social gains of the Revolution are embodied (§§118-20) in the rights to work, to paid vacations, to insurance against illness and old age, and to free dental and medical service, including access to hospitals and sanatoria. The social-insurance system, administered by the trade unions, and socialized medicine, directed by the Ministry of Health, are among the significant contributions of the Soviet State to the welfare of the people. The number of physicians increased from 20,000 in 1913 to 63,000 in 1928, 141,000 in 1941 (January 1), and 299,000 in 1955 (July 1), with lesser health workers, including *feldshers* (medical aides) and nurses, increasing from 393,200 in 1941 to 731,100 in 1955. Death rates declined from 18.3 per thousand population in 1940 to 9.6 in 1950, 9.0 in 1953, and 8.4 in 1955, while birth rates for the corresponding years were reported as 31.7, 26.5, 24.9, and 25.6.

Equality of rights for women, including equal access to all vocations and identical status with men as to salaries, vacations, social insurance, and education, plus "pre-maternity and maternity leave with full pay" (§122), is also a fact and not a fiction. Early Soviet legislation made marriage and divorce simple civil formalities, costing only a few rubles at the Registration bureaus (*Zags*), recognized no distinction between legitimate and illegitimate children, and permitted free abortions in public clinics. In a change of "line," decrees and laws of 1936 forbade abortions except for reasons of health. Under the impact of the fearful blood-letting of World War II, new legislation of 1943-4 made divorce expensive and difficult, imposed special taxes on the unmarried and the childless, and offered monetary rewards and honors to mothers of many children. While these statutes are still in force, abortion was again legalized in 1955. Any Soviet woman, married or unmarried, may by her own decision have an abortion without cost. Meanwhile, Western travelers in the U.S.S.R. are often shocked to see women sweeping streets, working in construction gangs, building houses, and performing other heavy tasks. But this phenomenon is merely visual evidence —along with many policewomen and numerous female bus-drivers, subway-operators, taxi-drivers, etc.—that equality of the sexes is a reality. By 1955, according to the handbook issued in Moscow by the Central Statistical Board, women comprised the following percentages of sundry vocations: health services, 85 (over two-thirds of Soviet physicians are women); restaurant workers, 83; teachers, 68; public administration, 49; industry, 45; transport and communications, 33; and construction, 31.

Amid so mixed a record of failures and successes, of pledges broken and of promises carried out, of rights betrayed and rights achieved, it is fitting to conclude our evaluation with the one duty of the State which has been most adequately fulfilled and is bright with hope for the future. §121: "Citizens of the U.S.S.R. have the right to education. . . ." Freedom from ignorance through the abolition of illiteracy has been achieved via the nation-wide network of ten-year public schools, combining elementary and secondary grades in one sequence and raising the number of pupils in attendance from 7,900,000 in 1914 to 34,800,000 in 1940. Falling birth rates and the decline of population during the years of war reduced the total to 28,200,000 in 1955. All Soviet children were going through seven grades by 1956. All would go through all ten grades by 1960, thus universalizing high-school education even more completely than in the U.S.A. Coeducation, introduced in 1918 and abolished in 1943, was restored in 1956-7. Early experimentation in "progressive" education gave way in the 1930's to an exacting discipline, which has never since been much modified, despite complaints in recent years that school children are overworked.

Mathematics and the natural sciences are the "core" of Soviet education in the upper grades. All pupils are required to choose English, French, or German in the fifth grade (Latin, Greek, Spanish, Italian, and other tongues are not taught below the university level) and to study their choice for six years—with graduates of the ten-year schools usually acquiring a good reading knowledge, though seldom an adequate speaking knowledge, of the language thus selected. German was the most popular choice before 1939.

English has been the favorite since 1945. A new network of highly selective "boarding schools" was established in 1956-7 on the model of English "public" and American private schools.

Beyond the ten-year schools Soviet higher education has taken flourishing form in a galaxy of trade schools, technical institutes, research centers, and universities, with the latter planned not for the few, as in Western Europe, but for the many, as in America. Small tuition fees were introduced in 1940 but were abolished in 1956-7. All Soviet youths with the requisite talents are encouraged to attend universities, granted scholarships and living stipends whenever their needs call for such support, and generously rewarded for outstanding achievement with honors, prizes, and vocational opportunities. Between 1940 and 1955 the graduates of institutes and universities waxed from 908,000 to 2,184,000, with engineers increasing from 289,000 to 585,900, economists and business specialists from 59,300 to 113,800, and teachers, librarians, and other "cultural workers" from 300,400 to 906,400. In 1955, 1,230,000 young people were full-time students at universities, as compared with 850,000 in 1950 and 590,000 in 1940 (U.S.A., 1954: 2,499,750). In 1955, 54,700 books were published in almost a billion copies, with even the most abstruse scientific works, however large the printing, being snatched up by an insatiable public within a few days in the innumerable bookstores and sidewalk stalls throughout the U.S.S.R. Public libraries numbered 277,000 with 527,000,000 books in 1940, and 392,000 with 1,351,000,000 books in 1955.

In short, Russia since 1917 has become educated as well as industrialized and urbanized. Stalin's totalitarian police state brought into being a community that can no longer be governed by the police methods of totalitarianism. In sundry ways, not yet altogether clear in 1957, the "dead letters" of the Constitution of 1936 were in painful process of having some breath of life infused into their empty symbols by the post-Stalin "collective" leadership. It is not fortuitous that, apart from the nearby Kremlin, the most impressive building in central Moscow, 40 years after 1917, is the Lenin State Library, claiming to be, with its 18,000,000 books, pamphlets, and periodicals, the largest library in the world, though singularly devoid of anti-Soviet works in any language. Neither is it accidental that the visitor who comes to Moscow by plane obtains his first glimpse of the Soviet capital, on the horizon of the Lenin Hills between the airport and the city, in the form of the 37-story tower (surrounded by a gigantic "suburban" development of huge apartment blocks, planned to house 200,000 people) of the new building of Moscow State University, opened in 1953. This imposing edifice, along with its adjuncts, is dedicated to physics, chemistry, biology, and allied sciences, with social studies and the humanities housed elsewhere in older academic structures within the city proper. The central citadel of learning, unquestionably the largest university building in the world, contains classrooms, lecture halls, laboratories, gymnasiums, and apartments for all of the faculty and much of the student body of 22,000. The Stalinist State, having in some measure expiated the crimes committed in its name by educating Russia, was in process, four decades after 1917, of ceasing to be a Stalinist State.

OFFICIAL RETURNS ON 1962 ELECTION TO SUPREME SOVIET

CENTRAL ELECTION COMMISSION*

REGISTERED VOTERS AND BALLOTS CAST

As previously reported, the elections to the Supreme Soviet of the U.S.S.R., held on March 18, 1962, were marked by the high political activity of the Soviet people. The election results demonstrated once again the lofty moral and political unity of Soviet society and the triumph of socialist democracy.

The Central Election Commission has compiled the final results of the elections. It has established that all district election commissions, in strict conformity with the Statutes on Elections, have counted the ballots and established the election results for each election district.

According to the figures of the district election commissions, the number of registered voters for the U.S.S.R. as a whole totaled 140,022,359, of whom 139,957,809, or 99.95%, voted in the elections.

The total number of voters and the number of ballots cast in the elections by Union republics are as follows:

| | 1962 ELECTION | | | 1958 |
UNION REPUBLIC	VOTERS REGISTERED	BALLOTS CAST	% OF VOTERS	% OF VOTERS
Russian Republic	78,725,696	78,683,883	99.95	99.96
Ukraine Republic	29,488,316	29,481,232	99.98	99.98
Belorussian Republic	5,346,550	5,344,434	99.96	99.99
Uzbek Republic	4,769,190	4,768,841	99.99	99.99
Kazakh Republic	6,264,564	6,263,398	99.98	99.99
Georgian Republic	2,643,145	2,643,060	99.99	99.99
Azerbaidzhan Republic	2,194,501	2,194,408	99.99	99.98
Lithuanian Republic	1,856,727	1,855,301	99.92	99.96
Moldavian Republic	1,864,015	1,862,582	99.92	99.97
Latvian Republic	1,593,258	1,590,601	99.83	99.92
Kirgiz Republic	1,246,959	1,246,539	99.97	99.99
Tadzhik Republic	1,158,487	1,158,436	99.99	99.99
Armenian Republic	1,063,553	1,063,288	99.98	99.98
Turkmenian Republic	914,965	914,903	99.99	99.99
Estonian Republic	892,433	886,903	99.38	99.66

* This is a translation of an official announcement that appeared in *Pravda* on March 21, 1962, covering the 1962 election to the Supreme Soviet. [The corresponding percentages for the 1958 election, taken from the official returns in *Pravda* on March 19, 1958, have been added by this editor.]

RESULTS OF ELECTIONS TO SOVIET OF THE UNION

Seven hundred ninety-one election districts were formed to conduct elections to the Soviet of the Union. Elections were held in all the election districts. A total of 139,210,431 persons, or 99.47% of those voting, voted for the candidates for Deputy to the Soviet of the Union. A total of 746,563 persons voted against them. On the basis of Art. 88 of the Statutes on Elections to the U.S.S.R. Supreme Soviet, 815 ballots were declared invalid.

All the candidates who ran received an overwhelming majority of the votes and were elected Deputies.

The results of the elections to the Soviet of the Union by republics are as follows:

UNION REPUBLIC	1962 ELECTION		1958 ELECTION
	BALLOTS CAST	% OF VOTERS	% OF VOTERS
Russian Republic	78,105,309	99.26	99.40
Ukraine Republic	29,413,239	99.77	99.83
Belorussian Republic	5,332,600	99.78	99.84
Uzbek Republic	4,754,004	99.69	99.80
Kazakh Republic	6,229,802	99.46	99.62
Georgian Republic	2,640,588	99.91	99.95
Azerbaidzhan Republic	2,189,614	99.78	99.75
Lithuanian Republic	1,853,451	99.90	99.91
Moldavian Republic	1,859,318	99.82	99.33
Latvian Republic	1,585,562	99.68	99.91
Kirgiz Republic	1,239,990	99.47	99.65
Tadzhik Republic	1,155,318	99.73	99.81
Armenian Republic	1,061,883	99.87	99.78
Turkmenian Republic	910,187	99.48	99.56
Estonian Republic	879,566	99.17	99.55

RESULTS OF ELECTIONS TO SOVIET OF NATIONALITIES

Six hundred fifty-two election districts were formed to conduct elections to the Soviet of Nationalities, including 375 election districts for elections to the Soviet of Nationalities from the Union republics, 220 from the autonomous republics, 40 from the autonomous provinces and ten from the national regions. Elections were held in all election districts. A total of 139,391,455 persons, or 99.60% of those voting, voted for the candidates for Deputy to the Soviet of Nationalities. A total of 564,155 persons voted against them. On the basis of Art. 88 of the Statutes on Elections to the U.S.S.R. Supreme Soviet, 706 ballots were declared invalid.

All the candidates who ran received an overwhelming majority of the votes and were elected Deputies.

The results of the elections to the Soviet of Nationalities by Union republics are as follows:

| UNION REPUBLIC | 1962 ELECTION | | 1958 ELECTION |
	BALLOTS CAST	% OF VOTERS	% OF VOTERS
Russian Republic	78,279,687	99.49	99.67
Ukraine Republic	29,419,223	99.79	99.86
Belorussian Republic	5,335,346	99.85	99.81
Uzbek Republic	4,752,605	99.66	99.81
Kazakh Republic	6,227,005	99.42	99.51
Georgian Republic	2,641,118	99.93	99.94
Azerbaidzhan Republic	2,189,283	99.78	99.84
Lithuanian Republic	1,853,301	99.90	99.89
Moldavian Republic	1,860,915	99.83	99.86
Latvian Republic	1,587,675	99.80	99.90
Kirgiz Republic	1,238,443	99.36	99.58
Tadzhik Republic	1,151,795	99.45	99.72
Armenian Republic	1,061,663	99.85	99.85
Turkmenian Republic	911,491	99.62	99.70
Estonian Republic	881,905	99.36	99.59

In the autonomous republics, autonomous provinces and national regions the total number of voters registered for elections to the Soviet of Nationalities from these autonomous areas was 12,057,479; of this number, 12,052,744, or 99.96%, voted. A total of 11,968,855 persons, or 99.30% of those voting, voted for the candidates for Deputy; 83,848 voted against them. On the basis of Art. 88 of the Statutes on Elections, 41 ballots were declared invalid.

Having examined the materials submitted by the district election commissions, the Central Election Commission, on the basis of Art. 38 of the Statutes on Elections, has registered the election of Deputies to the U.S.S.R. Supreme Soviet for all election districts.

A total of 1,443 Deputies have been elected, including 791 Deputies to the Soviet of the Union and 652 Deputies to the Soviet of Nationalities.

All the elected Deputies are candidates of the people's bloc of Communists and non-Party persons.

Chapter 11

MYTH AND REALITY:
SELF-DETERMINATION AND EQUALITY OF NATIONS

One of the proudest boasts of the U.S.S.R. is that "it has solved the national question—completely and finally." This thesis is elaborated by the distinguished Soviet editor, B. G. Gafurov, and challenged by the prominent American sociologist, Alex Inkeles. Despite their sharp differences, it is well to emphasize that, generally speaking, students of Soviet affairs credit the U.S.S.R., in the words of Alex Inkeles, with "substantial attainments" in the field of national relations.

It should be recalled that Lenin, as early as the turn of the century, supported recognition of "the equality of rights of all nationalities" including the right of self-determination. These "rights" were affirmed in the first program of the Party adopted in 1903, embodied in Soviet decrees after the Revolution, and appear in the Soviet Constitution. At the same time, it was Lenin's view that Marxism could not be reconciled with divisive, bourgeois nationalism, even in its "most 'just,' 'pure,' refined, or civilized" form. He confidently anticipated, as Professor Julian Towster explains in his pioneer study, Political Power in the U.S.S.R., *that the proletariat having attained power and eliminated oppression and friction would induce the nations of the earth voluntarily to "draw together, fusing their different cultures and languages into one common culture and language," to constitute "one, unified community of mankind." "In place of any nationalism," Lenin wrote in 1913, "Marxism proposes internationalism—the amalgamation of all nations in a supreme unity."*

Is there a basic inconsistency in Lenin's views? So some of the early Russian Marxists charged. And this, too, is the view of Professor Richard Pipes, author of The Formation of the Soviet Union, *who maintains that Lenin's theory of self-determination was, in essence, an "endeavor to reconcile two sets of mutually exclusive premises: those derived from Marxism and those supplied by political realities." Lenin, as a "realist," assailed the Bolsheviks, who anticipated that the proletarian power would abolish all*

333

*borders and create a supra-national state, as visionaries seeking a "pure"
instead of a "social" revolution. But, on the other hand, as a "Marxist,"
Lenin insisted that "the question of the right of self-determination" should
not be confused "with the question whether the secession of this or that
nation is expedient." The latter question must be decided by the Party "in
each individual case entirely independently, from the viewpoint of the
interests of the whole social development and of the interests of the proletariat's class struggle for socialism."*

*The careful reader will discern in the excerpt from the recently adopted
Program of the Communist Party—the third in its history—some of the
"dualism" to be found in Lenin's formulations on the national question.*

THE SOLUTION OF THE NATIONAL QUESTION

B. G. GAFUROV*

For centuries the best minds of mankind both in the East and in the
West dreamed of a brotherhood of peoples irrespective of nationality, race
or color. But the grim reality of the old world barred the implementation of
this dream.

In this connection I would like to start my lecture with a parable that is
common in the East. Two tribes dwelt on two opposite banks of a river.
For centuries they were at loggerheads with each other. Once, a peasant
from the tribe dwelling on the right bank met a wizard who said to him: "I'll
give you anything you wish, but under one condition—a member of the
other tribe dwelling on the left bank of the river will receive twice as much."
And the peasant answered: "Put out one of my eyes," wanting the wizard to
put out both eyes of his counterpart in the other tribe. Such is the bitter tale
of the formidable power of national enmity and hate that cripples human
life.

As is known, in the last century two men—the Frenchman Arthur de
Gobineau and the Germanized Englishman Houston Chamberlain—evolved
a most elaborate argument to substantiate the theory alleging that the
northern, or the so-called Nordic, race of dolichocephalic, blond-haired and
blue-eyed men is the most superior of all existing human races, and because
of merits inherent in it is the natural master of all other races and, above all,
of the colored ones. This theory was repeatedly lauded to the skies by various
ideologists and politicians, and received its most finished and tragic mani-

---

* Director of the Institute of Oriental Studies and chief editor of its periodical, *Sov-
remenniy vostok*. Mr. Gafurov has also been a member of the Central Committee of the
Communist Party. The selection is from a lecture delivered to the Diplomatic corps in
Moscow on October 12, 1961.

festation in the policies of Hitlerism. History proved the antiscientific, reactionary and anti-popular nature of this false theory. . . .

Even long before the October Revolution, Lenin and the Bolsheviks had worked out a comprehensive theoretical program on the national question in Russia. The main provisions of this program were: equality and sovereignty of all peoples of Russia; their right to free self-determination, including the right to secede; abolition of all national and religious restrictions and privileges; free development of national minorities and ethnographic groups.

Immediately after the victory of the October Revolution, the Communist Party set about to practically implement the program laid down on the national question. The Second All-Russian Congress of Soviets, on November 8, 1917, declared that it was the paramount task of Soviet power to insure to "all nations inhabiting Russia genuine right to self-determination." The solicitude of the Leninist Party for the establishment of complete equality of all nations in our country found reflection in the Declaration of Rights of the Peoples of Russia adopted by the Soviet Government on November 15, 1917. The Declaration solemnly confirmed the sovereignty and equality of these peoples, their right to self-determination including that to secede, abolished all national restrictions and privileges, guaranteed the all-round and free development of all nations and nationalities, however small. . . .

At a certain stage in the attainment of complete and all-round unity of the peoples of the country, the Eighth Congress of the Party [in 1919] recommended a federation of Soviet national republics. The federation was to be based on the well-known premise by V. I. Lenin who emphasized: "We want a voluntary union of nations; a union which would allow no coercion of one nation by another; a union which would be based on complete trust, clear awareness of fraternal unity and absolutely voluntary agreement. Such a union cannot be established at once; it should be built with the greatest possible patience and caution in order not to spoil everything, not to arouse distrust; to let distrust bred by centuries of landlords' and capitalists' oppression, of private property and enmity over its distribution and redistribution, be overcome." (V. I. Lenin, Letter to Workers and Peasants of the Ukraine. *Works,* Vol. XXX, p. 269.) The Union of Soviet Socialist Republics established in 1922 was precisely such a voluntary alliance of nations. . . .

In the years of Soviet power the formerly backward outlying areas of Russia have become prosperous industrial and agrarian republics. As a rule, the proportion of investments in the economy of the national republics exceeded the average for the Soviet Union as a whole, and this resulted in a quicker pace of their industrialization than that of the central areas of the country. The Communist Party radically changed the entire economics of the Soviet republics on the basis of socialism. It is particularly true regarding the Eastern republics of the USSR, where the working people made a direct

transition from patriarchal and feudal relations and colonial slavery to socialism, by-passing the capitalist stage of development. . . .

In the course of socialist construction achievements of historic significance were gained in the field of national relationship, their main characteristics being as follows:

1. The nationalities of the Soviet Union, who had not attained nation-
hood before the Revolution, have developed into nations under the banner
of the Soviets. If previously history knew the process of development of nations on the basis of the development of capitalist relations, the experience
of the Soviet Union proved that the development of capitalism is by no means
an indispensable condition of the development into nations of nationalities
that have not reached the stage of capitalism. Thus, for instance, the Tajik
nationality, where prior to the October Revolution feudal relations prevailed,
developed into a nation in this way.

The process of development of nations in the Soviet Union had many
peculiar and instructive features. Thus certain nationalities, speaking similar languages but historically self-determined a long time ago, developed
into different nations (the Tartars, Bashkirs, Kazakhs and Kirghiz). On the
other hand, nationalities speaking different languages but long brought
together by history (the Persian-speaking Tajiks, the Pamirs peoples, Yazgu-
lems, Yagnobs) developed into a single Tajik nation.

2. As a result of the effort of the Communist Party to eliminate economic and cultural inequality, there are no longer any backward nations in
the USSR.

3. The greatest achievement in the solution of the national question was
that national discord and enmity were replaced by fraternal friendship and
cooperation of all nations and nationalities of the Soviet Union. History
knows instances of peaceful coexistence of nations, of setting up of all kinds
of unions between them, but the unity of Soviet socialist nations is essentially
different from such alliances. The objective basis of the union of Soviet nations is the socialist ownership of the implements and means of production,
which is the dominant form of property in our land; socialist relations of
production, which are the relations of cooperation and mutual assistance of
people free from exploitation. It was the liquidation of the exploitation of
man by man, the doing away with social strife in the land of Soviets that ensured disappearance of national discord and establishment of friendship
among all peoples of the USSR.

Of historic importance was also the fact that the biggest and, economically and culturally, the most developed nation—the Russian nation—which
before the Revolution played the role of the ruling nation, now resolutely
and selflessly gave up its former privileged position. Moreover, the Russian
socialist nation made many efforts and sacrifices to help the formerly oppressed nationalities to develop into independent nations and to evolve their
own statehood, economy and culture.

Tremendous successes and gains scored in the field of economic, political and cultural development of nations and nationalities of the Soviet Union support the claim that in the course of building a socialist society, the national question in our country has been solved completely and finally. All this was achieved as the result of tremendous work on the part of the Party, the Soviet Government and the entire Soviet people.

Let us remember that Russia herself was an underdeveloped country. To build industry, a great effort was needed. We did not have a rich uncle to depend on; everything had to be done by our own hands. But even at the height of the Civil War, when the country's economy was completely dislocated, Lenin ordered that machines and factory equipment be sent to the national republics.

There was another big and complex problem—the training of personnel. Apart from highly skilled specialists, there was a lack of personnel with secondary-school education. Various short-term schools were opened. Thousands of boys and girls from the Central Asian republics were sent to the USSR textile industrial centers—Ivanovo-Voznesensk, Shuya, Serpukhov—where they learned from Russian weavers and spinners how to operate the textile machinery. On returning home they formed the nucleus of skilled personnel in local mills and factories. In that way, personnel and workers were trained simultaneously with the building of industrial enterprises. Great difficulties had to be surmounted by Russian specialists while building industry. Under extremely hard conditions they not only helped to build but also taught local personnel.

The degree of literacy was very low. In Tajikistan, for instance, there was only 0.5 per cent literacy. Therefore, the elimination of illiteracy was an indispensable condition for the development of a new, advanced economy.

After the end of the Civil War, feudal relations and survivals of the tribal system, rules of feudal and tribal law (Adah, Sharia, etc.) proved a grave obstacle in the way of building up a new life in the national republics.

In 1925-1926 agrarian and water reforms were carried out in Central Asia and other national republics which were of great import for the development of the productive forces and were instrumental in the growth of the political consciousness of the broad masses of people.

Feudal survivals were completely eliminated on the basis of mass cooperation in agriculture. The land was given to the tiller. Collectivization transformed small-scale, backward farming into a large-scale mechanized branch of the economy. An end was put once and for all to impoverishment, famine and epidemics—three features of village life in the East before the Revolution.

To promote the development of the economy and culture, it was necessary to combat both great-power chauvinism and local nationalism. In the late twenties the main danger came from great-power chauvinism, against which the main blow of the Communist Party was directed. But local nationalism too did tremendous harm to the interests of the people. The Party always encouraged Russian Communists to fight against great-power chauvinism in the first place, and the local workers to combat local nationalism. The tremendous organizational and cultural work of the Party for the international education of the masses resulted in the strengthening of friendship among all nations.

In the USSR a man, preaching national discord and enmity, asserting the exclusiveness of one people and haughtily and contemptuously treating people of other nationalities, is bound to be severely condemned by the Soviet public. The laws of our state punish any encroachment on the rights of Soviet nations and nationalities. Combating great-power chauvinism and local nationalism, the Party fought against both: the ignoring of local national characteristics and the over-accentuating of them. . . .

Much had to be done in order to do away with the feudal attitude toward women. In the national republics, where the bulk of the population were Moslems, women had a very low status. Polygamy still existed there. In the areas with settled population women had to wear all kinds of veils— *paranjas, chachvans* and *chadras*. They were 100 per cent illiterate.

Women's departments and councils were set up by the Party committees and conducted a great project of enlightenment and education. In 1926-1927 a broad campaign was developed against the veil. Hundreds of courageous, open-minded women publicly burned their veils, calling upon other women to follow their example. Despite the furious resistance of feudal elements, who killed dozens of women, hundreds of thousands of women threw off the veil and joined the ranks of the builders of the new life.

I could tell you a lot of interesting things about the way we succeeded in getting rid of the custom of wearing the veil. In the thirties and forties there were people who insisted on laws and decrees being passed prohibiting the veil. But the Soviet Government refused to follow their advice, and chose the way of education and explanatory work. It often happened that at the meetings where women were told of the harm of the custom of wearing veils they would throw them off, but, coming back home, put them on again. And we realized that it was not enough to persuade only women and that men also had to be appealed to.

Special schools, courses and technical schools for women were opened in the national republics. In the cities where silk and cotton mills were built, many women, throwing off the veil, entered them as workers. The fight for the emancipation of women was bitter; it required great effort. But now we are proud of the fact that millions of women have become educated and aware members of society. Thousands of women who hold a doctor's or master's degree now work as specialists in industry, agriculture and the arts.

Extremely impressive are our gains in the field of social, economic and cultural transformation in the Soviet national republics. I would like to cite only a few examples to give you an idea of the scale of these changes: In

Lenin and Stalin in 1922.

At a picnic party in Moscow are N. S. Khrushchev, G. Malenkov, and N. Bulganin, with foreign press correspondents.

Rules on elections to the Supreme Soviet are being read to collective farmers in Kirghiz.

A meeting of the Supreme Soviet of the Russian Socialist Federated Soviet Republic in the Kremlin.

Samuel Hendel

On a ferry along the river near Novgorod, 1960.

Samuel Hendel

Children in Zelenegorsk, 1960.

Red Square and the Lenin Mausoleum. From Lenin's tomb (lower right), Soviet officials review parades passing through the Square. In the center is the cathedral of St. Basil, begun by Ivan Grozny to commemorate the conquest of Kazan (1552), and now a museum. On the right is part of the historic Kremlin Wall.

Uzbekistan, which was formerly considered one of the backward regions of czarist Russia, there are now 1,400 large industrial enterprises. Uzbekistan's industrial output is exported to more than 40 countries. . . .

Besides the Academy of Sciences, there are in Uzbekistan the Academy of Agricultural Sciences, two universities, 32 higher educational establishments, and 102 technical schools. Uzbekistan has more than double the number of students per thousand of population of France and Italy, and has outstripped the United States and Great Britain in this respect too. Forty years ago the Kirghiz people had no written language of their own. At present the republic has 80 students per 10,000 of population, considerably more than France, Belgium and Italy.

In Turkmenia there are 17 doctors per 10,000 of population, while in the United States the figure is 12, in Great Britain and France—11.

Armenia, the formerly backward Transcaucasian land, has now become one of the most advanced Soviet republics as regards the level of economic and cultural development. At present it is a country of all-round electrification. In 1960 its per capita output of electricity was 1,478 kilowatt-hours, i.e., greater than that of Italy, Japan and Denmark. When we turn to Armenia's neighbors on the opposite bank of the Araks, we find that Turkey generates 15 times less electricity and Iran 32 times less than Armenia. . . .

When numerous local specialists were trained and acquired the necessary experience, excessive centralization and supervision on the part of the Union government became unnecessary. Our Party, on the initiative of Comrade N. S. Khrushchev, embarked on the policy of the further development of the Leninist principles of democratic centralism in the management of the national economy, of the extension of rights of the union republics. . . .

The extension of the rights of each Soviet republic in all spheres of state, economic and cultural activities has greatly enhanced the initiative of the masses in tackling the economic tasks of the republics and further consolidated the social and governmental system of the USSR. Important functions of the management of the huge economy were transferred to the local bodies. It is sufficient to mention that at present 94 per cent of the over-all industrial output of the country comes from enterprises which are the responsibility of the Councils of Ministers of the union republics.

Now I would like to dwell briefly on certain other points. There are some people in the West who speak much about "Russification" of the USSR's national republics. They often base their allegations on the fact that Russian is taught in the higher educational establishments and that certain republics switched over to the Russian script.

The charge of "Russification" is, of course, wrong and does not reflect the real state of affairs. About 50 nationalities of the USSR got a written national language for the first time only after the October Revolution. Books and magazines are published in 89 languages of the peoples of the

USSR. Even the nationalities numbering only 5-7 thousand people have their written languages and literatures. National operas and ballets are created, research works are written in national languages. Everything is being done in the Soviet Union to preserve and promote the development of national traditions. We collect and study rich collections of manuscripts of the peoples of the USSR. Hundreds of people are engaged in the collection and study of their folklore. Large-scale research is conducted in the fields of archaeology, ethnography and the classical literature of Soviet nations and nationalities.

The setup of the supreme legislative body of the country, the USSR Supreme Soviet, reflects the solicitude of the Soviet state for the needs and requirements of the peoples of the USSR. As is known, the Supreme Soviet consists of two chambers—the Soviet of the Union and the Soviet of Nationalities. All union republics, autonomous republics, autonomous regions and national territories are represented in the Soviet of Nationalities. The union republics, irrespective of the size of their territory and population, send the same number of deputies to the Soviet of Nationalities, namely—25; and the autonomous republics, autonomous regions and national territories—11, 5 and 1 respectively.

A high-powered Economics Committee has been established in the Soviet of Nationalities. Its task is to ensure the proper solution of problems of economic, social and cultural construction in the republics in accordance with their national and economic characteristics.

I believe that these facts are sufficient to refute the charges of "Russification." Complete equality of languages has always been ensured in our country, and in the future national languages will be developed and perfected. The Program of the CPSU states that it is our task "to continue promoting the free development of the languages of the peoples of the USSR and the complete freedom for every citizen of the USSR to speak and to bring up and educate his children in any language, ruling out all privileges, restrictions or compulsions in the use of this or that language." By virtue of the fraternal friendship and mutual trust of peoples, national languages are developing on a basis of equality and mutual enrichment.

The friendship of our peoples has withstood all trials. It has to be admitted even by those whose outlook is very far from being communist. The well-known American social scientist E. Franklin Frazier, author of the book *Racial and Cultural Contacts in the Contemporary World,* published in 1957, wrote that if someone were to try to find an answer to the question of whether the Russian policy solved the national problem, he would have to note that during World War II various peoples and nations remained loyal to the Soviet Union and fought enthusiastically to defend it. . . .

The USSR—a multinational state based on the friendship and brotherhood of nations—is a model of monolithic unity, indestructible strength and cohesion unprecedented in history. The peoples comprised in the Soviet

Union cannot conceive of being separated; they are full of inexhaustible vitality and creative power brought into being by the socialist system. The new Program of the Communist Party of the Soviet Union heralds the beginning of a new stage in the development of national relations in the USSR. . . .

The prophecies of the best minds of humanity, of great thinkers and poets about the era of equality and friendship of all nations have become true in the Soviet Union. It was not in vain that the Polish poet Mitskiewicz dreamed of "the future times when peoples, forgetting their quarrels, will unite as one great family." The bard of the Scottish people, Robert Burns, wrote of the day when all men will be brothers, and the great Arab thinker al Maari, who lived nine centuries ago, had a vision of a "pure land where human beings do not torture their like." These beautiful dreams have become a reality in our time, in our country.

SOVIET NATIONAL POLICY IN PERSPECTIVE

Alex Inkeles*

In the current atmosphere of "peaceful competition between systems," increasing emphasis is placed on the economic factor of production and consumption levels in comparisons of Soviet and non-Soviet achievement. In the process some observers have all but lost sight of the fundamental political, social and cultural characteristics that continue to differentiate the two systems. Among relevant issues one of importance is the status of the national and racial minorities in the Soviet Union. At a time when the Western democracies are granting full independent statehood to one after another of the formerly subject peoples of Africa and Asia, it seems particularly appropriate to inquire into the position of the Soviet minorities. Unfortunately, this subject has received less attention than it deserves, perhaps because many have uncritically accepted Moscow's claim that any issues of nationality and race have long since been successfully resolved. If this were true, Soviet policy would still merit close examination. The fact is, however, that despite some substantial attainments, the Soviet regime has far from solved the problem of minority status either to the satisfaction of the groups themselves or to the particular credit of the Soviet system.

In order to assess Soviet nationality policy intelligently, it is necessary to know certain distinctive historical and demographic facts about the minorities.

* Author of *Public Opinion in Soviet Russia* and co-author of *The Soviet Citizen*. The selection originally appeared in *Problems of Communism*, Vol. 9 (May-June 1960), pp. 25-34, and is reproduced with permission.

POPULATION PATTERNS

While the Great Russians are the single largest group in the Soviet Union, they hold only a precariously slim margin of numerical superiority over the combined population of the national minorities. Indeed, as a result of the rapid expansion of the Tsarist Empire, the Russians were formerly in a minority, comprising only 45 percent of the population in the 1897 census. The loss of certain territories during the Revolution and the Civil War somewhat redressed the balance, and by the 1926 census the Great Russians emerged as 52.9 percent of the total. With the apparent aim of widening this slight margin, the basis of classification was changed in the 1939 census: people were no longer asked what they regarded as their "ethnic origin" (*narodnost*), but rather what they thought of as their "nationality," the Russian term for which (*natsionalnost*) is closer in meaning to culture or citizenship than to race. With the aid of this device the regime was able to report a Russian majority of 58 percent in 1939.

The 1959 census—preliminary results of which have just been published —reveals a new downward ratio, undoubtedly due to the incorporation of the Baltic states, a section of Poland, and part of Bessarabia (Moldavia) since 1939. Today somewhat under 55 percent of the Soviet people think of themselves as Russian by nationality, and even fewer designate Russian as their native language.

The minorities generally live in homogeneous and compact groups on the outer edge of the central land mass which is the territory of the Great Russians. This basic demographic structure persists despite a great increase in the dispersion of peoples—especially of Russians—into other nationality areas during World War II and its aftermath. The 15 national republics strung around the outer borders of the Soviet Union constitute the overwhelming bulk, 80 percent or more, of the country's national minorities. In the northwest, the three Baltic republics include close to five million Latvians, Lithuanians and Estonians. On the western frontier there are some eight million Belorussians, and 37 million Ukrainians who, when added to the Russians, give the Soviet Union its overwhelmingly Slavic majority. On the same frontier are two and a quarter million Moldavians, in the republic of the same name, and almost one and a half million Poles, who for obvious reasons have no identifying territorial unit. Further to the south and east, along the Black Sea and in the Caucasus, there are numerous nationalities distributed in a complex pattern of settlement. These include the Georgians, Armenians and Azerbaijanians, each in their own republic and each more than two and a half million strong—as well as several million Tatars. In Central Asia, the four republics of the Turkmen, Uzbeks, Tadzhiks and Kirghiz, along with the people of adjoining Kazakhstan, contribute some 13 million Turkic people of Moslem faith. Other Moslems, living in areas further in from the border, include several million Volga Tatars and almost a million of the closely related Bashkirs. A neighboring area contains close to a million and a half Chuvash, a Christian and often Russianized remnant of the old Bolgar Empire on the Volga. Of the remaining larger nationalities, only the million and a quarter Mordvians and the two and a quarter million Jews are widely dispersed.

Some 85 percent of all the Great Russians live in the vast, sprawling Russian Soviet Federated Socialist Republic. The rest are spread throughout the surrounding ring of nationality areas, usually living in enclaves in the cities within a countryside that is solidly non-Russian. In this limited sense minority status is at least as typical of the Russian as any other Soviet nationality. Collectively, Russian groups constitute a median proportion of 13.5 percent of the population in the 14 republics other than the RSFSR. In certain areas, however, the influx of Russians has been far greater. In Kazakhstan, for example, the Russians are now the most numerous group (43 percent) of the population; together with other Slavic residents, the Ukrainians and Belorussians, they constitute a majority of the republic. Thus, the Kazakhs have become a minority in the area presumably set aside for them as a national home, and by process over which they have had little say and less control.

Most of the important minorities represent separate and distinct nationalities, with their own language and literature, and in many cases an earlier history of independent existence as a nation-state. Their sense of separate identity is intensified by the fact that ethnicity is generally linked with religious identification, without the cross-cutting of religion and race found in some lands. Thus, to be Russian is to be Orthodox, to be Polish, Catholic; Armenians are in the Armenian National Church and Georgians in the Georgian Church; and the Asiatic peoples, especially the Turkic, are overwhelmingly Moslem. It seems fairly clear that the last thing these people wish is the loss of identity as separate nationalities through absorption into the larger homogeneous culture of the Russian nation. Indeed, although there are often important historical ties which bind them to the center in Moscow, the nationalities seldom share much in common with other peoples of the Soviet Union beyond their minority status. How, then, did these diverse peoples all come together in common Soviet citizenship? The answer is not to be found, as in some other ethnically heterogeneous nations, in voluntary emigration or incorporation into Russia. It must be sought in the history of Russian state policy going back many centuries.

TSARIST EXPANSIONISM

Following their subjugation by the Khans, the Russian people lived for centuries under the rule of the Tatar hordes, compressed into a modest area in central Russia and cut off from other major Slavic groups such as the Poles and Ukrainians, who were variously under domination by peoples from the West, Scandinavia and the Baltic. The starting point of Russian colonialism may be taken as 1552, when Ivan the Terrible took Kazan, and thus liquidated the Tatar Khanate. The expansion of the previously small Muscovite state thus began with the incorporation of large numbers of Turkic peoples, especially from along the Volga and its tributaries. About a century later a comparable major movement to the west was completed when the left-bank regions of the Dnieper were established as a protectorate, bringing Cossack and Ukrainian peoples under Russian hegemony. Peter the Great added the peoples along the coast of the Baltic Sea. In her turn Catherine the Great made further acquisitions in the west, including parts of Poland, and drove all the way to the Black Sea in the south. The Caucasus was added later, and most of the rest of Turkestan was acquired by Alexander II to complete the movement by the end of his reign in 1881.

This extraordinary territorial expansion was estimated to have proceeded at the rate of 50 square miles a day over a period of 400 years, from the end of the 15th to the end of the 19th centuries. As pointed out earlier, it brought the Russians to the status of being a minority in the land they ruled. To speak of Russia as having a minority problem in the usual sense is therefore misleading. Russia was a huge colonial empire; but in distinction to the other empires of Europe, her colonial possessions were contiguous to the homeland. Thus she *incorporated* her possessions, her dependencies and satellites, within one continuous border, with the captive nations strung around the outer limits of the solid Great Russian core. It is impossible to understand the nationality problem in the Soviet Union without always keeping in mind that the Soviet regime inherited this "prison of nations" from the Tsars when it took power, and it had to operate within the framework thus set by history.

THE LENINIST FORMULA

In this situation, the Soviet regime has adopted an essentially dualistic attitude toward Tsarist expansionism: on the one hand, it has generally treated the conquest and incorporation of the minorities as an "historically progressive" policy; on the other hand, it has encouraged the myth that Tsarist treatment of the captive peoples was uniformly harsh, oppressive and reactionary, and that it was designed to destroy the character and individuality of the many groups which had come under the empire's sway. Actually Tsarist policy toward the subject minorities varied considerably at different times, depending on the political philosophy of the different rulers. It also varied with respect to different areas and groups. Most modern impressions of this policy tend to concentrate on the period of intensive suppression starting after the accession of Alexander III in 1881 and lasting until the revolution in 1905, after which a considerable liberalization again ensued. The depredations of Alexander's reign, especially the marked efforts at

Russification and the virtual driving underground of local cultural movements, left a lasting mark not only on world opinion but on the national groups, and this fact was soon to be of great importance to the as yet unborn Soviet government.

Considering how obvious a source of grievance against the Tsarist regime here lay ready for exploitation, it is striking that the Bolsheviks were so slow to realize its potentialities as an instrument for shaking the old order. But their whole philosophy inclined them to gloss over the nationality problem. It was a basic belief of Marxists that the path of history would lead toward ever larger, more homogeneous, centralized, industrial, political units which in time would yield to a world-wide "proletarian" society. The slogan "the proletariat has no fatherland" expressed the belief that nationalism, patriotism, regionalism, and similar attachments were part and parcel of the social pattern of bourgeois capitalism, which would somehow be outlived and sloughed off once socialism and then communism came to the world. Lenin himself gave virtually no attention to the nationality problem until 1913, when he was forced to turn to it both because of the growing popularity of the Bauer-Renner program and because of his own growing awareness that the success of his plans must reckon with the fact of national loyalties and aspirations.

The Bauer-Renner program, conceived to meet the multi-national situation facing the political parties in the Austro-Hungarian empire, proposed an unusual degree of autonomy for minorities in the conduct of their own affairs; had it been put into effect, it would have permitted a great multiplication of small and more-or-less exclusive national, religious and ethnic units. Lenin naturally viewed this program as a challenge to the principle of centralization which he had steadfastly espoused; but he was equally opposed to the alternative idea of federalism, again on grounds that it weakened the chances for the development of a truly international proletarian power. Forced to take a stand, he went to what he thought was the absolute heart of the matter, by basing his policy squarely *and exclusively* on the right of each nationality to so-called "self-determination." He was unwilling to consider any compromises which might weaken the power of a central Communist government. Any people or nation—theoretically, at least—had the right to secede from the larger society, but if it chose to remain it must accept the general system in its entirety, without demanding special status or privilege and without asking for a federal union:

The right to self-determination is an exception to our general thesis, which is centralism. This exception is absolutely necessary in the face of the Black Hundred type of Great Russian nationalism. . . . But a broad interpretation may not be made of an exception. There is *nothing*, absolutely nothing here, and there must be nothing here, but the *right* to secede.

Lenin felt that this acknowledgment of the abstract "right" to secede was necessary as a political maneuver. But at the same time—in a contradiction that no amount of esoteric language could hide—he held that any attempt at *actual* secession would be retrograde, anti-proletarian, bourgeois counterrevolution. He assumed, in short, that no one would want to *exercise* the right of secession should there be a proletarian revolution.

He proved completely wrong, although in this he had the company of most of the other political groups in Russia, all of whom inadequately assessed both the effect of Tsarist policy in hardening national feeling against *any* central Russian government, and the effect of the rapid social and cultural changes which were increasing national consciousness in many of the minority areas. In any event, the Bolshevik regime found, to its great embarrassment, that in most of the national areas of the former empire the local political leaders took their right of secession quite seriously. Even where complete separation was not their prime objective, the local leaders viewed themselves as equals with the leaders in Moscow, entitled on that basis to negotiate the nature of their nationality's participation in the new state.

The Bolsheviks did not hesitate to use the force of arms to meet this upsurge of independence, sending their Red Armies to regain control over most of the provinces of the former empire. Finland was allowed to slip away without any particular struggle, and Poland and the Baltic States were abandoned after unsuccessful military campaigns. But under the command of such well-known Communist figures as Frunze and Kuibyshev in Central Asia, Kirov and Ordzhonikidze in the north Caucasus, Kaganovich in Belorussia, and Mikoyan in Azerbaijan, almost all the other territories were recaptured by Soviet troops and turned over to the control of the local Communist parties, reliable subordinates of the central party apparatus in Moscow. The army which entered Georgia on February 16, 1921, and by February 25th once again placed the Communist flag over the capital Tiflis, fought the last major round in the effort to reintegrate the rebellious national areas.

The need for force to win back control of these areas brought home to the Soviet leaders the crucial nature of the nationality problem, and it is largely to this realization that we owe the particular forms which the so-called nationality policy of the Soviet Union has assumed. Rather than attempting to relate the explicit history of the policy, the writer will turn directly to a consideration of its overall features, giving the historical context as seems necessary. Perhaps the best approach is to pose four questions which would be important in evaluating the policy of any large-scale colonial power.

SELF-DETERMINATION: A PAPER RIGHT

1). The first question in such an assessment would be: to what extent does the country's nationality policy provide for gradual transition to separate statehood for the major national minorities whose culture, history, and socio-political and economic maturity make them reasonable candidates for such status?

The attainment of a condition of self-government and national independence has come to be accepted as a fundamental goal and an inalienable right of people all over the world. Since World War II we have witnessed a tremendous socio-political movement as virtually all the major colonial dependencies of the former British Empire, and to a lesser but striking degree of the French Empire, have achieved national independence. Any nation which tries to maintain control over a colonial area—or even to slow down the pace toward independence—invites serious criticism and often serious trouble; the crisis in Algeria is only the most striking and recent evidence of the explosive nature of this issue. It seems not at all inappropriate, therefore, to address the above question to the Soviet Union, particularly since it takes so much pride in pointing to the provision in its constitution which grants each of the constituent republics the ultimate right "freely" to secede from the Union. What, if anything, is done to implement this right in practice?

It may seem superfluous to observe, in the first place, that the Soviet regime in no way acts to encourage the secession of the minorities. In fact, one might well argue that no central government could be expected to take an active part in urging its constituent parts to achieve independence. The point is made here because there are those who apply a double standard on this score, criticizing other colonial powers for their lack of encouragement to independence movements, while turning a blind eye to Soviet practice.

It is of course one thing for a central government to encourage some part of a larger union to detach itself, and quite another to ask simply that minority peoples have the right to advocate and work peacefully for their eventual independence. Since the right of secession is constitutionally guaranteed in the Soviet Union, the right to pursue that goal would logically seem to follow. Yet even to advocate, let alone to work toward, the political independence of any area in the Soviet Union is unthinkable for the Soviet citizen. Such action is identified, both by law outside the constitution and by long practice of the secret police, as a counterrevolutionary crime against the state, warranting severe punishment. Almost every major purge trial has involved charges that the accused conspired to separate some national area from the Union. At various stages of Soviet history hundreds and thousands of officials, teachers, writers and other members of the intellectual classes of different national republics have been purged from the party and state apparatus, and/or sent into forced labor on charges of harboring "bourgeois nationalist leanings," the official term for identifying with the interests of one's national group and resisting abject subordination to the interests of the Moscow center.

In short, what the constitution says about the national question bears virtually no relationship to Soviet practice. Any lingering doubts on this score should have been destroyed by the action of the Soviet regime during

World War II, when it simply erased from the map and from the face of the earth four autonomous socialist republics—the Volga German, the Crimean Tatar, the Kalmyk, and the Chechen-Ingush. Although there was an announcement in the case of the Volga Germans that this action was taken in the interest of national security, and a belated statement that the Chechen and Crimean Tatars had collaborated with the Germans, not even this much explanation was given with regard to the Kalmyks.

Not only were the republics liquidated as political entities, but their millions of people were dispersed to distant regions of the Soviet Union. There were wide repercussions and revulsion against this act; among others, Tito of Yugoslavia went so far as to accuse the Soviet Union of genocide. Certainly the indiscriminate mass dispersion of a whole population because of acts of individuals, no matter how numerous, violated basic standards of humanity and made a mockery of Stalin's assertion that "the national question and the problem of collaboration among nations have been settled better [in the USSR] than in any other multinational state." It was not until after Stalin's death that some members of these nationalities were rehabilitated and partially restored to their former status.

CULTURAL SURVIVALS

2). The second broad question may be phrased: To what degree are the minorities permitted and facilitated in the free expression of their cultural heritage? First and foremost, this involves the right to use one's native tongue in all types of public and private communication and in the education of youth. Cultural expression also includes the preservation and further development of folk and tribal ways, including art forms, ceremonial and religious customs, the national costume, etc. In addition, some hold that free cultural expression should include the right to have economic and political forms of organization which are distinctive to a particular culture.

That the Soviet approach toward the cultural self-expression of the minorities has been unique is beyond doubt; whether it has been as liberal as is claimed is quite another question. The doctrinal explanation of Soviet policy rests in the distinction which is made between the content and the form of culture, expressed in the well-worn formula "national in form, socialist in content." In theory, this phrase means that the values and ideas of the socialist society should be uniform in every culture, though the means by which they are expressed may be—indeed, should be—of a traditional and indigenous nature. The vagueness of this formula, however, has left wide leeway in its application, and like most Soviet slogans it has become quite meaningless in practice.

Obviously it is important to know *which* institutions and distinctive cultural forms are allowed to persist, and how crucial to the integrity of the original culture are those which have been suppressed because they fall in the realm where "socialist" uniformity is required. In the Soviet totalitarian system, the model for society as developed in Moscow is so rigid and all-pervasive that very little has in fact been left that could qualify as being "national" without conflicting with what must be "socialist."

The outstanding survival has been the native languages. With one exception (Yiddish), the Soviet regime has made no attempt to eradicate local tongues; they are used in the educational system, in communications media, and in indigenous literature. Generally distinctive literary forms associated with the languages in such spheres as poetry, epic writing and drama have also been permitted. Another class of survivals which has suffered comparatively little interference is folk arts, including folk handicrafts and native art forms. Nor has there been much effort made to alter distinctive modes of native dress (except in the case of the Moslem veil for women, against which a rather successful campaign has been waged). These policies, it might be pointed out, parallel the practice adopted by most colonial powers.

If the Soviet attitude with respect to these several fundamentals of cultural expression has been generally permissive—and certainly represents a vast reform over the predatory Russification efforts of Alexander III—there is nevertheless much on the record to indicate that tolerance extends only as far as it suits the interests of the central authorities. Even in the matter of language, Moscow's actions have in some cases profoundly affected an indigenous culture. Much is made of the fact that the Soviets provided alphabets for several dozen languages which previously could not be written down, paving the way for newspapers and other literature in these tongues. Less is known of the fact that the Soviet regime used its power, against the overwhelming opposition of the local population, to force the abandonment of the religiously-sanctioned Arabic script used by the millions of Soviet Moslems. Not once but twice they did this, first introducing the Latin alphabet, and then in 1939 substituting the Cyrillic. Even the Tsars never dreamed of attempting such a victory for Russian culture among their subject Moslems.

Folk literature and art, too, have been subjected to interference and suppression whenever Moscow chose to see in their various forms any manifestations of "bourgeois nationalism." Frequently the regime has seized on old or new folk writings, dramas, operas, etc., condemning them for deviation from the official line, forbidding their production, and taking reprisals against their authors. The writing or presentation of native history in particular has suffered from intervention by the authorities, who insist that the Tsarist subjugation of the nationality areas be treated as "historically progressive." Among many such acts of repression, one of the more glaring examples was the dissolution of the entire cultural apparatus of the Soviet Jews—including their native theater, newspapers, publishing houses and writers' association—during the postwar wave of officially-inspired anti-Semitism; despite regime claims that no discrimination is practiced, nothing has ever been done to rectify this situation.

All of the minority religions have, of course, been the object of repressive measures. The fact that these moves have, from a doctrinal point of view, been part of the Communist campaign against religious belief *per se* (including the Russian Orthodox faith) has made little difference to peoples whose religion and nationality are closely identified. For them, the attack on religion has been simply another example of the effort of an alien regime to encroach on indigenous cultural patterns and to shackle national development.

In short, the Soviet attitude toward "national forms" in the cultural sphere has been one of tolerance when—but only when—tolerance has not interfered with the ideological or practical needs of the regime.

SYSTEM AND SACRIFICE

Outside of the specific areas of cultural expression mentioned above, few of the traditional ways of the minorities have been allowed to survive. In the political, economic, and generally the social spheres, the uniform institutions of Soviet society prevail in the form of the supreme ruling party, the bureaucratic administrative apparatus, the planned and centrally-controlled industrial economy, the collectivized peasant agriculture, and the ubiquitous instruments of ideological indoctrination and control. Thus Soviet nationality policy has allowed no recognition of the fact that economic, political and social forms of organization may be distinctive and indeed crucial elements in a particular national culture.

The imposition of the Soviet system involved a social and cultural revolution throughout Soviet-held territory. Among the more settled European or Europeanized populations, whose culture was already somewhat geared to the patterns of industrial society, the process of Sovietization was highly disruptive, but no more so than for the majority of the Great Russians—and perhaps even less so in the case, say, of Armenian traders than of the Russian peasants. But among the peoples of the more isolated, underdeveloped areas —mainly in Asia—the depredations caused by Sovietization and the enforced departure from traditional ways were of enormous magnitude.

An outstanding example is the case of the Kazakh people. Before collectivization the Kazakhs were either nomads, who relied extensively on the use of horses on the great Central Asian steppe, or recently-settled cattle and sheep herders. Their whole way of life was regulated by and within the tribal structure, especially the clan system. The attempt blindly to impose the pattern of collectivization on these people in the early 1930's met with intensive resistance, leading to an open struggle with the regime. The loss of life was staggering. While some of the Kazakhs escaped with their herds over the border into Chinese Sinkiang, the huge decimation of the population during this period was mainly due to deaths in the fighting or through starvation. Census figures for 1926 and 1939 show that in the interim the Kazakh population dropped from 3.967 to 3.098 million, an absolute decline of 869 thousand, or 22 percent. Calculating in what would have been an expectable rate of population growth under normal circumstances (on the basis of 15 percent for the Soviet population as a whole), the survivors in Kazakhstan were one and a half million fewer by 1939 than they should have been, a staggering deficit considering the overall size of the population. Moreover, in the course of the bitter struggle the greater part of the livestock on which the local economy had rested was lost, through retaliative slaughter on the part of the desperate natives, neglect of the herds while the men were off fighting, or in minor part, through migration. Taking the stocks in 1928 as a base, by 1934 only 25 to 50 percent of the cattle, 13 percent of the sheep, and 12 percent of the horses remained.

Although the stark statistics above are from official sources, the Soviet regime has never put forward any explanation of this chapter of its history. Unfortunately the statistics are little known to the world, and are seldom weighed in the balance when glib estimates are made in praise of "enlightened" Soviet nationality policy. Yet this case represents a relentless fulfillment of Stalin's instruction to the Communist Party in 1923, when he urged that Turkestan—which included Kazakhstan—be transformed into a model republic because of its revolutionary significance for Soviet Russia's eastern policy. He declared: "We have to fulfill this task whatever the price, without sparing efforts and without shrinking from sacrifices. . . ." Stalin, certainly, could never be accused of having shrunk from sacrifices in Kazakhstan.

EQUAL OPPORTUNITY

3). Turning to the third question under consideration, to what extent is Soviet nationality policy non-discriminatory—that is, to what extent does it offer members of the minority nationalties equal access to such benefits as the society provides for average citizens? Are opportunities for education, work, pay, social mobility, freedom of movement, and choice of residence the same for all or does the dominant group enjoy a favored status?

On the whole the record of the Soviet Union in these respects is good. The data which support this evaluation are based on republics as a whole, not on pure ethnic or national groups, so that the presence of large Russian and Ukrainian minorities in some of the national republics—and conversely of non-Russian minorities in the RSFSR—may distort the picture of Soviet accomplishment to some degree. Still, on the basis of a large number of indices, it seems clear that members of all nationalities (including the Great Russian) have received broadly equal treatment with respect to personal economic and social—if not political—opportunities. Allowance must be made, of course, for the fact that many of the minorities live in predominantly rural or backward regions whose development has expectably lagged

behind that of more urban or industrial areas; however, the *relative* position
of these groups has improved greatly since the prerevolutionary era.

Important among the indices considered here is the striking spread of
literacy among all groups of the Soviet population. In the intercensus period
from 1926 to 1939 the overall literacy rate in the Soviet Union rose from 51
to 81 percent. In certain national republics the low base at start made the
rise much more dramatic. For example, in the Central Asian Tadzhik
republic the rate of literacy increased from 4 to 72 percent, and in the
Azerbaijan republic from 25 to 73 percent. The preliminary release on the
1959 census does not provide data on literacy by nationality, but since the
All-Union rate is now reported to be 98.5 percent, it must be assumed that
the nationality areas have continued to advance in this respect. While the
Soviet definition of literacy is based on a very rudimentary level of learning,
and while some area improvement can be attributed to the influx of Russian
and other literates, the record of accomplishment is nevertheless substantial.

Data on improvements in education are closely related. In the area of
the five Central Asian Republics (including Kazakhstan) there were in 1914-
15 only 136,000 pupils in elementary and secondary schools, representing less
than half of one percent of the 9.6 million pupils in all Russia. By 1955-56
the parallel enrollment was 3.59 million, an increase by more than 25-fold;
this figure constituted about 13 percent of the total student enrollment in the
same grades, which is about the weight of the population of the Central
Asiatic republics in the Soviet population as a whole. Similar progress has
been made in higher education: whereas before the Revolution there were
virtually no higher school establishments in these areas, by 1955 local institutions had an enrollment of 155 thousand students, or about 9 percent of the
total higher school population in the USSR.

There are many other ways in which the Soviet regime has accorded
equal treatment to the minorities. Available data show that facilities such as
libraries, medical clinics, movie and dramatic theaters, sports stadia, clubs,
newspapers and journals, radio and television stations, *etc.*, have been provided in the nationality areas at close to the same per capita rate as in the
Great Russian area.

The sum indication of such statistical evidence is that minority members
(again, with the striking exception of Soviet Jews) do not suffer from any
discrimination insofar as educational training, economic opportunity, and
social benefits are concerned. This impression is supported by the testimony
of Soviet refugees. In the Harvard Project on the Soviet Social System, in
which this writer participated, questionnaires were submitted to several
hundred Ukrainians and to smaller groups of other nationalities—along
with Russians—all of whom had escaped from the Soviet Union. The replies
showed that people whose occupations had been on a comparable level had,
regardless of their nationality, been in very similar circumstances with respect
to income, opportunities for education, job satisfaction, and the general rate

of social mobility. Such similarity in living conditions produced similarity in values, attitudes and opinions, again cutting across national lines. In other words, class status rather than national identification determined what people found praiseworthy in the Soviet system and what they condemned. The Russian peasant described and criticized his life very much as did the Ukrainian, Georgian, Tatar or Kazakh peasant; similarly, professional people of different nationality evaluated their life situations in like terms and shared the same criticisms of the system. Such differences as did emerge between nationalities were largely a reflection of the varying class composition—in particular, the proportion of peasants—from group to group.

UNEQUAL INOPPORTUNITY

There was, however, one distinctive complaint voiced by those in the minority nationalities, and this on an issue of profound importance. The reader may have noted that all of the above examples of nondiscrimination have been confined to the economic and social spheres. In the political realm—in the structure of rule—a very different picture emerges. The crucial protest voiced in common by refugees from the minorities was that their people did not share equally in the direction of society and were not free to shape their culture along lines in keeping with native or indigenous traditions. Many saw themselves as still essentially vassals of a foreign power, as ruled by the alien Russian. The basis of these feelings is not just a matter of the sharp restrictions which, as we have seen, the regime places on the development of local nationalism. Just as important is the fact that the institutions of governance, both at the center and within the republics, have not included a proportionate representation of the minorities. The Communist Party has been predominantly a Russian party, with only a weak representation of the nationalities, while in the republics themselves the influence and indeed control of Russians and other outsiders sent in from Moscow has been painfully evident.

The composition of the supreme council of the party has reflected this imbalance during most of its history. Up to the time of its reorganization in 1952, the Politburo had altogether 28 members, of whom 16 were Russians and 8 more Russified Jews or Georgians. The people of 13 national republics, containing some 80 million of the population, never had representation on that body, including the third largest nationality, the Belorussians, and some 16 to 20 million Moslems. The 30 to 40 million Ukrainians were not represented after 1938, when the purges claimed the leading figures of Ukrainian nationality. The membership of the Presidium, which replaced the Politburo in 1952, has been somewhat more in proportion, but not markedly so. Of the 33 people who have served on the Presidium only 8—including Stalin before his death—have been non-Russians. The others are Beria (also Georgian), Kaganovich (Jewish), Mikoyan (Armenian), Korot-

chenko and Kirichenko (Ukrainians), Kuusinen (Finnish), and Mukhitdinov
(Uzbek). A number of minority members, however, have been appointed as
candidate (alternative) members of the Presidium.

The fact that Stalin himself was a Georgian by birth counts for little,
since like many of these leaders he thoroughly identified himself with the
Russians, a trait reflected in his extraordinary toast at the end of World
War II:

I should like to propose a toast to the health of our Soviet people, and above all of
our Russian people. I drink in particular to the health of the Russian people because it is the most outstanding of all the nations of the Soviet Union. . . .

The weakness of national representation has been evident not only at
the top of the power hierarchy, but in the rank-and-file of the party. In
proportion to population, the Communist Party is strongest in the predominantly Great Russian areas, weakest in the nationality regions. In Moscow
and Leningrad, for example, the ratio of local to total party membership is
more than twice that of local to total population; in republics like Tadjikistan the reverse applies. In fact, however, the disproportion is much greater,
since within the nationality areas, the party is not only small but includes a
substantial number of non-natives, preponderantly Russians. The exact
ratios are hard to estimate, since the party generally stopped publishing data
according to nationality by 1938. It is known, however, that as late as 1935
Tadzhiks and Turkmen—for example—constituted 75 percent of the population in the republics bearing their names, but only about 50 percent of the
party organizations.

Within the lower and middle ranks of the national parties, both the
rank-and-file and their officials are predominantly of native stock and speak
the native language (the same is even truer of the governmental apparatus).
But in the large urban centers, at the seats of power, the Russian image looms
large. Access to positions of power is comparatively limited to the native,
except insofar as he has become Russified—and in this case he is considered a
non-national who may be transferred to work anywhere within the Soviet
Union.

The fact that the party chief in the national areas has often been someone sent in from the outside has been perhaps the most important affront to
national pride and symbol of the alien nature of the party. The best example in this respect is the Ukraine, where the First Secretary of the Communist Party has almost always been a non-Ukrainian, even though sometimes vaguely connected with the Ukrainian area or nationality. Kaganovich,
who held the post in 1925-28, was a Russified Jew born in Belorussia. Kossior, who followed, was a Pole. The rest were Russians, and many never
even learned to speak Ukrainian with fluency, despite the fact that it was the
national tongue of some 40 million subjects. The only exception in the line
was Khrushchev's chosen successor in the post—his Ukrainian assistant
Kirichenko (who later rose to the Presidium but is now in disgrace).

ECONOMIC DEVELOPMENT POLICY

To pose the fourth and last question: has there been any economic exploitation of minority regions, by depletion of the land or other natural resources, by the carrying off of wealth produced in the area without sufficient compensation, or by the development of the region's economy in so special or limited a way as to subordinate it unduly to the productive needs and interests of the dominant majority?

In the Soviet case the answer to these questions is clear-cut: the regime's economic policy as a whole does not discriminate against the minority areas and their economic development in favor of the Great Russians. Soviet industrialization was, of course, based on forced savings, which the government extracted for investment at the cost of popular consumption. But the minorities were not asked to bear a disproportionate share of the resulting hardships of a depressed living standard. The burden fell on all; in fact, it might be argued that the Great Russian majority initially made the greater sacrifice in order to permit the development of the capital-hungry, economically backward areas.

One economist has estimated, for example, that while the all-Union living standard fell markedly during the 1930's, in the four republics of Central Asia (not counting Kazakhstan), it may actually have improved to a slight degree. At the time the local economy was undergoing rapid change, as indicated by the fact that industrial output, which had been negligible, multiplied between six and nine times over between 1928 and 1937. Such an increase could only have been accomplished by the substantial investment of capital drawn from other parts of the country and by the application of new technology. Such help was even more important to the agriculture of the region.

In the initial stage of European colonial development, substantial capital was invested in the colonies, but often only in order to create a one-crop economy that in the long run was economically disadvantageous to the local people. There was an element of this approach in the Soviet regime's insistence on the expansion of cotton acreage in Central Asia, usually at the expense of existing wheat crops. But the area was not treated simply as a vast cotton plantation for the rest of the Soviet Union. On the contrary, existing resources of other kinds were widely developed. A hydro-electric power industry was developed, the output of which increased 8.5 times over in the period 1928-37. Earlier virtually all cotton had been shipped to Russia to be made into textiles, which in turn had to be shipped back, but in the 1930's a substantial textile industry was established in Tashkent. Leather shoe-making was established to utilize the hides from the region's extensive herds. These efforts make it evident that capital was retained in the area and not syphoned off for accumulation at the center. The data already cited on the growth of education and other cultural and social facilities similarly indicate that a goodly share of the returns accrued from exploitation of the region's natural wealth was reinvested in raising standards in the region.

Although the central Asian case may be one of the more outstanding examples, it reflects the general pattern of Soviet policy in the economic development of backward areas. The allocation of investment during the process of economic expansion has not in any significant degree been guided by considerations of nationality, but rather by those of economic efficiency or the defense needs of the country. And the benefits—as well as the burdens —which have resulted from economic development have been more or less equally shared by all peoples of the Soviet Union.

A SUMMARY VIEW

The main features of Soviet nationality policy sketched above have been consistently manifested since at least the early 1930's. Although the program as a whole is often identified as "Stalinist" nationality policy, only minor modifications have taken place in the post-Stalin era. In line with the general relaxation of terror in the USSR, the most repressive policies *vis-à-vis* certain nationalities have been abandoned and some of the iniquities of Stalin's reign (*e.g.*, the dispersion of the Chechen-Ingush, Kalmyks, and so on) have been rectified. In addition, Khrushchev has shown more awareness of the requirements of good "public relations" by such gestures as personal visits to the nationality areas, the appointment of a Ukrainian to the top post in the Ukraine, and the nomination of representatives of the Central Asian peoples to the higher councils of the ruling Communist Party.

In all other respects, however, the present leadership has followed the pattern of the past. On the credit side of the record, this has generally meant equality of social and economic opportunity for the individual of minority status. On the whole it has also meant equal treatment of national groups with regard to the exploitation of resources and economic development on the one hand, and to the elaboration of certain cultural institutions on the other.

Against these features, other factors must be weighed. First, if equality of treatment has been the general rule in the above respects, the exceptions and departures have been numerous enough and in some cases so glaring as to demonstrate that the application of nationality policy remains a matter of arbitrary and expedient decision on the part of the regime. More important, however, are the moral and political issues which underly the question of minority rights. The basic fact—and no amount of achievement can obscure it—is that Soviet nationality policy has constituted a forceful imposition of social, political and economic forms by a powerful center upon a host of colonial subjects. If these people had little part in choosing their path of national development, they have as little freedom today to alter it.

NATIONAL RELATIONS IN THE COMMUNIST STAGE

New Program of the Communist Party*

The New Program of the Communist Party of the Soviet Union was adopted by the 22nd Congress on October 31, 1961. This is only the third program in the history of the Party; the others were adopted in 1903 (before it came to power) and in 1919. By its terms, it is designed "for the building of a communist society." The included excerpt reproduces the section of the program specifically concerned with "The Tasks of the Party in the Sphere of National Relations."

Under socialism nations flourish and their sovereignty is strengthened. The development of nations proceeds not along lines of strengthening national discord, national narrow-mindedness and egoism, as it does under capitalism, but along lines of their association, fraternal mutual assistance and friendship. The appearance of new industrial centers, the discovery and exploitation of natural resources, the plowing up of virgin lands and the development of all types of transport increase the mobility of the population and promote greater contact among the peoples of the Soviet Union. People of many nationalities live together and work in harmony in the Soviet republics. The boundaries between the Union republics within the U.S.S.R. are increasingly losing their former significance, since all the nations are equal, their life is organized on a single socialist foundation, the material and spiritual needs of each people are satisfied to the same extent, and they are all united into one family by common vital interests and are advancing together to a single goal—communism. Common spiritual features deriving from the new type of social relations and embodying the finest traditions of the peoples of the U.S.S.R. have taken shape in Soviet people of different nationalities.

Full-scale communist construction signifies a new stage in the development of national relations in the U.S.S.R. in which the nations will draw still closer together and their complete unity will be achieved. The building of the material and technical base of communism is leading to still closer association of the Soviet peoples. The exchange of material and cultural wealth among nations is becoming more and more intensive, and the contribution of each republic to the common cause of communist construction is increasing. Obliteration of distinctions between classes and the development of com-

---

* Reproduced, with permission, from *The Current Digest of the Soviet Press*, Vol. XIII (December 13, 1961), pp. 14-15. The new Communist Party Program appears in its entirety in *Current Soviet Policies—IV*, published by Columbia University Press from the translations of the *Current Digest.*

munist social relations is intensifying the social homogeneity of nations and contributing to the development of common communist traits in their culture, ethics and way of living, to a further strengthening of mutual trust and friendship among them.

With the victory of communism in the U.S.S.R., the nations will draw still closer together, their economic and ideological unity will increase and the communist traits common to their spiritual make-up will develop. However, the effacement of national distinctions, especially of language distinctions, is a considerably longer process than the effacement of class distinctions.

The Party approaches all questions of national relationships arising in the course of communist construction from the positions of proletarian internationalism and on the basis of unswerving application of the Leninist national policy. The Party permits neither the ignoring nor the overemphasis of national characteristics.

The Party sets the following tasks in the sphere of national relations:

(a) to continue the all-round economic and cultural development of all the Soviet nations and nationalities, ensuring their increasingly close fraternal cooperation, mutual aid, solidarity and closeness in all spheres of life and achieving the utmost strengthening of the Union of Soviet Socialist Republics; to make full use of and improve the forms of the national state system of the peoples of the U.S.S.R.

(b) in the economic sphere, to continue to pursue the line of comprehensive development of the economy of the Soviet republics; to ensure a rational geographical distribution of production and planned development of natural resources and to perfect the socialist division of labor among the republics, unifying and coordinating their labor efforts and properly combining the interests of the state as a whole and those of each Soviet republic. Since the expansion of the rights of the Union republics in economic management has yielded substantial favorable results, such measures may also be carried out in the future, with due regard to the fact that the creation of the material and technical base of communism will call for still greater interrelationship and mutual assistance among the Soviet republics. The closer the contact between nations and the greater the understanding of the countrywide tasks, the more successfully can manifestations of localism and national egoism be overcome.

For the successful accomplishment of the tasks of communist construction and the coordination of economic activities, interrepublic economic agencies (especially for such matters as irrigation, power grids, transport, etc.) may be set up in particular zones.

The Party will continue to follow a policy of ensuring the actual equality of all nations and nationalities with full consideration for their interests, devoting special attention to those areas of the country that are in need of more rapid development. Benefits growing in the process of communist construction must be fairly distributed among all nations and nationalities.

(c) to work for the further all-round flowering of the socialist culture of the peoples of the U.S.S.R. The vast scope of communist construction and the new victories of communist ideology are enriching the cultures of all the peoples of the U.S.S.R., cultures socialist in content and national in form. The ideological unity of the nations and nationalities is growing, and there is a rapprochement of their cultures. The historical experience of the development of socialist nations shows that national forms do not harden; they change, improve and draw closer together, shedding all obsolete features that conflict with the new living conditions. An international culture common to all the Soviet nations is developing. The cultural treasures of each nation are increasingly augmented by works of an international character.

Attaching decisive importance to the development of the socialist content of the cultures of the peoples of the U.S.S.R., the Party will promote their future mutual enrichment and rapprochement, the strengthening of their internationalist basis and thereby the formation of a future single worldwide culture of communist society. While supporting the progressive traditions of each people and making them the possession of all Soviet people, the Party will in all ways develop new revolutionary traditions of the builders of communism, traditions common to all nations.

(d) to continue ensuring the free development of the languages of the people of the U.S.S.R. and the complete freedom of each citizen of the U.S.S.R. to speak and to rear and educate his children in any language, ruling out all privileges, restrictions of compulsion in the use of this or that language. In the conditions of the fraternal friendship and mutual trust of peoples, national languages are developing on a basis of equality and mutual enrichment.

The existing process of voluntary study of Russian in addition to the indigenous language has favorable significance, since it facilitates mutual exchange of experience and the access of each nation and nationality to the cultural achievements of the other peoples of the U.S.S.R. and to world culture. The Russian language has, in effect, become the common medium of intercourse and cooperation among all the peoples of the U.S.S.R.

(e) to continue consistently applying the principles of internationalism in the field of national relations; to strengthen the friendship of peoples as one of the most important gains of socialism; to conduct an uncompromising struggle against manifestations and survivals of any kinds of nationalism and chauvinism, against trends of national narrow-mindedness and exclusiveness, idealization of the past and the veiling of social contradictions in the history of peoples, and against customs and ways that impede communist construction. The growing scale of communist construction calls for the continuous exchange of cadres among the nations. Any manifestations of national insularity in the rearing and employment of workers of different nationalities in the Soviet republics are impermissible. The elimination of manifestations of nationalism is in the interests of all nations and nationalities of the U.S.S.R. Each Soviet republic can continue to flourish and grow stronger only in the great family of fraternal socialist nations of the U.S.S.R.

Chapter 12

THE ROLE OF TERROR

In Chapter 6, entitled "Ends and Means," the discussion was concerned primarily with the theoretical position of Lenin and Trotsky on the interrelation of Marxist ends and revolutionary and terrorist means in the seizure and holding of power. In this section, we are principally concerned with the institutionalization of terror as a system of power in the U.S.S.R.

One of the most provocative explanations of the role of terror in a modern state appears in Barrington Moore, Jr., Terror and Progress, U.S.S.R. *He suggests that organized terror*

. . . does not stem from any particular type of economic structure, but from the attempt to alter the structure of society at a rapid rate and from above through forceful administrative devices. The essence of the situation appears to lie in the crusading spirit, the fanatical conviction in the justice and universal applicability of some ideal about the way life should be organized, along with a lack of serious concern about the consequences of the methods used to pursue this ideal. . . . The attempt to change institutions rapidly nearly always results in opposition by established interests. The more rapid and more thorough the change, the more extensive and bitter is the opposition likely to be. Hence organized terror becomes necessary. . . .

Whether spontaneous or forced, a rapid pace of change is likely to produce wide-spread human suffering. Hence the situation in which a socialist regime comes to power is crucial in determining the probabilities of terror, as is widely recognized in socialist writings. If the socialists are content to take over the situation left by their predecessors without making fundamental changes, relatively little terror may be needed. This was the situation originally anticipated in Marxist theory, where terror would merely brush away the remnants of the old order. If, on the other hand, socialism is to be dynamic after it has come to power, it is likely to require the constant application of terror, both against the population at large and dissidents within its own ranks. Its commitment to terror is as great as its commitment to change that goes against the habits and desires of various sectors of the population.

TERROR AS A SYSTEM OF POWER

MERLE FAINSOD*

Terror is the linchpin of modern totalitarianism. What distinguishes twentieth-century totalitarianism from earlier patterns of more primitive dictatorship is not the use of terror and a secret police as instruments of control but rather their high development as an organized system of power. With the emergence of totalitarianism, terror has become elaborately institutionalized, has developed its own bureaucratic apparatus and specialized professionalisms, and has spread its net over the whole range of society. The large-scale organizational rationalization of the totalitarian terror machine introduces a new dimension of cold-blooded efficiency and calculated violence in comparison with which even the Jacobin terror takes on the character of a spontaneous and chaotic *Jacquerie*.

This does not mean that terror is the only method by which a totalitarian regime maintains itself in power. Loyalty and devotion must also be elicited. The skillful totalitarian dictator weaves a complex web of controls in which indoctrination and incentives have their appointed places. Agitation and propaganda may rally fanatic support, and appeals to self-interest may enlist the energies of the ambitious and bind their fortunes to the regime. When discontent accumulates, "loyalty" to the regime may be consolidated by providing scapegoats on whom frustrated aggression may exhaust itself. The shrewd totalitarian dictatorship may go further and permit ventilation of grievances of a nonpolitical and nonorganized character. It may even institutionalize such expression as the Soviet dictatorship does when it sanctions criticism of bureaucratic malpractice or inefficiency. Such criticism may play a constructive role in strengthening the regime since it accomplishes the triple function of draining off aggression on the part of its subjects, prodding the bureaucracy to improve its performance, and sustaining the illusion that the supreme leadership is genuinely concerned about popular annoyances and vexations.

Yet ultimately the totalitarian dictator must depend on terror to safeguard his monopoly of power. Behind the totalitarian façade, the instrument of terror can always be found, ready for use when needed, operative, above all, even when not visible by the mere fact that it is known to exist.

* Professor of Government at Harvard University. Reprinted by permission of the publishers from chapter 13 of Merle Fainsod's *How Russia is Ruled* (Cambridge, Mass.: Harvard University Press, Copyright, 1953, by the President and Fellows of Harvard College). For footnote references, see original source.

Because the totalitarian regime provides no legitimate channel for the expression of political dissent, its constant concern is to prevent or eliminate its illegal existence. To accomplish this purpose, it recruits its specialists in espionage and terror and uses fear as a political weapon. The secret police becomes the core of totalitarian power, an omnipresent and pervasive force which envelops every sector of society in an ominous cloud of suspicion and insecurity. The task of the secret police is to serve as the eyes and ears of the dictatorship, as well as its sword. It must not only hear what people say; it must also be prepared to diagnose their souls and plumb their innermost thoughts. It must transform every citizen into a potential watchdog and informer to check and report on his friends and neighbors. It must sow distrust, for distrust will discourage organization and revolt.

THE DEFENSE OF TERROR

The practice of totalitarian terror generates its own underlying theoretical justifications. The role of terror in Communist ideology furnishes a prime example. Violence is accepted as implicit in the class struggle. As Lenin said in defending the dissolution of the Constituent Assembly, "Violence when it is committed by the toiling and exploited masses is the kind of violence of which we approve." This instrumental attitude toward violence prepares the way for its sanctification when employed by the Party in the name of the working class and by the Party leadership in the name of the Party.

The rationalization of terror embraces two central propositions. The first emphasizes the safety of the Revolution as the supreme law. In the words of Lenin, "The Soviet Republic is a fortress besieged by world capital . . . From this follows our right and our duty to mobilize the whole population to a man for the war." The second emphasizes the intransigence of the enemies of the Revolution, the necessity of crushing them completely if the Revolution itself is not to be destroyed. "What is the 'nutritive medium,' " asks Lenin,

which engenders counterrevolutionary enterprises, outbreaks, conspiracies, and so forth? . . . It is the medium of the bourgeoisie, of the bourgeois intelligentsia, of the kulaks in the countryside, and, everywhere, of the "non-Party" public, as well as of the Socialist-Revolutionaries and the Mensheviks. We must treble our watch over this medium, we must multiply it tenfold. We must multiply our vigilance, because counterrevolutionary attempts from this quarter are absolutely inevitable, precisely at the present moment and in the near future.

In essence, Stalin's defense of terror, delivered in an interview with a visiting Foreign Workers' Delegation on November 5, 1927, covers much the same ground, though with notably less frankness.

The GPU or Cheka is a punitive organ of the Soviet government. It is more or less analogous to the Committee of Public Safety which was formed during the Great French Revolution . . . It is something in the nature of a military-political tribunal set up for the purpose of protecting the interests of the revolution from attacks on the part of the counterrevolutionary bourgeoisie and their agents . . .

People advocate a maximum of leniency; they advise the dissolution of the GPU . . . But can anyone guarantee that the capitalists of all countries will abandon the idea of organizing and financing counterrevolutionary groups of plotters, terrorists, incendiaries, and bomb-throwers after the liquidation of the GPU . . . ?

. . . We are a country surrounded by capitalist states. The internal enemies of our revolution are the agents of the capitalists of all countries . . . In fighting against the enemies at home, we fight the counterrevolutionary elements of all countries . . .

No, comrades, we do not wish to repeat the mistakes of the Parisian Communards. The GPU is necessary for the Revolution and will continue to exist to the terror of the enemies of the proletariat.

The real significance of Stalin's theory of Soviet terror did not become fully manifest until the period of the Great Purge in the thirties. The liquidation of the Old Bolsheviks made it altogether clear that the salient role of terror in Stalinist ideology was to serve as a bulwark of defense for his own monopoly of Party leadership. Since this involved establishing a regime of terror within the Party, Stalin was faced with the problem of reconciling his innovation with the traditional notion that terror was reserved for the class enemy. The problem was neatly and ruthlessly solved by identifying any form of opposition to Stalin with counterrevolution and foreign espionage. The formula of capitalist encirclement proved elastic enough to embrace the enemy inside the Party as well as the enemy outside. Stalin put it as follows:

It should be remembered and never forgotten that as long as capitalist encirclement exists there will be wreckers, diversionists, spies, terrorists, sent behind the frontiers of the Soviet Union by the intelligence services of foreign states . . .

It should be explained to our Party Comrades that the Trotskyites, who represent the active elements in the diversionist, wrecking and espionage work of the foreign intelligence services . . . have already long ceased to serve any idea compatible with the interests of the working class, that they have turned into a gang of wreckers, diversionists, spies, assassins, without principles and ideas, working for the foreign intelligence services.

It should be explained that in the struggle against contemporary Trotskyism, not the old methods, the methods of discussion, must be used, but new methods, methods for smashing and uprooting it.

After the Great Purge, Stalin again faced the problem of reconciling the retention of these strong-arm methods with the claim that antagonistic classes had ceased to exist in the Soviet Union. In his report to the Eighteenth Party Congress in 1939, Stalin addressed himself to the issue, "It is sometimes asked: 'We have abolished the exploiting classes; there are no longer any hostile classes in the country; there is nobody to suppress; hence there is no more need for the state; it must die away— Why then do we not help our socialist state to die away? . . . Is it not time we relegated the state to the museum of antiquities?" Again Stalin rested his case for the retention of the terror apparatus on the allegation of capitalist encirclement:

These questions not only betray an underestimation of the capitalist encirclement, but also an underestimation of the role and significance of the bourgeois states and their organs, which send spies, assassins and wreckers into our country and are waiting for a favourable opportunity to attack it by armed force. They likewise betray an underestimation of the role and significance of our socialist state and of its military, punitive and intelligence organs, which are essential for the defense of the socialist land from foreign attack.

Writing in 1950, after a considerable expansion of Soviet power as a result of World War II, Stalin remained committed to "the conclusion that in the face of capitalist encirclement, when the victory of the socialist revolution has taken place in one country alone while capitalism continues to dominate in all other countries, the country where the revolution has triumphed must not weaken but must strengthen in every way its state, state organs, intelligence agencies, and army if it does not want to be destroyed by capitalist encirclement." Behind these rationalizations was the crystallization of a system of government in which terror had become the essential ingredient. Defended originally as an expression of the class interests of the proletariat, its edge was first turned against all opponents of Communist ascendancy and finally against any appearance of challenge to the domination of the ruling clique.

THE CREATION OF THE CHEKA

The genealogy of the Bolshevik apparatus of terror reaches back to the first weeks after the seizure of power. In pre-Revolutionary days, the Bolsheviks had occasion to acquire an intimate familiarity with the operations of the Tsarist *Okhrana* or secret police; the lessons they learned then were later to be applied and amplified. Lenin quickly decided that the Bolsheviks would have to develop their own Okhrana. In a memorandum dated December 19-20, 1917, he called on Dzerzhinsky, the commandant of Smolny, to organize the struggle against counterrevolution and sabotage. On December 20, the Council of People's Commissars approved a decree establishing the Cheka or All-Russian Extraordinary Commission. Dzerzhinsky was made the first chairman of the eight-member commission. One of its early acts was an appeal "to all local soviets to proceed immediately to the organization of similar commissions." Workers, soldiers, and peasants were instructed to inform the Cheka "about organizations and individual persons whose activity is harmful to the Revolution." At the same time, a system of revolutionary tribunals was established to investigate and try offenses which bore the character of sabotage and counter-revolution. The judges of the revolutionary tribunals were to fix penalties in accordance with "the circumstances of the case and the dictates of the revolutionary conscience."

In the confusion of the first months of the Bolshevik Revolution, terror was far from being a monopoly of the specialists in terror. The Cheka was still in its organizational phase, and its regime was singularly mild compared with what was to come. Acts of violence against the bourgeoisie were common, but they were usually committed by revolutionary mobs and undisciplined sailors and soldiers and were not ordinarily officially authorized and inspired. The early death sentences of the Cheka were imposed on bandits and criminals. As the White forces began to rally their strength, the Cheka spread its net more widely and turned to sterner measures. On February 22, 1918, the Cheka ordered all local soviets "to seek out, arrest, and shoot immediately all members . . . connected in one form or another with counterrevolutionary organizations . . . (1) enemy agents and spies, (2) counterrevolutionary agitators, (3) speculators, (4) organizers of revolt . . . against the Soviet government, (5) those going to the Don to join the . . . Kaledin-Kornilov band and the Polish counterrevolutionary legions, (6) buyers and sellers of arms to equip the counterrevolutionary bourgeoisie . . . all these are to be shot on the spot . . . when caught red-handed in the act."

The terror began to gather momentum. Gorky's newspaper *Novaya Zhizn'* (New Life) reported, "Executions continue. Not a day, not a night passes without several persons being executed." On the night of April 11, 1918, the Cheka staged a mass raid on anarchist centers in Moscow; several hundred were arrested and approximately thirty were killed while resisting arrest. Though the curve of Cheka activity was rising, its operations still remained on a limited scale.

The terror was given a sharp impetus by the effort of the Left SR's to seize power in Moscow soon after the assassination of the German Ambassador Mirbach on July 6, 1918. Large-scale arrests of Left SR's followed, and at least thirteen were shot. As the punitive actions of the Cheka increased, the SR's replied in kind. On August 30, 1918, Uritsky, the head of the Petrograd Cheka, was assassinated, and Lenin was seriously wounded. The attack on Uritsky and Lenin unleashed mass reprisals. In Petrograd alone, more than five hundred "counterrevolutionaries and White Guards" were immediately shot. The slaughter in Moscow included "many Tsarist ministers and a whole list of high personages." The President of the Provincial Soviet of Penza reported, "For the murder from ambush of one comrade, Egorov, a Petrograd worker, the Whites paid with 152 lives. In the future firmer measures will be taken against the Whites." The prominent Chekist Latsis declared,

We are no longer waging war against separate individuals, we are exterminating the bourgeoisie as a class. Do not seek in the dossier of the accused for proofs as to whether or not he opposed the soviet government by word or deed. The first question that should be put is to what class he belongs, of what extraction, what education and profession. These questions should decide the fate of the accused. Herein lie the meaning and the essence of the Red Terror.

The demonstrative massacres which followed the attack on Lenin were designed to strike fear into the hearts of all opponents of the Bolsheviks. The terror was mainly directed against the former nobility, the bourgeoisie, the landowners, the White Guards, and the clergy. But it was by no means confined to these groups. The SR's and Mensheviks, too, felt its sharp edge, and peasants who resisted the requisitioning of grain or who deserted from the Red Army were also among its victims. The Red Terror had its counterpart on the White side; the victims in this grim competition were numbered in the tens of thousands and perhaps hundreds of thousands.

As the Cheka broadened the scope of its activities, it also jealously resisted any interference with its claimed authority. Its tendency to set itself above and beyond the law aroused concern even in Bolshevik circles. At the Second All-Russian Conference of Commissars of Justice held in Moscow July 2-6, 1918,

Comrade Lebedev . . . pointed out that granting the necessity for the existence of the Extraordinary Commissions, it was nevertheless important to delimit their sphere of activity . . . Otherwise we shall have a state within a state, with the former tending to widen its jurisdiction more and more. . .

Comrade Terastvatsaturov said that . . . in the provinces the question of the activities of the Extraordinary Commissions is a very acute one. The Commissions do everything they please . . . The president of our Cheka in Orel said: "I am responsible to no one; my powers are such that I can shoot anybody."

The reply of Krestinsky, the Commissar of Justice, emphasized the difficulty of imposing restraints on the Cheka. "So long as the Cheka functions," concluded Krestinsky, "the work of justice must take a secondary place, and its sphere of activity must be considerably curtailed." The Cheka was vigorous and effective in asserting its prerogatives both against local soviet authorities and the Commissariat of Justice. The Chekist Peters put it bluntly, "In its activity the Cheka is completely independent, carrying out searches, arrests, shootings, afterwards making a report to the Council of People's Commissars and the Soviet Central Executive Committee."

After the end of the Civil War and the inauguration of the NEP, an effort was made to impose legal limits and restraints on Cheka operations. On the initiative of V. M. Smirnov, an Old Bolshevik of the Left Opposition, the Ninth Congress of Soviets, meeting in December 1921, adopted a resolution, which, after expressing gratitude for the "heroic work" of the Cheka "at the most acute moments of the Civil War," recommended that curbs be imposed on its powers.

THE GPU

On February 8, 1922, VTsIK (the All-Russian Central Executive Committee) issued a decree abolishing the Cheka and its local organs and transferring its functions to a newly created State Political Administration (GPU), which was to operate "under the personal chairmanship of the People's Commissar for Interior, or his deputy." . . .

The mass incidence of OGPU arrests during the period of the First Five Year Plan was most widely felt in the countryside. The commitment to collectivize and mechanize agriculture involved a decision to liquidate the kulaks as a class, on the ground that they were inveterate enemies of Soviet power and could be counted on to sabotage collectivization. Stalin estimated in November 1928 that the kulaks constituted about 5 per cent of the rural population, or more than one million of the twenty-five million peasant families. The OGPU was assigned the task of ejecting them from their land, confiscating their property, and deporting them to the North and Siberia. Some of the more recalcitrant were shot when they resisted arrest or responded with violence to efforts to dispossess them. The great majority became wards of the OGPU and were sentenced to forced labor in lumber camps or coal mines, or on canals, railroads, and other public works which the OGPU directed. At one stroke, the OGPU became the master of the largest pool of labor in the Soviet Union. Its own enterprises expanded rapidly to absorb them; those for whom no work could be found in the OGPU industrial empire were hired out on contract to other Soviet enterprises encountering difficulty in mobilizing supplies of free labor.

The mass deportation of the kulaks meant a tremendous growth in the network of OGPU forced labor camps. At the same time, the jurisdiction of the OGPU over ordinary criminals was enlarged. All prisoners serving sentences of more than three years were transferred to OGPU care, even if the crimes were not of a political character. No official statistics were made available on the population of the camps in the early thirties, but some indication of the magnitudes involved is provided by the fact that Belomor, the canal project connecting Leningrad and the White Sea, alone utilized more than two hundred thousand prisoners. By the end of the First Five Year Plan, forced labor had become a significant factor in manning the construction projects of the Soviet economy.

THE NKVD AND THE GREAT PURGE

The powers of the OGPU were concurrently enhanced. It was given authority to enforce the obligatory passport system introduced in large areas of the Soviet Union at the end of 1932. In July 1934 the OGPU was transformed into the People's Commissariat of Internal Affairs, or NKVD

The enlarged activities of the NKVD included responsibility for state security, all penal institutions, fire departments, police (militia), convoy troops, frontier guards, troops of internal security, highway administration, and civil registry offices (vital statistics). The reorganization of 1934-35 involved a consolidation of the repressive machinery of the Soviet state. For the first time, all institutions of detention were placed under one jurisdiction. The secret police and their supporting military formations were united with the ordinary police. A formidable structure of power was cemented.

Some contemporary commentators tended to view the reorganization as an effort to impose limits on the arbitrary authority of the secret police. The bases for these hopes were twofold. In July 1933 a new office, the Procuratorship of the U.S.S.R., was established, and among its duties was "the supervision . . . of the legality and regularity of the actions of the OGPU." The statute creating the NKVD appeared to restrict its judicial powers. A special council attached to the NKVD was vested with authority "to issue orders regarding administrative deportation, exile, imprisonment in corrective labor camps for a term not exceeding five years." No mention was made of any NKVD authorization to inflict the death penalty. The statute seemed clearly to imply that criminal cases not disposed of administratively by the NKVD were to be transferred to the courts for trail and that crimes such as treason and espionage, which involved the possibility of the death penalty, were to be triable by the Military Collegium of the Supreme Court or other military tribunals. Whatever may have been the intent behind these measures to restrict the NKVD, subsequent events testified to their futility. In the Great Purge touched off by the assassination of Kirov, legal forms lost all significance. The arbitrary power of the NKVD reached previously unattained heights; the "Yezhovshchina" (as the worst phase of the purge became known after its sponsor, the NKVD head Yezhov) entered the language as a symbol of lawlessness run riot.

Before 1934 the victims of the OGPU-NKVD were largely former White Guards, the bourgeoisie, political opponents of the Bolsheviks, Nepmen, members of the old intelligentsia, and kulaks. During the late twenties and early thirties, some members of the Trotsky-Zinoviev and Right oppositions were also arrested by the OGPU and condemned to administrative exile or confinement in political *isolators;* but as Anton Ciliga, who was sentenced to one of the latter, records, the political prisoners received "special treatment," had books at their disposal, held meetings and debates, published prison news sheets, and lived a relatively privileged existence compared with the wretched inhabitants of the forced labor camps. Until 1934, the Party was largely exempt from the full impact of the OGPU-NKVD terror; the relatively few oppositionists who were confined in OGPU prisons were still treated with comparative humanity.

In December 1934, when Kirov was assassinated by Nikolayev, allegedly a former member of the Zinoviev opposition, a new era in NKVD history opened. The "liberal" regime which the imprisoned "oppositionists" enjoyed came to an abrupt end. The concentrated power of the NKVD was now directed toward uprooting all actual or potential opposition in the Party. For the first time, the Party felt the full brunt of the terror.

The murder of Kirov was followed by drastic reprisals. Nikolayev and a group of his alleged confederates were charged with having formed a so-called Leningrad Center to organize the assassination and were condemned to death. More than a hundred persons who had been arrested prior to Kirov's death as "counterrevolutionaries" were promptly handed over to military commissions of the Supreme Court of the U.S.S.R. for trial, were found guilty of preparing and carrying out terrorist acts, and were instantly shot. This demonstrative massacre was accompanied by the arrest and imprisonment, on charges of negligence, of twelve high NKVD officials in Leningrad. In the spring of 1935, thousands and perhaps tens of thousands of Leningrad inhabitants who were suspected of harboring opposition sentiments were arrested and deported to Siberia. In the sardonic nomenclature of exile and concentration camp, they came to be referred to collectively as "Kirov's assassins."

Zinoviev, Kamenev, and all the principal leaders of the Zinoviev group were also arrested and transferred to the political *isolator* at Verkhne-Uralsk. During the summer of 1935, Zinoviev, Kamenev, and an assortment of lesser figures were secretly tried for plotting against the life of Stalin. According to Ciliga, "Two of the prisoners were shot: one collaborator of the G.P.U. and one officer of the Kremlin Guard. The others escaped with sentences ranging between five and ten years." Stalin, in addressing the graduates of the Red Army Academies at the Kremlin on May 4, 1935, observed,

> These comrades did not always confine themselves to criticism and passive resistance. They threatened to raise a revolt in the Party against the Central Committee. More, they threatened some of us with bullets. Evidently, they reckoned on frightening us and compelling us to turn from the Leninist road . . . We were obliged to handle some of these comrades roughly. But that cannot be helped. I must confess that I too had a hand in this.

During 1935 the purge gathered momentum, but its proportions were still relatively restricted. The dissolution of the Society of Old Bolsheviks on May 25, 1935, was an ominous portent of things to come. On May 13, some two weeks earlier, the Party Central Committee had ordered a screening of all Party documents in order to "cleanse" the Party of all opposition elements. As Zhdanov stated in a report at the plenum of the Saratov *kraikom,* "Recent events, particularly the treacherous murder of Comrade Kirov, show clearly how dangerous it is for the Party to lose its vigilance . . . I have to remind you that the murderer of Comrade Kirov, Nikolayev, committed his crime by using his Party card." By December 1, 1935, 81.1

per cent of all Party members had been subjected to screening, and 9.1 per cent of these were reported as expelled. On December 25 the Central Committee of the Party, dissatisfied with the modest results of the verification of Party documents, ordered a new purge. Beginning February 1, 1936, all old Party cards were to be exchanged for new cards; the issuance of new Party documents was to serve as the occasion for a rigorous unmasking of enemies who had survived the earlier screening. The bite of the first phase of the purge is indicated by the striking decline of Party membership from 2,807,786 in January 1934 to 2,044,412 in April 1936. In a little over two years, more than one out of every four members and candidates disappeared from the Party rolls. Their fate can be inferred from the diatribes which the Soviet press of the period directed against "wreckers, spies, diversionists and murderers sheltering behind the Party card and disguised as Bolsheviks."

The Great Purge reached its climax in the period 1936-1938. Its most dramatic external manifestation was the series of show trials in the course of which every trace of Old Bolshevik opposition leadership was officially discredited and exterminated. The first of the great public trials took place in August, 1936. Zinoviev, Kamenev, Ivan Smirnov, and thirteen associates were charged with organizing a clandestine terrorist center under instructions from Trotsky, with accomplishing the murder of Kirov, and with preparing similar attempts against the lives of other Party leaders. All sixteen were executed. In the course of the trial, the testimony of the accused compromised many other members of the Bolshevik Old Guard. A wave of new arrests followed. On August 23, 1936, Tomsky, hounded by a sense of impending doom, committed suicide.

In January 1937 came the Trial of the Seventeen, the so-called Anti-Soviet Trotskyite Center, which included such prominent figures as Pyatakov, Radek, Sokolnikov, Serebryakov, and Muralov. This time the accused were charged with plotting the forcible overthrow of the Soviet government with the aid of Germany and Japan, with planning the restoration of capitalism in the U.S.S.R., and with carrying on espionage, wrecking diversive, and terrorist activities on behalf of foreign states. Again, the trial was arranged to demonstrate that Trotsky was the *éminence grise* who inspired, organized, and directed all these activities. The prisoners in the dock fought for their lives by playing their assigned role in a drama designed to destroy Trotsky's reputation. Radek and Sokolnikov were rewarded with ten-year prison sentences. Two minor figures were also sentenced to long prison terms. The remaining thirteen were shot.

On June 12, 1937, *Pravda* carried the announcement of the execution of Marshal Tukhachevsky and seven other prominent generals of the Red Army "for espionage and treason to the Fatherland." This time no public trial was held. The Party press merely declared that the executed generals had conspired to overthrow the Soviet government and to reëstablish "the

yoke of the landowners and industrialists." The conspirators were alleged
to be in the service of the military intelligence of "a foreign government,"
to which they were supposed to have indicated their readiness to surrender
the Soviet Ukraine in exchange for assistance in bringing about the downfall of the Soviet government. Besides Tukhachevsky, the Deputy People's
Commissar of Defense, the list of the executed included General Yakir,
Commander of the Leningrad Military District; General Uborevich, Commander of the Western Military District; General Kork, Commander of
the War College in Moscow; General Primakov, Budënny's Deputy Commander of Cavalry; Feldman, head of the Administration of Commanding
Personnel in the Defense Commissariat; Putna, the former Soviet military
attaché in Great Britain; and Eideman, President of the Central Council
of *Osoaviakhim,* the civilian defense agency. Gamarnik, who served as the
Party's watchdog over the army in his capacity as head of the Political
Administration of the Red Army (PUR), committed suicide to avoid arrest.
The execution of Tukhachevsky and his associates was the prelude to a
mass purge of the Soviet armed forces in the course of which the top commanding personnel was particularly hard hit.

The slaughter of the Old Guard continued with the Trial of the
Twenty-one, the so-called Anti-Soviet Bloc of Rights and Trotskyites, in
March 1938. Among the prisoners in the dock were Bukharin, Rykov, and
Krestinsky, all former members of the Politburo; Yagoda, the former head
of the NKVD; Rakovsky, the former chairman of the Council of People's
Commissars in the Ukraine and Soviet ambassador to England and France;
Rosengoltz, the former People's Commissar of Foreign Trade; Grinko, the
former People's Commissar of Finance; and Khodjayev, the former chairman of the Council of People's Commissars of Uzbekistan. The indictment
against them embraced the usual combination of treason, espionage, diversion, terrorism, and wrecking. The bloc headed by Bukharin and Rykov
was alleged to have spied for foreign powers from the earliest days of the
Revolution, to have entered into secret agreements with the Nazis and
the Japanese to dismember the Soviet Union, to have planned the assassination of Stalin and the rest of the Politburo, and to have organized innumerable acts of sabotage and diversion in order to wreck the economic
and political power of the Soviet Union. If the testimony of Yagoda is to
be believed, he not only murdered his predecessor in office, Menzhinsky,
but also tried to murder his successor, Yezhov; he facilitated the assassination of Kirov, was responsible for the murder of Gorky, Gorky's son, and
Kuibyshev; he admitted foreign spies into his organization and protected
their operations; he planned a palace coup in the Kremlin and the assassination of the Politburo.

If these lurid tales strain the credulity of the reader, they nevertheless represent the version of oppositionist activity which Stalin and his faithful lieutenants found it expedient to propagate. Without access to the

archives of the Kremlin and the NKVD, it is doubtful whether the web of fact and fancy behind the show trials will ever be authoritatively disentangled. The hatred of the former leaders of the opposition for Stalin can be taken for granted. That their hatred carried them to the point of conspiring together to overthrow him is not unlikely, though the evidence adduced at the trails to support the charge is lame and unconvincing. What appears singularly implausible are the allegations that Old Bolsheviks who had given their lives to the Communist cause would plot with the Nazis to restore capitalism in the Soviet Union, would function as their puppets and espionage agents, and arrange to hand over large portions of the Soviet Union to them as compensation for dethroning Stalin. . . .

The crescendo of the Great Purge was reached in the second period, which extended from late September 1937, when Yezhov was appointed head of the NKVD, until the end of July 1938, when Lavrenti Beria was designated as Yezhov's deputy and eventual successor. The announcement of Yezhov's removal did not come until December, but meanwhile Beria assumed *de facto* command of the NKVD organization, and early in 1939 Yezhov disappeared and was probably liquidated.

The period of the Yezhovshchina involved a reign of terror without parallel in Soviet history. Among those arrested, imprisoned, and executed were a substantial proportion of the leading figures in the Party and governmental hierarchy. The Bolshevik Old Guard was destroyed. The roll of Yezhov's victims included not only former oppositionists but many of the most stalwart supporters of Stalin in his protracted struggle with the opposition. No sphere of Soviet life, however lofty, was left untouched. Among the purged Stalinists were three former members of the Politburo, Rudzutak, Chubar, and S. V. Kossior, and three candidate members, Petrovsky, Postyshev, and Eikhe. An overwhelming majority of the members and candidates of the Party Central Committee disappeared. The senior officer corps of the armed forces suffered severely. According to one sober account, "two of five marshals of the Soviet Union escaped arrest, two of fifteen army commanders, twenty-eight of fifty-eight corps commanders, eighty-five of a hundred and ninety-five divisional commanders, and a hundred and ninety-five of four hundred and six regimental commanders." The havoc wrought by the purge among naval commanding personnel was equally great. The removal of Yagoda from the NKVD was accompanied by the arrest of his leading collaborators, Agranov, Prokofiev, Balitsky, Messing, Pauker, Trilisser, and others. The Commissariat of Foreign Affairs and the diplomatic service were hard hit. Among the Old Guard, only Litvinov, Maisky, Troyanovsky, and a few lesser lights survived. Almost every commissariat was deeply affected.

The purge swept out in ever-widening circles and resulted in wholesale removals and arrests of leading officials in the union republics, secretaries of the Party, Komsomol, and trade-union apparatus, heads of industrial trusts and enterprises, Comintern functionaries and foreign Communists, and leading writers, scholars, engineers, and scientists. The arrest of an important figure was followed by the seizure of the entourage which surrounded him. The apprehension of members of the entourage led to the imprisonment of their friends and acquaintances. The endless chain of involvements and associations threatened to encompass entire strata of Soviet society. Fear of arrest, exhortations to vigilance, and perverted ambition unleashed new floods of denunciations, which generated their own avalanche of cumulative interrogations and detentions. Whole categories of Soviet citizens found themselves singled out for arrest because of their "objective characteristics." Old Bolsheviks, Red Partisans, foreign Communists of German, Austrian, and Polish extraction, Soviet citizens who had been abroad or had relations with foreign countries or foreigners, and "repressed elements" were automatically caught up in the NKVD web of wholesale imprisonment. The arrests mounted into the millions; the testimony of the survivors is unanimous regarding crowded prison cells and teeming forced labor camps. Most of the prisoners were utterly bewildered by the fate which had befallen them. The vast resources of the NKVD were concentrated on one objective—to document the existence of a huge conspiracy to undermine Soviet power. The extraction of real confessions to imaginary crimes became a major industry. Under the zealous and ruthless ministrations of NKVD examiners, millions of innocents were transformed into traitors, terrorists, and enemies of the people.

How explain the Yezhovshchina? What motives impelled Stalin to organize a blood bath of such frightening proportions? In the absence of revealing testimony from the source, one can only venture hypotheses. Stalin's desire to consolidate his own personal power appears to have been a driving force. The slaughter of the Bolshevik Old Guard may be viewed partly as a drastic reprisal for past insubordination; it was more probably intended as a preventive measure to end once and for all any possibility of resistance or challenge from this direction. The extension of the purge to the Stalinist stalwarts in the Party and governmental apparatus is much more difficult to fathom. It is possible that many fell victim to the system of denunciations in the course of which their loyalty to Stalin was put in question, that a number were still involved in official or personal relationships with former oppositionists, that some were liquidated because they displayed traces of independence in their dealings with the Supreme Leader, that others were merely suspected of harboring aspirations toward personal power, and that still others simply furnished convenient scapegoats to demonstrate the existence of a conspiracy that reached into the highest circles.

Implicit in any understanding of the Yezhovshchina is a theory of the role of terror in Stalin's formula of government. The consolidation of personal rule in a totalitarian system depends on the constant elimination of all actual or potential competitors for supreme power. The insecurity of the masses must be supplemented by the insecurity of the governing elite who surround the Supreme Dictator. The too strongly entrenched official with an independent base of power is by definition a threat to the dictator's total sway. The individuals or groups who go uncontrolled and undirected are regarded as fertile soil for the growth of conspiratorial intrigue. The function of terror thus assumes a two-fold aspect. As prophylactic and preventive, it is designed to nip any possible resistance or opposition in the bud. As an instrument for the reinforcement of the personal power of the dictator, it is directed toward ensuring perpetual circulation in the ranks of officeholders in order to forestall the crystallization of autonomous islands of countervailing force.

The manipulation of terror as a system of power is a delicate art. A dictator in command of modern armaments and a secret police can transform his subjects into robots and automatons, but if he succeeds too well, he runs the risk of destroying the sources of creative initiative on which the survival of his own regime depends. When terror runs rampant, as it did at the height of the Yezhovshchina, unintended consequences follow. Fear becomes contagious and paralyzing. Officials at all levels seek to shirk responsibility. The endless belt of irresponsible denunciations begins to destroy the nation's treasury of needed skills. The terror apparatus grows on the stuff on which it feeds and magnifies in importance until it overshadows and depresses all the constructive enterprises of the state. The dictator finds himself caught up in a whirlwind of his own making which threatens to break completely out of control.

As the fury of the Yezhovshchina mounted, Stalin and his intimates finally became alarmed. Evidence accumulated that the purge was overreaching itself and that much talent sorely needed by the regime was being irretrievably lost. The first signal of a change of policy was given in a resolution of the January 1938 plenum of the Party Central Committee entitled "Concerning the Mistakes of Party Organizations in Excluding Communists from the Party, Concerning Formal-Bureaucratic Attitudes toward the Appeals of Excluding Members of the VKP(b), and Concerning Measures to Eliminate these Deficiencies." The resolution identified a new culprit, the Communist-careerists, who sought to make capital out of the purge by securing promotions through provocatory denunciations of their superiors. It was these careerists, the resolution charged, who were primarily responsible for sowing suspicion and insecurity within Party ranks and for decimating the Party cadres. The resolution concluded with a ten-point program designed to put an end to mass expulsions and to secure the rehabilitation of former members who had been expelled as the result of slanders. The immediate effect of this resolution was to produce a new purge of so-called Communist-careerists. At the same time, the

Party press began to carry stories of the reinstatements of honest Communists who had been the unfortunate victims of unjustified denunciations.

The third and final phase of the Great Purge involved the purging of the purgers. In late July 1938 Yezhov's sun began to set when Beria took over as his deputy. In December, Yezhov was ousted as head of the NKVD and appointed Commissar for Inland Water Transport, from which post he soon disappeared unmourned but not forgotten. During the same month came the sensational announcement of the arrest, trial, and shooting of the head of the NKVD of Moldavia and a group of his examiners for extracting false confessions from innocent prisoners. The enemies of the people, it now appeared, had wormed their way into the NKVD apparatus itself and had sought to stir up mass unrest and disaffection by their brutal persecution of the guiltless.

It was now the turn of Yezhov and his collaborators to play the role of scapegoat for the excesses of the purge. A wave of arrests spread through the NKVD organization. The prisons began to fill with former NKVD examiners; many prisoners who had been tortured by these same examiners had the welcome experience of greeting their former tormentors as cellmates in prisons and forced labor camps. The "Great Change," as it was soon to become known, was marked by a substantial amelioration in prison conditions and examining methods. According to Beck and Godin, "Prisoners were released by the thousands, and many were restored to their old positions or even promoted." A new era appeared to have dawned.

Stalin now presented himself in the guise of the dispenser of mercy and justice. Excesses of the purge were blamed on subordinate officials who had exceeded their authority, saboteurs who had tried to break the indissoluble link which bound Leader and people, and careerists and counterrevolutionaries who had insinuated themselves into the Party and NKVD organizations in order to subvert and undermine the Soviet regime. At the Eighteenth Congress in 1939, Zhdanov reeled off case after case of so-called slanderers and calumniators who had tried to advance themselves in the Party by wholesale expulsions of honest Party members. Quoting from Stalin, he repeated, "Some of our Party leaders suffer from a lack of concern for people, for members of the Party, for workers . . . As a result of this heartless attitude towards people . . . discontent and bitterness are artificially created among a section of the Party, and the Trotskyite double-dealers artfully hook on to such embittered comrades and skillfully drag them into the bog of Trotskyite wrecking." Zhdanov called for a change in Party Rules to ensure "an attentive approach and careful investigation of accusations brought against Party members," which would "protect the rights of Party members from all arbitrary procedure," and "abolish the resort to expulsion from the Party . . . for trifling misdemeanours."

Thus, the pressure of the purge was temporarily relaxed as Stalin sought to enlist the energies and loyalties of the new governing elite whom he had promoted to positions of responsibility over the graves of their predecessors. Again, as in the collectivization crisis earlier, Stalin demonstrated his remarkable instinct for stopping short and reversing course at the brink of catastrophe.

The full circle of the Great Purge offers a remarkable case study in the use of terror. Arrests ran into the millions. The gruesome and harrowing experiences of the victims blackened the face of Stalinist Russia. The havoc wrought in leading circles appeared irreparable. Yet despite the damage and the hatred engendered, the dynamic momentum of the industrialization program was maintained. The arrests of responsible technicians and officials frequently produced serious setbacks in production, but as their replacements acquired experience, order was restored, and production began to climb again. While many functionaries reacted to the purge by shunning all responsibility, others responded to the fear of arrest by working as they had never worked before. Terror functioned as prod as well as brake. The acceleration in the circulation of the elite brought a new generation of Soviet-trained intelligentsia into positions of responsibility, and Stalin anchored his power on their support. Meanwhile, Stalin emerged from the purge with his own position consolidated. The major purpose of decapitating the Bolshevik Old Guard had been accomplished. Every rival for supreme power who was visible on the horizon had been eliminated. The Party and the nation were thoroughly intimidated. The purgers had been purged and the scapegoats identified. The ancient formula of protecting the infallibility of the Leader by punishing subordinates for their excessive ardor was impressively resurrected.

The moving equilibrium on which Stalin balanced his power structure entered a new phase. The temporary lifting of the blanket of fear was designed to restore morale, to revive hope and initiative, and to reforge the bonds between regime and people which the purge had dangerously strained. But the mitigation of the terror involved no abandonment of the system. For the totalitarian dictator, terror is an indispensable necessity, and its invocation is a guarantee that no organized force will rise to challenge his undisputed rule. The Stalinist refinement on the use of terror as a system of power involved oscillating phases of pressure and relaxation which varied with the dictator's conception of the dangers which he confronted. The essence of control was never abandoned. At the same time, when the pressure became too great, a mirage of security and stability was held out in order to enlist the energy and devotion of the oncoming generations. It is a system which devours many of its servants, but as in games of chance, since the winners and survivors are highly rewarded and cannot be identified in advance, the ambitions of the players are periodically renewed, and the regime bases its strength on their sacrifices.

As the Great Purge drew to a close, the major efforts of the NKVD were concentrated against elements which might prove unreliable in the event that the Soviet Union became involved in war. After the Soviet-Nazi pact and the partition of Poland, the NKVD undertook wholesale arrests in the newly occupied areas. The victims ran into the hundreds of thousands and included whole categories of people whose "objective characteristics" could be broadly construed as inclining them to anti-Soviet behavior. The great majority were deported to forced labor camps in the Soviet North, from which the survivors were amnestied by the terms of the Polish-Soviet pact concluded after the Nazi attack on the Soviet Union. The Soviet occupation of the Baltic States in June 1940 was also followed by large-scale NKVD arrests and deportations of so-called anti-Soviet elements.

After the Nazi invasion, the NKVD engaged in widespread roundups of former "repressed" people and others whose records aroused suspicion of disloyalty to the Soviet regime. The Volga-German Autonomous Republic was dissolved, and its inhabitants were dispatched to forced labor camps or exile in the far reaches of Siberia. With the turning of the tide at Stalingrad and the advance of the Soviet armies westward, the NKVD found new victims among the population of the reoccupied areas. Many were arrested on the ground of actual or alleged collaboration with the Germans, and the forced labor camps reaped a new harvest. A number of the national minorities served as a special target of NKVD retribution because of their alleged disloyalty. The Kalmyk and Chechen-Ingush Republics were dissolved. The Crimean Tatars were penalized for their "traitorous" conduct by the abolition of the Crimean Autonomous Republic. The Autonomous Republic of the Kabards and Bolkars was dismembered, leaving only the Kabardinian ASSR. Meanwhile, German war prisoners accumulated, and the NKVD took over the responsibility of running the camps in which they were confined.

After the capitulation of the Nazis, the NKVD confronted the vast new assignment of sifting the millions of Soviet citizens who found themselves in Germany and Austria at the end of the war. Most of them were war prisoners and *Ostarbeiter* who had been shipped west by the Germans as forced labor. Some, however, had retreated with the German armies in order to escape Soviet rule. Others had fought in Nazi military uniform or in separate anti-Soviet military formations such as the Vlasov Army. The latter when caught received short shrift; the great majority were executed. All of these elements on whom the NKVD could lay its hands were rounded up at assembly points and subjected to intensive interrogations by the NKVD before being shipped back to the Soviet Union. The NKVD followed a calculated policy of treating the "returners" as contaminated by their contact with the West. In order to isolate them from the Soviet populace, large numbers were dispatched to forced labor camps on suspicion of disloyalty or traitorous conduct.

Much less is known about police activities inside the Soviet Union since the end of the war. Large-scale deportations have been reported from the border areas of Esthonia, Latvia, Lithuania, Karelia, and the Western Ukraine; the native population has been shifted to remote areas in Siberia and replaced by Russians, frequently war veterans, brought in from other regions. From reports in the Soviet press of campaigns against collective farm abuses, of cases of venality and corruption among bureau-crats and industrial administrators, of purges of the Party apparatus and among intellectuals, it can be inferred that the secret police continues to claim its victims in widely diversified strata of Soviet society. While the available information is too sparse to justify any sweeping conclusions, there have been no indications thus far of any repetition of the mass retri-butions of the 1936-1938 period, except for the large-scale campaigns against so-called "untrustworthy" elements in the border regions. Elsewhere, if the testimony of escaped Soviet citizens is to be given credence, the secret police makes its presence felt by individual rather than group arrests. Its arbitrary power and pervasive organization help to sustain its reputation as the most feared weapon in the Soviet arsenal of power. . . .

FORCED LABOR

. . . Estimates of the number of people confined in forced labor camps in the Soviet Union run a wide gamut, even within the same period. The Soviet government has not seen fit to release any official statistics. Most estimates represent the guesses of former prisoners who escaped from the Soviet Union and whose personal experience was ordinarily confined to one or a few camps or even sections of camps. Beck and Godin, in an account of the Great Purge which is distinguished by its sobriety and restraint, estimated the total number of prisoners "living in detention under the NKVD" during the Yezhovshchina as between seven and four-teen million. Alexander Weissberg, a distinguished scientist who was im-prisoned in Kharkov during the Yezhovshchina, hazarded the guess that between 5 and 6 per cent of the local population was arrested in the 1937-1939 period. By projecting this percentage to the country at large, Weiss-berg arrived at a total of nine million arrests, of which two million repre-sented criminal charges and seven million were attributable to the purge. After reviewing a wide variety of estimates by former inmates of forced labor camps, Dallin and Nicolaevsky, in a work devoted exclusively to forced labor, concluded that the totals ranged in different periods from seven to twelve million. In the nature of things, these estimates are not susceptible to precise corroboration.

Perhaps the most revealing collection of unquestionably authentic data on the role of forced labor in the Soviet economy is contained in an official Soviet document entitled "State Plan of Development of the National Economy of the U.S.S.R. for 1941." This classified Soviet document, which was captured by the Nazis in the rapid advance of the first months of the war, contains a detailed statement of economic targets for 1941; it also includes a rich assortment of material on the economic activities of the NKVD. The 1941 plan lists a projected capital investment of 37,650,000,000 rubles, exclusive of capital investments of the Commissariats for Transportation, Defense, and Navy. Out of this sum, the NKVD accounted for 6,810,000,000 rubles, or about 18 per cent. In presenting the 1941 economic plan, Voznesensky, the chairman of Gosplan, reported the total capital investment planned for 1941 as 57,000,000,000 rubles. The NKVD share of this total was approximately 12 per cent. On the basis of the 1941 capital investment data, Naum Jasny reached the conclusion that the NKVD was expected to account for 17 per cent of the total 1941 construction and that the number of concentration camp inmates engaged in NKVD construction projects alone would approximate 1,172,000. The 1941 plan indicated that lumbering was the second most important industrial activity of the NKVD. The total share of the NKVD in this industry was about 12 per cent, but this percentage was substantially exceeded in the northern areas of the U.S.S.R. In Archangelsk *oblast,* it was 26 per cent; in the Khabarovsk *krai* and the Karelo-Finnish Republic, more than 33 per cent; in Murmansk *oblast,* more than 40 per cent; and in the Komi Autonomous Republic, more than 50 per cent. Other NKVD industrial targets mentioned in the plan included 5,300,000 tons of coal out of a total 191,000,000 tons; 250,000 tons of oil out of a total 35,000,000 tons; 150,000 tons of chrome ore out of a total of 370,000; and 82,000,000 bricks to be produced in the Khabarovsk and Maritime *krais.*

It should be noted that the captured version of the 1941 plan is incomplete. Data on gold production and armaments were not included and were apparently reserved for separate supplements which circulated among a very restricted group. Information from other sources indicates that gold mining was virtually an NKVD monopoly, the vast development in the Kolyma region was administered by the NKVD through its subsidiary *Dalstroi* and was largely manned by forced labor. On the basis of sober reading of the reports of former inmates of the concentration camps in the Kolyma area, it would appear that Dalstroi utilized from two hundred thousand to four hundred thousand forced laborers in the 1941 period. This, it should be stressed, is a conservative figure. The estimate of Dallin and Nicolaevsky runs from one and a half to two million prisoners.

The 1941 plan does not list the number of camp inmates. The data on the economic activities of the NKVD, however, make it possible to arrive at a fairly reliable estimate of approximately three and a half million. This total applies only to forced labor confined in prison camps under direct NKVD jurisdiction. It does not include persons hired out to other enterprises. It does not include persons sentenced to exile in remote areas who remained under NKVD supervision even though they lived and worked under the same conditions as the rest of the population. Nor does it include the arrested who were being held for investigation and sentence in remand prisons or those serving terms of confinement in ordinary prisons. It does not include workers penalized for tardiness or absenteeism by being compelled to work at their jobs at substantially reduced pay. And it takes no account of the degree of compulsion which is ordinarily attached to job assignments and transfers of so-called "free" labor in the Soviet system. It is obvious that estimates of "forced labor" will vary widely, depending on the categories which are included.

Since 1941, no authoritative internal source comparable to the State Plan has become available. The accounts of released prisoners for subsequent years indicate that large contingents of new forced laborers have been steadily flowing into the camps, but estimates must be speculative to a high degree, and no attempt will be made here to undertake even a crude estimate of the present population of the forced labor camps. Reports that the MVD has been charged with the sole responsibility for the building and operation of all atomic developments and the large-scale construction projects launched under the postwar Five Year Plans point toward a continuing reliance on forced labor as an essential aspect of the Soviet system.

The role of forced labor in the Soviet economy has given rise to sharp controversy. Those who view the concentration camps as an asset to the Soviet economy argue that the MVD derives a substantial profit from the exploitation of slave labor, that the productivity of the concentration camp inmates is considerably in excess of the cost of their upkeep, and that the profits realized from the use of slave labor are "an important element of the government's industrialization fund." The accelerated development of the Soviet North and other remote areas, it is contended, would have been impossible had the government been forced to rely on free labor.

Those who regard the concentration camps as a liability to the Soviet economy are usually ready to concede that the existence of large pools of forced labor has facilitated the exploitation of resources in regions where primitive conditions and hardships are barriers to the recruitment of free labor. But they also point out that the productivity of slave labor is considerably less than that of free workers and that the alleged profits involved disappear when full account is taken of the expense of maintaining the MVD apparatus, both outside and inside the camps. They also stress the high mortality rates in the camps and the great losses involved for the Soviet economy when scarce skilled workers, highly qualified engineers and other professionally trained experts, whose education has involved high costs for the state, are utilized as unskilled laborers.

The initial impetus for the establishment of concentration camps was provided by political rather than economic considerations. The arrests of hundreds of thousands or millions of Soviet citizens were not originally planned as a method of obtaining slave labor power. The large-scale economic enterprises of the NKVD-MVD were developed in order to exploit the prisoners whom the secret police had accumulated. As these enterprises were established, they acquired a momentum of their own. The manpower that they consumed had to be replaced by new contingents, and the NKVD-MVD encountered no great difficulty in finding pretexts for replenishments. A system of power in which the security of the leadership is founded on the insecurity of its subjects demands a continuous crop of fresh victims. The regime of forced labor serves to ensure that the leadership will at least derive some advantage from this process.*

THE HAZARDS OF TERROR

The reliance on terror as an instrument of dominion has its elements of danger. It is not easy to control. A secret police develops its own laws of growth. The more discord it discovers or develops, the more indispensable it becomes. Its tendency is always to extend its own sovereignty, to seek to emancipate itself from all external controls, to become a state within a state, and to preserve the conditions of emergency and siege on which an expansion of its own power depends. Once terror becomes an end in itself, there is no easy and natural stopping place. From the viewpoint of the leadership, there is an even greater worry, the fear that as the secret police apparatus emancipates itself from external controls, it becomes a menace to the security of the highest Party leaders themselves. It is a risk of which the Party leadership has been aware and against which it has taken precautions. Every effort is apparently made to ensure the subordination of the MVD to the central Party organization. Employees are required to be Party members. The secretaries of the Party organizations in the MVD are used as the eyes and ears of the Party Central Committee to ensure loyalty to the Party. The Special Section in the secretariat of the Central Committee is presumed to have a particularly close supervisory relationship to the secret police. Special groups of the Party Control Committee are assigned to watch over the MVD. In these and perhaps other ways, the Party leadership seeks to safeguard itself against the possibility that "the avenging sword of the Revolution" may turn against the revolutionary leadership itself.

Thus far, no head of the Soviet secret police has succeeded in using his position as a platform from which to strike out for supreme power. The first director of the Cheka and OGPU was Felix Dzerzhinsky, an Old Bolshevik of unimpeachable idealism whose whole career documented the

* Editor's footnote: Available evidence suggests that forced labor camps have been largely liquidated since the death of Stalin. But Professor Fainsod's account remains a vivid part of the historic tragedy.

proposition that there is no fanaticism so terrible as that of the pure idealist. Dzerzhinsky gave no evidence of Napoleonic ambitions and died in 1926 without attaining Politburo status. His successor, Menzhinsky, was a much lesser figure, and though he continued as head of the OGPU until 1934, he never moved beyond the second rank of Party leaders. Yagoda, who came next, was removed from office in 1936 and executed in 1938. His successor, Yezhov, was relieved of his duties in 1938 and disappeared in 1939, presumably a scapegoat for the excesses of the Great Purge. Neither Yagoda nor Yezhov could be counted in the front ranks of Party leaders. Beria, who succeeded Yezhov, was the first head of the NKVD to enter the Politburo, where he became an outstanding figure. His rise to power, however, gave every evidence of reflecting Stalin's tutelage rather than any independent leverage which his position as head of the NKVD afforded. Thus far, the vigilance of the ruling group has been proof against all dreams of utilizing the terror apparatus as the road to supremacy. The proposition that Beria may carve a new path has still to be tested.

Even if the Party leadership is successful in imposing its mastery on the secret police, there are other disadvantages in a regime of terror which are not so amenable to skillful manipulation. A system which relies on a large secret police as a basic core of its power is highly wasteful of manpower. The main occupation of the secret police is that of spying, investigating, examining, guarding, and controlling others. Large numbers of talented people are removed from productive work. There is always the hazard that the secret police will run amok and do serious and perhaps unintended harm to the productive and administrative machinery of the state. The atmosphere of universal suspicion which terror breeds is not ordinarily conducive to creative thinking and displays of individual initiative. If the weight of terror becomes too great and the penalty of any administrative failure or mistake is MVD detention, it becomes difficult to persuade people to take responsibility. Even those driven by fear of the secret police to work as they have never worked before begin to crack under the strain. It is no easy task to apply terror and at the same time to hold it in leash.

Perhaps the most subtle danger in a police regime of the Soviet type is its impact on the quality of political decisions at the very highest level. The MVD is one of the main pillars that sustains the regime. It is also a primary source of intelligence regarding both domestic and international developments. Since the MVD apparatus lives and grows on emergency and danger, its justification hinges upon the maintenance of a state of siege. Consequently, the intelligence that filters through the MVD to the top political leadership is apt almost unconsciously to emphasize the storms that are brewing, the plots against the regime, and sinister threats at home and abroad. The risk which the Party leadership faces is that it too will become the unconscious victim of the Frankenstein's monster which it has created. The ultimate hazard of terror as a system of power is that it ends by terrorizing the master as well as the slave.

[EDITOR'S NOTE: *On July 10, 1953, some few months after the death of Stalin on March 5, 1953, it was officially announced that Beria had been dismissed as head of the MVD and was being held for trial. On December 16, the Soviet State Prosecutor issued a statement that Beria (and accomplices) had confessed during the course of investigation to "having committed a number of State crimes." Among the crimes charged were that Beria had been "an agent of foreign capital, directed toward the subversion of the Soviet state" with links to foreign Intelligence services "as far back as the civil war"; had striven "to place the Ministry of Internal Affairs above the party and Government, to seize power and to liquidate the Soviet worker-peasant regime with a view to restoring capitalism and securing the revival of the bourgeoisie." It was also charged that Beria had attempted "to subvert the collective-farm system and to create food difficulties in our country" and "to sow hatred and discord between the peoples of the U.S.S.R."*

On December 23, it was briefly announced that the accused had been tried (behind closed doors) before a tribunal headed by Marshal Ivan S. Konev, that all had been found guilty, and shot.]

STALIN AND THE CULT OF THE INDIVIDUAL

NIKITA S. KHRUSHCHEV*

This denunciation of Stalin and of "the cult of the individual" was delivered on February 24-25, 1956, before a closed session of the XXth Congress of the Communist Party of the Soviet Union and first published in the United States, after release by the United States Department of State on June 4, 1956. Its authenticity has never been officially acknowledged. However, it has been widely credited in the Communist press of the world and was implicitly acknowledged by Anastas I. Mikoyan, First Deputy Premier of the U.S.S.R., on his visit to the United States. (See New York Times, January 19, 1959.)

In Russia itself, a long "Resolution of the Central Committee of the Communist Party of the Soviet Union," published in Pravda *on July 2, 1956, read in part: "For more than three years now our Party has been*

---

* First Secretary of the Communist Party of the Soviet Union and Chairman of the Council of Ministers of the U.S.S.R. The text of this speech is reprinted with permission in abridged form from the version published in *The New Leader* on July 16, 1956, and in its pamphlet titled "The Crimes of the Stalin Era," with the footnote annotations by Boris I. Nicolaevsky, author of *Letter of an Old Bolshevik* and co-author of *Forced Labor in Soviet Russia*.

*waging a consistent struggle against the cult of the person of J. V. Stalin,
persistently overcoming its harmful consequences. Naturally this question
occupied an important place in the work of the XXth Congress of the
CPSU and in its decisions." The next day,* Pravda *commented editorially,
"As is well known, at the XXth Congress of the Communist Party of the
Soviet Union the question of the cult of the individual and its consequences
was examined in detail."*

*It may be said, finally, that during visits made to the U.S.S.R. by this
editor in 1957 and 1960, every one with whom he raised the question seemed
aware of the document and its general contents.*

Comrades! In the report of the Central Committee of the party at the
20th Congress, in a number of speeches by delegates to the Congress, as
also formerly during the plenary CC/CPSU [Central Committee of the
Communist Party of the Soviet Union] sessions, quite a lot has been said
about the cult of the individual and about its harmful consequences.

After Stalin's death the Central Committee of the party began to implement a policy of explaining concisely and consistently that it is impermissible and foreign to the spirit of Marxism-Leninism to elevate one
person, to transform him into a superman possessing supernatural characteristics, akin to those of a god. Such a man supposedly knows everything,
sees everything, thinks for everyone, can do anything, is infallible in his
behavior. Such a belief about a man, and specifically about Stalin, was
cultivated among us for many years.

The objective of the present report is not a thorough evaluation of
Stalin's life and activity. Concerning Stalin's merits, an entirely sufficient
number of books, pamphlets and studies had already been written in his
lifetime. The role of Stalin in the preparation and execution of the
Socialist Revolution, in the Civil War, and in the fight for the construction
of socialism in our country, is universally known. Everyone knows this well.

At present, we are concerned with a question which has immense importance for the party now and for the future—with how the cult of the
person of Stalin has been gradually growing, the cult which became at a
certain specific stage the source of a whole series of exceedingly serious and
grave perversions of party principles, of party democracy, of revolutionary
legality.

Because of the fact that not all as yet realize fully the practical consequences resulting from the cult of the individual, the great harm caused by
the violation of the principle of collective direction of the party and because
of the accumulation of immense and limitless power in the hands of one
person, the Central Committee of the party considers it absolutely necessary to make the material pertaining to this matter available to the 20th
Congress of the Communist Party of the Soviet Union.

Allow me first of all to remind you how severely the classics of

Marxism-Leninism denounced every manifestation of the cult of the individual. In a letter to the German political worker, Wilhelm Bloss, Marx stated: "From my antipathy to any cult of the individual, I never made public during the existence of the International the numerous addresses from various countries which recognized my merits and which annoyed me. I did not even reply to them, except sometimes to rebuke their authors. Engels and I first joined the secret society of Communists on the condition that everything making for superstitious worship of authority would be deleted from its statute. . . ."

The great modesty of the genius of the Revolution, Vladimir Ilyich Lenin, is known. Lenin had always stressed the role of the people as the creator of history, the directing and organizational role of the party as a living and creative organism, and also the role of the Central Committee.

Marxism does not negate the role of the leaders of the working class in directing the revolutionary liberation movement. While ascribing great importance to the role of the leaders and organizers of the masses, Lenin at the same time mercilessly stigmatized every manifestation of the cult of the individual, inexorably combated the foreign-to-Marxism views about a "hero" and a "crowd," and countered all efforts to oppose a "hero" to the masses and to the people. . . .

During Lenin's life the Central Committee of the party was a real expression of collective leadership of the party and of the nation. Being a militant Marxist-revolutionist, always unyielding in matters of principle, Lenin never imposed by force his views upon his co-workers. He tried to convince; he patiently explained his opinions to others. Lenin always diligently observed that the norms of party life were realized, that the party statute was enforced, that the party congresses and the plenary sessions of the Central Committee took place at the proper intervals.

In addition to the great accomplishments of V. I. Lenin for the victory of the working class and of the working peasants, for the victory of our party and for the application of the ideas of scientific Communism to life, his acute mind expressed itself also in this—that he detected in Stalin in time those negative characteristics which resulted later in grave consequences. Fearing the future fate of the party and of the Soviet nation, V. I. Lenin made a completely correct characterization of Stalin, pointing out that it was necessary to consider the question of transferring Stalin from the position of the Secretary General because of the fact that Stalin is excessively rude, that he does not have a proper attitude toward his comrades, that he is capricious and abuses his power.

In December 1922, in a letter to the Party Congress,[1] Vladimir Ilyich wrote: "After taking over the position of Secretary General, Comrade Stalin accumulated in his hands immeasurable power and I am not certain

[1] The full text of this document is commonly known as "Lenin's Testament," although Lenin himself did not use that term. [It appears in Chapter 9 of this book.] [All footnotes are by Boris I. Nicolaevsky.]

whether he will be always able to use this power with the required care."

This letter—a political document of tremendous importance, known in the party history as Lenin's "testament"—was distributed among the delegates to the 20th Party Congress. You have read it and will undoubtedly read it again more than once. You might reflect on Lenin's plain words, in which expression is given to Vladimir Ilyich's anxiety concerning the party, the people, the state, and the future direction of party policy. . . .

This document of Lenin's was made known to the delegates at the 13th Party Congress, who discussed the question of transferring Stalin from the position of Secretary General. The delegates declared themselves in favor of retaining Stalin in this post, hoping that he would heed the critical remarks of Vladimir Ilyich and would be able to overcome the defects which caused Lenin serious anxiety.

Comrades! The Party Congress should become acquainted with two new documents, which confirm Stalin's character as already outlined by Vladimir Ilyich Lenin in his "testament." These documents are a letter from Nadezhda Konstantinovna Krupskaya to [Leo B.] Kamenev, who was at that time head of the Political Bureau, and a personal letter from Vladimir Ilyich Lenin to Stalin.

I will now read these documents:

LEV BORISOVICH! [2]
Because of a short letter which I had written in words dictated to me by Vladimir Ilyich by permission of the doctors, Stalin allowed himself yesterday an unusually rude outburst directed at me. This is not my first day in the party. During all these 30 years I have never heard from any comrade one word of rudeness. The business of the party and of Ilyich are not less dear to me than to Stalin. I need at present the maximum of self-control. What one can and what one cannot discuss with Ilyich I know better than any doctor, because I know what makes him nervous and what does not, in any case I know better than Stalin. I am turning to you and to Grigory [E. Zinoviev] as much closer comrades of V. I. and I beg you to protect me from rude interference with my private life and from vile invectives and threats. I have no doubt as to what will be the unanimous decision of the Control Commission, with which Stalin sees fit to threaten me; however, I have neither the strength nor the time to waste on this foolish quarrel. And I am a living person and my nerves are strained to the utmost.

N. KRUPSKAYA

Nadezhda Konstantinovna wrote this letter on December 23, 1922. After two and a half months, in March 1923, Vladimir Ilyich Lenin sent Stalin the following letter:[3]

[2] This letter has first come to light now. It has never before been mentioned in the literature of this field. It sheds considerable light on Stalin's real relations with Lenin in the last months of the latter's life. It shows that Stalin started baiting Krupskaya, Lenin's wife, immediately after Lenin suffered his second stroke (December 16, 1922) and systematically continued doing so right up to Lenin's death. . . .

[3] The existence of this letter was known from Trotsky's memoirs, but the full text has never previously been available. . . .

To COMRADE STALIN.
COPIES FOR: KAMENEV AND ZINOVIEV.
Dear Comrade Stalin!

You permitted yourself a rude summons of my wife to the telephone and a rude reprimand of her. Despite the fact that she told you that she agreed to forget what was said, nevertheless Zinoviev and Kamenev heard about it from her. I have no intention to forget so easily that which is being done against me, and I need not stress here that I consider as directed against me that which is being done against my wife. I ask you, therefore, that you weigh carefully whether you are agreeable to retracting your words and apologizing or whether you prefer the severance of relations between us.

SINCERELY: LENIN

MARCH 5, 1923

(Commotion in the hall.)

Comrades! I will not comment on these documents. They speak eloquently for themselves. Since Stalin could behave in this manner during Lenin's life, could thus behave toward Nadezhda Konstantinovna Krupskaya —whom the party knows well and values highly as a loyal friend of Lenin and as an active fighter for the cause of the party since its creation—we can easily imagine how Stalin treated other people. These negative characteristics of his developed steadily and during the last years acquired an absolutely insufferable character.

As later events have proven, Lenin's anxiety was justified: In the first period after Lenin's death, Stalin still paid attention to his advice, but later he began to disregard the serious admonitions of Vladimir Ilyich.

When we analyze the practice of Stalin in regard to the direction of the party and of the country, when we pause to consider everything which Stalin perpetrated, we must be convinced that Lenin's fears were justified. The negative characteristics of Stalin, which, in Lenin's time, were only incipient, transformed themselves during the last years into a grave abuse of power by Stalin, which caused untold harm to our party.

We have to consider seriously and analyze correctly this matter in order that we may preclude any possibility of a repetition in any form whatever of what took place during the life of Stalin, who absolutely did not tolerate collegiality in leadership and in work, and who practiced brutal violence, not only toward everything which opposed him, but also toward that which seemed, to his capricious and despotic character, contrary to his concepts.

Stalin acted not through persuasion, explanation and patient cooperation with people, but by imposing his concepts and demanding absolute submission to his opinion. Whoever opposed this concept or tried to prove his viewpoint and the correctness of his position was doomed to removal from the leading collective and to subsequent moral and physical annihilation. This was especially true during the period following the 17th Party Congress, when many prominent party leaders and rank-and-file party workers, honest and dedicated to the cause of Communism, fell victim to Stalin's despotism.

We must affirm that the party had fought a serious fight against the Trotskyites, rightists and bourgeois nationalists, and that it disarmed ideologically all the enemies of Leninism. This ideological fight was carried on successfully, as a result of which the party became strengthened and tempered. Here Stalin played a positive role.

The party led a great political-ideological struggle against those in its own ranks who proposed anti-Leninist theses, who represented a political line hostile to the party and to the cause of socialism. This was a stubborn and a difficult fight but a necessary one, because the political line of both the Trotskyite-Zinovievite bloc and of the Bukharinites led actually toward the restoration of capitalism and capitulation to the world bourgeoisie. Let us consider for a moment what would have happened if in 1928-1929 the political line of right deviation had prevailed among us, or orientation toward "cotton-dress industrialization," or toward the kulak, etc. We would not now have a powerful heavy industry, we would not have the *kolkhozes*, we would find ourselves disarmed and weak in a capitalist encirclement.

It was for this reason that the party led an inexorable ideological fight and explained to all party members and to the non-party masses the harm and the danger of the anti-Leninist proposals of the Trotskyite opposition and the rightist opportunists. And this great work of explaining the party line bore fruit; both the Trotskyites and the rightist opportunists were politically isolated; the overwhelming party majority supported the Leninist line and the party was able to awaken and organize the working masses to apply the Leninist party line and to build socialism.

Worth noting is the fact that, even during the progress of the furious ideological fight against the Trotskyites, the Zinovievites, the Bukharinites and others, extreme repressive measures were not used against them. The fight was on ideological grounds. But some years later, when socialism in our country was fundamentally constructed, when the exploiting classes were generally liquidated, when the Soviet social structure had radically changed, when the social basis for political movements and groups hostile to the party had violently contracted, when the ideological opponents of the party were long since defeated politically—then the repression directed against them began.

It was precisely during this period (1935-1937-1938) that the practice of mass repression through the Government apparatus was born, first against the enemies of Leninism—Trotskyites, Zinovievites, Bukharinites, long since politically defeated by the party—and subsequently also against many honest Communists, against those party cadres who had borne the heavy load of the Civil War and the first and most difficult years of industrialization and collectivization, who actively fought against the Trotskyites and the rightists for the Leninist party line.

Stalin originated the concept "enemy of the people." This term automatically rendered it unnecessary that the ideological errors of a man or men engaged in a controversy be proven; this term made possible the usage of the most cruel repression, violating all norms of revolutionary legality, against anyone who in any way disagreed with Stalin, against those who were only suspected of hostile intent, against those who had bad reputations. This concept "enemy of the people" actually eliminated the possibility of any kind of ideological fight or the making of one's views known on this or that issue, even those of a practical character. In the main, and in actuality, the only proof of guilt used, against all norms of current legal science, was the "confession" of the accused himself; and, as subsequent probing proved, "confessions" were acquired through physical pressures against the accused. This led to glaring violations of revolutionary legality and to the fact that many entirely innocent persons, who in the past had defended the party line, became victims.

We must assert that, in regard to those persons who in their time had opposed the party line, there were often no sufficiently serious reasons for their physical annihilation. The formula "enemy of the people" was specifically introduced for the purpose of physically annihilating such individuals.

It is a fact that many persons who were later annihilated as enemies of the party and people had worked with Lenin during his life. Some of these persons had made errors during Lenin's life, but, despite this, Lenin benefited by their work; he corrected them and he did everything possible to retain them in the ranks of the party; he induced them to follow him.

In this connection the delegates to the Party Congress should familiarize themselves with an unpublished note by V. I. Lenin directed to the Central Committee's Political Bureau in October 1920. Outlining the duties of the Control Commission, Lenin wrote that the commission should be transformed into a real "organ of party and proletarian conscience."

As a special duty of the Control Commission there is recommended a deep, individualized relationship with, and sometimes even a type of therapy for, the representatives of the so-called opposition—those who have experienced a psychological crisis because of failure in their Soviet or party career. An effort should be made to quiet them, to explain the matter to them in a way used among comrades, to find for them (avoiding the method of issuing orders) a task for which they are psychologically fitted. Advice and rules relating to this matter are to be formulated by the Central Committee's Organizational Bureau, etc. . . .

An entirely different relationship with people characterized Stalin. Lenin's traits—patient work with people, stubborn and painstaking education of them, the ability to induce people to follow him without using compulsion, but rather through the ideological influence on them of the whole collective—were entirely foreign to Stalin. He discarded the Leninist method of convincing and educating, he abandoned the method of ideological struggle for that of administrative violence, mass repressions and terror. He acted on an increasingly larger scale and more stubbornly through punitive organs, at the same time often violating all existing norms of morality and of Soviet laws.

Arbitrary behavior by one person encouraged and permitted arbitrariness in others. Mass arrests and deportations of many thousands of people, execution without trial and without normal investigation created conditions of insecurity, fear and even desperation.

This, of course, did not contribute toward unity of the party ranks and of all strata of working people, but, on the contrary, brought about annihilation and the expulsion from the party of workers who were loyal but inconvenient to Stalin.

Our party fought for the implementation of Lenin's plans for the construction of socialism. This was an ideological fight. Had Leninist principles been observed during the course of this fight, had the party's devotion to principles been skillfully combined with a keen and solicitous concern for people, had they not been repelled and wasted but rather drawn to our side, we certainly would not have had such a brutal violation of revolutionary legality and many thousands of people would not have fallen victim to the method of terror. Extraordinary methods would then have been resorted to only against those people who had in fact committed criminal acts against the Soviet system.

Let us recall some historical facts.

In the days before the October Revolution, two members of the Central Committee of the Bolshevik party—Kamenev and Zinoviev—declared themselves against Lenin's plan for an armed uprising.[4] In addition, on October 18 they published in the Menshevik newspaper, *Novaya Zhizn,* a statement declaring that the Bolsheviks were making preparations for an uprising and that they considered it adventuristic. Kamenev and Zinoviev thus disclosed to the enemy the decision of the Central Committee to stage the uprising, and that the uprising had been organized to take place within the very near future.

This was treason against the party and against the Revolution. In this connection, V. I. Lenin wrote: "Kamenev and Zinoviev revealed the decision of the Central Committee of their party on the armed uprising to Rodzyanko[5] and Kerensky[6] . . .." He put before the Central Committee the question of Zinoviev's and Kamenev's expulsion from the party.

However, after the Great Socialist October Revolution, as is known,

[4] Gregory E. Zinoviev (1883-1936) and Leo B. Kamenev (1883-1936), who in 1917 were members of the Party Central Committee, voted at this October 10, 1917 meeting against Lenin's proposal to organize an insurrection. . . .

[5] Mikhail V. Rodzyanko (1859-1924), President of the Third and Fourth Dumas, and a leader in the democratic February Revolution. He played a prominent role in its first days, but later vanished completely from the political scene. Lenin and other Bolsheviks concocted a completely false story that he had inspired behind-the-scenes reactionary forces which influenced the policies of the Provisional Government in 1917.

[6] Alexander F. Kerensky (born 1881) was President of the Provisional Government from July to October 1917.

Zinoviev and Kamenev were given leading positions. Lenin put them in positions in which they carried out most responsible party tasks and participated actively in the work of the leading party and Soviet organs. It is known that Zinoviev and Kamenev committed a number of other serious errors during Lenin's life. In his "testament" Lenin warned that "Zinoviev's and Kamenev's October episode was of course not an accident." But Lenin did not pose the question of their arrest and certainly not their shooting.

Or, let us take the example of the Trotskyites. At present, after a sufficiently long historical period, we can speak about the fight with the Trotskyites with complete calm and can analyze this matter with sufficient objectivity. After all, around Trotsky were people whose origin cannot by any means be traced to bourgeois society. Part of them belonged to the party intelligentsia and a certain part were recruited from among the workers. We can name many individuals who, in their time, joined the Trotskyites; however, these same individuals took an active part in the workers' movement before the Revolution, during the Socialist October Revolution itself, and also in the consolidation of the victory of this greatest of revolutions. Many of them broke with Trotskyism and returned to Leninist positions. Was it necessary to annihilate such people? We are deeply convinced that, had Lenin lived, such an extreme method would not have been used against any of them.

Such are only a few historical facts. But can it be said that Lenin did not decide to use even the most severe means against enemies of the Revolution when this was actually necessary? No; no one can say this. Vladimir Ilyich demanded uncompromising dealings with the enemies of the Revolution and of the working class and when necessary resorted ruthlessly to such methods. You will recall only V. I. Lenin's fight with the Socialist Revolutionary organizers of the anti-Soviet uprising, with the counterrevolutionary kulaks in 1918 and with others, when Lenin without hesitation used the most extreme methods against the enemies. Lenin used such methods, however, only against actual class enemies and not against those who blunder, who err, and whom it was possible to lead through ideological influence and even retain in the leadership. Lenin used severe methods only in the most necessary cases, when the exploiting classes were still in existence and were vigorously opposing the Revolution, when the struggle for survival was decidedly assuming the sharpest forms, even including a civil war.

Stalin, on the other hand, used extreme methods and mass repressions at a time when the Revolution was already victorious, when the Soviet state was strengthened, when the exploiting classes were already liquidated and socialist relations were rooted solidly in all phases of national economy, when our party was politically consolidated and had strengthened itself both numerically and ideologically.

It is clear that here Stalin showed in a whole series of cases his intolerance, his brutality and his abuse of power. Instead of proving his political correctness and mobilizing the masses, he often chose the path of repression and physical annihilation, not only against actual enemies, but also against individuals who had not committed any crimes against the party and the Soviet Government. Here we see no wisdom but only a demonstration of the brutal force which had once so alarmed V. I. Lenin.

Lately, especially after the unmasking of the Beria gang, the Central Committee looked into a series of matters fabricated by this gang.[7] This revealed a very ugly picture of brutal willfulness connected with the incorrect behavior of Stalin. As facts prove, Stalin, using his unlimited power, allowed himself many abuses, acting in the name of the Central Committee, not asking for the opinion of the Committee members nor even of the members of the Central Committee's Political Bureau; often he did not inform them about his personal decisions concerning very important party and government matters.

Considering the question of the cult of an individual, we must first of all show everyone what harm this caused to the interests of our party. Vladimir Ilyich Lenin had always stressed the party's role and significance in the direction of the socialist government of workers and peasants; he saw in this the chief precondition for a successful building of socialism in our country. Pointing to the great responsibility of the Bolshevik party, as ruling party of the Soviet state, Lenin called for the most meticulous observance of all norms of party life; he called for the realization of the principles of collegiality in the direction of the party and the state.

Collegiality of leadership flows from the very nature of our party, a party built on the principles of democratic centralism. "This means," said Lenin, "that all party matters are accomplished by all party members—directly or through representatives—who, without any exceptions, are subject to the same rules; in addition, all administrative members, all directing collegia, all holders of party positions are elective, they must account for their activities and are recallable."

It is known that Lenin himself offered an example of the most careful observance of these principles. There was no matter so important that Lenin himself decided it without asking for advice and approval of the majority of the Central Committee members or of the members of the Central Committee's Political Bureau. In the most difficult period for our

---

[7] This statement by Khrushchev is not quite true: Investigation of Stalin's terrorist acts in the last period of his life was initiated by Beria. On April 4, 1953, Beria announced the release of all those arrested in the so-called "doctors' plot" and the commitment for trial of those who fabricated it, led by Deputy Minister of State Security Ryumin, who was accused of torturing the prisoners (the first time such an accusation had been made openly against functionaries of the MGB). Khrushchev, who now depicts himself as having well-nigh initiated the probe of Stalin's torture chambers, actually tried to block it in the first months after Stalin's death.

party and our country, Lenin considered it necessary regularly to convoke congresses, party conferences and plenary sessions of the Central Committee at which all the most important questions were discussed and where resolutions, carefully worked out by the collective of leaders, were approved.

We can recall, for an example, the year 1918 when the country was threatened by the attack of the imperialistic interventionists. In this situation the 7th Party Congress was convened in order to discuss a vitally important matter which could not be postponed—the matter of peace. In 1919, while the civil war was raging, the 8th Party Congress convened which adopted a new party program, decided such important matters as the relationship with the peasant masses, the organization of the Red Army, the leading role of the party in the work of the soviets, the correction of the social composition of the party, and other matters. In 1920 the 9th Party Congress was convened which laid down guiding principles pertaining to the party's work in the sphere of economic construction. In 1921 the 10th Party Congress accepted Lenin's New Economic Policy and the historical resolution called "About Party Unity."

During Lenin's life, party congresses were convened regularly; always, when a radical turn in the development of the party and the country took place, Lenin considered it absolutely necessary that the party discuss at length all the basic matters pertaining to internal and foreign policy and to questions bearing on the development of party and government.

It is very characteristic that Lenin addressed to the Party Congress as the highest party organ his last articles, letters and remarks.[8] During the period between congresses, the Central Committee of the party, acting as the most authoritative leading collective, meticulously observed the principles of the party and carried out its policy. So it was during Lenin's life. Were our party's holy Leninist principles observed after the death of Vladimir Ilyich?

Whereas, during the first few years after Lenin's death, party congresses and Central Committee plenums took place more or less regularly, later, when Stalin began increasingly to abuse his power, these principles were brutally violated. This was especially evident during the last 15 years of his life. Was it a normal situation when over 13 years elapsed between the 18th and 19th Party Congresses, years during which our party and our country had experienced so many important events? These events demanded categorically that the party should have passed resolutions pertaining to the country's defense during the Patriotic War [World War II] and to peacetime construction after the war. Even after the end of the war a Congress was not convened for over seven years. Central Committee

---

[8] It was, of course, very characteristic of Lenin that he addressed his last articles, letters and notes to the Congress; but it is even more characteristic of the methods employed by the Communist dictatorship that these documents are still unpublished today under Khrushchev.

plenums were hardly ever called. It should be sufficient to mention that during all the years of the Patriotic War not a single Central Committee plenum took place. It is true that there was an attempt to call a Central Committee plenum in October 1941, when Central Committee members from the whole country were called to Moscow. They waited two days for the opening of the plenum, but in vain. Stalin did not even want to meet and talk to the Central Committee members. This fact shows how demoralized Stalin was in the first months of the war and how haughtily and disdainfully he treated the Central Committee members.

In practice, Stalin ignored the norms of party life and trampled on the Leninist principle of collective party leadership. Stalin's willfulness *vis-à-vis* the party and its Central Committee became fully evident after the 17th Party Congress which took place in 1934.

Having at its disposal numerous data showing brutal willfulness toward party cadres, the Central Committee has created a party commission under the control of the Central Committee Presidium; it was charged with investigating what made possible the mass repressions against the majority of the Central Committee members and candidates elected at the 17th Congress of the All-Union Communist Party (Bolsheviks).

The commission has become acquainted with a large quantity of materials in the NKVD archives and with other documents and has established many facts pertaining to the fabrication of cases against Communists, to false accusations, to glaring abuses of socialist legality, which resulted in the death of innocent people. It became apparent that many party, Soviet and economic activists, who were branded in 1937-1938 as "enemies," were actually never enemies, spies, wreckers, etc., but were always honest Communists; they were only so stigmatized and, often, no longer able to bear barbaric tortures, they charged themselves (at the order of the investigative judges—falsifiers) with all kinds of grave and unlikely crimes.

The commission has presented to the Central Committee Presidium lengthy and documented materials pertaining to mass repressions against the delegates to the 17th Party Congress and against members of the Central Committee elected at that Congress. These materials have been studied by the Presidium of the Central Committee.

It was determined that of the 139 members and candidates of the party's Central Committee who were elected at the 17th Congress, 98 persons, *i.e.,* 70 per cent, were arrested and shot (mostly in 1937-1938). (Indignation in the hall.) What was the composition of the delegates to the 17th Congress? It is known that 80 per cent of the voting participants of the 17th Congress joined the party during the years of conspiracy before the Revolution and during the civil war; this means before 1921. By social origin the basic mass of the delegates to the Congress were workers (60 per cent of the voting members).

For this reason, it was inconceivable that a congress so composed would have elected a Central Committee a majority of whom would prove to be enemies of the party. The only reason why 70 per cent of Central Committee members and candidates elected at the 17th Congress were branded as enemies of the party and of the people was because honest Communists were slandered, accusations against them were fabricated, and revolutionary legality was gravely undermined.

The same fate met not only the Central Committee members but also the majority of the delegates to the 17th Party Congress. Of 1,966 delegates with either voting or advisory rights, 1,108 persons were arrested on charges of anti-revolutionary crimes, *i.e.*, decidedly more than a majority. This very fact shows how absurd, wild and contrary to common sense were the charges of counterrevolutionary crimes made out, as we now see, against a majority of participants at the 17th Party Congress. (Indignation in the hall.)

We should recall that the 17th Party Congress is historically known as the Congress of Victors. Delegates to the Congress were active participants in the building of our socialist state; many of them suffered and fought for party interests during the pre-Revolutionary years in the conspiracy and at the civil-war fronts; they fought their enemies valiantly and often nervelessly looked into the face of death.

How, then, can we believe that such people could prove to be "two-faced" and had joined the camps of the enemies of socialism during the era after the political liquidation of Zinovievites, Trotskyites and rightists and after the great accomplishments of socialist construction? This was the result of the abuse of power by Stalin, who began to use mass terror against the party cadres.

What is the reason that mass repressions against activists increased more and more after the 17th Party Congress? It was because at that time Stalin had so elevated himself above the party and above the nation that he ceased to consider either the Central Committee or the party.

While he still reckoned with the opinion of the collective before the 17th Congress, after the complete political liquidation of the Trotskyites, Zinovievites and Bukharinites, when as a result of that fight and socialist victories the party achieved unity, Stalin ceased to an ever greater degree to consider the members of the party's Central Committee and even the members of the Political Bureau. Stalin thought that now he could decide all things alone and all he needed were statisticians; he treated all others in such a way that they could only listen to and praise him.

After the criminal murder of Sergei M. Kirov, mass repressions and brutal acts of violation of socialist legality began. On the evening of December 1, 1934 on Stalin's initiative (without the approval of the Political Bureau—which was passed two days later, casually), the Secretary of the Presidium of the Central Executive Committee, Yenukidze, signed the following directive:

1. Investigative agencies are directed to speed up the cases of those accused of the preparation or execution of acts of terror.

2. Judicial organs are directed not to hold up the execution of death sentences pertaining to crimes of this category in order to consider the possibility of pardon, because the Presidium of the Central Executive Committee of the U.S.S.R. does not consider as possible the receiving of petitions of this sort.

3. The organs of the Commissariat of Internal Affairs are directed to execute the death sentences against criminals of the above-mentioned category immediately after the passage of sentences.

This directive became the basis for mass acts of abuse against socialist legality. During many of the fabricated court cases, the accused were charged with "the preparation" of terroristic acts; this deprived them of any possibility that their cases might be re-examined, even when they stated before the court that their "confessions" were secured by force, and when, in a convincing manner, they disproved the accusations against them.

It must be asserted that to this day the circumstances surrounding Kirov's murder hide many things which are inexplicable and mysterious and demand a most careful examination. There are reasons for the suspicion that the killer of Kirov, Nikolayev, was assisted by someone from among the people whose duty it was to protect the person of Kirov.

A month and a half before the killing, Nikolayev was arrested on the grounds of suspicious behavior but he was released and not even searched. It is an unusually suspicious circumstance that when the Chekist assigned to protect Kirov was being brought for an interrogation, on December 2, 1934, he was killed in a car "accident" in which no other occupants of the car were harmed.[9] After the murder of Kirov, top functionaries of the Leningrad NKVD were given very light sentences, but in 1937 they were shot. We can assume that they were shot in order to cover the traces of the organizers of Kirov's killing. (Movement in the hall.)

Mass repressions grew tremendously from the end of 1936 after a telegram from Stalin and [Andrei] Zhdanov, dated from Sochi on September 25, 1936, was addressed to Kaganovich, Molotov and other members of the Political Bureau. The content of the telegram was as follows:

We deem it absolutely necessary and urgent that Comrade Yezhov be nominated to the post of People's Commissar for Internal Affairs. Yagoda has definitely proved himself to be incapable of unmasking the Trotskyite-Zinovievite bloc. The OGPU is four years behind in this matter. This is noted by all party workers and by the majority of the representatives of the NKVD.[10]

[9] Kirov did not permit a secret-police guard to be maintained around him, but he had in his office in Leningrad's Smolny Institute an elderly man named Borisov who acted more or less as his orderly. This Borisov would have been a most inconvenient eye-witness for the organizers of the murder. On December 2, he was called to the Leningrad NKVD to receive orders; on the way, he was killed in an auto crash in which no one else was injured. This mysterious episode was noted in a number of accounts of the Kirov murder; Khrushchev's report provides further confirmation.

[10] This telegram is an exceptionally important document, showing that Stalin felt that mass repressions within the Communist party were four years overdue—that is, they

Strictly speaking, we should stress that Stalin did not meet with and, therefore, could not know the opinion of party workers.

This Stalinist formulation that the "NKVD is four years behind" in applying mass repression and that there is a necessity for "catching up" with the neglected work directly pushed the NKVD workers on the path of mass arrests and executions.

We should state that this formulation was also forced on the February-March plenary session of the Central Committee of the All-Union Communist Party (Bolsheviks) in 1937. The plenary resolution approved it on the basis of Yezhov's report, "Lessons flowing from the harmful activity, diversion and espionage of the Japanese-German-Trotskyite agents," stating:

> The plenum of the Central Committee of the All-Union Communist Party (Bolsheviks) considers that all facts revealed during the investigation into the matter of an anti-Soviet Trotskyite center and of its followers in the provinces show that the People's Commissariat of Internal Affairs has fallen behind at least four years in the attempt to unmask these most inexorable enemies of the people.

The mass repressions at this time were made under the slogan of a fight against the Trotskyites. Did the Trotskyites at this time actually constitute such a danger to our party and to the Soviet state? We should recall that in 1927, on the eve of the 15th Party Congress, only some 4,000 votes were cast for the Trotskyite-Zinovievite opposition while there were 724,000 for the party line. During the 10 years which passed between the 15th Party Congress and the February-March Central Committee plenum, Trotskyism was completely disarmed; many former Trotskyites had changed their former views and worked in the various sectors building socialism. It is clear that in the situation of socialist victory there was no basis for mass terror in the country.

Stalin's report at the February-March Central Committee plenum in 1937, "Deficiencies of party work and methods for the liquidation of the Trotskyites and of other two-facers," contained an attempt at theoretical justification of the mass terror policy under the pretext that as we march forward toward socialism class war must allegedly sharpen. Stalin asserted that both history and Lenin taught him this.

Actually Lenin taught that the application of revolutionary violence is necessitated by the resistance of the exploiting classes, and this referred to the era when the exploiting classes existed and were powerful. . . .

Stalin deviated from these clear and plain precepts of Lenin. Stalin put the party and the NKVD up to the use of mass terror when the exploiting classes had been liquidated in our country and when there were no serious reasons for the use of extraordinary mass terror.

---

should have begun in 1932, when Stalin first demanded execution of members of the opposition group headed by Ryutin, Gorelov and others but was defeated both in the Politburo and at the Central Committee plenum which met from September 28 to October 2, 1932. On Stalin's demand, Henry Yagoda was removed from the post of People's Commissar for Internal Affairs and, on September 26, 1936, replaced by Nikolai I. Yezhov.

This terror was actually directed not at the remnants of the defeated exploiting classes but against the honest workers of the party and of the Soviet state; against them were made lying, slanderous and absurd accusations concerning "two-facedness," "espionage," "sabotage," preparation of fictitious "plots," etc.

At the February-March Central Committee plenum in 1937 many members actually questioned the rightness of the established course regarding mass repression under the pretext of combating "two-facedness." . . .

Using Stalin's formulation, namely, that the closer we are to socalism the more enemies we will have, and using the resolution of the February-March Central Committee plenum passed on the basis of Yezhov's report, the *provocateurs* who had infiltrated the state-security organs together with conscienceless careerists began to protect with the party name the mass terror against party cadres, cadres of the Soviet state and the ordinary Soviet citizens. It should suffice to say that the number of arrests based on charges of counterrevolutionary crimes had grown ten times between 1936 and 1937.

It is known that brutal willfulness was practiced against leading party workers. The party statute, approved at the 17th Party Congress, was based on Leninist principles expressed at the 10th Party Congress. It stated that, in order to apply an extreme method such as exclusion from the party against a Central Committee member, against a Central Committee candidate and against a member of the Party Control Commission, "it is necessary to call a Central Committee plenum and to invite to the plenum all Central Committee candidate members and all members of the Party Control Commission"; only if two-thirds of the members of such a general assembly of responsible party leaders find it necessary, only then can a Central Committee member or candidate be expelled.

The majority of the Central Committee members and candidates elected at the 17th Congress and arrested in 1937-1938 were expelled from the party illegally through the brutal abuse of the party statute, because the question of their expulsion was never studied at the Central Committee plenum.

Now, when the cases of some of these so-called "spies" and "saboteurs" were examined, it was found that all their cases were fabricated. Confessions of guilt of many arrested and charged with enemy activity were gained with the help of cruel and inhuman tortures.

At the same time, Stalin, as we have been informed by members of the Political Bureau of that time, did not show them the statements of many accused political activists when they retracted their confessions before the military tribunal and asked for an objective examination of their cases. There were many such declarations, and Stalin doubtless knew of them.

The Central Committee considers it absolutely necessary to inform the Congress of many such fabricated "cases" against the members of the party's Central Committee elected at the 17th Party Congress.

An example of vile provocation, of odious falsification and of criminal violation of revolutionary legality is the case of the former candidate for the Central Committee Political Bureau, one of the most eminent workers of the party and of the Soviet Government, Comrade Eikhe who was a party member since 1905. (Commotion in the hall.)

Comrade Eikhe was arrested on April 29, 1938 on the basis of slanderous materials, without the sanction of the Prosecutor of the U.S.S.R., which was finally received 15 months after the arrest.

Investigation of Eikhe's case was made in a manner which most brutally violated Soviet legality and was accompanied by willfulness and falsification.

Eikhe was forced under torture to sign ahead of time a protocol of his confession prepared by the investigative judges, in which he and several other eminent party workers were accused of anti-Soviet activity.

On October 1, 1939 Eikhe sent his declaration to Stalin in which he categorically denied his guilt and asked for an examination of his case. In the declaration he wrote: "There is no more bitter misery than to sit in the jail of a government for which I have always fought."

A second declaration of Eikhe has been preserved which he sent to Stalin on October 27, 1939; in it he cited facts very convincingly and countered the slanderous accusations made against him, arguing that this provocatory accusation was on the one hand the work of real Trotskyites whose arrests he had sanctioned as First Secretary of the West Siberian Krai [Territory] Party Committee and who conspired in order to take revenge on him, and, on the other hand, the result of the base falsification of materials by the investigative judges.

Eikhe wrote in his declaration:

. . . I am now alluding to the most disgraceful part of my life and to my really grave guilt against the party and against you. This is my confession of counterrevolutionary activity. . . . The case is as follows: Not being able to suffer the tortures to which I was submitted by Ushakov and Nikolayev—and especially by the first one—who utilized the knowledge that my broken ribs have not properly mended and have caused me great pain, I have been forced to accuse myself and others.

The majority of my confession has been suggested or dictated by Ushakov, and the remainder is my reconstruction of NKVD materials from Western Siberia for which I assumed all responsibility. If some part of the story which Ushakov fabricated and which I signed did not properly hang together, I was forced to sign another variation. . . .

It would appear that such an important declaration was worth an examination by the Central Committee. This, however, was not done, and the declaration was transmitted to Beria while the terrible maltreatment of the Political Bureau candidate, Comrade Eikhe, continued.

On February 2, 1940 Eikhe was brought before the court. Here he did not confess any guilt and said as follows:

In all the so-called confessions of mine there is not one letter written by me with the exception of my signatures under the protocols, which were forced from me. I have made my confession under pressure from the investigative judge, who from the time of my arrest tormented me. After that I began to write all this nonsense. . . . The most important thing for me is to tell the court, the party and Stalin that I am not guilty. I have never been guilty of any conspiracy. I will die believing in the truth of party policy as I have believed in it during my whole life.

On February 4 Eikhe was shot. (Indignation in the hall.)

It has been definitely established now that Eikhe's case was fabricated; he has been posthumously rehabilitated.

Comrade Rudzutak, candidate-member of the Political Bureau, member of the party since 1905, who spent 10 years in a Tsarist hard-labor camp, completely retracted in court the confession which was forced from him. The protocol of the session of the Collegium of the Supreme Military Court contains the following statement by Rudzutak:

. . . The only plea which he places before the court is that the Central Committee of the All-Union Communist Party (Bolsheviks) be informed that there is in the NKVD an as yet not liquidated center which is craftily manufacturing cases, which forces innocent persons to confess; there is no opportunity to prove one's non-participation in crimes to which the confessions of various persons testify. . . .

He was not even called before the Central Committee's Political Bureau because Stalin did not want to talk to him. Sentence was pronounced on him in 20 minutes and he was shot. (Indignation in the hall.)

After careful examination of the case in 1955, it was established that the accusation against Rudzutak was false and that it was based on slanderous materials. Rudzutak has been rehabilitated posthumously.

The way in which the former NKVD workers manufactured various fictitious "anti-Soviet centers" and "blocs" with the help of provocatory methods is seen from the confession of Comrade Rozenblum, party member since 1906, who was arrested in 1937 by the Leningrad NKVD.

During the examination in 1955 of the Komarov case Rozenblum revealed the following fact: When Rozenblum was arrested in 1937, he was subjected to terrible torture during which he was ordered to confess false information concerning himself and other persons. He was then brought to the office of Zakovsky,[11] who offered him freedom on condition that he make before the court a false confession fabricated in 1937 by the NKVD concerning "sabotage, espionage and diversion in a terroristic center in Leningrad." (Movement in the hall.) With unbelievable cynicism, Zakovsky told about the vile "mechanism" for the crafty creation of fabricated "anti-Soviet plots."

[11] Leonid Zakovsky, one of the most prominent figures in the *Yezhovshchina,* was chief first of the Leningrad section (1934-38) and then of the Moscow section of the NKVD. He was notorious for his merciless employment of torture followed by execution. After Yezhov's removal and Beria's rise to power, Zakovsky was arrested and disappeared.

"In order to illustrate it to me," stated Rozenblum, "Zakovsky gave me several possible variants of the organization of this center and of its branches." . . . Said Zakovsky:

You, yourself, will not need to invent anything. The NKVD will prepare for you a ready outline for every branch of the center; you will have to study it carefully and to remember well all questions and answers which the Court might ask. This case will be ready in four-five months, or perhaps a half year. During all this time you will be preparing yourself so that you will not compromise the investigation and yourself. Your future will depend on how the trial goes and on its results. If you begin to lie and to testify falsely, blame yourself. If you manage to endure it, you will save your head and we will feed and clothe you at the Government's cost until your death.

This is the kind of vile things which were then practiced. (Movement in the hall.) . . .

Many thousands of honest and innocent Communists have died as a result of this monstrous falsification of such "cases," as a result of the fact that all kinds of slanderous "confessions" were accepted, and as a result of the practice of forcing accusations against oneself and others. . . . In those years repressions on a mass scale were applied which were based on nothing tangible and which resulted in heavy cadre losses to the party.

The vicious practice was condoned of having the NKVD prepare lists of persons whose cases were under the jurisdiction of the Military Collegium and whose sentences were prepared in advance. Yezhov would send these lists to Stalin personally for his approval of the proposed punishment. In 1937-1938, 383 such lists containing the names of many thousands of party, Soviet, Komsomol, Army and economic workers were sent to Stalin. He approved these lists.

A large part of these cases are being reviewed now and a great part of them are being voided because they were baseless and falsified. Suffice it to say that from 1954 to the present time the Military Collegium of the Supreme Court has rehabilitated 7,679 persons, many of whom were rehabilitated posthumously.

Mass arrests of party, Soviet, economic and military workers caused tremendous harm to our country and to the cause of socialist advancement. Mass repressions had a negative influence on the moral-political condition of the party, created a situation of uncertainty, contributed to the spreading of unhealthy suspicion, and sowed distrust among Communists. All sorts of slanderers and careerists were active.

Resolutions of the January plenum of the Central Committee, All-Union Communist Party (Bolsheviks), in 1938 had brought some measure of improvement to the party organizations. However, widespread repression also existed in 1938.[12] . . .

[12] Khrushchev gives a completely incorrect appraisal of the decisions adopted by the January 1938 Central Committee plenum. The published version of one resolution did contain criticism of several incorrect expulsions from the Party, but the criticism was

Facts prove that many abuses were made on Stalin's orders without reckoning with any norms of party and Soviet legality. Stalin was a very distrustful man, sickly suspicious; we know this from our work with him. He could look at a man and say: "Why are your eyes so shifty today?" or "Why are you turning so much today and avoiding to look me directly in the eyes?" The sickly suspicion created in him a general distrust even toward eminent party workers whom he had known for years. Everywhere and in everything he saw "enemies," "two-facers" and "spies." Possessing unlimited power, he indulged in great willfulness and choked a person morally and physically. A situation was created where one could not express one's own will.

When Stalin said that one or another should be arrested, it was necessary to accept on faith that he was an "enemy of the people." Meanwhile, Beria's gang, which ran the organs of state security, outdid itself in proving the guilt of the arrested and the truth of materials which it falsified. And what proofs were offered? The confessions of the arrested, and the investigative judges accepted these "confessions." And how is it possible that a person confesses to crimes which he has not committed? Only in one way —because of application of physical methods of pressuring him, tortures, bringing him to a state of unconsciousness, deprivation of his judgment, taking away of his human dignity. In this manner were "confessions" acquired.

When the wave of mass arrests began to recede in 1939, and the leaders of territorial party organizations began to accuse the NKVD workers of using methods of physical pressure on the arrested, Stalin dispatched a coded telegram on January 20, 1939 to the committee secretaries of *oblasts* and *krais,* to the central committees of republic Communist parties, to the People's Commissars of Internal Affairs and to the heads of NKVD organizations. This telegram stated:

The Central Committee of the All-Union Communist Party (Bolsheviks) explains that the application of methods of physical pressure in NKVD practice is permissible from 1937 on in accordance with permission of the Central Committee of the All-Union Communist Party (Bolsheviks) . . . It is known that all bourgeois intelligence services use methods of physical influence against the representatives of the socialist proletariat and that they use them in their most scandalous forms.

The question arises as to why the socialist intelligence service should be more humanitarian against the mad agents of the bourgeoisie, against the deadly enemies of the working class and of the *kolkhoz* workers. The Central Committee of the All-Union Communist Party (Bolsheviks) considers that physical pressure should still be used obligatorily, as an exception applicable to known and obstinate enemies of the people, as a method both justifiable and appropriate.

curious: The plenum found that Party organizations had been guilty of expelling people on false denunciations "by masked two-facers," but that the NKVD organs led by Yezhov had exposed these criminal attempts and, after rehabilitating the innocent victims, punished the culprits. In other words, this was a resolution which praised the Yezhov purge. Khrushchev had to falsify his account because it was at this plenum that he himself was first elected a candidate member of the Politburo.

Thus, Stalin had sanctioned in the name of the Central Committee of the All-Union Communist Party (Bolsheviks) the most brutal violation of socialist legality, torture and oppression, which led as we have seen to the slandering and self-accusation of innocent people. . . .

The power accumulated in the hands of one person, Stalin, led to serious consequences during the Great Patriotic War.

When we look at many of our novels, films and historical "scientific studies," the role of Stalin in the Patriotic War appears to be entirely improbable. Stalin had foreseen everything. The Soviet Army, on the basis of a strategic plan prepared by Stalin long before, used the tactics of so-called "active defense," *i.e.,* tactics which, as we know, allowed the Germans to come up to Moscow and Stalingrad. Using such tactics, the Soviet Army, supposedly thanks only to Stalin's genius, turned to the offensive and subdued the enemy. The epic victory gained through the armed might of the land of the Soviets, through our heroic people, is ascribed in this type of novel, film and "scientific study" as being completely due to the strategic genius of Stalin. . . . What are the facts of this matter?

[Editor's note: Khrushchev proceeds to show that Stalin ignored repeated warnings of impending German attack and adds that "despite these particularly grave warnings, the necessary steps were not taken to prepare the country properly for defense and to prevent it from being caught unawares."]

The result was that already in the first hours and days the enemy had destroyed in our border regions a large part of our Air Force, artillery and other military equipment; he annihilated large numbers of our military cadres and disorganized our military leadership; consequently we could not prevent the enemy from marching deep into the country.

Very grievous consequences, especially in reference to the beginning of the war, followed Stalin's annihilation of many military commanders and political workers during 1937-1941 because of his suspiciousness and through slanderous accusations.[13] During these years repressions were instituted against certain parts of military cadres beginning literally at the company and battalion commander level and extending to the higher military centers; during this time the cadre of leaders who had gained military experience in Spain and in the Far East was almost completely liquidated.

The policy of large-scale repression against the military cadres led also to undermined military discipline, because for several years officers of all

---

[13] We now know from revelations by former members of the German secret police that Stalin wiped out a vast part of the command personnel of the Red Army on the basis of false documents which Stalin's personal secretariat had received from Nazi agents. The false documents on the basis of which Marshal Tukhachevsky and his closest colleagues were executed were turned over by Nazi agents to L. Z. Mekhlis, a trusted member of Stalin's personnel secretariat, who flew to Berlin for that purpose in May 1937.

ranks and even soldiers in the party and Komsomol cells were taught to
"unmask" their superiors as hidden enemies. (Movement in the hall.) It
is natural that this caused a negative influence on the state of military discipline in the first war period.

And, as you know, we had before the war excellent military cadres
which were unquestionably loyal to the party and to the Fatherland. Suffice
it to say that those of them who managed to survive, despite severe tortures
to which they were subjected in the prisons, have from the first war days
shown themselves real patriots and heroically fought for the glory of the
Fatherland; I have here in mind such comrades as Rokossovsky (who, as
you know, had been jailed), Gorbatov, Meretskov (who is a delegate at
the present Congress),[14] Podlas (he was an excellent commander who perished at the front), and many, many others. However, many such commanders perished in camps and jails and the Army saw them no more.

All this brought about the situation which existed at the beginning of
the war and which was the great threat to our Fatherland. It would be incorrect to forget that, after the first severe disaster and defeat at the front,
Stalin thought that this was the end. In one of his speeches in those days he
said: "All that which Lenin created we have lost forever."

After this Stalin for a long time actually did not direct the military
operations and ceased to do anything whatever. He returned to active
leadership only when some members of the Political Bureau visited him
and told him that it was necessary to take certain steps immediately in
order to improve the situation at the front.

Therefore, the threatening danger which hung over our Fatherland
in the first period of the war was largely due to the faulty methods of
directing the nation and the party by Stalin himself.

However, we speak not only about the moment when the war began,
which led to serious disorganization of our Army and brought us severe
losses. Even after the war began, the nervousness and hysteria which Stalin
demonstrated, interfering with actual military operation, caused our Army
serious damage.

Stalin was very far from an understanding of the real situation which
was developing at the front. This was natural because, during the whole
Patriotic War, he never visited any section of the front or any liberated
city except for one short ride on the Mozhaisk highway during a stabilized
situation at the front. To this incident were dedicated many literary works
full of fantasies of all sorts and so many paintings. . . .

[14] Marshal Konstantin K. Rokossovsky, [formerly] Poland's Defense Minister, was arrested in 1937 in Leningrad, where he was a corps commander. He was repeatedly subjected to brutal beatings in the course of interrogation and then sent to a concentration
camp, from which he was released shortly before the outbreak of war in 1941. The same
fate overtook the other military commanders mentioned by Khrushchev: Colonel-General
Alexander V. Gorbatov, now commander of the Baltic Military District; Marshal Kirill
A. Meretskov, now commander of the Northern Military District, and many others.

The tactics on which Stalin insisted without knowing the essence of the conduct of battle operations cost us much blood until we succeeded in stopping the opponent and going over to the offensive.

The military know that already by the end of 1941, instead of great operational maneuvers flanking the opponent and penetrating behind his back, Stalin demanded incessant frontal attacks and the capture of one village after another.

Because of this, we paid with great losses—until our generals, on whose shoulders rested the whole weight of conducting the war, succeeded in changing the situation and shifting to flexible-maneuver operations, which immediately brought serious changes at the front favorable to us.

All the more shameful was the fact that, after our great victory over the enemy which cost us so much, Stalin began to downgrade many of the commanders who contributed so much to the victory over the enemy, because Stalin excluded every possibility that services rendered at the front should be credited to anyone but himself.

Stalin was very much interested in the assessment of Comrade Zhukov as a military leader. He asked me often for my opinion of Zhukov. I told him then, "I have known Zhukov for a long time; he is a good general and a good military leader."

After the war Stalin began to tell all kinds of nonsense about Zhukov, among others the following, "You praised Zhukov, but he does not deserve it. It is said that before each operation at the front Zhukov used to behave as follows: He used to take a handful of earth, smell it and say, 'We can begin the attack,' or the opposite, 'The planned operation cannot be carried out.'" I stated at that time, "Comrade Stalin, I do not know who invented this, but it is not true." It is possible that Stalin himself invented these things for the purpose of minimizing the role and military talents of Marshal Zhukov.

In this connection, Stalin very energetically popularized himself as a great leader; in various ways he tried to inculcate in the people the version that all victories gained by the Soviet nation during the Great Patriotic War were due to the courage, daring and genius of Stalin and of no one else. . . .

Not Stalin, but the party as a whole, the Soviet Government, our heroic Army, its talented leaders and brave soldiers, the whole Soviet nation—these are the ones who assured the victory in the Great Patriotic War. (Tempestuous and prolonged applause.) . . .

Comrades, let us reach for some other facts. The Soviet Union is justly considered as a model of a multinational state because we have in practice assured the equality and friendship of all nations which live in our great Fatherland.

All the more monstrous are the acts whose initiator was Stalin and which are rude violations of the basic Leninist principles of the nationality policy of the Soviet state. We refer to the mass deportations from their native places of whole nations, together with all Communists and Komsomols without any exception; this deportation action was not dictated by any military considerations.

Thus, already at the end of 1943, when there occurred a permanent break-through at the fronts of the Great Patriotic War benefiting the Soviet Union, a decision was taken and executed concerning the deportation of all the Karachai from the lands on which they lived.

In the same period, at the end of December 1943, the same lot befell the whole population of the Autonomous Kalmyk Republic. In March 1944, all the Chechen and Ingush peoples were deported and the Chechen-Ingush Autonomous Republic was liquidated. In April 1944, all Balkars were deported to faraway places from the territory of the Kabardino-Balkar Autonomous Republic and the Republic itself was renamed the Autonomous Kabardian Republic.[15]

The Ukrainians avoided meeting this fate only because there were too many of them and there was no place to which to deport them. Otherwise, he would have deported them also. (Laughter and animation in the hall.)

Not only a Marxist-Leninist but also no man of common sense can grasp how it is possible to make whole nations responsible for inimical activity, including women, children, old people, Communists and Komsomols, to use mass repression against them, and to expose them to misery and suffering for the hostile acts of individual persons or groups of persons.

After the conclusion of the Patriotic War, the Soviet nation stressed with pride the magnificent victories gained through great sacrifices and tremendous efforts. The country experienced a period of political enthusiasm. The party came out of the war even more united; in the fire of the war, party cadres were tempered and hardened. Under such conditions nobody could have even thought of the possibility of some plot in the party.

And it was precisely at this time that the so-called "Leningrad affair" was born. As we have now proven, this case was fabricated. Those who innocently lost their lives included Comrades Voznesensky, Kuznetsov, Rodionov, Popkov, and others.

As is known, Voznesensky and Kuznetsov were talented and eminent leaders. Once they stood very close to Stalin. It is sufficient to mention that Stalin made Voznesensky first deputy to the chairman of the Council of Ministers and Kuznetsov was elected Secretary of the Central Committee. The very fact that Stalin entrusted Kuznetsov with the supervision of the state-security organs shows the trust which he enjoyed.

How did it happen that these persons were branded as enemies of the people and liquidated?

---

[15] Khrushchev does not mention two Soviet republics liquidated during the war on Stalin's orders whose populations were deported to Siberia and Kazakhstan, *i.e.*, the autonomous Volga German and Crimean Republics.

Facts prove that the "Leningrad affair" is also the result of willfulness which Stalin exercised against party cadres. Had a normal situation existed in the party's Central Committee and in the Central Committee Political Bureau, affairs of this nature would have been examined there in accordance with party practice, and all pertinent facts assessed, as a result, such an affair as well as others would not have happened.

We must state that, after the war, the situation became even more complicated. Stalin became even more capricious, irritable and brutal; in particular his suspicion grew. His persecution mania reached unbelievable dimensions. Many workers were becoming enemies before his very eyes. After the war, Stalin separated himself from the collective even more. Everything was decided by him alone without any consideration for anyone or anything. . . .

The question arises: Why is it that we see the truth of this affair only now, and why did we not do something earlier, during Stalin's life, in order to prevent the loss of innocent lives? It was because Stalin personally supervised the "Leningrad affair," and the majority of the Political Bureau members did not, at that time, know all of the circumstances in these matters and could not therefore intervene. . . .

The willfulness of Stalin showed itself not only in decisions concerning the internal life of the country but also in the international relations of the Soviet Union.

The July plenum of the Central Committee studied in detail the reasons for the development of conflict with Yugoslavia. It was a shameful role which Stalin played here. The "Yugoslav affair" contained no problems which could not have been solved through party discussions among comrades. There was no significant basis for the development of this "affair"; it was completely possible to have prevented the rupture of relations with that country. This does not mean, however, that the Yugoslav leaders did not make mistakes or did not have shortcomings. But these mistakes and shortcomings were magnified in a monstrous manner by Stalin, which resulted in a break of relations with a friendly country.

I recall the first days when the conflict between the Soviet Union and Yugoslavia began artificially to be blown up. Once, when I came from Kiev to Moscow, I was invited to visit Stalin, who, pointing to the copy of a letter lately sent to Tito, asked me, "Have you read this?"

Not waiting for my reply, he answered, "I will shake my little finger—and there will be no more Tito. He will fall. . . ."

Let us also recall the "affair of the doctor-plotters." (Animation in the hall.) Actually there was no "affair" outside of the declaration of the woman doctor Timashuk, who was probably influenced or ordered by someone (after all, she was an unofficial collaborator of the organs of state security) to write Stalin a letter in which she declared that doctors were applying supposedly improper methods of medical treatment.

Such a letter was sufficient for Stalin to reach an immediate conclusion that there are doctor-plotters in the Soviet Union.[16] He issued orders to arrest a group of eminent Soviet medical specialists. He personally issued advice on the conduct of the investigation and the method of interrogation of the arrested persons. He said that the academician Vinogradov should be put in chains, another one should be beaten. Present at this Congress as a delegate is the former Minister of State Security, Comrade Ignatiev. Stalin told him curtly, "If you do not obtain confessions from the doctors we will shorten you by a head." (Tumult in the hall.)

Stalin personally called the investigative judge, gave him instructions, advised him on which investigative methods should be used; these methods were simple—beat, beat and, once again, beat.

Shortly after the doctors were arrested, we members of the Political Bureau received protocols with the doctors' confessions of guilt. After distributing these protocols, Stalin told us, "You are blind like young kittens; what will happen without me? The country will perish because you do not know how to recognize enemies."

The case was so presented that no one could verify the facts on which the investigation was based. There was no possibility of trying to verify facts by contacting those who had made the confessions of guilt. We felt, however, that the case of the arrested doctors was questionable. We knew some of these people personally because they had once treated us. When we examined this "case" after Stalin's death, we found it to be fabricated from beginning to end. . . .

In organizing the various dirty and shameful cases, a very base role was played by the rabid enemy of our party, an agent of a foreign intelligence service—Beria, who had stolen into Stalin's confidence. In what way could this *provocateur* gain such a position in the party and in the state, so as to become the First Deputy Chairman of the Council of Ministers of the Soviet Union and a member of the Central Committee Political Bureau? It has now been established that this villain had climbed up the Government ladder over an untold number of corpses. . . .

The indictment in the Beria case contains a discussion of his crimes. Some things should, however, be recalled, especially since it is possible that not all delegates to the Congress have read this document. I wish to recall Beria's bestial disposition of the cases of Kedrov,[17] Golubev, and Golubev's

[16] The case of the "doctors' plot" was concocted on Stalin's orders in the winter of 1952-53 by the then Minister of State Security, S. D. Ignatiev, and his deputy, Ryumin. Several dozen of the leading doctors in Moscow were arrested, headed by the top specialists of the Kremlin hospital who treated Stalin and all the Soviet chieftains. They were officially charged with using improper medical techniques in order to murder their patients. Specifically, they were accused of having poisoned Andrei A. Zhdanov and Alexander S. Shcherbakov and of attempting to poison Marshals Konev, Vasilevsky, Govorov and others. . . .

[17] Mikhail S. Kedrov (1878-1940), a Bolshevik since the early 1900s, was in 1907-08 director of the legal Bolshevik publishing house in St. Petersburg, which published among other works the first collection of Lenin's political articles, *During Twelve Years.* . . .

adopted mother, Baturina—persons who wished to inform the Central Committee concerning Beria's treacherous activity. They were shot without any trial and the sentence was passed *ex post facto,* after the execution.

Here is what the old Communist, Comrade Kedrov, wrote to the Central Committee through Comrade Andreyev (Comrade Andreyev was then a Central Committee secretary):

> . . . My torture has reached the extreme. My health is broken, my strength and my energy are waning, the end is drawing near. To die in a Soviet prison, branded as a vile traitor to the Fatherland—what can be more monstrous for an honest man? And how monstrous all this is! Unsurpassed bitterness and pain grips my heart. No! No! This will not happen; this cannot be, I cry. Neither the party, nor the Soviet Government, nor the People's Commissar, L. P. Beria, will permit this cruel, irreparable injustice. I am firmly certain that, given a quiet, objective examination, without any foul rantings, without any anger and without the fearful tortures, it would be easy to prove the baselessness of the charges. I believe deeply that truth and justice will triumph. I believe. I believe.

The old Bolshevik, Comrade Kedrov, was found innocent by the Military Collegium. But, despite this, he was shot at Beria's order. (Indignation in the hall.)

Beria also handled cruelly the family of Comrade Ordzhonikidze. Why? Because Ordzhonikidze had tried to prevent Beria from realizing his shameful plans. Beria had cleared from his way all persons who could possibly interfere with him. Ordzhonikidze was always an opponent of Beria, which he told to Stalin. Instead of examining this affair and taking appropriate steps, Stalin allowed the liquidation of Ordzhonikidze's brother and brought Ordzhonikidze himself to such a state that he was forced to shoot himself.[18] (Indignation in the hall.)

Beria was unmasked by the party's Central Committee shortly after Stalin's death. As a result of the particularly detailed legal proceedings, it was established that Beria had committed monstrous crimes and Beria was shot.

The question arises why Beria, who had liquidated tens of thousands of the party and Soviet workers, was not unmasked during Stalin's life. He was not unmasked earlier because he had utilized very skillfully Stalin's weaknesses; feeding him with suspicions, he assisted Stalin in everything and acted with his support.

Comrades: The cult of the individual acquired such monstrous size chiefly because Stalin himself, using all conceivable methods, supported the glorification of his own person. This is supported by numerous facts. One of the most characteristic examples of Stalin's self-glorification and of

[18] Official Soviet statements during the past three years have gradually lifted the veil of secrecy from the death of Grigory K. (Sergo) Ordzhonikidze (1886-1937). The original version published in the Soviet press attributed his death on February 18, 1937 to heart disease. This can now be finally discarded—as can any confidence in the official bulletins of Soviet doctors. Nor can one trust the latest statement, that he shot himself. . . .

his lack of even elementary modesty is the edition of his *Short Biography*, which was published in 1948.

This book is an expression of the most dissolute flattery, an example of making a man into a godhead, of transforming him into an infallible sage, "the greatest leader, sublime strategist of all times and nations." Finally, no other words could be found with which to lift Stalin up to the heavens.

We need not give here examples of the loathesome adulation filling this book. All we need to add is that they all were approved and edited by Stalin personally and some of them were added in his own handwriting to the draft text of the book.

What did Stalin consider essential to write into this book? Did he want to cool the ardor of his flatterers who were composing his *Short Biography?* No! He marked the very places where he thought that the praise of his services was insufficient. . . . Thus writes Stalin himself:

> Although he performed his task as leader of the party and the people with consummate skill and enjoyed the unreserved support of the entire Soviet people, Stalin never allowed his work to be marred by the slightest hint of vanity, conceit or self-adulation. . . .
> Stalin's military mastership was displayed both in defense and offense. Comrade Stalin's genius enabled him to divine the enemy's plans and defeat them. The battles in which Comrade Stalin directed the Soviet armies are brilliant examples of operational military skill. . . .

And when Stalin himself asserts that he himself wrote the *Short Course of the History of the All-Union Communist Party (Bolsheviks)*, this calls at least for amazement. Can a Marxist-Leninist thus write about himself, praising his own person to the heavens?

Or let us take the matter of the Stalin Prizes. (Movement in the hall.) Not even the Tsars created prizes which they named after themselves. . . .

And was it without Stalin's knowledge that many of the largest enterprises and towns were named after him? Was it without his knowledge that Stalin monuments were erected in the whole country—these "memorials to the living"? . . . Consider, yourself, was Stalin right when he wrote in his biography that ". . . he did not allow in himself . . . even a shadow of conceit, pride, or self-adoration"? . . .

In speaking about the events of the October Revolution and about the Civil War, the impression was created that Stalin always played the main role, as if everywhere and always Stalin had suggested to Lenin what to do and how to do it. However, this is slander of Lenin. (Prolonged applause.)

I will probably not sin against the truth when I say that 99 per cent of the persons present here heard and knew very little about Stalin before the year 1924, while Lenin was known to all; he was known to the whole party, to the whole nation, from the children up to the graybeards. (Tumultuous, prolonged applause.)

All this has to be thoroughly revised so that history, literature and the fine arts property reflect V. I. Lenin's role and the great deeds of our Communist party and of the Soviet people—the creative people. (Applause.)

Comrades! The cult of the individual has caused the employment of faulty principles in party work and in economic activity; it brought about rude violation of internal party and Soviet democracy, sterile administration, deviations of all sorts, covering up the shortcomings and varnishing of reality. Our nation gave birth to many flatterers and specialists in false optimism and deceit.

We should also not forget that, due to the numerous arrests of party, Soviet and economic leaders, many workers began to work uncertainly, showed over-cautiousness, feared all which was new, feared their own shadows and began to show less initiative in their work.

Take, for instance, party and Soviet resolutions. They were prepared in a routine manner, often without considering the concrete situation. This went so far that party workers, even during the smallest sessions, read their speeches. All this produced the danger of formalizing the party and Soviet work and of bureaucratizing the whole apparatus.

Stalin's reluctance to consider life's realities and the fact that he was not aware of the real state of affairs in the provinces can be illustrated by his direction of agriculture. All those who interested themselves even a little in the national situation saw the difficult situation in agriculture, but Stalin never even noted it. Did we tell Stalin about this? Yes, we told him, but he did not support us. Why? Because Stalin never traveled anywhere, did not meet city and *kolkhoz* workers; he did not know the actual situation in the provinces. . . .

And when he was once told during a discussion that our situation on the land was a difficult one and that the situation of cattle breeding and meat production was especially bad, a commission was formed which was charged with the preparation of a resolution called "Means toward further development of animal breeding in *kolkhozes* and *sovkhozes*." We worked out this project.

Of course, our proposals of that time did not contain all possibilities, but we did chart ways in which animal breeding on *kolkhozes* and *sovkhozes* would be raised. We had proposed then to raise the prices of such products in order to create material incentives for the *kolkhoz,* MTS [machine-tractor station] and *sovkhoz* workers in the development of cattle breeding. But our project was not accepted and in February 1953 was laid aside entirely.

What is more, while reviewing this project Stalin proposed that the taxes paid by the *kolkhozes* and by the *kolkhoz* workers should be raised by 40 billion rubles; according to him the peasants are well off and the *kolkhoz* worker would need to sell only one more chicken to pay his tax in full.

Imagine what this meant. Certainly, 40 billion rubles is a sum which the *kolkhoz* workers did not realize for all the products which they sold to the Government. In 1952, for instance, the *kolkhozes* and the *kolkhoz* workers received 26,280 million rubles for all their products delivered and sold to the Government.

Did Stalin's position, then, rest on data of any sort whatever? Of course not. In such cases facts and figures did not interest him. If Stalin said anything, it meant it was so—after all, he was a "genius," and a genius does not need to count, he only needs to look and can immediately tell how it should be. When he expresses his opinion, everyone has to repeat it and to admire his wisdom.

But how much wisdom was contained in the proposal to raise the agricultural tax by 40 billion rubles? None, absolutely none, because the proposal was not based on an actual assessment of the situation but on the fantastic ideas of a person divorced from reality. . . .

If we are to consider this matter as Marxists and as Leninists, then we have to state unequivocally that the leadership practice which came into being during the last years of Stalin's life became a serious obstacle in the path of Soviet social development. Stalin often failed for months to take up some unusually important problems, concerning the life of the party and of the state, whose solution could not be postponed. During Stalin's leadership our peaceful relations with other nations were often threatened, because one-man decisions could cause, and often did cause, great complications.

In the last years, when we managed to free ourselves of the harmful practice of the cult of the individual and took several proper steps in the sphere of internal and external policies, everyone saw how activity grew before their very eyes, how the creative activity of the broad working masses developed, how favorably all this acted upon the development of economy and of culture. (Applause.)

Some comrades may ask us: Where were the members of the Political Bureau of the Central Committee? Why did they not assert themselves against the cult of the individual in time? And why is this being done only now?

First of all, we have to consider the fact that the members of the Political Bureau viewed these matters in a different way at different times. Initially, many of them backed Stalin actively because Stalin was one of the strongest Marxists and his logic, his strength and his will greatly influenced the cadres and party work.

It is known that Stalin, after Lenin's death, especially during the first years, actively fought for Leninism against the enemies of Leninist theory and against those who deviated. Beginning with Leninist theory, the party, with its Central Committee at the head, started on a great scale the work of socialist industrialization of the country, agricultural collectivization and the cultural revolution.

At that time Stalin gained great popularity, sympathy and support.

The party had to fight those who attempted to lead the country away from the correct Leninist path; it had to fight Trotskyites, Zinovievites and rightists, and the bourgeois nationalists. This fight was indispensable. Later, however, Stalin, abusing his power more and more, began to fight eminent party and Government leaders and to use terroristic methods against honest Soviet people. . . .

In the situation which then prevailed I have talked often with Nikolai Alexandrovich Bulganin; once when we two were traveling in a car, he said, "It has happened sometimes that a man goes to Stalin on his invitation as a friend. And, when he sits with Stalin, he does not know where he will be sent next—home or to jail."

It is clear that such conditions put every member of the Political Bureau in a very difficult situation. And, when we also consider the fact that in the last years the Central Committee plenary sessions were not convened and that the sessions of the Political Bureau occurred only occasionally, from time to time, then we will understand how difficult it was for any member of the Political Bureau to take a stand against one or another unjust or improper procedure, against serious errors and shortcomings in the practices of leadership. As we have already shown, many decisions were taken either by one person or in a roundabout way, without collective discussion. . . .

One of the oldest members of our party, Klimenti Yefremovich Voroshilov, found himself in an almost impossible situation. For several years he was actually deprived of the right of participation in Political Bureau sessions. Stalin forbade him to attend the Political Bureau sessions and to receive documents. When the Political Bureau was in session and Comrade Voroshilov heard about it, he telephoned each time and asked whether he would be allowed to attend. Sometimes Stalin permitted it, but always showed his dissatisfaction.

Because of his extreme suspicion, Stalin toyed also with the absurd and ridiculous suspicion that Voroshilov was an English agent. (Laughter in the hall.) It's true—an English agent. A special tapping device was installed in his home to listen to what was said there. (Indignation in the hall.) By unilateral decision, Stalin had also separated one other man from the work of the Political Bureau—Andrei Andreyevich Andreyev. This was one of the most unbridled acts of willfulness.

Let us consider the first Central Committee plenum after the 19th Party Congress when Stalin, in his talk at the plenum, characterized Vyacheslav Mikhailovich Molotov and Anastas Ivanovich Mikoyan and suggested that these old workers of our party were guilty of some baseless charges. It is not excluded that had Stalin remained at the helm for another several months, Comrades Molotov and Mikoyan would probably have not delivered any speeches at this Congress.

Stalin evidently had plans to finish off the old members of the Political

Bureau. He often stated that Political Bureau members should be replaced by new ones.

His proposal, after the 19th Congress, concerning the election of 25 persons to the Central Committee Presidium, was aimed at the removal of the old Political Bureau members and the bringing in of less experienced persons so that these would extol him in all sorts of ways. We can assume that this was also a design for the future annihilation of the old Political Bureau members and, in this way, a cover for all shameful acts of Stalin, acts which we are now considering.

Comrades! In order not to repeat errors of the past, the Central Committee has declared itself resolutely against the cult of the individual. We consider that Stalin was excessively extolled. However, in the past Stalin doubtless performed great services to the party, to the working class and to the international workers' movement.

This question is complicated by the fact that all this which we have just discussed was done during Stalin's life under his leadership and with his concurrence; here Stalin was convinced that this was necessary for the defense of the interests of the working classes against the plotting of enemies and against the attack of the imperialist camp.

He saw this from the position of the interest of the working class, of the interest of the laboring people, of the interest of the victory of socialism and communism. We cannot say that these were the deeds of a giddy despot. He considered that this should be done in the interest of the party, of the working masses, in the name of the defense of the revolution's gains. In this lies the whole tragedy! . . .

We should, in all seriousness, consider the question of the cult of the individual. We cannot let this matter get out of the party, especially not to the press. It is for this reason that we are considering it here at a closed Congress session. We should know the limits; we should not give ammunition to the enemy; we should not wash our dirty linen before their eyes. I think that the delegates to the Congress will understand and assess properly all these proposals. (Tumultuous applause.)

Comrades! We must abolish the cult of the individual decisively, once and for all; we must draw the proper conclusions concerning both ideological-theoretical and practical work. It is necessary for this purpose:

First, in a Bolshevik manner to condemn and to eradicate the cult of the individual as alien to Marxism-Leninism and not consonant with the principles of party leadership and the norms of party life, and to fight inexorably all attempts at bringing back this practice in one form or another.

To return to and actually practice in all our ideological work the most important theses of Marxist-Leninist science about the people as the creator of history and as the creator of all material and spiritual good of humanity, about the decisive role of the Marxist party in the revolutionary fight for the transformation of society, about the victory of communism.

In this connection we will be forced to do much work in order to examine critically from the Marxist-Leninist viewpoint and to correct the widely spread erroneous views connected with the cult of the individual in the sphere of history, philosophy, economy and of other sciences, as well as in literature and the fine arts. It is especially necessary that in the immediate future we compile a serious textbook of the history of our party which will be edited in accordance with scientific Marxist objectivism, a textbook of the history of Soviet society, a book pertaining to the events of the Civil War and the Great Patriotic War.

Secondly, to continue systematically and consistently the work done by the party's Central Committee during the last years, a work characterized by minute observation in all party organizations, from the bottom to the top, of the Leninist principles of party leadership, characterized, above all, by the main principle of collective leadership, characterized by the observance of the norms of party life described in the statutes of our party, and, finally, characterized by the wide practice of criticism and self-criticism.

Thirdly, to restore completely the Leninist principles of Soviet socialist democracy, expressed in the Constitution of the Soviet Union, to fight willfulness of individuals abusing their power. The evil caused by acts violating revolutionary socialist legality which have accumulated during a long time as a result of the negative influence of the cult of the individual has to be completely corrected.

Comrades! The 20th Congress of the Communist Party of the Soviet Union has manifested with a new strength the unshakable unity of our party, its cohesiveness around the Central Committee, its resolute will to accomplish the great task of building communism. (Tumultuous applause.)

And the fact that we present in all their ramifications the basic problems of overcoming the cult of the individual which is alien to Marxism-Leninism, as well as the problem of liquidating its burdensome consequences, is an evidence of the great moral and political strength of our party. (Prolonged applause.)

We are absolutely certain that our party, armed with the historical resolutions of the 20th Congress, will lead the Soviet people along the Leninist path to new successes, to new victories. (Tumultuous, prolonged applause.)

Long live the victorious banner of our party—Leninism! (Tumultuous, prolonged applause ending in ovation. All rise.)

Chapter 13

THE PROBLEM OF SUCCESSION

<hr>

Harrison E. Salisbury explains what he regards as a "fatal flaw in the Soviet system," namely, that Russia has developed no constitutional means resting on popular participation and consent for transmitting governmental power. He queries whether "a modern technological state" can afford "the fantastic price of a murderous struggle for power each time a transition in leadership is required."

FATAL FLAW IN THE SOVIET SYSTEM

HARRISON E. SALISBURY*

Today, the whole world once ruled by Stalin with an iron hand is in a state of profound transition. Within the Soviet Union itself there has been a continuous process of change since Stalin's death. In the hinterland even more powerful forces for change are at work. Two events have directed attention with special force toward a re-examination of the factors which underlie what is gradually revealing itself as a general crisis of communism.

The first of these events was the leadership crisis in Moscow [in 1957]. This struggle for power, from which Nikita S. Khrushchev, with the aid of Marshal Georgi K. Zhukov, emerged victorious, again emphasized that communism as it developed under Stalin in Russia is not a genuine system of government but merely a mechanism of rule. It has no formal structure for transferring power peacefully and smoothly from one leader or group of leaders to another. The only way a new ruler can arise is by a test of force. Whether, in a nuclear age, Russia or any nation can afford to be governed

* Formerly the *New York Times* correspondent in Moscow. The selection is from *New York Times Magazine*, August 25, 1957, pp. 13 ff. By permission of *The New York Times* and Harrison E. Salisbury.

by so primitive a method is one of the questions which thoughtful Europeans are studying with especial care.

The second event which has placed communism as a means of government under new scrutiny is the publication of the fascinating analysis by the eccentric former Yugoslav Communist leader, Milovan Djilas, which he calls "The New Class." It is Mr. Djilas' conclusion that communism has given birth to a new class of Communist bureaucrats whom he regards as the worst class of all time, worse than the bourgeoisie whom they replaced or the feudal lords who preceded the bourgeoisie.

The Djilas critique appears at a special moment in history—a moment when the educated, knowledgeable peoples of many countries in Eastern Europe are themselves asking how much longer they must suffer a kind of government which falls vastly short of their expectations and needs. There are young people in many East European countries, including some within the Soviet Union, who have been challenging the basic postulates of Communist rule as it has long been practiced.

There are writers and poets who are writing novels and sonnets whose themes come closer and closer to being: "How long, O Lord, how long?" One does not need to agree with Djilas to understand readily that he has given voice and form to the bitter antagonism which communism has aroused against itself among many peoples.

The reason for this general crisis of communism lies in a basic flaw in the Soviet scheme: It constitutes a rule without a system, a meting out of justice without laws, a land where, in the end, only the man with the loaded revolver says who is the boss.

The transfer of power from one ruler to another has always been a risky thing in Russia. There was no well-established tradition under the Czars. Violence, more often than not, attended the accession of a new ruler to the throne. Indeed, an acid-penned English observer once noted that in England the throne descends by the law of primogeniture; in Russia by the law of regicide. Russian history is pockmarked with "times of trouble," "false Czars," murders of the sovereign by his son and murders of the heir apparent by the sovereign.

Peter the Great, aware of the problem (and himself the murderer of his own heir apparent, his eldest son) sought to remedy the situation by giving each sovereign, in effect, the right to designate his successor. This reform, like so many Russian reforms, had little merit. Sovereigns died suddenly— by poison, by the dagger or even of natural causes—and had no time, in most cases, to name their successors. Inheriting this tradition of tyranny and violent power transfers, the Communists tended to succumb to the mores of the country rather than to create a new tradition of their own.

Lenin himself, before he died in 1924, was probably the first to realize that the rule which the Bolshevik party was imposing on Russia did not constitute a genuine system of government. The Communist party which he had created as an underground, fighting organization with a single purpose —the overthrow of the Czar and the carrying out of the Revolution—was now, after the November *coup d'état,* civil war and foreign intervention, settling down to the tasks of civil reorganization and the reconstruction of a very backward country.

The Communist party was still a lean fighting élite with military rules and spartan discipline. To try to use this small vanguard to rule a vast country was something like putting a commando unit in charge of General Motors.

Alongside the party stood the hollow shell of conventional government apparatus—a council of ministers (then called "commissars"), the usual departments and offices and a flowering bureaucracy. This apparatus had been inherited, by and large, complete with civil servants, from the Czarist regime. It continued to do business very much as it had under the Czars. Given the necessary powers, it could, after a fashion, have administered the affairs of the Soviet Union.

Lenin had no illusions about the "government." He described it as "the same Russian apparatus * * * taken over from Czarism and only thinly anointed with Soviet holy oil." As he watched its workings in Moscow he asked, a little plaintively, "If we take that huge bureaucratic machine, that huge pile, we must ask: Who is directing whom?" He made no secret of his fear that, because of their low level of "culture," the Bolshevik cadres would be swamped by the traditional Russian bureaucracy, just as the Mongol invaders were swamped by the superior culture of the Chinese kingdom they conquered.

Mainly for this reason the Communists have always tried to keep real power concentrated inside the party. The real decisions of state have been made not in the Council of Commissars or Ministers—the Government— but in the Politburo or the Central Committee of the party.

This division and confusion of authority prevented the establishment of a traditional line through which power might be conveyed. It tended to make the Government little more than a facade. "Everything that comes up in the Council of People's Commissars is dragged before the Politburo," Lenin said in despair. This meant that even the smallest questions had to go to the very pinnacle of power before being decided. Lenin blamed himself because, as both Chairman of the Council and Chairman of the Politburo, he formed a personal bridge between the shell of Government and the power of the party.

"The leading comrades take shelter behind commissions," he wrote. "The devil himself would lose his way in this maze of commissions. Nobody knows what is going on, who is responsible; everything is mixed up and finally a decision is passed to the effect that everybody is responsible."

Lenin saw that to a great extent these ills stemmed from the fact that "there is only one Government party at the head of affairs in our country." But he was not able to invent a solution because he was not willing to permit any transfer of power out of the hands of the dynamic élite which he had created in the name of the Communist party.

One of the devices which Lenin invented to give his revolutionary corps a greater cohesion and discipline was a procedure called "democratic centralism." Democratic centralism meant, in essence, that free discussion was permitted within a party group until a question was decided. But once the decision was taken each member was pledged to support it with all his power regardless of his previous attitude. This was a rigid military rule and it gave the small revolutionary corps a power far beyond its numbers.

But, although the party did not appreciate the importance of this, democratic centralism, combined with the monopolistic role of the Communist party, established an impenetrable barrier against the evolution of any system of checks and balances. It was made to order for the evolution and persistence of personal dictatorship.

Lenin did not see or did not wish to see the fatal consequences of the rule of democratic centralism. But he did see that conditions within the party were leading directly toward a split and a bitter personal fight for power. He saw the intrigues of Stalin, analyzed the weaknesses of Trotsky, dispassionately evaluated the other Communist party leaders and sought to warn his followers against the inevitable struggle. But the corrective measures which he proposed (such as doubling the size of the Central Committee) were unrealistic, his warnings were ignored or minimized, and Stalin ruthlessly utilized the mechanism of the party and the ritual of its combat discipline to rout his opponents and establish as tyrannical a dictatorship as any of his Czarist predecessors.

In many ways the enervating dichotomy of the party and Government grew worse under Stalin, who demonstrated complete disinterest in any theory of government. For years he ruled the country while nominally holding only the general secretaryship of the Communist party. His cabinet ministers had no more real power than tailors' dummies. Stalin gave Russia a constitution (written by Bukharin just before Stalin had him arrested, tried and executed), but even though he attached his own name to it Stalin paid no heed to its provisions. He often announced changes in government statutes over the signature of the Central Committee of the Communist party. Sometimes, he used both party and Government signatures. There was no rhyme or reason about this. It seemed to depend on which rubber stamp his hand first touched.

Nor is there any indication that Stalin ever gave serious thought to the problem of the transfer of power after his death. Like many a tyrant before him, Stalin found the thought of his death abhorrent. He did not think about it nor did he make any move to prepare the Soviet state for this event. Thus, Stalin's death in 1953 confronted Russia with the precise dangers which had preoccupied Lenin's thoughts in his last months, a generation before. There was still no system for selecting a successor.

Personally aware of the enormously evil consequences of the power struggle which Stalin had waged, the new post-Stalin leaders embarked on a policy which they called "collective leadership." Their watchword was "*kollektivnost,*" and they cited many quotations from Lenin in support of the virtues of rule by the party's Central Committee.

But behind these verbal trappings began almost immediately a time of test and challenge to determine which of the leaders had actually inherited substantial elements of the great power which Stalin had gathered. The principal elements of this power were vested in the Communist party organization, the Government bureaucracy, the secret police and the army.

The first test of strength may have come over power in the party. Just eight days after becoming Premier of the Soviet Government, Georgi M. Malenkov resigned as party secretary. This opened the way for Nikita S. Khrushchev to gain control of the party secretariat and, like Stalin, to use the secretariat to capture the party organization.

A second show of strength occurred late in June, 1953, when Police Chief Lavrenti P. Beria defied a demand to submit his police to the direction of the "collective leadership." He paid for his defiance with his arrest and eventual execution along with a group of his top aides.

The army, led by Marshal Georgi K. Zhukov, provided the force which enabled the "collective leadership" to cope with Beria. Part of its price for this aid was liquidation of the secret police as a basis of political power.

Having lost his party base Malenkov then sought to build up the power and prestige of the Government; but this effort was doomed to failure because of the built-in Soviet bias which vests all real authority in the party.

It was only by this series of tests that the Soviet leaders were able to judge their own respective strengths. After Malenkov peacefully stepped down as Premier in February, 1955, the dominance of Premier Nikolai A. Bulganin and Party Secretary Khrushchev became more pronounced, although it still appeared that the Soviet group might actually be evolving a new kind of rule, a sort of Communist board of governors. Precedent was against them, but the idea was not completely impossible. Venice was ruled for some 200 years by a similar system.

Without the handicap of a "democratic centralism," without the tradition of a single party, without the long history—both Czarist and Communist —which equated opposition with conspiracy against the state, the experiment might have worked. But the odds were against it. Under Soviet conditions a high-level power contest is not like a friendly game of penny ante in which there is one good-sized winner, several who come out a few dollars ahead, one man who winds up even and two or three moderate losers. The Soviet version is cutthroat—one man after another is eliminated until a final showdown in which the winner takes all.

One day right in the midst of his June struggle with Malenkov, Molotov, Kaganovich and Shepilov, Khrushchev took a couple of hours out to give an interview to a Japanese newspaper man. What Khrushchev called the "law of the jungle" was very much on his mind. He was talking, ostensibly, about the world situation. But, in the light of the struggle he was going through, events much closer to home may have colored his remarks.

"Here is the real law of the jungle," Khrushchev said. "I am strong and you are weak—therefore you must bow to me. We do not want to be like lambs who are defenseless against wolves. But lambs and wolves live in the same world. And wolves by right of strength devour lambs. We do not want to be in the position of lambs. We must have teeth so that the wolves will know that they will not get away with an attack * * * without a mark. The wolves may lose their skins and, perhaps, even their heads * * *."

Such a life, Khrushchev said two or three times, is intolerable. "It is impossible to be guided by the law of the jungle that right is strength, and to dictate one's will to others * * * people want peace and quiet * * * The chief thing is to listen attentively to the voice of the people and not to permit mistakes which damage mutual relations between the leaders and the people. We are confident that it is impossible to rule the people only by force, to hold the population in terror."

The battle in which Khrushchev was then engaged was one in which only the law of the jungle applied. He came out on top—with the aid of Marshal Zhukov. Thus, by the very act of victory the stage is set for another eventual test of power—between Khrushchev and Zhukov.

This may not come. The two men may exercise restraint. Their policies may be identical and their personalities complementary. But the rule of democratic centralism will tend to make sharper differences which arise. And the inadmissibility of opposition groups or opposition opinions will constantly tend to split leader from leader until only one remains.

In the end, of course, Khrushchev or Zhukov will be replaced by a newer, younger man, succeeding to the scepter of power either through the intervention of death or through the gradual weakening of the dictator with the onset of age.

There is, however, another alternative. It may be that over the long period of years the Russian people are gradually beginning to tire of a method of rule which is so arbitrary and inflexible. There is a great weariness with the "law of the jungle" reflected in Khrushchev's statement to the Japanese newspaper man. And this weariness may be shared by many of his countrymen.

The Russian dictatorship, contrary to popular supposition, is not immune to the trends of public opinion. In fact, since the death of Stalin it has been assiduous in courting Soviet opinion. No one has gone to greater efforts in this direction than Khrushchev himself. He has tried to link his fortunes with all of the things which he thinks the Soviet people want—peace, a better and easier life, relaxation of police rule, more personal liberty, more money for the farmer and more meat for the factory worker.

The time may be at hand when Soviet citizens can and will insist that their rulers begin to observe the rules and procedures laid down in the Soviet Constitution. The Constitution is not the most democratic in the world, but it does provide a system of government which should function fairly well and even fairly representatively—if the Soviet leaders ever permitted it to be tried out.

The Communist party structure, with its tight leadership control, proved itself an excellent instrument for revolution and for conducting a war (its pyramid of power resembles that of an army and general staff). But as a peacetime organ it is subject to the same conflicts and uncertainties as a military junta. It is made to order for internecine strife and intrigue.

Today the question is being posed in ever stronger terms to the Soviet public and to their leaders: Can a modern technological state afford the fantastic price of a murderous struggle for power each time a transition in leadership is required? Whether Russia can survive many more such contests becomes increasingly doubtful.

EDITOR'S NOTE: Pravda *reported on July 15, 1957, that Marshal of the Soviet Union, Georgi K. Zhukov, in a speech delivered in Leningrad had supported the ouster of Malenkov, Kaganovich, and Molotov from high office and had stated: "As you know, this anti-Party group resisted the measures for a decisive rise in agriculture. Its members objected especially to the slogan 'catch up with the United States of America in the near future in the per capita production of meat, milk and butter,' put forward by the Central Committee on the initiative of Nikita Sergeyevich Khrushchev, a slogan which was unanimously approved by all the Soviet people. The anti-Party group opposed expanding the political, economic and legislative powers of the Union republics, apparently not wanting to give up the powers it had held for nearly 30 years . . . and stubbornly resisted the measures pursued by the Party for eliminating the consequences of the cult of the individual leader, particularly the disclosure and calling to account of those mainly responsible for violation of legality in the past."*

Subsequently, on November 2, 1957, the Central Committee of the Communist Party of the Soviet Union announced that its plenary meeting late in October had adopted a resolution which "has excluded Georgi K.

Zhukov from membership of the Presidium of the Central Committee and from the Central Committee of the Communist party." It further noted that "of late former Defense Minister Comrade Zhukov has violated the Leninist party principles of guiding the armed forces, pursued a policy of curtailing the work of party organizations, political organs, and military councils, of abolishing the leadership and control of the party, its Central Committee and Government over the Army and Navy."

The announcement continued: "The plenary meeting . . . has established that the cult of Comrade Zhukov's personality was cultivated in the Soviet Army with his personal participation. With the help of sycophants and flatterers, he was praised to the sky in lectures and reports, in articles, films and pamphlets, and his person and role in the Great Patriotic War were over-glorified." He was charged with lack of "modesty," with imagining "that he was the sole hero of all the victories achieved by our people and their armed forces under the Communist party's leadership," and with being "a politically unsound person, inclining to adventurism. . . ." It was stated that "the decision was adopted unanimously by all the members and alternate members of the Central Committee and the members of the Central Auditing Commission. It was approved by all the military men, Communist party and Government executives present at the meeting."

The following day Marshal Ivan S. Konev wrote in Pravda: *"One should not forget that Comrade Zhukov occupied the high position of Chief of General Staff during the period immediately preceding the war, and bore a considerable share of the responsibility for the condition of the Soviet armed forces and their ability to meet Fascist aggression." While Stalin's "incorrect assessment . . . lay at the bottom of the serious miscalculations," "serious responsibility for the fact that the troops of our military frontier areas were taken unaware by the sudden attack of the Fascist army also falls upon the Chief of General Staff, Comrade Zhukov. . . ."*

On March 27, 1958, the Supreme Soviet unanimously elected Khrushchev Chairman of the Council of Ministers to succeed Bulganin, who had submitted his resignation. Khrushchev remained Party Secretary as well. On September 6, 1958, Radio Moscow briefly announced that the Central Committee of the Communist Party had "relieved Nikolai A. Bulganin of his duties as a member of the Presidium of the Central Committee of the Communist Party of the Soviet Union." His decline dated from June 1957 when he had stood with Malenkov, Molotov, and Kaganovich in their unsuccessful challenge to Khrushchev.

It was subsequently revealed that the "anti-Party group" in 1957 had also included K. Ye Voroshilov, M. G. Pervukhin, and M. Z. Saburov—a clear majority of seven of the Presidium's eleven members. Khrushchev

*turned defeat into victory when he persuaded the Party's Central Committee
to reverse the Presidium. Each of Khrushchev's 1957 opponents was, in the
course of time, "exposed" and ousted from any position of real importance.
As an aftermath of the October 1962 Cuba crisis, however, Voroshilov appears to have regained a measure of power. (For Khrushchev's and other
comments on the "anti-Party group" at the 22nd Party Congress, see "The
Party Crisis and Epilogue on Terror" herein.)*

THE CASE OF KHRUSHCHEV

BOHDAN R. BOCIURKIW*

*Why should internecine struggles for power within the U.S.S.R. interest
and concern the Western student? The matter has, I believe, been well put
by Robert Conquest in the final paragraph of his book* Power and Policy in
the USSR. *He suggests that such study "gives us priceless insights into not
only the nature of the Soviet political world but also the special characteristics of the members of the Soviet ruling group." Moreover, their "basic habits
of thought and modes of action are likely to manifest themselves in international affairs as well."*

*While Professor Bociurkiw agrees with Harrison Salisbury that the de-
mise of Khrushchev will produce another "crisis," he suggests that the
U.S.S.R. has demonstrated its capacity to "compensate for the mortality of
rulers by the vitality of a party machine" that has made its secretarial apparatus "the central avenue of political succession in the Soviet Union."*

The mode of succession has long been recognized as one of the principal
factors in determining the stability of a given political system and a key
datum in the analysis of power relations within such a system.[1] Essentially,
the problem can be stated as involving (*a*) the technique of choosing a successor to a political leader, and (*b*) the successor's legitimization in the legal,
traditional, or charismatic sense. This paper will deal primarily with the
technique of succession in the Soviet system, touching only marginally on
the question of legitimization. While drawing analogies from the post-Lenin
succession crisis, the paper will attempt to identify the factors that shaped the
nature and the course of the post-Stalin power struggle and the technique

---

* In the Department of Political Economy, University of Alberta. Professor Bociurkiw's
remarks were originally presented as a paper at a meeting of the Canadian Political Science
Association on June 9, 1960, and were reprinted in *The Canadian Journal of Economics and
Political Science*, Vol. 26 (Nov., 1960), pp. 575-591. The selection is reproduced here (with
some authorized footnote deletions) by permission of the journal and author.

[1] For a general discussion of the problem, see F. M. Watkins, "Political Succession,"
Encyclopaedia of the Social Sciences (New York, 1934), XIV, 441-3.

that ensured Khrushchev's victory over his rivals. Needless to say, limitations of evidence have introduced a considerable speculative element into the discussion, and some of the generalizations are therefore, at best, only tentative hypotheses that will have to be tested against such empirical evidence as may become available in the future.

Although modern constitutionalism has largely resolved the problem of succession by legally defining the technique of succession and making the technique the criterion of legitimacy, the very nature of the totalitarian dictatorship that emerged in Russia after 1917 precludes a constitutional solution to the problem. ". . . dictatorship," Lenin wrote in 1920, "means neither more nor less than unlimited power resting directly on force, not limited by anything, not restrained by any laws or any absolute rules." [2] He left no doubt that the "dictatorship of the proletariat" was to be exercised not by the proletarians themselves, but by their self-appointed "vanguard" —a militant, monolithic Communist party, infallible by virtue of its command of the scientific key to the past, the present, and the heavenly city of the future. Lenin's theory of the party contained the seeds of personal dictatorship *within* and *over* the party. As Trotsky had observed prophetically in 1904, Lenin's "democratic centralism" meant that "the organization of the party substitutes itself for the party, the Central Committee substitutes itself for the organization, and finally the dictator substitutes himself for the Central Committee."

Yet the notion of a single, all-powerful dictator fits badly into the Marxist framework of thought which assigns the history-making role to the classes or, in the Leninist version, to the party as a whole. It is not surprising, then, that Soviet political and constitutional theory consistently shied away from the question of what happens when a personal dictator, the unique *"Vozhd'* of the Party and the people," disappears from the lonely summit of Soviet power. The subterfuge employed from time to time by Soviet writers was to dismiss the problem of succession by piously insisting that leadership of the party has always been "collegial" or "collective," residing in the regularly re-elected Central Committee (or the Politburo) and hence self-perpetuating. When Stalin's heirs officially admitted that "collective leadership" was but a fiction during most of the late dictator's reign, Soviet writers readily agreed that the "cult of the personality" (the official euphemism for Stalin's despotism) was a "deviation from the Leninist principle of collegiality"; accordingly, the whole problem of the succession was reduced, in Soviet theory, simply to the "restoration of collective leadership."

Lenin, despite an awareness of his unique role as an undisputed leader of the party and state, never ventured beyond the formula of "collective leadership" as the answer to the problem of succession in the Soviet system.

[2] In his "K istorii voprosa o diktature" in *Sochineniia* (3rd ed.), XXV, 441. For the sense in which "totalitarian" is used in this paper, see Z. Brzezinski, "Totalitarianism and Rationality," *American Political Science Review*, L, no. 3, Sept., 1956, 754.

While composing his famous "testament" in the winter of 1922-3, he declined to take advantage of his great authority to designate an heir, save in a negative sense; having noted that "Comrade Stalin . . . has concentrated enormous power in his hands," he proposed to the Central Committee that Stalin be removed from the office of General Secretary. Otherwise, Lenin's "will" alternated rebuke with praise for his closest associates in order to disqualify any one of them from claiming personal leadership, and to show, at the same time, that each was indispensable in the collective leadership of the party. Well aware of the conflict between Trotsky and Stalin, Lenin advised doubling the membership of the Central Committee in order to dilute the differences between them and to avert the danger of a split in the party.

As it happened, Stalin indeed amassed "enormous power" in the party machine and was able to suppress the publication of the "testament." [3] Not only did he retain his office;[4] he also used the device suggested by Lenin—the enlargement of the Central Committee—to pack that body with his own supporters so as ultimately to destroy the "collective leadership" and to establish absolute personal control over both party and state. Unwittingly, Lenin also provided Stalin with another legitimate weapon against the "collective leadership." In 1921, striving to maintain a monolithic party against a growing factionalism (which could have evolved into a sort of multi-factional democracy within the party), Lenin drafted the resolution "On Party Unity." Adopted after a bitter debate at the Tenth Party Congress, the resolution outlawed "all factional activities" within the party and made them punishable by "immediate and unconditional expulsion." The banishment of organized differences of opinion left the *apparat* as the only active element in the party and the sole bearer of the correct "general line." It is not surprising that the same resolution was invoked again by Khrushchev in June, 1957, to justify the expulsion of his opponents from the Presidium and the Central Committee.

I

When Stalin died in 1953 he did not, as far as can be established, leave behind anything resembling Lenin's "testament." Nor did he clearly designate any one of his lieutenants as his sole successor, although his favourite at that time, Georgii Malenkov, his deputy in the Secretariat and the Cabinet, may have been considered by the aging dictator as the best man to succeed him. Indeed, the obscure manœuvres preceding Stalin's death and the de-

---

[3] Although Lenin's "testament" was read (as a secret party document) to separate delegations attending the 1924 Congress (*ibid.*, 260), its full text was not published in the U.S.S.R. until June, 1956 (in *Kommunist*).

[4] Ironically, with the help of his future victims, Zinoviev and Kamenev (see John S. Reshetar, Jr., *A Concise History of the Communist Party of the Soviet Union* (New York, 1960), 188-98).

velopments at the Nineteenth Party Congress in 1952 tend to support such speculation.[5]

It is nevertheless clear that if it was Stalin's intention to invest Malenkov as his heir the dictator's death occurred before power could be transferred to Malenkov and his rivals eliminated. The latter were apparently still powerful enough to frustrate Malenkov's bid for a direct succession by forcing him to accept the formula of "collective leadership" personified in the *troika* of Malenkov, Beria, and Molotov.[6]

The inception of "collective leadership" in 1953 attested to the fluidity of the Soviet institutional arrangements and constitutional norms. Within less than twenty-four hours after Stalin's death, the new leadership, in clear violation of the party's statute and the constitution, decreed sweeping changes in the structure and composition of the central organs of the party and government.[7] What emerged from this marriage of expedience and "revolutionary legality" was a state-party-police oligarchy, centred in the

[5] After Zhdanov died in 1948, Malenkov was clearly accorded precedence over such durable lieutenants of Stalin as Molotov, Beria, Kaganovich, and Mikoyan; from 1949 on, the latter were gradually removed from the important government posts they had occupied for many years. Malenkov's strategic position as Stalin's deputy in the Secretariat and the Cabinet was further enhanced at the Nineteenth Party Congress in 1952; not only was he chosen to deliver the report of the Central Committee (the function that Stalin had performed at every congress since 1925), but the old Politburo was replaced by a much larger and, inevitably, ineffectual body—the Presidium of the thirty-six members and candidates. More ominous portents of the forthcoming transition of power were the purges of the "Zhdanovites" and Beria's supporters, followed in January, 1953, by the announcement of the notorious "doctors' plot" which, while implicitly aimed at Beria, presaged a sweeping purge in the highest echelons of the party. According to Khrushchev, "Stalin evidently had plans to finish off the old members of the Political Bureau. He often stated that Political Bureau members should be replaced by new ones. His proposal, after the Nineteenth Congress, concerning the selection of 25 persons to the Central Committee Presidium, was aimed at the removal of the old Political Bureau members. . . . We can assume that this was also a design for the future annihilation of the old Political Bureau members. . . ." (Khrushchev's "secret speech" at the Twentieth Congress, February, 1956, cited in Wolfe, *Khrushchev and Stalin's Ghost*, 244). Later, in his 1957 speech, Khrushchev elaborated: "Occupying a high post in the Party and the State, Comrade Malenkov not only failed to restrain I. V. Stalin, but very cleverly made use of Stalin's weaknesses and habits during the last years of his life. In many instances he pushed him into such acts which deserve to be severely condemned." ("Za t'esnuiu sviaz' literatury i iskusstva s zhizniu naroda," *Kommunist*, no. 12, Aug., 1957, 20.)

[6] The existence of such a *troika* was nowhere confirmed in official Soviet sources, but the special prominence accorded these three men (in contrast to the rest of the Presidium) at Stalin's funeral, in the Soviet press, etc., led most Western students to assume that the long Bolshevik tradition of triumvirates in the party leadership was being followed.

[7] In an attempt to "legalize" the succession, an unprecedented joint meeting of the Central Committee of the party, the Council of Ministers, and the Presidium of the Supreme Soviet was summoned at the Kremlin immediately after Stalin's death; yet in changing the *structure* of the central organs of the party and government and replacing Shvernik with Voroshilov as the nominal head of the state, the meeting clearly usurped the prerogatives of the Supreme Soviet and the party Congress. The rationale behind these measures was stated in the resolution of this joint meeting, announced in *Pravda* on March 6, 1953: ". . . to ensure an uninterrupted and correct leadership over all life in the country, which in turn calls for the greatest unity of leadership, the prevention of any kind of disorder and panic. . . ."

much smaller Presidium of the Central Committee and largely overlapping the revamped Presidium of the Council of Ministers. Malenkov emerged as *primus inter pares,* combining, as Stalin before him, the offices of Premier and ranking Secretary of the Central Committee; the other two triumvirs— Beria and Molotov, the First Deputy Premiers—regained control of the police and the Foreign Ministry respectively. The remaining members of the party's Presidium were each assigned an important post in the Cabinet, except for the second secretary of the party, Nikita Khrushchev, who was to "concentrate on work in [the Secretariat of] the Central Committee." [8]

At the time of Stalin's death, given the relative power standing of his lieutenants, their mutual distrust, and yet their common concern for the preservation of the régime, "collective leadership" indeed appeared as the only immediate solution to the problem of succession. Moreover, Stalin's position, "achieved as a consequence of a protracted historical process . . . was not simply a post in a table of organization that can be mechanically filled." [9] The synthetic charismatic image of Stalin, blown up to heroic proportions, left too great a psychological vacuum to be filled at once by any of the men who had grown up in his shadow. Compared to the overbearing stature of "the greatest genius of all time," and "the Lenin of today," Stalin's disciples could not but appear as small and colourless men.

And yet the "collective leadership," while following the precedent set by the *troika* of Stalin, Zinoviev, and Kamenev in 1923-4,[10] could not but have been aware of the fate that befell the post-Lenin "collective leadership"; Stalin's heirs must have understood the inherent instability of such a structure of leadership and the inner compulsion of the system begotten by Lenin and Stalin to seek culmination in a single, all-powerful dictator. Thus in March, 1953, Stalin's lieutenants faced a dilemma; the maintenance of the régime and of its continued dynamic called for a unity of thought and action which an oligarchy could not provide, and yet the realization of such unity in the form of a personal dictator meant the downgrading and the possible liquidation of his former peers. Much of the subsequent struggle in the Kremlin can be explained in terms of the tension between these two negative alternatives and the futile search for a resolution of the dilemma.

The crucial events which doomed Malenkov's bid for the succession and established some sort of balance of power within the "collective leadership" occurred during the first nine days after Stalin's death. It seems that the cavalier manner in which the changes of March 6, 1953, were effected in the leadership of party and state, the ominous power axis between Premier-Secretary Malenkov and Beria's police machine, as well as the initial build-up of

[8] *Ibid.* Voroshilov (Chairman of the Supreme Soviet Presidium); Bulganin (First Deputy Premier; Defense Ministry); Kaganovich (First Deputy Premier; no specific portfolio); Mikoyan (External and Domestic Trade). Saburov and Pervukhin were given consolidated industrial ministries.

[9] W. W. Rostow, *The Dynamics of Soviet Society* (New York, 1953), 178.

[10] See Reshetar, Jr., *Concise History,* 189-203.

Malenkov in the Soviet propaganda media as Stalin's successor[11] alarmed the majority in the Presidium and the Central Committee.[12] At the Plenum of the Central Committee on March 14 they were able to persuade or compel Malenkov to divest himself of his function as the ranking Secretary of the Central Committee; his place was filled by Khrushchev, presumably regarded as a more trustworthy upholder of the principle of "collective leadership." [13] It is, nevertheless, possible that, if given the choice between his two offices, Malenkov himself would have decided to keep the premiership. It must be remembered that, since the war, Stalin had consistently emphasized the government and the police as his main levers of control, and had reduced the influence of the party, especially over the secret police.[14] It may be that Malenkov hoped to continue this trend (as was indeed suggested by his subsequent tactics) and to return the Secretariat to the purely administrative status it had had before Stalin made it his springboard to power. As long as he could rely on Beria's apparatus of coercion, this prospect seemed plausible.

Malenkov, it appears, misconstrued the subtle but extremely important shift that had taken place in the balance of power. With the "collective leadership" split into shifting factional alignments the Central Committee re-emerged, after two decades of insignificance, as the arbiter and the court of appeal in the Presidium struggles; the statute of the party suddenly acquired real significance as the "rules of the game" and the frame of reference for the succession controversies, and, inevitably, as a weapon which could be used to factional advantage.

Beria's manoeuvres during the spring of 1953, apparently designed to set the stage for his own bid for dictatorial power,[15] brought together Malenkov

[11] In its first few issues immediately after Stalin's death *Pravda* displayed Malenkov's photographs and contained frequent quotations from his speeches; its celebrated photomontage on March 10 showing Malenkov in the company of Stalin and Mao abruptly ended the "cult of Malenkov's personality."

[12] According to Giuseppe Boffa, an Italian Communist journalist who served as a Moscow correspondent for *L'Unità* from 1953 to 1958, Khrushchev "revealed" at the Plenum of January, 1955, that "at Stalin's death Malenkov and Beria had jointly shuffled the main organs of control, even before the Presidium was called together. The Central Committee was in fact faced with a *fait accompli*. Considering the gravity of the moment, no one raised any objections; but so singular a procedure could not easily be forgotten." (*La Grande Svolta* (Rome, 1959), 29) Boffa's report has not yet been corroborated by official Soviet statements, but Khrushchev had alluded more than once to the close relations between Malenkov and Beria (see, e.g., his speech "Za tesnuiu sviaz' . . . ," *Kommunist*, no. 12, 1957, 20).

[13] The reshuffle was not announced in *Pravda* until March 21, 1953.

[14] According to a well-informed Polish defector, party organizations in the secret police during the last years of the Stalin era were *not* subordinated to the Central Committee, but to the Ministry of State Security (S. Bialer, "But Some Are More Equal than Others," *Problems of Communism*, March-April, 1960, 48).

[15] Between April and June, 1953, Beria not only tried to win personal popularity for such measures as amnesty and the repudiation of the "doctors' plot," but put his followers back in control of the party organizations in Georgia and Azerbaijan, and placed his own men in charge of the republican ministries of internal affairs; his boldest move (one which

and the rest of the Presidium in an anti-Beria coalition which successfully foiled (reportedly with the help of the army) what looked like an imminent *coup d'état*. The immediate consequence of Beria's fall was the elimination of the secret police as a major factor in the succession struggle and the emergence of the military as a new element in the configuration of power. The "Beria affair," attributed to the weakness of the party's control over the police, weakened Malenkov's position and strengthened that of Khrushchev, who hastened to place his adherents in charge of the purged police. His new prominence was formally recognized in his election as the First Secretary of the party at the Plenum held in September, 1953.[16]

Before long, the now triumphant "collective leadership" was torn by the conflict between Khrushchev and Malenkov. Ostensibly concerned with policy and centring on the relative importance of heavy industry, consumer goods, and agriculture,[17] the conflict resulted in a new alignment in the Presidium. With Khrushchev shrewdly manipulating the "conservative" and the military elements,[18] and winning over or purging Malenkov's followers in the party and the Central Committee, Malenkov found himself increasingly isolated in the party councils. He was defeated at the Plenum of the Central Committee in January, 1955,[19] and in February was replaced by Marshal Bulganin,[20] Khrushchev's nominee.

Having now emerged as the leading figure in the Presidium, Khrushchev soon manœuvred the remaining member of the initial *troika,* Viacheslav Molotov, into an untenable position on foreign policy (especially on Yugoslavia) which led to Molotov's condemnation at the Plenum of July, 1955,[21]

---

was certain to consolidate his opponents in Moscow) was to expose "Russification" in the Ukraine and Lithuania, and to replace Russians with native Communists in the leading party organs in these republics. See F. F., "The Fall of Beria and the Nationalities Question in the USSR," *World Today,* Nov., 1953, 481-97, and B. Nikolaievsky, "Znacheniie d'ela Beria," *Sotsialisticheskii Vestnik,* Jan., 1954, 3-7.

[16] See *Pravda,* Sept. 13, 1953.

[17] See Malenkov's speech to the Supreme Soviet on August 8, 1953 (*Pravda,* Aug. 9, 1953) calling for development of light industry and the food industries "at the same rate as heavy industry"; Khrushchev's report at the Plenum of the Central Committee in September, 1953 (*ibid.,* Sept. 15, 1953) stressing heavy industry as the "only material basis of socialism" and calling for a rapid development of agriculture as a prior condition to increased production of consumer goods; and a signed article by Shepilov ("Generalnaia liniia partii i vulgarizatory marksizma," *ibid.,* Jan. 24, 1955) condemning the former policy though not naming Malenkov.

[18] See R. Lowenthal, "Crisis in Moscow," *Problems of Communism,* May-June, 1955, 1-8. It seems that Molotov and Kaganovich supported Khrushchev against Malenkov, as did Bulganin and the military circles.

[19] Apparently, in addition to his "error" on the question of heavy *vs.* light industry, Malenkov (as Stalin's deputy in the Secretariat) was also charged with responsibility for failures in agriculture and (jointly with the "Beria gang") with masterminding the "Leningrad Affair" (the purge of the Zhdanovites) in 1949. See S. Bialer, "I Chose Truth," *News From Behind the Iron Curtain,* Oct., 1956, 6-7, and Boffa, *La Grande Svolta,* 28-30.

[20] For Malenkov's "confession" which accompanied his "resignation" from the post of Premier, see *Pravda,* Feb. 10, 1955.

[21] "Comrade Molotov's mistaken policy regarding Yugoslavia was unanimously condemned by the plenary session of the Party Central Committee in July, 1955" (*Voprosy Istorii KPSS,* Jan., 1957, 6).

and his subsequent removal from the Foreign Ministry.[22] The same Plenum also decided to convene the Twentieth Party Congress in February, 1956 (ahead of schedule), and, without waiting for it to convene, elected two of Khrushchev's supporters (Kirichenko and Suslov) to the Presidium and added three of his protégés (Aristov, Belaiev, and Shepilov) to the Secretariat.[23]

Indirect election of the delegates to the Congress provided an opportunity for a far-reaching purge among the lower officials of the party; as a result many of the *raion,* city, and *oblast'* secretaries were now replaced by Khrushchev's partisans. Not surprisingly, the Congress was well packed with his supporters, the result being the election of a solid majority for him in the enlarged Central Committee.[24] The highlight of the Congress, and the most dramatic development since the death of Stalin, was of course Khrushchev's so-called secret speech "On the Cult of Personality and Its Consequences." Western commentators are still arguing about the motives behind this shattering attack on Stalin, but its significance, in our opinion, may be described as follows:

(*a*) By attacking Stalin's despotism and, especially, his persecution of loyal Communists, Khrushchev pledged himself not to repeat the dictator's crimes and errors.[25] To underline his "respect" for "collective leadership," Khrushchev refrained from using his strength at the Congress to remove his rivals from the Presidium.

(*b*) By pointedly referring to his rivals' close collaboration with Stalin, Khrushchev implicated them in Stalin's crimes;[26] at the same time, he proclaimed his own innocence (as well as Bulganin's and Mikoyan's), and, indeed his covert opposition to Stalin.[27]

(*c*) By ascribing some of the worst features of the Stalinist era to the latter-day deterioration in Stalin's character, the influence of the "Beria gang," and the exigencies of war, Khrushchev attempted to protect the doctrinal infallibility of the party and to exonerate the Soviet system from responsibility for the crimes and errors of the late dictator.

[22] Molotov was largely relieved of the conduct of Soviet foreign policy from that time on, but his resignation was made public only in 1956, to coincide with Marshal Tito's visit to the U.S.S.R. Prior to that, he had been compelled to write a humiliating letter to the party's ideological journal, confessing his "theoretically fallacious and politically harmful" views on the "question of construction of socialist society in the USSR"; see *Kommunist,* no. 14, Sept. 1955, 127-8.

[23] *Pravda,* July 13, 1955.

[24] At the Twentieth Party Congress, some 111 (or 44 per cent) of the 255 full and alternate members of the new Central Committee—now increased from 125 to 133 full members, and from 111 to 122 alternate members—were elected for the first time (see Embree, *Soviet Union,* 331-2). Of the old Control Commission (thirty-seven members) twelve were removed and thirty-eight new members added. See A. Avtorkhanov, *Stalin and the Soviet Communist Party* (Munich, 1959), pp. 356-7.

[25] Wolfe, *Khrushchev and Stalin's Ghost,* 102, 244.

[26] In particular, Malenkov, Molotov, Kaganovich, and, obviously, Beria.

[27] Wolfe, *Khrushchev and Stalin's Ghost,* 240. Later, the Central Committee's resolution of June 30, 1956, spoke of the "Leninist core of leaders within the Central Committee" as a counterweight to Stalin (*Pravda,* July 2, 1956).

(*d*) By repudiating the Stalin myth, Khrushchev sought to legitimize his claim to the succession (as well as his venturesome domestic and foreign policies) in terms of a "return to Leninism" and to the "true faith" and "original" norms of party and state life.

Khrushchev's renunciation of the dogmatism and repressiveness of the Stalin era may also have aimed at reinvigorating the party, releasing the arrested dynamic energies of the Soviet society, filling the gap between the ruling minority and the masses, and providing a new basis for relations between the Soviet Union and the "fraternal socialist countries."

The unintended consequences of this attack on Stalin—ideological confusion and unrest at home and in the satellites, culminating in the Polish "October" and the Hungarian revolution, as well as turmoil and defection in Western Communist parties—was seriously threatening Khrushchev's position in the Presidium by the winter of 1956-7.[28] It is a measure of his tactical prowess that as early as February, 1957, he had not only recovered from this crisis, but had also struck back at his critics with bold proposals for a sweeping decentralization of economic management, which were aimed, incidentally, at his rivals' remaining basis of power—the bureaucratic and managerial élite. In May, 1957, Khrushchev's "Theses" were made into law, with the result that the newly formed economic regions were placed under the close supervision of the territorial party apparatus. Thus, like the police, the huge administrative-managerial machine, so much emphasized under Stalin, was clearly reduced to secondary importance in the last round of the succession struggle.

The showdown came at the meetings of the Presidium and the Central Committee in June, 1957. A variety of motives—opposition to Khrushchev's "de-Stalinization" campaign, resentment over his domestic and foreign policies, personal grudges, and, above all, a belated recognition that the enormous concentration of power in his hands was rapidly transforming the "collective leadership" into a fiction—brought together the "liberal" Malenkov, the "conservatives" Molotov and Kaganovich, and Khrushchev's recent allies, Bulganin and Shepilov. At least two other members[29] of the Presidium failed to give their support to Khrushchev, so he was confronted with a hostile majority in the Presidium, intent on removing him from the Secretariat.[30] In-

---

[28] See Avtorkhanov, *Stalin and the Soviet Communist Party*, 349-52. It seems that Khrushchev's proposal for administrative-managerial decentralization was voted down at the Plenum of the Central Committee in December, 1956. (Significantly, it was Bulganin rather than Khrushchev who presented the report, "On the Improvement of Economic Leadership," to that Plenum.) See *Pravda*, Dec. 25, 1956.

[29] Saburov and Pervukhin, as disclosed at the 1959 Party Congress. See *Pravda*, Jan. 30-Feb. 5, 1959.

[30] To conceal from the public the fact that the majority in the Presidium had turned against Khrushchev, only Malenkov, Molotov, Kaganovich, and Shepilov were at first identified as members of the "anti-party group"; Bulganin's name was added as late as the fall of 1958, and Saburov and Pervukhin were first publicly attacked only at the Twenty-First Congress in January-February, 1959.

voking the party statute and the 1921 resolution against factionalism, Khrushchev successfully appealed to the Presidium's nominal parent body—the Central Committee. The Committee was dominated by Khrushchev's partisans so the initial advantage enjoyed by the hostile coalition vanished. In June the Plenum expelled what now became the "anti-party group" [31] from the leading party and state organs, replacing them with Khrushchev's loyal lieutenants.

For all practical purposes, this Plenum marked the end of "collective leadership" in the Presidium[32] and signalled the rapid eclipse of the Central Committee. The Presidium, now dominated by Khrushchev's *apparatchiki*, was reduced to a sort of enlarged plenum of the Secretariat.[33] The events of June, 1957, closed the succession crisis; Khrushchev had emerged as the undisputed winner and the personal leader of the party and state. True, one obstacle to dictatorship had yet to be swept away, for the military, though consistently supporting Khrushchev, had acquired enough power and prestige to become a potential threat to him. Marshal Zhukov's demotion from his party and government posts in October, 1957,[34] symbolized the removal of the army from political influence and the restoration of effective party control over the military. To bring his official position into accord with his vast

[31] On the eve of the public announcement of the "anti-party group's" defeat and expulsion, *Pravda* (July 3, 1957) carried an ominous editorial article ("Leninskoe edinstvo Partii-istochnik ee nepobedimoi sily") which provided a "definition" of "anti-party views": "To determine the edge separating the party from the anti-party [views] there is a firm and faithful criterion: it is the [party] statute, programmatic rules, decisions of the party, its whole, more than half-century old, experience. . . ." Moreover, the article continued, "in our socialist country there is not and cannot be a social basis for the emergence within the party of tendencies and factions hostile to Leninism. . . . Lenin accorded special importance to the leading core of the party, its Central Committee. He . . . in every way protected it from the influence of purely personal and accidental circumstances [and] skilfully prevented the possibility of violation of its unity. These Leninist traditions [are] an inviolable law, binding our party [and] all Communists."

[32] In fact, since 1957, the expression "collective leadership" has come to be applied more and more to the "Central Committee headed by N. S. Khrushchev."

[33] By May, 1959, nine out of fourteen full members and one of the nine alternate members of the Presidium were secretaries of the Central Committee. A significant reshuffle of the top personnel of the party at the Plenum in May, 1960, reduced the number of Central Committee secretaries to five; thus, in the present fifteen-man Presidium there are five such secretaries, two officials of the Central Committee's Bureau for the Russian Republic, and one republican party secretary; the seven alternate members of the Presidium include three republican secretaries and one *obkom* secretary. See *Pravda,* May 5, 1960.

[34] He was removed from the Ministry of Defence, the Presidium, and the Central Committee by the Plenum of the Central Committee which met on October 29, 1957; *Pravda* announced his removal from the Cabinet on October 27, but did not publish the communiqué about the Plenum and his removal from the party leadership until November 3. Zhukov was accused of "Bonapartism": ". . . he took the line aiming at the separation of our armed forces from the Communist party, at the weakening of the party organizations and actual liquidation of political organs in the Soviet army. . . . [He displayed] a tendency to view the Soviet armed forces as his patrimony . . . [strove] to escape from the control of the Central Committee, . . . [fostered] the cult of his [own] personality" ("Kommunisticheskaia partiia-rukovodiashchaia sila sovetskogo obshchestva," *Kommunist,* no. 16, Nov., 1957, 10-11). See also *Partiinaia zhizn',* no. 21, Nov., 1957, 48-57.

power, Khrushchev had himself elected Premier (in place of Bulganin) at the session of the Supreme Soviet in March, 1958.[35] Stalin's two principal offices whose separation in March, 1953, symbolized the emergence of "collective leadership" were now reunited in the hands of his fittest lieutenant.

The Extraordinary Twenty-First Party Congress that assembled in January, 1959, can well be compared with Stalin's "Congress of Victors," in January, 1934.[36] It "legitimized" Khrushchev's ascendance as a single leader, not yet a *Vozhd'*, but already the *rukovodit'el* and the "head of the Central Committee," to whom "personally" all the major achievements of the post-Stalin era were now ascribed.[37] The "Congress of the Builders of Communism" provided Khrushchev with the appropriate stage for claiming yet another of Stalin's functions, that of supreme theoretician of the régime. His report to the Congress was met by the familiar chorus of sycophant praise, as an "example of the creative development of Marxist-Leninist theory," a "living incarnation of the Leninist idea," a "magnificent symphony of Communist construction." [38]

The acclamation of Khrushchev at this Congress as the "faithful disciple of Lenin" and a "model of Leninist leadership" [39] resembled Stalin's attempts after Lenin's death to establish his "apostolic succession" from the charismatic founder of Bolshevism. The "pseudo-charismatic" image of Stalin, extending beyond his death, played a considerable role in the succession struggle as a symbol manipulated to personal advantage by both Malenkov[40] and Khrushchev.[41] The negative connotations and synthetic genesis of the Stalin myth were, it seems, among the considerations that led Khrushchev to shatter it in his "secret speech" of 1956. Following the attempts, evident in the Soviet press from March, 1953, to "transfer" the charisma from Stalin to

[35] *Pravda,* March 28, 1958.

[36] The speakers echoed, almost word by word, Stalin's boast of 1934, which ran: "The present Congress takes place under the flag of the complete victory of Leninism, under the flag of the liquidation of the remnants of the anti-Leninist groups. . . . It must be admitted that the Party today is united as it has never been before." Cited in M. Fainsod, *How Russia Is Ruled* (Cambridge, Mass., 1954), 47-8.

[37] Indeed, the proceedings of the Congress show that Khrushchev was "personally" credited for achievements in such areas as agriculture, the anti-alcohol campaign, the armed forces, nuclear research, chemical industry, construction, cultivation of cotton, educational reform, electric power, literature, cultural development of the nationalities, "socialist legality," science, and astronautics. See *Pravda,* Jan. 29-Feb. 6, 1959.

[38] *Ibid.*

[39] Kapitonov's speech; see *ibid.,* Jan. 30, 1959.

[40] See above, n. 11; in his speech at Stalin's funeral, Beria addressed Malenkov as a "talented disciple of Lenin and a faithful companion-in-arms of Stalin"; similar phrases appeared in the Soviet press in the first week after Stalin's death.

[41] On Khrushchev's manipulation of the Stalin "myth" see Rush, *Rise of Khrushchev,* 6-20. On December 21, 1954, the East German *Taegliche Rundschau* published a photomontage showing Khrushchev and Bulganin in the company of Stalin, Zhdanov, and Voroshilov at a session of the Supreme Soviet in 1938. Malenkov was removed from the original photograph and Khrushchev and Bulganin substituted (see Embree, *Soviet Union,* 164). Khrushchev's defence of the traditional emphasis on heavy industry was, apparently, closely related to the initial attempts to identify himself with Stalin.

the Central Committee and the party as a whole,[42] Khrushchev, after 1956, consistently sought identification with the "positive" and more "genuine" charismatic image of Lenin. Yet, despite a concerted publicity campaign to establish his claim to "discipleship" and "reincarnation" of Lenin, Khrushchev's personality, past history, and *modus operandi* seem to typify him more as a "bureaucratic" than "charismatic" leader.[43]

II

Shifting alignments and continued friction within the short-lived "collective leadership" reflected the futile search of Stalin's heirs for an alternative to personal dictatorship. The alternative of stable majority rule in the Presidium proved to be incompatible with the logic of Soviet totalitarianism.[44] The rise of Khrushchev to the position of undisputed control of the main instruments of Soviet power ensured what the "collective leadership" could not offer—unity of command, ideological certainty, a dynamic and flexible leadership, and a tangible focus of loyalty.

This inner compulsion of totalitarianism to concentrate authority in the hands of a single leader was obviously only one of several factors responsible for the rise of Khrushchev. It does not explain why it was Khrushchev rather than Malenkov or Beria, initially the two most powerful contenders for Stalin's mantle, who took advantage of this objective tendency. Such interdependent factors as personalities and policies combined with the changing configurations of personal cliques and functional "interest groups" at the apex of the Soviet pyramid to shift the balance of power in Khrushchev's favour. Miscalculation and over-confidence on the part of Malenkov and Beria also played a part in forging coalitions that frustrated their bids for power and placed the much more inconspicuous and cautious Khrushchev in charge of the party machinery. Once entrenched in the crucial position of First Secretary, Khrushchev proved himself a brilliant student of Stalin in the arts of political warfare.

[42] See, e.g. editorial "Monolitnoe edinstvo i splochennost' partii i naroda" in *Kommunist*, no. 4, March, 1953, 23-32, which states: "The C. C. [Central Committee] is rightly regarded as the incarnation of the wisdom of the Party, its gigantic experience. . . ." See also J. Towster, "The Soviet Union After Stalin," *American Slavic and East European Review*, XIII, no. 4, Dec., 1954, 471-99.

[43] This observation may be substantiated by such evident traits of Khrushchev's personality as his pragmatism (*praktitsism*) and extrovert behaviour, his apparent lack of *mystique*, as well as his career as an *apparatchik* who rose to power through a succession of secretarial offices. His emphasis on expertness and specialization of the party officials and his disparagement of theory in favour of "practical results" also point in this direction. On his political career, see William K. Medlin, "Khrushchev," *Russian Review*, XVII, no. 4, 1958, and XVIII, nos. 1-3, 1959.

[44] To quote one of the sharpest observers of the Soviet scene, "the concept of collective leadership endured as long as there was a relative equilibrium of power within the Soviet leadership, *preventing* the formation of a working majority. The process of elimination before such a 'working' majority could be formed, left—in the end—a 'majority of one,'" that is, Khrushchev. Bialer, "But Some Are More Equal than Others," 47.

There are, indeed, some striking analogies between the techniques used by Stalin in the 1920's and those used by Khrushchev.

(*a*) Having established themselves as Secretary, both Stalin and Khrushchev used the broad powers of this office over the nomination, confirmation, cooptation, and dismissal of party officials to pack the local and territorial secretariats and bureaux with their own supporters. They were able thereby to secure the control of the party's electoral machinery and, through it, control of the Congress and the Central Committee. Thus they could deprive their opponents in the Politburo-Presidium of support in the nominally superior party organs; and by invoking certain party rules and resolutions at the appropriate moment, they could isolate, discredit, and finally remove their adversaries from leading positions.

(*b*) Capitalizing on the party prerogatives of *nomenklatura* (patronage)[45] both Stalin and Khrushchev placed their adherents in charge of the governmental and police organs, the army, and the media of communication and indoctrination. By depriving their opponents of institutional support outside the party hierarchy, both men used these institutions to their own advantage. Khrushchev, in particular, relied on the party's monopoly of propaganda to silence or distort the arguments of his critics, and to compromise them before the public.[46]

(*c*) As Stalin had before him, Khrushchev successfully played off his principal rivals against each other by manipulating the issues calculated to incite animosities among them, and he shrewdly alternated concessions and persuasion with threats and political blackmail [47] to split and demoralize the opposition. Indeed the talents the two men shared—talents for intrigue and manipulation, for dissimulation and conspicuous unpretentiousness—were of decisive importance in the initial stages of their drive for power, when they were still overshadowed and outnumbered by more prominent aspirants to Soviet leadership.

It would be, however, an over-simplification to explain Khrushchev's rise merely in terms of dissimulation, manipulation, and demagogy. Al-

---

[45] For a discussion of this crucial instrument of party control, see: D. J. R. Scott, *Russian Political Institutions* (London, 1958), 181-2; John A. Armstrong, *The Soviet Bureaucratic Elite* (New York, 1959), 76-7; and M. Fainsod, *Smolensk under Soviet Rule* (Cambridge, Mass., 1958), 64-6, 86-8.

[46] Thus, immediately after the Plenum of June, 1957, the whole party *agit-prop* apparatus was mobilized to "explain" the decisions of the Plenum and to discredit members of the "anti-party group" who, on the other hand, were denied any means of stating their case or justifying their actions. According to *Partiinaia zhizn'* (no. 13, July, 1957, 15), within less than three weeks over 3 million party members took part in special meetings condemning the "factionalists," over 660,000 members delivering speeches against the "anti-party group."

[47] The taking over by his *apparatchiki* of the secret police files and the personal secretariat of Stalin supplied Khrushchev with enough ammunition to compromise (and to intimidate) any of Stalin's former lieutenants. Witness, for example, his use of the "now discovered" party documents in his "secret speech" or of the "'Leningrad Affair" evidence against Malenkov.

though he lacked Stalin's theoretical mind, Khrushchev had other qualities that helped to tip the scales in his favour—political instinct, a capacity for facing the burning issues of the day and translating them into bold and imaginative programmes,[48] and a peculiar mixture of ideological revivalism, folksiness, and pragmatic common sense.

Nor must the similarities in the techniques employed by Stalin and Khrushchev blind us to substantial differences in other aspects of the two successions crises. In contrast to the "pre-totalitarian" conditions existing at the time of Lenin's death, the character of the post-Stalin succession struggle reflected the tremendous centralization of authority in the upper layers of the Soviet political structure, as well as the conditioned conformity of the party rank and file. At no time during the 1950's did there emerge anything that resembled the great ideological debate of the 1920's, when the opposing factions reached down into the party ranks and published their appeals and platforms. The post-Stalin struggle was conducted in the secretive circle of the Presidium and the Central Committee. The echoes of this muted conflict reached the outer world in the carefully edited and invariably biased versions issued by the winning side—the faction controlling the party *apparat* and propaganda media—and only then when losers were to be publicly exposed, slandered, and condemned. The regimented "public" outwardly gave its habitual and invariably "unanimous" endorsement to each of the successive casualty reports, varying its applause for the winners in accordance with their latest rank.

The functional structures of the régime—the huge state bureaucracy, the police, and the army—unlike those of the 1920's now entered into the struggle for power; they "participated," however, not as autonomous power groups but rather as manipulatable instruments of uncertain strength, split at the top by conflicting loyalties, and subject to shifting allegiance depending on the policies and power configurations of the day. Their upper layers having been absorbed into the party, these functional groupings could not be opposed to the party; as a rule, what really mattered were the cross-functional and cross-institutional hierarchies culminating in one of the several power figures in the Presidium, and only these power figures had any chance of success.[49] The party, having become both a participant in and the arena of the succession struggle, had shown itself hardly immune to factionalism, and far less monolithic than it had professed to be.

It is in trying to tackle this crucial question of factionalism[50] that we

---

[48] Let us mention only such programmes as the opening of virgin lands, managerial and administrative decentralization, dissolution of the machine-tractor stations, educational reform, reorganization of the judiciary and the police and (in the field of foreign policy) reconciliation with Yugoslavia, the "peaceful coexistence" campaign combined with an all-out economic offensive, and the proposal for total disarmament.

[49] See Armstrong, *Soviet Bureaucratic Elite,* 146.

[50] On the ramifications of this problem see Daniel Bell, "Ten Theories in Search of Reality" in A. Dallin, ed., *Soviet Conduct in World Affairs* (New York, 1960), 25-6.

become painfully aware of the limitations of our knowledge about developments *inside* party councils. What were the foci around which factions
formed in the Presidium and the Central Committee? What caused their
disintegration and the crystallization of new alignments? Khrushchev, for
example, reached back for support and trusted assistants into the personal
machines he had built over the years of his secretaryship in the Ukrainian
and Moscow party organizations.[51] But we have also seen that many of those
who had for a long time been lieutenants and protégés of Malenkov, Kaganovich,[52] and Beria defected to Khrushchev, just as, at the critical moment—
before the Plenum of June, 1957—some of Khrushchev's own protégés joined
the ranks of his opponents. Personal likes and dislikes, self-interest, cynicism,
deception, intimidation, and fear cannot fully explain these phenomena; we
must also make some allowance for the real differences over policy and ideology as well as for such human factors as imagination, loyalty, and courage.

The struggle did not proceed in a social vacuum. Although society
could not legitimately determine the choice of Stalin's successor, such considerations as the popular expectations of change and the people's desire for
greater security, a relaxation of controls, and a more decent standard of living could not but influence the nature and the outcome of the struggle in the
Kremlin. All three major contenders for the succession—Malenkov, Beria,
Khrushchev—addressed themselves to the grievances and aspirations of
particular social groups, hoping to win support by praise, promises, and
concessions. Thus while Malenkov strove for the support of the Soviet
intelligentzia and the urban consumers, Beria sought to identify himself
with the grievances of the non-Russian nationalities: Khrushchev, while
showing no scruples about appropriating his rivals' programme, assiduously
courted the long-neglected lower strata of Soviet society—the peasantry and
the factory workers.[53] The submission of his major policy proposals for
"popular discussion" (which he could guide and censor through his control of the party propaganda machinery) was a manœuvre which he used
repeatedly to win popularity and strengthen his hand against his critics
in the Presidium.[54]

Nor can we, in reviewing the post-Stalin succession struggle, discount a
few other factors whose relative weight cannot be established with any

[51] On Khrushchev's Ukrainian machine and some of his former lieutenants in the
Ukrainian Communist party, whom he promoted and used during his struggle for power,
see Armstrong, *Soviet Bureaucratic Elite*, 146-51.

[52] Ironically, Khrushchev himself had for a long time been Kaganovich's protégé; it was
through the latter that he first rose to prominence in the Moscow apparatus during the
1929-37 period.

[53] His measures to reinvigorate the trade unions and to increase their influence on factory management, as well as to narrow the differences in pay and salaries, his attacks on
"bureaucracy" and the "petty-bourgeois" tendencies of the Soviet intelligentzia, and his
interest in educational reform with its emphasis on manual work and technical training—
all can be related to his "proletarian" orientation.

[54] E.g., in connection with industrial-managerial decentralization, dissolution of the
machine-tractor stations, educational reform, etc.

precision. What we have in mind is the role played by the Soviet satellites and allies, especially China, as well as the impact of the world situation. One can assume that the anticipated reaction of the "fraternal People's China," the posture of the Western powers, and the nature of the problems to be solved inside and outside the Soviet bloc must have weakened the chances of some and strengthened those of other contenders for the Soviet leadership.

III

The régime's survival through the two succession crises points to an essential difference between the earlier forms of dictatorship and their modern totalitarian counterparts. The latter, as Soviet experience illustrates, can compensate for the mortality of rulers by the vitality of a party machine that has successfully destroyed or absorbed traditional social structures. As Sigmund Neumann has clearly brought out in his *Permanent Revolution,* the tenacity of totalitarian dictatorships derives from a "party machine which represents the life-line of the present-day autocracies. . . . The existence of a machine promises the survival of autocratic rule beyond the life span of its creators. . . ." [55]

The question of a successor to Stalin seems now to be closed. Although Khrushchev's present position resembles that of Stalin in 1930-4, it is by no means certain that he aspires to the kind of despotic power that Stalin exercised after the Great Purges. Khrushchev's personality, the changed context of his authority, and the tendencies released by the upheavals since Stalin's death make unlikely a complete return to Stalinism.

Khrushchev is sixty-six years old, and it should not be long before the question of succession is reopened in the Soviet Union. Although it is reported that Khrushchev has referred to Frol Kozlov as his possible successor,[56] it is highly doubtful whether the apostle of "socialist legality" and "party democracy" would resort to an unprecedented formal designation of an heir. Pragmatist that he is, Khrushchev should realize the futility of testaments in totalitarian dictatorships. Should he die before stepping aside for a man of his choice, we can expect another crisis, a new "collective leadership" taking over the reins of authority, fighting it out, and producing in the end, through the familiar process of elimination, a new personal dictator. The winner in this struggle is not likely to be the most obvious candidate or the most brilliant of the dictator's lieutenants, but again a "dark horse" candidate, the "unostentatious master of the [party] machine." [57] Khrushchev's reforms, which have reasserted the party's supremacy over society and strengthened the control of the party apparatus over the other func-

---

[55] New York, 1942, viii-ix.

[56] See H. E. Salisbury, "After Khrushchev, Who?" *Saturday Evening Post,* March 5, 1960, 19-21, 84-6.

[57] Neumann, *Permanent Revolution,* 95.

tional hierarchies of the system, have indeed made the secretarial machine of the party the central avenue of political succession in the Soviet Union.

THE PARTY CRISIS AND EPILOGUE ON TERROR

NIKITA S. KHRUSHCHEV*

Some insight into the nature, implications and consequences of the critical struggle for power within the Party in 1957 may be gleaned from an analysis of Nikita S. Khrushchev's final speech to the 22nd Party Congress.

In an earlier address to the Congress, Khrushchev had explained the reasons which had led to the denunciation of Stalin in 1956:

What would have become of the Party and the country had the cult of the individual not been condemned, had its harmful consequences not been removed and the Leninist standards of Party and government activity not restored? The result would have been a cleavage between Party and people, grave violations of Soviet democracy and revolutionary legality, slower economic progress, a lower rate of communist construction and hence a deterioration of the people's standard of living. In the sphere of international relations, the result would have been a weakening of Soviet positions on the world scene and a worsening of relations with other countries, which would have had dire consequences. That is why criticism of the cult of the individual and the elimination of its consequences were of the utmost political and practical importance.

In his final address to the Congress on October 27, 1961, Khrushchev reiterated and elaborated on some of the charges made against Stalin in his 1956 "secret" speech. On this occasion, however, his remarks were at an open session and were published throughout the U.S.S.R. Also subjected to vitriolic denunciation and linked with Stalin's crimes—or, at the very least, with an unwillingness to expose them and alter Stalin's course—were "the anti-Party group headed by Molotov, Kaganovich and Malenkov."

During the proceedings, speaker after speaker mounted the rostrum and vied with each other in loosing fierce invective against "the anti-Party group" which included senior old Bolsheviks, two former Premiers, and a former Marshal of the Soviet Union. Typical remarks, to "stormy applause," were the following: "Molotov, Malenkov and Kaganovich—these slugs— should not have been trusted"; Kaganovich is a degenerate, in whom there has been nothing Communist for a long time"; "on Malenkov's conscience lies the deaths of totally innocent people and numerous repressions." They were called "swamp creatures . . . used to slime and mud," a "contemptible

* First Secretary of the Communist Party and Chairman of the Council of Ministers of the U.S.S.R. The selection is reproduced, with permission, from a translation of his address of October 27, 1961, in *The Current Digest of the Soviet Press*, Vol. XIII (Dec. 13, 1961), pp. 27-31. The address appears in its entirety in *Current Soviet Policies—IV*, published by Columbia University Press from the translations of the *Current Digest*.

group of factionalists . . . and miserable clique of oppositionists." Although reference was made to a letter of Molotov's to the Congress, it was not published. Nor were members of the so-called anti-Party group permitted to present their case to the Congress or to the Russian people (except for a humiliating letter of apology from Voroshilov).

Western scholars on the whole are convinced that a victory for the "anti-Party group" would have prevented or delayed such relaxation as has taken place in the U.S.S.R., and brought a more intransigent and obdurate foreign policy. (In this editor's opinion, the relaxation should not be dismissed or denigrated.) Nonetheless, the lack of any real opportunity for defeated leaders in the U.S.S.R. to publicly voice their opposition and dissent suggests that Soviet society bears little resemblance to the Western conception of democracy and, it is appropriate to add, to the Marxist-Leninist theoretical conception of "proletarian democracy."

It is interesting to speculate on what the Russian people would have been told about Khrushchev (and his supporters) if the "anti-Party group" had prevailed in 1957. It may be asserted confidently that in no event would Khrushchev have received the opportunity to reply.

Comrades! The 22nd Congress can be called with perfect justice a congress of monolithic unity of the Leninist party and of complete unanimity and solidarity. . . .

Many comrades who have spoken here have angrily condemned the anti-Party subversive activity of the handful of factionalists led by Molotov, Kaganovich and Malenkov. Our whole party and the entire people have rejected these schismatics who opposed everything new and who wished to restore the defective methods that reigned under the cult of the individual. They wanted to return to those days, so difficult for our party and our country, when no one was ensured against arbitrariness and repressions. Yes, Molotov and the others wanted precisely that.

We resolutely reject such methods of leadership, if they may be so called. We stand and we shall continue to stand firmly on the position that inner-Party affairs must be solved on the basis of Leninist norms, on the basis of the methods of persuasion and broad democracy. (*Applause.*) The Party's strongest weapon is its ideology, the great teaching of Marxism-Leninism, which has brought many glorious victories to the Party, to the Soviet people and to the whole international Communist movement. (*Prolonged applause.*)

Is it possible for different opinions to appear in the Party at various periods of its activity, especially during transitional stages? Yes, it is possible. What should be done, then, with those who express their own opinion, different from that of others? Our stand is for the application in such cases not of repressions but of Leninist methods of persuasion and explanation. . . .

In the years following Lenin's death, the Leninist norms of Party life were grossly distorted in the conditions of the Stalin cult. Stalin elevated limitations on inner-Party and Soviet democracy to the status of norms of inner-Party and state life. He crudely flouted the Leninist principles of leadership and permitted arbitrariness and abuses of power.

Stalin could look at a comrade sitting at the same table with him and say: "Your eyes are shifty today," after which it could be assumed that the comrade whose eyes were supposedly shifty was under suspicion.

Comrade delegates! I wish to tell the Congress how the anti-Party group reacted to the proposal that the question of abuses of power in the period of the cult of the individual be placed before the 20th Party Congress.

Molotov, Kaganovich, Malenkov, Voroshilov and others categorically objected to this proposal. In answer to their objections they were told that if they continued to oppose the raising of this question, the delegates to the Party Congress would be asked to decide the matter. We had no doubt that the Congress would favor discussion of the question. Only then did they agree, and the question of the cult of the individual was presented to the 20th Party Congress. But even after the Congress, the factionalists continued their struggle and obstructed in every possible way the clarification of the question of abuses of power, fearing that their role as accomplices in the mass repressions would come to light.

The mass repressions began after the murder of Kirov. A great deal of effort is still necessary to determine fully who was guilty of his death. The more deeply we study the materials relating to Kirov's death, the more questions arise. . . . There are still many, a great many, unclarified circumstances in this and other similar cases.

Comrades! It is our duty to make a thorough and comprehensive study of all such cases rising out of the abuse of power. Time will pass, we shall die, we are all mortal, but as long as we continue to work we can and must find out many things and tell the truth to the Party and the people. We are obliged to do everything possible to establish the truth now, for the greater the length of time that separates us from these events, the more difficult will it become to re-establish the truth. It is now too late to bring the dead back to life, as the saying goes. But it is necessary that all this be recorded truthfully in the history of the Party. This must be done so that phenomena of this sort can never be repeated in the future. (*Stormy, prolonged applause.*)

You can imagine how difficult it was to solve these questions when the Presidium of the Central Committee included people who had themselves been guilty of abuses of power, of mass repressions. They stubbornly resisted all measures aimed at exposing the cult of the individual and then opened up a struggle against the Central Committee, wishing to change the composition of its leadership, to change the Leninist Party policy, the course laid down by the 20th Congress.

Naturally, they did not want to investigate cases of this sort. You have heard Comrade Shelepin's speech. He told the Congress many things, but needless to say he told by no means all that has now come to light. Thousands of completely innocent people perished, and each person is a whole story. Many Party, government and military figures perished.

Of course, those people in the Presidium of the Central Committee who had been responsible for violations of legality and mass repressions resisted in every possible way the exposure of arbitrary acts in the period of the cult of the individual, and then they launched an anti-Party factionalist struggle against the leadership of the Central Committee, concentrating their fire primarily against me personally, as First Secretary of the Central Committee, inasmuch as it had fallen to me in the line of duty to raise these questions. It was necessary to accept blows and to reply to these blows. (*Stormy, prolonged applause.*)

The participants in the anti-Party factionalist group hoped to seize leadership in the Party and the country and to remove the comrades who were exposing the criminal actions committed in the period of the cult of the individual. The anti-Party group wanted to place Molotov in the leadership. Then, of course, there would have been no exposures of these abuses of power.

Even after the 20th Congress had condemned the cult of the individual, the anti-Party group did all in its power to prevent the exposure from going any further. Molotov said that in large matters there may be bad things and good. He justified the actions that had taken place in the period of the cult of the individual and claimed that such actions are possible and that their repetition in the future is possible. Such was the course of the anti-Party factionalist group. This is not a simple aberration. It is a calculated, criminal and adventurist position. They wanted to divert the Party and the country from the Leninist path, they wanted to return to the policy and methods of leadership of the period of the cult of the individual. But they miscalculated. The Central Committee, our whole party and the entire Soviet people, administered a decisive rebuff to the anti-Party group and exposed and smashed the factionalists. (*Stormy, prolonged applause.*)

People have spoken here with pain about many innocent victims among outstanding Party and government figures. Such outstanding military commanders as Tukhachevsky, Yakir, Uborevich, Kork, Yegorov, Eideman and others fell victim to the mass repressions. They had been worthy people of our army, especially Tukhachevsky, Yakir and Uborevich, who had been brilliant military leaders. Later Blyukher and other outstanding military commanders fell victim to the repressions. . . .

Many splendid commanders and political officials of the Red Army were executed. Here among the delegates there are comrades—I do not wish to name them so as not to cause them pain—who spent many years in prison. They were being "persuaded"—persuaded by quite definite techniques—

that they were either German or British or some other kind of spies. And several of them "confessed." Even in cases when such people were told that the accusation of espionage had been withdrawn, they themselves insisted on their previous testimony, because they believed it was better to stand on their false testimony in order to put an end as quickly as possible to the torment and to die as quickly as possible. . . .

I knew Comrade Yakir well. I knew Tukhachevsky too, but not as well as Yakir. In 1961, during a conference in Alma-Ata, his son, who works in Kazakhstan, came to see me. He asked me about his father. What could I tell him? When we investigated these cases in the Presidium of the Central Committee and received a report that neither Tukhachevsky nor Yakir nor Uborevich had been guilty of any crime against the Party and the state, we asked Molotov, Kaganovich and Voroshilov:

"Are you for rehabilitating them?"

"Yes, we are for it," they answered.

"But it was you who executed these people," we told them indignantly. "When were you acting according to your conscience, then or now?"

But they did not answer this question. And they will not answer it. You have heard the notations they wrote on letters received by Stalin. What can they say?

In his speech to the Congress, Comrade Shelepin has told you how these finest representatives of the Communist Party in the Red Army were killed. He also read Comrade Yakir's letter to Stalin and the recommendations on this letter. It should be said that at one time Yakir was highly esteemed by Stalin. It may be added that when Yakir was shot he exclaimed: "Long live the Party, long live Stalin!"

He had so much faith in the Party, so much faith in Stalin that he never permitted himself the thought that a deliberate injustice was being committed. He believed that certain enemies had found their way into the NKVD agencies. When Stalin was told how Yakir had behaved before his death, he cursed Yakir. . . .

The fate of Alyosha Svanidze, the brother of Stalin's first wife, who was less well known to the broad circles of our party, was also tragic. He had been an old Bolshevik, but Beria made it appear, through all kinds of machinations, that Svanidze had been planted near Stalin by the German intelligence service, although he was a very close friend of Stalin's. And Svanidze was shot. Before the execution, Svanidze was told that Stalin had said that if he asked for forgiveness he would be pardoned. When Stalin's words were repeated to Svanidze, he asked: "What am I supposed to ask forgiveness for? I have committed no crime." He was shot. After Svanidze's death, Stalin said: "See how proud he is: He died without asking forgiveness." It never occurred to him that Svanidze had been above all an honest man.

Thus many completely innocent people perished. That is what the cult of the individual means. That is why we cannot show the slightest tolerance toward abuses of power.

Comrades! The Presidium of the Congress has received letters from old Bolsheviks in which they write that in the period of the cult of the individual outstanding Party and state figures, such loyal Leninists as Comrades Chubar, Kossior, Rudzutak, Postyshev, Eikhe, Voznesensky, Kuznetsov and others, died guiltless.

The comrades propose that the memory of the outstanding Party and state figures who fell victim to completely unjustified repressions in the period of the cult of the individual be perpetuated. We believe this proposal to be a proper one. (*Stormy, prolonged applause.*) It would be advisable to charge the Central Committee that will be elected by the 22nd Party Congress with deciding this question positively. Perhaps a monument should be erected in Moscow to the memory of the comrades who fell victim to arbitrary rule. (*Applause.*)

In the conditions of the cult of the individual the Party was deprived of normal life. People who usurp power cease being accountable to the Party, they escape from under its control. Herein is the greatest danger of the cult of the individual. The situation in the Party must always be such that every leader is accountable to the Party and its agencies, and the Party can replace any leader when it considers this necessary. (*Applause.*)

Now, since the 20th Congress, Leninist principles of Party life and collective leadership have been restored in the Party. The new Party Program and Statutes give legal force to propositions that restore the Leninist norms of Party life and preclude the possibility of relapses into the cult of the individual.

The 20th Congress of our party condemned the cult of the individual, restored justice and demanded that the distortions that had taken place be eliminated. The Party Central Committee adopted resolute measures to prevent a return to arbitrariness and lawlessness. The anti-Party group of Molotov, Kaganovich, Malenkov and others resisted in every possible way the implementation of these measures.

The factionalists undertook an attempt to seize the leadership and to steer the Party away from the Leninist path. They prepared reprisals against those who defended the course set by the 20th Congress. When the anti-Party group was smashed, its participants expected that they would be treated in the same way they had dealt with people at the time of the cult of the individual and in the way they hoped to deal with those who favored the restoration of Leninist norms of Party life. . . .

I want to talk particularly about Comrade Voroshilov. He has been approaching me and telling me about his tribulations. His state of mind is understandable, of course. But we are political leaders and we cannot be guided by feelings alone. Feelings may differ, and they can be deceptive. Here at the Congress Voroshilov listens to the criticism directed against him and walks around like a beaten man. But you should have seen him at the time when the anti-Party group raised its hand against the Party. Then Voroshilov was a man of action; he came forth, if not on horseback, at least in his full regalia, in battle dress, so to speak. . . .

Comrade Voroshilov committed grave errors. But I believe, comrades, that he must be treated differently than the other active participants in the anti-Party group—than Molotov, Kaganovich and Malenkov, for instance. It must be said that in the course of the bitter struggle with the factionalists during the early part of the June plenary session of the Central Committee, when Comrade Voroshilov saw the monolithic unity of the Central Committee members in the struggle against the anti-Party group, he apparently became aware that he had gone too far. Voroshilov understood that he had joined with men who were fighting against the Party, and he condemned the actions of the anti-Party group and admitted his mistakes. He thereby in some measure helped the Central Committee. We cannot underestimate this step on his part, comrades, because at the time this was a support for the Party. . . .

Comrade Voroshilov has been sharply criticized; this criticism was just, for he had committed grave mistakes and Communists cannot forget them. But I believe that our approach to Comrade Voroshilov should be considerate, that we should show magnanimity. I believe that he sincerely condemns his actions and repents them. (*Applause.*)

Kliment Yefremovich Voroshilov has lived many years and has done much good for our party and people. I want to say that when the Central Committee considered Comrade Voroshilov's request that he be relieved of the duties of Chairman of the Presidium of the U.S.S.R. Supreme Soviet for reasons of health, the members of the Central Committee, despite the mistakes he had committed, spoke warmly about him. In May, 1960, in recognition of his services to the Party and the state, the Presidium of the Supreme Soviet awarded Kliment Yefremovich Voroshilov the title Hero of Socialist Labor. (*Applause.*)

I believe that Kliment Yefremovich will, together with us, actively fight for the cause of our party. (*Stormy applause.*)

Comrades! The 22nd Congress has confirmed with full force that the course of the 20th Party Congress, the course of the restoration and further development of Leninist norms of Party and state life, the course of raising the leading role of the Party and the creative activeness of the popular masses, is the only correct course. The 22nd Congress is confirming this beneficial course. The Party Program and Statutes and the resolutions of the Congress set forth new guarantees against relapses into the cult of the individual. The role of the Party as the great inspiring and organizing force in the building of communism is rising higher still.

I would like to say a few words about the following question. In many speeches at the Congress, and not infrequently in our press as well, when mention is made of the activity of our party's Central Committee a certain special emphasis is placed on me personally, and my role in carrying out major Party and government measures is underlined.

I understand the kind feelings guiding these comrades. Allow me, however, to emphasize emphatically that everything that is said about me should be said about the Central Committee of our Leninist party and about the Presidium of the Central Committee. (*Stormy, prolonged applause.*) Not one major measure, not one responsible pronouncement has been carried out upon anyone's personal directive; they have all been the result of collective deliberation and collective decision. (*Stormy applause.*) And this concluding speech, too, has been considered and approved by the executive collective. (*Prolonged applause.*) Our great strength, comrades, lies in collective leadership, in collegial decisions on all questions of principle. (*Stormy applause.*)

No matter what abilities this or that leader may possess, no matter what contributions he may make to the cause, he cannot achieve true and lasting success without the support of the collective, without the most active participation of the whole Party and of the broad popular masses in the implementation of adopted measures. This must be clearly understood and constantly borne in mind by all. (*Applause.*)

Communist leaders are strong through the activity of the masses they lead. If they correctly understand and express the interests of the Party, the interests of the people, if they struggle for these interests without sparing their strength, their energy and even their life, if they are inseparable from the Party in great matters and in small, just as the Party is inseparable from the people, such leaders will always be supported by the Party and the people. And the cause for which such a leader fights will inevitably triumph. (*Prolonged applause.*) . . .

While resolutely pronouncing themselves opposed to all the disgusting phenomena of the cult of the individual, Marxist-Leninists have always recognized and will continue to recognize the authority of leaders.

But it would be incorrect to single out this or that leader, to set him apart from the executive collective or to exalt him inordinately. This is contrary to the principles of Marxism-Leninism. It is known with what impatience Marx, Engels and Lenin spoke out against those who eulogized their contributions. Yet it is difficult to overestimate the great role of the founders of scientific communism, Marx, Engels and Lenin, and their contributions to the working class and to all mankind. (*Prolonged applause.*)

Feelings of self-praise and any special emphasis on or excessive exaggeration of the role of individual leaders are utterly alien to true Marxist-Leninists. They find it simply insulting when someone tries obtrusively to set them apart, to isolate them from the executive nucleus of comrades. (*Stormy applause.*)

We Communists highly value and support the authority of correct and mature leadership. We must safeguard the authority of the leaders who are recognized by the Party and the people. But each leader must also understand the other side of the matter—never to plume himself on his position, to remember that in holding this or that post he is merely fulfilling the will of the Party and the will of the people, who may have invested the greatest power in him but never lose control over him. (*Applause.*) The leader who forgets this pays heavily for his mistake. I would add that he will pay while he is alive, or even after his death the people will not forgive him, as has happened with the condemnation of the cult of Stalin. (*Applause.*) A person who forgets that he is obliged to fulfill the will of the Party and of the people cannot, properly speaking, be called a true leader; there must be no such "leaders" either in the Party or in the state apparatus. (*Applause.*)

Of course, for many reasons great power is concentrated in the hands of the man who holds an executive post. A leader advanced by the Party and the people must not abuse his power. In the reports to the Congress you have heard about the measures that we have implemented and that we shall carry out in order that a revival of the ugly phenomena of the cult of the individual may never recur in the future. But there is one thing that no statutory provision can prescribe: The collective of leaders must thoroughly understand that a situation must not be permitted to arise whereby any authority, even the most deserving one, can cease to heed the opinions of those who have advanced him. (*Applause.*)

It is wrong, comrades, it is simply impossible to permit the inception and development of instances when the merited prestige of an individual may assume forms in which he fancies that everything is permissible to him and that he no longer has need of the collective. In such a case this individual may stop listening to the voices of other comrades who have been advanced to leadership, just as he was, and may begin suppressing them. Our great teacher V. I. Lenin resolutely fought against this, and the Party paid too dear a price for not heeding his wise counsel in good time.

So let us be worthy disciples of Lenin in this important matter. (*Stormy, prolonged applause.*)

Chapter 14

WHO RULES IN RUSSIA?

Few serious students of Soviet affairs would maintain that significant political power resides in the mass of the Russian people—except in an inchoate sense—or even in the millions of Communist Party members as a whole. While E. H. Carr and Milovan Djilas, in the excerpts that follow, both see power concentrated in a ruling group which, in Carr's phrase, "finds its institutional embodiment in the Party," they disagree on whether there may be said to be a ruling class in Russia and on the extent to which there is fluidity in Soviet society and the ruling group.

Whatever potential may have existed at the time of the death of Stalin in 1953 for a challenge to the dominance of the Communist Party by the government machine, the secret police, the army, or other forces, it is now abundantly clear that the hegemony of the Party is firmly established. As Merle Fainsod wrote, speaking generally, "the major thrust of the Khrushchev reforms has been to reinforce the authority of the party apparatus in every direction."

Parenthetically, typical of the Communist need to relate practice to theory is Khrushchev's justification of the primacy of the Party. In an interview with Iverach McDonald, foreign editor of The Times of London, on January 31, 1958, Khrushchev linked decentralization of industry with the transition to a communist society under which "many organs of state administration will gradually wither away. Thus the army, the court, the Prosecutor's office and other organs will wither away." He further maintained that "Already now social life is developing exactly along lines following from the theoretical principles of Marxism-Leninism," and added:

So, in these conditions, in order to utilize most rationally the available material and other resources, the Party's role is increasing. The Party has a stronger foundation than the government organs. It has arisen and exists not as a result of some obligations of a legislative kind. Its development is conditioned by circumstances following from political views of people, that is, from propositions of a moral factor. And humanity will always need moral factors.

The Communist Party is organized and presumably governed by its "Rules"—although obviously they imposed no barrier to Stalin's despotism. The New Rules (adopted at the 22nd Party Congress in October 1961) are, in form, the most thoroughgoing and far-reaching revision since the first all-Union Rules were adopted in 1925. Probably the most important change is found in Article 25, which reads as follows:

The principle of systematic turnover of the membership of Party bodies and of continuity of leadership is observed in elections of Party bodies.

At all regular elections of the Central Committee of the C.P.S.U. and its Presidium, not less than one-fourth of the membership shall be newly elected. Presidium members shall as a rule be elected for not more than three successive terms. Particular Party workers may, by virtue of their recognized authority and high political, organizational or other abilities, be successively elected to executive bodies for a longer period. In such cases, election requires a majority of at least three-fourths of the votes cast by closed ballot.

At least one-third of the members of the Central Committees of the Union-republic Communist Parties and of territory and province committees chosen at each regular election, and one-half of the members of region, city and district Party committees and the committees and bureaus of primary Party organizations, shall be new members. Furthermore, members of these executive Party bodies may be elected for not more than three successive terms. The secretaries of primary Party organizations may be elected for not more than two successive terms.

A meeting, conference or Congress may, in consideration of the political and work qualities of an individual, elect him to an executive body for a longer period. In such cases election requires that not less than three-fourths of the Communists participating in the voting cast their ballots for him.

Party members who are not re-elected to an executive Party body on the expiration of their terms may be re-elected in subsequent elections.

Philip E. Mosely notes in his analysis of the 22nd Party Congress that this change is "supposed to broaden the recruitment of new leaders and to undercut the tendency of Party bureaucrats to dominate their local units and muzzle criticism." He emphasizes that while tenure of office for leaders is "as a rule" to be restricted to three successive terms, Party officials of "recognized authority and high political, organizational or other abilities" may be exempted from the limitation. The fact is, Mr. Mosely maintains, that during the turnover in the upper ranks of the Party in recent years, "Khrushchev has reinforced his control over the entire apparatus of power."

Professor Jan F. Triska in a recent book, Soviet Communism: Program and Rules, *finds the differences between the old and new Rules "significant." The 1961 Rules are "anti-Stalinist in spirit, broaden what the communists call 'inner-Party democracy,' de-emphasize the authoritarian role of the top Party bodies and limit their members' tenure in office, somewhat encourage criticism from below, and make the Party seem less conspiratorial and absolutist." However, he believes that mandatory turnover linked to the exception for leaders of "recognized authority" may very well "have been intended by Khrushchev to serve as a periodic, institutionalized, legitimate purge of his actual or potential rivals in the Party."*

Whether the promise of diffusion of power within the Communist Party will be realized remains to be seen.

WHO RULES IN SOVIET SOCIETY?

E. H. CARR*

The victors of 1917 thought they were establishing a dictatorship of the proletariat, or, a shade more realistically, a dictatorship of the proletariat and the peasantry. Just as the peasants were encouraged to seize the land, so the workers were encouraged to take over the factories. "Workers' control" was the slogan of the hour. Workers' control did not work, and without it the dictatorship of the proletariat ceased to be a reality and became a symbol. It was replaced by what? The answer is clear. By the dictatorship of the party (a phrase used at the time by Lenin and others, though afterwards rejected as heretical) and later by the dictatorship of the party machine. In other words, if we want to identify the ruling group in Soviet society, we have to look not for a class but for a party.

The Marxist class analysis of society was a product of the nineteenth century. Few people are convinced by the famous generalization with which the Communist Manifesto opens, that all history has been the history of class struggles. Marx took what he correctly diagnosed as the most significant feature of contemporary society in Western Europe and sweepingly extended it to other periods, where its application was by no means so clear. Marx never explained what he meant by a class: it probably seemed so obvious a phenomenon of the world in which he lived as not to require definition. But I will take Lenin's definition: "Classes are groups of people of such a kind that one group can appropriate the labor of another, thanks to the difference of their position in the specific structure of the social economy."

This takes account of the two cardinal factors in class. Class is primarily based on common economic interest, but it also acquires a quasi-permanent character conferred on it by social tradition or convention. I have never been altogether happy about the application of the class analysis to countries like the United States where, for historical reasons, this quasi-permanent character is weak or non-existent, or to countries like Czarist Russia where the major divisions of society were not economic, but legal and constitutional; and I feel sure that it is altogether misleading as an explanation of the structure of Soviet society. There is no ruling class in Soviet Russia.

* Fellow, Trinity College, Cambridge. Author of the monumental *A History of Soviet Russia; Studies in Revolution; The Soviet Impact on the Western World,* and many scholarly articles on Soviet affairs. The selection is from *The Nation,* Vol. 181 (October 1, 1955), pp. 278-280. By permission.

There is a ruling group which finds its institutional embodiment in the party.

This is, I think, significant. A class is an economic formation, a party a political formation. I shall not argue that economic factors play a smaller role in the life of society than in the nineteenth century. But what I would maintain is that the clear-cut line of demarcation between economics and politics which dominated all economic thinking in the nineteenth century, including that of Marx, is out of date. In Soviet Russia, at any rate, economics means politics, and the structure of Soviet society must be analyzed in terms not of economic class but of political party.

As I have said, the dictatorship of the proletariat was replaced by the dictatorship of the party when workers' control collapsed in the factories. And workers' control collapsed because the workers lacked the necessary technical engineering and managerial skills. One of the first tasks of the party, of the ruling group, was to find the technicians and white-collar workers of all grades to put industry back into production; and the attitude to be adopted to these "specialists," as they were called, was a constant pre-occupation of party literature. And when, a few years later, the even more desperate problem was tackled of mechanizing agriculture and introducing modern methods of cultivation, the difficulty once more was to provide not only machinery but skilled personnel to use it and organize its use. It was precisely those specialists who, being indispensable to the regime, came to occupy a leading—and sometimes equivocal—position in the ruling group of what was still called a workers' state; and to study the party's attitude toward them is an important part of the analysis of Soviet society.

From the outset the attitude of the party toward specialists was utterly different from its position on the nepmen. The nepmen, and *a fortiori* the *kulak,* was *ex hypothesi* an enemy of the regime, pursuing aims incompatible with it, tolerated only so long as he had to be. A loyal nepman or a loyal *kulak* was an impossibility; no nepman or *kulak* could conceivably be admitted to the party. The specialist, on the other hand, though by his origins he might be a class enemy like the nepman, was pursuing the aims of the regime whose servant he was. His origins might make him suspect. But he could be, and often was, loyal; and as time went on more and more specialists became party members. Thus, for the specialist, origin was not the determining factor. He might be bourgeois by origin but he was not bourgeois in function. He did not enjoy the economic independence of the *entrepreneur*. On the contrary, he was politically dependent on the government and on the party. If he was successful, success was rewarded not by increased profits but by promotion to a bigger and better job. The soft-pedalling of world revolution, the proclamation of "socialism in one country," and the policy of industrialization eased the process of the assimilation for the specialist. By the end of the nineteen-twenties he had become, by and large, a loyal servant of the regime; the avenues of promotion and of party membership were wide open to him.

I do not think that up to this time the specialist had any important influence on decisions of policy. These were still taken by the old party leadership, by the survivors of the pre-revolutionary party intelligentsia. But in the nineteen-thirties, when a new generation grew up which had never known pre-revolutionary Russia, and when sons of workers had clambered up the educational ladder to the top, the distinctions began to fade. The taint of bourgeois origin was no longer acutely felt; and the whole group of white-collar workers—party officials, government officials, managers, technicians, teachers, doctors, lawyers, and intellectuals of all kinds—began gradually to coalesce. Official pronouncements began to extol the member of this new intelligentsia; the Stalin constitution enfranchised him irrespective of his origin; the party statute of 1939 gave him a status in the party side by side with the worker and the peasant.

It is in this new intelligentsia, recruited from different class origins, and not constituting a class in the Marxist or Leninist sense of the term, that we must look for the ruling group in Soviet society. This is the group which has substituted itself for the dictatorship of the proletariat; the only theoretical justification for the substitution is that its *raison d'etre* and its purpose—the cementing force which holds it together—is the industrialization of the country. In this respect, it still carries the dynamic of the proletarian revolution; and to this long-term purpose the immediate welfare of the worker, to say nothing of the peasant, will be ruthlessly sacrificed. The ruling group remains pledged to the eradication of everything bourgeois from Soviet society. It if still tolerates a handful of nepmen, it tolerates them because it must. It is engaged in a desperate uphill struggle to turn the *kolkhoz* worker into a good Socialist—a struggle only halted by the still more desperate need to induce him to feed the towns for a meager return in the form of consumer goods. This is the core of the problem which any ruling group that stands for industrialization has to face.

One more question: How far does this ruling group constitute a closed and privileged social order? . . . Every ruling group looks after its own, including its own children; and, when good educational facilities are scarce, it will see to it that its children get the best. But the essential facts about Soviet society is that it is the society of an expanding economy; and educational facilities, too, are expanding rapidly. In an expanding society policies of exclusion do not work and do not last. The child of the worker does not, it is true, start level with the child of the party official or of the industrial manager. But the gulf is not unbridgeable, and it seems likely to narrow if the Soviet economy continues to expand at anything like its present rate. So long as this goes on, Soviet society and the ruling group will remain fluid and we shall see further changes. Meanwhile, we only confuse ourselves by attempting to equate the present regime in Russia with anything we have seen in the past—whether with a Czarist autocracy or with a Victorian bourgeoisie. It is a new phenomenon in history, with new merits and new vices, and we had better try to see it for what it is.

THE NEW CLASS

Milovan Djilas*

Everything happened differently in the U.S.S.R. and other Communist countries from what the leaders—even such prominent ones as Lenin, Stalin, Trotsky, and Bukharin—anticipated. They expected that the state would rapidly wither away, that democracy would be strengthened. The reverse happened. They expected a rapid improvement in the standard of living—there has been scarcely any change in this respect and, in the subjugated East European countries, the standard has even declined. In every instance, the standard of living has failed to rise in proportion to the rate of industrialization, which was much more rapid. It was believed that the differences between cities and villages, between intellectual and physical labor, would slowly disappear; instead these differences have increased. Communist anticipations in other areas—including their expectations for developments in the non-Communist world—have also failed to materialize.

The greatest illusion was that industrialization and collectivization in the U.S.S.R., and destruction of capitalist ownership, would result in a classless society. In 1936, when the new Constitution was promulgated, Stalin announced that the "exploiting class" had ceased to exist. The capitalist and other classes of ancient origin had in fact been destroyed, but a new class, previously unknown to history, had been formed. . . .

The roots of the new class were implanted in a special party, of the Bolshevik type. Lenin was right in his view that his party was an exception in the history of human society, although he did not suspect that it would be the beginning of a new class.

To be more precise, the initiators of the new class are not found in the party of the Bolshevik type as a whole but in that stratum of professional revolutionaries who made up its core even before it attained power. . . .

The once live, compact party, full of initiative, is disappearing to

* Partisan leader during the war and former Vice-President of Yugoslavia under Tito, he broke with Yugoslav Communism and was expelled from the Party in 1954. He is presently in prison as a result of attacks on the Yugoslav regime. The selection is from the book and chapter titled *The New Class* (New York: Frederick A. Praeger, Inc., 1957). By permission of the publisher.

become transformed into the traditional oligarchy of the new class, irresistibly drawing into its ranks those who aspire to join the new class and repressing those who have any ideals.

The party makes the class, but the class grows as a result and uses the party as a basis. The class grows stronger, while the party grows weaker; this is the inescapable fate of every Communist party in power. . . .

The movement of the new class toward power comes as a result of the efforts of the proletariat and the poor. These are the masses upon which the party or the new class must lean and with which its interests are most closely allied. This is true until the new class finally establishes its power and authority. Over and above this, the new class is interested in the proletariat and the poor only to the extent necessary for developing production and for maintaining in subjugation the most aggressive and rebellious social forces. The monopoly which the new class establishes in the name of the working class over the whole of society is, primarily, a monopoly over the working class itself. . . .

As defined by Roman law, property constitutes the use, enjoyment, and disposition of material goods. The Communist political bureaucracy uses, enjoys, and disposes of nationalized property.

If we assume that membership in this bureaucracy or new owning class is predicated on the use of privileges inherent in ownership—in this instance nationalized material goods—then membership in the new party class, or political bureaucracy, is reflected in a larger income in material goods and privileges than society should normally grant for such functions. In practice, the ownership privilege of the new class manifests itself as an exclusive right, as a party monopoly, for the political bureaucracy to distribute the national income, to set wages, direct economic development, and dispose of nationalized and other property. This is the way it appears to the ordinary man who considers the Communist functionary as being very rich and as a man who does not have to work. . . .

Membership in the Communist Party before the Revolution meant sacrifice. Being a professional revolutionary was one of the highest honors. Now that the party has consolidated its power, party membership means that one belongs to a privileged class. And at the core of the party are the all-powerful exploiters and masters. . . .

In Stalin's victory Trotsky saw the Thermidoric reaction against the revolution, actually the bureaucratic corruption of the Soviet government and the revolutionary cause. Consequently, he understood and was deeply hurt by the amorality of Stalin's methods. Trotsky was the first, although he was not aware of it, who in the attempt to save the Communist movement discovered the essence of contemporary Communism. But he was not capable of seeing it through to the end. He supposed that this was only a momentary cropping up of bureaucracy, corrupting the party and the revolution, and concluded that the solution was in a change at the top, in a "palace revolution." When a palace revolution actually took place after Stalin's death, it could be seen that the essence had not changed; something deeper and more lasting was involved. The Soviet Thermidor of Stalin had not only led to the installation of a government more despotic than the previous one, but also to the installation of a class. . . .

Without relinquishing anything it created under Stalin's leadership, the new class appears to be renouncing his authority for the past few years. But it is not really renouncing that authority—only Stalin's methods which, according to Khrushchev, hurt "good Communists." . . .

In view of the significance of ownership for its power—and also of the fruits of ownership—the party bureaucracy cannot renounce the extension of its ownership even over small-scale production facilities. Because of its totalitarianism and monopolism, the new class finds itself unavoidably at war with everything which it does not administer or handle, and must deliberately aspire to destroy or conquer it. . . .

The fact that the seizure of property from other classes, especially from small owners, led to decreases in production and to chaos in the economy was of no consequence to the new class. Most important for the new class, as for every owner in history, was the attainment and consolidation of ownership. The class profited from the new property it had acquired even though the nation lost thereby. The collectivization of peasant holdings, which was economically unjustified, was unavoidable if the new class was to be securely installed in its power and its ownership. . . .

The establishment of the ownership of the new class was evidenced in the changes in the psychology, the way of life, and the material position of its members, depending on the position they held on the hierarchical ladder. Country homes, the best housing, furniture, and similar things were acquired; special quarters and exclusive rest homes were established for the highest bureaucracy, for the elite of the new class. The party secretary and the chief of the secret police in some places not only became the highest authorities but obtained the best housing, automobiles, and similar evidence of privilege. Those beneath them were eligible for comparable privileges, depending upon their position in the hierarchy. The state budgets, "gifts," and the construction and reconstruction executed for the needs of the state and its representatives became the everlasting and inexhaustible sources of benefits to the political bureaucracy. . . .

Open at the bottom, the new class becomes increasingly and relentlessly narrower at the top. Not only is the desire necessary for the climb; also necessary is the ability to understand and develop doctrines, firmness in struggles against antagonists, exceptional dexterity and cleverness in intra-party struggles, and talent in strengthening the class. . . .

Just as under Stalin, the new regime, in excuting its so-called liberalization policy, is extending the "socialist" ownership of the new class. Decentralization in the economy does not mean a change in ownership, but only gives greater rights to the lower strata of the bureaucracy or of the new class. If the so-called liberalization and decentralization meant anything else, that would be manifest in the political right of at least part of the people to exercise some influence in the management of material goods. At least, the people would have the right to criticize the arbitrariness of the oligarchy. This would lead to the creation of a new political movement, even though it were only a loyal opposition. However, this is not even mentioned, just as democracy in the party is not mentioned. Liberalization and decentralization are in force only for Communists; first for the oligarchy, the leaders of the new class; and second, for those in the lower echelons. This is the new method, inevitable under changing conditions, for the further strengthening and consolidation of monopolistic ownership and totalitarian authority of the new class. . . .

The new class instinctively feels that national goods are, in fact, its property, and that even the terms "socialist," "social," and "state" property denote a general legal fiction. The new class also thinks that any breach of its totalitarian authority might imperil its ownership. Consequently, the new class opposes *any* type of freedom, ostensibly for the purpose of preserving "socialist" ownership. Criticism of the new class's monopolistic administration of property generates the fear of a possible loss of power. . . .

In defending its authority, the ruling class must execute reforms every time it becomes obvious to the people that the class is treating national property as its own. Such reforms are not proclaimed as being what they really are, but rather as part of the "further development of socialism" and "socialist democracy." . . .

This is a class whose power over men is the most complete known to history. For this reason it is a class with very limited views, views which are false and unsafe. Closely ingrown, and in complete authority, the new class must unrealistically evaluate its own role and that of the people around it.

Having achieved industrialization, the new class can now do nothing more than strengthen its brute force and pillage the people. It ceases to create. Its spiritual heritage is overtaken by darkness.

While the new class accomplished one of its greatest successes in the revolution, its method of control is one of the most shameful pages in human history. Men will marvel at the grandiose ventures it accomplished, and will be ashamed of the means it used to accomplish them.

When the new class leaves the historical scene—and this must happen—there will be less sorrow over its passing than there was for any other class before it. Smothering everything except what suited its ego, it has condemned itself to failure and shameful ruin.

KHRUSHCHEV'S PARTY CONGRESS

PHILIP E. MOSELY*

During the Party Congress, which met in the new Kremlin theater from October 17 through October 31, 1961, the attention of the world was divided almost equally between the vivid and almost daily attacks on the "antiparty group" of Khrushchev's repentant and unrepentant rivals and the clear if somewhat muffled Sino-Soviet divergences over revolutionary strategy. The first of these "sensations" was obviously orchestrated in advance, and each spokesman for the central leadership was assigned a larger or smaller dose of "revelations" to pepper up the otherwise somewhat routine speeches. The second, which came to a head early in a dispute over the future treatment of the recalcitrant Albanian Party, was clearly unplanned, and it has left a wide-open field for speculation about its implications for the future.

The questions that most concern people living beyond the writ of Communist power are somewhat different, and to them only indirect answers are suggested by the published reports of the Congress proceedings. One of them is: Has the struggle for leadership in the Soviet Party been ended, or is Khrushchev's power challenged from within? Another: Is his dominance of the Communist bloc stronger or weaker than it was in December 1960, at the issuance of the Declaration of Eighty-one Parties? And finally: Does the Congress offer any useful clues to Khrushchev's strategy and tactics of the next few months in the sphere of world politics?

The adoption of the new Party Program "for the building of Communism" in the next 20 years sets very high, popular and impressive goals for the Soviet economy. [Editor's note: See chapter titled "The Road To Communism."] Thrusting to one side doctrinaire disputes over whether the collective farms should be merged into the system of state farms, and whether or not to prohibit the free market for the sale of surplus foodstuffs, the program promises to maintain strong incentives of differential wages for better work, but it also provides for a gradual expansion of "free" services to be provided out of the state budget. For example, textbooks and other school supplies, which have been provided free of charge for almost 100 years in America, will also be made available free after a few years to Soviet schoolchildren. On the whole, the economic goals reflect the more realistic approach to management and investment that has been increasingly emphasized in Soviet pronouncements and practice since Stalin's death. They

---

* Director of Studies, Council on Foreign Relations; former Director of the Russian Institute, Columbia University; author of *The Kremlin and World Politics* and other works. The selection is from an article of the same title that appeared in *Foreign Affairs*, Vol. 40 (Jan. 1962), pp. 183-188, and is reproduced with the permission of the journal and author. Copyright held by Council on Foreign Relations, Inc., New York.

include, especially after 1970, a steady rise in the production of consumer goods, to a level closer to that of other advanced industrial societies.

Some significant changes were introduced into the draft program as a result of widespread discussions between July and October. Khrushchev now states that, instead of providing adequate housing for all badly-housed families during the decade of the 1970s, this is to be accomplished during the 1960s. Since one-quarter of new capital investment is now going into the construction of housing, this promise, which was greeted by prolonged applause, will require some marked shifts in the allocation of resources. Of course, the problem can be met in part by changing the definition of what constitutes "adequate" housing. On the other hand, the finding of a solution has been complicated by the larger-than-planned influx of people into the cities. In his report of October 17, Khrushchev admitted that by 1966 "the urban population will have increased by about fifteen million more than had been estimated; consequently, even more houses will be required."

Numerous other proposals were rejected by the leadership. In view of the great increase planned in heavy and extractive industries, in consumer goods, foodstuffs and housing, Khrushchev was understandably reluctant to endorse a wide range of special benefits such as shortening work hours for mothers of small children and abolishing night work for women workers. These would, he said, require "further study."

A second major line of internal development, as laid down in the process of "achieving Communism," is the abandonment of the dictatorship of the proletariat; no longer suited to the needs of Soviet society, it is to be gradually transformed into a "general-people's state." In effect, this means that more and more of the people, whether Party members or not, are to be drawn into active participation in a wider range of local decisions, inspections and other activities. Through their recently expanded commissions, local and regional Soviets are to enroll many more citizens in the tasks of supervising and improving education, public health, housing and retail marketing. The role of trade unions, cultural societies and even the new parent-teachers' associations is to be enlarged. One legacy from iron-fisted rule from above has been the timidity and passivity of ordinary citizens in combating inefficiency and protesting injustices. The new trend broadens and dramatizes the efforts that have been made over the past several years, again mainly "from above," to elicit more initiative from below, but without really lessening the extreme centralization of the system.

There may be more substance in the changes that have now been incorporated into the Statutes of the Communist Party. The amended procedures for admitting and expelling members seem designated procedures to enhance the role of rank-and-file members, grouped in more than 300,000 primary Party organizations. These provisions, together with new rules requiring a periodic turnover in the membership of Party committees at local, county and regional levels, are supposed to broaden the recruitment of new leaders and to undercut the tendency of Party bureaucrats to dominate their local units and muzzle criticism. In presenting the amendments, which had been approved at a secret meeting of the Central Committte, Frol Kozlov laid special stress on secrecy of voting in choosing members of local and regional Party committees. His announcement that the Central Committee had rejected numerous proposals for reinstituting the "mass purges" or periodic review of all Party membership, so typical of Stalin's time, was greeted with "prolonged applause."

Throughout the Khrushchcv and Kozlov reports on the Statutes, the emphasis was on a slogan that is as old as the dictatorial Party itself, "criticism and self-criticism." To publicize the new methods of rule, even the theater has been mustered into service over the last five or six years. One example of Khrushchevian reëducation is the popular play "Battle Along the Road," which last spring was playing in 46 different theaters at one time. In this play, by Galina Nikolaeva, two types of factory managers, the Stalinist and the Khrushchevian, wrestle for the leadership of an important factory. The struggle between the old and the new, the gradual intervention of the workers as an almost faceless but discriminating judge, and the final and "wise" decision by "the Central Committee," pictured as an offstage *deus ex machina,* obviously involve the hopes and fears of the audience as a real problem of Soviet life, however melodramatic it may seem to an outsider.

In appealing for greater "activism" by both Party members and loyal and hardworking citizens, the Party leadership sets definite limits to these initiatives. "Increase the responsibility of the primary Party organizations," they say in effect, but in the next breath Kozlov reminded the Congress that "the C.P.S.U. is not a federation of parties or party committees; it is a centralized organization." While urging every opportunity "for a free and businesslike discussion of questions relevant to Party policy," Kozlov denounced any attempt to form factions or cliques. Even discussion has narrow limits. "Naturally one must not allow a situation to come about in which the Party can be drawn into a sterile discussion at the whim of some small group of muddle-headed or immature people, in which individual antiparty elements can undertake actions leading to the subversion of party unity." Basically the leadership is urging the middle ranks of the Party to throw off their fear or friendship for the petty bosses above them and to speak their minds, and thus to help the top leadership meet its goals more efficiently than in the past. "Democracy" in the Western sense is not one of those goals.

II

Even more completely than the Twentieth and Twenty-first Congresses, the Twenty-second was "Khrushchev's Congress." Since the purge of the "antiparty group" in June 1957, and the dismissal of Marshal Zhukov in

October of that year, the Party-Presidium has been completely "his" presidium and the Central Secretariat has been "his" secretariat. During the steady turnover in the upper ranks of the Party over the past four years, Khrushchev has reënforced his control over the entire apparatus of power. Since February 1956 the membership of the Party has grown by some 2,500,000, from 7,215,000 to 9,716,000 and over 200,000 members have been expelled. Why, in the light of the consolidation of his power, did Khrushchev devote so much time at the Congress to denouncing his former rivals for power?

One explanation that has been put forward is that somehow Molotov, Kaganovich, Malenkov and Voroshilov are still active contenders for power, that they retain a large potential following within the Party, and that a further purge, on a substantial scale, may follow this public attack on them, on their crimes during the Stalin era, and on the policies that they are accused of advocating. This seems most improbable. If the "antiparty group" was not able to muster its forces better in June 1957, when its members were still close to the levers of power, how much strength can it summon now, after it has been scattered and reviled? Its fate was actually determined by January 1955, and it was sealed by the failure of its attempt, in February 1956, to prevent Khrushchev from delivering his secret anti-Stalin speech to the Twentieth Congress.

In most respects the recent attacks on Stalin constitute a relatively restrained and unmelodramatic re-run of the famous "secret speech," perhaps expurgated for wider distribution at home and abroad. Significantly, each spokesman of the central apparatus—Presidium and Secretariat—was assigned some part of the denunciatory material, perhaps to demonstrate the solidarity of the leading group, perhaps to make each of their speeches that much more stirring to the Congress. A few additional details were offered on Stalin's actions, particularly on his alleged planning of the Kirov murder in 1934. The most striking addition to the "chamber of horrors" was the painstaking and direct linking of the "antiparty group" with the crimes of the Stalin era. Anyone living abroad is bound to ask a further question: "But will not people in the Soviet Union associate Khrushchev with the same misdeeds? Will they not recall the long years in which he served and praised Stalin no less faithfully and obsequiously than did his defeated rivals?"

Some, possessed of longer memories or feeling somewhat freer now to make cynical comments about the leaders, will no doubt do so, but this is of no political importance. After the Congress of February 1956 the "secret speech" was read by or to all members of the Party, and even to millions of nonparty activists, and to Communist leaders outside the Soviet Union. The shock has long since been absorbed by them, and the differences between the Stalin and Khrushchev methods of rule have been drilled into them for several years. By naming scapegoats for the Stalinist crimes, Khrushchev actually makes it easier for himself and the Party members to localize the diffused sense of shared guilt in a few powerless individuals. The fact that for long years these same individuals wielded, even by delegation, the heavy hand of monolithic power makes their downfall and Khrushchev's contrasting image of success and benevolence a more convincing part of a mammoth "morality play," Communist-style.

Since the Congress provided no opportunity for genuine debate or discussion, any more than in Stalin's day, its effectiveness as a transmission belt of Party directives was enhanced by the drama of "crime and punishment" played out on its stage. The anti-Stalinist tirades spelled out, probably with a substantial dose of exaggeration, the differences over recent and future policies. Khrushchev was, it now appears, full of good ideas as early as 1950 and 1951 for improving agriculture and housing; Molotov and Kaganovich frustrated these proposals. In 1957 they also opposed his program for partially decentralizing the management of the economy. Molotov resisted bitterly Khrushchev's attempts to develop a more relaxed system of control over the Communist bloc and his efforts to enhance Soviet influence beyond the area of the Leninist writ through personal contacts with foreign statesmen. Molotov underestimated the growing might of the Soviet Union and therefore rejected Khrushchev's foreign policies as dangerous to its survival as a state and a revolutionary ideology. Far from repenting of his dogmatism, Molotov wrote the Central Committee just before the Congress, according to Satiukov, to denounce most of the new policies; his letter has, of course, not been made public.

By spelling out in his own words the sharp differences between his own policies and those of the "antiparty group," Khrushchev has given a clearer focus to his own policies and has sent the delegates home with a vivid picture of the "perils of Pauline" that the party has escaped. Like other congresses since Lenin's death, the latest one did not actually shift power from one leader or group to another; it merely registered and consolidated a previous shift of power that had already been carried out by the top leadership through its exclusive power of promotion and demotion. It has not laid down new policies or even debated them; it has received, for transmission down the line, the codified policies already worked out and applied by the leadership. The basic message its members have taken home is that Khrushchev intends to continue the gradual broadening of responsibilities and initiatives downward within the Party; that no drastic changes in the system are being planned; that the relaxation of tension between the ruling group and the people at large is going to be continued; that the Soviet Party intends to assert its dominance over the bloc; and that Khrushchev is confident that outside the bloc the growing Soviet military might and his own more flexible political strategy will enable him to make important and eventually decisive gains for Communism without involving his people in a nuclear war.

VII

THE SOVIET ECONOMIC SYSTEM

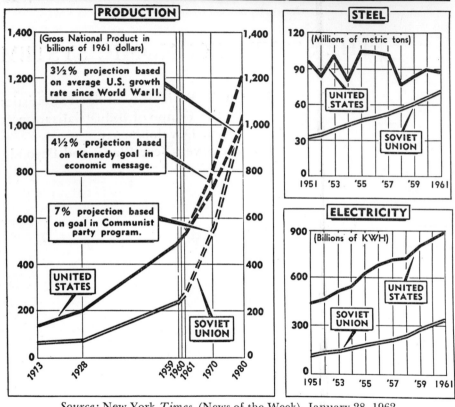

Source: New York *Times* (News of the Week), January 28, 1962

EDITOR'S NOTE: *By way of introduction to the several sections concerned with the Soviet Economic System, it must be emphasized that there is in the U.S.S.R. a close interdependence and interrelationship, both in theory and practice, between economics and politics—beyond anything known to the capitalist world. It must be said, too, that the belief of Russian leaders (and of many Russian people) in the ultimate triumph of socialism throughout the world is predicated, in major part, upon what they regard as the demonstrated superiority—and, hence, the ultimate irresistible appeal—of the socialist economic system over capitalism. Typical, for example, were the statements made by Khrushchev in a recent interview with the correspondent of* Figaro:

We, Communists, are convinced that mankind's only right path is the path of socialist development. Socialism expresses the vital interests of the people, of all men and women who live not by exploiting working people, but by their own labor. It brings the peoples deliverance from social and national oppression, from the horrors of unemployment and the arbitrary rule of a handful of monopolists who usurped all the wealth of a country. We are convinced that the peoples of all countries will come to socialism, to Communism, but when and how—this is the internal affair of each people.

M. A. Suslov stated at the 20th Congress: "The urge of the peoples to socialism is irresistible, the attractive power of the socialist ideas increases from day to day, and the process will be accelerated by the continued achievements of socialism in our country, China and all the People's Democracies."

Obviously these claims deserve the most careful analysis even though the merits of a system rest on bases which transcend the purely economic.

Chapter 15

ON THE RELIABILITY OF SOVIET STATISTICS

There is no intention to suggest that the question of the reliability of Soviet statistics—an extremely difficult and complex problem—can be resolved by reference to the three brief excerpts that appear in the following pages. It was simply considered desirable to give some indication—from opposing vantage points—of the complexities of the problem and the dangers of easy and shallow judgments. The interested reader will find some suggestions for further reading in the bibliography.

COMMENT ON SOVIET ECONOMIC STATISTICS

MAURICE DOBB*

The view that all Soviet figures are naturally suspect, designed as propaganda-instruments to deceive the unwary, is no longer seriously held, and scarcely merits attention here. Though commonly met with in uninformed circles before the war, it was seldom if ever accepted, at any rate in its crude form, by anyone with much experience of handling Soviet statistics and submitting them to normal tests of consistency.[1] Gaps there were, of course (which grew larger towards the end of the 'thirties for security reasons), and continuous series were difficult to construct in many cases owing to changes of base and of definition. A notable post-war gap

---

* Lecturer and Fellow of Trinity College, Cambridge. The selection is from *Soviet Studies*, Vol. 1 (1950), pp. 18-19, by permission, and from *Soviet Economic Development Since 1917* (London: Routledge & Kegan Paul Ltd., 4th ed., 1957), pp. 330-332, by permission of the publisher and of International Publishers, New York.

[1] Cf. Dr. A. BAYKOV: "I do not share the view that Soviet statistical and other sources are less reliable than those published in other countries. On the contrary, systematic study over a number of years has convinced me that they can be used to analyse the economic process . . . of the U.S.S.R. with the same degree of confidence as similar sources published in other countries." (*The Development of the Soviet Economic System* xiv.)

has been the absence of regular annual output figures of particular industries (although these can to some extent be deduced from the published index-figures which have 1945 as a base, and from information as to the relationship of post-war output to 1940 output). But such difficulties are met with in varying degrees in the handling and interpretation of the published data of all nations. And although in some respects Soviet published data before the war were deficient by comparison with this country [England], in other directions they were more plentiful.[2]

One deficiency that aroused much comment in the West during the 'thirties and was often cited as a reason for suspicion, was the absence of any index number of general prices; the publication of such indices having been discontinued in the early years of the first Five-Year Plan. This deficiency is qualified, however, by two considerations. Firstly, we have now learnt from our own experience of recent years that price-indices have very restricted meaning and limited use in conditions of rationing and controlled prices and wide dispersion of price-movements,[3] and that they may be positively misleading at a time when consumption-habits are subject to considerable change. Secondly, value-data concerning production were generally given in "constant prices of 1926-27," and accordingly did not depend on the use of a price-index for conversion from money into real terms when comparing the value-data for different years. What this meant was that the constituent items of the total in question (e.g. for some branch of industry) for any year were valued at the prices ruling in the base year; 1926-27 being chosen as this base year on the ground that it was the first "normal" year after the reconstruction-period following the war and civil war, when prices had been restored to some kind of normal relationship with one another. This practice of valuing output in different years in the prices of a single year is now familiar to us in this country; seeing that it has become the practice since the war in our own official statistics to express the gross value of consumer goods and services (i.e. consumers' expenditure) "in 1938 prices." . . .

In conclusion one should perhaps mention that criticism during recent years among Western economists in relation to Soviet economy has largely been directed towards the valuation of gross industrial output in terms

[2] The fullest collection of quantitative data is the 500-page *Socialist Construction: a Statistical Abstract* (in both Russian and English) of 1936. For the years subsequent to 1936 nothing of the kind was published; and one had to rely on particular sets of published figures (e.g. of output of selected industries).

[3] In U.S.S.R. between 1929 and 1934, there was not only a spread between the price-movements of rationed and unrationed commodities, but multiple prices for the *same* commodity according to whether it was bought "on the ration" or "off the ration" (the Soviet ration-system taking the form of a minimum quota to which one was entitled at a fixed "ration price"; additional amounts being purchasable, if available, at a much higher price), and in the case of the latter according to the market in which it was purchased (e.g. in the "closed co-operative," the State "commercial stores" or on the free market).

of which official calculations of growth-rates have been expressed. The practice of valuing industrial output in "constant prices of 1926-7" has been criticised on the ground that it gives an "upward bias" to the valuation of the increase since, according to the price-structure prevailing in 1926-7, products like tractors, motor-cars and machine-tools that were destined to show the highest rates of increase, were highly-priced relatively to other things and hence highly-weighted in the resulting index. To this has been added the charge that new products, introduced into production after the base year (1926-7), were valued at the *current* price-level of the year of their introduction, and that since there was price-inflation after 1929 this meant that these new products were given an exaggerated weight in the index compared with older products. The author has made his own comments elsewhere[4] on this controversy. It is undeniable, of course, that measurement of the change in an output-total will be very different when conducted in the different price-structures of various years (the problem is well-known to statisticians under the name of the Paasche-Laspeyres discrepancy —the discrepancy between valuing a change according to the prices of the end-year or the beginning-year of the period in question—and is by no means confined to the statistics of industrial production in the U.S.S.R.).[5] It is also probably true that valuation at the prices of an early year yields a higher rate of increase than valuation at the prices of a later year in a period of rapid industrial development.

What this Western controversy has tended to conceal is that, even when allowance has been made for such discrepancy and for such criticisms, the magnitude of the qualification involved is not very great compared with the rate of growth that is in question—it does not go beyond 25 or 30 per cent. for the period of the First and Second Five Year Plans (to which criticisms chiefly apply). An American economist has recently attempted to construct an index of his own of Soviet industrial output, using for this purpose wages and salaries prevailing in the year 1934 as weights instead of selling-prices seven years before. The result is to show an annual rate of growth of industrial output from 1928-1937 of about 14 per cent., or for the decade as a whole slightly less than a fourfold increase, compared with an increase of five-and-a-half times shown by the official index.[6] Such a rate of increase represents almost a doubling of output

[4] In *The Review of Economics and Statistics*, Feb., 1948, and in his *On Economic Theory and Socialism* (London, 1955), 247-53.

[5] An American calculation of the output of items of machinery in U.S.A. has shown that a valuation in prices of 1899 yields a *fifteen*-fold increase between 1899 and 1939 and no more than a *two*-fold increase when valued in prices of 1939. (A. Gerschenkron, *A Dollar Index of Soviet Machinery Output, 1927-8 to 1937*, California, 1951, 52).

[6] D. R. Hodgman, *Soviet Industrial Production 1928-1951* (Cambridge, Mass., 1954). This rate of increase comes remarkably close to the results of a calculation of the unweighted average of quantity-increases of basic metal-fuel-power output made by the present writer (*op. cit.*, 119-23). For the period between 1937 and 1951 Prof. Hodgmen's index shows a somewhat larger discrepancy from the official index than for 1928-37 (but

every quinquennium and is something very much larger than has previously been attained by other countries.

This controversy, however, is to-day only of historical interest, since the method of valuation in 1926-7 prices was terminated with the Fourth Plan. Since 1950 industrial output has been calculated in terms of the prices of a particular month or year of the quinquennium in question:[7] throughout the Period of the Fifth Plan in terms of the prices of January 1, 1952 (new products of subsequent years and "that part of production which is not reckoned in natural units" being reduced to the basis of January 1, 1952 by an index of the average price-changes of the remaining output of the enterprise or industry in question);[8] and for the Sixth Plan in terms of the prices prevailing on July 1, 1955.[9] The method of valuing output, in up-to-date (but "constant") prices, has accordingly been assimilated to the method previously adopted for valuing investment at the prices prevailing in a given year of the quinquennium in question.

PROBLEMS OF ANALYZING AND PREDICTING SOVIET BEHAVIOR

John S. Reshetar*

SOVIET STATISTICS

The amount of available statistical data regarding the Soviet economy and what it can produce has dwindled to a small fraction of what it was. The statement of the First Five Year Plan comprised more than 1700

---

then his data for this period are much more scanty): his index shows a doubling of output between 1937 and 1951 as against an increase of three times according to the official index. Another American, G. Grossman, has made an estimate for national income as a whole (including, e.g., agriculture), and reaches a figure of 6.5-7 per cent. as the annual rate of increase between 1928 and 1937. This compares with 3 per cent. for U.S.A. between 1929 and 1950 (*Soviet Economic Growth,* ed. A. Bergson, Evanston and New York, 1953, 9). In this case the discrepancy from the official estimate was much greater, the latter being more than double the former.

[7] I.e. of wholesale (*optovie*) prices, *without* turnover tax.

[8] *Planovoe Khoziaistvo,* 1952, No. 1, 77-9; cf. also G. I. Baklanov, *Promishlennaia Statistika* (Moscow, 1953), 123, where the defects of measurement in 1926-7 prices are explicitly mentioned, including the difficulty of valuing new products, but without any indication of the net effect of these defects.

[9] *Voprosi Ekonomiki,* 1955, No. 8, 74-5. Output in 1955 was to be valued both at January 1952 prices and in July 1955 prices so as to link the index-series relating to the past quinquennium with the new one.

---

* Department of Political Science, University of Washington in Seattle. The selection is from pp. 48-51 of *Problems of Analyzing and Predicting Soviet Behavior* by John S. Reshetar. Copyright 1955 by Random House, Inc. Reprinted by permission of Random House, Inc.

pages, while those of the Fourth and Fifth Plans were published as small pamphlets. A decree of June 9, 1947, increased the amount of economic information which must not be published and made the divulging of such information a serious offense punishable by imprisonment. Not since 1929 has the Soviet regime published a cost-of-living index such as that prepared by the United States Bureau of Labor Statistics. Besides the paucity of data there is a deliberate effort on the part of the regime to exaggerate economic growth by the use of such propaganda devices as the increase in terms of percentages with a period and base year which will give the impression of phenomenal growth. Thus Malenkov, speaking at the Nineteenth Party Congress in October 1952, boasted that Soviet industrial production had increased more than twelvefold between 1929 and 1951 while that of the United States had only doubled during the same period.

One can also question the value of some Soviet statistics in view of the known falsification of production reports by the administrators of economic enterprises in order to make it appear that production goals have been fulfilled or overfulfilled. Indeed, the constant preoccupation of the Soviet leadership with production goals and the use of figures referring to goals as well as to actual achievements of the economy serve to confuse the picture. While the falsification of production data is discouraged by the central statistic-gathering authorities (since it compounds the difficulties of the forecasting which a fully planned economy requires) they are not in a position to prevent it because the system of incentives and sanctions in the Soviet Union is such as to encourage this practice. Another difficulty is that Soviet statistics, to the extent that they are accurate, reflect production in quantitative terms but tell little or nothing about the quality of the commodities being produced.

Soviet statistics can also be misleading when the particular concept upon which the statistical formulation is based has doubtful validity. Thus statistics regarding Soviet grain production have been based on the concept of "biological yield" rather than "barn yield"—although the regime is presumably attempting to rectify this. This has importance because the concept of "biological yield" represents unharvested grain in the field, while that of "barn yield" represents the actual amount of grain harvested. The use of the former concept after 1933, first with a deduction for losses during harvesting and later without any such deduction, has given to Soviet grain statistics an inflated character, since there has frequently been a great difference in the Soviet Union between the amount of grain on the sheaf and the amount actually harvested. Another Soviet statistical concept which is unique is that of national income. In the Soviet Union this includes only the production and distribution of goods and omits all services, whether rendered by the government or by individuals, such as are an integral part of the American concept of national income.

A related problem is that of the price indices used for determining

gross industrial production in the Soviet Union. The value of the industrial output was determined for more than two decades in terms of
"constant" 1926-1927 ruble prices. Serious difficulties arose, however,
when new products were added to the Soviet industrial output and could
not be given prices in terms of 1926-1927 rubles because they were not being
produced at that time. Instead, these new commodities were given arbitrary
prices at the time they were first produced on a large scale during the Five
Year Plans. (Such commodities were often produced at a very high cost in
the beginning because of inefficiencies in production methods.) This practice
led to the introduction of an inflationary bias into the indices and to the
exaggeration of Soviet statements regarding increases in individual output.
Thus the value of Soviet industrial production was inflated to make it
appear that the system had produced more goods than it had in fact.
Another factor which "increased" industrial production was the transfer of
such activities as fishing and forestry from agriculture to industry.

Use of this index of industrial production by Soviet economists and
planners involved many difficulties, since it was not a homogeneous index:
goods which were being produced in 1926-1927 (as contrasted with products
introduced in later years) were included in the index at their prices during
that base period. Thus there was lack of comparability within the index.
In an effort to remedy this the Soviet regime in 1949 abandoned the index
based on 1926-1927 ruble prices and shifted to the use of current wholesale prices. In 1952 the new index was regularized in terms of wholesale
prices prevailing on January 1 of that year, and it was decreed that new
goods produced by the economy after 1952 were to be given "comparable
1952 prices" in terms of the prices which have been assigned in the 1952
index to similar goods. However, the inflationary nature of the earlier
index, which exaggerated Soviet economic development, was retained,
since Soviet economists were told that in comparing production of years
following 1952 with that of the years prior to 1950, they must accept the
production data of the pre-1950 period as reflected in the old index.

The propaganda aspect of certain Soviet economic and statistical practices is also well illustrated in the case of the valuation of the ruble. The
Soviet regime carried out a currency reform in December 1947, issuing one
new ruble for ten old rubles in circulation. Deposits remained unchanged
up to the amount of 3000 rubles; larger sums on deposit in banks were
revalued at lower rates. This measure was designed to wipe out the accumulated cash reserves held by peasants and tradesmen of the more
conventional and black-market variety. At that time the ruble was declared
to be worth 19 cents (5.3 rubles to the dollar) at the official rate of exchange.
However, since foreign trade is a monopoly of the state in the Soviet Union,
this figure was meaningless. The rate of exchange for diplomats was reduced from 12 to 8 rubles to the dollar. Actually the ruble has been worth
little more than three cents or, at the most five cents. A subsequent

"revaluation" of the ruble was decreed in March 1950, when it was given an arbitrary value of 25 cents. The special diplomatic rate of exchange was abolished, thus adding greatly to the maintenance costs of foreign embassies in Moscow. The ruble was also declared at that time to be based on gold instead of on the dollar, but it was not made convertible into gold internally. This action was accompanied by a propaganda claim that the value of the ruble had "increased" while other currencies—such as the British pound and the French franc—had suffered a decline through devaluation.

The difficulty in determining the real value of the ruble has been increased by the Soviet regime's refusal to allow any free exchange of currencies and its insistence upon an artificial and ridiculously high rate of exchange. This has led to numerous comparisons between American and Soviet prices—which have appeared in the American press—based on the simple conversion of Soviet prices into dollars at the official rate of exchange of four rubles to the dollar. A more meaningful approach involves a very complex analysis aimed at determining the real value of the ruble in terms of what can be purchased with it. This, of course, entails a close study of price levels as related to wage and salary scales and market supplies. Prices have fluctuated widely in the Soviet Union, and for some commodities, such as rye bread, have increased by as much as 3500% over a period of twenty-two years, with increases in the money wage lagging far behind. Price cuts since December 1947, when rationing was abolished, have reduced this percentage increase substantially. Prices of other commodities increased tremendously in the 1930s and during World War II, but less than for rye bread.

Although we know the price which Soviet subjects pay for rye bread today as compared with that of 1928 or 1946, as well as for other commodities, we do not know the price of a Soviet tank or jet airplane. This lack of data regarding the whole price structure of the Soviet economy is one of the difficulties encountered in attempting to estimate the meaning of the Soviet military budget. We know the size of the expenditure for the Soviet military establishment in billions of rubles, but we encounter serious difficulties in estimating its significance and all of its implications, or in making comparisons between the Soviet military budget and the budgets of other states. Since we do not know enough about the cost factor, it makes little sense to convert the ruble sum into dollars at the official rate of exchange or at an arbitrary rate and make a comparison on a strictly monetary basis. Indeed, it is likely that one ruble is worth more than another in the Soviet economy, and the ruble used to purchase a tank or artillery piece may be worth much more than that used to purchase a home appliance. Thus a reduction in the military budget in monetary terms may not mean a reduction in armaments if the cost of heavy industrial goods has been substantially reduced at the same time.

Another problem is encountered if the amount appropriated for the Soviet military budget is taken as a percentage of the total state budget and then compared with the military expenditures in the budgets of non-Soviet states. The difficulty stems from the fact that the Soviet state budget includes many forms of capital investment not to be found in the budgets of non-Soviet governments and embraces a far greater percentage of the national income. This tends to minimize the military budget and makes it possible for Soviet statisticians to "prove" that other states are spending "more" for armaments percentagewise than the Soviet Union, in terms of the total state budget. An additional factor which prevents exact comparisons is the unusually low pay of Soviet rank-and-file military personnel as contrasted with that of the armies of other states. There is also the very real possibility of hidden appropriations in the Soviet state budget which are actually military in character but are included under capital investment (as, for example, the construction of munitions plants) or under "education" as part of the military training program.

Soviet demographic statistics also have their lacunae. There are few data available between the censuses of 1926 and 1939, and Soviet writers hesitate to use what there are because of the deficit caused by famine during the collectivization in 1932-1933. The census of 1937 was declared to be the work of "wreckers" and was suppressed, probably because it revealed the high mortality rate during the famine to a greater extent than did the census of 1939. The fact that important data of this kind can be suppressed by the regime makes it necessary for the scholar to extrapolate and interpolate on the basis of the meager data which are available.

Economists who study the Soviet system have attempted to fill the gaps in their data by developing estimates based on a variety of assumptions as well as upon rule of thumb guesses. Some economists, notably Colin Clark and Naum Jasny, have been critical of some of the assumptions which other economists have employed in utilizing Soviet statistics. Yet the obvious as well as the concealed pitfalls in work with Soviet statistics should not be regarded as precluding their use if adequate attention is given to the biases inherent in them.

INTERPRETING SOVIET STATISTICS

NAUM JASNY*

In spite of the immense amount of research into the Soviet economy being done in the United States, the sputniks came as a complete surprise except to a very few. The explanation lies largely in the bias both of those who are unwilling to give the Soviet régime due credit for its achievements, and those whose sympathies tend in the opposite direction. In either case the prevalence of wishful thinking, and the readiness of the opportunist to fall in with it, can clearly have deplorable results.

During many years of Stalin's reign and for some time thereafter almost no statistics were released in the USSR. This policy was changed in 1956, and since then a great volume of statistics has been published. They are markedly selective; for example estimates of the population, both total and sub-divided into rural and urban, were published in 1956, but the age and sex composition was withheld. Among the items not covered at all or only inadequately covered by Soviet statistics are such important items as nominal wages and indices of farm production, not to speak of practically everything connected with the armed forces. A reasonably correct official price index exists only for the retail prices of consumer goods in 1947-57, with 1940 as the base year; lack of information about prices will, it is expected—and with justification—prevent even a superficial analysis of the most important economic items, such as the budget.

The nature of Soviet statistics is in itself controversial. One extreme, and perhaps the less dangerous one, is represented by those who believe that *all* Soviet statistics are falsified. The other camp insists that Soviet statistics are not false, but that their acknowledged defects arise from methodological deficiencies. In fact, Soviet statistics cover the full range from correct to falsified, with every kind of intermediate grade in between. Concealment of the methods of calculating the data, and of all the details of the calculations (for national income, for example, only one figure is announced for each year), frequent unannounced changes in concepts and coverage, and last but not least, the marked element of distortion introduced by the language used in commenting on the statistics, immensely enhance the difficulties.

The degree of distortion in Soviet statistics depends in the first place on

* Author of *The Socialised Agriculture of the USSR; The Soviet Economy during the Plan Era; The Soviet Price System;* and many other works. The selection is from an article which originally appeared in *Soviet Survey* (now *Survey*), No. 26 (Oct.-Dec. 1958), pp. 9-14, and is reproduced here by permission.

the importance that an item has in Soviet propaganda and on the extent to which reality departs from the Soviet rulers' wishes or from what they want the reality to be believed to be. Other differences in reliability are related to the time factor. Correct statistics have a much greater propaganda value than false statistics; hence the release of false statistics declines in periods favourable for the régime, and soars in unfavourable periods.

The idea that all Soviet statistics are a falsification is obviously absurd. It is held mainly by strangers in the field of statistics, or by those with an anti Soviet attitude who give free rein to their fantasy in describing what is going on (or not going on) in the USSR. This is of course much easier than making the sustained effort needed to separate the wheat from the chaff in Soviet data.

The idea that Soviet statistics do not contain falsifications—the other extreme—could have grown up only at a time when the study of the Soviet economy in the West was in its early stages. It is for reasons unconnected with research that the idea has survived until today. If this attitude towards Soviet statistics has not made the analytical work of its adherents entirely valueless, this is because they have largely disregarded the distorted official data—sometimes to an even greater extent than the present writer does.

The bulk of Soviet statistics, so far as they are released at all, are correct. Their shortcomings, if any, consist in unexpected and unannounced changes in concepts. Transport statistics, for example, seem to be entirely correct. Statistics of industrial production *in physical terms* are almost completely correct as well. Soviet statistics of acreages under cultivation and livestock herds have never been seriously doubted (possibly only because of the inability to provide proof of their unreliability).

On the other hand, most of the statistics relating to aggregate quantities, such as the indices for national income and industrial production, are incorrect. Although such data may not cover a large number of categories, they are precisely the figures to which a statesman, scholar, or journalist would in the first place turn.

Falsification reaches astronomical dimensions in statistics of real wages and real incomes. The great achievements of the USSR in industrialisation were obtained by imposing immense sacrifices on the population. Even Khrushchev admitted as much in his speech on the expansion of output of textiles and shoes in May 1958 (*Pravda,* 10 May 1958). Nevertheless, Soviet statistics are made to demonstrate immense increases in real wages and real incomes of the peasants. For example, the fantastic claim was officially made that in one year only (1948) real wages more than doubled, although such an increase is physically impossible; the actual growth is unlikely to have exceeded 15 per cent. In 1939 it was announced that real wages had more than doubled during the second five year plan; a rise of 25 per cent would have been more in line with facts. To reinforce this claim the turnover in State and co-operative trade in 1928-40 (which did not increase at constant prices by much more than 50 per cent) was advertised as having grown 4.6-fold.[1]

Falsifications and exaggerations are, in fact, strewn over the whole economy. An astonishing case was a table in an official statistical handbook, *Socialist Agriculture,* (Moscow, 1939) reproduced in 1948 by M. M. Lifits, Minister of Trade, in his pamphlet *Soviet Trade.* It showed a rapid rise in per capita sales of the most important consumers' goods by the peasants in 1933-38. The table left no doubt that physical quantities were involved. Only after several years of work did the present writer realise that the quantities sold were measured in rubles of rapidly declining purchasing power.

The Soviet economy has shown great rates of growth since 1946. In the decade before the war, only the years 1934-36 were of similar nature. The period of the great purges, 1936-40, were years of near stagnation, while the period of full-scale collectivisation, connected with the drive to industralise (the years 1930-32), was characterised by rapidly declining rates of growth. As might be expected, statistics covering the good periods showed in general only relatively moderate exaggerations and occasionally there were no exaggerations at all. On the other hand, the indices for the unfavourable periods are as a rule exaggerated immensely. Long-range indices for the most important items, such as national income, industrial output and investment, embody all—even the most stupendous—exaggerations of the unfavourable periods and consequently they too are greatly exaggerated.[2]

Unexpected and usually unannounced changes in concepts are most frequent in regard to farm products. For about 20 years, until 1954, the Soviets operated with the so-called 'biological' or 'factual' yield of grain (for a somewhat shorter period for other crops); this departed from reality by quite substantial but never announced percentages. Recently some non-meat food was included in the estimates of meat production to make them more presentable. The milk covered by statistics was also recently expanded, without any explanation or announcement.

The idea that the errors in Soviet statistics are not deliberate implies that the Moscow central statistical office is staffed by infants. The people working there are better statisticians than most of those analysing Soviet statistics in the West. They know better than most Western analysts the weak spots in their statistics, the great extent of falsifications, the immense contradictions between them. Most Soviet statisticians would be only too happy to release honest statistics, but they operate on orders and have no choice. They may and no doubt do congratulate themselves on the great effectiveness of

[1] In 1956, the percentage increase claimed in retail trade in 1928-40 was scaled down—without any comment—to a 2.3-fold rise.

[2] Actually the statistics for the years since 1951 are much more reliable than those for 1940-50. While the rates of growth in 1946-50 were very high, the deprivations of the population were immense, and this too is a factor tending to produce greatly exaggerated statistics in the USSR.

Soviet propaganda. The Soviet 1956 statistical handbook was published in many hundreds of thousands of copies in many languages—three editions in English alone. (Both I and my publisher would be satisfied if a few thousand copies of my *Commentary* on this handbook were to be sold.) The immensely distorted indices for the aggregates mentioned above are also repeated in virtually every speech and article, certainly in every book.

The methods used in the tiresome and frustrating work of checking Soviet data vary. Here only the most important will be discussed.

The Soviet economy, as that of any other country, represents a body with an endless web of inter-connected links. Many farm products serve as the raw materials of the food industries. The output of these reaches the consumer via the retail trade. In between these two series of linked stages is the operation of the transport system. In short, there is a chain in which each stage is tied in with the preceding and the succeeding link. Other examples of such important chains of inter-connected links are: iron ore and coking coal—pig iron—steel—machinery—investment in equipment, or building materials—construction as part of investment.

In dealing with the economy of a country with good statistics, an analyst will devote attention to such chains and inter-connections only in specific cases, for example, when he is interested in the proportions of total farm output reaching the market. In general the existence of proper tie-ins is taken for granted. In work on the Soviet economy, examination of the tie-ins (most frequently the ascertainment of their insufficiency) is a major, if not the major, tool.

The degree of inexactness varies in each chain from link to link, from zero in some cases to immense proportions in others. Proper tie-ins between the individual links may consequently be absent, sometimes glaringly absent. The table on p. 34 of *Economy of the USSR in 1956,* the official statistical handbook (this is the basic table of the handbook), gives the Major Indicators of Development of the National Economy of the USSR in 1913-56. Some of the indicators for 1956 (1913 and 1928 = 100) in the table are as follows:

	1913-56	1928-56
Numbers of wage and salary earners	443	446
Fixed investment of the State	—	3527
Basic funds	1480	1089
National income	1922	1615
Gross industrial production	3021	2288
Freight transports (5 carriers)	1136	1092

Of the six series, two, those of wage and salary earners and freight transports, are reasonably correct. The other four indices are extremely high relative to those for wage and salary earners and freight transports. The contradiction in regard to the number of wage and salary earners cannot be cleared up by general considerations. It is obvious, on the other hand, that gross industrial production could not have increased in 1928-56 more than twice as much as freight transports. The transport system is engaged primarily in transporting industrial goods and the raw materials required for them. Moreover, the five carriers for which the index is calculated do not include transport by horse, which declined greatly over the period. Similarly, home industry, which is as a rule conducted without or with relatively little use of transport by the five registered carriers, was still quite important in 1928, but has been greatly reduced since. Transports by the five carriers must consequently have grown substantially more than industrial production.

The official indices for gross industrial production and freight transports by the 5 carriers imply that raw materials and finished industrial goods were making their own way from the farm to the factory, from factory to factory, and from factory to retail stores. This does not occur even in a socialist state, and since the index for freight transports is accepted as correct, the index showing a roughly eight-fold increase in industrial production in 1928-56, calculated by D. Shimkin *et al.* of the U.S. Bureau of Census as well as by this writer, appears to accord well with the roughly 11-fold increase in freight transports by the 5 carriers.

The official claim of a 16-fold growth in national income in 1928-56, makes even less sense relatively to the 11-fold increase in freight transports by the 5 carriers, than does the 23-fold increase in industrial output. Again it may be said that, all things considered, the 4.5-fold increase in national income calculated by this writer, and the even smaller percentage rises calculated by other analysts, seem to tie in well with the officially calculated 11-fold increase in freight transports by the 5 carriers.

Most of the marked discrepancies between individual links in the chains and conditions point to distortions. Few of them yield reasonably exact data, as for example, determination of the grain harvest from the utilisation end. Usually only a broad idea is obtained, indicating the direction in which research must be conducted.

Statistics of the national economy are normally prepared by statistical organisations. Since research on the Soviet economy in the West is mostly conducted by individuals or at best by small groups, the handling of even the available material causes great difficulties which are aggravated by the Soviet habit of concealment (wise from the Soviet point of view). A really thorough covering of the whole economy is impossible in these conditions. The choice for the Western analyst is usually between having relatively more thorough results, at prohibitive costs and with a long delay, and the use of short-cut methods (basing indices on small samples, employing semi-detective methods such as pinning down the implications, not intended for disclosure, in statements, etc.). Judiciously handled, short-cut methods yield satisfactory results, but very few analysts are able to make use of them, especially in the field of Soviet economics, and the results obtained by those who are qualified for such tasks are looked upon with more or less distrust. If this were not so, a discussion would not have been conducted in 1957-58 in the pages of *The Times* on the reliability of the funny Soviet index of industrial production (torn to shreds by Colin Clark as far back as 1939, as well as by his numerous successors thereafter).

Whatever findings on the Soviet economy are available are at best incomplete, and the disagreements between Western students in some cases substantial. The growth of national income in the five years 1951-55, for example, is estimated by this writer at 9 per cent per year (the official figure is 11.5 per cent). Probably not many of his colleagues would agree with this estimate. The estimate of 6-7 per cent per year is generally accepted in the United States.

One of the easiest tasks is a rough calculation of real paid-out wages. Nominal wages, even when they were concealed, could have been roughly estimated from one or another tied-in item, such as retail trade. Most prices of consumer goods and services can be found, too, although a great deal more time is needed for this task than most analysts are prepared to devote. A usable index for Soviet real wages was not calculated before 1951. Calculation of peasants' incomes meets with the difficulty, which cannot be entirely surmounted, of estimating the output from their private plots and livestock; there has been a complete black-out on this since 1940. With the prices used for the index of real wages, an index of retail prices can be constructed (by changing weights), but only one attempt has been made so far, and even this needs revision.

Official estimates of the real grain crops have not been disclosed even now. The present writer's estimate for the years before World War II turned out to be accurate, while those for the post-war years were too high. Still, it was useful to have the estimate of the 1950 grain crop of 92 million tons, in face of the official estimate of 124.5 million tons, although the crop later turned out to have been equal only to about 80 million tons (implied in official data), or 85 million tons (this writer's latest estimate).[3] Calculation of the grain crops does not actually meet with serious difficulties for one who is familiar with the utilisation of grain; there are only six items (food, feed, seed, technical uses, foreign trade, and waste) to consider. With the relatively small number of important farm products, and with the data on acreages and livestock herds usually available, even estimating the index for farm production available for sale and for consumption in the farm home is really not a very big task.

The calculation most frequently attempted has been that of industrial production. It has been undertaken for both gross and net output, and both by more thorough and by short-cut methods. A full coverage is impossible because of the absence of data on the output of armaments and of the great

---

[3] The Soviets do not mind underestimating an item for former years, if by so doing they can claim greater rates of growth in more recent years.

variety of machines produced and the frequent changes in models. Impressively, the results reached by most analysts for the period 1928-50 are fairly close to each other. A successful appraisal of the growth in industrial output in 1928-37 was even reached by something resembling a trick (evaluating a contradiction between two widely-diverging estimates of the share of Soviet industrial production in total world production in the same year in two different editions of the same official statistical handbook).

There are numerous factors causing considerable difficulties in estimating construction and investment. But too great errors can be avoided, because changes in investment more or less parallel changes in construction, and for construction a good check is available in the output of building materials. The main difficulties are encountered in estimating the shift of investment from 1928, when the private sector accounted for a large part of total investment, and, say, 1932, by which time this share had dwindled greatly. There are also great distortions in the official data pertaining to changes in investment during the purges (1936-40) and the subsequent years until 1946, distortions which it is not easy to eliminate completely.

All estimates of Soviet national income thus far made in the West have been produced by crude methods. The results differ greatly, depending on the selection of weights. Still, with due allowance made for this fact, the estimates do give a fair order of magnitude,[4] while the official index for, say, 1928-55, is exaggerated more than two-fold.

In conclusion, it seems to me that I may have taken too lightly those questions on which my own mind has been made up, and that therefore the task will look too easy. I really do not see how an outsider can find his way among the various estimates, official and unofficial. Machinery output represents almost 40 per cent of total Soviet industrial production. According to official calculations, the production of machinery (including other metal-processing) grew from 1950 to 1955, a period of considerably improved Soviet statistics, by as much as 120 per cent. One organisation devoted to research into the Soviet economy has given, for the output of machinery (excluding armaments) an increase of 14 per cent (1928 weights) or 23 per cent (1955 weights) in those years. Statisticians in the U.S. Bureau of Census calculated for the output of machinery, including armaments, an increase of 72 per cent for the same period. (Let it be added that the output of armaments is unlikely to have grown during the period in question much more than the average for all machinery.) There you are: 120, 72, 14 or 23. Take your choice.

---

[4] An account of estimates of the growth of national income and industrial output by the various western analysts, and their comparison with the official estimates, is to be found in N. Jasny, *The 1956 Soviet Statistical Handbook—A Commentary* (Michigan State Press, 1957), pp. 32-33 and 57. The interested reader is referred to this source for information on the work of other analysts who helped to raise the iron curtain on the economic front.

Chapter 16

On the Tempo of Industrialization

The tremendous advances which have made the U.S.S.R. the second mightiest industrial nation in the world were achieved in an incredibly short period of time and with the imposition of tremendous hardships and sacrifices. Stalin offers his explanation and justification of the methods and tempo involved, and Bertrand de Jouvenel raises some questions about the necessity for the sacrifices imposed.

ON SOVIET INDUSTRIALIZATION

Joseph V. Stalin

THOSE WHO FALL BEHIND GET BEATEN *

It is sometimes asked whether it is not possible to slow down the tempo somewhat, to put a check on the movement. No, comrades, it is not possible! The tempo must not be reduced! On the contrary, we must increase it as much as is within our powers and possibilities. This is dictated to us by our obligations to the workers and peasants of the U.S.S.R. This is dictated to us by our obligations to the working class of the whole world.

To slacken the tempo would mean falling behind. And those who fall behind get beaten. But we do not want to be beaten. No, we refuse to be beaten! One feature of the history of old Russia was the continual beatings she suffered because of her backwardness. She was beaten by the Mongol khans. She was beaten by the Turkish beys. She was beaten by the Swedish feudal lords. She was beaten by the Polish and Lithuanian gentry. She was beaten by the British and French capitalists. She was beaten by the Japanese barons. All beat her—because of her backwardness, military backwardness,

* From a speech at the First All-Union Conference of Managers of Socialist Industry, February, 1931.

481

cultural backwardness, political backwardness, industrial backwardness, agricultural backwardness. They beat her because to do so was profitable and could be done with impunity. Do you remember the words of the prerevolutionary poet: "You are poor and abundant, mighty and impotent, Mother Russia." Those gentlemen were quite familiar with the verses of the old poet.* They beat her, saying: "You are abundant," so one can enrich oneself at your expense. They beat her, saying: "You are poor and impotent," so you can be beaten and plundered with impunity. Such is the law of the exploiters —to beat the backward and the weak. It is the jungle law of capitalism. You are backward, you are weak—therefore you are wrong; hence, you can be beaten and enslaved. You are mighty—therefore you are right; hence, we must be wary of you. That is why we must no longer lag behind.

In the past we had no fatherland, nor could we have one. But now that we have overthrown capitalism and power is in our hands, in the hands of the people, we have a fatherland, and we will defend its independence. Do you want our socialist fatherland to be beaten and to lose its independence? If you do not want this you must put an end to its backwardness in the shortest possible time and develop genuine Bolshevik tempo in building up its socialist system of economy. There is no other way. That is why Lenin said on the eve of the October Revolution: "Either perish, or overtake and outstrip the advanced capitalist countries."

We are fifty or a hundred years behind the advanced countries. We must make good this distance in ten years. Either we do it, or we shall be crushed. This is what our obligations to the workers and peasants of the U.S.S.R. dictate to us.

But we have other, still more serious and more important, obligations. They are our obligations to the world proletariat. They coincide with our obligations to the workers and peasants of the U.S.S.R. But we place them higher. The working class of the U.S.S.R. is part of the world working class. We achieved victory not solely through the efforts of the working class of the U.S.S.R., but also thanks to the support of the working class of the world. Without this support we would have been torn to pieces long ago. It is said that our country is the shock brigade of the proletariat of all countries. This is a fitting definition. But this imposes very serious obligations upon us. Why does the international proletariat support us? How did we merit this support? By the fact that we were the first to hurl ourselves into the battle against capitalism, we were the first to establish a working-class state, we were the first to start building socialism. By the fact that we are doing work which, if successful, will change the whole world and free the entire working class. But what is needed for success? The elimination of our backwardness, the development of a high Bolshevik tempo of construction. We must march forward in such a way that the working class of the whole world, looking at us, may say: This is my vanguard, this is my shock brigade, this is my work-

* Nekrasov, "Who Is Happy in Russia?" (1876)—Editor's note.

ing-class state, this is my fatherland; they are promoting their cause, which is *our* cause, and they are doing this well; let us support them against the capitalists and promote the cause of the world revolution. Must we not live up to the hopes of the world's working class, must we not fulfil our obligations to them? Yes, we must if we do not want utterly to disgrace ourselves.

Such are our obligations, internal and international. As you see, they dictate to us a Bolshevik tempo of development.

I will not say that we have accomplished nothing in regard to economic management during these years. In fact, we have accomplished a good deal. We have doubled our industrial output as compared with the prewar level. We have created the largest-scale agricultural production in the world. But we could have accomplished more had we tried hard during this period really to master production, the technique of production, the financial and economic side of it.

In ten years at most we must make good the distance which separates us from the advanced capitalist countries. We have all the "objective" possibilities for this. The only thing lacking is the ability to take proper advantage of these possibilities. And that depends on us. *Only* on us! It is time we learned to take advantage of these possibilities. It is time to put an end to the rotten policy of noninterference in production. It is time to adopt a new policy, a policy adapted to the present times—the policy of *interfering in everything*. If you are a factory manager, then interfere in all the affairs of the factory, look into everything, let nothing escape you, learn and learn again.

PREPARATION FOR DEFENSE *

What material potentialities did our country command before the Second World War? To help you examine this point, I shall have to report briefly on the work of the Communist Party in preparing our country for active defense.

If we take the figures for 1940, the eve of the Second World War, and compare them with the figures for 1913—the eve of the First World War— we get the following picture. In 1913 our country produced 4,220,000 tons of pig iron, 4,230,000 tons of steel, 29 million tons of coal, nine million tons of oil, 21,600,000 tons of marketable grain and 740,000 tons of raw cotton. Those were the material potentialities with which our country entered the First World War. Such was the economic base of old Russia which could be drawn upon for prosecution of the war.

Now as regards 1940. In the course of that year our country produced 15 million tons of pig iron, or nearly four times as much as in 1913; 18,300,000 tons of steel, or nearly four and one half as much as in 1913;

* The balance of the excerpt is from Stalin's speech delivered in Moscow on February 9, 1946.

166 million tons of coal, or more than five and one-half times as much as in 1931; 31 million tons of oil, or nearly three and one-half times as much as in 1913; 38,300,000 tons of marketable grain, or nearly 17 million tons more than in 1913; 2,700,000 tons of raw cotton, or more than three and one-half times as much as in 1913. Those were the material potentialities with which our country entered the Second World War. Such was the economic base of the Soviet Union which could be drawn upon for prosecution of the war. The difference as you see is tremendous.

Such an unprecedented increase in production cannot be regarded as the simple and usual development of a country from backwardness to progress. It was a leap by which our Motherland was transformed from a backward into an advanced country, from an agrarian into an industrial country.

FIVE-YEAR PLANS

This historic transformation was accomplished in the course of three Five-Year Plan periods, beginning with 1928, the first year of the First Five-Year Plan. Up to that time we had to concern ourselves with rehabilitating our ravaged industry and healing the wounds received in the First World War and the Civil War. Moreover, if we bear in mind that the First Five-Year Plan was fulfilled in four years, and that the fulfillment of the Third Five-Year Plan was interrupted by war in its fourth year, we find that it took only about 13 years to transform our country from an agrarian into an industrial one. It cannot but be admitted that 13 years is an incredibly short period for the accomplishment of such an immense task. . . .

METHODS OF INDUSTRIALIZATION

By what policy did the Communist Party succeed in providing these material potentialities in the country in such a short time? First of all, by the Soviet policy of industrializing the country.

The Soviet method of industrializing the country differs radically from the capitalist method of industrialization. In capitalist countries industrialization usually begins with light industry. Since in light industry smaller investments are required and there is more rapid turnover of capital and since, furthermore, it is easier to make a profit there than in heavy industry, light industry serves as the first object of industrialization in these countries.

Only after a lapse of much time, in the course of which light industry accumulates profits and concentrates them in banks, does the turn of heavy industry arrive and accumulated capital begin to be transferred gradually to heavy industry in order to create conditions for its development.

But that is a lengthy process requiring an extensive period of several decades, in the course of which these countries have to wait until light industry has developed and must make shift without heavy industry. Naturally, the Communist Party could not take this course. The Party knew that a war was looming, that the country could not be defended without heavy industry, that the development of heavy industry must be undertaken as soon as possible, that to be behind with this would mean to lose out. The Party remembered Lenin's words to the effect that without heavy industry it would be impossible to uphold the country's independence, that without it the Soviet order might perish.

Accordingly, the Communist Party of our country rejected the "usual" course of industrialization and began the work of industrializing the country by developing heavy industry. It was very difficult, but not impossible. A valuable aid in this work was the nationalization of industry, and banking, which made possible the rapid accumulation and transfer of funds to heavy industry. There can be no doubt that without this it would have been impossible to secure our country's transformation into an industrial country in such a short time.

AGRICULTURAL POLICY

Second, by a policy of collectivization of agriculture.

In order to do away with our backwardness in agriculture and to provide the country with greater quantities of marketable grain, cotton, and so forth, it was essential to pass from small-scale peasant farming to large-scale farming, for only large-scale farming can make use of new machinery, apply all the achievements of agronomical science and yield greater quantities of marketable produce.

There are, however, two kinds of large farms—capitalist and collective. The Communist Party could not adopt the capitalist path of development of agriculture, and not as a matter of principle alone but also because it implies too prolonged a development and involves preliminary ruination of the peasants and their transformation into farm hands. Therefore, the Communist Party took the path of the collectivization of agriculture, the path of creating large-scale farming by uniting peasant farms into collective farms.

The method of collectivization proved a highly progressive method not only because it did not involve the ruination of the peasants but especially because it permitted, within a few years, the covering of the entire country with large collective farms which are able to use new machinery, take advantage of all the achievements of agronomic science and give the country greater quantities of marketable produce. There is no doubt that without a collectivization policy we could not in such a short time have done away with the age-old backwardness of our agriculture.

ON THE CHARACTER OF THE SOVIET ECONOMY

Bertrand de Jouvenel[*]

Man is free to choose his purpose: but once wedded to a purpose, he is bound to the conditions of its fulfillment. The avowed purpose of the Soviet government is to bring Russian industrial power, in the shortest possible time, to parity with that of the United States. There is nothing specifically "communist" in this purpose. Indeed it stands in stark contradiction to the Marx-Engels picture of a communist economy which would not be concerned with building-up of capacities but with their full employment for the consumer satisfaction of the workers. The purpose of the Soviet government might just as well be that of a modern Colbert whom we can imagine presiding over the eventually blended destinies of the six European nations which have begun to associate in the Coal-Steel Community.[1]

It is worth stressing that the Soviet program is the conscious and systematic imitation of something which exists, but which was not brought about either consciously or systematically. Take, for instance, steel: steel capacity did not, in the U.S., reach its successive levels because someone enjoying supreme power had decreed that steel capacity should reach such a level by such a date, but additions to capacity occurred in response to demands made upon it by steel-consuming industries, which, in turn, attuned their capacities to rising demand, ultimately consumer demand. There is no question in Russia of steel capacity growing under the prodding of demand: it must grow, period. Evidently if the growth of steel capacity is regarded as an end in itself, it can be best served by reserving all the steel presently produced for the building of more steel capacity.

This is, of course, driving things to the extreme; but it can serve at least to stress the orientation of Russian industry. Russian industry is, to a considerable degree, employed in producing industrial capacity. Of course every industrial nation has some part of its industrial plant engaged in producing plant and equipment. This is necessary in order that plant and equipment which wears down or becomes outdated can be replaced,

* French political philosopher and economist. Author of *Power* and of *Sovereignty*. The selection is excerpted from the *Bulletin of the Atomic Scientists,* Vol. 13 (November 1957), pp. 327-330. By permission of the publication and the author.
    [1] These nations, France, Western Germany, Italy, Belgium, the Netherlands, Luxembourg, muster together 160 million inhabitants. They are however far poorer in natural resources than either the U.S. or the U.S.S.R.

and so that in every field the productive apparatus can be enlarged and improved.

But in Russia the production of plant and equipment has absolute priority, which is understandable enough, given the aim, which is to reach a stated level of productive capacity. According to the statistical publication which the Soviet government has recently brought out, industrial production in Russia consisted of consumer goods in the proportion of 66.7% in 1913, of 60.5% in 1928 (when total industrial production was no greater than in 1913, as far as one can tell on other authorities), and the proportion of consumer goods in total industrial production fell successively to 29.4% in 1955, the last figure given, producers' goods having risen to 70.6% of total industrial production. The Russian publication also gives indexes of growth of the two sectors of industry: all outside experts agree that these indexes are fantastically exaggerated, but the relation between the two indexes may presumably be trusted. From 1928 to 1955 it is claimed that the sector producing means of production multiplied its output almost 39 times, while the sector producing consumer goods multiplied its own output only 9 times.

The much faster expansion of the sector producing means of production has been obtained by a priority which is perhaps the decisive feature of the Russian economy. That sector, which bears the A label in Russian economic vocabulary (as against the B label for consumer goods industries) is bidden to produce means of production for itself instead of producing them for the consumer goods industries. The Soviet reasoning is that providing plant and equipment to consumer goods industries competes with providing the same to producer goods industries, and that the faster the A sector grows, the easier it will be for it then to fill out the voids existing in the plant and equipment of the consumer goods industries.

The logic of this reasoning cannot be attacked. It is quite true that the more steel that goes into not only motorcars but also the motorcar industries, the less there is available for building steel furnaces and hydraulic presses; and that the sooner you have a great deal of the latter, the easier you will find it to equip the motorcar industry.

Russian economic history from 1928 to date can be contrasted with American economic history up to 1914 as a thing different in kind: building as against growing. In the process of growth, the bones and the flesh develop together. In building, you first construct the skeleton, then you put on the flesh: that is the Russian formula—which is incidentally convenient for purposes of world power since it gives you means of war far in advance of your means of comfort.

INVESTMENT, SAVING, AND POLITICAL STRUCTURE

An economy is most easily understood if you analyze it in terms of concrete goods. The manpower of Russian industry has risen from less than 4 million in 1928 to approximately 18 million in 1956: this is about the same manpower as that of American industry. Russian industry however produces less of everything, and the difference in amounts produced is far more pronounced in consumer goods than it is in investment goods. There are indeed some investment goods which are produced in greater quantities in the U.S.S.R. than in the U.S. In other terms, the percentage of resources going into investment activities is much higher in Russia than in America. If this fact is formulated in the language of national financial accounting, we have to say that the rate of investment within the industrial product is very much higher in Russia than in the U.S. . . .

Marx's critique of the capitalist system was based upon his postulate that the whole of added value belonged by right to the workers: and therefore the distribution of profits was an expropriation of the workers. It was an injustice, but at the same time it was necessary. Only through profits, as he clearly saw, could there be reinvestment, building up of the productive apparatus. Therefore this injustice would have to endure until the productive apparatus had been sufficiently built up. When no further capital investment was necessary, then the capitalist would become un-necessary. But he would not readily perceive his redundance; therefore he would have to be forcibly done away with. His redundance would be revealed by the fact that he would be able to find no productive employment for the capital arising out of profits: opportunities to invest would have withered away, and therefore his levy upon added value would be useless and nefarious, depriving the working consumers of the buying power needed to absorb rising production.

The historical necessity of the capitalist's disappearance was based primarily upon the postulate, widely prevalent in Marx's day, of the dwindling opportunities for productive investment: this is to be found in Ricardo. It was based also on the assumption that capitalists would not allow workers to get directly or indirectly (through government redistribution) a rising share of added value. On the other hand, the capitalist was held necessary for the process of accumulation because Marx could not imagine (and here he was no doubt right) that the workers, if they received the whole of added value, would be willing to save a large part of it for investment.

The class struggle was regarded by Marx as a struggle over "value added," the workers wishing to obtain the whole of it and to apply it to consumption, the capitalists wanting to retain as much of it as possible, and to apply it to investment. The workers were bound to win this fight, but not as long as it was socially useful that accumulation should proceed. And therefore it was also a historical necessity that capitalists should retain their power to make profits as long as accumulation had to proceed.

COMMUNISM AS SUPER-CAPITALISM

When things are looked at from this angle, it becomes quite clear that the Soviet government plays the part of the capitalist as seen by Marx. Just as Marx pictured the capitalist, the government gives the workers the smallest possible share of "added value" and retains the largest possible share in order to apply it to investment. No doubt a true democracy of workers would, within an individual company, assign a far greater part of the financial product to wages, and, within the nation, address a far larger share of activities to consumption-serving activities. This tendency must be overcome in the interests of accumulation, and therefore there must be a despotic authority to do it.

No such thing was conceived by Marx. While this point cannot be stressed here, it may be mentioned that the term, "dictatorship of the proletariat," was not understood by Marx to connote the strengthening of the state's power; the state, on the contrary, had to be destroyed root and branch, and by "dictatorship of the proletariat" Marx meant that workers' councils should be bound by no law until the liquidation of the privileged classes had been completed.

What interests us here however is simply the fact that in order to obtain rapid accumulation of productive assets, it is necessary to tilt the balance of power against the workers' eagerness to consume. This tilting was achieved in capitalist society, as Marx saw it, by the economic power of the capitalists, able to employ workers at a mere living wage. Why were they able to do so? As Marx saw it in England, there were three contributing factors: firstly, the rapid influx of candidates for industrial employment, due in small part to the rise in population and in major part to the flight from the fields. Secondly, because the capitalists owned the means of production and were free to give or deny employment: they held the whip-hand. Thirdly, they were able to do this because of the backing which the capitalists received from the state, which was a "class-state," the state of the capitalist class.

It is quite clear that in the capitalist countries of our day, there is no excess offer of manpower, thanks to policies of full employment. It is also clear that the government has ceased to be the whole-hearted supporter of the employers as against the employees. Insofar as it departs from neutrality it does so in espousing the interests of the employees. Under such conditions, the ownership of the means of production does not give the capitalists the whip-hand over the workers, the power to dictate the share these will get.

On the other hand, we do find in Russia the precipitate influx of workers depressing the labor market which Marx observed in England in his day, and which led to the "hard times" described by Dickens. And we do find the solidarity between employers and government which Marx thought characteristic of capitalist society: this solidarity is based on the fact that the employers are the instruments of government, which is completely at one with them.

We are therefore tempted to conclude that Soviet communism as we see it today is a synthetic version of early industrial capitalism.

ARE THESE SACRIFICES NECESSARY?

A question, however, arises, which does not seem to have been asked in the leading circles of Soviet Russia: was it really necessary to reproduce, as it were systematically, all the most regrettable traits of capitalist growth, to condense and accentuate them? This is surely a relevant question, when Soviet economic development is imposed as a model upon the satellite European nations, accepted as a model by the leaders of Communist China, and suggested as a model for the underdeveloped countries of the world. There is no more urgent task for Western economists than to give an answer to this question, as upon this answer may turn the choices made by leaders of the uncommitted areas of the world.

Obviously, an adequate answer cannot be offered here. Some rough suggestions may, however, be put forward for further thought. To begin with, it is a puzzling fact that while the purpose of the Soviet leaders has been to repeat the American performance, their concept of procedure has not been taken from direct pondering of American growth but at second hand from Marx's analysis of British industrial growth. . . .

Such a study would no doubt have brought to the fore, among other points, the enormous part played in American industrial growth by the high and rising productivity in agriculture, a feature to which American industrial workers owed their initially high living standards. The lack of any reference to the American experience seems all the more absurd on the part of the Russian leaders, since what they wished to emulate was the U.S., and since the natural resemblance of the U.S.S.R. physical data was plainly to the U.S. and not to Britain. This neglect can be explained by mental enslavement to the Marxian model.

But let us take up the problem from another angle, and make the questionable assumption that the basic equipment of the U.S.S.R. could not have been built up to its present pitch in the given period of time by any other procedure than that which was adopted.[2] Then the discussion

[2] We can note this analogy in respect of steel production: in Russia it rose from 4.5 million tons in 1928 to 45 million tons in 1955. In the U.S. it rose from 4.5 million tons in 1894 to 45 million tons in 1917.

might turn upon the question whether so steep a rise by so arduous a path was a desirable thing.

Let us further assume that Russia persists in its procedure of rapid growth, and therefore catches up with the U.S.[3] in basic capacities by a certain date T, and in production of consumer goods by a certain later date T'. Is anyone ready to argue that the total welfare of the Russian people between the years 1928 and T' will have been maximized by the procedure followed? Is it not far more plausible that the total welfare of the generations concerned would have been greater if a less arduous path had been followed?

It is natural to discount very distant satisfactions as against immediate satisfactions. Tinbergen has produced striking estimates of such discounting.[4] Acting as self-constituted "representatives" of the Russian people, the Soviet leaders seem to have turned things the other way round and to have set future satisfactions at a premium as against the present. But have they really reasoned in this manner? And have they not rather thought in terms of equalization of power?

For over a century, starting with Sismondi if not earlier,[5] there has been a ceaseless critique of capitalism, arguing that its unquestionable achievements in the building up of capacities were not worth the price paid in the uprooting and hustling of men, that in fact men would have been better off, and happier with a more leisurely pace of change than that forced upon them by capitalists and their sales pressure. It is interesting to find the communists enamored of the buildup achieved by the hated and despised capitalism, to the point of thinking that its speedy emulation justifies greater pressure upon men than was ever exerted under capitalism.

[3] As far as one thinks of consumer goods, one should, of course, picture the catching up as involving equalization of consumer goods per capita; if one thinks of power, then the catching up is to be thought of as merely the equality of productive capacities between the two nations, regardless of differences in population.

[4] See Tibergen's remarkable article in the *Economic Journal*, December 1956.

[5] One might say that this critique starts with Rousseau's *Discourse on the Sciences and the Arts*.

Chapter 17

RECENT DEVELOPMENTS

This section presents the viewpoints of three specialists on Soviet affairs on recent economic developments in the U.S.S.R. The first, by Maurice Dobb, an acknowledged Marxist, is largely—but not entirely—an historical account. Joseph A. Kershaw's analysis covers essentially the decade after the war. Professor Robert W. Campbell is concerned with the special problems of agriculture in the U.S.S.R.

It is not suggested, of course, that the positions represented in this and earlier sections exhaust the range of views on the Soviet economic system. But they do at least have the merit of presenting some varying positions on a subject of great intricacy and controversy.

FROM THE FOURTH FIVE-YEAR PLAN
TO THE SIXTH

MAURICE DOBB*

I

The reconstruction years, following the ravages of war and military occupation, were neither easy nor untroubled; and the first two years, in particular, of the Fourth Plan were ones of acute difficulties and of intense hardship. 1946 was overshadowed by a crop-failure due to what was officially described as "the worst drought in our country for the last fifty years"; and it was also a year of reconversion of industry from a war-time to a peace-time basis, as a result of which industrial production fell below the pre-war level by about a quarter (and consumer goods production by considerably more than this—probably by as much as a third or even two-

* Lecturer and Fellow at Trinity College, Cambridge. Author of *Political Economy and Capitalism; Studies in the Development of Capitalism;* and *On Economic Theory and Socialism.* The selection is from chapter 13 of *Soviet Economic Development Since 1917* (London: Routledge & Kegan Paul Ltd., 4th ed., 1957), by permission of the publisher and of International Publishers, New York.

fifths).[1] It seems likely that the grain harvest in 1946 was only about a half of the pre-war level; and since fodder-grains were particularly affected, there was a serious setback to the recovery of livestock (and especially pigs) from devastating war-time losses.[2] In reporting six years later to the 19th Party Congress Malenkov was to state that "the war retarded our industrial development for eight or nine years, that is, approximately two five-year plans." [3]

The following year 1947, however, witnessed considerable improvement. Firstly there was a large improvement in the harvest: grain-yields per hectare were said to have been restored to their pre-war level and the grain crop to be larger than the year before by as much as 58 per cent. (the sugar-beet crop was nearly three times that of 1946). Industry had surmounted most of the dislocations attendant upon reconversion and re-tooling; and industrial production as a whole had recovered to more than 90 per cent. of the pre-war level (heavy industry to just above it; but consumer goods production was still some 20 per cent. below it). In 1948 it was announced that for the first time industrial production had passed the pre-war level in the course of that year, although it was not until the end of 1949 that industrial output in the devastated western areas (where the bulk of consumer goods industries were located) was restored to pre-war.

In view of the improvement in the situation in 1947, derationing of foodstuffs was undertaken in December of that year, and coupled with it a monetary reform designed to reduce the amount of money in circulation (expanded by some two and a half times during the war),[4] by the issue of new money to replace the depreciated war-time rouble. The official decree of December 11 announcing the change contained this explanation: "During the years of the Patriotic War the expenditure of the Soviet State on maintenance of the Army and on the development of the war industry rose sharply. The enormous war expenditure demanded the issue for circulation of large amounts of money . . . At present, when the transfer to open trade at unified prices has become the task of the day, the great amount of money issued during the war hampers the abolition of the rationing system, since the surplus money in circulation inflates market prices, creates an exaggerated demand for goods, and increases the opportunities for speculation."

A leading object of the change was, no doubt, to tax hoarded stocks

---

[1] Cf. G. Malenkov, *Report to the Nineteenth Party Congress* (Moscow, 1952), 53. The production indices (1940 = 100) for 1945 and 1946 were here given as 92 and 77 respectively for "All Industry," and 112 and 82 respectively for "Production of Means of Production." Also cf. A. Bergson, J. H. Blackman and A. Erlich, "Post-war Economic Reconstruction and Development in the U.S.S.R." in *Annals of the American Academy of Political and Social Science,* May 1949, 59, 62.

[2] *Ibid.,* 62-3.

[3] G. Malenkov, *op. cit.,* 52.

[4] N. Voznesensky, *War Economy of the U.S.S.R. in the period of the Patriotic War* (Moscow, 1948), 111.

of money accumulated (largely, though not entirely, in the countryside) by war-time sales of scarce foodstuffs at greatly inflated prices (e.g. on the collective farm markets and by private speculation). A central feature of the monetary reform was that the new money was exchangeable for the old at parities that varied according to different categories. *Cash* holdings were exchangeable on the basis of ten old notes to one new; whereas savings bank deposits under 3,000 roubles were exchangeable on a one-one basis (with deposits of over 3,000 at progressively less favourable ratios). State bonds of recent loan issues were exchangeable for a new conversion loan (carrying 2 per cent. interest) at a ratio of one rouble of the new loan for three of the old; the reason for this discrimination as officially given being that "a considerable part of the State Loans were created during the war, when the purchasing power of money fell, whereas after the currency reform the State will redeem that debt with full-value roubles." [5] But while the main burden of the change was borne by hoarders of cash, the level of wage and salary payments remained unaffected (except for a raising of the very lowest wage categories). The new uniform retail prices were fixed at a level intermediate between the former ration prices and the higher "commercial prices" at which off-ration purchases could be made in the State shops. It seems probable that the result was to reduce the urban cost of living by approximately a half compared with what it had been in the years prior to the monetary reform.[6] Thereafter the policy was adopted of making successive price-reductions (while keeping money wages more or less stable) as increased supplies of consumers' goods became available; the result of this series of price-reductions being to bring the retail price-level by the end of 1954 to about 20 per cent. above the immediate pre-war level (i.e. 1940) and the level of real wages (excluding the value of free services) to about 65 per cent. above pre-war (i.e. 1940).[7] It seems probable that the average real income of the collective farm peasantry rose during this period by rather more than that of industrial and other workers.

The progress of reconstruction in the course of 1948 was sufficient to justify the hopes on which the monetary reform was based; and of the agricultural situation at the end of that year the Central Statistical Ad-

[5] Decree of Dec. 11, 1947.

[6] M. C. Kaser, "Soviet Statistics of Wages and Prices," in *Soviet Studies* (University of Glasgow), Vol. VII, No. 1, 39. On the eve of the monetary reform retail prices were about three times the level of 1940; while the average level of money wages was less than double pre-war.

[7] *Ibid.*, 42-3; *Politicheskaia Ekonomia: Uchebnik* (Moscow, 1954), 462. Including the value of free services, the average real income of workers was almost double pre-war and between three and four times the level of 1947. An article in *Planovoe Khoziaistvo*, 1955, No. 4, 8, claimed that by 1955 real wages had reached a level of 90 per cent above 1950. The recently published *Narodnoe Khoziaistvo S.S.S.R.* (Moscow, 1956) gives for 1955 an index number of retail prices in State shops of 138 (1940 = 100) and for prices in Kolkhoz markets of 111 (1940 = 100). It is to be noted that prices in 1940 were appreciably above the level of 1937 and real wages lower. A comparison with 1937 instead of 1940 would therefore yield a rather smaller increase than the above mentioned.

ministration was able to report that "despite unfavourable weather conditions in most of the Volga regions, the gross grain harvest practically
reached the pre-war level of 1940, while average grain yields per hectare
exceeded the pre-war level." [8] As regards livestock, the number of cattle and
of sheep and goats was said to have been restored to the pre-war level by
the end of the year, although not yet the number of cows or the number of
pigs. Industrial output showed the remarkably large rise of 27 per cent.
over the previous year. Altogether during these first three years of the Five
Year Plan some 4,000 industrial plants had been put into operation, of
which about a half were completed in the course of 1948.

The main targets of the Five Year Plan were actually attained ahead
of time, and the overall industrial target set for 1950 was exceeded by 17
per cent. The Report on the Fulfilment of the Fourth Five Year Plan,
issued by Gosplan and the Central Statistical Board in April 1951, announced that the plan had indeed been completed in four years and a
quarter.[9] Industrial output in 1950, the last year of the plan, stood at 73
per cent. above 1940, with capital goods about double but consumer goods
no more than 23 per cent. above pre-war. Ferrous metals exceeded the
pre-war level by 45 per cent., coal by 57, oil by 22 and electricity by 87, but
textiles, clothing, footwear and other light industries only by 17 per cent.
Grain output, although short of the plan-target, was some 5 million tons
above 1940. More surprisingly it was announced that the total head of
productive livestock, sharply reduced during the war, was restored, and
in 1950 increased by 4 per cent. compared with 1940 in all categories of
farming.[10] However, while cattle and sheep and goats were above the
pre-war level, cows and pigs were still below (horses were also very substantially below), as the following table shows:[11]

LIVESTOCK NUMBERS
(in millions)

	1940 (post-war territory)	1950
Cattle	54.5	57.2
of which:		
Cows	27.8	24.2
Pigs	27.5	24.1
Sheep and Goats	91.6	99.0
Horses	20.5	13.7

[8] Report on the Fulfilment of the State Plan for 1948.

[9] See *Planovoe Khoziaistvo*, 1951, No. 2, 3-13.

[10] Report of Gosplan and Central Statistical Board on "Results of the Fulfilment of
the Fourth Five-Year Plan."

[11] Cf., "Results of the Fulfilment of the State Plan for 1950" (Report of Central
Statistical Administration, § IV; United Nations Economic Commission for Europe, *Economic Survey of Europe in 1950* (Geneva, 1951), 40, and *Economic Survey of Europe in
1951* (Geneva, 1952), 134.

As was to transpire in the course of the next few years, the failure of grain and livestock to recover as rapidly as industrial production was to be the crucial limiting factor upon the rise in the standard of life in the course of the 1950's.

II

Details of the Fifth Plan were not publicly announced until just before the 19th Party Congress in October, 1952.[12] Its two main features were: (1) a rate of increase of industrial production of 72 per cent. over the quinquennium, which was lower than that of previous plans (even somewhat lower than in the unfinished Third Plan);[13] (2) a narrowing of the divergence between the rates of growth of the two main departments or sectors of industry producing capital goods and consumer goods: output of the former was to grow by 80 per cent, and of the latter by 65 per cent., whereas, by contrast, between 1928 and 1940 the former grew about double as fast as the latter. The result was accordingly to place more emphasis on raising the level of consumption.

If we take some individual commodities for which quantity figures were given, we find that ferrous metals, fuel and power are listed for increases close to the average for industry in general; the exception to this being coal, the figure for this (43 per cent.) being lower than in previous plans (oil, however, was equivalently higher). Non-ferrous metals, on the other hand, such as copper, lead, zinc, tin and aluminium were scheduled for considerably higher rates of increase. For grain an ambitious target of a 40-50 per cent. increase was set, and a similar figure for gross agricultural output; the intention being that this increase should come mainly from higher yields rather than from extended acreage (the "Directives on the Plan" stating that "the main task in the sphere of agriculture still remains the raising of the yields of all agricultural crops"). Similarly in industry prime emphasis was placed on a rise in labour productivity (of approximately 50 per cent.), while the rise in the number of "factory and office workers" over the quinquennium was set at 15 per cent. In this connection Mr. Malenkov in his report to the 19th Party Congress claimed that "labour productivity in industry increased 50 per cent. between 1940 and 1951" and that this accounted for two-thirds of the rise of industrial output over that period.

Investment in house-building was to be raised, and urban housing financed by the State was to be higher by about a fifth (measured in floorspace provided) than in the previous quinquennium of reconstruction. During the period of the Fourth Plan about 100 million square metres of

[12] See "Directives of the Plan" in *Planovoe Khoziaistvo*, 1952, No. 4, 4-25.

[13] A quinquennial increase of 72 per cent. represents an annual (compound) rate of 12 per cent., which is to be compared with 18.3 per cent. between 1928 and 1940 according to the official index (on which see below, 330-2) and 20 per cent. in the concluding three years of the Fourth Plan.

floor-space were built by "State enterprises, institutions and local Soviets, and also by the population of towns and workers' settlements with the aid of State credits." [14] This was equivalent to about 2½ million small flat-dwellings of 2 rooms *plus* kitchen and bathroom. In addition, about 2,700,-000 rural houses were built. The new Plan mentioned a figure of 105 million square metres for urban building by State organisations alone (i.e. excluding building "by the population of towns and workers' settlements with the aid of State credits," which had previously accounted for some 12 per cent. of the whole); but it was silent about the volume of rural building.[15]

The successive price-cuts and the rise in the standard of life from 1949 onwards has been mentioned in the previous section. In the course of 1953 a new emphasis on raising living-standards came into official pronouncements and policy. The price-reductions announced in the spring of that year were larger than usual, and had the effect of increasing consumers' purchasing power probably by a sixth. Retail turnover, measured in constant prices, was at any rate greater by 15 per cent. in the first half of the year compared with the corresponding period of the previous year, and State Loan issues during the year were reduced by more than a half. In the autumn a series of Ministerial Decrees were issued to improve incentives to agricultural production (by tax revisions and price-adjustments), to increase the supply of foodstuffs to the urban population and to raise the targets for the output of consumer goods in the two concluding years of the Fifth Plan. This was the first occasion on which revision of a Plan in the middle of a quinquennium had been in favour of consumer goods industries (in the pre-war period such a revision had invariably been at the expense of this sector of industry and in favour of heavy industry under the pressure of rearmament). In the second half of 1953 the output of consumers' goods increased by 14 per cent. over the same period of the previous year, or by more than the increase of industrial output in general.[16] There was talk of giving priority to light industries in the supply of personnel, of materials, of power and of equipment and repairs; and in the course of the year about 300 new industrial enterprises producing consumer goods were brought into operation and some 6,000 new shops were opened; while a decree of October 23 outlined a programme for building 40,000 new shops and 11,000 new restaurants in the course of the next three years. At the same time there were adjustments in the import-programme to provide more room for the import of consumer goods.

It was to transpire, however, that the position in agriculture during

[14] *Planovoe Khoziaistvo*, 1951, No. 2, 13.

[15] *Planovoe Khoziaistvo*, 1952, No. 4, 21; U.N. Economic Commission for Europe, *Economic Survey of Europe since the War* (Geneva, 1953), 49.

[16] Indeed from 1951 to 1954 the growth-rates of capital-goods and consumer-goods industries were identical. 1937 was the only year previously when consumer goods had increased faster than capital goods.

the early years of the '50's had in crucial respects actually deteriorated. The head of cattle declined between 1950 and 1953 (the fall being among those privately owned, which was not compensated by the increased number in the ownership of State and collective farms), and the number of cows remained below, not only the 1928 level, but also the (lower) 1940 level. Supplies of meat and milk to the towns remained practically stationary over the years 1950, 1951 and 1952. Sheep and goats (which are mainly owned by State or collective farms) increased by only 10 per cent. over the three years and even pigs by no more than 18 per cent. A leading reason was shortage of fodder. Grain output in these years showed no improvement, being on the average of 1951-53 only 3 to 4 per cent. above 1950, which as we have seen was very little above the pre-war level. Sugarbeet and raw cotton did only a little better, and the output of flax declined drastically. This was the reason for renewed attention to agriculture, to overcome this grave "agricultural lag"; which took the form, not only of increased investments in agriculture in the next two years and improved procurement-prices to farmers for grain, vegetables and livestock, but a campaign to encourage the extension of maize cultivation and the "virgin lands campaign" to bring under the plough over the next three years some 70 million acres (30 million hectares) of steppeland in Siberia and Kazakhstan, thereby increasing the sown area of the country by about a sixth (of which by the end of 1954 rather more than a half had already been ploughed-up).

In the last year of the quinquennium these measures were to bear fruit in an increase of grain production to 29 per cent above 1950, and in quite remarkable recoveries in sugar-beet and flax (although not in cotton or potatoes which suffered in 1950 from weather conditions). By 1955 the number of cows had recovered to above the pre-war level, and of all cattle to above even the 1928 level; while the number of pigs had doubled over the quinquennium and the number of sheep had grown by 50 per cent. The data on livestock are summarised in the following table:[17]

As regards industrial output, the quinquennium showed a rather greater increase both in total output and in industrial consumer goods than had been set in the plan-targets. The total increase from 1950 to 1955 was 85 per cent. as against a planned increase of 72; while the increase in the consumer goods sector was 76 per cent., compared with a planned increase of 65. The capital goods industries still held the lead (although a comparatively small one) with a 91 per cent. increase, compared with a plan-target of 80. The result was to raise the level of industrial output to more than double the pre-war level, and even industrial consumer goods

[17] Report of N. S. Khrushchev to the 20th Party Congress, Feb. 14, 1956; Results of the Fulfilment of the Fifth Five-Year Plan; U.N. Economic Commission for Europe, *Economic Survey of Europe in 1953* (Geneva, 1954), 52, and *Economic Survey of Europe in 1955* (Geneva, 1956), 170.

LIVESTOCK NUMBERS
(*million head, on present territory*)

	1928 end of	1940 end of	1945 end of	1950 end of	1951 end of	1952 end of	1953 Oct. 1st	1954 Oct. 1st	1955 Oct. 1st
Cattle	66.8	54.5	45.3	57.2	58.8	56.6	63.0	64.9	67.1
of which: Cows	33.2	27.8	—	24.2	24.8	24.3	26.0	27.5	29.2
Pigs	27.4	27.5	3.4	24.1	26.7	28.5	47.6[2]	51.1	52.1
Sheep and Goats . . .	114.6	91.6	56.0	99.0	107.5	109.9	114.9[3]	117.5[3]	124.9[3]
Horses	36.1	20.5	9.1	13.7	14.6	15.3	—	—	—

[2] Nearly the whole of this very surprising increase came from those privately owned, which almost trebled in number within less than a year.

[3] Sheep only. Mr. Khrushchev in his report gave 50 per cent. as the increase of sheep between 1950 and 1955; and it seems probable that the inclusion of goats in the later years would raise the figures as stated by about one-sixth.

to double the pre-war level. The rise of the national income over 1940 was officially stated as being 80 per cent., and "the turnover in State and Co-operative retail trade during the same period more than doubled." [18] House-building in towns (including building on private account with the aid of State credits) amounted to about 154 million square metres of floor-space, or some 50 per cent. more than in the previous quinquennium; while rural house building, at 2.3 million houses, was smaller by about half a million than it had been during the period of the 4th Plan.[19]

Detailed increases for particular products can be seen from the output table that is given below. It may serve to put them in historical perspective if one points out that the general growth-rate of industrial output over this quinquennium, although lower than in the pre-war decade, represents a rate of growth some 50 per cent. above that attained by capitalist economies in the past during exceptional boom periods (e.g. Japan between 1907 and 1913, U.S.A. between 1885 and 1889 and the United Kingdom in the immediate post-war years). It is more than three times the average rate of industrial growth in U.S.A. between 1899 and 1937, three times the rate of growth of industrial production in the countries of Western Europe between 1950 and 1955, and double that in U.S.A. during the same period.

It should, perhaps, be mentioned that in the concluding years of this quinquennium some important changes were introduced into the machinery and methods of planning, especially in relation to agriculture. These changes were in the direction of decentralisation, with less detail specified

[18] Report on the Results of the Fulfilment of the Fifth Five Year Plan.
[19] *Planovoe Khoziaistvo*, 1956, No. 2, 7.

in the central plan, greater discretion to lower levels likely to be more in touch with the actual situation in their regions or their special branches of industry, and more reliance on economic incentives as a way of getting things done, with less reliance on "administrative" methods and compulsion. In 1953 a start was made by introducing simplified planning methods in agriculture (previously there had been 200 or more targets for each collective farm in the annual plan), with a decentralisation to the provincial administration (where in future detailed plans for individual farms are to be worked out) and greater discretion to the farm management to decide questions about production on the basis of appropriate financial incentives. In 1954 the functions of Gosplan were narrowed somewhat in order to concentrate attention "on the cardinal questions of the national economy —the establishment of proper proportions in the development of individual branches, the elimination of bottlenecks, the maximum utilisation of the reserves available in the national economy"; and measures were taken "to cut the list of targets approved in the annual plan, both in industrial and agricultural production." [20] This was done under the slogan of "encouraging creative initiative and a struggle against bureaucracy in all its forms and manifestations." [21] Later, some economic Ministries were transferred from the All-Union to the Republican level, and Gosplan itself was divided into two (in May, 1955), the one body to be responsible for the preparation and operation of the annual plans (*Gosekonomkomissia*) and the other to confine itself to long-term planning (*Gosplan*).

RECENT TRENDS IN THE SOVIET ECONOMY

JOSEPH A. KERSHAW*

It is now a decade since World War II came to a conclusion. That conflict inflicted great punishment on the Soviet economy. The valuable industrial and agricultural areas of the west and southwest were laid waste once by the Soviet armies retreating eastward, and again by the German armies retreating westward. This destruction, coupled with the intensive use of capital during the war and the failure to replace a good deal of it, could not help weakening the economy seriously.

[20] G. M. Malenkov in speech to the Soviet of Nationalities, April 26, 1954.
[21] *Ibid.*

* Economist, Rand Corporation, where he has supervised research on the Soviet economy. The selection originally appeared in the *Annals of the American Academy of Political and Social Science,* Vol. 303 (January 1956), pp. 37-49. By permission.

It is true that by the end of the war reconstruction had already begun in a serious way. Nonetheless, the economy in 1945 was considerably smaller by almost any measure than it had been five years earlier. Casualties had been high, the people were tired, farms were depleted of their best manpower, and the nonagricultural labor force had been reduced by the operation of the draft. With the possible exception of Germany and Poland, the Soviet economy enjoyed the dubious distinction of having suffered more than any other as a result of the war.

The details of economic development following the conclusion of the war are not well known to Western scholars. The broad outlines, however, are unmistakable, and there is rather general agreement that the recovery has been little short of remarkable. The Soviet economy is now the world's second mightiest, and the scars of the war that ended just one short decade ago have all but disappeared.

The main purpose of this paper is to examine some recent trends in the Soviet economy, especially from the viewpoint of their influence on Soviet rates of growth. To do this, we shall have to look at the growth rates in effect before Stalin's death in order to evaluate the influence of the post-Stalin changes. We shall also want to speculate on future developments in the economy with particular emphasis on the probabilities that rates of growth in the future will or will not vary significantly from those that have characterized the past.

DIMENSIONS OF SOVIET GROWTH

While there is general agreement that Soviet growth since the end of the war has been rapid, there is some disagreement as to just how rapid it has been. This disagreement stems in part from the fact that there are serious conceptual difficulties in describing the growth of an economy; in the case of the Soviet Union there is the added difficulty that the Soviet authorities have restricted the amount of data made available to Western and, perhaps, Soviet scholars. The Iron Curtain has not been able to impose a blackout, since a centrally directed economy requires the existence of considerable amounts of data for the implementation of its own instructions; many of these data cannot be kept from the eyes of the West, but quantitatively and qualitatively the statistical dim-out has been impressive.

The Russians have published data on Soviet national income for some time, but those who have studied the data and the concepts and practices of Soviet national income statistics find it impossible to accept the rates of increase implied by these data.[1] There has been as yet no definitive Western study indicating the rate of growth of the Soviet economy as a

[1] Paul Studenski and Julius Wyler, "National Income Estimates of Soviet Russia— Their Distinguishing Characteristics and Problems," *American Economic Review*, Vol. 37, No. 2 (May 1947), pp. 595-610.

whole. We are not able, therefore, to describe the dimensions of Soviet growth with either exactness or confidence. But we do have estimates that are plausible.

Several years ago, at a conference of economists who are students of the U.S.S.R., Professor Gregory Grossman set forth an estimate of the growth of the Soviet economy which may be taken as of the right order of magnitude, at least pending the completion of more definitive studies. Professor Grossman found that the annual rate of growth of the Soviet economy before World War II was 6.5 to 7 per cent.[2] In the postwar period, but with the exception of the immediate postwar years when reconstruction obviously meant a rapid rate of growth, the annual rate of growth of national income seems to have been about the same. There is some discernible tendency for this rate to slacken off, but more will be said on the subject on a later page.

To some, this sort of percentage rate of increase sounds fairly modest. It is, however, large by any standards of Western experience. It may be well to keep in mind that such a rate implies a doubling in size every eleven years. Perhaps more germane is a comparison of rates of increase of the United States economy. Most American economists, when they think about the future of the United States economy, think in terms of growth rates on the order of 2.5 to 3 per cent a year. This, for example, is the range used by President Truman's Materials Policy Commission and by Gerhard Colm in a recent publication of the National Planning Association.[3] There have been occasions when the United States growth rate has been higher than 3 per cent, but there have seldom if ever been occasions when, over a prolonged period of time, the growth rate in this country has approximated that which has apparently been maintained in the Soviet Union since 1928, with the exception, of course, of the war years.[4]

But there is a real question as to whether a growth rate for the Soviet economy as a whole is the significant figure to look for. For one thing, the total economy is made up of many sectors which grow at very disparate rates. This creates serious statistical problems, and casts real doubt on the significance of a single growth rate. Moreover, when comparisons are made between two economies with rather different structures, there is a serious question as to the meaning of over-all rates of increase.

Significance of industry and agriculture in total economy

This leads to the desirability of examining separate sectors of the economy separately. Among those which might be examined, two sectors—

[2] A. Bergson (Editor), *Soviet Economic Growth* (Evanston, Ill.: Row, Peterson and Company, 1953), p. 9.

[3] G. Colm, *The American Economy in 1960* (National Planning Association, 1952), p. 19.

[4] See, for example, Simon Kuznets, *National Product Since 1869* (New York: National Bureau of Economic Research, Inc., 1946), p. 119; also see the Grossman chapter in A. Bergson (Editor), *op. cit.* (note 2 *supra*), p. 12.

industry and agriculture—are of particular interest in themselves, because of their importance in the total economy, and because of economic relationships between them. The output of industry, or rather its relative size and rate of increase, is the magnitude of greatest interest to us when we attempt to assess the degree and rate of industrialization. Furthermore, industrial strength determines economic strength, at least in the short run when capability to make war (cold or hot) is the central issue. It is the output of the basic industries like coal, machinery, electric power, steel, and petroleum that we are really interested in when we are thinking of the comparative size of the Soviet economy and economies of the West.

On the other hand, the ability of an economy to satisfy its people becomes important in the longer run. And here, though industry too supplies consumer goods, the success of industry in this respect rests, in a virtually closed economy like the U.S.S.R., on success in agriculture. Furthermore, in a developing economy, it is agriculture which supplies an important part of the growing industrial labor force and which, to do so, requires an increasing amount of machinery.

Thus, we are led to examine the industrial and agricultural sectors of the Soviet economy. Perhaps the most important characteristic of these sectors is that they are growing at vastly different rates. To some extent this is a result of deliberate policy, but in a very important sense it is not. In any case, the difficulties of talking about growth of the total economy are perhaps best illustrated by pointing out that the total economy is made up, among other things, of a sector (industrial output) which has grown at a very rapid rate for twenty-five years, and another sector (agriculture) which has grown at a very modest rate.

Industry

Turning first to the industrial sector, we find rates of increase that are consistently and outstandingly high. The most careful study of this sector has been that by Professor Donald Hodgman.[5] He has accumulated indices of physical output for as many industrial commodities as he could find, and has combined these indices with an approximation to value-added weights, to get an over-all index of physical production. His index is a good deal more comprehensive for the years before World War II than for the period since the end of the war. Nonetheless, it shows that industrial production (again with the exception, of course, of the war years) increased during the prewar period at a rate of approximately 15 per cent per year,[6] and for the postwar years, until the death of Stalin, at a rate of

[5] Donald Hodgman, *Soviet Industrial Production 1928-51*. Cambridge, Mass.: Harvard University Press, 1954.

[6] Hodgman's index is for large-scale industry only. Since small-scale industry grew less rapidly, Hodgman's index overstates growth of total industry before the war, perhaps by two or three percentage points. Incidentally, the cited rate applies to the 1928-37 period. In the three years before the war the rate fell rapidly as the economy began to

10 per cent. As in the case of national income, these are rates of increase
that are rarely if ever known in Western economies.[7]

For the postwar period the Hodgman index probably understates the
annual growth rates. This is because the commodities he is able to include
are mostly basic ones; very few of the more fabricated items like machinery
appear, and it is these which have grown most. It is not clear, therefore,
that Hodgman's postwar 10 per cent is really lower than his prewar 15 per
cent.

What *is* clear is that the rates are still high. Six years ago THE ANNALS
devoted an issue to the Soviet Union. The article on the Soviet economy
contained a table showing physical outputs for a selected list of commodities. When one compares these with the 1954 output, one finds that
the increases imply annual growth rates of between 10 and 20 per cent in
almost every case.[8] Rapid growth in industry has been and is unmistakable.

Agriculture

The situation in agriculture is quite different. Agriculture has been
much in the news of late, and most of the leaders of the U.S.S.R. have been
clearly anxious about the general agricultural situation. In brief, the
increase in output of most agricultural commodities in the last twenty-five
years has scarcely kept pace with the increase in population, so that
agricultural output per capita is no greater than it was before the period of
the Five Year Plans began.

Two major items of agricultural output are grain and livestock. The
Russians have put great emphasis on the need to increase the output of
both these items, but with marked lack of success. Grain output for 1954
was less than in 1937, much less on a per capita basis;[9] and in the mid-1950's
per capita grain output was below even the 1928 level. The livestock situation was no better. In no year since 1950 has the stock of cattle been as
large as it was in 1928 and, while there have been some recent successes in
increasing the number of hogs, it is clear that the output of meat and

---

mobilize. One other study may be cited here. Professor Gerschenkron, using 1939 dollar
price weights, computed an index of heavy industrial production (more specifically
machinery, iron and steel, coal, petroleum products, and electric power) for the period
1928/29 to 1937. His index increases at an annual rate of 17.8 per cent. *Review of
Economics and Statistics,* Vol. 37, No. 2 (May 1955), p. 126.

[7] It is possible that Japan, in the latter part of the nineteenth century, may have
enjoyed comparable growth rates.

[8] The 1948 data came from Abram Bergson, James Horton Blackman, and Alexander
Erlich, "Postwar Economic Reconstruction and Development in the U.S.S.R.," THE
ANNALS, Vol. 263 (May 1949), p. 56. The 1954 data were compiled by Nancy Nimitz from
scattered Soviet sources.

[9] These developments have to be interpreted with care, since there is less current use of
grain in feeding horses now that tractors have replaced so many horses. But even so, more
grain is urgently needed, as is indicated by the 1960 planned output, which is a third
larger than 1950.

dairy products per capita is not as large as it was in 1928.[10] All in all, the Soviet diet has unquestionably deteriorated.[11] . . .

One should note that the lack of real progress in agriculture has come about not because the sector has been starved by the planners, for in one sense at least agriculture has been favored. There has been a consistent policy of directing appreciable proportions of total Soviet investment into agriculture. There has been a good deal of discussion about the need to mechanize, and a good deal of bragging about the extent of mechanization on the farm. Indeed, the primitive agriculture of the late 1920's has been very substantially transformed through the investment program that has been a central part of all the Five Year Plans.

In one sense, agriculture has made a real contribution. One output of Soviet agriculture is labor. In good part, the investment in agriculture which has looked toward mechanization has had as its main purpose the release of labor from the land. We shall discuss this at a later point, but it may be noted here that the Soviet countryside constituted and perhaps still constitutes a large reservoir of labor for the rapidly expanding Soviet industry. Soviet agriculture in this regard has succeeded in supplying large quantities of labor. Most of the productivity increases have resulted in freeing labor from the land rather than in increasing output on the land. To a certain extent, this is a choice that the planners have made, although it will be pointed out later that they are faced with serious constraints in their exercise of choice.

EXPLANATION OF HIGH RATE OF INDUSTRIAL GROWTH

The consistently high rate of industrial growth in the U.S.S.R. is something which has a quite plausible explanation. Part of this lies in the distinction between the institutions of a centrally planned economy and a market economy. In a market economy such as the United States or the United Kingdom, there is a rather effective way in which the people as consumers, savers, and investors determine the over-all allocation of resources. This mechanism is by no means perfect, and it is of course seriously interrupted in times of war and major depression but, by and large, the people through the marketplace determine the way in which the society allocates its resources. In their performance of this function, the people are guided by their own efforts to derive the greatest possible utility from the fruits of their own labor. In other words, the important thing is the preferences of the people themselves.

[10] Two RAND "RM" studies, one published and one forthcoming, bear on these difficulties. Both are by Nancy Nimitz. "Statistics of Soviet Agriculture," RM-1250, has been published.

[11] The loss in calories has been made up to a considerable extent (perhaps completely) by the rapid growth in output of potatoes and vegetables. But the change in diet has been quite involuntary.

In a centrally directed economy, the situation is very different. The dictator decides how he wants the resources of the economy allocated, and then proceeds to do so by direction. In the case of the U.S.S.R., the planners decide that they are more interested in the production of heavy industrial goods than in the production of consumer goods. They are able to implement this decision by various techniques: by subsidies on industrial goods, for example, or by high taxes on consumer goods. So long as they exercise effective control over the people, they can continue to allocate the resources of the economy in a way at variance with what the people themselves would decide if they had any real choice in the matter.

It is clear from the statements of the Soviet leaders that they consciously set out in 1928, through the device of the Five Year Plans, to build up the heavy industrial sector of the economy at the expense of the consumer. A recent *Pravda* editorial puts it this way: "Heavy industry has always been and continues to be the basis of the constant development of our national economy. The Communist party has always considered rapid development of heavy industry its main task." [12] In other words, the emphasis on heavy industry has been a deliberate policy for a long period of time. The driving force has been an unswerving desire to "catch up with the West." In a perverse sort of way, the basest villain of them all, the United States, has been the ideal.

In pursuing these goals, the U.S.S.R. has had a number of advantages. For one thing, he who starts late can copy. It is clear that the Russians have practiced emulation, either by importing engineering skill and exploiting it, or by the cruder technique of purchasing equipment from abroad and imitating it. Whatever form it took, emulation has made it easier to take initial strides more rapidly than the pioneer, who had to learn as he progressed.

A second important factor has been the vast reservoir of labor on the countryside. The process of industrial growth in any country is accomplished by a rapid shift of labor from agriculture to industry, and the Soviet Union has been no exception. The only peculiar feature of the Soviet experience is that there still exists a very large agricultural labor force in spite of the large industrial advances that have already been made. At the present time the Soviet regime still has around half of its total labor force in agriculture; the corresponding figure in the United States is about 10 per cent. Millions of people have already moved from the farm and, if solutions to the basic agricultural problems are found, the flow of labor from the farm to the city can remain high. This flow is of course in addition to the increase that results from the growth in population.

Much should also be made of the absence of the business cycle in the U.S.S.R. Prolonged periods of depression such as that in the 1930's in the

[12] *Pravda*, March 7, p. 1. Translated by *Current Digest of the Soviet Press*, April 13, 1955, p. 19.

United States can and do interrupt industrial progress. In the Soviet Union, the institutional arrangements are such that periods of this sort have not occurred and will not occur in the future. To be sure, Soviet society has its disadvantages, some of them coming about for the same reason that business cycles do not, but from this one difficulty, at least, it is free.

Soviet Investment Policy

But the most important determinant of the high rate of industrial growth is certainly to be found in Soviet investment policy. There are two things about this investment policy that are deserving of emphasis. Both are the results of conscious decisions of the economic planners.

TYPICAL POSTWAR DISTRIBUTION OF INVESTMENT BY SECTORS, U.S.A. AND U.S.S.R.

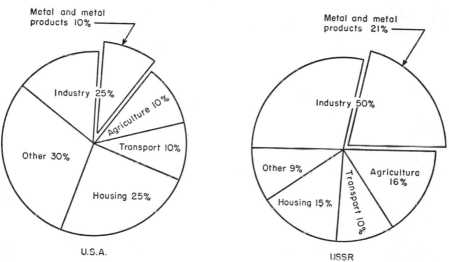

(From *Annals of the American Academy of Political and Social Science.* **Vol. 33,** January, 1956, pp. 37-49)

The first is that the rate of investment (that is, the ratio of gross investment to gross national product) has been consistently high. More specifically, for the last twenty-five years, with the exception of the war years, the Soviet government has, year after year, allocated 20 per cent or more of the economy's total resources to investment. This is a percentage which the United States and other Western countries equal on occasion, when economic activity is at very high levels. The difference is that in the U.S.S.R. it happens every year, and no Western economy has had this experience.

The second feature regarding Soviet investment is equally important. Of the resources that are invested, a far larger proportion than is true in our case goes into heavy industry. For each unit of total investment, therefore, the payoff in terms of continued high rates of increase of industrial output is high. Whereas in the United States a good proportion of investment goes into things like luxury hotels, laundry facilities, and the like, the Russians devote every possible kopeck of their investment to electric power, steel, chemicals, and so forth. The accompanying pie chart contrasts the postwar Soviet and American practices.

The effect of these two peculiar features of Soviet investment is a continuous plowing back of resources into those areas which in turn create more resources which can be plowed back. This reflects itself in the rate of increase of industrial production, and largely accounts for its being high. It may be noted that there is no real reason why both the rate and the direction of investment should not be continued in the future as they have been in the past for an indefinite period. That is to say, there is nothing inherent in what is going on which says that there must be a change at any foreseeable date. It is possible, of course, that the policy which has dictated the nature of investment may be changed.

THE ECONOMY AT STALIN'S DEATH

It may be appropriate to summarize the situation in 1953 which had resulted from the general trends that have been thus far described. Several features stand out.

In the first place, the Russians had managed to build up a very strong industrial base. In most of the important commodities, they were second only to the United States. In spite of the terrible devastation of the war, they had managed by 1948 or so to recover their prewar position, and then had pushed ahead so that by 1953 they had passed England, France, Germany, and all others except the United States.

Secondly, and paradoxically, in spite of all this, the Soviet economy in a very real sense was still an agricultural economy. In many ways, the proportion of an economy's labor force engaged in agriculture is a measure of its stage of development, and it is noteworthy that this proportion in the U.S.S.R. was still around half in 1953.

In 1953 the Soviet people were still experiencing a very low standard of living. The emphasis on heavy industry, which has been discussed, had as a natural result a standard of living which was bound to be very low. Actually, it appeared for many years as though the Five Year Plans regarded consumption as the residual claimant, while the planners determined the rate of investment that they wanted largely in terms of what they could get away with in denying consumption to the people.

In the two or three years before 1953, the standard of living had been permitted to turn rather sharply upward. It is interesting to speculate on why this should have been done, and even more interesting to wonder whether the trend will continue To be sure, it may be that some of the increase is illusory, since about this time stories of queuing up and bare shelves began to creep into the press.

Real wage comparisons with the West are, of course, extremely difficult. Nonetheless, it may be interesting to point to some research under way at the RAND Corporation, which compares the ruble prices of a substantial number of consumer goods and service items with dollar prices in the United States of the same or comparable items. When this is done, a 1950 ruble-dollar price ratio for consumer goods, including food, services, and manufactured goods, comes out to 20 to 1 when United States weights are used, and 15½ to 1 when Soviet weights are used. In 1950 the average wage in the U.S.S.R. was something like 7,500 rubles, in the United States about $3,000. The Soviet worker's real wage in 1950, then, was some one-sixth to one-eighth that of the American, depending on the weighting system used.[13]

Finally, we may note that the Soviet economy at the time of Stalin's death was supporting a substantial military establishment. Some four million men were reputed to be in uniform, and the Korean experience had indicated a modern military technology to be characteristic of Soviet military equipment. The Russians had exploded their first A-bomb three and a half years previously, and were soon to begin talking about their prowess in the manufacture of H-bombs.

As nearly as we can calculate, the proportion of total resources in the U.S.S.R. going into the military establishment in 1953 was around 15 per cent. It is important to understand the meaning of this, since there has apparently been a good deal of uninformed speculation about it recently. It should be clear that resources spent for the military, unlike those devoted to capital goods, are not productive. A blast furnace can be used to produce something else, a military tank cannot.[14] To this extent, therefore, the Soviet economy like any other is penalized by the resources it allocates to the military. The military is competing for resources with other sectors of the economy. It does not follow, however, that the drain is necessarily serious, so long as the total is rising and the military sector does not rise more than proportionately. Indeed there is no reason to assume that the Soviet leaders could not go on indefinitely devoting a given percentage of their total resources to the military or spending resources equal in amount to those they were spending in 1953. To repeat, what is spent on the military cannot be spent on investment or for consumers, but there is nothing to indicate that the drain represented by the military program at the stated level threatens to bring about economic collapse in any sense.

[13] For trends in real wages, see Janet Chapman, "Real Wages in the Soviet Union, 1928-1952," *Review of Economics and Statistics,* Vol. 36, No. 2 (May 1954), pp. 134-56.

[14] It does produce "national security." There is no intent to imply that military production is necessarily wasteful. The point is that military end items, unlike capital goods, do not produce additional economic goods.

MALENKOV-KHRUSHCHEV CHANGES

The end of an era occurred in March 1953 with the death of Stalin. There followed two years during which Malenkov was at least nominally in charge. Then in February 1955 Malenkov was succeeded by Bulganin or Khrushchev or both. When Malenkov's economic program began to emerge, it appeared to constitute a real break with the immediate past. Its main outlines were as follows. There was to be a sharp shift in the distribution of investment, away from heavy and toward light industry and trade. Much more of the fruits of the economy were to be distributed to the people. In fact, promises to the consumer were lavish and, to some of us, seemed surprisingly specific. Finally, the ever-present problem of agricultural output was given even more emphasis, and price and tax policies were altered to improve the earnings of farmers and to give them incentive to produce more.

It was not apparent in 1953, and still is not, how much of all this was propagandistic and how much was substantive. A great deal was made of the fact that aircraft factories had been instructed to begin turning out aluminum pots and pans. Indeed, extremely large percentage increases in things like television sets and other durables were enthusiastically reported in the press. Large percentage increases in many of these things were in fact achieved, but since the base figures from which these percentage outputs were measured were in most cases extremely small, these "triumphs" are not to be taken very seriously.

It is not easy to determine what really did happen during this period, but the data at hand point toward the tentative conclusion that changes in the structure of the economy were minor and unimportant. The revolution, if it was ever really intended, failed to come off.

If we look at the official Soviet indices of gross industrial output in the 1950's, we find that the ratio of increases in the producers' goods area to those in the consumers' goods area remained practically constant from 1951 through 1954. It is true that the latter half of 1953 indicates that the increase in consumers' goods was a bit higher than it had been earlier; but by 1954, the year in which these changes should have been reflected in the statistics, there is a decline in this rate. It is possible that the time required for true structural shifts was more than Malenkov had at his disposal. Whatever the cause, the shift did not take place, and there was, therefore, no appreciable interruption to the economic trends we have been discussing.

Although there is little evidence of such structural shifts, Malenkov was more successful in keeping his promise to improve the lot of the consumer. This appears to have been done in two ways. In the first place, there was apparently a significant drawing down of state reserves of various sorts. In the second place, there was an increase in the volume of imports that took place, beginning in the middle of 1953, and a simultaneous and substantial increase in the proportion of total imports made up of foods and consumers' goods.[15]

With the ascendancy of Bulganin and Khrushchev in 1955, Malenkov's agricultural reforms were intensified, but other parts of his program were repudiated. Bulganin reproached Malenkov specifically for what he termed errors in policy inherent in using the state reserves for current consumption.[16] The much-publicized charges of having corrupted true party ideology by asserting that the time had come to let light industry expand at a faster rate than heavy industry were explicitly directed at political unknowns, but undoubtedly were aimed at Malenkov, and whoever were his major henchmen in the intended reversal of economic policy. The announcement by Bulganin of the annual 1955 Plan targets for industry left no doubt that heavy industry was to continue to receive favored treatment, and the rate of increase for consumer goods was planned at only about half what had actually been achieved in this field in 1954. We may summarize the experience of the Malenkov interregnum by hazarding the opinion that the changes that took place were much less important, at least in areas other than agriculture, than we thought might be the case, and in fact had a minor impact on the course of economic development.

Change in Economic Policy?

By way of pure speculation, it may be said that a genuine change in economic policy is not completely unlikely in the future. The current soft international policy seems to have a logical counterpart in an economic policy favoring the consumer, and there are some who are expecting the change to take place if the current softness in international dealings continues. It may be interesting to consider briefly what might happen if this consumer goods reorientation should appear. A successful program would certainly have interesting propagandistic effects throughout the world. We may ask, then, what would be the result of a sincere and prolonged attempt on the part of the Soviet economic planners to move their economy away from the heavy industrial economy toward one that emphasized the output of consumer goods. It seems fairly clear that rather startling improvements in the standard of living in the near future could be achieved. Among other reasons, this could be expected because most of the small amount of consumers' goods capital in the U.S.S.R. is obsolete, worn out, and inefficient. As a result, its replacement by new equipment would bring about very substantial increases in the productivity of these industries. In the economist's lingo, the marginal productivity of capital in the consumers' goods industries must be regarded as very high.

[15] Cf. the article by O. Hoeffding in this issue of *The Annals*.
[16] *Pravda*, February 10, 1955, p. 1.

The probability is that the resulting rapid increases in the standard of living could be expected to continue for some years. Following this, however, there would be an inevitable slowdown in the rate of increase. One reason for this is that a great deal of consumer capital is very costly. All of the capital for consumer services in cities, for instance, is costly to install, and has little immediate payoff. Streets, transportation facilities, sewers, and so on are of this sort. The construction of housing in the U.S.S.R. before the war did not keep pace with the growth of the urban population, and yet the improvement of housing facilities is essential to a balanced increase in the standard of living. A housing program designed to obtain accommodations merely approaching the decency level would require a tremendous investment effort in the U.S.S.R.[17]

There is another factor which would tend to bring a slowdown in due course. De-emphasis of heavy industry would mean that a larger proportion of the output of industry would be consumed. When output is consumed it cannot be used to make more output, except of course insofar as it increases the productivity of labor. The output of capital goods industries, on the other hand, is used directly to make more goods. One type of industrial output therefore produces satisfaction for consumers, whereas the other produces measurable outputs for statistical series. Paradoxically, consumers' goods production is analogous to military production. Both are consumed directly and add nothing in direct ways to the future output of the economy. Last but not least, the hypothesized policy would presuppose genuine success in expanding agricultural production, to supply more food and raw materials for consumer goods. Reliance on imports is an unlikely alternative, as we suggest below.

It is difficult, if not impossible, to quantify the course of action just described in general terms. It is also difficult to say what the propagandistic effects of a rather rapidly and continually increasing standard of living would be. It would seem, however, that they should be considerable, particularly in countries like France and Italy, where the standard of living is not high and is not increasing rapidly. And they ought to be very substantial in many of the Asian countries, where freedom means a good deal less than it does in the West and where the competition of the Communistic versus the capitalistic societies is being closely watched. Indeed, it does not appear at all clear that an economic course of this sort, perhaps coupled with a substantial decline in the military claims on the economy, would be less dangerous to the West than the piling up of impressive growth rates in steel, electric power, machinery, and chemicals.

[17] For a summary of the housing situation, see Timothy Sosnovy, *The Housing Problem in the Soviet Union*. New York: Research Program on the U.S.S.R., 1954.

POSSIBILITIES FOR FUTURE GROWTH

We turn now to a look into the future, and an attempt to assess the probability of continued future growth. We assume, of course, that hot war does not break out. We also assume that the Soviet leaders have debated the matters referred to in the immediately preceding paragraphs and have decided to retain the present policy of building up the industrial base as rapidly as is consistent with political stability.

The first thing to say is that at some time in the future, if the time has not already arrived, a modest decline in the *rate* of industrial growth may be expected to take place. The chief reason for this expectation is that there has to be a time when the rate of release of labor from agriculture to industry must decline. This is true if only because there will always have to be some agricultural labor on the farm, and the withdrawal, therefore— and the curve indicating withdrawal—will level out in asymptotic fashion. The flow of labor from agriculture to industry can be expected to continue, therefore, but beyond some point at a diminishing rate.

Actually, the data seem to indicate that a decline in the rate of growth of nonagricultural labor has already set in. Between 1928 and 1937 the annual rate of increase of workers and employees was about 10 per cent. In the 1950's it is only about half that. Much the same changes have been taking place in the number of industrial wage earners, which means workers in manufacturing, mining, and electric power production.

Recent Soviet statements have stressed that the cities cannot in the future count on an influx of peasant labor at the rate which formerly prevailed. The decline has created a considerable campaign in recent years for a more rapid increase in labor productivity, in particular through the introduction of new techniques. The campaign has not been wholly success-ful; the official statistics indicate that the labor productivity goals will not be met by 1955. This has been partly compensated for by an overfulfillment of the nonagricultural labor force goal. This type of compensation cannot continue indefinitely, of course. As a consequence we can expect to see the beginnings of a reduction in the rate of increase of industrial output.

In spite of this, there is reason to believe that the rate of increase can remain above that in the West almost indefinitely. It may be noted, parenthetically, that this does not mean greater absolute increases, at least not necessarily so for some period of time. But the investment policy, in terms of both rate and direction of investment, should be sufficient to maintain rates of growth in industry which are higher than those that prevail in Western nations. And unless the Soviets run into a genuine bottleneck, this inequality can remain indefinitely.

Bottlenecks

We turn now to the bottleneck possibility. There is a good deal of loose thinking on this matter. At various times we are told that the Soviet economy is in danger of imminent collapse because the military burden is excessive, or because the transportation situation is acutely critical, or because it lacks crude oil—and there are many other culprits. It is important to recognize that in any society which is proceeding at forced draft, there will always be one or more bottlenecks operating somewhere. It is not easy to plan the detailed growth process of a large and complex economy. The planner who seeks to maximize the rate of growth has as his ideal a situation where everything in the economy is equally critical at any given moment. If his plan results in surpluses in any parts of the economy, this is a sign to him that he is not planning well. If everything is in equally short supply, this means that he is using to the fullest everything that is being produced.

Now it is clear that no planner can be efficient enough to maintain a situation of this sort at all times. What actually happens, therefore, is that on occasion the economy seems to be held up by a shortage of freight cars or locomotives. There will be other years when rolling stock cannot move because of lack of petroleum; there will be shortages of skilled labor in certain industries where the needs have not been foreseen sufficiently far in advance; and so on. To a considerable extent, the Russians could overcome some of these difficulties, at modest cost, by maintaining fairly substantial inventories, although there is little evidence of what their practices are. But to become true bottlenecks, these difficulties would have to be more than temporary, and there seems to be almost no difficulty that, given time, cannot be alleviated by a reallocation of effort. One needs, therefore, to place in proper perspective the continual minor crises that are likely to occur and not regard them as evidences of imminent breakdown.

Agriculture a Real Difficulty

There is one sector which is different from others and which, because of this difference, may turn out to constitute a genuine brake on economic development. We refer to agriculture. . . .

The great thing that sets off agriculture from other parts of the economy is its dependence upon natural factors. There is scarcely any limit to the production of most industrial commodities if the planners devote enough effort to it. There is a very real limit to the production of agricultural commodities. Man can, it is true, alter nature to some extent, but it is hard to get around the fact that the endowment by nature of agricultural resources in the U.S.S.R. is very poor. The latitudinal position of the great bulk of Soviet land is such that the growing season is very much shorter than it is, for example, in United States agricultural areas. There are very few agricultural areas in the U.S.S.R. where the average annual rainfall is as high as twenty inches. Also, the quality of the land itself in Soviet Russia is poor. All this means that the best agricultural lands in the U.S.S.R. more nearly resemble North Dakota than Iowa.

This niggardliness of nature goes far to explain the dramatic efforts that have been made in recent years to reclaim vast quantities of land, to institute very large programs of reforestation for wind sheltering, to create the huge irrigation projects of which we have heard so much, and so on. All of these things will certainly help, but they are all expensive and the payoffs are limited. The niggardliness of nature likewise helps explain why the Russians still have half of their labor force in agriculture. One Russian farmer feeds himself and three other Russians. One American farmer feeds himself and twenty other Americans, and he embarrasses his government by insisting on producing "too much." The disposal of agricultural surpluses is a problem with which the Soviet planners would love to be faced.

To an undetermined extent, the organization of Soviet agriculture contributes to its inefficiency. The state and collective farm system is such that it is very difficult for any farmer to relate the income he receives and the effort he puts into the farm. Incentives toward hard work are so indirect as to be virtually nonoperative; the government has not helped by its practice of procuring at very low prices and under compulsion a good proportion of total output. There is no simple solution to this problem.

The population in the U.S.S.R. is increasing at a rate of about 1.5 per cent per year. Soviet agricultural output, therefore, has to increase this much simply to maintain per capita consumption at its current low levels. But this is not enough. If the Soviet economy is to continue to grow, output must increase even more in order to produce surpluses. Furthermore, this must be done with less manpower than is now available, since the growth of industry requires a continuous flow of labor from the countryside. The experience of Soviet agriculture raises serious question as to whether the planners are going to be able to solve the problems that are becoming increasingly critical. If they do not solve these problems, it seems clear that the rate of growth of the economy as a whole, and of the industrial sector, must slow down. . . .

There is, of course, one obvious method of solving agricultural problems. The British pointed the way in 1846 when it had become clear that British farmers were unable to feed the British people. In that year the Corn Laws were repealed; and the British changed their policy from one of self-sufficiency to one of ever increasing reliance on international trade. This avenue is open to the Russians. There is no reason, for example, why they should not import their cotton, and use the land in the U.S.S.R. devoted to raising cotton for raising food. There is no reason why they should not go farther and import their grain or their beef in trade for manufactured goods. The probability of their doing so, of course, is very low, since it is a cardinal sin according to their ideology to make themselves dependent upon outsiders. Nevertheless, the possibility is there, and one cannot but watch with fascination for signs that international trade is increasing on a substantial scale.

THE SPECIAL CASE OF AGRICULTURE

Robert W. Campbell[*]

Agriculture is a special case, probably the most inefficient branch of the Soviet economy, and it merits separate consideration. The collective farm system, at least in the form in which it has existed in the Soviet Union until recently, has clearly been a very ineffective institution for stimulating efficiency or technical progress in agriculture. This form for organizing agriculture was really adopted more for its virtues as a means of forcing tribute from the peasants than as a tested device for assuring efficiency in agricultural production. The statistics show that it has indeed failed in the latter role; over most of the period of Soviet industrialization the collective farm system has offered an insuperable obstacle to improvements in productive efficiency. While in other branches the Soviet economy began to overtake other countries in terms of productivity levels, agriculture scarcely advanced beyond the precollectivization levels of productivity. This is true in both the main branches of agriculture, crop production and animal husbandry.

In crop production the two most important inputs are land and labor, and there are two kinds of input-output ratios which should be considered— output per unit of land (yields) and output per man-hour (labor productivity). The yields for the four most important crops of the Soviet Union are compared with yields in the United States in Chart 4.2. (The chart shows average yields over the five-year period, 1953-57. Yields are much affected by the weather, and in any given year the yield may be considerably above or below the long-term average. The use of an average yield over a period of several years eliminates most of this variation to give a more accurate picture.) In all cases the Soviet yields are less than half those in the United States. The most important of these four crops is grain, which includes wheat, corn, rye, barley, oats, and a few other minor grains. The dominant place of grain in Soviet crop production is indicated by the fact that it has accounted for something between 65 and 70 per cent of the total Soviet sown

[*] Professor of Economics, Indiana University. The selection is from his *Soviet Economic Power*, 1960, pp. 70-77, and is reprinted by permission of and arrangement with Houghton Mifflin Company, the authorized publishers.

area in recent years. All together the four crops listed account for about 80 per cent of the Soviet sown area, and the rough figure of 40 per cent that emerges from the chart can be looked upon as a valid generalization for virtually all of Soviet crop production.

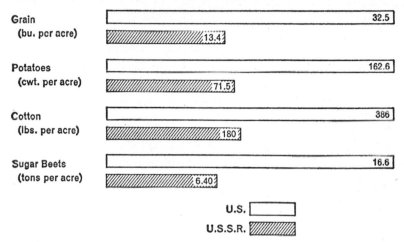

Grain (bu. per acre) — 32.5 / 13.4

Potatoes (cwt. per acre) — 162.6 / 71.5

Cotton (lbs. per acre) — 386 / 180

Sugar Beets (tons per acre) — 16.6 / 6.40

U.S. / U.S.S.R.

CHART 4.2. *Comparative Yields in U.S. and Soviet Crop Production, 1953-57.*

Yields are affected by many factors outside the control of planners, of course, and so are not a direct indication of relative efficiency. The climatic and soil conditions of Soviet agriculture are probably somewhat less favorable for crop production than those which American farmers enjoy—Soviet agriculture suffers a handicap in terms of the fertility of the soil, the length of the growing season, the average rainfall, and other such factors. Nevertheless, much of the difference in yields can only be explained as the result of the ineffectiveness of the Soviet system. The reasons for low yields in Soviet agriculture have been widely investigated with the following conclusions:

1. The Russians have not emphasized the high-yielding grains enough in the overall pattern. For instance, corn has a much higher yield per acre than other grain crops, and the heavy emphasis on corn in the United States (38 per cent of the area sown to all grains as against only about 7 per cent in the U.S.S.R.) brings up our average grain yield relative to the Russians'. If corn had the same subordinate place in our pattern of crop production, our average yield for all grain would be only about 20-21 bushels per acre rather than 32.5.

2. The quality of tractor work on collective farms has often been very low—plowing, seeding, and harvesting have all been done carelessly. Moreover, poor timing of tractor work lowers yields. The soil must be worked at the right time to kill weeds and accumulate maximum moisture, and harvesting has to be done at the proper time to avoid losses. Until recently these mechanized operations were carried out for the collective farms on a contract

basis by the Machine Tractor Stations (MTS) rather than by the collective farms themselves, and the MTS never performed this work very conscientiously. Their performance was judged by how much area they got over, rather than by how well they did the work, and so they had little incentive to do a good job. The collective farmers had no power to penalize the MTS for poor work.

3. Another factor which the Russians are now talking about a great deal is the poor planning of the assignment of crops to different areas of the country. Any given region is much more suitable in terms of its soil and climatic conditions for the production of some crops than others, and the crops should be distributed among regions accordingly. But this distribution was never carefully planned.

These three factors are only a few among many affecting yields, and in many other ways as well the collective farm-MTS combination simply has not done as good a job as the individual farming system of the United States.

In animal production the crucial input is the number of livestock, but the productivity of the animals depends on how they are fed and looked after, and how rapidly they gain weight, on their average weight at time of slaughter, on selectivity in breeding, and on a number of other such factors. Some comparison of Soviet output per animal with ours reveals a great deal about the efficiency of their livestock operations. A comparison of U.S. and Soviet agriculture for several animal productivity ratios is shown in Chart 4.3. (As

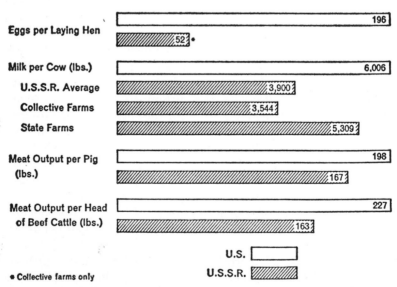

CHART 4.3. *Comparison of Animal Productivity in U.S. and Soviet Agriculture.*

in the case of crop yields, the chart gives averages for a number of years, to eliminate the influence of temporary fluctuations.) In all the indicators Soviet performance is considerably below American. Particularly interesting is the comparative performance of the collective farms, as distinguished from the state farms and the private-plot agriculture of the collective farmers. The worst performance in comparison with U.S. levels shown in the chart is for egg production on collective farms, and the milk yields per collective farm cow are far below the yields obtained on the state farms. In animal husbandry it is particularly important that the farmer have some personal interest in his work. The almost complete absence of such interest on the part of the collective farmers in their work for the collective has resulted in gross inefficiency in the area of animal production. The collective farmers have reserved their efforts more for the animals they are allowed to keep on their private plots.

For both crop production and animal husbandry, labor is the second important input, and so we are interested in labor productivity in agricultural operations. Chart 4.4 shows some interesting figures on the input of man-hours per unit of output for the United States, as compared with those for the collective farms and state farms in the Soviet Union. These figures represent fantastically low levels of labor productivity, but there is no possible charge of bias here, since they were revealed by Khrushchev himself in a speech in 1958.

It is difficult to understand how labor productivity can be so low in Soviet agriculture. The levels of productivity in state farms are bad enough, though they are at least in the same ball park as the relative labor productivities suggested above for industry. But some of the figures for the collective farms are simply incredible—it is hard to conceive how the Russians can spend so much time in these operations. In the case of grain for instance, the ground is plowed, planted, and harvested for the most part by machines, and surely the Russians do not have seven men riding every tractor. The figures for the care of livestock are almost unbelievable. Imagine, for instance, an American farm boy, a member of the 4-H Club, who spends most of his time taking care of some prize beef cattle. It is hard to imagine any circumstances under which it would require fourteen collective farmers to replace his labor in taking care of these cattle. But that is what Khrushchev has said.

In trying to explain the low productivity of labor and land in Soviet agriculture, it is possible to point to some more or less objective conditions that cause or would result in low levels of productivity. For instance, the low level of labor productivity is partly the result of the low level of mechanization of Soviet agriculture. The relatively smaller amount of power and equipment which the Soviet farmer has to work with is well demonstrated by the figures of Table 4.1.

Another factor is the relatively minor use of fertilizer and chemical agents such as pesticides, fungicides, and weed killers. In 1956, for instance, Soviet agriculture used only 48 pounds of mineral fertilizer per acre of sown area while American farmers used 133 pounds. The total consumption of pesticides and other chemical preparations in agriculture in the United States in 1956 was about one and one-half million tons, whereas in the U.S.S.R., with a sown area larger by about a third, consumption was probably no more than about a tenth of this.

Hence, low productivity is in part the result of factors over which Soviet planners have little control, and one must be careful in drawing conclusions

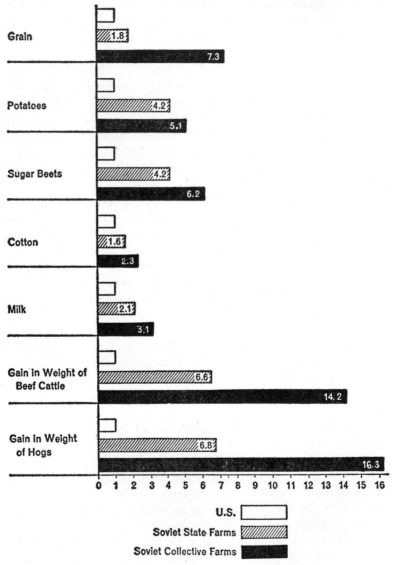

CHART 4.4.   *Soviet and U.S. Labor Requirements per Unit of Agricultural Output*
(*U.S. = 1*).

about agricultural efficiency on the basis of the above figures on productivity. For instance, the low level of mechanization is not just a matter of inefficiency or incorrect planning. Capital for investment is still relatively scarce in the Soviet economy, and the amount that can be devoted to investment in machinery for agriculture or in rural electrification is limited. But at the same time most economists would support the assertion that the Russians

TABLE 4.1.   RELATIVE AVAILABILITY OF POWER AND EQUIPMENT IN U.S. AND SOVIET AGRICULTURE (1956 FIGURES)

	U.S.	U.S.S.R.
Number of tractors (millions)	4.558	.866
Number of horses (millions)	3.751	13.2
Number of trucks (millions)	2.850	.588
Electricity consumed (billion KWH)	22.2	5.4

have invested billions of rubles in projects elsewhere in the economy that gave them a much smaller increment of output or a smaller saving of labor than they could have gotten for the same investment in agriculture. So there is surely some wasteful inefficiency involved here. The low consumption of fertilizers and chemical-control agents is more clearly a failure to make use of the most efficient way of achieving agricultural output. The gains from greater use of fertilizer and chemical agents would have far exceeded the costs. Even acknowledging the differences in the objective conditions under which agriculture must work in each country, the conclusion seems inescapable that the Soviet Union wastes resources in agriculture on a massive scale. The overall economic development of the U.S.S.R. would have been even greater in the past forty years than it has been if this waste in agriculture had been controlled.

It would be unwarranted to conclude that Soviet agriculture cannot do better in the future than in the past. Soviet agricultural performance has been the result of egregiously bad policy with regard to incentives, planning, the relationship with the MTS, marketing, and many other features of the regime's agricultural program. After Stalin died in 1953, agriculture has been given much more attention, particularly since Khrushchev has assumed unchallenged leadership. He is familiar with agricultural problems, and much concerned to mend the errors of the past. He has launched some drastic policy changes, including raising farm income greatly to increase incentives, abolishing the MTS and handing the machinery over to the collective farms, instituting cost accounting on collective farms, and many other new departures. In response to the new policies, most of the indicators of agricultural performance described above have improved markedly in the past five or six years. Poor performance is not necessarily an inherent feature of Soviet agriculture, and there are prospects for fairly rapid improvement in this sector of the economy.

Chapter 18

THE SEVEN-YEAR PLAN—AND BEYOND

The Soviet Seven-Year Plan—and the nature and implications of the Soviet economic challenge—are the focal concerns of this chapter. Of related significance are a number of economic developments in the U.S.S.R., some ante-dating and some post-dating the inauguration of this Plan.

In September 1957, the government of the U.S.S.R. officially scrapped the sixth Five-Year Plan (which had been announced at the 20th Party Congress in 1956) and advised that it was substituting a Seven-Year Plan to begin in 1959. Two months earlier, a major reorganization and decentralization of the economy had been launched. With few exceptions, industrial and building enterprises were transferred to approximately 100 newly formed Regional Economic Councils, with the stated intention of eliminating waste and overlapping, improving coordination, initiative, and cooperation at the local level, and reducing unproductive bureaucratic staffing at the center.

In February 1962, however, in the attempt to solve difficulties engendered by the decentralization, the country was reorganized into 17 major economic regions, headed by coordinating and planning councils, for purposes of long-term development and planning. Furthermore, in November 1962 the 100-odd Regional Economic Councils were drastically reduced in number and brought under control of a new, central, powerful Council of the National Economy. Concomitantly, the Communist Party apparatus (except at certain of its pinnacles) was divided into parallel organizations, one to be concerned with industry and the other with agriculture. The Party itself was invested with a greatly expanded role in directing the economy.

522

In April 1958, with a view to improving agricultural production, the Central Committee of the Communist Party and the Council of Ministers jointly put into operation a far-reaching scheme proposed by Khrushchev to permit and encourage collective farms to purchase and maintain their own tractors, combines, and other machinery. The machine and tractor stations —which exercised such vast political as well as economic power—were reorganized and reduced to repair and technical service stations. On March 1, Pravda had editorially described the proposal as part of "a broad movement to overtake the United States in the next few years in the per capita production of meat, milk and butter." It had further explained that,

Under the present conditions—when the collective farms have matured and become strong, when the fundamental issue of the Party's domestic policy is the drive for higher productivity of labor—the technical servicing of the collective farms by the machine-and-tractor stations can no longer satisfy the requirements resulting from the growing collective-farm production and is beginning to hinder the progress of the productive forces in agriculture. The fact that there are two masters over one plot of land, to wit, the collective farm and the machine-and-tractor station, does away with personal responsibility, interferes with the more efficient and rational employment of tractors and other machinery, and also the punctual observance of the time-table of farming jobs.

There can be little doubt that one of the most troublesome and persistent problems for the U.S.S.R., as Professor Campbell has shown, has been to raise agricultural output. Following the 22nd Party Congress, in March of 1962, a plenary meeting of the Central Committee of the Party was called with the main purpose of obtaining "a mighty upsurge of agriculture." "We must regard the further progress of agriculture, increase in the output of foodstuffs," Khrushchev told the plenum, "as a matter of vital concern for the whole Party, for the whole nation." If this task is not solved, he added, "we shall confront the country with great difficulties and the course of building communism will be seriously damaged."

A number of recommendations were adopted including a call for technical reorganization, condemnation of the grass rotation system in favor of planting of "more productive feed crops," expansion and construction of storage facilities, a program for an "adequate" supply of machinery and fertilizers, and for greater "material incentive" to both collective and state farmers.

It is clear that, under the leadership of Khrushchev, the U.S.S.R. is using the viability of a planned economy and political dictatorship to embark upon large-scale programs to increase both industrial and agricultural productivity—with potential economic and political benefits and risks which are, as of now, not clearly calculable.

SUMMARY OF SEVEN-YEAR PLAN
FOR 1959-1965

The New York Times

On November 14, 1958, the Central Committee of the Communist Party of the U.S.S.R. proposed a new economic Seven-Year Plan for nationwide discussion prior to submission to the 21st Party Congress which met early in 1959 and adopted the Plan. This summary of the basic objectives of the Plan appeared in the New York Times *on November 15, 1958, and is presented here with its permission.*

The Plan envisages an 80 per cent increase in gross industrial production, a 65 per cent increase in consumer goods, and a 70 per cent increase in agricultural output. An average of at least 40 per cent increase in real income is promised and a vast housing program to ease the critical shortage.

HEAVY INDUSTRY

Heavy industrial output by 1965 will increase 85 to 88 per cent. Production of steel will reach 86 to 91 million metric tons, an increase of 56 to 65 per cent over 1958. Pig iron will reach 65 to 70 million tons, increasing 65 to 77 per cent. Rolled steel will reach 65 to 70 million tons, an increase of 52 to 64 per cent. Raw iron ore will reach 230 to 245 million tons to yield 150 to 160 million tons of marketable ore.

Aluminum production is to increase 180 per cent over 1958, refined copper 90 per cent and other nonferrous metals "considerably."

At least 140 large chemical enterprises are to be completed and 130 others will be modernized to meet previously announced goals for considerable increases in chemical and synthetic fiber production.

Oil and gas will become the dominant fuels.

Electric power production is to increase 100 to 120 per cent for a 1965 output of 500 to 520 billion kilowatt-hours.

LIGHT INDUSTRY

Light industry's gross output is to increase about 50 per cent.

Production of cotton fabrics is to increase from 5.8 billion meters in 1958 to 7.7 or 8 billion in 1965. Woolen fabric output is to rise from 300 million to 500 million meters. (One meter equals 39.37 inches.)

One hundred fifty-six "major light-industry factories" are to be built and 114 that already have been begun will be completed. Output of household goods is to be doubled.

FOOD INDUSTRY

State food enterprises are to turn out 6,130,000 metric tons of meat by 1965, an increase of 117 per cent over 1958; 1,006,000 tons of butter, a 60 per cent increase; 13,546,000 tons of milk products, up 125 per cent; up to ten million tons of ground beet sugar, an increase of up to 94 per cent; 1,975,000 tons of margarine, up 62 per cent, and 4,626,000 tons of fish, up 62 per cent.

AGRICULTURE

The total volume of agricultural production will increase by 70 per cent.

The yields per acre of major farm products in 1965, the Government said, will exceed the 1957 yields per acre in the United States.

CAPITAL INVESTMENT

Capital investments in 1959-65 are scheduled to increase by 80 per cent over 1951-1958. Investments in rubles planned for some sectors of the economy were listed as follows (4 rubles to $1 at the official exchange rate):

Ferrous metals industry, 100 billion; chemical industry, 100 to 105 billion; oil and gas industries, 170 to 173 billion; coal industry, 75 to 78 billion; power industry, 125 to 129 billion; wood and paper industry, 58 to 60 billion; light and food industries, 80 to 85 billion; housing and municipal construction, 375 to 380 billion; agriculture 150 billion, and railroads, 110 to 115 billion.

TRADE

Retail trade is to increase 57 to 62 per cent. Trade with other Communist countries is to increase more than 50 per cent.

WELFARE

The national income is to increase 62 to 65 per cent. Real wages are to increase at least 40 per cent and pensions are to be improved. A thirty-five-hour work week of five or six days "is to be introduced" apparently in some industries.

EDUCATION

A compulsory eight-year school program will replace the current seven-year schools in the countryside and the ten-year schools in the cities. All basic schooling is to combine vocational and academic training.

SCIENCE

Large-scale research programs are to be undertaken, especially in areas of immediate practical value. Physicists are to concentrate on problems of cosmic rays, nuclear reactions and semi-conductors. Mathematicians are to work on computing machines and chemists on the theory and practice of creating new synthetic materials.

[Editor's Note: In the Report for the Central Committee of the Communist Party delivered to the 22nd Party Congress, Khrushchev claimed that although the Plan had envisaged only an 8.3 per cent average annual growth in industrial output in the first three years, the actual growth had been about 10 per cent. "That is how we 'miscalculated' when drawing up the Seven-Year Plan! We are not ashamed to admit such 'miscalculations,'" he said, and added, "and let those who prophesied the failure of our plans think of a way out of the bog into which they have floundered; that is not our headache."]

RUSSIA'S BOLD PLAN

Harry Schwartz*

The political, propaganda and economic challenge posed by the new Soviet Seven-Year Plan for 1959-65 is the most ambitious such document ever unveiled by the Kremlin.

Premier Nikita S. Khrushchev boasted some time ago that this new plan would "astonish" the world when it was made public. On this score, at least, he proved a prophet. The astonishment was generated, of course, by the boldness of the goals he set.

The full extent of Mr. Khrushchev's audacity can be summed up simply: If the targets outlined by him for 1965 and 1970 are actually attained on schedule, then in the next decade or so the Communist world will clearly have won the economic competition with the West and, quite possibly, the political and propaganda contest for the allegiance of the uncommitted under-developed nations of Asia, Africa and Latin America as well. Conversely, of course, by setting such ambitious goals, Premier Khrushchev created the risk that a gross failure to reach them would have major undesirable consequences for the Soviet regime at home and abroad.

* Economist, specializing on Soviet affairs, *New York Times.* Author *of Russia's Soviet Economy.* The article originally appeared in the *New York Times,* November 16, 1958. Reprinted by permission.

THE MAIN TARGETS

This conclusion emerges from an examination of the main targets he set for 1965 and 1970:

By 1965, Mr. Khrushchev predicted, the Communist bloc as a whole will have greater industrial production than the rest of the world put together, while the Soviet Union will have sharply reduced the substantial economic lead over it held by the United States. During the next seven years, he asserted, the Soviet people can produce and have far more of everything—steel, machine tools, homes, television sets, food—than they have ever produced or had before.

By 1970, he added, the Soviet people will have the highest standard of living in the world, and in addition will be out-producing the United States both in absolute terms and on a per capita basis. Implied in this, of course, is the notion that by 1970 the Communist world as a whole will be so far ahead of the free world in production that the free world will have no chance of ever catching up, at least so long as it stubbornly refuses to enter the Communist "paradise."

Apparently spurred by recent Soviet economic and scientific successes, Premier Khrushchev has obviously decided to gamble in the grand manner, seeking a quick victory for his cause.

THE ASSETS

Let us look initially at the assets which have encouraged this gamble:

(1) There is the enormous mineral wealth of the Soviet Union, far exceeding that of the United States. With respect to iron ore, oil, bauxite, coal, and many other such commodities, the Soviet Union has the raw material base to support a much larger industrial production.

(2) The Soviet Union is today one of the most technologically advanced nations in the world. There can be little doubt that Premier Khrushchev intends to harness the most modern available technology—from automatic factories run by computers to the latest achievements of polymer chemistry and nuclear physics—to raise labor productivity and production rapidly.

(3) The Soviet population is still a tractable labor force which does not indulge in strikes, slowdowns, feather-bedding or other production-restricting activities. Moreover, the Soviet population is today better educated—and therefore potentially more productive—than ever before in Russian history.

(4) The Soviet economy seems not subject to recessions or depressions such as have historically interrupted the production progress of non-Communist countries. Each year since 1946 Soviet industry has produced more than the year before, and there is no present reason to suppose that this steady upward movement will not continue.

(5) Mr. Khrushchev has produced a set of agricultural reforms—higher prices for farmers, the virgin-lands and corn-raising programs, and the like, which have finally ended the post-war stagnation of Soviet agriculture. The farmers of Russia had never produced so much as they have in recent years, particularly in 1956 and this year.

THE OBSTACLES

These assets, however, must be balanced against the obstacles in Premier Khrushchev's way:

(1) To realize his production targets, the Soviet economy will have to receive enormous capital investments for new factories, mines, railroads, and the like. Yet at the same time Mr. Khrushchev is committed to an enormous housing construction program, to providing a rapidly rising living standard and to permitting reduced hours of work—there is even pressure for a five-day week. Moreover, he presumably plans continued large expenditures on arms production and space exploration. It is far from clear that even the vast Soviet resources are adequate to do all these things simultaneously. Shortage of capital forced the abandonment in September, 1957, of the original sixth Five-Year Plan for 1956-60. The same problem may recur.

(2) Many of the richest raw material sources found by Soviet geologists in recent years are in the thinly populated areas of the Urals. To realize the plans for exploiting these resources by creating giant new production complexes in Siberia will require the movement of large numbers of workers there from European Russia. Short of using compulsion on a Stalinist scale, can the required number of workers be induced to migrate?

(3) In the years immediately ahead, the number of new entrants to the Soviet labor forces will be cut sharply from past years because of the greatly reduced birth rate in the period of World War II. Thus the question of the overall adequacy of the labor supply arises. It is already likely that Moscow's educational reform that will send youngsters to work after they have finished only elementary school is a move prompted by the seriousness of this problem.

(4) Premier Khrushchev is counting on getting some of the capital he needs and on being able to reduce prices to consumers in the belief that the efficiency of Soviet farming will soon improve sharply. He expects this will reduce production costs and permit him to lower the prices farmers are paid for the produce they grow. But will the Soviet farmers accept such price cuts?

(5) At a minimum Mr. Khrushchev's ambitious plans presuppose some important political conditions that cannot be taken for certain. They assume there will be no very heightened international tension that will require sharply stepped up military preparedness. They assume there will be no more catastrophes like the Polish and Hungarian revolts requiring direct Soviet military intervention and the large scale pouring in of Soviet goods to quiet discontent.

WHAT THE WEST FACES

At the very least, realization of the problems before the Soviet economy should warn against any facile assumption that the Khrushchev goals are certain to be met on schedule. Yet even taking account of these problems, the assets seem substantial enough to suggest that rapid and substantial Soviet economic progress will continue over the next decade or so. On this assumption certain difficult problems seem likely to assume great urgency for the West in the years ahead.

One is the problem of counteracting the impression made on underdeveloped countries if there is anything like the rapid progress in the Soviet Union and the Communist bloc that Premier Khrushchev envisages. That problem might well become insoluble, and Soviet victory assured, if rapid Communist progress were to be accompanied by anything resembling a serious depression or recession in the West.

If realized, a sharply higher Soviet living standard would increase the political attractiveness of the Communist system, not only in the underdeveloped nations but even in the poorer countries of Western Europe such as Italy.

A second problem is likely to be that of meeting the greatly increased Communist military strength that may emerge as the Communist bloc increases its output of steel and other basic materials and equipment.

A third problem is the very much greater competition Western businessmen are likely to face in world markets as the flood of Communist goods mounts. The unhappy experiences this last year of free world producers of aluminum, tin and platinum—who have seen their prices reduced by sudden Soviet sales campaigns—may well be repeated in many key international markets.

PROGRESS UNDER THE PLAN

Central Statistical Board of U.S.S.R.*

The selection is from the Report of the U.S.S.R. Council of Ministers' Central Statistical Administration which appeared in late January 1962. While the Report is specifically concerned with performance for the year 1961, it covers progress made under the Plan in more general terms, as well.

* From a translation appearing in *The Current Digest of the Soviet Press*, Vol. XIV (Feb. 21, 1962), pp. 14-18. With permission. Charts (but not summaries) have been omitted.

The working people of the Soviet Union marked the past year—the year of the historic 22nd Party Congress—with new successes in the development of the economy and in the rise of the well-being cultural level of the people.

I. INDUSTRY

Workers in industry overfulfilled the annual plan for the total volume of industrial output. The output of products grew 9.2% in comparison with the 1960 level, including—according to preliminary data—10% in the production of means of production (Group A) and 6.6% in consumer items (Group B).

The assignments of the seven-year plan are being fulfilled successfully. Gross industrial output has increased 33% in the past three years, instead of the 27% called for in the control figure estimates of the seven-year plan for these years. Approximately 19,000,000,000 rubles' worth of above-plan industrial output was produced in the three years. The seven-year-plan assignments for these years were overfulfilled in the output of pig iron by 1,600,000 tons, steel by 9,200,000 tons, rolled metal by 7,900,000 tons, steel pipe by 670,000 tons, iron ore by 9,000,000 tons, oil by 10,500,000 tons, farm machinery by more than 350,000,000 rubles, precast reinforced concrete by 10,000,000 cubic meters, cotton, wool and linen fabrics by 1,200,000,000 linear meters, leather footwear by 67,000,000 pairs and furniture by more than 350,-000,000 rubles, as well as in a number of other types of output.

All the Union republics overfulfilled the annual plan for industrial output as a whole and in a number of major types of production. While the plan was successfully fulfilled for industry as a whole, the nonfulfillment of the plan by a number of enterprises was a serious shortcoming.

In comparison with the preceding year, the gross output of ferrous and nonferrous metallurgy increased 10%, the fuel and power industry 7%, machine-building and metalworking 16%, the chemical industry 14%, the building materials industry 12%, the lumber, paper and wood-processing industry 5%, light industry and the production of cultural and household articles 5% and the food industry 7%.

The output of products of heavy industry increased substantially. Production rose by the following amounts over the 1960 totals: pig iron, 4,100,000 tons; steel, 5,400,000 tons: rolled metal, 4,300,000 tons; steel pipe, 550,000 tons; iron ore, 11,800,000 tons; oil, 18,000,000 tons; gas, 13,700,000,-000 cubic meters; electric power, 34,700,000,000 kwh.; cement, 5,300,000 tons; and reinforced concrete, 6,000,000 cubic meters. While the total output of the chemical industry rose 14%, the output of synthetic resins and plastics increased by 22%.

Although output grew in comparison with 1960, the plan for the smelting of pig iron and steel and for the production of rolled metal, steel pipe, individual machines and chemical and oil equipment was somewhat under-

Students in the foreground of the skyscraper building of the University of Moscow.

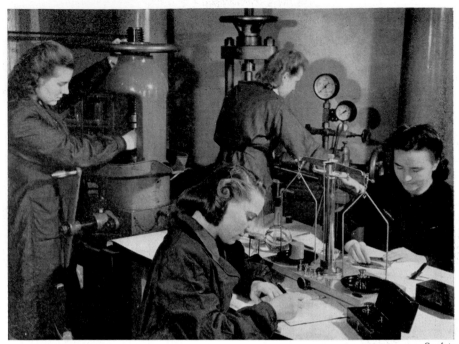

Geology students at work in a laboratory of a Soviet university.

Magnitorsk, Urals. Workers on their way home after their work shift.

In the Kuban area, 1958.

A Kazakh child reading from the book of Jambul, a celebrated folk bard, to an aged collective farmer.

Reception in honor of Soviet cosmonauts A. Nikolaev and P. Popovich, 1962.

Igor Stravinsky, American composer and conductor, returns for cultural exchange visit, after 48-year absence from Russia. He is being greeted by T. Khrennikov of the composers' union, 1962.

fulfilled; the plan for the output of newsprint, typographical paper and other types of products was not fulfilled.

Output of consumer goods increased as follows: leather footwear by 23,000,000 pairs, knitted undergarments and outer garments by 22,000,000 pieces, television sets by 223,000 units, refrigerators by 157,000, washing machines by 390,000, furniture by 175,000,000 rubles, whole milk products by 749,000 tons, granulated sugar by 2,100,000 tons, canned goods by 695,-000,000 cans. Larger amounts of still other popular consumer commodities were produced.

Considerable work has been done in the development and introduction of new machinery and advanced technology, in integrated mechanization and automation of production and in the creation of the latest machines, mechanisms and equipment that facilitate and replace human labor. . . .

At the same time, some economic councils and enterprises are not fulfilling the established plans for working out designs for and organizing and mastering the production of new types of machines, equipment and instruments and for removing from production equipment and articles of obsolete design.

The use of equipment in industry improved in comparison with 1960. At enterprises of ferrous metallurgy, the coefficient of utilization of blast furnace capacity improved by 1.6%. The amount of steel smelted per square meter of hearth space of Martin furnaces increased by 2.6%. The proportion of the most economical types of fuel—oil and gas—in the total output of fuel grew from 38% to 43%. . . .

Labor productivity rose in comparison with 1960 by more than 4%, while the length of the working day for workers and employees decreased. Taking into account the reduction of the working day, hourly labor productivity increased by 11%.

As a result of the rise in the volume of production, shipments and trade, approximately 6% more profits were obtained for the national economy than in 1960. However, the accumulations plan was not fulfilled; at the same time, many industrial enterprises and a number of economic councils fell short of fulfilling the plan for increasing labor productivity and decreasing production costs.

In 1961 the Soviet Union achieved new successes in peaceful economic competition with the United States of America. While the 1961 growth in industrial production in the U.S.S.R. amounted to 9.2%, in the U.S.A. production increased only 1%. For the same period, steel output in the U.S.S.R. rose 8% and in the U.S.A. declined 1.7%; electric power output rose 12% in the U.S.S.R. and only 4% in the U.S.A.; and oil output rose 12% and 2.5% respectively.

The relative output of major types of production in the U.S.A. and the U.S.S.R. in 1961 is characterized by the following data: steel, 90,500,000 tons in the U.S.A. and 70,700,000 tons, or 78% of American output, in the

U.S.S.R.; cement, 54,000,000 tons and 50,900,000 tons, or 94%, respectively; cotton fabrics (coarse), 8,400,000,000 square meters and 5,300,000,000 square meters, or 63%; woolen fabrics, 270,000,000 square meters and 355,000,000 square meters, or 131%; leather footwear, 610,000,000 pairs and 442,000,000 pairs, or 73%; and granulated sugar (from domestic raw materials), 3,700,000 tons in the U.S.A. and 6,100,000 tons, or 164% of American output, in the U.S.S.R.

In 1961 the total volume of industrial production in the U.S.S.R. amounted to more than 60% of the output of industry in the U.S.A.

II. AGRICULTURE

The implementation of highly important measures outlined by the Party and government for an upsurge in agriculture was of decisive significance to the further increase in the output of agricultural products.

In 1961 the areas planted to all agricultural crops totaled 204,600,000 hectares, as against 203,000,000 hectares in 1960, an increase of 1,600,000 hectares.

The areas planted to grain crops totaled 128,300,000 hectares, as against 121,700,000 hectares in 1960. More wheat, corn for grain, groat and leguminous crops, cotton, sugar beets and sunflowers were sown. The area planted to corn for grain totaled 13,200,000 hectares, as against 11,200,000 hectares in 1960. The total area planted to corn in 1961 was 25,700,000 hectares.

However, a substantial amount (47,600,000 hectares) of our planted area is occupied by plantings of low-yield crops, such as grasses and oats.

Substantial work has been done to create conditions for the rapid development of animal husbandry. The data of the Jan. 1, 1962, inventory show that the number of livestock of all types increased substantially.

The growth in the size of the herd of cattle and pigs was greater than the growth for any other postwar year: 6,100,000 for cattle and 7,700,000 for pigs. The number of cows increased by 1,500,000 in the course of the year and the number of sheep and goats by 3,800,000. The overwhelming proportion of this growth is occurring in the communal livestock herd on collective and state farms.

The output of milk in 1961 increased by 800,000 tons and of eggs by 1,500,000,000; meat output increased somewhat. However, the rate of growth of the output of livestock products for the country as a whole does not correspond to the level necessary for satisfying the demands of the population. The opportunities for strengthening the fodder base and for a more rapid growth on this basis of the output of livestock products are still not used in due measure.

State purchases of livestock products in 1961 increased as follows: milk, 2,000,000 tons; eggs, 924,000,000; and wool, 11,000 tons. Meat purchases declined somewhat.

Collective and state farms are playing a decisive part in state purchases. Their share in total state purchases: livestock, 89%; milk, 94%; eggs, 66%; and wool, 85%.

III. TRANSPORT

Maritime transport fulfilled the plan for coastal cargo movement 110% and the plan for overseas cargo volume 105%; in all types of navigation cargo movement increased 20%.

Air transport fulfilled the plan for passenger traffic 104%; passenger traffic increased 36% over the 1960 figure.

In the past three years freight movement in all types of transport increased 25%, as against the 20% envisioned for these three years in the seven-year plan.

By the end of the year, more than 42,000 km. of railroads had been converted to electric and diesel traction. Railroad freight movement by electric and diesel traction increased by 24% and constituted 51.5% of the total railroad freight movement, as against 43% in 1960 and 26% in 1958.

Railroad transport fulfilled and overfulfilled the plan for shipments of the major types of freight: hard coal, petroleum products, ores, ferrous metals and grain cargo. The assignment for increasing the weight of freight trains and the sector (commercial) speed of freight trains and for raising labor productivity was fulfilled; the average distance of freight shipments declined. At the same time, the assignment for reducing the turnaround time of freight cars and the idleness of cars during freight operations and at service yards was unfulfilled. . . .

The truck pool of common-carrier transport increased by 11% in the course of the year, and centralized freight hauls rose 15%. Work continued on merging trucking lines, but in a number of economic councils, ministries and departments the amalgamation of small trucking lines is still being carried out slowly, and truck idleness and empty runs of trucks are still extensive.

IV. CAPITAL CONSTRUCTION

Major production capacities in all branches of the national economy were put in operation through capital investments. The total volume of basic funds put to use was 8% more than in 1960.

In 1961 more than 800 major new state industrial enterprises and a large number of shops at existing enterprises went into operation. More that 7,000,000 kw. of new capacity was put in operation at power plants. . . .

In ferrous metallurgy, new capacities were put in operation as follows: for iron smelting, 2,000,000 tons; for steel smelting, 4,800,000 tons; and for rolled metal production, 2,900,000 tons. The Central Ore-Enriching Combine, with a capacity of 9,000,000 tons of iron ore a year, went into operation in the Krivoi Rog Basin.

New enterprises and shops went into operation in the chemical industry, including capacity for producing 3,100,000 tires a year.

New gas and oil pipelines totaling 7,800 km. in length went into operation. The plan for putting gas pipelines into operation in 1961 was over-fulfilled.

A large number of precast reinforced-concrete plants and plants for producing large panels housing construction plants was built. New capacity for producing 5,000,000 tons of cement annually was started up in the cement industry.

Capacity at enterprises of light industry and the food industry increased substantially. At textile enterprises, about 500,000 spindles and 8,000 looms were installed in 1961. Capacity for producing more than 13,000,000 pairs of shoes a year went into operation at shoe factories. At sugar refineries, capacity for refining about 300,000 centners of beets a day was started up. New grain elevators and granaries with a total storage capacity of 3,500,000 tons were built.

Nine hundred and ninety-nine kilometers of new railroad were opened for use and 1,860 km. of railroad were electrified. The electrification of a major trunkline, the Moscow-Baikal, was completed.

At the same time, the annual plan for putting capital funds to use and for starting up some capacities was not fulfilled.

The total volume of capital investments of state and cooperative organizations (not counting collective farm capital investments) was 32,500,000,000 rubles. Collective farms also made capital investments on a large scale. Capital investments from funds provided for in the state plan rose 9% over 1960.

The annual plan for capital investments was 95% fulfilled; in construction and installation work it fell 5% short of fulfillment and in equipment 4%. Nevertheless, capital investments were larger than specified for 1961 in the seven-year plan.

Capital investments increased as against 1960 in ferrous and nonferrous metallurgy by 8%; in the oil and gas industry by 8%; in power plant construction by 7%, including 10% for thermal power stations; in machine building by 14%; in the chemical industry by 13%; in the building materials and construction industry by 1%; in light industry by 18%; in transport and communications by 4%; and in agriculture by 22%.

Contract organizations increased the volume of construction and installation work 7%, but the plan for contract work was not fulfilled. . . .

Labor productivity in construction rose 3.5%. Taking into account the reduction of the working day, hourly labor productivity rose approximately 12%.

At the same time, construction has not yet outgrown the ruinous practice of scattering funds among countless construction projects, many supplier enterprises are not fulfilling plans for delivery of equipment to construction sites on time, and in a number of cases design organizations are furnishing construction projects with technical documentation tardily. Machines and mechanisms on hand at construction sites are not used at full capacity, and in connection with this some labor-consuming jobs are performed manually.

Many construction organizations did not fulfill the plan for increasing labor productivity and the assignment for lowering the cost of construction and installation work.

V. RISE IN PEOPLE'S LIVING STANDARD AND CULTURAL LEVEL

According to preliminary data, the U.S.S.R. national income in 1961 was more than 153,000,000,000 rubles, an increase of 7% over 1960, in comparable prices.

As a result of the growth of the national income, accumulations in the national economy increased and the living standard of the Soviet people rose both through a growth in direct recompense for labor and through an increase in the public consumption funds.

The population received 26,400,000,000 rubles from the public consumption funds for public education, medical services, social security and various payments and benefits, as against 24,500,000,000 rubles in 1960.

The number of workers and employees in the national economy in 1961 averaged 66,000,000, an increase of 3,950,000 over the 1960 figure.

As in 1960, there was no unemployment in the country.

The average wage of workers and employees increased 4% over 1960, while the length of the working day decreased. The incomes of collective farmers obtained from the communal economy of the collective farms also increased somewhat. . . . By the start of 1962, more than 40,000,000 workers and employees were working under new wage terms.

In accordance with the decisions of the Fifth U.S.S.R. Supreme Soviet, the gradual abolition of taxes on workers and employees continued. On Oct. 1, 1961, the collection of taxes on wages of 60 rubles a month or less was discontinued altogether and the tax rates on wages of 61 to 70 rubles a month were reduced by an average 40%. As a result, the take-home pay of workers and employees increased by an additional 400,000,000 rubles (on a yearly basis).

The population's deposits in savings banks continued to grow. By the end of 1961 deposits totaled 11,700,000,000 rubles, and the number of depositors reached 52,700,000.

The volume of retail sales for state and cooperative trade was 80,200,-000,000 rubles. As compared with 1960, the retail trade volume increased by 2,500,000,000 rubles, or by 4% in comparable prices. However, the annual retail trade plan was not fulfilled in 1961.

While the plan for trades as a whole was not fulfilled, the public catering plan was overfulfilled. As against 1960, the public catering trade volume increased 6%, in comparable prices.

The consumers' cooperative system sold, at local market prices, 847,-000,000 rubles' worth of food products, purchased from collective farmers or received on commission from the collective farms. As compared with 1960, the volume of these sales rose 8%, in comparable prices.

The sales of individual types of goods in state and cooperative trade changed as follows (in percent of 1960): meat, sausage products and other meat products, 96; fish, herring and other fish products, 105; butter, 101; vegetable oil, 109; milk and milk products, 110; cheese, 111; eggs, 115; sugar, 110; confectionery products, 104; tea, 104; vegetables, 107; citrus fruits, 108; fresh fruit, 117; fabrics, 94; clothing and underwear, 106; knitted items, 103; hosiery, 106; leather footwear, 110; porcelain, china and glassware, 103; soap, 106; furniture, 113; sewing machines, 99; refrigerators, 130; washing machines, 130; vacuum cleaners, 111; clocks and watches, 89; motorcycles and motor scooters, 108; bicycles and motor bicycles, 101; radios and radiophonographs, 101; television sets, 116; and passenger cars, 89.

The population's demands for a number of food products were not met. Many industrial and trade enterprises did not pay due attention to raising the quality and improving the assortment of a number of goods of popular consumption, especially clothing, footwear and fabrics, and as a result goods unwanted by the public lay for long periods on the store counters.

In the sphere of foreign trade, the Soviet Union continued to expand its economic ties with foreign countries. The foreign trade turnover was 10,500,000,000 rubles, an increase of 4% over 1960. . . .

Further successes were achieved in the sphere of cultural construction.

The number of students, including all types of study, was 56,000,000. In 1961 work continued on the further reorganization of the public education system. By the end of the year about 40,000 primary and seven-year schools had been reorganized as eight-year schools.

The number of students in general schools was 39,000,000, or almost 3,000,000 more than in the preceding academic year. About 1,000,000 persons received diplomas, among them 375,000 who obtained a secondary education without leaving production at schools for working and rural youth. By the start of the academic year, the country had more than 20,000 general-education labor polytechnic secondary schools, at which approximately 1,500,000 upper-grade students were undergoing production training. More than 173,-000 young men and women graduated from secondary schools with production training and received vocational preparation along with their diplomas.

The number of boarding schools and extended-day schools and groups increased. At the start of the current academic year, about 1,500,000 pupils were included in boarding schools and extended-day schools and groups.

The number studying in higher and specialized secondary educational institutions is 5,000,000, of whom 2,600,000 are in higher educational institutions. In 1961 more than 750,000 young specialists graduated from higher educational institutions and technicums; 320,000 of these had received a higher education, including 120,000 engineers.

Correspondence and evening education underwent further development. The number of persons studying without leaving production at higher and specialized secondary educational institutions and at general-education schools for working and rural youth was 5,900,000, including 2,600,000 at higher schools and technicums. Of the students admitted to day branches of higher schools, 167,000, or 60% of the total number, have had at least two years of practical work experience.

The network of scientific institutions continued to develop and improve. The number of scientific workers increased to 400,000 by the end of the year.

Service to the population by cultural-enlightenment institutions improved. In the course of the year the country's film studios completed 135 feature films, including 111 art films and 24 newsreels, documentaries and popular science films. The number of screen installations was 113,000, an increase of 10,000 over the 1960 figure. The film audience came to more than 3,800,000,000, while attendance at the theater, concerts and circuses was 250,000,000.

The circulation of books published in 1961 was 1,200,000,000 copies; the circulation of newspapers, magazines and other periodical publications increased.

Housing, cultural and service construction was carried out on a large scale. Apartment houses with a total space of 80,000,000 square meters, or about 2,200,000 well-appointed apartments, built with state funds and with public funds in cities and workers' settlements were opened for tenancy in 1961. State housing construction accounted for 57,000,000 square meters of housing opened for tenancy, 5% more than in 1960; however, the plan for housing construction was not fulfilled. The urban population built housing with a total space of 23,000,000 square meters with the aid of state credits.

In addition, collective farmers and the intelligentsia built more than 4,500,000 dwellings in the rural localities with the aid of state credits and with aid from the collective farms.

State capital investments in the construction of institutions of enlightenment, culture, science, art and public health increased. In the course of the year 13% more general-education schools were built with funds allocated in accordance with the state plan than were built in 1960. A substantial number of boarding schools, preschool children's institutions, hospitals and polyclinics, sanatoriums, rest homes, motion picture theaters and other cultural and cultural-enlightenment institutions were built. At the same time, in a number of republics and provinces the plan for opening such institutions was not fulfilled.

Medical help to the population continued to improve. The network of hospitals, maternity homes, dispensaries, children's and women's consultation centers, sanitary-prophylactic and other public health institutions was expanded. The number of beds in hospitals increased by almost 111,000 over the 1960 total and in sanatoriums, rest homes and homes for pensioners by almost 20,000; the number of children in nurseries and kindergartens increased by more than 580,000. The number of doctors increased by more than 20,000.

The improvement in the material well-being of the working people and of medical services to the population has ensured a high birth rate and a steady decline in the mortality rate of the population, especially infant mortality. The Soviet Union remains the country with the lowest over-all mortality rate in the world.

According to preliminary data, the U.S.S.R. population as of Jan. 1, 1962 was approximately 220,000,000.

The results of fulfillment of the state plan for the development of the national economy in 1961—the third year of the seven-year plan—attest to the fact that the Soviet people, under the leadership of the Communist Party, have achieved wonderful new successes in the development of all branches of the national economy and are successfully fulfilling and overfulfilling the seven-year plan, which is a large stride in the cause of creating the material and technical base for communism.

THE SOVIET ECONOMIC CHALLENGE

Robert W. Campbell[*]

To summarize succinctly the varied elements of the discussion, it is perhaps appropriate to recall our description of the Soviet economy as "totalitarianism harnessed to the task of rapid economic growth." Rapid expansion of economic power has been the primary goal of the Soviet planners, and they have created a set of economic institutions that would enable them to realize this objective. The resulting economic system may be ineffective in some ways, but it has made possible the achievement of the

* Professor of Economics, Indiana University. The selection is from his *Soviet Economic Power*, 1960, pp. 187-198, and is reprinted by permission of and arrangement with Houghton Mifflin Company, the authorized publishers.

main goal. The Russian economy is still a long way behind ours in terms of total output, and in terms of the productivity of the resources employed in it. Nevertheless, it outperforms ours significantly in terms of growth, and the rate of improvement of many of its productivity indicators exceeds ours.

As a result the Russians have gained on us markedly in terms of economic power in the past thirty years. The operation of this economy is somewhat marred in the short run by irrationalities in planners' decisions and by waste, but a real breakthrough in effectiveness of organization and decision-making one of these days is not an unlikely possibility. The period since Stalin's death in 1953 has been a time of ferment in economic theorizing and economic administration in the Soviet Union. The Russians seem to be groping their way toward greater rationality in the mechanisms of planning and decision-making. The record of Soviet economic performance has been achieved by the employment of methods and institutions repugnant to us. Indeed the whole history seems to be based on a perverted conception of objectives. Russian planners have failed to grasp the notion that economic power is only a means to an end, and that the objective should be the maximum satisfaction of the wants of the population. This is a valid objection to the Soviet economic system, but does not alter the facts of its performance as measured by other criteria.

It is this picture of growth that underlies the statement in the introduction that the Soviet Union is capable of giving the United States serious competition both in terms of military effort and in terms of winning admirers and imitators in the underdeveloped countries of the world. The level of general economic power which the Soviets have reached, plus the controls which the planners exercise over its use, enables the Soviet regime, either now or in the near future, to engage in programs rivaling ours in these areas.

The question most pertinent to our deliberations is how the Soviet economy will perform in the future. It is with regard to the future that we still have some freedom to act, to make adjustments in our attitudes and policies to deal as best we can with Soviet economic rivalry. Will the future favor the Russians in this economic competition, or will it bring an accumulation of obstacles to continuation of their past record? Has their rapid growth been uniquely a function of the stage of development through which they have been passing, or can it continue indefinitely in the future? Is there anything we can do to influence their rate of growth, and are there ways we can accelerate ours? Partial answers to these questions have been essayed in the course of the discussion. Considered all together they suggest that there is no really compelling reason to conclude that Russian growth must slow down markedly in the future, though there is enough uncertainty about some growth factors, such as progress in technology, to admit the possibility of some retardation.

THE SEVEN-YEAR PLAN

A more concrete appreciation of the near-term prospect for their expansion can be gained by examining the targets set for the Soviet economy in the Seven-Year Plan. In this document Soviet planners have given us a blueprint of their expected growth over the seven years from 1959 through 1965, and though there is no reason to expect that this plan will be fulfilled precisely, it is still a reasonably accurate guide to their prospective development. The Seven-Year Plan envisages increases in industrial output at the rate of 8.6 per cent per year. This means that in 1965, the output of industry will be nearly 80 per cent again as great as it was in 1958. The targets for agriculture are particularly impressive, with total output scheduled to increase by 70 per cent. Detailed targets specify that grain output should increase from something like 120 million tons in recent years to about 175 million tons in 1965, meat output from current levels of 6-7 million tons to 16 million, milk from an output of 55 million tons in 1957 to 100 million tons. There are also to be large increases in the production of sugar beets, hides, cotton, wool, and other commodities such as these, used as raw materials for the branches of industry producing consumer goods. If these targets are actually achieved, agriculture will experience a growth which is probably greater than that which has occurred in the previous forty years of Soviet power.

There is even promised an improvement in the housing situation. The Seven-Year Plan envisages raising the amount of housing space in urban areas in 1965 to 1.6 times what it was in 1958. Finally Khrushchev has promised that the Russians are going to produce this expanded output with less effort on the part of each worker than in the past. The length of the working day is now in the process of being cut from 8 hours to 7 hours, and by 1962, this is to result in a 40-hour workweek for all Soviet workers. By 1965 there will be a transition to a 35-hour workweek. Thus increases in material production and consumption are supposed to be graced by increases in leisure as well. The Russian workers have long been oppressed by a long working day, with only one day off per week, and these promises must sound good to them.

Now, these appear to be ambitious goals, and Khrushchev has implied that they are so ambitious as to inspire disbelief. He has also said that they represent such a forward leap that their mere enunciation would strike fear into the hearts of the capitalists. But Khrushchev is given to exaggeration, and one can be pardoned for seeking an alternative evaluation. Are the targets attainable, and what will they do to the relative positions of the United States and the Soviet Union? It seems likely that the basic elements of the plan can probably be accomplished, though past experience raises the suspicion that there may be disappointments in such elements as housing, in agriculture, and in reduction of the workweek. It has been commented that this is a well-thought-out plan, and that it appears to have been worked over much more carefully than its ill-fated predecessor—the Sixth Five-Year Plan. That plan was overambitious, and not enough care was taken to make certain that its goals were attainable with the resources provided. As a result it had to be abandoned in mid-course and replaced with the Seven-Year Plan.

Comparison of the two plans shows that in some ways the present plan is a conservative one, and suggests an emphasis on realistic projection by the planners rather than mechanical extrapolation of past rates of growth. By comparison with previous achievements, it actually represents something of a slowdown, and hence probably recognizes the operation of some factors that will have an adverse effect on expansion. The rate of growth of industrial output, for instance, is planned to be rather less than it has been over the last ten years.

The most apparent threat to the achievement of the goals for 1965 is the labor situation. Soviet planners are facing the prospect of a labor shortage resulting from the low birth rates during the war years. The number of young people now entering the working age is small compared to the past, and so increments in the labor force will be hard to achieve. The leaders hope to forestall such a bottleneck by bringing a greater percentage of the population into the labor force. For instance, one of the aims of the drastic reorganization of the educational system is to direct young people into the labor force at an earlier age than formerly, and to put pressure on them to go directly to jobs from graduation, rather than waiting around hoping to get into higher educational institutions. But however successful these efforts may turn out, the achievement of the output goals will be impossible without very large increases in labor productivity. The plan schedules a much slower growth of the labor force than of output. It is clear that the planners expect to achieve increased labor productivity by accelerated technical progress. New capacity is to have much higher standards of labor productivity than present capacity, and in addition an extensive program is planned to modernize existing plants and replace present equipment with more advanced models.

Large increases in other kinds of productivity are expected as well. For instance, it is planned that as the result of the introduction of new equipment in the electric power industry the consumption of fuel in the generation of electric power will decline from 1.29 to 1.11 pounds of coal per kilowatt-hour. This will mean a saving by 1965 of millions of tons of coal. Many other targets for such input savings are also specified in the plan. Likewise the planners hope that the productivity of capital can be increased significantly. Recent Soviet economic discussions reveal a strong emphasis on finding innovations that will make capital savings possible. As an illustration, huge economies in capital are expected from changes in fuel policy. The capital investment per BTU produced per year is much less for oil and gas than for coal. By reducing the share of coal in the total production of fuel to only 50 per cent, and raising the share of natural gas from 8 to 25 per cent, many billions of rubles worth of investment resources will be saved.

The plan also calls for big savings in capital from building larger power stations. It is claimed that the investment per kilowatt of installed capacity is much less in the very large stations being planned now than it has been in the smaller ones built in the past. By making this kind of savings in the creation of new capacity, the planners think that they can stretch their capital resources to cover extensive replacement of obsolete equipment in existing plants. Modernization of existing facilities will be an important ingredient in achieving the goals for labor productivity which the plan specifies.

In agriculture the achievement of the goals is predicated on the success of Khrushchev's radical changes in agricultural organization. Agriculture has been a field of major concern to him, and he has sponsored a series of reforms, such as a new price policy, abolition of the machine tractor stations, and the new land policy, which have already led to rapid improvement in agricultural performance. In the light of the successes which this program has already achieved, the goals of the Seven-Year Plan do not seem so unrealistic as they otherwise might.

Assuming that the Russians fulfill this program, what progress will they have made toward their goal of catching up with the United States? What will have happened to the relative positions of the Soviet and U.S. economies by 1965? The answer obviously depends on how well our economy performs over the same period. Although we can certainly expect output to grow during these seven years, it is impossible to predict by how much.

An answer is also made difficult by the differential lag which the Russians suffer in different sectors. They are much further behind in some areas of the economy than in others. Still, a revealing indication of how the fulfillment of the goals of the Seven-Year Plan will change the relative positions of the two economies is obtained by projecting our industrial output to 1965 and comparing it with the expected Soviet level then. If it is assumed that industry in the United States will continue to expand at the rate of about 4 per cent that has characterized the postwar period, and that the rate of growth planned by the Russians for their industry is actually achieved, their industrial output will rise from about 45 per cent of ours at the beginning of the seven-year period to about 61 per cent at the end. In other words they will still be a long way behind us (and even further behind in terms of *per capita* output, it may be added), though they will certainly have made a remarkable gain on us.

Needless to say only a part of this industrial output is intended for the purpose of improving the economic welfare of the population, and Soviet consumption levels are still going to lag incomparably far behind ours. With all industrial output increasing by about 80 per cent, production of consumer goods will grow by only 62 to 65 per cent, while nonconsumer goods grow

much faster. Sales of all kinds of goods to the population is planned to increase in volume by about 60 per cent, though this is the sort of statistical
indicator that the Soviet statisticians are tempted to exaggerate.

In agriculture, it seems unlikely that they will match our per capita
levels of consumption of the main agricultural outputs, and the composition
of their agricultural output will be markedly inferior to ours from the dietary
point of view. Nevertheless, they will have made a big relative gain.

In housing, likewise, they will remain on an incomparably lower level.
Even if the targets for housing construction are fulfilled, and past experience
makes this outcome suspect, the housing space per urban dweller in the Soviet
Union cannot possibly increase to more than about 10 square meters. Translated into more familiar terms, this is a space approximately 10 feet by 10
feet, and under Soviet definitions this allotment of housing space includes
kitchens, baths, stairwells, and hallways. Thus the vision of overtaking the
American standard of living which Khrushchev has held out to the Russian
people is a false one. He has talked as though American-style abundance was
in sight for the Soviet population, and has embellished the vision with some
misleading comparisons, such as per capita butter production in the two
countries, but it is perfectly clear that even by 1965, the Soviet citizen is still
going to be living an impoverished life by American standards.

It would be foolish, however, for us to take relative consumption levels
as the main criterion for evaluating the catching-up process. As has been
stated earlier, the rivalry between these two economic systems in the world
today is not centered around winning the allegiance of the Soviet citizenry,
but around growth *per se,* especially growth in industrial production, to impress the outside world, to make possible expanded trade, credit and technical assistance, and to support the expensive military effort that each considers
essential to offset the power of the other. Perhaps the best gauge of this
general production capacity is industrial output, and the gain from 45 per
cent of ours at the beginning of the Seven-Year Plan period to something like
61 per cent in 1965 is striking evidence that in the area where it counts the
most, the gap between the two economics will have become disturbingly
narrower.

LONG-TERM PROSPECTS

The Seven-Year Plan projects Soviet expectations only a relatively short
distance into the future. Is it possible to forecast in a general way what the
longer-term prospects might be? Will the Seven-Year Plan be followed by a
succession of others, each bringing the Soviet Union closer to its goal of overtaking the United States? Any answer to this question must be extremely
conjectural, but it may be useful to look at some possibilities. Let us begin
with the prospects for industrial growth.

Considering how much Soviet industry will gain on American in seven years, how many years might it take before the Russians' industrial output would be equal to ours? As we turn to longer perspectives we must forego any attempt at precise forecasts, but the arithmetic of the catching-up process can be sketched out on a do-it-yourself basis. Table 9.1 summarizes a wide range of possibilities in this industrial competition. Across the top of the table are shown a number of alternative rates of growth for U.S. industry, and the numbers down the side embrace the possible range of rates for Soviet industrial growth. If it is assumed that Soviet industrial output is now 45 per cent of ours, then the figures in the body of the table show for any given pair of growth rates how many years would be required for Soviet industrial output to match ours. One can choose the assumptions he likes, but even if one believes that the Soviet rate of growth will be only 7 per cent (remember that the plan for the next 7 years is 8.6 per cent), and that ours will stay at 4 per cent, then Soviet industrial output will match ours within three decades. And if one takes a less optimistic view of the relative rates of growth, say 3 per cent for the United States and 8 per cent for the Soviet Union, the catching-up period is shortened to two decades.

It is not hard to draw conclusions as to what such a change would mean in world influence, ability to extend foreign assistance, to explore space, to engage in military programs, or to improve the Soviet standard of living.

TABLE 9.1.   YEARS REQUIRED FOR SOVIET INDUSTRIAL
OUTPUT TO MATCH U.S. OUTPUT

Average Annual Rate of Growth (per cent) → ↓	U.S.		
	2	3	4
Soviet 7	19	24	32
8	16	19	24
9	14	16	20

When we go from a single component of the national output, such as industrial production, to a forecast of the future course of the more comprehensive aggregate of gross national product, the picture becomes further blurred by the intrusion of more variables, such as differences in rates of growth between sectors and the interaction between them as the composition of GNP changes. Despite these complications, it is reasonable to expect that it will take the Russians rather longer to catch up with us in terms of GNP than in terms of industrial output, since the Soviet-American differential in rates of growth is probably less for GNP than for industrial output alone.

One reason for the relatively low rate of industrial growth in our country compared to the Soviet Union is that once the production of industrial goods per capita reaches certain levels, needs for additional output take new directions, and the pressure for growth shifts to other sectors, such as trade, services, and government. In their concentration on industrialization as the major objective, Soviet planners have neglected other sectors and the relatively low rates of growth of these sectors temper the differential between the two countries in overall growth. Nevertheless, the Soviet gross national product has grown faster than ours in the past, and even if it slows down somewhat in the future, there will probably remain some differential in favor of the Russians. The estimated rate of growth of Soviet GNP in the past suggests that a growth of 5 per cent per year might be a reasonable projection for the future, as against the 2.5 to 3 per cent that is considered the long-term prospect for our economy.

What this rate of growth means can be illustrated in the following manner: Soviet GNP has been divided up among competing ends in the past more or less as shown in Table 9.2. Because of the peculiarities of the ruble price structure underlying Soviet economic magnitudes, there are many theoretical difficulties in calculating the allocation of Soviet GNP by end use in such a way that it can justifiably be compared with ours. Hence the figures of Table 9.2 must be considered as only approximate. Nevertheless it is clear

TABLE 9.2. DISTRIBUTION OF SOVIET GNP
BY END USE (IN PER CENT)

Consumption of households	45
Investment	25
Military	15
Other government	15
Total	100

enough that the Soviet pattern differs markedly from the American in its neglect of consumption for greater emphasis on military and investment uses. The share of consumption in the Soviet economy is less than 50 per cent of the total output, whereas the share of consumption in the economy of the United States in recent years has been slightly above 65 per cent.

Consider what a year's growth of 5 per cent of GNP would enable the Soviet regime to do in any of these areas. Thinking of the growth as a more or less amorphous increment to output, we can imagine its being applied to alternative uses. For instance, if growth takes the form of an increased provision of consumer goods and services, consumption levels of the population could be improved quite rapidly. Devotion of all growth to consumption would make it possible to increase consumption levels by about 10 per cent per year. This would be a spectacular increase, as can be judged by the fact that the prosperous postwar period has enabled the United States to raise personal consumption by a little less than 3 per cent per year. On the other hand, such massive redirection of emphasis would very quickly slow down the rate of growth of GNP. In less than a decade it would so alter the proportion between consumption and investment in the economy that expansion would have to decelerate. There is no reason to expect the Soviet regime to change the emphasis so drastically, but even if consumption is allotted a share of the increment proportionate to its present role in GNP, consumption levels can rise appreciably.

Alternatively, channeling the increment primarily to military purposes could give an even bigger percentage increase from year to year in this area than in consumption. Finally, this increment is so large relative to the present magnitude of the Soviet foreign assistance program (foreign assistance being by the best estimate less than one-tenth of a per cent of Soviet GNP) that if the regime were willing to allocate even a small fraction of its annual growth to expansion of economic aid, its present amount could be multiplied many times.

Actually the planners do not have nearly so much flexibility as these calculations demand. They are not perfectly free to dispose of the increase in output just as they would like to. The speed with which they could translate growth in GNP into improvements in the standard of living, for instance, is limited by the problem of converting resources from one use to another. Increases in consumption require the growing of more agricultural produce, and expansion of capacity for producing manufactured consumer goods. The goods going into other uses, such as economic aid, foreign trade, military power, and investment, are more nearly convertible among themselves, although there would be bottlenecks in individual industries if the planners tried to alter proportions too rapidly. Nevertheless, the essential point to be made here is that rapid growth of the gross national product means that the Soviet leaders have at their disposal each year a sizable increment in output which they can use to increase the scope of their operations in any of these areas.

Implications for the economic policy of the United States from this description of the Soviet economic challenge can best be left to the reader's own judgment. The explanation of how the Russians have managed to grow so fast makes one conclusion fairly obvious. There is not much we can do to affect the Soviet rate of growth. Their rapid expansion comes from factors internal to their economic system, and is independent of any actions we might take. The half of the competition over which we have some control is the performance of our own economy, and even to some extent the economies of the entire non-communist world. How much of an effort we should make to increase our own growth, what directions this growth should take, and the choice of means by which we might stimulate growth involve unsettled questions of economic policy and questions of values, which can be resolved only by extended public debate. Recognition of the seriousness of Soviet economic rivalry should encourage us to make the effort.

VIII

THE IMPACT AND THE PROSPECTS
OF THE SOVIET SYSTEM

"It is not technical and economic innovations but the human aspects of a society that matter."

KARL KAUTSKY

"Without freedom, heavy industry can be perfected but not justice or truth."

ALBERT CAMUS

"Let us not, having criticized the Russian Communists all these years for being too totalitarian, pour scorn and ridicule upon them the moment they show signs of becoming anything else."

GEORGE F. KENNAN

Chapter 19

SOCIAL WELFARE AND ITS MOTIVATIONS

In setting this discussion, as it originally appeared in Problems of Communism, *the editor stated that "within recent years the U.S.S.R. has made notable progress, as compared with the past, in meeting some of the basic needs of its long-deprived population." He then posed a series of questions, to which Mr. Nove addressed himself, and which provided the basis for the ensuing comments. It seems appropriate to reproduce those questions:*

"What is the significance of the Soviet leaders' seeming preoccupation with material welfare? How is it to be explained? Is the regime truly abandoning its traditional overwhelming emphasis on heavy industrial growth, which has for many decades reduced the satisfaction of consumer needs to a place—at best—of secondary importance? If the proportion of consumer goods vs. producers' goods is indeed changing in favor of the former, if we are witnessing a shift from 'socialist accumulation' to 'socialist abundance,' does this not of necessity imply a fundamental transformation of the economic structure of the Soviet Union, as well as of its political system and political goals? Or are we to conclude that a totalitarian system is quite compatible with a relatively 'enlightened' consumer-oriented economy?"

SOCIAL WELFARE IN THE U.S.S.R.

ALEC NOVE*

As some critics see it, the Soviet state is exclusively an organ of oppression. The motivations of its leaders, they believe, are to be found solely in the pursuit of world revolution, of national aggrandizement, of personal power—or of all these at once. The attitude of the Soviet leaders toward

* British economist at the London School of Economics and Political Science; author of numerous studies on the Soviet economy. The selection is from "Social Welfare in the USSR," *Problems of Communism,* Vol. IX (Jan.-Feb. 1960), pp. 1-10. By permission.

their own people is often represented as if it were mainly inspired by the objective of keeping the mass of Soviet citizens on the lowest possible living standard consistent with the necessity of providing minimum work incentives.

Hence such critics are inclined to view all Soviet measures which seem to increase public welfare as "concessions" wrung from a reluctant regime by irresistible force of circumstance or popular pressure. It is but a short step from this view to the conclusion that such measures are, in themselves, proof of the regime's weakness or instability. If more was done to improve welfare in the first years after Stalin's death, these critics might argue, it was only because the struggle for power among Stalin's successors was undecided, and because the police apparatus had lost much of its capacity to intimidate. Inversely, now that Khrushchev has become unquestioned boss, they should logically expect a return to the old ways.

The purpose of the present article is to inquire into the validity of such interpretations of the "welfare" aspect of Soviet rule. But it is necessary first of all to define the area of discussion. To take a negative approach, the author does not propose to discuss such matters as wage rates and consumer goods production. It is acknowledged fact that real wages in the Soviet Union have been rising slowly but steadily, that peasant incomes and retail trade turnover have gone up, and that the present Soviet leadership has declared its intention to continue this process through the period of the Seven-Year Plan (1959-65). It is also true that the upward trend in these areas is highly relevant to welfare in the general sense and should be duly noted. In the present paper, however, attention will be concentrated rather on activities of a more direct "public welfare" nature, *i.e.*, on the various social services (health, education, *etc.*), on housing and such other state measures as affect the everyday life of Soviet citizens.

A LOOK AT THE RECORD

Before inquiring into the question of motivation, it is also necessary to set forth a few facts showing what actually *has* been done, or is being done, by the Soviet Union in the area of welfare. Such a survey of the record may best begin with a look at budget allocations for social and cultural expenditures during the 1950-59 period, presented in the accompanying table. Keeping the general trend toward increased outlays in mind, the individual categories of welfare listed are reviewed below with particular attention as to whether or not there has been any recent change of policy.

Health

There is no evidence that Soviet policy in this field has undergone any basic change in recent years. Vigorous efforts to expand medical and health services were already a feature of Stalin's reign, and the progress that was achieved is clearly indicated by the fact that the Soviet Union, as the following figures attest, has since 1951 boasted a larger number of doctors per thousand inhabitants than most Western countries:

USSR (1951)	13.9
USSR (1957)	16.9
United States (1954)	12.7
United Kingdom (1951)	8.8
West Germany (1955)	13.5

(Source: *Dostizheniia sovetskoi vlasti za 40 let* [The achievements of the Soviet Government in 40 years], Moscow, 1957, p. 348).

Thus, while the 1957 and 1959 budget figures show relatively sharp increases in health expenditures, it is clear that these are not a new departure in Soviet policy, but rather a continuation of past trends.

It is true that the equipment of many Soviet hospitals is antiquated, that drugs are often scarce, and that the general level of health facilities is not up to the best Western standards. Nevertheless, a great deal has certainly been done to spread hygiene, combat epidemics, and reduce infant mortality. The services of state doctors and hospitals are free, although most medicines have to be bought by the patient.

U.S.S.R. SOCIAL-CULTURAL BUDGET: 1950-59
(*in billions of rubles*)

	1950	1953	1957	1959
Total Health	21.4	24.2	38.3	44.0
(of which)				
Hospitals & clinics, urban	10.3	12.3	18.6	—
Hospital & clinics, rural	2.6	3.1	4.6	—
Total Education	56.9	61.1	80.7	94.3
(of which)				
General schooling (a)	30.4	32.2	37.6	—
Higher and technical	18.3	19.3	24.2	—
Science and research (b)	5.4	6.2	13.6	23.1 (c)
Total Social Security	22.0	22.8	52.8	88.2
Total Social Insurance	12.7	16.2	23.5	—
Total Maternity Assistance	1.2	4.5	5.2	5.5
Total, Social-Cultural	116.7	128.8	200.5	232.0

Source: *Raskhody na sotsialno-kulturnye meropriiatia po gosudarstvennom byudzhetu SSSR* (Expenditures for Social-Cultural Measures in the State Budget of the USSR), Moscow, 1958; also Finance Minister Zverev's speech, reported in *Pravda*, December 23, 1958.

Notes: (a) Includes kindergarten and adult education. (b) As most all-Union expenditures for science and research are kept secret, no complete breakdown of this item is given in the budget, but nuclear research is doubtless a major element. The item as a whole has practically no relevance for "welfare" in any sense. (c) Part of the big increase in 1959 is accounted for by a change in definition hinted at in Zverev's budget speech.

Education

Here again, recent Soviet policy has not basically altered Stalin's approach insofar as the latter aimed at a large-scale expansion of the educational system, but there have been important changes in emphasis and direction. Thus, the decision of the 20th CPSU Congress (February 1956) to extend full-time secondary education to all has since been modified in favor of part-time education after the age of 15, and Khrushchev's reform of higher education also seems likely to result in a reduction of the number of *full-time* university students. It is not, of course, within the scope of the present article to discuss the detailed causes and consequences of Khrushchev's reforms of Soviet education. Regardless of the effect they may have on academic standards, however, it can be stated that these reforms are unlikely to result in any modification of the upward trend in Soviet educational expenditures (except for a possible large saving in student stipends).

One notable reason for this assumption is the evident rise in the school building program, partly as a result of an overdue effort to remedy the overcrowding which at present necessitates a two-shift, and sometimes even three-shift, system of attendance, and partly to set up the new-type boarding schools in which Khrushchev plans to train the "new Soviet man." It is only fair to add that, in contrast to the continuing shortage of physical facilities, the situation of Soviet schools with regard to the ratio of teachers to pupils compares very favorably with that in many other countries including the United States, as evidenced by the following figures:

	PUPILS	TEACHERS	PUPILS PER TEACHER
	(in thousands)		
USSR (1956-57)	30,127	1,811	16.6
United States (1955)	30,531	1,135	26.9
United Kingdom (1956)	7,981	309	25.8

(Sources: For the USSR *Dostizheniia.* . . . p. 274; for the US and UK, *United Nations Statistical Yearbook*, 1958.)

Mention should also be made of the Khrushchev leadership's action in 1956 to abolish all fees in schools and universities, which reversed one of Stalin's counter-reforms. It will be recalled that free education had been a feature of the Soviet regime from the beginning and was explicitly guaranteed by the 1936 Stalin constitution. Despite the constitutional guarantee, however, educational charges were imposed in the top three grades of secondary schools and in universities by a simple decree of the Council of Ministers in 1940. Although the action did not have such a serious effect on university students because of the fact that the large majority were receiving stipends from which the fees simply were deducted, its impact on children of poor families enrolled in secondary schools, where stipends were not payable, was much more severe. Without doubt the restoration of free education was a highly popular act.

Social Insurance, Social Security, and Pensions

Sick-pay benefits in the Soviet Union have long been on a relatively generous scale, and there have been no significant changes in rates of payment in recent years, although overall expenditures for this purpose have increased as a result of the upward trend in total numbers of employed and in the average wage. As part of the campaign launched in the 1930's to reduce the high rate of labor turnover, full rates of sick pay were made conditional upon a minimum period of work in the same enterprise or office, except in cases where workers had transferred under official orders. These rules remain in force, although with some modifications in favor of the worker.

Provided he is a trade-union member, a worker who falls ill is paid the following proportions of his actual earnings (non-members receive one-half these rates, subject to the minima referred to below):

Years of Service	% of Earnings
Less than 3	50
3-5	60
5-8	70
8-12	80
More than 12	90

Present regulations provide for minimum monthly payments of 300 rubles in towns and 270 rubles in rural areas, and a maximum payment of 100 rubles per day.* Those who are injured at work or suffer from diseases caused by their work are entitled to sickness benefits at the rate of 100 per cent of their earnings regardless of length of service. Where a worker leaves his job of his own volition, he is not entitled to sickness pay for ordinary illness until a period of six months has elapsed, but this limitation does not apply (since February 1957) to cases of accident or disease caused by a person's work.[1] Of course, the social insurance rates described here apply only to disability for a limited period of time, permanent disablement being dealt with under pension regulations.

The maternity benefit rate itself also has not been changed in recent years, but in 1956 the period of paid maternity leave was lengthened to 112

* To give the reader some idea of the purchasing power of the ruble, here are the official Soviet prices (in rubles) of a few representative commodities (per kilogram in the case of food, unless otherwise stated): chicken, 16.5; beef (stewing), 12; pork, 19.5; average fish, 11; butter, 28; milk, 2.2 per liter; eggs (10), 7.5; rye bread, 1.24; potatoes, 1; cabbage, 1.5-2; coffee, 40; wool-mixture blanket, 100+; cotton print dress, 200; wool dress, 475; man's overcoat, 720; man's all-wool suit, 2,000; shoes (adequate), 200; bicycle, 450-600; motorcycle, 4,200; radio, 400; washing machine, 2,250; family divan, 1,300; toilet soap, (bar) 2.2; lipstick, 4.5-6. Source: Lynn Turgeon, "Levels of Living, Wages and Prices in the Soviet and United States Economies," *Comparisons of the United States and Soviet Economies,* Joint Economic Committee of the US Congress, US Government Printing Office, Washington, 1959, pp. 335-36.—Ed.

[1] These details are taken from S. A. Mitin (ed.), *Spravochnik po trudui zarabotnoi platy v stroiteltsve* (Reference Book on Labor and Earnings in Construction), Moscow, 1957, pp. 438-41.

days.[2] This was, in effect, a return to the regulation which had been in force up until 1938, when the period of maternity leave was reduced from 112 to 70 days. . . .

The reform of 1956, while reducing certain very high pensions, established an all-round minimum old-age pension of 300 rubles per month for those qualified by length of service, an advance of great importance. In addition, it put into effect a new scale of payments benefiting lower-paid workers, so that those earning up to 350 rubles per month now receive pensions amounting to 100 per cent of earnings, with progressively smaller percentages for those with higher earnings, and with a maximum overall ceiling of 1200 rubles per month. An average worker earning, say 750 rubles per month qualifies for a pension of 487 rubles under the new rules, as against probably only 200 under the old.[3] One offsetting feature of the reform is that working pensioners are no longer permitted to receive full pensions on top of their wages.[4] (This provision, together with the better pension rates, has very probably encouraged many old people to retire.) On balance, however, the net gain to Soviet pensioners can readily be measured by the increase in pension expenditures shown in the following table (in billions of rubles):

	1950	1956	1957 (prelim.)	1958 (plan)
Total pensions	30.1	36.5	59.9	66.0
(of which)				
Non-working pensioners	8.7	12.6	27.6	34.2
Working pensioners	4.7	5.1	5.3	5.8
Ex-military & families	15.6	17.5	23.5	23.4

(Source: A. Zverev, in *Planovoe Khoziaistvo*, No. 12, 1957, p. 24.)

The improvement in old-age pension benefits was accompanied by substantial increases in pensions for those suffering permanent disability of varying degrees and for dependents, the increases reportedly amounting to 50-65 per cent.[5] Further sizable increases in minimum pension rates have been also promised under the Seven-Year Plan, along with a raising of minimum wages. No doubt exists regarding the general popularity of these measures.

There has also been a good deal of talk about extending social insurance and pension rights to collective farmers, who have thus far never enjoyed them. Some farms are reported to have adopted a system of paying fixed amounts of money and produce to their sick and aged members, which represents a step forward from the normal collective farm practice of ex-

[2] G. A. Prudenski (ed.), *Voprosy Truda v SSSR* (Problems of Labor in the USSR), Moscow, 1958, p. 66.

[3] Prudenski, *op. cit.*, p. 357.

[4] The normal payment to working pensioners is now only 150 rubles per month.

[5] See *Vedomosti Verkhovnovo Soveta* (Supreme Soviet Gazette), July 28, 1956.

tending relief to such members out of a small fund set aside for this purpose. Cases where fixed payments have been instituted are still the exception since the vast majority of collective farms do not yet have sufficient revenues for this purpose, but it is a fact that the number of such exceptions is steadily growing, and the extensive publicity given to them in the Soviet press indicates that the new system is officially regarded as a desirable development.

It must be noted that, at present, all such payments are made out of the resources of each farm, and that the state has no responsibility, financial or otherwise. However, as the regime's policy toward the peasants is, in principle, to reward regular collective work with regular pay, and to bring the status of the peasant gradually closer to that of the industrial worker, it seems to follow that the state eventually will have to accept some responsibility for at least ensuring that the collective farms are financially capable of providing social-insurance benefits. This is all the more necessary because the collective farms have now absorbed the workers of the disbanded Machine Tractor Stations, who were promised the continuation of the benefits they formerly enjoyed as state employed workers. It is too soon, however, to say how the problem will be tackled.

OTHER WELFARE BENEFITS

Holidays

Turning to other kinds of social welfare benefits for state-employed persons, there appears to have been no appreciable change in the rules governing paid holidays, which already were on a fairly generous scale under Stalin. These regulations compare favorably with those of West European countries, especially for workers in what are deemed to be arduous or unhealthy occupations. For example, miners, steel workers, and bus drivers are allowed up to four weeks of paid vacation per year. Overall statistics showing the distribution of the total working force according to numbers of paid (working-day) holidays per year are as follows:

Days of Vacation	% of Total Workers
12	43
15	12
18	11
21	3
24	19
Over 24	12
	100%

(Source: *Vestnik Statistiki*, No. 10, 1958, Statistical Supplement.)

A less desirable feature of the Soviet holiday system is the practice of spreading vacations over the whole year, so that many are on vacation when the weather is unfavorable. There is also a grave shortage of holiday accommodations: despite the existence of much-publicized trade-union rest homes charging low prices, these can accommodate only a small fraction of the workers.

Working Time

There has been significant improvement in respect of hours of labor, although here again the reform effected by the present leadership so far represents, in large part, a return to the more liberal regulations which prevailed prior to Stalin's oppressive labor legislation of 1938-40. A 1940 decree lengthened the standard workday from seven to eight hours, increasing total hours for the six-day work week to 48. This remained unchanged until 1956 when the Khrushchev leadership, implementing its promise at the 20th Party Congress to reduce working hours, took an initial step to cut down Saturday work to six hours, leaving most of the afternoon free and thus creating the beginnings of a Soviet "weekend."

During 1957-58 further reductions of working hours were made effective in certain industries, notably mining and metallurgy.[6] These were followed by still greater promises at the 21st Party Congress in January 1959, when the leadership explicitly pledged a standard 40-hour week (and a 35-hour week in unhealthy occupations) by no later than 1962, with further reductions to follow later in the decade. There was even talk of achieving "the shortest working week in the world" by 1967. The promises have been so definite and attended by such great publicity that it will be hard indeed for the leadership to go back on its word, except in the event of dire emergency. Reduced hours are in fact already being put into effect in several key industries. A statement jointly issued by the CPSU Central Committee, the Council of Ministers, and the central trade union organization, and published in the Soviet press on September 20, 1959, announced a detailed time schedule for the gradual extension of the seven-hour day to "all workers and employees in the national economy." (With six-hour Saturdays, this will reduce the standard working week to 41 hours.) The process began October 1, 1959, and is to be completed in the fourth quarter of 1960.

Some Western critics, pointing to the fact that planned productivity increases are greater than would be necessary to compensate for the reduction of working hours, conclude from this that the reform is in some way not genuine since there will have to be greater intensity of effort in the shortened work period.[7] Such a view hardly seems justifiable. It is obvious, in the first place, that a shorter working week requires greater work intensity and higher productivity not only in Russia but in the United States or any

---

[6] See *Pravda*, January 27, 1958, and November 4, 1958.

[7] This was argued, for instance by Dr. E. Kux, writing in the *Neue Zürcher Zeitung* (December 16, 1958), in tones suggesting that the reform was practically a fraud.

other country. If output per hour remained the same while hours were reduced by 15 per cent, then—other things being equal—total output would go down by 15 per cent and everyone would be correspondingly poorer, a situation which no one could possibly want. Nor is it true that the Soviet Union intends to increase productivity solely, or even mainly, by imposing heavier physical burdens on labor. This is quite evident from the great attention being paid to the mechanization of labor-intensive processes, especially in auxiliary occupations (loading, moving of materials, *etc.*).

The charge that weekly wages are being cut as part of the reduction in working hours is equally untenable. The fact that a major reform of the Soviet wage system has coincided with the reduction of the working week makes it difficult to determine the precise effect of either change, but average wages appear in any event to be displaying their usual tendency to rise slowly. Thus, the cut in the working week is as genuine as these things can be in an imperfect world. Those who assert the contrary are guilty of using against the Soviet Union the very same—quite unfounded—arguments by which Soviet propagandists seek to explain away the reduction of the working week in the United States.

Other Employment Reforms

Brief mention should also be made of recent steps extending the special privileges of juvenile workers. Since May 1956 workers between the ages of 16 and 18 have enjoyed a working day shortened to six hours, with extra piecework pay to make up any loss in earnings. In addition they are allowed a full month's vacation each year and special facilities for study.[8] These privileges have, indeed, caused many managers to try to avoid employing juveniles—a tendency which has aroused official criticism and contributed to the difficulties experienced by high school graduates in seeking employment.[9] The compulsory drafting of young people into labor reserve schools, introduced in October 1940, had already been terminated by a decree of March 18, 1955, and has been replaced by voluntary recruitment.

For another thing, the worker's right to change his occupation, while not explicitly recognized, has been made more real by the present regime's abolition, in 1957, of criminal penalties for leaving one's job without permission. These penalties, as well as others for worker absenteeism and unpunctuality, had been instituted by decree in 1940. Although the decree gradually became a dead letter under Stalin's successors and was no longer mentioned in Soviet legal textbooks from 1954 on, it apparently survived on the statute books until 1957.

In still another reversal of Stalinist policy, the 1936 decree which required the rural population to give six days' unpaid labor per year for work-

[8] A. I. Denisov (ed.), *Trudovoe Pravo* (Labor Law), Moscow, 1959, p. 441.
[9] A decree to combat this was issued by the party Central Committee and the government on September 12, 1957.

ing on roads was repealed by the present leadership in November 1958. Instead, responsibility for building and repairing local roads has been placed on the "collective farms, state farms, industrial, transport, building and other enterprises and organizations." Of course, the job still has to be done, but presumably the individual is now entitled to be paid for doing it.

Wage Questions

Although wages as such are outside the province of this discussion, it may be useful to refer briefly to changes in this field insofar as they are indicative of political attitudes. The practice of the Stalin period was to maximize wage differentials, which indeed reached record dimensions; on the contrary, the trend in recent years has been in the opposite direction. In 1956, a minimum wage law was adopted, fixing a floor of 300-350 rubles per month in urban areas and 270 rubles in the country. The measure particularly benefited the appallingly underpaid groups of auxiliary personnel (janitors, cleaners, messengers, etc.) and the lowest grades of shop assistants, railroad workers, and others. This process of raising the level of the lowest-paid workers is to continue. The decree on the Seven-Year Plan provides for increasing the minimum wage to 400-450 rubles monthly during 1959-62, and to 500-600 rubles during 1963-65, as well as for a consequential (but smaller) upward revision of the pay of middle-grade workers. Since the average increase in all money wages is to be only 26 per cent, it is evident that the spread between top and bottom will be sharply reduced.

This policy is reflected in other aspects of wage reform now in progress. Apart from introducing smaller differentials in basic rates, the reforms are tending to eliminate the more exaggerated forms of progressive piecework bonuses, which will cut down disparities in actual earnings. The gap between skilled and unskilled workers' pay on collective farms is also being significantly reduced.[10] There have apparently been cuts in very high salaries, such as those of government ministers and university professors. (Though no statement to this effect seems to have appeared in print, the cuts are apparently a matter of general knowledge in the Soviet Union and have been confirmed to the writer several times.) The relative position of the lowest-paid has also been improved as a result of a decree of March 23, 1957, reducing direct taxation on incomes below 450 rubles per month. All this certainly does not indicate that the Soviets are embracing hitherto-condemned "petty-bourgeois egalitarianism," but it does show that the *excessive* inequalities of the Stalin era are being corrected.

Housing

Something must also be said about housing, since the fact that rents in the Soviet Union are far too low to bear any relation to housing costs justi-

[10] Some farms are adopting a pay ratio for unskilled as against skilled labor of 1:3 instead of the previously "recommended" 1:5. See *Voprosy Ekonomiki*, No. 2, 1959, p. 114.

fies treating it as a social service rather than as a species of commercial transaction. At 1.32 rubles per square meter per month (somewhat higher for
new apartments in some cities), rents are generally insufficient even to cover
bare maintenance, which may explain why this is so often neglected.[11] At
the same time, the miseries caused by the shortage of housing and consequent
overcrowding are too well known to require comment here. Khrushchev has
declared that his aim is eventually to provide a separate apartment for every
Soviet family instead of the single room which is the usual situation today.
It is evident from the housing provisions of the Seven-Year Plan, however,
that the separate apartments will be very small by Western standards: the
plan calls for the construction of 15 million apartment units with a total
floor space (including corridors, bathroom and kitchen) of 650-60 million
square meters—or, at most, 44 square meters (430 square feet) per apartment.
A British working-class family would be shocked at having to live in so little
space. Still, no one can doubt that Soviet citizens will be much happier if and
when each family can have its own front door and no longer have to share
the kitchen with several neighbors.

There is no question about the sharp acceleration of housing construction under the post-Stalin leadership. This is fully evident from the following figures showing housing space (excluding private rural housing) completed in four different years from 1950 to 1958, and the Seven-Year Plan
goals:

YEAR	TOTAL	STATE	URBAN PRIVATE
	(in million sq. meters of total space)		
1950	24.2	17.8	6.4
1953	30.8	23.2	7.6
1957	52.0	38.5	13.5(a)
1958	70.1	45.6	24.5(a)
1959 (plan)	80.0	—	—
1960 (plan)	101.0	—	—
1959-65 plan, total	650-60.0	—	—
do., annual average	93.0	—	—

(Source: *Vestnik Statistiki*, No. 5, 1959, p. 94). (a) These figures
include private house-building by state-employed persons engaged in agriculture and forestry.

Despite the sharply-increased effort since Stalin's death, it is clear that
there is still a very long way to go before tolerable housing conditions will
be achieved, since a large part of new construction is necessary merely to
keep pace with urban population growth. It has been pointed out that the
Soviet *per capita* rate of house-building, even allowing generously for peasant construction, remains below that of the (West) German Federal Repub-

[11] In Moscow, for example, the average revenue from tenants for rent and "other items"
is 1.75 rubles per square meter, while running costs, inclusive of capital repairs, average
4.31 rubles per square meter. See *Novyi Mir*, No. 10, 1959, p. 211.

lic.[12] Nonetheless, the facts reveal considerable progress in the USSR. The ambitious plans for rebuilding villages in connection with Khrushchev's contemplated revival of the *agrogorod* necessarily call for a still greater expansion of housing construction in rural areas, although the financial burden involved is to be shouldered by the collective farms.

Services

Finally, brief mention must be made of improvements in badly needed consumer services—restaurants, cafes, shops, repair facilities and the like. This is a very backward sector of Soviet life. To cite just one example, an article in *Pravda* (March 14, 1959) estimated the total capacity of shoe-repair establishments in the Russian republic (RSFSR) at 15 million pairs annually, although 100 million pairs of new shoes are sold each year and may be presumed to require repair at least once annually. A recent decree embodied plans for increasing the turnover of service and repair shops of all kinds to 10.3 billion rubles in 1961, as against 6.2 million rubles in 1958.[13] There have also been measures to increase the number of shops and restaurants.

MOTIVATIONS OF RECENT POLICY

This, then, is the actual Soviet record in social welfare. It suggests, first of all, that even under Stalin's rule much attention was paid to the expansion and improvement of health services and education, and fairly generous rules adopted in regard to such things as sickness benefits and paid vacations. In the late 1930's, however, some steps backward were taken, particularly affecting hours of labor, maternity leave, and the worker's right to change his occupation, and it was only after Stalin's death that moves got underway to restore the conditions which had prevailed until the mid-1930's. In the last few years, the record shows, much more has been or is being done to improve old-age pensions and disability pay, to reduce working hours, to build more housing, and to provide more consumer services, even though the Soviet citizen certainly still has—and probably will continue to have—much to complain about.

Only the willfully blind will refuse to take all this seriously. But more than *what* has been done, the vital question is *why* has it been done, and what significance, if any, do these developments have from the standpoint of assessing the nature of the Soviet system? No single, definitive answer is possible of course, but here, for what they may be worth, are a few thoughts on the subject.

While it is arguable that the Soviet rulers do as little as possible for the citizen in order to devote the largest possible share of national resources to heavy industry and weapons, such a formulation begs the question. One

---

[12] S. Wolk, in *Bulletin* (of the Munich Institute for the Study of the USSR), No. 5, 1959.
[13] *Pravda,* March 13, 1959.

could reverse it and say that they devote as much as possible to improving the citizen's lot, subject to the necessary investment in heavy industry and weapons—which would sound better from the Soviet point of view, but mean equally little. Is the glass half-full or half-empty? In any case, neither formulation explains why more is being done for the Soviet citizen today than in the past.

One relevant factor may simply be that the USSR is now powerful enough economically to permit the diversion of an increasing amount of resources to the satisfaction of the needs of its citizens, without curtailing ambitious plans for the expansion of heavy industry. To carry out the first Five-Year Plan (1928-32), Stalin found it necessary to reduce living standards drastically, but it would be foolish to take this to be what lawyers term "evidence of system." It is obviously no part of Communist ideology to make people poorer; on the contrary, communism lays great stress on abundance. The "abundance" of communism may well be—in the author's opinion it definitely is—a meaningless, even nonsensical concept, but it surely was the intention of all Soviet leaders, including even Stalin, to raise living standards at some future date, once the painful sacrifices of "primitive accumulation" were no longer necessary. The Soviet citizen was, and still is, denied adequate housing, but it would be a mistake to conclude that the leadership believes in bad housing in the same sense that it believes in the undesirability of private peasant enterprise. Soviet leaders have been willing to sacrifice a generation, to neglect urgent needs for years, but it would be patently foolish to represent them as favoring poverty and hardship as such. They surely would concede, and even advocate, improvements in popular welfare if doing so would not interfere with the pursuit of their basic aims.

Before leaving the subject of ideology, two other points are worth making. One is the enormous attention which Communists always pay to education: however they may twist its content to suit their purposes, they have invariably lavished resources on its development, whether under Stalin or under his successors. It is true that this effort is due, in part, to the urgent need of developing technical skills, but this is far from the whole explanation. Indeed, the promise made at the 20th Congress to extend full-time secondary education to all went far beyond practical necessities, and its implementation even tended to aggravate social tensions, which was one reason for Khrushchev's subsequent counter reforms.

The second point is the great importance, from the standpoint of Communist ideology, of appearing to be doing something to improve the lot of the working masses. Even when nothing or little is actually being done, the party leaders must of necessity claim to be acting in that direction. Too great a contrast between words and deeds, however, can lead to general cynicism, as in fact it did under Stalin. Khrushchev is now engaged in an evident effort to revive the fervor of the party and to replace passive bureaucratism with initiative. It is reasonable to suppose, therefore, that with this aim in view he wants to show that the party is genuinely doing something to carry out its promises to the people.

One example of this ideological influence is the regime's insistence, for political reasons, on cheap bread and low rents even when these are economically irrational and administratively inconvenient. Thus, Khrushchev recently reasserted the *political impossibility* of raising bread prices despite the fact that, at these prices, it pays to feed bread rather than regular cattle feed to private livestock. In short, cheap bread is essential to the party's outward picture of itself.[14]

THE ROLE OF INCENTIVES

Other factors, too, have a bearing on the regime's attitude in regard to welfare. For a number of reasons too complex to be analyzed here, the functioning of the Soviet economy is coming to depend more on incentives and less on compulsion. Prisoners can be kept working even when forced to live in overcrowded barracks on a minimum diet, but unless there is some emergency to spur them free men work better when they can expect to live better by greater effort. To achieve the leadership's ambitious plans, better work, more efficient organization, more initiative at the grass roots are all objective necessities. To some extent, of course, this was also true under Stalin and was acted upon, as evidenced by the lavish rewards given to Stakhanovites. But few analysts question that there has been a shift toward much *greater* reliance on incentives in recent years, paralleled by a scaling down of the number and powers of the police. To give but one of many examples of how this works in practice, the author, during a tour of the Soviet Union, was shown a new apartment block in Kiev, which he was told was being erected by the building industry for its own workers because, now that they could change employment without incurring criminal penalties, they would not remain in the industry "unless we replaced the barracks and hostels with decent housing."

Of course, people's attitudes and expectations are relevant to the efficacy of incentives as well as to political stability. The more the Soviet Union boasts of its great technical progress, of its Sputniks and moon rockets, of its equality with or superiority over the United States in weapons, the more impatient its citizens become with their backward living conditions, and the less reasonable it seems to them that nothing drastic is done to improve them. Confronted by such a popular state of mind, an intelligent leadership is likely to see the wisdom of taking some action to satisfy it.

[14] This picture has been obscured in the West by denunciations of an allegedly huge Soviet turnover tax on bread. Although it is true that the tax was for years the major constituent of the price of bread, the reason for this was that the tax was calculated on the basis of a ridiculously low procurement price for grain. The real economic incidence of the tax was not on consumers, but on the producers—the peasants.

The increasing range of contacts between Soviet citizens and foreigners plays a dual role in this process. Many more Soviet citizens are now learning at first or second hand how the other side lives, and this affects their own expectations. Then, too, with the increasing flow of foreign visitors to Russia, it must certainly appear politically advantageous to the leadership to impress them with higher standards of living. This is much more than a matter of impressing unsophisticated tourists from the West, who can if necessary be fobbed off with Potemkin villages. Much more important are the thousands of students and others from underdeveloped countries, as well as from the Soviet Union's own allies, who actually spend some time living among the Russians and cannot help learning the truth. Khrushchev is well aware that relative living standards will play an important role in the world impact of the two opposed systems.

SOME POINTS OF LOGIC

For all its simplicity, one should not overlook still another point: Khrushchev wants to be popular. He may genuinely care to reduce poverty, or he may be acting on the basis of cold political calculation—it does not matter which. He may even aspire to go down in history as the man who brought prosperity to the Soviet people—on the foundations laid by his grim predecessor. There are some Western observers who seem to shy away from even considering such motives possible, as if to do so would label them as pro-Soviet. This is clearly an illogical attitude. What is primarily objectionable about the Soviet system is its totalitarian character, its lack of intellectual and political freedom; and this character is not directly affected by the shortening of working hours or the provision of a separate apartment for every family.

It is indeed true that certain features of the Soviet economy are inconsistent with the proper satisfaction of consumer demand. It may also be true that the ultimate logic of a better-educated and materially more satisfied citizenry is incompatible with the totalitarian one-party state. Let us hope that it will prove so. But that is no reason for closing one's eyes to the realities: much is being done on the Soviet "welfare" front, and there is no sign that Khrushchev's consolidation of his political power will cause any change in this respect, especially since the policies being followed must, in his judgment, appear rational, right and necessary.

WHY THE CHANGES?

Solomon M. Schwarz*

In his introductory remarks, Mr. Nove takes issue with some anonymous critics who, it would appear, have put forward rather peculiar answers to the question. As Mr. Nove formulates it, "such critics are inclined to view all Soviet measures which seem to increase public welfare as 'concessions' wrung from a reluctant regime by irresistible force of circumstances or popular pressure." The accent is—perhaps with a tinge of irony—on "concessions."

The fact is, however, that once the polemics and the "concessions" are put aside, the arguments of "irresistible force of circumstances" and "popular pressure" assume considerable weight. In fact, this may be said of the argument of "irresistible force of circumstances" by itself, since "popular pressure," as will be shown, is often (not always!) only a part, a concomitant, or, if you will, a derivative of the "irresistible force of circumstances."

What is this force which, especially in the last decade, has so deeply influenced the development of the Soviet Union and—to remain within the frame of Mr. Nove's topic—has made the improvement of public welfare so necessary and, indeed, so unavoidable? The answer may be reduced to a simple formula: *the USSR has become a modern industrial state, but the great majority of its working population lived until recently, and to a lesser degree continues to live today, under conditions characteristic of economically backward countries.* It is this simple yet fundamental fact—perhaps *the greatest internal contradiction of Soviet life*—which in the past few years has, with "irresistible force," influenced the entire course of development in the USSR. And it is this contradiction which has engendered not only economic and social but, to some degree, even political adjustments to the conditions and requirements of a modern industrial society.

Again confining our analysis to Mr. Nove's topic, it is important to point out that a modern industrial state can function properly only if it possesses a working class that enjoys a relatively high standard of living, tolerable working conditions, and access to educational opportunities. Ineluctably, a modern working class will also demand more and more freedom. These are not merely social imperatives finding their expression in social tensions and pressures: they are also economic imperatives—that is, necessary preconditions for the required rise in the quality and productivity of labor. It is these economic imperatives which, as will be shown, have played the most important role in recent developments.

* Author of *The Jews in the Soviet Union* and of *Labor in the Soviet Union*. The selection is from *Problems of Communism*, Vol. IX (Jan.-Feb. 1960), pp. 10-12. By permission.

A few examples will illustrate this point. They are taken not from the field of social welfare *stricto sensu*—i.e., not from the field of "fringe benefits," in popular American terminology—but from the general area of labor relations, where the causalities of the development appear more clearly.

Throughout the 1930's, that is, during the first decade of intensive Soviet industrialization, Russian workers were subjected to extraordinary strains which became even more exacerbated during World War II. To further industrial development under general conditions of misery and deprivation, the Soviet government provided relatively better conditions for a small number of highly skilled workers, thus in effect creating a privileged class at the expense of the vast majority of the population. The policy of extreme wage-differentiation, which would have been unthinkable in any advanced industrial country, was for many years hailed as a true expression of socialism in action—in contrast, of course, to the "capitalist wage policy," supposedly based on the "levelling" principle. In the last decade, however, this wage policy became more and more of a handicap to further industrial development, making impossible a rational organization of labor. Its continuation caused a creeping demoralization, an increasing tendency to resort to ruses and stratagems of all sorts—in short, a situation harmful to labor and management alike.[1] In 1956 this unique "socialist" wage policy was finally buried, and the Soviet authorities set about reorganizing the wage system, cutting down the extraordinarily high earnings of some privileged workers, and raising the wages of the underprivileged ones. . . .

One more example. Under Stalin, Soviet labor relations came to be based not on a free labor contract but on compulsion. The development in the direction of greater compulsion was climaxed by a decree of the Supreme Soviet of the USSR, dated June 26, 1940, which deprived employees of the right to terminate their employment of their own volition, invested managers with virtually unrestricted power to hire and fire at will, and made not only unauthorized departure but even lateness in reporting for work (by as little as twenty minutes!) subject to criminal punishment. In the postwar years, however, the Soviet leadership came to realize the impossibility—and, from a practical standpoint, the undesirability—of keeping the entire working population in a straitjacket, and it gradually relaxed its labor practices—characteristically, without issuing any open instructions to this effect. It was not until three years after Stalin's death, in April 1956, that the basic provisions of the 1940 decree were finally rescinded.[2] To quote Mr. Nove, "the functioning of the Soviet economy is coming to depend more on incentives and less on compulsion." This, indeed, is the essence of *any* modern industrialism, to which the Soviet system can no longer claim exception.

[1] On this subject, see "Blat is Higher than Stalin!," by Joseph Berliner, *Problems of Communism*, January-February 1954.

[2] A thorough examination of this development will be found in "Recent Trends in Soviet Labor Policy," by Jerzy G. Gliksman, *Problems of Communism*, July-August, 1956.

The need to adjust Soviet realities to the imperatives of modern industrialism is thus the *main* cause of the recent development of social welfare in the USSR. Yet one more factor should also be mentioned, namely, *the change of generations,* the importance of which must not be underrated. Those who were children at the beginning of World War II are now in their early and middle thirties. Those who were in their teens are now in their late thirties. Together with their juniors, they comprise the most active segment of the working population, the great majority in the newly developed eastern areas. With the exception of the 1948-53 period, which embraced the so-called *"Zhdanovshchina,"* the hysterical "vigilance" campaign of 1952, and the ominous "doctors' plot" in January 1953, the Soviet youth and young adult population of today have grown up in a relatively relaxed political atmosphere. The horrors of the prewar decade are relatively unfamiliar to them. In their feelings, in their thoughts, in their attitudes they differ considerably from their elders—those who were psychologically mutilated during the long years of unmitigated terror. The urgent needs and demands of these young people—voiced or still in the process of germination—create those social pressures which, in addition to the economic imperatives described above, are exercising such a profound influence on the evolving Soviet system.

FACTS AND POLEMICS

Bertram D. Wolfe*

Mr. Nove has done a useful job in bringing together in one place so many facts on social welfare in the Soviet Union, and in showing, on the whole, a trend toward more education, better health conservation, some improvement in housing, less draconic labor laws than in Stalin's last years, and a lessening of extreme differentiation in wages in favor of the most poorly paid. I think that in some cases he has taken official statement for fact, and promise for performance, but on the whole his picture is undoubtedly correct, and no useful corrections could be offered in so brief a space as a commentary affords. This comment, therefore, is limited to two general points: 1) The historical framework in which these changes should be viewed; and 2) the polemical use Mr. Nove has tried to make of his material.

* Author of *Three Who Made a Revolution; Khrushchev and Stalin's Ghost;* and *Communist Totalitarianism.* The selection is from *Problems of Communism,* Vol. IX (Jan.-Feb. 1960), pp. 12-13. By permission.

1). The Historical Framework

Most writing on the Soviet era suffers from a lack of consideration of the earlier history of Russia; the history of the postwar upsurge of other war-ruined countries such as Germany and Japan; and the history of industrialization in general.

Thus our whole perspective on the rate of recovery and industrial expansion in post-World War II Russia is altered if we stop to consider the faster rate of recovery and expansion of, let us say, Germany and Japan during the same period.

Or again, in examining the Soviet Union's rate of industrial growth, we get a fresh perspective if we examine the history of the sudden march of other countries into industrialism. Thus in the period 1860-1900, Russian industrial productivity increased more than seven times, German almost five times, French two and one-half times, English a little over twice. When we attempt to evaluate Soviet industrial growth at various periods, we must regard it in the context of these comparative figures.

It is no less interesting to examine the standard of living during the industrial upsurge in Tsarist Russia. There were two distinct periods so far as labor was concerned. In the decade of the 1890's, the upsurge of industry was accompanied, and in fact partly achieved, by a fall in the standard of living. But in the next decade, the still more stormy advance was accompanied by a *rise* in the standard of living. May this not be characteristic of the earlier and later phases of industrialism under any socio-political system?

The same applies to such "welfare" features as health. When Mr. Nove retreats from the comparative figure on doctors (of little meaning, incidentally, unless we define the degree of training) to the sounder "nevertheless a great deal has certainly been done to spread hygiene, combat epidemics, and reduce infant mortality," is it not incumbent on us to remember that medical progress is fatefully easier and cheaper than industrial progress, and that this generalization on hygiene, epidemics and infant mortality applies even to the most underdeveloped countries? [1]

Again, does not advancing industrialism—under any "system"—require more literate, better-trained workers? In the Khrushchev era, for the first time in the history of the Soviet Union, there is a shortage of the rural "reserve" population which hitherto has made up any deficiency of capital investment per worker and productivity per worker. Does this not make mandatory more capital investment per head? And more "investment" in the training of "human capital"? Do not these questions on the historical framework of industrialization take precedence over an examination of the special role of totalitarianism in shaping industrialization?

When Mr. Nove comes to the proportions of the national product

---

[1] This is the source of the "population explosion" in underdeveloped countries.

devoted to consumers' goods on the one hand and "power" goods (means of production plus military might) on the other, his question ("Is the glass of water half-full or half-empty?") is anything but helpful. For if we compare a society which devotes $\frac{3}{4}$ of its GNP to consumption and $\frac{1}{4}$ to expansion of production with a society which reverses these fractions, then the question of whether the glass is $\frac{1}{4}$ full or $\frac{3}{4}$ full is far from meaningless to those who drink.

2). Totalitarianism and the Motives of the Rulers

Mr. Nove says that the "purpose" of the article is to inquire into the validity of some interpretations of the interrelations between the sector devoted to "welfare" and the sector devoted to the expansion of power. But some of the "interpretations" he chooses seem to border on the fatuous.

Thus his first target (sentence one) is those "who see the Soviet state as exclusively an organ of oppression." But is it not ABC that we are dealing with the greatest managerial and ownership state in all history? If there are any serious students of Soviet affairs who do not know that, do we need all of Mr. Nove's statistical ammunition on "welfare" when we can dispose of it by the simple reminder that a state which seeks to own and run everything must be primarily an organ of the administration of the economy itself?

In sum, I find the factual material which Mr. Nove has assembled highly useful. His interpretation of the facts he has assembled is weakened by the failure to put them into the perspective of the history of modern industrialization, and of the features common to industrializing societies whatever their political form—republic, monarchy, limited despotism and totalist despotism.

As for the polemical framework, it is scarcely worthy of the material he has been at pains to assemble. The analysis of the nature of totalitarianism is an even more difficult subject, and one on which far less progress has been made than on the analysis of industrialization—or, for that matter, on the problems of how much of the Soviet product is devoted to the expansion of "power," and how much to "welfare." Indeed, it is even difficult to decide such a simple question as the degree to which such a "welfare" feature as health is also a "power" problem, for does not any modern state need healthy soldiers, schooled workingmen, and at least some measure of mass acceptance of things as they are?

IDEOLOGY, POWER AND WELFARE

Richard Lowenthal[*]

In my opinion, Mr. Nove has performed a most useful service in pointing out that the achievement of substantial improvements in the welfare standard (and, by extension of the same argument, also in the general living standard) of Soviet citizens can be explained, and the possibility of further improvements admitted, *without assuming a basic change in the political and ideological motivations of the ruling Communist Party and its leaders.* I am not quite sure whether this was Mr. Nove's main intention; I feel certain that it is the general upshot of his argument, and its great merit.

The people's welfare is not, of course, the principal moving force of the Soviet economy, any more than it is of the capitalist economy. The principal moving force of the Soviet economy has been and remains power, just as the principal moving force of the capitalist economy has been and remains profit. But once we clear our minds of both Communist and capitalist cant, it is obvious that this formulation does not imply the impossibility of welfare improvements under Communist dictatorship, just as it does not imply a "law of absolute and relative impoverishment of the proletariat" under capitalism.

There are two reasons for this. The first is that, given the achievement of a certain degree of capital accumulation and productivity, it becomes possible for both economic systems to satisfy secondary objectives as well. The second is that the nature of the modern industrial process—independent of the economic and political systems—increasingly requires educated workers with a sense of responsibility regarding the maintenance of their tools and the quality of their output. For building pyramids in Egypt or railway lines in Arctic Russia, it may be just as effective (and certainly cheaper) to employ masses of underpaid and undernourished laborers as it is to maintain a well-fed and well-trained working class. For operating modern machinery efficiently, however, you need the latter, particularly if the birthrate and the influx of manpower from the countryside slows down; and that means a guaranteed minimum standard, plus incentives.

The transformation of living and working conditions in post-Stalin Russia, which has included the welfare measures noted by Mr. Nove, thus amounts to a somewhat belated adjustment by the USSR to the stage of "industrial maturity" it has already reached. The adjustment has not conflicted with the ideological and power objectives of the regime; in fact,

[*] Political analyst; author (under the name of Paul Zering) of *Jenseits des Kapitalismus (Beyond Capitalism)*. The selection is from *Problems of Communism*, Vol. IX (Jan.-Feb. 1960), pp. 18-21. By permission.

as Mr. Nove points out, Soviet action to improve welfare has satisfied certain low-priority propaganda objectives without hampering in the slightest the high-priority pursuit of producers' goods, armaments, and so on. All this parallels corresponding developments at corresponding stages in the history of the older capitalist-industrial countries.

In most of the advanced industrial countries of the West, however, the pursuit of profit is modified not only by the need to keep the labor force efficient and responsible, but also by two other major factors. One is the existence of political democracy, including the role played by independent trade unions and political labor groups. The other is the ideology of consumption. These two modifying factors have no parallel in the Soviet Union; on the contrary, they are incompatible with the power structure and ideology of any Communist party dictatorship. It follows that the pressure for higher standards of living and consumption is less strong in the Soviet Union and its satellites than in democratic industrial countries, and that the improvement is likely to remain within narrower limits than in democratic countries with comparable productivity.

Mr. Nove points out that there is no need to *assume* the existence of democratic pressures in Russia in order to explain what has happened. There is also no *evidence* for the existence of such pressures, except for the mass strikes in the slave labor camps during the immediate post-Stalin years, and possibly some pressure among the ruling group for increased personal security. There has been no sign of independence on the part of the party-controlled "trade unions," and no hint of giving them any bargaining rights in determining the wage level fixed by the plan: as for the peasants, they are not even "organized" (in unions) as a class. To grant such rights to independent pressure groups would, of course, be the beginning of the end of the totalitarian power structure, unless these rights were quickly revoked again—witness Gomulka's Poland after October, 1956.

The ideology of consumption, as widely held in advanced capitalist countries, maintains that the demand of consumers is the ultimate driving force of capitalist economies. This is a misleading picture of reality, partly because capitalist production tends to create its own demand by "synthesizing wants," and partly because a growing sector of effective demand emanates from public funds and is directed to goods which either do not enter private consumption at all, such as armaments, or are not individually paid for, such as public education, roads, and so on. But the ideological stress on consumption, together with the capitalist producers' continuous efforts to create new wants, tends to reinforce democratic demands for an ever higher minimum standard. Hence the tendency of democratic capitalist societies not only to provide the workers with the minimum required for training and incentives, but to channel at least part of all productivity gains into mass consumption.

Of course, Communist ideology also proclaims that abundant satisfaction of all wants is the ultimate purpose of the economic system; and the recent stress on catching up with American consumption has made this utopian vision appear more concrete and practical. Yet the Stalinist principle of continued priority for heavy industry has not been abandoned either in theory or in practice; nor could an economic system of total planning, in which literally all demand emanates from the state, ever become dependent on "want creation" to the extent that characterizes the American economy. No doubt the Soviet rulers are genuinely interested in increasing mass consumption, and there is little question that within the limits set by higher priority objectives, and given normal circumstances, they should be able to do so. But the idea that because of their propagandist promises they are "committed" to a consumption race with the United States, whatever its effect on their other objectives—an idea frequently advanced in current discussion on the prospects of "peaceful coexistence," though not of course in Mr. Nove's paper—overlooks the fact that the Soviet system has neither the political mechanism of democratic pressures, nor the economic mechanism of partial dependence on demand, which would give such promises the weight of a "commitment" in democratic capitalist conditions.

Assuming, therefore, that continued economic growth in the USSR will make further improvement of welfare and consumption standards possible, the actual rate of such improvement will depend not only on the total rate of growth, but also on the changing allocation of resources between consumption on the one hand, and such competing claims as continued investment, development aid (particularly to the countries within the Soviet bloc) and armaments on the other. This is not the place, nor am I competent, to give an estimate of the likely development in regard to such allocation. But it may be confidently asserted that as long as the totalitarian power structure and its ideological dynamics last, the share of individual consumption in the national product will continue to be far below that in the capitalist democracies—just as it is now, after all the recent improvements.

Against this, a view now fashionable in Western discussions on the future of the Soviet Union contends that the very emergence there of a modern industrial economy based on material incentives and a high level of technical education, and "committed" to rising consumption standards, is bound to erode the ideological dynamism of the regime, as traditional ideological goals come to be replaced in the minds of its rulers and managers by the material standards of efficiency and affluence familiar in the West. The obvious objection to this latest revival of 19th-century materialist optimism is that it completely neglects the experience of Nazi Germany. I do not, of course, equate the ideological goals and political methods of Mr. Khrushchev with those of Hitler; if they were the same, we should probably all be dead by now. The relevance of Nazi experience lies not in the particular content and direction of its ideological dynamism, but in the fact that the pursuit of dynamic ideological goals, *whatever their content,* proved compatible with the conditions of a highly developed industrial country under totalitarian rule.

REPLY TO MY CRITICS

ALEC NOVE*

I am very grateful to those who criticized my article "Social Welfare in the USSR.". . .

I did not examine "the historical framework of industrialization," or specifically "the special role of totalitarianism in shaping industrialization," to the apparent dissatisfaction of Mr. Wolfe (from whom I quote these phrases), because I was not asked to write about them, though I do indeed take these things very seriously in their proper context.

His more relevant criticisms puzzle me, because I very largely agree with him. He accuses me of failing to see that totalitarian "power" considerations could be consistent with increased attention to welfare. Yet the basic implication of my entire article, as was correctly observed by Mr. Lowenthal, was that a shift to more welfare can be explained "without assuming a basic change in the political and ideological motivations of the ruling Communist Party and its leaders." Certainly, given the general situation confronting them and the various technical, social and political factors involved, the party leadership is wise, from its own point of view, in sharply increasing welfare appropriations. To say so is the clear purpose of the final sentence of my article. Then what is Mr. Wolfe attacking? The dichotomy between "power" and "welfare" is not of my making; it is surprisingly common among the less thoughtful critics of Soviet policies. It is certainly not "bordering on the fatuous" (his words) to point out that many in the West still believe the propaganda stereotype to the effect that Soviet leaders pursue power to the constant and deliberate detriment of welfare. It is important to note that this interpretation leads logically to seeing the provision of more pensions or houses, or relaxation of labor restrictions, as *signs of political weakness,* because they are taken to represent reluctant yielding to pressure from below. This view is thought by many to be held to this day by Dr. Adenauer, and to have been held by Mr. Dulles. I believe these arguments to be wrong, and note with pleasure that Mr. Wolfe agrees with me.

I am also delighted to find Mr. Wolfe saying that the Soviet state "must be primarily an organ of the administration of the economy itself." If I had

* The selection is from *Problems of Communism,* Vol. IX (May-June 1960), pp. 49-51. By permission.

made so sweeping a generalization, I would have been accused of *déformation professionnelle*, perhaps not altogether unjustly. Mr. Wolfe also criticizes me for failing to see that increased welfare goes with developing industrialization. Yes, to some extent it does, and references to this (*e.g.,* in connection with education) did appear in my article. Firstly, however, the fact remains that in relation to national income the Soviet Union spends far more on health, education and so on, than highly industrialized Western countries do, and it is therefore wrong to assume that her present rate of spending is in some sense economically predetermined, regardless of political decision or system of government; secondly, *pace* Rostow, it is possible to argue that the USSR, as distinct from Western countries, can hold down living standards despite achieving a high level of industrialization—therefore we cannot assume what must be proved; and, thirdly, long-term tendencies inherent in establishing a relationship between industrial society and welfare cannot help to explain an important shift in policy of which the most significant developments were concentrated into the years 1956-59. Less "basic," more prosaic, reasons must be considered. . . .

I have very little disagreement with Mr. Solomon Schwarz. He stresses the tension caused by the contrast between backward living standards and modern industrial technology, and indeed I made the same point in my paper. The resultant social attitudes and expectations are part of the situation to which the Soviet leadership seeks to adapt its policy. In that sense, there is indeed a species of unorganized pressure from below, since failure to respond would lead to tensions and perhaps trouble. Yet the process is rightly described by Mr. Schwarz as due more to what he calls "economic imperatives": the leaders find that it is necessary and right, from their point of view, to act in the way they do. In *this* sense, they do not make "concessions," which suggests a forced compromise, any more than a sensible general who feeds his men properly makes a "compromise" with the troops. . . .

Whether improved living standards would contribute to lessening of tension and of totalitarian ideology is a matter which Mr. Lowenthal tends to rule out of court. Indeed, the experience of Nazi Germany shows that an educated and technically advanced country can be totalitarian. This disposes of anyone's delusion about some *inevitable* development towards freedom, but surely there is more to be said. If Soviet totalitarianism is historically connected with social tensions, if the size and power of the police had some relation with the scale on which people were compelled to do things they disliked, then the increased attention to welfare and the decrease in the powers of the police are also connected. It needs fewer police to supervise an increase than a decrease in wages. While none of this leads necessarily to the solution of any international or internal problem, evolution in this direction can surely be taken seriously as a ground for hope.

Mr. Lowenthal bases the assertion that the Soviet government is not "committed" to carrying out its promises—*i.e.*, that it is free to reverse its policies—on the lack of institutional safeguards. In a superficial "power" sense, he is right. There is no *institutional* check to prevent Khrushchev from decreeing a 20 per cent wage cut, or ordering that no pensions be paid to those entitled to them, or indeed doing many other things which manifestly he will not do without some very strong publicly-defensible reason. I would ask Mr. Lowenthal to ponder over Mr. Schwarz's "economic imperatives." Undeniably, Khrushchev has a greater possibility of neglecting public opinion, or of molding it, than has any Western statesman. Undoubtedly, in some last-resort situation, he would sacrifice non-priority objectives to the survival of party power. But, looking at the present situation realistically, is it really useful to say that he could at any time reverse his welfare policies? Apart from anything else, why on earth should he? . . .

There is in the Soviet system a lack of political and economic responsibility to the ordinary citizen, which still remains. It is an important social and political fact that the top leadership in the USSR is to a great extent free from any organized pressure from below, and that it has been able to neglect with impunity the urgent needs of the people if it considered it in its own interest to do so. So thoroughly was the system designed to prevent the emergence of social pressure-groups, that the regime itself suffers from the unresponsiveness and irresponsibility of local officials. It is hard to see how these defects can be cured without genuine accountability to the electorate (or to trade union membership), which would be inconsistent with party control. The local official charged with looking after the citizens remains primarily responsible to the all-powerful local party secretary and not to his constituents. The result is to distort even such desirable phenomena as housing drives. Unfinished houses are reported as completed, even though the unfortunate tenants cannot live in them, because local officialdom is responsible not to them but to those authorities above them who desire to report the fulfillment of the housing plan. Nor does the economic system "transmit" consumer demand effectively to the planners or the producers. This is why further travel along the road of welfare improvements might lead to conflict with the organizational basis of the Soviet regime. Personally I hope it will.

Chapter 20

THE GOVERNORS AND THE GOVERNED

The impact of the Soviet system upon the values, "inarticulate major premises," beliefs, loyalties, habits, and social behavior of the Soviet people —and the people's reaction back upon the Soviet system —are the principal subjects considered in this section. As Wright W. Miller tells us in his perceptive study Russians as People, *"in Russia the history, even more than in other countries, is inherent in the people."*

The selection from Bauer, Inkeles, and Kluckhohn is based largely on data obtained from probing and systematic inquiries put to Soviet refugees. The article by the anonymous "L," on the other hand, does not purport or appear to be based on any methodical survey. Nonetheless, it was undoubtedly written by someone familiar with the Russian scene. It constitutes an appraisal of life and thought in the U.S.S.R. with which many Western observers would undoubtedly substantially agree. Another account, which is intimate, personal and moving, is furnished by David Burg.

It would be erroneous to suppose, however, that all non-Communist observers of the U.S.S.R. share the view expressed in these articles. Some would not agree, for example, that "for the average citizen, political loyalty to the regime is a strange compound of apathy, passive acceptance, and cynicism." Some, like Sir John Maynard, have maintained that the Soviet system brought to the Soviet people "what they earnestly desire"—"economic security and an economic and social levelling." Another writer, Edward Hallett Carr, spoke of the high degree of "moral fervour for the social purposes of Soviet policy which is . . . generated among the citizens of the Soviet Union." These statements, to be sure, were written some years ago—before the purges of the Stalin era were exposed in all their massive ugliness. But it would be unwise to underestimate (or overestimate) the ability of the Soviet leaders to find suitable rationalizations and open up new great vistas. Whether the New Party Program (see "The Road to Communism") represents such a new vista remains to be seen.

HOW THE SOVIET SYSTEM WORKS

Raymond A. Bauer, Alex Inkeles, and Clyde Kluckhohn*

In an introductory chapter, the authors explain that the book "represents an attempt to assess the social and psychological strengths and weaknesses of the Soviet system from the perspective of a unique body of data—interviews with hundreds and questionnaires administered to thousands of refugees from the Soviet Union, in Europe and the United States, in 1950 and 1951." They add that their conclusions are not based on the special data of the project alone; they have drawn "equally on regularly published works on the Soviet Union." "Developments since Stalin's death," they maintain, "do not make our conclusions obsolete, but verify them."

The authors were aware of the danger of biases and undertook "to take them adequately into account in our analysis." However, they assert that "to regard our sample as representing only a tiny special and disaffected minority would be contrary to fact. Only a minority of our respondents (about 40 per cent) claim to have fled the Soviet Union voluntarily."

To keep our summary brief and succinct we have elected to forego a running commentary on the interrelations of our findings and to present instead a series of short discrete paragraphs. . . .

1. Ideology plays a distinctive role in Soviet society. As an instrument of policy, it is carefully manipulated by the leaders to implement their program both at home and abroad. At the same time, it importantly influences the thinking and behavior of the leaders. This ideology cannot, of course, be simply read out of a book. Rather, it is an amalgam of formal and openly expressed principles, informal and covertly held ideas which are nevertheless consciously shared by the elite, principles of action which are merely implicit and often not consciously formulated by the leadership, and lessons learned from experience in the hard school of Soviet politics. Correct interpretation of Soviet behavior, adequate assessment of their intentions, or accurate prediction of their probable behavior cannot be made without weighing the role of ideological factors together with "objective conditions" as an influence on the actions of the leaders.

2. The long-range goals of Soviet policy are importantly influenced by ideological considerations, and appear to be generally directed toward

* Reprinted by permission of the publisher from chapter 23 of *How the Soviet System Works* (Cambridge, Mass.: Harvard University Press, Copyright, 1956, by The President and Fellows of Harvard College).

maintaining and substantially strengthening the present structure of Soviet society and toward creating a world predominantly, if not wholly, Communist under Soviet leadership or hegemony. Current policy is, of course, always considerably influenced or determined by the actions of the United States and other nations involved in the total international scene and by practical considerations arising from the resultant balance of forces. In addition, the regime's long-range policy appears subject to the important reservation that every precaution should be taken to avoid immediate and major risks to the security of the home base. Thus, ultimately, the domestic requirements of the system set an absolute limit on the degree of risk undertaken in foreign affairs. Nevertheless, many of the difficulties on the domestic front stem from the regime's ambitious foreign policy goals and the consequent commitments to offensive and defensive preparedness, which strain the resources of the system to the utmost.

3. While the long-range goals of the leadership are highly stable, there have been, from a shorter-term point of view, enough sudden alternations in both domestic and foreign policy, both between rigidity and flexibility and between two drastically contrasting courses of policy and action, to justify naming "cyclical behavior" one of the most distinctive operating characteristics of the Soviet system. This adds an important element of insecurity to the life situations of both the elite and the rank and file, which the regime may exploit to its advantage, but which also makes it more difficult for the Soviet citizen to regard the system with equanimity.

4. In large measure, the internal problems of the regime stem from the leaders' persistent tendency to overcommit the system's resources. The system involves, in effect, permanent rationing and perpetual mobilization. Goals are invariably set too close to the theoretical capacity of the available resources in the effort to stimulate each unit to maximum output. Furthermore, effective expenditures of energy are usually characterized by mass assault on a single objective or a relatively narrow range of objectives, while other considerations are ignored until their sheer neglect causes sufficient problems so that they, in turn, rise to a high position on the scale of priorities and become the focus of mass assault. As a result, despite the extensive machinery of allocation, there are always localized scarcities of resources, resulting in hoarding and inevitable costs in the form of malcoördination of effort. Overcontrol and overcentralization are therefore chronic features of the system.

5. Both because of their addiction to rational planning and because of their conviction that "everyone who is not completely for us is against us," the ruling elite have made tremendous efforts to stamp out growing centers of independent power and communication. Their success, however, is not complete, particularly with regard to the military, who retain continuing capabilities for independent action and are possessed of notably increased relative power and prestige.

6. The needs of the citizen are relatively low in the priority scheme of the leaders. Nevertheless, the individual is recognized as the most flexible resource in the system. The regime is therefore necessarily concerned with the morale of the population—not as an objective in itself but as an unavoidable prerequisite to effective economic production and military preparedness. The regime's objective is to extract from the citizen a maximum of effort with a minimum of reward. The purge and the terror are the standard instruments for insuring unhesitating obedience to central command. But to maximize incentive the regime also relies heavily on sharply differentiated material and social rewards. Further, it may periodically relax the pressure and make a show of concern for popular welfare when the results of increased pressure appear to have passed the point of diminishing returns.

7. Certain features of Soviet society win strong, widespread support and approval. These are notably the welfare-state aspects of the system, such as the health services, government support of the arts, and public educational facilities. In addition, the regime is credited with major achievements in the technological development of the country, in which Soviet citizens take obvious pride. The armed might and international prominence of the regime are recognized and held somewhat in awe. The depth of loyalty to "the motherland" is an outstanding sentiment in all classes of the population, irrespective of religion, political attitudes, and personality structure. This is coupled with a genuine fear of foreign aggression. These sentiments are strongest in the heartland of Great Russia, but they prevail generally.

8. Our data show that ignorance and distorted views of the outside world are deeper and more widespread—even among the intelligentsia—than heretofore had been realized by most students of the U.S.S.R. It is almost impossible to exaggerate the ignorance of the outside world prevalent among Soviet citizens. And, while feelings toward the American people and toward certain American achievements have distinctly positive elements, there is a general distrust of American intentions and a fear of "capitalist aggression." Most attitudes toward the West change after emigration, but not in a uniformly favorable direction.

9. The general features of Soviet life and the Soviet system that are most intensely resented are the low standard of living, the excessive pace of everyday life, the invasion of personal privacy, and the "terror," i.e., the threat of arbitrary political repression. We found little concern with "civil liberties" per se, and little pressure toward a democratic form of government. The specific institution most resented was the collective farm, which all groups, virtually without distinction and nearly unanimously, want eliminated. There was strikingly little complaint about the factory system other than dislike of harsh labor-discipline laws, which now are no longer being stringently enforced.

10. Hostility is directed mainly toward the regime—the actual people in power—rather than toward the idea of a welfare state with high concentration of economic and social as well as political power in the hands of a few men. There is a strong tendency for the rank-and-file citizen to establish a "we-they" dichotomy, in which "they" are the people, regardless of rank, who are closely identified with the regime. In general, but not exclusively, this distinction tends to correspond to that between Party and non-Party personnel, although some members of the Party are accepted in the "we" category. In any event, wherever the line is drawn, "we" see "them" as having no regard for "our" feelings, depriving "us" of just rewards, terrorizing "us" without cause, and generally failing to show proper trust and respect for the citizenry. All classes appear to channel much of their hostility and aggression in this way. Indeed, many of the routine daily frustrations of life are charged to the regime because the immediate source of those frustrations is defined as a representative of "them."

11. The conflict over straightforward matters of policy, which creates a gulf between the leaders and the rank and file, is aggravated by the important psychological differences which separate the elite and the masses. The masses remain rather close to the traditional picture of Russian character. They are warm-hearted, impulsive, given to mood swings, and contradictory in behavior. The goal of the elite is the rather puritanical "new Soviet man": disciplined, working steadily and consistently, subordinating personal conduct and motivation to the requirements of Party discipline. It appears that the Soviet leaders have succeeded to a certain degree in developing among the elite a considerable proportion of people of an externally disciplined and driving character, and their patterns of behavior add to the sense of alienation felt by many of the rank and file toward the leaders.

12. Despite the high level of dissatisfaction and discontent, there seems to be only a relatively small amount of disaffection and disloyalty. The life histories of our respondents left little doubt of the extent to which most of them were unhappy about many aspects of their life situations. But these same life histories indicated that most of the citizens of the U.S.S.R. feel helpless in the face of the power of the state and desire only to live peacefully. There is scant evidence for the view that more than a very tiny part of the population would, except under conditions of extreme crisis, take appreciable risks to sabotage the regime or to aid Western democracy.

13. Certain traumatic experiences, such as being arrested, had less effect than we had anticipated. Being arrested has virtually no impact on a person's general social and political attitudes and values. The individual does not generalize his experience to the point of revising his judgment concerning the kind of society in which he lives or would want to live. Arrest, however, does increase the *intensity* of his hostility *to the regime.* Further-

more, arrest—whether his own, or that of a family member—makes him anxious about his own future, and thereby increases the probability of his leaving the Soviet Union voluntarily if the opportunity arises.

14. Degree of dissatisfaction with, or even disaffection from, the system does not necessarily detract from the energy with which a person does the job assigned to him by "the system." The disaffected person often does his job well and may work with a little extra energy, either because he feels he has to prove himself or because he finds comfort in his work. Thus, the fact that the Soviet system tends to produce dissatisfaction in its citizens does not in itself mean that it gets less effective work from them. This applies, however, mainly in the professional and white-collar classes. In the working class and the peasantry there appears to be a fairly direct relation between the individual's level of satisfaction and the quality and quantity of his work.

15. The Soviet elite, a markedly privileged social class, inevitably has a vested interest in maintaining and perpetuating the system. This tendency, however, varies with different individuals and under various combinations of circumstances and is partly counterbalanced by one or more of the following factors: (a) the conviction that the ruling clique is acting contrary to the interests of the nation-state; (b) the conviction that the regime has betrayed the humane goals of Marxism; and (c) personal insecurity. On the other hand, even when these factors are operative, the conflicted members of the elite often fall into line of their own choice because of deep-rooted attitudes, such as suspicion of foreigners and their motives; belief that, after all, national patriotism and loyalty to the regime are inextricably linked; acceptance of Communist ideology; a conspiratorial mentality; and the habit of disciplined obedience.

16. A Soviet citizen's social class and his occupation largely determine both his opportunities for advancement and his attitudes toward the Soviet system, as well as his general social and political values. The individual's social position is more important than such factors as nationality or arrest history in affecting his hostility toward, passive acceptance of, or positive identification with the regime. Members of the intelligentsia, being the more favored beneficiaries of the system, understandably show substantial satisfaction with the conditions of daily life and with opportunities for development and advancement. They are generally the persons most accepting of the broad outlines of Soviet society, with the exception of its political patterns which hit them especially hard owing to the greater surveillance to which the regime subjects them and their work. At the other pole, the peasant emerges as the "angry man" of the system, strongly rejecting most of its features, convinced of his exploitation, resentful of his deprivation of goods and opportunities, and outraged by the loss of his autonomy. The workers shared many attitudes and life experiences with the peasants, thus forming a broad manual group which can regularly be distinguished from the non-

manual. The workers are, on the whole, less intense and resentful than the peasants and generally accept the sociopolitical structure of the Soviet factory as natural and proper.

17. It has been asserted that the Soviet youth, although showing a strong early allegiance to the regime, have a high probability of becoming disaffected as they mature and experience the full dimensions of the regime. Our materials indicate that there is a period of crisis in the relation of youth to the regime as the individual reaches maturity, but that only a small minority actually turn against the system because of disillusionment. In most instances, they are able to reconcile their conflicts. Furthermore, the younger generation is coming to accept as natural many aspects of Soviet life and the Soviet system against which the older generation rebelled. The youth is relatively unlikely to turn against the regime, in spite of experiences that Americans would think would lead to disaffection.

18. The individual's nationality appears to play a lesser role in determining his attitudes toward the regime than has often been supposed. Indeed, people in the same occupation or social group hold essentially the same attitudes and values regardless of nationality, and those in the national minorities feel the same resentments toward the regime and experience the same dissatisfactions with the system as do all other citizens of the U.S.S.R. Generally, therefore, nationality is only a secondary, contributing cause for disaffection. There is a distinctive nationality feeling in sections of many national groups, however, and this national identification is supported by a sense of oppression and resentment of Great Russians.

19. Certain scholars had advanced the plausible and provocative thesis that political domination within the Soviet system was threatened by a "managerial revolution." Our data, however, indicate that technical and managerial personnel, having a stake in the existing system, have developed an interest in maintaining it in predominantly its present form. They are concerned mainly with reducing interference and extreme pressure from the center and in improving the system and making it work more smoothly. They feel that they can obtain the rewards they deserve without the risks involved in ownership.

20. The Project findings yield strong evidence as to the importance of informal mechanisms in the operation of a society that, on the surface, appears and pretends to be highly centralized, controlled, and rationalized. The rank-and-file citizen learns to apply complicated techniques of accommodation and evasion in order to carry on his day-to-day affairs and to maintain himself in reasonably successful, or at least untroubled, adaptation to the regime. In this he is often aided by others—doctors, for example—who serve as buffers between him and the pressures of the system. In addition, "localism" or "familism," the tendency for local loyalties and informal mutual protective associations to develop on the local level as defense against the pressures of the center, plays a major role. In fact,

Soviet society works as well as it does only because of the existence of a series of informal, extralegal practices which are tolerated, up to a point, by the regime, even though officially disapproved. Nevertheless, these informal adjustive mechanisms create problems for the leadership as well as facilitating the functioning of the society in significant respects.

21. The life histories of our respondents indicate that the stability of the Soviet system involves a nice balance between the powers of coercion and the adjustive habits of the Soviet citizenry. The stability of the system and of the citizen's loyalty depend to a high degree on the citizen's own belief in the stability of that system and on his having no alternative but to adjust to the system. For the average citizen, political loyalty to the regime is a strange compound of apathy, passive acceptance, and cynicism. Among the elite groups, some individuals are conforming loyalists to the system; some, the "careerists," are really loyal only to themselves; more than a few are loyal to Communist "ideals." Our pessimistic finding is that the new regime can gain much more solid popular support if it supplies more consumer goods and better housing, eases up on the terror, makes some concessions to the peasants, and relieves somewhat the frantic pace at which all the population has been driven. Such a change of policy would not only alleviate many of the day-to-day grievances of the citizen, but also change his basic image of the regime as a harsh and depriving force. These may be precisely the lines along which the current regime is proceeding.

THE NEW SOVIET MAN

"L" *

It might be supposed that as a result of so many years of Stalinist conditioning the new Soviet man would be a new creature, as different from his Western counterpart as the Soviet system differs from Western forms of government. But this has not, in fact, turned out to be so. In so far as recent conversations of mine with students, clerks in shops, taxi-drivers and stray acquaintances of all sorts can convey a just impression, the result is a kind of arrested infantile development, not a different kind of maturity.

In the Soviet Union today one finds the conditions that are often found to prevail in organizations in which degrees and types of responsibility are very sharply defined—strictly disciplined schools, armies or other rigid hierarchies in which the differences between the governors and the governed

* Anonymous. The article originally appeared under the title "The Soviet Intelligentsia" in *Foreign Affairs*, Vol. 36 (October 1957), pp. 122-130. Copyright held by Council on Foreign Relations, New York. By permission.

are extremely precise. Indeed, the chasm between the governors and the governed is the deepest single division noticeable in Soviet society; and when one speaks to Soviet citizens it soon becomes quite clear to which of the two groups they belong. Honest public discussion, either of the ends for the sake of which the new society supposedly exists, or of the more important means supposedly adopted for the forwarding of those ends, is equally discouraged on both sides of this great dividing line. The work of the ant-hill must be done, and anything that wastes time or creates doubts cannot be permitted. But the consequences in one case are somewhat different from those in the other.

Let me begin with the governed. Those who have no ambition themselves to become governors, and have more or less accepted their position in the lower ranks of the Soviet hierarchy, do not seem to be deeply troubled about public issues. They know they cannot affect those issues in any case, and discussion of them is, moreover, liable to be dangerous. Hence when they touch upon them at all they speak with the gaiety, curiosity and irresponsibility of schoolboys discussing serious public issues outside their ken, more or less for fun, not expecting to be taken too seriously, and with a pleasing sense of saying something daring, near the edge of forbidden territory. Such people cultivate the private virtues, and retain those characteristics that were so often noted as typically Russian by foreigners before. They tend to be amiable, spontaneous, inquisitive, childlike, fond of pleasure, highly responsive to new impressions, not at all blasé, and, having been kept from contact with the outside world for so long, essentially Victorian and prudishly conventional in their outlook and tastes. They are not as terrified as they were in Stalin's day, when no one knew what might not happen to him, and no effective appeal to any institutions of justice was possible. The tyrant is dead, and a set of rules and regulations rule in his place.

The rules are exceedingly harsh, but they are explicit, and you know that if you transgress them you will be punished, but that if you are innocent—if you live a very careful and circumspect life, take no risks, see no foreigners, express no dangerous thoughts—you can reasonably count on being safe and, if arrested, on a reasonable chance of clearing up the misunderstanding and regaining freedom. The justice of the rules themselves is not, one finds, much discussed. The question is not asked whether they are good or bad. They appear to be taken for granted, like something from on high, on the whole disagreeable, and certainly not believed in with the kind of religious devotion expected of good Communists, but, since they are clearly not alterable by the governed, accepted by them almost like the laws of nature.

Taste remains simple, fresh and uncontaminated. Soviet citizens are brought up on a diet of classical literature—both Russian (which is almost unrestricted now) and foreign—mainly of authors held to be of "social significance": Schiller, Dickens, Balzac, Stendhal, Flaubert, Zola, Jack London, plus "boy scout" novels celebrating the social virtues and showing how vice is always punished in the end. And since no trash or pornography or "problem" literature is allowed to distract them, the outlook of the pupils in this educational establishment remains eager and unsophisticated, the outlook of adolescents, sometimes very attractive and gifted ones. At the marvellous exhibition of French art in the Hermitage in Leningrad, Russian visitors (according to at least one foreigner who spoke to several among them) admired few pictures after the eighteen-fifties, found the Impressionists, particularly Monet and Renoir, difficult to like, and quite openly detested the paintings of Gauguin, Cézanne and Picasso of which there were many magnificent examples. There are, of course, Soviet citizens with more sophisticated tastes, but few and far between, and they do not advertise their tastes too widely.

Students are encouraged to take interest in scientific and technological studies more than in the humane ones, and the closer to politics their fields of study are, the less well they are taught. The worst off are, therefore, the economists, modern historians, philosophers and students of law. A foreign student working in the Lenin Library in Moscow found that the majority of his neighbors were graduate students, preparing theses which consisted largely of copying passages from other theses that had already obtained doctorates and, in particular, embodying approved quotations from the classics—mainly the works of Lenin and Stalin (still Stalin in 1956)—which, since they stood the test of many examinations, represented the survival of the fittest. It was explained to this foreign student that without these no theses could hope to pass. Evidently both examinees and examiners were engaged in an unspoken understanding about the type of quotations required, a quota of these being a sine qua non for obtaining a degree. The number of students reading books was very small in comparison with those reading theses, plus certain selected copies of *Pravda* and other Communist publications containing quotable official statements of various kinds.

In philosophy the situation is particularly depressed. Philosophy—that is, dialectical materialism and its predecessors—is a compulsory subject in all university faculties, but it is difficult to get any teacher of the subject to discuss it with any semblance of interest. One of these, perhaps in an unguarded moment, went so far as to explain to a puzzled foreign amateur of the subject that under the Tsarist régime a clergyman was expected to visit every form in the school, say, once a week, and drone through his scripture lesson, while the boys were expected to sit quiet. They were scarcely ever asked to answer questions; and, provided they gave no trouble, did not interrupt or give vent to aggressively anti-religious or subversive thoughts, they were by tacit consent permitted to sleep through the hour

—neither side expecting to take the other seriously. The official philosophers were the cynical clergy of today. Lecturers on dialectical materialism simply delivered their stock lectures, which had not altered during the last 20 years—ever since debates between philosophers had been forbidden even within the dialectical materialist fold. Since then the entire subject had turned into a mechanical reiteration of texts, whose meaning had gradually evaporated because they were too sacred to be discussed, still less to be considered in the light of the possibility of applying them—except as a form of lip service—to other disciplines, say, economics or history.

Both the practitioners of the official metaphysics and their audiences seem equally aware of its futility. So much could, indeed, be admitted with impunity, but only by persons of sufficient importance to get away with it: for example, by nuclear physicists whose salaries are now probably the highest of all, and who apparently are allowed to say, almost in public, that dialectical—and indeed all—philosophy seems to them meaningless gibberish upon which they cannot be expected to waste their time. Most of those who have spoken to teachers of philosophy in Moscow (and a good many Western visitors have done so by now) agree that they are one and all passionately interested to know what has been going on in the West, ask endless questions about "Neo-Positivism," Existentialism and so on, and listen like boys unexpectedly given legal access to forbidden fruit. When asked about progress in their own subject, the look of guilty eagerness tends to disappear, and they show conspicuous boredom. Reluctance to discuss what they know all too well is a dead and largely meaningless topic before foreigners who are not expected to realize this is almost universal. The students make it all too clear that their philosophical studies are a kind of farce, and known to be such, that they long to be allowed to interpret and discuss even such old-fashioned thinkers as Feuerbach or Comte, but that this is not likely to be found in order by those in authority. Clearly "the governed" do not seem to be taken in by what they are told. The philosophy students know that the philosophy dispensed to them is petrified nonsense. The professors of economics, for the most part, know that the terminology they are forced to use is, at best, obsolete.

At a wider level, it is difficult to find anyone with much belief in the information that comes from either their own newspapers or radio, or from abroad. They tend to think of it as largely propaganda, some of it Soviet, some of it anti-Soviet, and so to be equally discounted; and they avert their thoughts to other fields in which freer discussion is possible, mainly about issues of personal life, plays, novels, films, their personal tastes and ambitions and the like. On all these subjects they are fresh, amusing and informative. They suffer from no noticeable xenophobia. Whatever they might be told by the authorities, they hate no foreigners. They do not even hate the Germans, against whom there really was strong feeling of a personal kind in 1945-46, and certainly not the Americans, even though they fear that because of the quarrels of governments, the Americans may make war upon them; but even this is viewed more like the possibility of an earthquake or some other natural cataclysm than something to which blame attaches. Those who ask questions about current politics usually show little bias, only the curiosity of bright, elderly children. Thus the taxi-driver who asked his passenger if it was true that there were two million unemployed in England, and upon learning that this was not so, replied philosophically, "So they have lied about this too," said so without the slightest indignation, not even with noticeable irony, very much like someone stating a fairly obvious fact. It was the Government's business to dispense these lies, he seemed to say (like that of any Ministry of Propaganda in wartime), but intelligent persons did not need to believe them. The amount of deception or illusion about the external world in large Soviet cities is not as high as is sometimes supposed in the West— information is scanty, but extravagant inventions are seldom believed. It seems to me that if by some stroke of fate or history Communist control were lifted from Russia, what its people would need would be not reëducation—for their systems have not deeply absorbed the doctrines dispensed —but mere ordinary education. In this respect they resemble Italians undeluded by Fascism, rather than Germans genuinely penetrated by Nazism.

In fact, the relative absence of what might be called Communist *mystique* is perhaps the most striking fact about the ersatz intelligentsia of the Soviet Union. No doubt many convinced Marxists exist in Poland and Jugoslavia and elsewhere; but I cannot believe that there are many such in the Soviet Union—there it has become a form of accepted, and unresisted, but infinitely tedious, official patter. What writers and intellectuals desire—and those who have made their protests at recent meetings of writers' unions and the like are symptomatic of this—is not so much to be free to attack the prevailing orthodoxy, or even to discuss ideological issues, but simply to describe life as they see it without constant reference to ideology. Novelists are bored, or disgusted, with having to put wooden, idealized figures of Soviet heroes and villains into their stories and upon their stages; they would passionately like to compose with greater—if still very naïve—realism, wider variety, more psychological freedom. They look back with nostalgia to what seems to them the golden age of the Leninist twenties, but not beyond, which is different from seething with political revolt. The writers—or, at any rate, some of them—wish to discuss or denounce bureaucracy, hypocrisy, lies, oppression, the triumphs of the bad over the good, in the moral terms to which even the régime ostensibly adheres. These moral feelings, common to all mankind, and not heterodox or openly anti-Marxist attitudes, are the form in which the Hungarian revolt seems to have been acclaimed or condemned, and in which the new novel (almost worthless as literature, but

most important as a social symptom) that has stirred everyone so deeply—
"Not by Bread Alone," by Dudintsev—is written and discussed.[1]

The governed—the subject population—are for the most part neither
Communist believers nor important heretics. Some, perhaps the majority,
are discontented; and discontent in totalitarian states is ipso facto political
and subversive. But at present they accept or at any rate passively tolerate
their Government—and think about other things. They are proud of Russian economic and military achievements. They have the charm of a shel-
tered, strictly brought up, mildly romantic and imaginative, somewhat
boyish, deeply unpolitical group of simple and normal human beings who
are members of some ruthlessly ruled corporation.

As for the governors, that is a different story. Individually ruthless and
anxious to get on, they seem agreed that Communist language and a certain
minimum of Communist doctrine are the only cement that can bind the
constituent parts of the Soviet Union, and that to modify these too greatly
would endanger the stability of the system and make their own position
excessively precarious. Consequently they have managed to translate the
thoughts in their heads into a reasonable imitation of Communist terminology, and seem to use it in their communication with each other as well
as foreigners. When you ask them questions (and it is always clear whether
or not one is talking to a member of the upper tiers of the hierarchy or
someone who is aspiring to get there, if only from his looks and the tone
of his voice and the clothes he wears and other less palpable things) they
launch into something which at first seems a mere propagandist turn; then
gradually one realizes that they believe in what they are saying in much
the same way as a politician in any country can be said to believe in a
performance which he knows that he manages well, which he has adjusted
to his audience, upon which his success and career depend, which has
patently become bound up with his whole mode of self-expression, possibly
even to himself, and certainly to his friends and colleagues.

I do not believe that a double morality prevails in the Soviet Union:
that the Party leaders or bureaucrats talk in the consecrated mumbo jumbo
to their subjects, and then drop all pretense and talk cynical common
sense to each other. Their language, concepts, outlook are an amalgam
of both. On the other hand, again perhaps like that of the Russian bureaucrats of old, and of certain types of political manipulators and power-
holders everywhere, their attitude toward their own official doctrine, but
still more toward the beliefs of the outside world, is often skeptical and,
indeed, cynical. Certain very simplified Marxist propositions they certainly
do hold. I think they genuinely believe that the capitalist world is doomed
to destruction by its own inner contradictions; that the proper method of

[1] Nor does the "oppositionist" literary almanac *Literaturnaya Moskva* do more than
this: it is neither for "pure" art nor for some alternative political policy, however covertly.
Its "suspect" articles cry out for human values.

assessing the power, the direction and the survival value of a society is by asking a certain type of "materialistic" economic or sociological questions (taught to them by Lenin), so that the answers to these questions play a decisive part in the conception and formulation of their own most crucial political and economic policies. They believe that the world is marching inexorably towards collectivism, that attempts to arrest or even modify this process are evidence of childishness or blindness, that their own system, if only it holds out long enough against capitalist fury, will triumph in the end, and that to change it now, or to retreat too far simply in order to make their subjects happier or better, might mean their own doom and destruction, and—who knows?—perhaps that of their subjects too. In other words, they think in terms of Marxist concepts and categories, but not in terms of the original Marxist purposes or values: freedom from exploitation, or coercion, or even the particular interests of groups or classes or nations, still less in terms of the ultimate ideals: individual freedom, the release of creative energy, universal contentment and the like. They are too tough and morally indifferent for that. They are not religious; but neither are they believers in some specifically proletarian morality or logic or historical pattern.

Their attitude towards intellectuals can be compared in some degree to that of political bosses everywhere: it is, of course, largely conditioned by the tone set by the leaders—the members of the Central Committee of the Communist Party. The majority of these, in addition to their suspicion of those who are concerned with ideas in any form as a perpetual source of potential danger, feel personally uncomfortable with them, and dislike them for what can only be called social reasons. These are the kind of reasons for which trade unionists in all countries sometimes feel a combined attitude of superiority and inferiority to intellectuals—superiority because they think themselves more effective, experienced and with a deeper understanding of the world gained in a harder school, and inferior socially, intellectually and because they feel ill at ease with them. The group of roughnecks who preside over Russia's fortunes—and one glance at the Politbureau (now called the Presidium) makes it clear that they are men happier at street corner meetings or on the public platform than in the study—look upon intellectuals with the same uneasy feeling as they look on the better-dressed, better-bred members of the foreign colony— diplomats and journalists—whom they treat with exaggerated and artificial politeness, envy, contempt, dislike, intermittent affability and immense suspicion. At the same time they feel that great nations must have important professors, celebrated artists, cultural trappings of an adequate kind. Consequently they pay the topmost practitioners of these crafts high salaries, but cannot resist, from sheer resentment, an irresistible desire to bully and, from a deep, jealous sense of inferiority, the temptation to knock them about, kick them, humiliate them in public, remind them forcibly of the chains by which they are led whenever they show the least sign of independence or a wish to protect their own dignity.

Some intellectuals do, of course, themselves belong to the upper rungs of the hierarchy; but these are looked on by the bulk of other intellectuals either as semi-renegades and creatures of the Government, or else as blatant political operators or agitators, required to pose as men of learning or creative artists. The difference between genuine writers who can talk to other writers in normal human voices, and the literary bureaucrats—a difference, once again, between the governors and the governed—is the deepest single frontier in Soviet intellectual life. It was one of the former—the governors —who, talking not ostensibly about himself but about intellectuals in general, told a visiting American journalist not to think that Soviet intel-lectuals as a class were particularly keen about the granting of greater personal freedom to the workers and peasants in the Soviet Union. He said, in effect, that if they began giving liberties too fast, there might be too much unruliness—strikes, disorder—in the factories and the villages; and the intelligentsia, a most respected class in Soviet society, would not wish the order from which they very rightly get so much—above all, prestige and prosperity—to be jeopardized. "Surely you understand that?" he asked.

So far, then, have we travelled from the nineteenth century, when the whole of Russian literature was one vast, indignant indictment of Russian life; and from the agonies and enthusiasms and the bitter, often desperate, controversies and deadly duels of the twenties and early thirties. A few pre-Stalin men of letters survive, great names, but few and far between; they are half admired, half gaped at as semi-mythical figures from a fabu-lous but dead past. Bullying and half-cynical semi-Marxist philistines at the top; a thin line of genuinely civilized, perceptive, morally alive and often gifted, but deeply intimidated and politically passive, "specialists" in the middle; honest, impressionable, touchingly naïve, pure-hearted, in-tellectually starved, non-Marxist semi-literates, consumed with unquench-able curiosity, below. Such is Soviet culture, by and large, today.

THE VOICE OF A DISSENTER: AN INTERVIEW WITH A GRADUATE OF MOSCOW UNIVERSITY

DAVID BURG*

INTERVIEWER: You were born in Moscow?

BURG: Yes, in 1933, the year of the great Russian famine—although I

* David Burg is the pen name of a young Russian scholar who left the U.S.S.R. late in 1956. The selection is from an article by the same title which appeared in *Harper's Magazine*, Vol. 222 (May 1961), pp. 122-131. By permission.

didn't learn there had been a famine until I was seven years old and in the first grade at school.

INTERVIEWER: Your teacher told you?

BURG: No. During the war we were evacuated for a few months to a town on the Kazakh border. At school there I sat at the same desk as a girl named Zina and it seemed to me that her face was terribly pale, and I asked her why. She said, "Well, I was born in the hunger year of 1933, and that's why." Her parents had told her how horrible it had been—millions of people had died. But it was all news to me.

INTERVIEWER: Your own family was well situated then in Moscow and not affected?

BURG: Yes, they were professional people, well educated and well off. We lived in a three-room apartment, a very rare thing which we owed to my grandfather. He'd been the chief engineer when the apartment house was built. And so he got a three-room apartment to himself. We all lived there —father, mother, and two grandparents. My father worked as an economist, a specialist in labor planning. My mother once taught school. . . .

INTERVIEWER: Could you describe how your attitudes toward the regime formed as you were growing up?

BURG: I can never remember *liking* the way things were. I started having trouble as early as the seventh grade when we had lessons in the Constitution of 1936—Stalin's Constitution. I started asking nasty questions: "Why hasn't there been a Party Congress for such a long time? Why is it that the freedom of assembly guaranteed in the Constitution isn't practiced?" and so on.

INTERVIEWER: How did you know these things? Because of your parents' skepticism about the regime?

BURG: No—I think they were obvious. My parents, as a matter of fact, tried to protect me from anti-Soviet influences. For instance, they wouldn't have a radio set, so that I wouldn't be able to listen to foreign radio stations. When I was in the seventh grade I saved up my lunch money and bought a radio set of my own—which caused a big row in the family. They didn't like the idea of my having a radio set—I was in enough difficulty as it was.

INTERVIEWER: What sort of difficulty, exactly?

BURG: When I first started raising embarrassing questions, the teacher —a very nice and conscientious woman—tried to argue me out of it, and then she called in my parents for a private talk, which was very decent of her because she simply could have reported the whole thing to the secret police. Then a big scene followed at home:

"What are you doing? Do you want to send us all away to the camps? You're a grown boy—you've got to understand these are questions one doesn't ask.". . .

INTERVIEWER: How much enthusiasm for the regime did you find among the students and teachers in high school?

BURG: Foreigners seem to meet a lot of these enthusiasts. I met some of them later in life but not very many. The atmosphere in that Moscow high school, certainly, was neither very dedicated nor enthusiastic so far as the regime was concerned. I don't mean to imply it was one of conscious opposition—it wasn't. It was rather an attempt to *step aside* from all the propaganda and slogans and Komsomol work. For instance, one was aware that some of the teachers were trying to avoid letting literature become something to be read by parrots who would see only what the Central Committee had programmed for them—they really tried to teach the literature itself. And it seemed to me that one teacher in particular, a young woman, tried to give us more knowledge of history than you could find in the texts.

As for the students, there was a distinct atmosphere of boredom at the Komsomol meetings. Endless propagandistic talk of national aims, the duties of youth, the same phrases repeated over and over again, and most felt it was a tremendous waste of time. Nothing happened that anyone really cared about much, in a personal way—apart from the pressure to be a good, hard-working student.

INTERVIEWER: What, in fact, did they care about?

BURG: Above all, the boys cared about sports—for instance, soccer—and about their friends, their girls, their hobbies, their studies, and their reading. For most of the students, those things were far more real than what went on in the Komsomol meetings.

INTERVIEWER: But how do you explain the motives of those who do get involved in Party work at young ages?

BURG: Perhaps the most obvious explanation is that some have a strong *libido dominandi*—a will to power, a desire to organize and manipulate, and the Komsomol organization in the school is a fine vehicle for it.

Then you find those who are not awfully good at school but who want to get on—to make up for their inability to get high grades or be tremendous athletes. And so they try to show their talent for Komsomol work—a first-class Komsomol performance can help them on their way later in life, and they know it.

INTERVIEWER: One gets the impression of a determinedly nonpolitical atmosphere amongst the majority of the high-school students.

BURG: No, that's not quite accurate. There was a strangely split atmosphere, and in a way politics was omnipresent. Not only at Komsomol meetings but even in private one had to be on guard against saying unorthodox things. . . .

INTERVIEWER: How did the Party apparatus and the Komosomol bear on the life of the university? Did you find more or less the same system applied as in high school?

BURG: I should say it was very different. First of all, the political pressure was much, much greater. Remember this was still under Stalin— around 1952. Even the most casual remark would be brought up at a

Komsomol meeting and you would be accused of ideological error. The Komsomol leaders were capable of being far more ruthless. . . .

INTERVIEWER: Apart from attending meetings, what else did you have to do?

BURG: There was tremendous pressure—which did not exist in high school—to participate in "social work" while you were at the university. This meant, for example, going out every month and lecturing groups of workers—at that time we would go to the building site of the new University of Moscow. If you didn't do it, there was a good chance that you might be thrown out of the university. We were supposed to tell these laborers how lucky they were to be citizens of the first proletarian state. Or we were supposed to educate them for the coming elections.

INTERVIEWER: Were you supervised when you gave these talks? What did the workers make of them?

BURG: No one supervised us, but that didn't make them less unpleasant. The workers lived in barracks, in dreadful poverty, with men and women separated and many people to a room. Some complained that they had to wait years to marry, for lack of a place to live. I had known poor peasants before—as I've told you—but this was my first close contact with actual workers, and I was appalled by the conditions and felt ashamed and awkward. They would sometimes listen to you sullenly and ask questions: "You say we have the best system of health in the world—why do I have to wait three weeks to see a doctor? By that time my hand is so swollen I can't work for three months. Is it even worse in other countries?". . .

INTERVIEWER: To what extent did students engage in criticism of the regime amongst themselves?

BURG: From 1951 to 1954, practically all of us showed to the world a completely straight Communist face. You confined any critical views of the regime to your closest friends and even then unpleasant things sometimes happened. The danger of arrest and deportation was immediate. At times I thought: I am, if not a completely isolated person, perhaps a real white raven among the flock of good and orderly black crows. And I remember once theorizing to myself: Perhaps you think the way you do because of the generations of faulty bourgeois background behind you.

I was, frankly, very surprised to discover in 1955 and 1956, after the "Thaw" began, that there were a great number of other small circles of friends, thinking in much the same way, who had been cut off from each other.

INTERVIEWER: How did you become aware of the "Thaw"? Did it follow close after Stalin's death?

BURG: Not immediately—there was a short period of groping confusion. Then in the winter of '55 all of a sudden people started to talk about things they would never have mentioned previously. About art for instance. Painters who had always hidden their work because it was abstract or unorthodox would hold semiprivate exhibitions. You would hear by word of mouth that they were showing in their studio, and you would go, and find others. I once went to such an exhibition and found there a student whom I'd always considered to be a straight Party-liner—he wasn't at all. And gradually there was more talk about politics, especially after the Twentieth Party Congress in 1956 when Khrushchev made his famous denunciation of Stalin. One heard names like Bukharin and Trotsky that had been unmentionable before. I remember going to the apartment of a good friend and seeing a picture of Trotsky on the wall. I thought I was going mad. He said, "Well, I've been hiding this picture long enough. Now I want to flaunt it, at least for a while."

INTERVIEWER: Did the students discuss the immediate struggle for power after Stalin died—Beria, Malenkov, Khrushchev, and so on?

BURG: That was the sort of thing that remained confined to very close friends even after the Twentieth Party Congress. What we did talk about openly was the past of the Communist Party, especially the purges of the Party and intellectual leaders in the 'thirties. I remember one incident in particular that caused a huge shock to many of us. It involved Gronsky who had been a member of the Central Committee of the Party in the 'thirties and an editor of the literary magazine *Novy Mir*. In 1937 or 1938 he simply disappeared along with many others. And then in 1956 he was suddenly back in Moscow and was allowed to give a speech to a group of graduate students, and I went to the meeting to listen. Now perhaps you have never heard of Gronsky but he is quite a man—of peasant origin, he is simple and straightforward in his way, and cruel and dedicated and honest, typical of many of the old unsophisticated Bolsheviks who were eliminated by Stalin in the thirties. It was an experience simply to see him speaking in Moscow.

But what he said was, to us, astounding. He said that when Bukharin was arrested in 1937, he, Gronsky, had stood up in a meeting of the Central Committee and told Stalin that Bukharin may have had the wrong political view but he could *not* have been a traitor, because he had worked with him for twenty years and knew that Bukharin was a man of complete honesty. And Stalin looked at him and, in his heavy Georgian accent, had given orders that Gronsky be allowed to see Bukharin in Lefortovo prison, which is renowned as the most horrible prison in Moscow, the prison of torture.

And so Gronsky went and saw Bukharin and he challenged him to say that he was innocent but he found him terribly changed, completely broken. Bukharin looked at the ground—he had always looked people straight in the eye—and he said yes, yes, it was true, he was a traitor and an agent.

Now Gronsky still could not believe this, but after Bukharin was taken away, he was arrested himself, and they subjected him to week after week of awful torture and beating. But he would not sign a confession, he said, because: "How could I deceive the Party? I could not do it."

Later, Gronsky said, he was put in the same cell with one of the former chiefs of the Leningrad secret police who had confessed and Gronsky asked him if his confession was true. And the secret police chief had said: "You are probably the last man I'll talk to—they'll kill me soon. I tell you, there isn't a word of truth in the whole thing."

And then Gronsky said, "And what do you think, boys, what did I do? Do you think I took pity on him? No. I stood up and I socked him in the eye. I told him, 'What kind of a Bolshevik are you, deceiving the state in this way? The Party brought you so high and you are betraying the Party now'."

Gronsky was sent to Siberia for nineteen years, and now he was back. And by telling us experiences such as this he was trying to help the Party.

INTERVIEWER: How did the audience react to that speech?

BURG: The students who heard it were deeply shaken. They'd never heard *anyone* speak like that. As we were filing out, a Komsomol secretary —the last man from whom one would have expected protest—pointed up at Stalin's statue which loomed very large on the staircase and he said, "Why don't we throw this bastard out the window, Comrades?" But he didn't do anything. However, I know that at the Moscow Conservatory at the time, a portrait of Stalin actually was cut to shreds with knives.

THE POETRY OF PROTEST

INTERVIEWER: You've said that various attitudes, formerly hidden, started to be expressed more openly. What were they?

BURG: It seemed to me that among the intellectuals, there were four main dissenting attitudes. By far the most widespread was the one expressed by the popular young poet Evtushenko: "Comrades, let us give to the words their original meaning." That is, let us return to the original ideals of the Bolshevik revolution, let us go "back to Lenin," as some say. They hold that power should be returned to the people who should be able to elect representatives to local governing authorities—the soviets; these soviets should in turn elect higher organs of government right on up to the Council of Ministers—a quite decentralized system you see. Of course soviets exist today but they have no power, and the Council of Ministers is in the hands of the Party apparatus. The Party, in the view of this group, should stay a leading force, but instead of suppressing opposition, it must constantly regain the confidence of the masses, winning its position democratically over and over again.

INTERVIEWER: Against the opposition of another party?

BURG: Well, that's it. These people talk only about inner Party democracy—genuine discussion *within* the Party on large political issues. Of course they believe in doing away with cultural regimentation—all the dissenting intellectuals are for that. But they are unequivocally for a centrally planned economy—they believe a market economy would lead to inequality. In short what you have here is a group that would like to revive the egalitarian spirit of the revolution and turn it against the present regime.

INTERVIEWER: To a Westerner, it is particularly interesting that a poet should be the voice of significant political dissent.

BURG: Well, Evtushenko is the sort of poet you do not find in the West today—a poet of civic protest although some of his poems are lyrical and unpolitical. Perhaps he could be compared to Béranger or the Chartist poets, although he is less rhetorical. But he has a fresh and vigorous and lucid style, and his work has had an enormous vogue—his verses were bought up as soon as they appeared. Every little high school student felt it his duty to quote him, correctly or incorrectly.

INTERVIEWER: Did this neo-Bolshevism you speak about remain on the level of parlor and dormitory discussion—or did it ever express itself in some sort of action?

BURG: There have been a few incidents, most of them after I left the country; but they do indicate that something is going on. During the anniversary celebration of the Revolution in 1958 there was an attempt by some students in Leningrad to organize a demonstration. Some of them—not completely sober—climbed a decorative column near the Stock Exchange and started shouting, "Long Live the Hungarian Revolution! Down with the Government of the Fatties! Long Live Inner Party Democracy!" That sort of thing.

And earlier, in the history faculty of the University of Moscow, a dozen or so students started distributing leaflets directly to the workers in the district, attacking Khrushchev personally and calling for inner-Party democracy. A direct appeal to the proletariat, you see, quite in keeping with neo-Bolshevik ideology. They were arrested in the summer of 1957 and given three to eight years in prison—relatively mild sentences, if one considers the past. And in the fall of 1959 *Izvestia* carried a report of the arrest of a similar group which was meeting often and preparing to distribute leaflets.

INTERVIEWER: In all this, Khrushchev appears as a villain?

BURG: Oh yes. For the young intelligentsia, Khrushchev is one of those people to whom Stalin offered one of half-a-million jobs—a residue from the previous era. He really doesn't communicate to the intellectuals, I think, except for the endless jokes about him—obscene and otherwise. That is true for all the dissenters of the intelligentsia, neo-Bolshevik or not.

INTERVIEWER: What are some of the others?

BURG: Exactly opposed to the neo-Bolsheviks, you find a cult of the West—a sort of Utopian vision of capitalism as a "river of milk with banks of jam" as a Russian proverb puts it. You find this among some of the *stilyagi*—the so-called zoot-suiters and teddy-boys in the cities. These tend to be either the highly privileged sons of the very rich, or in contrast, the delinquent sons of poor urban workers. This sort of person isn't very political—he finds the regime dreary and oppressive and bad and simply assumes, or dreams, that what comes from the West must be good. Therefore he says he is anti-socialist and pro-capitalist.

You also find a kind of pro-capitalism among the students of the scientific technical colleges, at for instance the Moscow Institute of Aviation, an extremely well-regarded school whose standing might be compared to your M.I.T. Again the students aren't very sophisticated politically. Technological accomplishment, democracy, cultural freedom—all are lumped together for them in a Utopian picture of Western countries. But I never heard a concrete plan for converting Russia to a capitalist economy.

Then there is a third attitude which might be called "liberal socialism." These intellectuals are closer to the thinking of the revisionists in Poland. The Bolshevik idea was wrong, they argue, but socialism in Russia is inevitable and desirable.

So they would like to reform the country on the basis of a democratically run multi-party system, a socialist market economy, and cultural freedom. One heard such ideas as this: Industries would be owned through stock companies in which the workers would hold shares, and a workers' council would actually run each industry. Some of the most careful thinking goes along those lines.

Finally, among the intellectuals, you find a fourth attitude which has an old history in Russia—and that is nihilism: Life for the nihilists is a hopelessly shifting swamp of quicksand and all social systems can only end in horror and cruelty. "We should try to destroy the regime in Russia," a nihilistic student once told me, "but we should be *very* reserved about any millennium, any suggestion of a better life to come."

INTERVIEWER: You've been talking about dissenting views among the students and intellectuals. Were you aware of such views among the rest of the population?

BURG: Outside the intelligentsia in Russia, the most definite feeling of resistance you find is among the peasants. When I would visit the Russian countryside, I would meet hard resentment against city boys who are well fed and well dressed and wear a tie. In the countryside you sometimes encounter deep-seated hatred for the regime, and you sense the possibility of what Pushkin called "Russian mutiny, ruthless and senseless"—not a coherent plan but a sullen inchoate desire to throw over the whole social structure and to begin working from scratch toward some vague kind of muzhik's paradise.

But quite aside from the peasant hatreds, you do sense throughout Russia an attitude which is, really, the most widespread and formidable kind of dissent—the common feeling of stolid refusal on the part of the people to let the political aims of the regime seize hold of their private lives. Many people would describe themselves as good Soviet citizens; they might defend

Soviet foreign policy. But they refuse to go to the virgin lands or to develop Siberia or to sacrifice their leisure for "social works"; they dodge the relocation of young specialists. In short, despite the regime's demand of absolute "sacrifice of the personal for the common goal," they refuse to think in political terms and instead concentrate on their home life, their children, their sports, on simply trying to enjoy themselves.

This is not a consciously political attitude—it is, let us say, an existential attitude. But it runs very deep, and I believe it provides a kind of nourishing ground for the frankly political attitudes I described before.

INTERVIEWER: How widespread, proportionally, would you say, is active political thinking among the students?

BURG: I never took a Gallup Poll, of course, but I would guess about half the students in the universities are more or less nonpolitical. About 40 per cent, I think, do have consciously dissenting political views. And about 10 maybe 15 per cent are Party activists—professional idealists, you might say. . . .

TIGHTENING THE SCREWS

INTERVIEWER: Observing the Thaw and the Khrushchev regime from the West, do you feel that decision [the Thaw] has been confirmed?

BURG: Yes, particularly in the last year. But this business of the Thaw is very complex. It is a nice image but it involves many elements: the power struggle at the top, the intrigues within the Party, the pressure from the masses below for a better life, the craving of the intellectuals for more freedom. You have to take it all into account to understand any single policy.

As far as the condition of the masses is concerned, I think one can generalize and say that from 1953 to 1958, there was constant progress—more consumer goods, more housing, more food, and so on. For the intellectuals, of course, 1956 and 1957 were the freest years.

INTERVIEWER: You mean particularly freedom to publish.

BURG: Yes, but not only that. Evtushenko's poetry was published and Dudintsev's novel, *Not by Bread Alone*. And Ehrenburg's *Thaw* even before that—all of them frankly implying criticism of the regime. But public discussions went further. Evtushenko got up at a meeting of the Writers' Union and said, "We are *not* going to let those who would return to old times have their way. We'll rap their knuckles." And this summed up the illusory confidence of the opposition. For in 1958, the screws were tightened. Khrushchev met with a group of writers at one of his dachas and said that the Hungarian revolution would have been avoided if some of the early troublemakers had been shot. "*Our hand is not going to tremble*," he said. (At that point, I'm told, a woman writer fainted away.)

And after that, the liberal publishing policy stopped and instead of dealing with broad and burning social topics, literary discussion became much more technical and oblique—which kinds of artistic forms were "modern" and which were not, for example.

To be sure, there was still a spectrum of views: For instance, the magazine *Novy Mir* would take a more liberal line; the newspaper *Literature and Life,* a viciously reactionary one. It was nothing like the freedom of 1957 and 1958, but at least until 1960 hints of opposition were tolerated.

INTERVIEWER: And then?

BURG: And then came what has come to be called the U-turn in Soviet internal policy—although in fact it was taking place before the U-2 flight occurred. Suddenly the old Stalinist phrases reappeared: "the necessity for a new moral stimulus to labor," for example, which translated means that instead of stimulating productivity by making available more consumer goods, the administration would rely more heavily on coercion.

During 1960 and 1961 there have been crackdowns on private building —which grew considerably in the late 'fifties—and on private agriculture and private ownership of all sorts. There have been repressive measures against people doing work not deemed "socially useful"—for example, those who aren't employed by the state but make a living selling flowers or vegetables, from private plots, in the Moscow market. In short, the Party seems to have sensed a significant part of economic life slipping out of its control, and so it chose to tighten its grip, even though it meant slowing down the rise in living standards.

INTERVIEWER: What have been the effects on cultural life?

BURG: Curiously, the signs that a drastic suppression of cultural life may be on the way came after the economic measures I've mentioned—in fact, they are appearing right now, in the winter of 1960-61. One strong sign was the firing in December of Smirnov, the editor of the *Literary Gazette,* and his replacement by a downright Stalinist. I would fear that in the coming year we will see much more pressure on writers and artists and scholars generally to conform.

INTERVIEWER: You draw a dark picture.

BURG: Yes, but after telling you these grim stories, I would end on an optimistic note. For despite all the repression in Russia, perhaps the most significant thing is that Orwell's *1984* has not come to pass there. Despite the immense power of the Party, strong currents of independent and dissident thought have continued to flow in Russia, and there is no reason to think they will not continue to do so, short of a great purge. The intellectuals, the people, have not been able to break the power of the Party apparatus and they may not be able to do so for a long, long time, if ever. But neither has the Party been able to break all of them or their minds or their hopes.

INTERVIEWED BY R. B. SILVERS

Chapter 21

TWILIGHT OF TOTALITARIANISM?

*A seriously controverted question today—and one that is pregnant
with consequences for much of the world—is whether we are witnessing,
since the death of Stalin, the twilight of totalitarianism in the U.S.S.R.
or simply a form of relaxation which will leave the basic foundations of
Soviet despotism undisturbed.*

*This is not simply a matter of idle speculation, since our policies must
necessarily be affected by our evaluation of the nature, scope, future course,
and durability of Soviet totalitarian controls.*

*The four contributors to this discussion present variant and, to some
extent, conflicting positions.*

RUSSIA IN TRANSITION

Isaac Deutscher*

1

Who would still maintain nowadays that Soviet society has emerged
from the Stalin era in a state of petrified immobility, decayed and incapable
of inner movement and change? Yet, only a short time ago this was
the opinion commonly accepted; and a writer who defied it and claimed
that, despite all appearances to the contrary, the Soviet universe did move
seemed to argue from mere faith or wishfulness. Yes, the Soviet universe
does move. At times it even looks as if it were still a nebula unsteadily

* Author of *Stalin: A Political Biography*, and *The Prophet Armed*. Reprinted by
permission of Coward-McCann, Inc., from chapter 1 of *Russia in Transition* by Isaac
Deutscher. Copyright 1957 by Hamish Hamilton, Ltd. This essay was written January 1,
1957.

revolving around a shifting axis—a world in the making, rumbling with the tremor of inner dislocation and searching for balance and shape.

It is the twilight of totalitarianism that the U.S.S.R. is living through. Again, how many times have not "political scientists" told us that a society which has succumbed to totalitarian rule cannot disenthrall itself by its own efforts, and that such is "the structure of Soviet totalitarian power" (the like of which, it was said, history has never seen before!) that it can be overthrown only from the outside by mighty blows delivered in war. Yet, it is as a result of developments within the Soviet society that Stalinism is breaking down and dissolving; and it is the Stalinists themselves who are the subverters of their own orthodoxy.

It is nearly four years now since the U.S.S.R. has ceased to be ruled by an autocrat. None of Stalin's successors has "stepped into Stalin's shoes." Government by committee has taken the place of government by a single dictator. A French writer, still somewhat incredulous of the change, recalls that in Rome, when a Caesar died or was assassinated, his head was struck off the public monuments but "Caesar's body" was left intact until another head was put on it. Yet, in Moscow not one but many heads have been put on Caesar's body; and perhaps even the "body" is no longer the same. It is pointless to argue that it makes no difference for a nation whether it lives under the tyranny of an autocrat or under that of a "collective leadership." The essence of collective leadership is dispersal, diffusion, and therefore limitation of power. When government passes from one hand into many hands it can no longer be exercised in the same ruthless and unscrupulous manner in which it was exercised before. It becomes subject to checks and balances.

It is not only Caesar's head that has vanished. What used to be his strong arm, the power of the political police, is broken. The people are no longer paralyzed by fear of it. The stupendous machine of terror which overwhelmed so many people with so many false accusations and extorted so many false confessions of guilt, the machine which looked like an infernal *perpetuum mobile* at last invented by Stalin, has been brought to a standstill. Stalin's successors themselves have stopped it, afraid that even they would be caught by it; and they can hardly bring it back into motion, even if they wished to do so—the rust of moral opprobrium has eaten too deep into its cogs and wheels.

Nearly dissolved is also the Stalinist *univers concentrationnaire,* that grim world of slave labor camps which in the course of several decades sucked in, absorbed, and destroyed Russia's rebellious spirits and minds, leaving the nation intellectually impoverished and morally benumbed. Rehabilitated survivors of the Great Purges of the 1930's have returned from places of exile. There are, unfortunately, few, all too few, of them; and some may be broken and exhausted men. Yet, few as they are and such as they are, they are a leaven in the mind of post-Stalinist society—a reproach and a challenge to its disturbed conscience. Multitudes of other deportees have been allowed to leave concentration camps and to settle as "free workers" in the remote provinces of the north and the east. Temporarily or finally, the nightmare of mass deportations has ceased to haunt Russia.

The mind of the nation has stirred to new activity. Gone are the days when the whole of the Soviet Union was on its knees before the Leader and had to intone the same magic incantations, to believe in the same bizarre myths, and to keep its thoughts tightly closed to any impulse of doubt and criticism. To be sure, it is only slowly and painfully that people recover in their minds from monolithic uniformity and relearn to think for themselves and express their thoughts. Yet, a diversity of opinion, unknown for decades, has begun to show itself unmistakably and in many fields. A fresh gust of wind is blowing through the lecture halls and seminars of universities. Teachers and students are at last discussing their problems in relative freedom from inquisitorial control and dogmatic inhibition. The Stalinist tutelage over science was so barbarous and wasteful, even from the State's viewpoint, that it could no longer be maintained; and so it is perhaps not surprising that scientists should have regained freedom. What is more startling and politically important is the freedom for people to delve into the Soviet Union's recent history—a freedom still limited yet real. In Stalin's days this was the most closely guarded taboo, because the Stalin legend could survive only as long as the annals of the revolution and of the Bolshevik Party remained sealed and hidden away, especially from the young, who could find in their own memories no antidote to it.

Even now the annals have not been thrown open indiscriminately. They are being unsealed guardedly, one by one. The historians reveal their contents only gradually and in small doses. (The history of the October Revolution is still told in such a way that the giant figure of Trotsky is kept out of it—only his shadow is allowed to be shown casually, on the fringe of the revolutionary scene. But if Hamlet is still acted without the Prince of Denmark, the text of the play is becoming more and more authentic, while in Stalin's days the whole play, with the Prince cast as the villain, was apocryphal.) Every tiny particle of historical truth, wrested from the archives, is political dynamite, destructive not only of the Stalin myth proper, but also of those elements of orthodoxy which Stalin's epigoni are anxious to conserve. The old-Bolshevik heresies, of which even the middle-aged Russian of our days has known next to nothing, and the authors of those heresies, the ghostly apostates and traitors of the Stalin era, are suddenly revealed in a new light: the heresies can be seen as currents of legitimate Bolshevik thought and as part and parcel of Russia's revolutionary heritage; and the traitors—as great, perhaps tragic, figures of the revolution.

The rehabilitation, even partial, of past heresy militates against wholesale condemnation of present and future heresy. It corrodes the very core of orthodoxy to such an extent that the ruling group shrinks from the consequences. But the ruling group is no longer in a position to stop the process of Russia's historical education which forms now the quintessence of her political education.[1]

This is not the place to discuss further the intellectual ferment of the post-Stalin era, described elsewhere in this volume.[2] Suffice it to say, that in its initial phases de-Stalinization has been or was primarily the work of the intelligentsia. Writers, artists, scientists, and historians have been its pioneers. Their demands have coincided, at least in part, with the needs and wishes of the managerial groups and of influential circles in the party leadership. This accounts for the peculiarly limited, administrative-ideological character of the reforms carried out. Yet, as at the turn of the century, the intelligentsia has acted once again as the *burevestnik,* the storm finch. Its restlessness augurs the approach of an upheaval in which much wider social forces are likely to come into play.

2

The new working class which has emerged from the melting-pot of forced industrialization is potentially a political power of a magnitude hitherto unknown in Russian history. There are now in the U.S.S.R. four to five times as many industrial workers as there were before the revolution and even in the late 1920's. Large scale industry then employed not much more than three million wage laborers. It now employs at least fifteen million (not counting transport workers, state farm laborers, the medium and higher technical personnel, etc.). The working class has not only grown in size; its structure and outlook, too, have changed. These are not the old Russian workers who combined exceptional political *élan* with technological backwardness and semi-illiteracy. This, in its main sections, is a highly advanced working class which avidly assimilates skills and absorbs general knowledge. Among the young who now enter industry many have gone through secondary education. The change may be illustrated by the following comparison: about a quarter of a century ago as many as 75 per cent of the workers employed in engineering were classed as unskilled and only 25 per cent as skilled. In 1955 the proportion was exactly reversed: 75 per cent were skilled men and only 25 per cent re-

---

[1] It is difficult to find an analogy in any other nation at any time for so close an interdependence of history and politics as that which exists in the U.S.S.R. at present. The controversies of Soviet historians which preceded the 20th Congress foreshadowed Khrushchev's and Mikoyan's revelations at the Congress; and it was no matter of chance that even before Khrushchev, at the Congress itself, Professor Pankratova, an historian, made one of the most startling pronouncements. Since then the historians' disputes have gone on almost uninterruptedly.

[2] See the essay "Post-Stalinist Ferment of Ideas," p. 52 [of *Russia in Transition*].

mained unskilled. The relation is certainly not the same in other industries: engineering represents the most progressive sector of the economy. But the situation in this sector is highly significant, if only because engineering employs about one-third of the industrial manpower and accounts for about one-half of the total gross industrial output of the U.S.S.R.

The power of the Soviet bureaucracy was originally rooted in the weakness of the working class. The Russian proletariat was strong enough to carry out a social revolution in 1917, to overthrow the bourgeois regime, to lift the Bolsheviks to power, and to fight the civil wars to a victorious conclusion. But it was not strong enough to exercise actual proletarian dictatorship, to control those whom it had lifted to power, and to defend its own freedom against them. Here is indeed the key to the subsequent evolution or "degeneration" of the Soviet regime. By 1920-1921 the small working class which had made the revolution shrank to nearly half its size. (Not more than $1\frac{1}{2}$ to 2 million men remained then in industrial employment.) Of the rest many had perished in the civil wars; others had become commissars or civil servants; and still others had been driven by famine from town to country and never returned. Most factories were idle. Their workers, unable to earn a living by productive work, traded in black markets, stole goods from the factories, and became *déclassés*. As the old landlord class and the bourgeoisie had been crushed, as the peasantry was inherently incapable of assuming national leadership, and as the industrial working class was half dispersed and half demoralized, a social vacuum arose in which the new bureaucracy was the only active, organized, and organizing element. It filled the political vacuum and established its own preponderance.

Then, in the course of the 1920's, the working class was reassembled and reconstituted; and in the 1930's, the years of forced industrialization, its numbers grew rapidly. By now, however, the workers were powerless against the new Leviathan state. The bureaucracy was firmly entrenched in its positions, it accumulated power and privileges and held the nation by the throat. The working class could not at first derive strength from its own growth in numbers. That growth became, on the contrary, a new source of weakness. Most of the new workers were peasants, forcibly uprooted from the country, bewildered, lacking habits of industrial life, capacity for organization, political tradition, and self-confidence. In the turmoil of the Second World War and of its aftermath, society was once again thrown out of balance. It is only in this decade, in the 1950's, that the vastly expanded working class has been taking shape and consolidating as a modern social force, acquiring an urban industrial tradition, becoming aware of itself, and gaining confidence.

This new working class has so far lagged behind the intelligentsia in the political drive against Stalinism, although it has certainly had every sympathy with the intelligentsia's demand for freedom. However, the workers cannot possibly remain content with the administrative-ideological limitations of the post-Stalinist reform. They are certain to go eventually beyond the intelligentsia's demands and to give a distinctive proletarian meaning and content to the current ideas and slogans of democratization. Their thoughts and political passions are concentrating increasingly on the contradiction between their nominal and their actual position in society. Nominally, the workers are the ruling power in the nation. In the course of forty years this idea has been ceaselessly and persistently instilled into their minds. They could not help feeling edified, elevated, and even flattered by it. They cannot help feeling that they should, that they ought, and that they must be the ruling power. Yet, everyday experience tells them that the ruling power is the bureaucracy, not they. The bureaucracy's strong arm has imposed on them the Stalinist labor discipline. The bureaucracy alone has determined the trend of economic policy, the targets for the Five-Year Plans, the balance between producer and consumer goods, and the distribution of the national income. The bureaucracy alone has fixed the differential wage scales and wage rates creating a gulf between the upper and the lower strata. The bureaucracy has pulled the wires behind the Stakhanovite campaigns and, under the pretext of socialist emulation, set worker against worker and destroyed their solidarity. And, under Stalin's orders, it was the bureaucracy, aided by the labor aristocracy, that conducted a frenzied and relentless crusade against the instinctive egalitarianism of the masses.

Until recently the bureaucracy itself was subject to Stalin's whimsical terror and suffered from it even more than the working class did. This veiled, up to a point, the contrast between the theoretical notion of the proletarian dictatorship and the practice of bureaucratic rule. In their prostration before the Leader, worker and bureaucrat seemed to be equals. All the stronger did the beginning of de-Stalinization expose the contrast in their real positions. De-Stalinization was, at first, an act of the bureaucracy's self-determination. The civil servant and the manager were its first beneficiaries: freed from the Leader's despotic tutelage they began to breathe freely. This made the workers acutely aware of their own inferiority. However, the bureaucracy could not for any length of time reserve the benefits of de-Stalinization exclusively for itself. Having emancipated itself from the old terror, it willy-nilly relieved of it society as a whole. The workers too ceased to be haunted by the fear of the slave labor camp. Since that fear had been an essential ingredient of the Stalinist labor discipline, its disappearance entailed the end of that discipline. Malenkov's government proclaimed the obsolescence of the Stalinist labor code. That Draconic code had played its part in breaking the masses of the proletarianized peasantry to regular habits of industrial work; and only to those masses, bewildered and helpless, could it be applied. Vis-à-vis the new working class it was becoming increasingly useless and ineffective. A freer climate at the factory bench had indeed become the prerequisite for a steady rise in labor productivity and higher industrial efficiency.

Nor could the worker remain content merely with the relaxation of factory discipline. He began to use his freshly won freedom to protest against the pre-eminence of the managerial groups and of the bureaucracy. By far the most important phenomenon of the post-Stalin era is the evident revival of the long-suppressed egalitarian aspirations of the working class.

From this point the workers' approach to de-Stalinization begins to diverge from that of the intelligentsia. The men of the intelligentsia have been intensely interested in the political "liberalization," but socially they are conservative. It is they who have benefited from the inequalities of the Stalin era. Apart from individuals and small groups, who may rise intellectually above their own privileged position and sectional viewpoint, they can hardly wish to put an end to those inequalities and to upset the existing relationship between various groups and classes of Soviet society. They are inclined to preserve the social *status quo.* For the mass of the workers, on the other hand, the break with Stalinism implies in the first instance a break with the inequalities fostered by Stalinism.

It should not be imagined that the renascent egalitarianism of the masses is politically articulate. It has not yet found any clear and definite expression on the national scale. We know of no resolutions adopted by trade unions or by workers' meetings protesting against privilege and calling for equality. The workers have not yet been free enough to voice such demands or to make their voices heard. They may not even have been capable of formulating demands as people accustomed to autonomous trade-union and political acitvity would do. It is more than thirty years since they had ceased to form and formulate opinions, to put them forward at meetings, to stand up for them, to oppose the views of others, to vote, to carry the day, or to find themselves outvoted. It is more than thirty years since as a class they had ceased to have any real political life of their own. They could hardly recreate it overnight, even if those in power had put no obstacles in their way. Consequently the new egalitarianism expresses itself only locally, fitfully, and incoherently. It is only semiarticulate. It works through exercising pressure at the factory level. Its manifestations are fragmentary and scattered. Yet it makes itself felt as the social undertone to de-Stalinization, an undertone growing in volume and power.

Many recent acts of official policy have clearly reflected this egalitarian pressure from below. For the first time since 1931 the government has tackled a basic reform of wages; and although the reform has not yet taken final shape, the reversal of the antiegalitarian trend is already clearly discernible. Hitherto the piece rate has formed the basis of the whole wage system: at least 75 per cent of all industrial wages were, until quite recently, made up of piece rates, because these lend themselves much more easily than time rates to extreme differentiation. Within this system the so-called progressive piece rate was favored most of all, a method of payment under which the Stakhanovite producing 20, 30, and 40 per cent above the norm of output earned not just 20, 30, and 40 per cent more than the basic pay, but 30, 50, 80 per cent or even more. This method of payment, glorified in Stalin's days, as the supreme achievement of socialism, has now been declared as harmful to the interests of industry and workers alike. The grossly overadvertised Stakhanovite "movement" has been given a quiet burial. The time wage has again become the basic form of payment. It would be preposterous to see in this a triumph of socialism. Both the piece wage and the time wage—but the former much more than the latter —are essentially capitalist forms of payment; and it is only a measure of the retrograde character of some aspects of Stalin's labor policy that the return to the time wage should be regarded as progress. Yet progress it marks. It shows that workers no longer respond to the crude Stalinist appeal to their individual acquisitiveness which disrupted their class solidarity and that the government has been obliged to take note of this.

The year 1956 brought two further significant acts of labor policy: a rise by about one third in the lower categories of salaries and wages; and a new pension scheme with rates of pensions drastically revised in favor of workers and employees with low earnings. While in the Stalin era the purpose of almost every government decree in this field was to increase and widen the discrepancies between lower and higher earnings, the purpose of the recent increase has been to reduce such discrepancies.

The reawakening egalitarianism has likewise affected the government's educational policy. Beginning with the school year 1956-1957, all tuition fees have been abolished. It should be recalled that these had first been abolished early in the revolution, when Lenin's government pledged itself to secure free education for all. Poverty, cultural backwardness, and extreme scarcity of educational facilities made universal free education unattainable. The pledge remained nevertheless an important declaration of purpose. Stalin then reintroduced fees for secondary and academic education. Only the bureaucracy and the labor aristocracy could afford paying; and so education was almost defiantly reserved as a privilege for the children of the privileged. The tuition fee extended to the ranks of the young generation the social differences which Stalin's labor policy fostered among their parents. It tended to perpetuate and deepen the new stratification of society. On this ground Stalin's Communist critics, especially Trotsky, charged him with paving the way for a new bourgeoisie. All the more significant is the present abolition of all fees. This renewed pledge of universal free education, given by Stalin's successors, is of far greater practical value than was Lenin's pledge, because it is backed up by a tremendously expanded and still expanding school system. Even so, Soviet society has still a long way to go before it achieves genuine equality in

education. Only in the towns are there enough secondary schools to take
in all children—in the country there will not be enough of them before
1960 at the earliest. Universal academic education is *Zukunftsmusik*. All
the same, the abolition of school fees is the rulers' tribute to the new
egalitarianism. . . .

3

Of Stalin it has been said that like Peter the Great he used barbarous
means to drive barbarism out of Russia. Of Stalin's successors it may be
said that they drive Stalinism out of Russia by Stalinist methods.

The procedures of de-Stalinization are characterized by ambiguity, tor-
tuousness, and prevarication. At first it was allegedly only a matter of doing
away with the "cult of the individual," the grotesque adulation of the
Leader. When the issue was first posed, in the spring of 1953, even the
name of the "individual" who had been the object of the cult was not
mentioned; and up to the Twentieth Congress, up to February 1956, the
press still extolled the great Apostolic succession of "Marx-Engels-Lenin-
Stalin." The cult was abandoned, yet it was kept up. But having made
this first step, Stalin's successors could not help making the next one as
well. They had to denounce the Leader's "abuses of power." They denounced them piecemeal and shrunk from saying frankly that these were
Stalin's abuses. They found a scapegoat for him. As Beria had for fourteen years been Stalin's police chief, the responsibility for many of Stalin's
misdeeds could conveniently be placed on him.

For a time this particular scapegoat was constantly held before the
eyes of Russia and the world—until it refused to do service. For one thing,
Stalin could not be dissociated from the man who had for so long been
his police chief. For another, many of the worst "abuses," to mention only
the Great Purges of 1936-1938, had occurred before Beria took office in
Moscow. The denunciation of Beria implied the denunciation of Stalin
himself; and it led directly to it. It was as if the scapegoat had returned
from the wilderness to drag the real and the chief sinner down the steep
slope. It threatened to drag others as well. Malenkov, Khrushchev, Kaganovich, Molotov, Voroshilov, had all been Beria's close colleagues and
associates. The more they revealed of the horrors of the past, the stronger
grew their urge to exonerate themselves and to find a new scapegoat—this
time for themselves. That new scapegoat was none other than Stalin. "It
was all his fault, not ours" was the *leitmotif* of Khrushchev's secret speech
at the Twentieth Congress. "It was all his fault," *Pravda* then repeated
a hundred times, "but nothing has ever been wrong with our leading cadres
and with the working of our political institutions."

It was a most hazardous venture for Stalin's ex-associates to try and
acquit themselves at his expense. This scapegoat too—and what a giant

of a scapegoat it is!—is returning from the wilderness to drag them down. And so they are driven to try to re-exonerate Stalin, at least in part, in order to exonerate themselves.

Such attempts at "tricking history" and playing blindman's buff with it are all in good Stalinist style. In effect, Stalin's successors avoid telling the truth even when, on the face of it, truth should reflect credit on them. Their first move on their assumption of power was to repudiate the "doctors' plot." Yet, to this day they have not told the real story of that last great scandal of the Stalin era. What was hidden behind it? Who, apart from Stalin, staged it? And—for what purpose? Khrushchev's "secret" speech has not yet been published in the Soviet Union, a year after it was made; [nor by the date of publication of this volume]; and this despite the fact that its contents have in the meantime been shouted from the housetops outside the Soviet Union. Special commissions have been at work to review the many purges and trials and to rehabilitate and set free innocent victims. But their work has remained a secret. Not even a summary account of it has been published to explain officially the background, the motives, the dimensions, and the consequences of the purges. Masses of slave laborers have been released from concentration camps; and many prisoners have regained freedom under a series of amnesties. Yet, not a single announcement has been made to say how many convicts have benefited from the amnesties and how many have left the concentration camps. The present rulers are so afraid of revealing the real magnitude of the wrongs of the Stalin era, that they dare not even claim credit for righting the wrongs. They must behave like that "honest thief" who cannot return stolen goods to their owner otherwise than stealthily and under the cover of night.

How many of the "stolen goods" have in fact been returned?

The break with Stalinism was initiated under the slogan of a return to the "Leninist norms of inner party democracy." The Twentieth Congress was supposed to have brought about the practical restitution of those norms. Yet to anyone familiar with Bolshevik history it is obvious that this was far from being true. The Congress adopted all its resolutions by unanimous vote, in accordance with the best Stalinist custom. No *open* controversy or *direct* clash of opinion disturbed the smooth flow of its monolithic "debates." Not one in a hundred or so speakers dared to criticize Khrushchev or any other leader on any single point. Not a single major issue of national or international policy was in fact placed under discussion.

The change in the inner party regime has so far consisted in this: major decisions of policy are taken not by Khrushchev alone and not even by the eleven members of the Presidium but by the Central Committee which consists of 125 members (or 225 if alternate members are included). Inside that body free debate has apparently been restored; and differences of opinion have been resolved by majority vote. Only to this extent have

"Leninist norms" been re-established. But under Lenin the differences in the Central Committee were, as a rule, not kept secret from the party or even from the nation at large; and the rank and file freely expressed their own views on them. The post-Stalinist Central Committee has never yet aired its differences in the hearing of the whole party. Thus, only the upper hierarchy appears to be managed more or less in the Leninist way. The lower ranks are still ruled in the Stalinist manner, although far less harshly. In the long run the party cannot remain half free and half slave. Eventually the higher ranks will either share their newly won freedom with the lower ranks, or else they themselves must lose it.

4

Within the Soviet Union de-Stalinization has so far been carried out as a reform *from above,* a limited change initiated and controlled at every stage by those in power. This state of affairs has not been accidental. It has reflected the condition of Soviet society both *"above"* and *"below,"* in the first years after Stalin.

Above—powerful interests have obstructed reform, striving to restrict it to the narrowest possible limits, and insisting that the ruling group should in all circumstances hold the initiative firmly and not allow its hands to be forced by popular pressure. The attitude of the bureaucracy is by its very nature contradictory. The need to rationalize the working of the state machine and to free social relations from anachronistic encumbrances has induced the bureaucracy to favor reform. Yet, at the same time the bureaucracy has been increasingly afraid that this may imperil its social and political preponderance. The labor aristocracy has been troubled by a similar dilemma: It has been not less than the rest of the workers interested in doing away with the old terroristic labor discipline; but it cannot help viewing with apprehension the growing force of the egalitarian mood; and it resents the changes in labor policy which benefit the lower-paid workers without bringing compensatory advantages to the higher-paid. The various managerial groups and the military officers' corps are guided by analogous considerations; and they are, above all, anxious to maintain their authority. The attitude of these groups may be summed up thus: Reform from above? Yes, by all means. A revival of spontaneous movements from below? No, a thousand times no!

Below—everything has so far also favored reform from above. Toward the end of the Stalin era the mass of the people craved for a change but could do nothing to achieve it. They were not merely paralyzed by terror. Their political energy was hamstrung. No nation-wide, spontaneous yet articulate movements rose from below to confront the rulers with demands, to wrest concessions, to throw up new programs and new leaders, and to alter the balance of political forces. In 1953-1955 political prisoners and deportees struck in the remoteness of subpolar concentration camps, and these strikes led to the eventual dissolution of the camps. This was a struggle on the submerged fringe of the national life; but whoever has any sense of Russian history must have felt that when political prisoners were in a position to resume, after so long an interval, the struggle for their rights, Russia was on the move. Then the year 1956 brought much agitation to the universities of Leningrad, Moscow, and other cities. However, these and similar stirrings, symptomatic though they were, did not as yet add up to any real revival of the political energies in the depth of society.

It is not only that the working class had lost the habits of independent organization and spontaneous action. Stalinism had left a gap in the nation's political consciousness. It takes time to fill such a gap. It should be added that the gap is only relative. It is not by any means a vacuum. By spreading education, by arousing the people's intellectual curiosity, and by keeping alive the socialist tradition of the revolution, be it in a distorted and ecclesiastically dogmatic version, Stalinism has in fact accumulated many of the elements that should eventually go into the making of an extraordinarily high political consciousness. But Stalinism also forcibly prevented these elements from coalescing and cohering into an active social awareness and positive political thought. It increased enormously the potential political capacities of the people and systematically prevented the potential from becoming actual. Stalinist orthodoxy surrounded the nation's enriched and invigorated mind with the barbed wire of its canons. It inhibited people from observing realities, comparing them, and drawing conclusions. It intercepted inside their brains, as it were, every reflex of critical thought. It made impossible the communication of ideas and genuine political intercourse between individuals and groups. De-Stalinization has given scope to these constrained and arrested reflexes and has opened for them some channels of communication. This does not alter the fact that the people entered the new era in a state of political disability, confusion and inaction; and that any immediate change in the regime, or even in the political climate, could come only through reform from above.

Reform from above could be the work of Stalinists only. Had any of the old-Bolshevik oppositions—Trotskyist, Zinovievist, and Bukharinist—survived till this day, Khrushchev, Bulganin, Voroshilov & Company would surely have long since been removed from power and influence; and anti-Stalinists would have carried out de-Stalinization wholeheartedly and consistently. But the old oppositions had been exterminated; and new ones could not form themselves and grow under Stalinist rule. Yet the break with Stalinism had become a social and political necessity for the Soviet Union; and necessity works through such human material as it finds available. Thus, the job which it should have been the historic right and privilege of authentic anti-Stalinists to tackle has fallen to the Stalinists themselves, who cannot tackle it otherwise than halfheartedly and hypocritically. They have to undo much of their life's work in such a way as not to bring about their own undoing. Paradoxically, circumstances have forced Malenkov and Khrushchev to act, *up to a point,* as the executors of Trotsky's political testament. Their de-Stalinization is like the "dog's walking on his hinder legs." It is not done well; but the wonder is that it is done at all! [3] . . . No one, however, can foresee the actual rhythm of historic developments. In moments of great crises spontaneous mass movements *do* run ahead of all political groups, even the most radical ones, and of their programs and methods of action. So it was in Russia in February 1917. The workers then found in the Soviets, the Councils of *their* deputies, the institutions within which they learned to harmonize impulse and thought, to test conflicting programs, and to choose leaders. Of those institutions Stalinist Russia preserved no more than the name and the dead shells. Yet in the memory of the working class the Soviets have survived as *the* instruments of socialist government and self-government, *the* organs of a "workers' state." Even in Hungary, amid all the confusion of revolution and counterrevolution, the insurgent workers hastily formed their Councils. Any political revival in the working class of the U.S.S.R. is almost certain to lead to a revival of the Soviets which will once again become the testing ground of political programs, groups, and leaders, and the meeting place of spontaneous movements and political consciousness.

Whatever the future holds in store, a whole epoch is coming to a close—the epoch in the course of which the stupendous industrial and educational advance of the U.S.S.R. was accompanied by deep political lethargy and torpor in the masses. Stalinism did not and could not create that state of torpor; it spawned on it and sought to perpetuate it but was essentially its product. Basically, the apathy of the masses resulted from the extraordinary expenditure of all their energies in the great battles of the revolution. The aftermath of the French revolution was likewise one of a deadening lassitude in which the people "unlearned freedom," as Babeuf, who was so close to the masses, put it. Christian Rakovsky, recalling in his exile at Astrakhan in 1928, Babeuf's remark, added that it took the French forty years to relearn freedom. It has taken the Soviet people not less time—but there is no doubt that they are at last relearning freedom.

---

[3] History knows quite a few instances in which necessity worked through the most unsuitable human material when none other was available. Of course, whenever conservative rulers had to carry out progressive reforms, their work was self-contradictory and patchy; and it accumulated difficulties for the future. In my *Russia: What Next?* (1953), analyzing the social circumstances which would drive Stalin's successors to break with Stalinism, I compared their position with that of Czar Alexander II, the First Landlord of All the Russias, who, in conflict with the feudal landlord class and with himself, emancipated Russia's peasants from serfdom. Another example is Bismarck, the leader of the Junker class who transformed and adapted feudal Germany to the needs of bourgeois development. . . .

THE DURABILITY OF SOVIET DESPOTISM

BERTRAM D. WOLFE*

At every turn the historian encounters the unpredictable: contingency; historical accident; biological accident intruding itself into history, as when the death of a history-making person brings a change of direction; changes of mood; emergence of new situations; sudden leaps that seem to turn an accretion of little events into a big one; the complicated interaction of multiple determinants on every event; the unintended consequences of intended actions.

Still, history is not *so* open that any event is just as likely as any other. As in the flux of things we note continuing structures, as in biology we note heredity as well as variation and mutation, so in history there is an inter-relation between continuity and change.

Though all lands go through a history, and all orders and institutions are subject to continuous modification and ultimate transformation, there are some social orders or systems that are more markedly dynamic, more open, more mutable, even self-transforming, while others exhibit marked staying powers, their main outlines continuing to be discernibly the same through the most varied vicissitudes.

It may be difficult to determine except in retrospect just when a system may be said to change in ways so fundamental as to signify its transformation; still, it is possible and necessary to distinguish between self-conserving and self-transforming systems, between relatively open and relatively closed societies, and between changes so clearly of a secondary order that they may be designated within-system changes, and those so clearly fundamental that they involve changes in the system or basic societal structure. That this distinction may in practice be hard to make, that there may be gradations and borderline cases and sudden surprises, does not relieve us of this obligation. Merely to reiterate endlessly that all things change, without attempting to make such distinctions, is to stand helpless before history-in-the-making, helpless to evaluate and helpless to react.

* Author of *Three Who Made a Revolution; Six Keys to the Soviet System;* and *Khrushchev and Stalin's Ghost.* The selection is reprinted from the article by the same title in *Commentary,* Vol. 24 (August 1957), pp. 93-103. By permission of *Commentary* and the author. The article was first presented as a paper to open a Conference on Changes in Soviet Society Since Stalin's Death, held June 24 to 29, 1957, at Oxford University, under the sponsorship of St. Antony's College in association with the Congress for Cultural Freedom.

If we look at the Roman Empire, say from the time of Julius Caesar to the time of Julian the Apostate, or perhaps from Augustus to Romulus Augustulus, we can perceive that for three or four centuries, despite its many vicissitudes and changes, it continued in a meaningful and determinable sense to be the Roman Empire. In similar fashion we can easily select a good half millennium of continuity in the Byzantine Empire. Or if we take one of the most dynamic regions, Western Europe, in one of its more dynamic periods, we can note that monarchical absolutism had a continuity of several centuries. This is the more interesting because monarchical absolutism, though it was one of the more stable and monopolistically exclusive power systems of the modern Western world, was a *multi-centered system* in which the monarch was checked and limited by his need of support from groups, corporations, and interests that were organized independently of the central power: the castled, armed, and propertied nobility; the Church with its spiritual authority; the burghers of the wealthy, fortified towns.

It is the presence of these independent centers of corporate organization that makes Western monarchical absolutism an exception among the centralized, long-lasting power systems. It was these limiting forces that managed to exact the charters and constitutions, the right to determine size and length of service of armed levies, size and purpose of monetary contributions, thus ultimately transforming the absolute monarchy into the limited, constitutional monarchy of modern times. And it is from our own Western history, with its exceptional evolution, that we derive many of our unconscious preconceptions as to the inevitability, sweep, and comparative ease of change. To correct our one-sided view it is necessary to compare the characteristics of multi-centered Western absolutism with other, more "complete" and "perfected" forms of single-centered power and despotism.*

In the *samoderzhavie* of Muscovy we find a more truly single-centered power structure, stronger, more completely centralized, more monopolistic, more despotic, more unyielding in its rigid institutional framework than was the absolutism of Western Europe. The Czar early managed to subvert the independent boyars and substitute for them a state-service nobility. The crown possessed enormous crown lands and state serfs. Bondage, both to the state and to the state-service nobility, was instituted by the central power and adjusted to the purposes of the recruiting sergeant and the tax-gatherer. When the Emancipation came, in the 19th century, it was a state-decreed "revolution from above" (Alexander's own words for it), and

---

* This comparison is a central part of Karl A. Wittfogel's *Oriental Despotism: A Comparative Study of Total Power* (Yale, 1957). His attention is centered on the countries in which "the state became stronger than society" because of the need to undertake vast state irrigation and flood control works by *corvée* organization of the entire population, with the consequent assumption of enormous managerial functions. But his study is full of insights into modern, industry-based totalitarianism highly suggestive for the purposes of our theme.

carried with it state supervision and the decreeing of collective responsibility to the village *mir*.

To this universal state-service and state-bondage, we must add the features of Caesaro-papism: signifying a Czar and a state-dominated church. And the administrative-military nature of the Russian towns checked the rise of an independent burgher class.

Industrialization, too, was undertaken at the initiative of the state. From Peter I to Nicholas II, there were two centuries of state-ordained and -fostered industrialization; the state-owned and -managed basic industry —mining, metallurgy, munitions, railroad construction and operation—and some commercial monopolies, all crowned with a huge state banking and credit system.

The rudiments of a more multi-centered life were just beginning to develop in this powerful, single-center society when World War I added to the managerial state's concerns the total mobilization of men, money, materials, transport, and industry.

The "model" country in this new form of state enterprise was wartime Germany. The system of total management by the state for total war has been variously, but not very intelligibly, termed "state capitalism" and "state socialism." In any case, Lenin was quick to welcome this development as the "final transition form." In it, as in the heritage from the Czarist managerial autocratic state itself, he found much to build on in making his own transition to the new totalitarianism.

From Ivan the Terrible on, for a period of four centuries, "the state had been stronger than society" and had been ruled from a single center as a military, bureaucratic, managerial state. Amidst the most varied vicissitudes, including a time of troubles, wars, conquests, invasions, peasant insurrections, palace revolutions and revolutions from above, the powerful framework endured. Weakenings of the power structure, even breaches in it, were followed by a swift "restoration" of its basic outlines. When the strains of a world war finally caused its collapse, there came a brief interlude of loosening of the bonds. Then Lenin, even as he revolutionized, likewise "restored" much of the four-century-old heritage. Indeed, it was this "socialist restoration of autocracy" which Plekhanov had warned against, as early as the 1880's, as a danger inherent in the longed-for Russian revolution. He admonished the impatient Populists that unless all the bonds were first loosened and a free "Western" or "bourgeois-democratic" order were allowed to develop and mature, the seizure of power by would-be socialists could not but lead to a restoration of Oriental, autocratic despotism on a pseudo-socialist foundation with a pseudo-socialist "ruling caste." Things would be even worse, he warned Lenin in 1907, if this new "Inca ruling caste of Sons of the Sun" should make the fatal mistake of nationalizing the land, thus tightening even more the chains that bound the peasant to the auto-cratic state.

The term "Oriental despotism" applied to Russia in the course of this controversy among Russian socialists serves to remind us that there are yet more durable social formations with even greater built-in staying powers than those we have so far noted. These reckon their continuity not in centuries alone but even in millennia. As a Chinese historian once observed to me: "Your Renaissance was a fascinating period. We had seven of them." If we substitute restoration for renaissance, both in the sense of restoration of vigor and restoration of basic structure, he was right. For though China suffered upheavals, invasions, conquests, falls of dynasties, rebellions, interregnums, and times of trouble, a Chinese villager or a Chinese official of the 19th century, if transported to the China of two thousand or more years ago, would have found himself in a familiar institutional and ideological environment.

With the exception of Western monarchical absolutism, what all these enduring social structures had in common was a single power center, a managerial state, a lack of independent social orders and forms of property, an absence of checks on the flow of power to the center and the top, and an overwhelmingly powerful, self-perpetuating institutional framework.

Modern totalitarianism, I believe, is one of these comparatively closed and conservative societies, with a powerful and self-perpetuating institutional framework calculated to assimilate the changes which it intends and those which are forced upon it, in such fashion that—barring explosion from within or battering down from without—they tend to remain *within-system* changes in an enduring system.

At first glance the word conservative may seem out of place in speaking of a society that is organized revolution. And indeed there is a striking difference between Communist totalitarianism and all previous systems of absolute, despotic, undivided (and, in that sense, total) power. For whereas despotism, autocracy, and absolutism were bent on preserving the status quo, Communist totalitarianism is dedicated to "the future." This powerful institutional structure which tolerates no rival centers of organization has a vested interest in keeping things in flux. The omnipotence of state and ideology is maintained by carrying on a permanent revolution. Like Alexander's it is a revolution from above. But unlike Alexander's, its aim is nothing less than to keep a society atomized and to create, as rapidly and as completely as the recalcitrant human material and the refractory surrounding world will permit, a new man, a new society, and a new world.

Like the earlier systems referred to, it possesses a state that is stronger than society. Like them it represents a system of total, in the sense of undivided, power. Like them it lacks any organized and institutionalized checks on the flow of power to the top. Like them, it possesses a state-centered, state-dominated, state-managed, and, for the first time, a completely state-owned economy.

But if the other societies are distinguished by the high specific gravity of state ownership, state control, and state managerial function within the total activity of society, under Communist totalitarianism state ownership and state managerialism aspire to be total in a new sense. In the other cases, we have been contemplating total power in the sense of undivided power: power without significant rival centers of organization. But now, to the concept of *undivided power,* we must add that of *all-embracing power.*

No longer does the state limit itself to being "stronger than society." It now strives to be *coextensive* with society. Whereas the earlier power systems recognized certain limitations on their capacity to run everything, leaving room, for example, for pocket-handkerchief farms and the self-feeding of the *corvée* population, for private arts and crafts unconnected with the managerial concerns of the state, for certain types of private trade, and even finding room for village communal democracy under the watchful eye of the state overseer—what Wittfogel has aptly called "beggars' democracy"—the new totalitarianism strives to atomize society completely, to coordinate the dispersed villages into its centralized power system, to eliminate even the small private parcel of the *kolkhoznik,* already reduced from a "pocket handkerchief" to a mere swatch.

For the first time a total-power system in the earlier sense of undivided and unchallenged power aspires to be totalist or totalitarian in the further sense of converting the state-stronger-than-society into the state-coextensive-with-society.

We cannot deduce much from a comparison with other modern totalitarianisms. For historical and physical reasons Italian Fascism was more totalist in aspiration than in realization. And, though Nazism and Stalinist Communism suggestively moved towards each other, Nazism did not last long enough to complete its evolution. But it did live long enough to dispose of certain illusions concerning the supposed incompatibility of totalitarianism with certain aspects of modern life.

Thus it is widely held that the monopoly of total power and the attempt to embrace the totality of social life and activity are incompatible with the complexity of modern industry and advanced technology. But Germany adopted totalitarianism when it was the foremost country of Europe in industry and technology.

Indeed, it is precisely modern technology, with its all-embracing means of communication, its high-speed transmission of commands and reports and armed force to any point in a country, its mass-communication and mass-conditioning techniques and the like, which for the first time makes it possible for total (undivided) power to aspire to be totalist (all-embracing) power. That is what Herzen foreboded when he wrote: "Some day Jenghis Khan will return with the telegraph." If total power tends to arise wherever the state is stronger than society, totalitarian power can aspire to prevail over a great area and in great depth only where the state is both stronger than society and in possession of all the resources of modern technology.

Closely akin to the illusion of the incompatibility of totalitarianism with modern technology is the view that totalitarianism is "in the long run" incompatible with universal literacy, with advanced technological training, and with widespread higher or secondary-school education. Once more it is Germany that serves to remind us that one of the most highly literate and technologically trained peoples in the history of man adopted totalitarianism. Nay more, modern totalitarianism *requires* that everybody be able to read so that all can be made to read the same thing at the same moment. Not the ability to read, but the ability to choose between alternative types of reading, is a potential—and only a potential—liberating influence.

II

When Stalin died in 1953, Bolshevism was fifty years old. Its distinctive views on organization, centralization, and the guardianship or dictatorship of a vanguard or elite date from Lenin's programmatic writings of 1902 (*Where to Begin; What Is to Be Done?*). His separate party machine, which he controlled with an authoritarian hand, dates from the Bolshevik-Menshevik split of 1903 in the Russian Social Democratic party.

During these fifty years Bolshevism had had only two authoritative leaders, each of whom set the stamp of his personality upon it. Lenin, as we have suggested, inherited much from Czarist autocracy, yet his totalitarianism is different in principle from the old Muscovite despotism. He regarded himself as an orthodox Marxist, building upon and enlarging some aspects of Marx's conceptions while ignoring, altering, or misrepresenting others. His Marxism was so different from Marx's that a not unfriendly commentator, Charles Rappoport, called it *Marxisme à la Tartare*. Stalin's Leninism, in turn, differed enough from Lenin's that we might term it *Marxisme à la mode caucasienne*. Yet there is discernibly more continuity between Stalin and Lenin than between Lenin and Marx. The changes Stalin introduced involved the continuation and enlargement of certain elements in Lenin's methods and conceptions, along with the alteration of others. He inherited and used, now in Leninist, now in his own "Stalinist" fashion, an institutional framework involving a party machine, a state machine, a doctrine of infallibility, an ideology, and the determination to extend the totalization of power, to transform the Russian into the "New Communist Man," and win the world for Communism.

With Stalin's death, once more there are new leaders or a new leader. It is impossible to believe that this new personal imprint will not make alterations in Stalinism as Stalin did in Leninism.

But it seems to me useful, after four years of unsystematic talk about changes, that we should remind ourselves that the "new men" are not so new, that they have inherited a going concern, and that actually we are

confronting changes within a single-centered, closed, highly centralized
society run by a power that is both undivided and all embracing. And we
should remind ourselves, too, that such societies as I have classed it
with have tended to exhibit built-in staying powers and a perdurability
despite changes like the death of a despot, an oligarchical interregnum, or
a struggle for succession.

These "new men" are, of course, Stalin's men. They would not now
have any claim to power over a great nation were it not that they managed
to be the surviving close lieutenants at the moment of Stalin's death. It
is my impression that they are smallish men. There is a principle of selection in personal despotisms which surrounds the despot with courtiers,
sycophants, executants, and rules out original and challenging minds. This
almost guarantees a crisis of succession where there is no system of legitimacy,
until a new dictator emerges. Moreover, the heirs are no longer young
(Khrushchev is sixty-three), so that a fresh crisis of succession may well
supervene before the present muted and restricted crisis is over.

I would not write these "smallish men" too small, however, for when you
have a sixth of the earth, 200,000,000 population, and a total state economy
and a great empire to practice on, you learn other trades besides that of
courtier or faction lieutenant. Even so, not one of them at present exhibits
the originality and the high charge of energy and intellect that characterized
Lenin, or the grosser but no less original demonic force of Stalin.

Whenever a despot dies, there is a universal expectation of change. The
new men have had to take account of it, and have taken advantage of it to
introduce changes which the old tyrant made seem desirable even to his
lieutenants: they have taken advantage of the expectation of change to
rationalize elements of a system which has no organized, independent forces
which might change it from below, and to make limited concessions while
they are consolidating their power. But the institutional framework they
have inherited is one they intend to maintain.

Some parts of this power machine are now more than a half century
old, others date from 1917, others from the consolidation of the Stalinist
regime in industry, agriculture, politics, and culture in the 30's. But even
these last have been established for more than two decades.

What the epigoni have inherited is no small heritage: a completely
atomized society;* a monolithic, monopolistic party; a single-party state;
a regime of absolute force supplemented by persuasion or by continuous
psychological warfare upon its people; a managerial bureaucracy accustomed
to execute orders (with a little elbow room for regularized evasion); a
centrally managed, totally state-owned and state-regulated economy including farms, factories, banks, transport and communications, and all trade
domestic and foreign; an established dogmatic priority for the branches of

---

* This does not apply to the Soviet empire but only to the Soviet Union. In general
I have omitted any consideration of the empire here.

industry which underlie the power of the state; a bare subsistence economy for the bulk of the producers; a completely statized and "collectivized" agriculture which, though it has never solved the problem of productivity, threatens to reduce even the small parcel to a mere "garden adornment"; a powerful, if one-sided, forced tempo industry centralized even beyond the point of rationality from the standpoint of totalitarianism itself; the techniques and momentum of a succession of Five Year Plans of which the present is the sixth; a completely managed and controlled culture (except for the most secret recesses of the spirit which even modern technology cannot reach); a monopoly of all the means of expression and communication; a state-owned system of "criticism"; an infallible doctrine stemming from infallible authorities, interpreted and applied by an infallible party led by an infallible leader or a clique of infallible leaders, in any case by an infallible "summit"; a method of advance by zigzags toward basically unchanging goals; a system of promotion, demotion, correction of error, modification of strategy and tactics and elimination of difference by fiat from the summit, implemented by purges of varying scope and intensity; a commitment to continuing revolution from above until the Soviet subject has been remade according to the blueprint of the men in the Kremlin and until Communism has won the world.

It is in this heritage that these men were formed. In this they believe. It is the weight and power and internal dynamics of this heritage that in part inhibit, in part shape such changes as these men undertake, and enter as a powerful influence into the changes which they make involuntarily.

It would require a separate study to attempt an inquiry into what is fundamental to totalitarianism, so that a change in it would represent a "change in the system," and what is of a more superficial order, so that a change may readily be recognized as a "within-system" change.* Here we shall have to limit ourselves to a glance at a few post-Stalin political developments. The first change that obtrudes itself is "collective leadership."

The party statutes do not provide for an authoritative leader, a dictator or *vozhd*. Just as this, the most centralized great power, still professes to be federal, a mere union of autonomous republics, so the party statutes have always proclaimed party democracy and collective leadership.

It was not hard to predict that Stalin's orphaned heirs would proclaim a collective leadership at the moment of his death, even as they began the maneuvers that led to the emergence of a still narrower ruling group (triumvirate, duumvirate) and a muted struggle for the succession. Stalin, too, for a half decade found it necessary to proclaim a collective leadership

* At the Oxford Conference to which this paper was presented, Leonard Schapiro offered a brief and simple criterion of distinction between within-system changes and changes in the system. He said: "Any changes which leave undisturbed the monopoly of power by the party and its leaders may be regarded as a 'within-system' change. Any firm limitation upon this monopoly of power would represent a 'change-in-the-system.'"

and pose as its faithful wheelhorse, and took a full decade before he killed his first rivals.

Stalin's successors had the same reasons as he for proclaiming the collective leadership of the Politburo, and some additional ones as well. The harrowing and demoralizing experiences of the 30's, the signs of the beginnings of a new mass purge (in the "poison doctors' case") a few months before Stalin's death, the terror that gripped even his closest collaborators, and their justified fears of each other—all combined to make necessary the proclamation of a "collective leadership."

There is nothing inherently incompatible with total, undivided power, nor with totalitarian, all-embracing power, in the rule of an oligarchy, or in an interregnum between dictators or despots. What is noteworthy here is the swiftness with which the first triumvirate (Malenkov, Molotov, Beria) were demoted, compelled to confess unfitness, and, in the case of Beria, killed. It took Stalin ten years to shed the blood of potential rivals or aspirants to power; Beria disappeared in a few months. In less than two years the skeptical were obliged to recognize that Khrushchev was "more equal than the others" and was making all the important programmatic declarations.* Those who follow the Soviet press can perceive that Khrushchev is already the *Khozyain* (Boss), though not yet the *Vozhd* (Führer, Duce, Charismatic Leader).

This is not to say that Khrushchev must necessarily emerge as the undisputed and authoritative leader in the sense that either Stalin or Lenin was. Combinations and counter-forces in the oligarchy and limitations in his own capacity may check or slow or, in view of his age, even nullify the manifest trend. But triumvirates, duumvirates, directories are notoriously transitional in the succession to a despot where there is no legitimacy in providing a successor, and no checks against the flow of power to the top. Moreover, the whole dynamics of dictatorship calls for a personal dictator, authoritarianism for an authority, infallible doctrine for an infallible interpreter, totally militarized life for a supreme commander, and centralized, undivided, all-embracing, and "messianic" power for a "charismatic" symbol and tenant of authority. Unless the "collective leadership" should broaden instead of narrowing as it already has, unless power should flood down into the basic units of the party (which was not the case even in Lenin's day), and then leak out into self-organizing corporate bodies independent of the state, restoring some initiative to society as against the state—in short, unless the whole trend of totalitarianism is not merely slowed (as may be expected during an interregnum) but actually reversed, there is good reason to regard a "directory" or a "duumvirate" as transitory.

* For a time Bulganin made the "purely" economic pronouncements, but that period seems to have ended with the Twentieth Congress.

Both purge and terror were instituted by Lenin and "perfected" and "over-perfected" by Stalin. Leaving on one side the purely personal element (paranoia and relish for vengeance), both purge in the party and terror in society as a whole serve many of the "rational" purposes of the totalitarian regime: the establishment of the infallibility of the party, of its summit, and its doctrine; the maintenance of the party in a "state of grace" (zeal, doctrinal purity, fanatical devotion, discipline, subordination, total mobilization); the atomization of society as a whole; the breaking up of all non-state conformations and centers of solidarity; the turn-over in the elite, demotion of deadwood and promotion of new forces; the supplying of scapegoats for every error and for signaling a change of line; the maintenance of the priority of heavy industry, of forced savings for capital investment, of unquestioned command and relative efficiency in production, of "collectivization" in agriculture, of control in culture, and a number of similar objectives of the totalist state.

All of these institutions have been so well established that to a large extent they are now taken for granted. Stalin himself promised in 1939 that there would never again be a mass purge. Except in the case of the army and the Jewish writers, the purge became physically more moderate, until, with increasing marks of paranoia, Stalin gave every sign of opening another era of mass purge a few months before his death. The first thing the heirs did as they gathered round the corpse was to call off the purge, both because it had no "rational" purpose and because it had threatened to involve most of them.

But it would be a mistake to believe that the "moderated" purge can be dispensed with. In the preparation of the 20th Congress the heirs showed how well they had mastered the "Leninist norms," according to which every congress since the 10th had been prepared for by a prior purge of the party organization. All the regional secretaries and leading committees were "renewed," 37 per cent of those who attended the 19th Congress disappeared from public view, 44 per cent of the Central Committee failed to be elected as delegates or to be re-elected to the new Committee. All we can say is that the purge today resembles those of Stalin's "benign" periods or of Lenin's day. Yet the liquidation of Beria and at least twenty-five of his friends shows that the techniques of the blood purge have not been forgotten. That the party ranks breathe easier and are glad of the self-denying ordinance of the leaders in the struggle for position we do not doubt. But there is no evidence that the party ranks ordered this change, or could do so, or would venture to try.

The terror in society as a whole has also diminished. No longer are there such bloody tasks as forced collectivization to carry through. Habitual obedience, the amnesties and concessions of an interregnum, the shortage of manpower for industry, agriculture, and the army because of continued expansion, and the deficit of wartime births that should now have been reaching the labor age—these and many other things account for the fact that artists and writers, workmen and peasants and managers, do not at this moment feel that public reproof (which they are very quick indeed to heed) must necessarily be followed by incarceration in the concentration camp. In a time of manpower shortages, the fact that the concentration camp is the most wasteful and least productive way of exploiting manpower is especially felt. The camps are gentler now, yet they are there. Their size is shrinking, yet no one dares to propose their abolition or even to take public notice of them. Even as this paper is being prepared, at least one new class of young people, the rebellious student youth, is being moved in increasing numbers into the camps.

The police has been downgraded and, in a regime so in need of naked force, the army has been upgraded: i.e. given more internal political functions. The public prosecutors have been given more control of trials and pre-trial inquisitions—like making the fox the guardian of the chicken coop. There are some other minor legal reforms. Above all there has been much fuss made about a promise to codify and regularize the laws.

This new code was begun in Stalin's last months. It was promised "within sixty days" by Lavrentii Beria when his star seemed in the ascendant. It has not been promulgated yet, four years after Stalin's and almost four years after Beria's death. Sight unseen, we can predict that the new code will not touch the foundations of the totalist state: it will not alter the subservience of courts and laws and prosecutors and judges and police to the will and purposes of the oligarchy or the single leader. It is necessary to remember that any total power, and *a fortiori* any totalist power, may obey its own laws whenever it suits it to do so without giving those laws power over itself or making them into limitations upon its powers. A power center that is both legislator and administrator and judge and enforcer and even self-pronounced infallible "critic" of its own acts, may declare any activity it pleases a crime. In the Soviet Union, even loyalty to the underlying principles on which the state itself was founded has been declared a degrading crime and punished with incredible cruelty. How easily this totalist state may set aside its laws and negate its most solemn and "binding" promises is evidenced anew—after the proclamation of "socialist legality"—by the sudden repudiation by the "workers' state" of the state debt owed to the workers themselves, without so much as the possibility of anybody making a murmur. The owners of the repudiated bonds, in which they had invested their now wiped out compulsory savings, were even obliged to hold meetings and pass resolutions in which to express their delight at being expropriated.

The longer such a regime endures the more it has need of regularization of the duties and expectations of its subjects, even as it keeps up undiminished its powers of sudden reversal and unpredictable and unlimited intervention. The only guarantee against a totally powerful state is the existence of non-state organizations capable of effective control of or effective pressure on the governmental power. Otherwise, to attempt to check, or limit, or even question is to invite the fury of exemplary punishment.

"Betwixt subject and subject [Locke wrote of the defenders of despotism], they will grant, there must be measures, laws and judgments for their mutual peace and security. But as for the ruler, he ought to be absolute, and is above all such circumstances; because he has the power to do more hurt and wrong, it is right when he does it. To ask how you may be guarded from harm or injury on that side . . . is the voice of faction and rebellion. . . . The very question can scarcely be borne. They are ready to tell you it deserves death only to ask after safety. . . ."

It is well for us to remember that the most despotic rulers have on occasion handed down elaborate law codes. The famous and in many ways justly admired Roman Code was compiled and proclaimed only after the emperor himself had become a god, no longer subject to question or limitation, only to worship. Though laws must multiply and be regularized so that the subjects may know what is expected of them and what they can count on in their relations with each other wherever the central power is unaffected, the lack of independent courts, of independent power groups or corporate bodies, of an independent press and public opinion, deprives these laws of any binding force upon the rulers. In Communist totalitarianism, the place of imperial divinity is taken by the infallibility of doctrine, the dogmatic untouchability of the dictatorship, the infallibility of the masters of the infallible doctrine, and by such spiritual demiurges as "revolutionary consciousness," "historical necessity," and "the interests of the revolution and of the people." Those who *know* where History is going surely have the right and duty to see to it that she goes there.

"The scientific concept, dictatorship," Lenin reminds us with beautiful simplicity, "means neither more nor less than unlimited power, resting directly on force, not limited by anything, not restricted by any laws or any absolute rules. Nothing else but that."

And to Commissar of Justice Kursky, when he was elaborating the first legal code, Lenin wrote:

"[My] draft is rough . . . but the basic thought, I hope, is clear: openly to set forth the proposition straightforward in principle and straightforward politically (and not merely in the narrow juridical sense) which motivates the *essence* and *justification* of terror, its necessity, its limits.

"The court should not eliminate the terror: to promise that would be either to deceive oneself or to deceive others, but should give it a foundation and a legalization in principle, clearly, without falsification and without embellishment. It is necessary to formulate it as broadly as possible, for only a revolutionary consciousness of justice and a revolutionary conscience will put conditions upon its application in practice, on a more or a less broad scale."

In these regards the new men do not have to "return to Leninist norms," for they have never been abandoned for a moment.

If we can hope for, even perhaps count on, the diminution of the apocalyptic element in the ideology of a going, long-lasting society, we must remind ourselves that Leninism was peculiar in that its central "ideas" were always ideas about organization, and they have been strengthened rather than weakened in the course of time.

Bolshevism was born in an organizational feud about the definition of a party member, and who should control a paper (*Iskra*) which should act both as guardian of the doctrine and organizational core of the party. "Give me an organization," Lenin wrote at the outset of his career as a Leninist, "and I will turn Russia upside down." The organization he wanted, he explained, must be one in which "bureaucratism" prevailed against "democratism," "centralism" against "autonomy," which "strives to go from the top downward, and defends the enlargement of the rights and plenary powers of the central body against the parts." When at the 1903 Congress an exalter of the Central Committee urged that it should become the "omnipresent and one," the all-pervasive, all-informing and all-uniting "spirit," Lenin cried out from his seat: *"Ne dukh, a kulak!"* ("Not spirit, but fist!"). The idea of the rule of the elite, the idea of a vanguard party, the idea of the hatefulness of all other classes and the untrustworthiness of the working class, the idea that the working class too required a dictator or overseer to compel it to its mission—it is amazing to note that these "ideas" about organization form the very core of Leninism as a special ideology. Far from "eroding" or growing "weak" and merely "decorative," it is just precisely these structural principles which have grown and expanded, and become systematized.

Resentments, discontent, longing for a less oppressive regime and an easier lot exist under despotisms, autocracies, total-power states, and totalist states, even as in other social orders. Indeed, whenever hope or expectation stirs they are apt to become endemic and intense. The problem of "state-craft" in a despotism is that of preventing the discontent and longing from assuming *organized* form. Since the totalist state penetrates all social organizations and uses them as transmission belts (destroying whatever organization it cannot assimilate to its purposes and structure), it is particularly adapted to keeping discontent fragmented and unorganized.

By 1936, Lenin's central idea of an elite, single-centered dictatorship had gotten into the "most democratic constitution in the world" as Article 126, which proclaimed the party to be "the vanguard of the working people and the leading core of all organizations both social and state." And last summer, when Khrushchev and the rest were summing up the discussion over Stalin, they declared in *Pravda:* "As for our country, the Communist Party has been and will be the *only master* of the *minds,* the *thoughts,* the *only spokesman, leader and organizer* of the people" (my italics).

It is foolhardy to believe that they did not mean it, self-deluding to persuade ourselves that the forces pressing for concessions within the country are likely to find the road open to separate and effective corporate organization, which is the condition precedent to the development of a limited, multicentered state and a society which is stronger than it.

Even before Stalin died, we got evidence that the spirit of man is wayward and not as easily subjected as his body—the mass desertions at the war's end; the escape of millions who "voted with their feet" against totalitarianism; the two out of three "Chinese volunteers" in the Korean prison camps who preferred exile under precarious and humiliating "displaced person" conditions to return to their native scenes and homes. Since Stalin's death there have been East Berlin and Pilsen, Poznan and Vorkuta, Warsaw and Budapest, to prove that men will sometimes stand up unarmed to tanks and cannon and machine guns. They have proved too that the armies of the conquered lands have never been the pliant instruments of the Kremlin that faint-hearted men thought they were.

We have seen that forty years of *Gleichschaltung,* corruption, and terror have not rooted out of the artist the ineradicable notion that sincerity to his creative vision is more to be desired than *partiinost* and *ideinost.* We have seen that the youth—although the faint-hearted had thought they would be turned off the conveyer-belt as "little monsters"—are born young still, and therefore plastic, receptive, questioning, capable of illusion and disillusion, of "youthful idealism" and doubt and rebellion. Now the expulsions among the university youth are for the first time providing a pariah elite as a possible leadership to future undergrounds which may form under even this most efficiently regimented of societies.

I have never for a moment ceased to cast about for grounds of hope: that weaker heirs might make less efficient use of the terrible engines of total power; that a struggle or series of struggles for the succession might compel a contender to go outside the inner circles and summon social forces in the lower ranks of the party or outside of it into some sort of independent existence; that the army, disgraced as no other in all history by the charge that it gave birth to traitors by the thousands in its general staff, might develop sufficient independence from the party to make it a rival power center or an organized pressure body; that intellectuals, technicians, students might somehow break through the barriers that hinder the conversion of discontent into an organized, independent force.

But if I put the emphasis on the nature of the Soviet institutional framework and its built-in staying powers, it is by way of bending the stick in order to straighten it out. For the Western world has found it hard (or so it has seemed to me) to gaze straight and steadily at the head of Medusa, even if only in the reflecting shield of theoretical analysis. Brought up in a world of flux and openness, we find it hard to believe in the durability of despotic systems. Our hopes and longings are apt to betray us again and again into a readiness to be deceived by others or to deceive ourselves. And the "journalistic" nature of our culture has made us too ready to inflate the new because that alone is "news," while we neglect to put it into its tiresomely "repetitious" historical and institutional setting.

From the NEP to Socialism in One Country; from the Popular Front and Collective Security to the Grant Alliance and One World; from Peaceful Coexistence to the Geneva Spirit—the occupational hazard of the Western intellectual has been not to read too little but to read too much into planned changes, involuntary changes, and even into mere tactical maneuvers and verbal asseverations.

Each has been hailed in turn as the softening of the war of the totalist state on its own people and the world, as the long awaited "inevitable change" or "fundamental transformation"; "the sobering that comes from the responsibilities of power"; the "response to the pressure of the recognition of reality"; the growing modification of totalist power by "a rationalist technocracy"; the sobering "effect of privilege upon a new privileged class"; the "rise of a limited and traditionalist despotism"; a "feeling of responsibility to Russia as against World Revolution"; the "quiet digestion period of a sated beast of prey" no longer on the prowl; the "diffusion of authority which could lead to a constitutional despotism"; the "mellowing process that sooner or later overtakes all militant movements"; the second thoughts on the struggle for the world which have come at long last "from a recognition of the universal and mutual destructiveness of nuclear war"; the "inevitable work of erosion upon the totalitarian edifice." (Each of these expressions is quoted from some highly respected authority of Soviet affairs in the Anglo-Saxon world.)

Because of the nature of our mental climate and our longings, because too of the injection of "revolutionary methods" into diplomacy in a polarized and antagonistic world, the danger does not lie in a failure on our part to watch for change, nor in a failure to "test"—though generally without sufficient skepticism—the meaning of each verbal declaration. No, "the main danger," as the Communists would say, has not lain in insensitivity to hope, but in too ready self-deception.

SOVIET SOCIETY IN TRANSITION

Raymond Aron*

The future development of Soviet society is manifestly one of the most crucial issues under investigation by social scientists today. Studies in this field are necessarily speculative not only for the obvious reason that they deal with future unknowns but because there has been so little opportunity for outsiders to familiarize themselves with the Soviet-Russian reality. Social scientists face a further difficulty in that there are several possible—and somewhat incompatible—approaches, or bases, for an interpretation of Soviet society.

Studies to date have proceeded along three principal avenues of approach, investigating Soviet society, first, as an industrial civilization; second, as a totalitarian system (dealt with as a unique phenomenon without historical precedent); third, as the successor to Tsarist Russia (with stress laid on aspects of cultural continuity between past and present). Any of these conceptual approaches can lead to confusion in attempts to predict the Soviet future. In the first instance, little is known as yet about the laws of economic development in a system of the Soviet type. Analyses stressing the totalitarian aspect often suffer for lack of a clear definition of totalitarianism itself (e.g., does it date back to Lenin or just to Stalin?). As for the continuity approach, stress on the constant factors in Russian culture as a key to the future can too easily lead to underestimation or disregard of the impact of economic and political changes.

Synthesizing the issues implied by these three approaches, the basic question to be answered may be phrased: To what extent, if any, will the development of industrial civilization bring about an evolution of the Soviet totalitarian regime and of the social forms inherited from the past? What direction will this evolution take? Some observers, in attempting to answer this question, have put forward theses based on one or another of the above schemes of interpretation in virtual disregard of the issues raised by the others.

Two such theses are worth mention as categorical and contradictory extremes of opinion; both, in this writer's view, are invalid. One asserts that the stupendous development of productive forces in the Soviet Union will pave the way to democracy; the other, that the totalitarian regime is invulnerable to economic forces.

* Professor of Sociology at the Sorbonne. Author of *The Opium of the Intellectuals* and *A Century of Total War*. The selection is from *Problems of Communism*, Vol. VI (November-December 1957), pp. 5-9. By permission.

EXTREMIST THEORIES

The first of these has been expounded in particularly crude terms by Mr. Isaac Deutscher. His formation lends itself to numerous objections, raised so often already that they can be dealt with briefly here. The explanation that terrorism and ideological orthodoxy are determined solely by the needs of primary accumulation or of the Five-Year Plans runs up against the incontrovertible fact that the great purge of 1936-38 took place after the first Plan had already been carried out and the collectivization of agriculture completed. The terror that accompanied the latter may, at a stretch, be attributed to economic "necessities," but this explanation cannot apply to the great purge, during which millions of real and imagined opponents, faithful Bolsheviks and even Stalinists were thrown into prison.

The tremendous development of Soviet productive forces, on which neo-Marxists always dwell as a portent of the better life to come, is of course no fiction. By and large, however, it applies only to heavy industry. The lot of the Soviet citizenry has remained relatively unaffected, since the living standard is determined not by *per capita* production but by the value of goods intended for consumption by individuals. Considering additionally the lag in agricultural output, it is unlikely that the Soviet planners can greatly increase the purchasing power of the population in the foreseeable future.

In any thesis on the Soviet future, the meaning of the word "democracy" is crucial. If by democracy is meant the organized competition of parties— as it seems to in Deutscher's formulation—then there is no obvious connection between democracy and economic progress. But it is absurd to insist on rigid and unalterable concepts of democracy in its Western form (characterized by multi-party systems, legislative representation, intellectual liberties, *etc.*) as opposed to totalitarianism (characterized by the single party, ideological terrorism, police controls, *etc.*). Neither Western democracy nor Stalinist totalitarianism can be considered as fixed entities, as "historic atoms" which cannot be transmuted. Thus, if it is illogical to assert that totalitarianism will develop into full-fledged democracy with the development of productive forces, it is just as illogical to exclude dogmatically a softening up of totalitarianism.

This is the weakness of the second theory, opposite to Mr. Deutscher's, which asserts that totalitarianism is invulnerable to outside forces. It is usually posited as part of a political and almost metaphysical interpretation of totalitarianism, conceived of as a disease which is liable to infect any modern society—even though, so far, only Russia and Germany have experienced it in "pure" form. Its proponents argue that although totalitarianism is favored by certain economic and social circumstances, it is essentially something political and ideological. It is supposed to be the outcome of an obsessive drive of a group of people bent on shaping society according to their own ideology. The power of a single party, ideological orthodoxy, police terror, the creation of a world of superimposed conventional meanings, with no reference to the real world and yet forced on the masses as something truer than reality—all these features, we are told, are linked together and constitute the characteristics of a global, or self-contained, phenomenon—a phenomenon which has emerged and will eventually disappear, but which it would be idle to expect to return to normality by gradual stages.

In this definition of totalitarianism, three of the above features are essential: ideological orthodoxy, police terror, and world-wide victory or else apocalyptic collapse. These three elements are said to be closely linked. The will to set up an arbitrary and often absurd ideology as The Truth necessitates the recourse to police inquisition, which is used for hunting not only enemies, but also heretics. The truth of the ideology can triumph only when it is no longer rejected by anybody. So long as there is opposition anywhere, communism will not be entirely true, because its truth will still clash with reality, and its compete truth depends on its universal application. Thus communism is in a constant state of war with unbelievers both inside and outside its borders. The greater the progress, the more it is impelled to struggle, for nothing has been achieved so long as something still remains to be done. This line of analysis affords an explanation for the great purge having descended upon Soviet society after the completion of rural collectivization; the latter is viewed not as an economic and rational—however ruthless—measure, but as the expression of a policy which is *alien* to economic rationalism, and is intelligible only in terms of an ideological and emotional logic.

This kind of interpretation, which Hannah Arendt has developed with great skills, seems to me to be dangerous. It amounts to creating a certain ideal type, a kind of essence of totalitarianism—and to assuming, thereupon, that the regime, both in the present and in the future, must conform to this type or this essence. If the Soviets behaved as "perfect" totalitarians, as Miss Arendt understands the word, then it is quite true that we could expect no normalization or evolution of the Soviet regime. The real question is, however, whether the regime has even been completely totalitarian, whether the "essense" has not simply been created by theorists like Miss Arendt on the strength of certain historically-observed and historically-explicable phenomena. The Soviet regime *became* totalitarian by degrees, under the influence of certain circumstances. Why, then, could it not cease to be totalitarian, or become less totalitarian under the influence of other circumstances?

THE IMPACT OF ECONOMIC DEVELOPMENT

Once the extremes of the neo-Marxist and the totalitarian theory have been rejected, it must be decided what either of them can contribute to a logical assessment of the Soviet future. What transformations, social and economic, are brought about by the development of productive forces? What is the likely effect of these transformations on the political regime? To what extent is totalitarianism (or certain totalitarian elements) inseparable from the regime, regardless of economic progress?

There are at least three important social and economic consequences of the development of productive forces. The first is a rise in the general level of culture and the creation and development of an intelligentsia, whose broad base—in addition to traditional cultural and professional elements—is the swelling ranks of technical and managerial specialists who man the economy. It is as true for the Soviet Union as for the West that modern industry requires a higher proportion of technicians and specialized "cadres" than in the past, and Soviet statistics show a steady increase in the proportion of intelligentsia to the whole working population.

Even outside this intelligentsia with its higher-level specialization, the priority given to production and to productivity is bound to encourage the spread of specialized training and of technical education. More than half the Soviet labor force is at present employed in industry or its auxiliary services, and more than half the population is urban. This urban population can read and write, and it is no longer as cowed—or as malleable—as it was in the early years of Stalin's reign.

The second consequence of industrial development, closely related to the first, is an increase in the economic wants and demands of the population. In the Soviet Union, the development of productive forces has not been accompanied by a corresponding rise in the standard of living of the masses. The concentration of capital investments in heavy industry, the failures in agriculture, and the housing shortage have meant that the average citizen is worse housed, worse fed and less well-dressed than the average citizen of the West, even in some of the less prosperous countries. In recent years, however, there has been some improvement in material conditions, and various pressures have led the regime to pay some limited deference to consumer needs. The indications are that this limited satisfaction of certain wants has whetted the population's appetite for more goods. In particular, the intelligentsia has shown increasing eagerness to acquire commodities typical of the way of life of the Western bourgeois (durable consumer goods, automobiles, refrigerators, etc.).

The third consequence of developing productive forces is a trend toward a more rational economy. Over the last thirty years, the Soviet economy has become not only more powerful but technologically far more complex. To what extent and how long the crude planning methods of the first Five-Year Plans can continue to be applied is a highly complicated and controversial issue. Yet the general direction of evolution seems fairly clear to this writer. As shortages become less severe, the consumers' choice will tend to be of growing importance to the market. Technological complexity will strengthen the managerial class at the expense of the ideologists and the militants, at any rate on the enterprise level, if not on the state level. The decentralization of industrial administration, in reinforcing the managerial elements, should reduce the part played by fear and coercion in the Soviet management of an industrial society.

STABILIZING FORCES IN SOVIET SOCIETY

While the rate at which any of these social and economic trends will develop is hard to foresee, certain political implications seem clear. Briefly, it is the writer's view that none of these trends—toward a higher cultural level, toward increasing popular demands, or toward a more rational economy—constitutes a threat to the basic organization of the Soviet state or society.

Apart from its peculiarly totalitarian features, Soviet society is essentially bureaucratic and hierarchical, just as was prerevolutionary Russian society. The reliance of an industrial society on a state bureaucracy with vested interests—under a system which prevents the formation of organized opinion or pressure through professional groups, genuine trade unions, or political parties—obviously creates a certain tendency toward stability. A further stabilizing factor is class mobility; since the intelligentsia is expanding with each generation, it can absorb the ablest children of the masses without the regime's having to resort to purge or to demotion of the children of the already privileged.

As noted above, there is bound to be some tension between the economic desires of the masses and the intelligentsia, on one hand, the exigencies of regime policy on the other (requiring the continued priority of heavy industry). There is probably also a latent conflict between the desire for rationality and security on the part of the managerial and technocratic elements, and the desire for power and prestige on the part of the party men. But such conflicts do not imply any explosions or fundamental changes in the society.

In short, there is nothing to indicate that economic progress will force the ruling class, composed of party men and higher-level bureaucrats, to authorize the creation of rival forces—in the form of either parties or workers' trade unions. And there is nothing to indicate that such a challenge can come from below; neither the masses nor the intelligentsia have the means of overriding the ban on organized pressure groups. The leadership seems quite capable of maintaining the principle of the single hierarchy, of the single party, and of the legal *status quo* of the ruling bureaucracy. If any basic change is to take place, it will have to occur *within* the ruling elite—*i.e.,* inside the Communist Party.

EVOLUTION AND THE REGIME

What can be said, then, of the effects of progressing industrialization on the Communist regime itself, and specifically on those aspects of the regime which have come to be identified as "totalitarian." The question may be discussed under several heads: 1) Will the internal structure of the party undergo basic changes as a result of the spontaneous evolution of the economy and the society? 2) Will ideology continue, in the long run, to play the same role as it has in the past? 3) Is the movement still inspired by the same boundless ambition, by the same violence, or may it be expected eventually to rest content with what it is—that is, something less than universal?

The most crucial change in the party structure of recent years—the substitution of collective leadership for one-man dictatorship—is attributable to an historical event, to the death of an individual, rather than to the evolution of either the society or the regime. Nevertheless, the change was, in a way, logical. For the very nature of Stalin's power—or his misuse of it—dictated against the rise of a single successor. None of the members of the Presidium could face without anxiety the prospect of a repetition of the process whereby Stalin, little by little, had liquidated virtually all of the men who had once been his allies in the party leadership.

Some observers have held that Khrushchev's increasing domination of the ruling clique has already put an end to collective leadership. But Khrushchev has had to lean heavily on the support of allies to push through his policies, and in this sense group rule certainly continues. Acting as a group of leaders, the Presidium has appeared to be less indifferent to public demands, less able or less determined to carry out programs regardless of cost, than was Stalin with his unlimited personal power.

Whether further fundamental changes will take place in the structure and balance of power within the party is a matter of conjecture at this stage. However, it is worth noting that Khrushchev effected his purge of the so-called "anti-party" leaders last June through appeal to the Central Committee, over the objections of a majority of the Presidium. Before that time the Presidium appeared to be just as independent of the Central Committee as Stalin had been. Since the authority of the proletariat originally passed from the party to the Politburo (*i.e.,* Stalin) *through* the Central Committee, it is interesting to speculate on whether the reverse could take place. So far, there is no sign that any such basic shift in power is in the offing; if it were to occur, however, it would be directly attributable to the struggle for power rather than to broader forces of evolution.

The changeover from personal to collective leadership has been accompanied by the mitigation or abandonment of certain aspects of totalitarian rule. Perhaps the epitome of totalitarianism, certainly the feature most frequently mentioned, is the instrument of the purge, characterized by a combination of arbitrary police action (pragmatically unjustifiable), ideological terrorism and pure fantasy, defined by the inquisitor-theologians as more real than reality itself. The confession trials were the symbolic expression of this aspect of totalitarianism.

The collective leadership has renounced such excesses, and in doing so has revealed that it was never taken in by the mad logic of Stalinist ideological terrorism. At the same time, it may reasonably be objected that Khrushchev has not hesitated, on occasion, to employ it himself, as for instance when he has called Beria an "imperialist agent" or the Hungarian revolution a "counterrevolution." This leads us to perhaps the most crucial issue under consideration in this paper: that is the future role of ideology in the evolving Soviet society.

A TREND TOWARD SKEPTICISM?

Communist ideology is based on a few simple ideas: the party *is* the proletariat; the seizure of power by the party is the *sine qua non* for the establishment of socialism. In places where the party has not taken over power, capitalism reigns and the masses are exploited. The inevitable culmination will be the extension throughout the world of regimes similar to the Soviet regime.

As is frequently pointed out, this orthodoxy has little connection with either Marx *or* reality. A society which has developed a great industrial complex side by side with a relentlessly low standard of living resembles what Marx called capitalism: a welfare state, albeit "capitalist," in which the additional resources accruing from technical progress are used for the benefit of the masses, does not. The dialecticians have been obliged to place an arbitrary interpretation on facts, often at variance with the most obvious reality. The element of fantasy in the great trials is merely the supreme expression of this logic.

It is the writer's belief that Soviet society, with the improvement in its standard of living, its culture and its technology, not only is becoming economically more rational, but must in the long run lose its ideological fervor. As it makes further progress and becomes more stable, as its technical level draws closer to that of industrialized Western societies, so both its militants and the people at large are bound to incline to some degree of skepticism. They will come to admit certain incontestable facts, such as the plurality of methods of industrialization, the raising of the standard of living in the West, *etc*. As soon as Polish writers and educators were able to talk freely, they proceeded to admit these facts and to escape from the absurd logic of Communist ideology. . . .

THE PROSPECTS FOR A FREER SOCIETY

When making a simplified analysis, a distinction can be drawn between three different kinds of freedom: firstly, what Montesquieu called security; secondly, the freedom the Hungarian intellectuals claimed, namely, the right to tell the truth about everything; and finally, Rousseau's freedom, participation in sovereignty, represented in the twentieth century by free elections and the multiparty political system.

Individual security is, as a rule, most favored by a parliamentary type of government. But many nondemocratic regimes give a fairly broad measure of security to those who do not engage in politics. The Tsarist regime, during its final period, interfered little with the life and liberty of citizens who minded their own business. In the Soviet Union, the insecurity of the Stalin era appears to have been greatly lessened by Stalin's successors. But as long as the Soviet regime continues to apply political sanctions in order to make the economy work, as long as it demands unquestioning respect for the dogma, the Soviet citizen will not be able to enjoy a true or stable measure of security.

To what extent could intellectuals and ordinary Soviet citizens be allowed to enjoy the second kind of freedom—to tell the truth about things, to exchange ideas, to visit the capitalist West, *etc*? In the writer's view, the regime could, without endangering its own safety, grant musicians, painters and writers, more freedoms than it does at present. But the word "could" here has a double application; the question is whether the leaders of the regime and the party could bring themselves to grant such freedoms. Again, as long as they believe in their dogma, they will not allow it to be discussed, and there will be a harness on truth. Yet even if they themselves become skeptical, would they admit it publicly? For the future this is a matter of speculation; for the present, they certainly would not dare to do so. For even though there may be a tendency in Russia to evolve into a semi-ideological technocracy, the dogma is still a vital factor in less-advanced Communist countries and is crucial in justifying the unity of the socialist camp. To hope that the dogma will fade out in the near future would be over-optimistic.

In the long run, however, this writer holds to his view that increasing ideological skepticism is inevitable among both the leaders and the masses. Already the problems of Soviet planning are completely out of touch with the official economic textbooks, which are simplified versions of *Das Kapital*. Though tribute may still be paid to Marx, the day may come when an industrial society, concerned more with efficiency than with orthodoxy, will cease to follow the Lenin-Stalin ideology. Revolutionary fervor—though revived by the successes of communism in Asia and the Middle East—is nevertheless bound, in the end, to die down, and probably to die out.

Will the Soviet citizen eventually obtain Rousseau's freedom—participation in sovereignty—through either the development of factions within the party, or perhaps even the emergence of a multiparty system? The prospect of any move toward full-fledged political freedom in the Western style is so far beyond the scope of present or even predictable evolutionary trends that speculation would be foolish. Only time and the forces already at work in Soviet society will provide the clues to Russia's political future.

THE CONFUSION OF ENDS AND MEANS

George F. Kennan*

This selection is from a speech delivered by Ambassador George F. Kennan on September 21, 1959, to a seminar on "Industrial Society and the Western Political Dialogue," sponsored by the Congress for Cultural Freedom at Rheinfelden, Switzerland. It must be emphasized that Ambassador Kennan's remarks were made as comments on Professor Raymond Aron's paper, read at the Rheinfelden seminar, and not in relation to the article of Professor Aron's which appears in this volume.

Professor Raymond Aron poses, first of all, the question as to the true aims of Soviet power. Is the goal of Soviet policy, he asks, the welfare of the individual, and is its totalitarian character to be regarded only as a means to the rapid achievement of this end? Or has the totalitarianism become an end in itself, so that the ultimate aim is merely, as he put it, "to bring about total tyranny in the name of abundance and liberation"?

What I should like to say is that I doubt that we can usefully pose this question so sharply, or invite so clean and tidy an answer. Russia is a country of contradictions; and the history of Soviet power is one long record of the confusion of ends and means.

When the Russian Revolution occurred, Russia already was, and had been for some three or four decades, in a process of quite rapid evolution away from the archaic political and social institutions of Tsardom, in the direction of the modern liberal state. The development of a firm judicial

---

* United States Ambassador to Yugoslavia; formerly ambassador to the U.S.S.R.; author of *Russia and the West Under Lenin and Stalin* and of many other books and articles on the U.S.S.R. The material herein is reproduced with the permission of Ambassador Kennan and the Congress for Cultural Freedom.

system was far advanced; a beginning had been made toward the development of local self-government; public opinion was becoming a force to be reckoned with. There is no reason to doubt that this represented the natural and underlying trend of Russian society in this century—a movement occurring somewhat later in time than, but otherwise not dissimilar from, comparable movements in other western countries—a normal response, actually, to the introduction of popular education and to other stimuli of the modern age. While this long-term trend of Russian society was interrupted by the Revolution and its consequences, I can see no reason to doubt that it still represents the direction in which, over the long run, Russia must move.

Despite Lenin's intolerant temperament and the doctrinaire authoritarianism with which he governed his own party, there can, I think, be no question of the fundamental idealism of his purpose at the time of the Revolution. It was certainly with reluctance and with heaviness of heart that he was obliged to concede, initially, the necessity of the terror. One can argue that terror is the inevitable outcome of any attempt to put a utopian vision into practice by the use of political authority; and with this, I would agree. But I doubt that Lenin was himself aware of this. The Bolshevik movement was betrayed into terrorism and brutality by the strange sequence of events which carried it suddenly into power, contrary to its own expectations, in a single country where its active popular support was minimal, and where even the class it professed to represent—the proletariat—was only a tiny minority among the working masses. It was from this predicament that the early Bolsheviki hoped to be rescued by a general European revolution—and were not. They then found themselves confronted with the choice of resorting to terror or resigning what they believed was their natural and appointed place in history. Having no religious scruples that could have warned them against placing the ends before the means, they chose the terror.

Now the instruments of coercion, once created, have a tendency to find their own natural master. In Russia's case this was, of course, Stalin. It was with him that brutality was made into an end in itself. It was he who introduced the characteristic distortions of modern totalitarianism: the punishment of people not for the things they had done but for the things they might be presumed capable of doing; the substitution of blackmail for justice; the elevation of denunciation to the status of the highest civic duty; the cultivation of the anonymity and mystery and unpredictability of the punishing power; the creation of an artificial hell in the form of the forced labor and concentration camps; the reduction of the population, in short, to a state of general dread and mutual distrust.

It is idle to ask whether, for Stalin, happy prospects loomed at the end of this monstrous process of degradation. It was the only way he knew to protect his personal position and the integrity of his rule. Among a portion of the officials of Party and police, it came to be taken as the normal way of government. To the people at large, however, to the intelligentsia above all, and even to a considerable portion of the Party, it was not only hateful but a source of shame and humiliation vis-à-vis the outside world, particularly the foreign socialist parties. Among those who took this position, Khrushchev occupied a prominent place, but he was by no means alone in this feeling, even within the Presidium of the Party. Most of his senior colleagues were prepared to concede that a large portion of Stalin's methodology was unhealthy and undesirable, though they often differed over the question as to how much of Stalinism ought to be discarded and how much to be retained.

What we now see in the Soviet Union represents a compromise among these differing views; the liberalization has scarcely gone as far as some would have liked to see it go. Nevertheless, it has gone so far as to represent a highly significant departure from Stalinism and an essential alteration of the nature of the regime. The regime has, to be sure, not barred itself in any legal or constitutional way from resuming former practises: it simply does not apply them. But the aversion to these practises is still strong in the older generation; and a younger generation is growing up which is habituated to a greater freedom and to greater expectations of personal comfort than they could have dreamed of some years ago. It would be extremely difficult, today, to turn the clock back.

A distinction must of course be made here (and it is one highly relevant to Aron's question) between the system prevailing in the Soviet Union proper and that prevailing in outlying parts of the Soviet Empire. We must recognize that in certain of these regions, notably Eastern Germany, Czechoslovakia and Hungary, the movement away from Stalinism has been not nearly so marked as in the Soviet Union itself. And we must ask ourselves: does this greater totalitarianism of the periphery of Soviet power represent a deliberate policy? Is it a condition which the Soviet leaders have deliberately cultivated, and are yearning to impose elsewhere? Or is it a response, involuntary and perhaps reluctant, to external necessities?

Here, too, the pattern is confused. There are still Stalinists in Moscow who would no doubt find quite normal the manner in which Eastern Germany is now governed, and would be happy to see the same principles applied elsewhere. But it is also clear that this view has not always prevailed. There are significant variations within the satellite area itself. The regions where Stalinist controls are most firmly maintained are those which are most neuralgic from the standpoint of the cold war. The Soviet Government, significantly, has not found it necessary to impose the Stalinist pattern on Finland, although that country has been for fifteen years fully and helplessly exposed to the full force of Soviet power.

We note, too, that where a local communist regime has had the courage, as in Poland, to repudiate of its own accord the excesses of Stalinist police terror, and to persist stoutly in this repudiation, Moscow has not seriously interfered. The crucial limit of Russian patience, to judge from the Hungarian experience, relates less to the extent of internal liberalization in a satellite country (provided, of course, the formal devotion to socialist principle is maintained) than to the degree of fidelity to the international security arrangements of which Moscow is the center. Had the Nagy regime not moved, in 1956, to denounce the Warsaw Pact, in circumstances which gave the Russians no assurance whatsoever that Hungary, if permitted to take this step, would not end up by joining the Atlantic Pact instead, it is not at all certain that the final Soviet intervention would ever have occurred.

If we weigh these various circumstances, we see that where strongly totalitarian features of government have endured in the Communist orbit, this has been for reasons having to do partly with the peculiarities of the local situation, or, in even greater part, with the pressures and necessities of the cold war. In neither case would the controlling factor appear to have been any such thing as a disposition on the part of the Soviet leadership to inflict these totalitarian devices for their own sake.

The picture, I reiterate, is not a simple one. On countless occasions, when I have been asked which of two seemingly contradictory and incompatible realities is true in the Soviet Union, I have been obliged to say: both. This, too, is one of these instances.

There are still Stalinists in the Soviet Union—people who, from habit, from fear, or from limitation of vision, can think in no terms other than those of absolute domination, and for whom the utopian end-product of socialism has become indistinguishable from a state of total political slavery.

But these are only a portion of the leadership. They do not command the confidence of the oncoming student generation. Their views are not the ones that have prevailed in recent years. From the long-term and short-term standpoints they would appear to be on the side of the waning, not the waxing trends of Russian life.

In the main, the goals and trends of Russian communism lie along the same path as those of western liberal-industrialism. What divides the two worlds is not a difference in aim—what divides them is fear, timidity, the unsolved problem of eastern Europe, and the unhappy dynamics of a weapons race so absorbing that both sides tend to forget the issues of its origin. . . .

Let us remember, first of all, that authoritarianism, in one form or another, has been throughout the ages the normal lot of mankind. It is true that people of my generation in America were brought up to believe that liberal democracy, on the Anglo-Saxon pattern, was the final product of political enlightenment—a system which had a potential universal validity and to which all societies ought properly to tend. But the events of the last 40 years have taught us better; and today many of us would be inclined to regard **our own** institutions as at best a happy aberration, enjoyed by certain peoples who had their political origins on the shores of the English channel and the North Sea, connected specifically with the traditions of mercantile sea power rather than land power, of doubtful applicability in a wider geographic sphere, and plainly subject to the discipline of evolution in time. We could attach, therefore, no absolute positive value to these institutions, much as we may cherish them ourselves.

And conversely, just as we would attribute no absolute *positive* value to our own institutions, so we could attribute no absolute *negative* value to those of the Russians. These latter, as we have just noted, are now embraced in a process of evolution. They are changing, and we cannot yet know the full measure of the change. And besides, the differences that divide these institutions from our own are relative, not absolute. Aron does well to single out the one-party regime, the suppression of criticism, and the systematic cultivation of falsehood as features of Soviet power that contrast basically with what we have in the West. But the deliberate cultivation of falsehood seems to me to be undergoing, as a governmental policy, a process of severe erosion. The temper of Soviet youth and the pressures of the time are all against it. I cannot imagine that it can be long continued in the manner of the past. And as for the one-party system: it must be contrasted, unfortunately, with precisely that segment in the political life of the West which is itself today most subject to question, most doubtful in point of adequacy to the needs of the time: the system of political parties and the parliamentary institutions through which they find their expression. In the doctrinal sense, we in America also have in certain respects a one-party system: for the two parties are ideologically undistinguishable; their pronouncements form one integral body of banality and platitude; whoever does not care to work within their common framework is also condemned, like the non-party person in Russia, to political passivity—to an internal emigration.

I would not wish to be misunderstood at this point. I would be the last to deny the validity of relative distinctions. I find our system, for all its short-comings, vastly preferable to that which confronts it on the Communist side—if only because it interposes no political barriers to the freedom of the mind.

Chapter 22

THE ROAD TO COMMUNISM

The New Party Program of the Communist Party of the Soviet Union concludes with the ringing declaration, "THE PARTY SOLEMNLY PROCLAIMS: THE PRESENT GENERATION OF SOVIET PEOPLE SHALL LIVE IN COMMUNISM!"

What is the meaning of "communism" as distinguished from the "socialism" which has allegedly "triumphed in the Soviet Union completely and finally"? What are its premises, promises, and portents? What are the prospects of its being achieved in "the present generation" in the U.S.S.R.? These are questions to which Harry Schwartz and Robert C. Tucker address themselves.

In this editor's opinion, the Program, however great the difficulties and questionable the prospects of fulfillment, must be thought of, inter alia, as a statement of national and international purpose designed to serve a dual and, at times, conflicting role: to conform to the elitest leaders' conceptions of "the bright future of all mankind" but, at the same time, to respond to the hopes, aspirations and expectations of the Soviet people.

"COMMUNISM—THE BRIGHT FUTURE"

NEW PROGRAM OF THE COMMUNIST PARTY*

INTRODUCTION

The Great October Socialist Revolution ushered in a new era in the history of mankind, the era of the downfall of capitalism and the establish-

* Reproduced, with permission, from *The Current Digest of the Soviet Press,* Vol. XIII (Dec. 6, 1961), p. 3, and Vol. XIII (Dec. 13, 1961), pp. 3-4, 9-12, 13, 14, 16, 20-21. The new Communist Party Program appears in its entirety in *Current Soviet Policies—IV,* published by Columbia University Press from the translations of the *Current Digest.*

ment of communism. Socialism has triumphed in the Land of Soviets and has achieved decisive victories in the people's democracies; it has become a practical cause to hundreds of millions of people and the banner of the revolutionary movement of the working class of the whole world.

More than 100 years ago Karl Marx and Friedrich Engels, the great teachers of the proletariat, wrote in "The Communist Manifesto": *"A specter is haunting Europe—the specter of communism."* The courageous and selfless struggle of the proletarians of all countries has brought mankind nearer to communism. First tens and hundreds of people, then thousands and millions, inspired by the ideals of communism, stormed the old world. The Paris Commune, the October Revolution and the socialist revolutions in China and in a number of other countries of Europe and Asia—these are the major historical stages in the heroic battles fought by the international working class for the victory of communism. A very long road, a road drenched in the blood of fighters for the people's happiness, a road of glorious victories and temporary setbacks was traversed before *communism, which once seemed a mere dream, became the greatest force of modern times and a society that is being built up over vast areas of the globe.*

At the beginning of the 20th century, the center of the international revolutionary movement shifted to Russia. Russia's heroic working class, led by the party of Bolsheviks headed by Vladimir Ilyich Lenin, became the vanguard of this movement. The Communist Party inspired and led the socialist revolution; it was the organizer and leader of the first workers' and peasants' state in history. The shining genius of Lenin, the great teacher of the working people of the whole world whose name will live forever, illumines mankind's road to communism.

The Leninist party of Communists, emerging into the arena of political struggle, raised high over the world the banner of revolutionary Marxism. Marxism-Leninism became the powerful ideological weapon for the revolutionary transformation of society. At each historical stage the party, guided by the teachings of Marx, Engels and Lenin, accomplished the tasks scientifically formulated in its Programs.

In adopting its *first Program* at its Second Congress, in 1903, the Bolshevist party called on the working class and all the working people of Russia to struggle for the overthrow of the tsarist autocracy and then of the bourgeois system and for the establishment of the dictatorship of the proletariat. In February, 1917, the tsarist regime was swept away. In October, 1917, the proletarian revolution destroyed the capitalist system so hated by the people. *A country of socialism came into being for the first time in history. The creation of a new world began.*

The first Program of the Party had been carried out.

In adopting the *second Program* at the Eighth Congress, in 1919, the Party set the task of building a socialist society. Treading unexplored paths and overcoming difficulties and hardships, the Soviet people, under the leadership of the Communist Party, carried out the plan for socialist construction drawn up by Lenin. *Socialism triumphed in the Soviet Union completely and finally.*

The second Program of the Party has also been carried out.

The very great revolutionary feat accomplished by the Soviet people roused and inspired the masses of the people of all countries and continents. A mighty cleansing thunderstorm is sweeping across the world marking the springtime of mankind. *The socialist revolutions in countries of Europe and Asia led to the formation of a world socialist system.* A powerful wave of national-liberation revolutions is sweeping away the colonial system of imperialism.

One-third of mankind is building a new life under the banner of scientific communism. The first detachments of the working class to have broken away from the oppression of capitalism are facilitating the victory of new detachments of their class brothers. The world of socialism is expanding, the world of capitalism is shrinking. Socialism will inevitably succeed capitalism everywhere. Such is the objective law of social development. Imperialism is powerless to check the irresistible process of liberation. . . .

Today the Communist Party of the Soviet Union (C.P.S.U.) is adopting its third Program, a program for the building of a communist society. The new Program creatively generalizes the practice of socialist construction, it takes account of the experience of the revolutionary movement throughout the world, and, expressing the collective thought of the Party, it defines the chief tasks and basic stages of communist construction.

The supreme goal of the Party is to build a communist society on whose banner will be inscribed, "From each according to his abilities, to each according to his needs." The Party's slogan, "Everything in the name of man, for the benefit of man," will be put into effect in full.

The Communist Party of the Soviet Union, true to proletarian internationalism, always follows the militant slogan "Proletarians of all countries, unite!" *The Party considers communist construction in the U.S.S.R. as the Soviet people's great internationalist task,* in keeping with the interests of the world socialist system as a whole and with the interests of the international proletariat and all mankind.

Communism accomplishes the historic mission of delivering all men from social inequality, from all forms of oppression and exploitation, from the horrors of war, and affirms on earth Peace, Labor, Freedom, Equality, Brotherhood and Happiness for all peoples. . . .

COMMUNISM—THE BRIGHT FUTURE OF ALL MANKIND

The building of a communist society has become the immediate practical task of the Soviet people. The gradual evolution of socialism into communism is an objective law; it has been prepared by the whole preceding development of Soviet socialist society.

What is communism?

Communism is a classless social system with a single form of public ownership of the means of production and full social equality of all members of society; under it, the rounded development of people will be accompanied by growth of productive forces on the basis of constantly developing science and technology, all the springs of public wealth will yield abundantly, and the great principle "From each according to his abilities, to each according to his needs" will be applied. Communism is a highly organized society of free, socially conscious working people in which public self-government will be established, in which labor for the good of society will become a prime, vital need in everyone, a necessity recognized by all, and the abilities of each person will be employed to the greatest benefit of the people. . . .

Under communism there will be no classes and the socio-economic and cultural distinctions and differences in living conditions between town and countryside will disappear; the countryside rises to the level of the city in the development of productive forces, the nature of work, the forms of production relations, living conditions and the well-being of the population. With the victory of communism mental and manual labor in people's production activity will merge organically. The intelligentsia will cease to be a distinct social stratum, and manual workers will have risen in cultural and technological level to the level of mental workers.

Thus communism will end the division of society into classes and social strata, whereas the whole history of mankind, with the exception of its primitive period, has been a history of class society. Division into opposing classes led to the exploitation of man by man, class struggle and antagonisms among nations and states.

Under communism all people will have equal status in society, will stand in equal relation to the means of production, will enjoy equal conditions of work and distribution, and will participate actively in the management of public affairs. Harmonious relations will be established between the individual and society on the basis of unity of public and personal interests. For all their tremendous diversity, the requirements of people will express the healthy, reasonable requirements of persons of rounded development.

The goal of communist production is to ensure the constant progress of society and to provide each of its members with material and cultural benefits according to his or her growing needs, individual requirements and tastes. People's requirements will be met from public sources. Articles of personal use will come into the full ownership of each member of society and will be at his disposal.

Communist society, based on highly organized production and advanced technology, changes the character of work but does not release the members of society from work. By no means will it be a society of anarchy, idleness and inactivity. Every able-bodied person will participate in social labor and thereby ensure the steady growth of the material and spiritual wealth of society. Thanks to the change in the nature of labor, its greater mechanization and a high degree of consciousness, the inner need to work for the public benefit voluntarily and according to inclination will burgeon in all members of society.

Communist production demands high organization, precision and discipline, which are ensured not by compulsion but on the basis of understanding of public duty, and are determined by the whole way of life in communist society. Labor and discipline will not be a burden to man; labor will cease to be merely a source of livelihood—it will turn into a genuinely creative process and a source of happiness.

Communism represents the highest form of organization of the life of society. All production units, all self-governing associations will be harmoniously linked by a common planned economy and a single rhythm of social labor.

Under communism nations will draw closer and closer together in all spheres on the basis of a complete identity of economic, political and spiritual interests, of fraternal friendship and cooperation.

Communism is the system in which free men's abilities and talents and their best moral qualities blossom and fully show themselves. Family relations will be completely freed from material considerations and will be based entirely on mutual love and friendship.

Defining the basic tasks to be accomplished in building a communist society, the Party is guided by V. I. Lenin's inspired formula: *"Communism is Soviet rule plus the electrification of the whole country."*

As a party of scientific communism, the C.P.S.U. sets the tasks of communist construction and carries them out as the material and spiritual prerequisites are prepared and mature; in doing this, the C.P.S.U. is guided by the fact that one cannot leap over essential stages in development, any more than one can halt at an achieved level and check progress. The tasks of building communism are accomplished in successive stages.

In the current decade (1961-1970) the Soviet Union, creating the material and technical base of communism, will surpass the strongest and richest capitalist country, the U.S.A., in per capita production; the people's material well-being and cultural and technical level will rise substantially, everyone will be assured a material sufficiency; all collective and state farms will become highly productive and highly profitable enterprises; the demand of the Soviet people for well-appointed housing will in the main be satisfied; hard physical labor will disappear; the U.S.S.R. will become the country with the shortest working day.

By the end of the second decade (1971-1980) the material and technical base of communism will be created that will ensure an abundance of material and cultural benefits for the whole population; Soviet society will

come right up to the stage of application of the principle of distribution ac
cording to needs, and there will be a gradual transition to a single form of
public ownership. Thus a *communist society will be built in the main in
the U.S.S.R.* The construction of communist society will be completed in the
subsequent period.

The majestic edifice of communism is being erected by the persevering
labor of the Soviet people—the working class, the peasantry and the intelligentsia. The more successful their work, the closer the great goal—the
building of communist society. . . .

THE TASKS OF THE PARTY IN IMPROVING THE MATERIAL WELL-BEING OF THE PEOPLE

The heroic labor of the Soviet people has created a powerful and comprehensively developed economy. There is now every possibility of rapidly
improving the well-being of the whole population—workers, peasants and
intelligentsia. The C.P.S.U. sets a task of world-historic importance—*to
ensure a living standard in the Soviet Union higher than that of any capitalist country.*

This task will be accomplished by: (a) raising individual payment according to the quantity and quality of work, coupled with reduction of
retail prices and the abolition of taxes paid by the public; (b) increasing
the public funds of consumption earmarked for satisfying the requirements
of members of society irrespective of the quantity and quality of their labor
—that is, free of charge (education, medical treatment, pensions, maintenance of children at children's institutions, transition to cost-free use of
public utilities, etc.).

The rise in the real earnings of the population will be more than
covered by a rapid increase in the amount of commodities and services and
by extensive development of housing, cultural and service construction.

The Soviet people will be more prosperous than the working people in
the developed capitalist countries even if average incomes are equal, since
in the Soviet Union the national income is distributed in the interests of all
the members of society and there are no parasitic classes, as in the bourgeois
countries, that appropriate and squander immense wealth plundered from
millions of working people.

The Party proceeds from Lenin's thesis that communist construction
should rest on the principle of material incentive. In the coming 20 years
payment according to one's work will remain the principal source for satisfying the material and cultural needs of the working people.

At the same time the disparity between high and comparatively low
incomes must gradually shrink. Greater and greater masses of unskilled
workers and employees will become skilled, and the diminishing difference
in labor skills and productivity will be accompanied by a steady reduction of

disparities in the level of pay. As the living standard of the entire population rises, low income levels will approach the higher and the disparity between the incomes of peasants and workers, of low-paid and high-paid working people, and of the populations of different parts of the country will gradually decline.

Meantime, as the country advances toward communism, personal needs will be increasingly met out of public consumption funds, whose rate of growth will exceed the rate of growth of individual payment for labor. The transition to communist distribution will be completed after the principle of distribution according to work entirely exhausts itself—that is, when there is an abundance of material and cultural benefits and labor becomes a prime necessity of life for all members of society.

A. Provision of a High Level of Income and Consumption for the Whole Population; Development of Trade

The national income of the U.S.S.R. will increase almost 150% in the next ten years and about 400% in 20 years. Per capita real income will increase by more than 250% in 20 years. In the first ten years the real incomes of all workers and employees (including public funds) per employed person will be on the average almost double, while the incomes of workers and employees in lowpaid categories will approximately triple. Thus by the end of the first decade there will no longer be low-paid groups of workers and employees in the country.

On the basis of higher rates of growth of the labor productivity of collective farmers, their real incomes will rise more rapidly on the average than the incomes of workers and will, on an average per working person, more than double in the next ten years and increase more than fourfold in 20 years.

The pay of such numerically large strata of the Soviet intelligentsia as engineers and technicians, agronomists and zoo-technicians, teachers and medical and cultural workers will rise considerably.

As the incomes of the population grow, *the general level of public consumption will rise rapidly*. The entire population will be able to satisfy amply its demand for high-quality and varied food products. The share of livestock products (meat, fats, dairy products) and of fruit and high-grade vegetables in the public diet will rise substantially in the near future. The demand of all sections of the population for high-quality consumer goods— well-made and attractive clothing, footwear and goods for improving and adorning the daily life of Soviet people, such as comfortable modern furniture, improved household articles, a wide range of goods for cultural purposes, etc.—will be amply satisfied. Production of automobiles for the public will be considerably expanded.

The output of consumer goods must fully meet the growing consumer demand and must conform to its changes. The timely output of goods in accordance with the varied demand of the public, taking into account local, national and climatic conditions, is an imperative requirement for all the consumer industries.

Soviet trade will be further developed as a necessary condition for satisfying the growing requirements of the public. Good trade facilities will be arranged in all sections and populated points of the country, and progressive forms of service for the public will be widely applied. The material and technical base of trade—the network of stores, warehouses, refrigeration plants and vegetable storage facilities—will be expanded.

The consumer's cooperatives, which are called upon to improve trade in the countryside and to organize the marketing of farm surpluses, will be developed. Collective farm trade will also retain its importance.

The second decade will see an abundance of material and cultural benefits for the whole population, and the material prerequisites will be created for the transition in the subsequent period to the communist principle of distribution according to need.

B. Solution of the Housing Problem and Improvement of Living Conditions

The C.P.S.U. sets the task of solving the most acute problem in the improvement of the well-being of the Soviet people—the housing problem. The housing shortage will be ended in the course of the first decade. Those families that still live in overcrowded and poor housing will receive new apartments. By the conclusion of the second decade every family, including newlyweds, will have a well-appointed apartment meeting the requirements of health and cultured living. Peasant houses of the old type will in the main be replaced by new, modern dwellings, or where possible they will be rebuilt with necessary conveniences. In the course of the second decade housing will gradually be made rent-free for all citizens.

Urban development, architecture and planning are assuming great importance in creating modern, convenient cities and other populated points, as well as production, residential and public buildings, that are economical to build and maintain. Cities and settlements should represent rational, integrated organization of production zones, residential areas, a network of public and cultural institutions, service enterprises, transport, engineering installations and a power system ensuring the best conditions for the work, life and relaxation of people.

An extensive program of communal construction and of improvements in all cities and workers' settlements will be carried out in the coming period; this will require completion of their electrification, the necessary provision of gas, telephone service, public transport facilities, water supply and sewer systems, and measures for the further improvement of living conditions in cities and other populated points—including tree planting, pond building and a determined struggle against air, soil and water pollution.

Well-appointed small and medium-sized cities will be increasingly developed, making for better and healthier living conditions.

Public transport facilities (streetcars, buses, trolleybuses and subways) will become free in the course of the second decade, and at the end of it such public utilities as water, gas and heating will also be free.

C. Reduction of Working Hours and the Further Improvement of Working Conditions

In the coming ten years the country will change to a *six-hour working day* with one day off a week or a *35-hour working week* with two days off, and in underground work and hazardous jobs to a five-hour working day or a 30-hour, five-day working week.

On the basis of a corresponding rise in labor productivity, transition to a still shorter working week will be begun in the second decade.

The Soviet Union will thus have the world's shortest and at the same time most productive and highest-paid working day. Working people will have much more leisure time, and this will create additional conditions for improving their cultural and technical level.

The length of the annual paid vacations of working people will be increased in addition to the reduction in the working day. The minimum vacation for all workers and employees will gradually increase to three weeks and then to one month. Paid vacations will gradually be extended to collective farmers also.

Comprehensive improvement of working conditions to make work healthier and easier constitutes an important task in improving the well-being of the people. Modern labor safety and hygienic measures to prevent occupational injuries and diseases will be introduced at all enterprises. Night shifts will gradually be abolished at enterprises, except for those where around-the-clock operation is required by the technological process or the need to serve the population.

D. Health Care and Increasing Longevity

The socialist state is the only state that undertakes to protect and constantly improve the health of the whole population. This is provided for by a system of socio-economic and medical measures. An extensive program of measures will be carried out to prevent and decisively reduce illness, wipe out mass contagious diseases and further increase longevity.

The needs of the urban and rural population for all forms of highly qualified *medical care* will be met in full. Accomplishment of this task calls for the extensive construction of medical institutions, including hospitals and sanatoriums, the equipment of all medical institutions with modern apparatus, and regular medical checkups for the entire population. Special emphasis must be given to extending the urban and rural network of mother-and-child health institutions (maternity homes, medical consultation centers, children's sanatoriums and hospitals, forest schools, etc.).

In addition to the existing free medical services, sanatorium accommodations and medicines will be provided for the sick free of charge.

In order to afford the people an opportunity for recreation in an out-of-town environment, rest homes, boarding houses, country hotels and tourist camps will be built where working people will be accommodated at a reasonable charge or—by way of a bonus—at a discount or free.

The Party considers one of the most important tasks to be ensuring the upbringing from earliest childhood of a physically strong young generation, harmoniously developed physically and spiritually. This requires the utmost encouragement of all forms of mass sport and physical culture, including at schools, and the drawing of broader and broader strata of the population, particularly the youth, into the physical culture movement.

E. Improvement of Everyday Conditions and of the Position of Women; Maintenance of Children and Disabled Persons at Public Expense

The vestiges of the unequal position of women in domestic life must be completely eliminated; all social and living conditions must be provided to enable women to combine happy motherhood with increasingly active and creative participation in social labor and public activities and in scientific and artistic pursuits. Women must be given relatively lighter and at the same time sufficiently well-paid jobs. Maternity leave will be of longer duration.

It is essential to provide conditions to reduce and lighten woman's work in the home and later to make possible the replacement of this work by public forms of satisfying the everyday material needs of the family. Toward this end, improved, inexpensive domestic machines, appliances and electrical devices will be widely introduced in households, and the public's needs for service enterprises will be fully met in the next few years.

The extension of *public catering*—including dining rooms at enterprises and institutions and in big apartment houses—until it meets the demands of the population requires special attention. The service in dining rooms and the quality of food must be radically improved, so that dinners in the dining rooms will be tasty and nourishing and will cost the family less than meals cooked at home. Price reductions in public catering will keep ahead of price reductions for food products in the stores. Thanks to all of this, public catering will be able to take a preponderant place over home cooking within ten to 15 years.

The transition to free public catering (midday meals) at enterprises and institutions and for collective farmers at work will begin in the second decade.

To provide a happy childhood for every child is one of the most important and noble tasks of building a communist society. The further extensive development of the network of children's institutions will make it possible for more and more families, and in the second decade for every family, to keep children and adolescents free of charge at children's institutions if they so desire. The Party considers it necessary to do everything possible to satisfy fully the need for preschool institutions within the next few years.

In town and countryside the need for nurseries, kindergartens, playgrounds, extended-day schools and Young Pioneer camps will be satisfied fully and without charge; there will be mass extension of boarding schools with free maintenance; free hot lunches will be served at all schools, and extended school hours with free dinners for school children will be introduced; and school uniforms and textbooks will be issued without charge.

As the national income grows state agencies, the trade unions and the collective farms will in the course of the 20 years gradually undertake the maintenance of all citizens incapacitated through old age or disability. Sickness and temporary disability grants and old age pensions will be extended to collective farmers; old age and disability pensions will be raised. In town and countryside the network of well-appointed homes for the aged and invalids will be greatly extended to provide free accommodations for all applicants.

By fulfilling the tasks set by the Party for the improvement of the well-being of the people, the Soviet Union will make considerable headway toward the practical realization of the communist principle of distribution according to needs.

At the end of the 20 years public consumption funds will account for approximately half of the total real income of the population. This will make it possible to provide at public expense:

—free maintenance of children at children's institutions and boarding schools (if parents wish);

—material security for non-able-bodied persons;

—free education at all educational institutions;

—free medical care for all citizens, including the supply of medicines and treatment of the sick at sanatoriums;

—rent-free housing and, later, free public utilities;

—free public transport;

—free provision of some types of everyday services;

—steady reduction of charges for, and partially free, use of rest homes, boarding houses, tourist camps and sports installations;

—increasingly broad provision of the population with benefits, privileges and stipends (grants to unmarried mothers, stipends for students);

—gradual change-over to free public catering (midday meals) at enterprises and institutions and for collective farmers at work.

The Soviet state will thus present to the world a model of truly full and all-embracing satisfaction of the growing material and cultural requirements of man. The faster the productive forces of the country and labor productivity grow and the more broadly the creative energy of the Soviet people comes into play, the faster will the living standard of Soviet people improve.

The planned program can be successfully fulfilled under conditions of peace. Complications in the international situation and the resultant necessity of increasing defense expenditures may retard fulfillment of the plans for improving the people's well being. A lasting normalization of international relations, reduction of military expenditures, and in particular the realization of general and complete disarmament under an appropriate agreement among states would make it possible considerably to surpass the plans for raising the working people's living standard.

The fulfillment of the vast program for improving the well-being of the Soviet people will have world-historic significance. The Party calls on the Soviet people to work perseveringly, with inspiration. Every working person must do his duty in the building of a communist society, in the struggle to fulfill the program for improving the people's well-being.

TASKS OF THE PARTY IN THE SPHERES OF STATE CONSTRUCTION AND THE FURTHER DEVELOPMENT OF SOCIALIST DEMOCRACY

The dictatorship of the proletariat, born of the socialist revolution, has played a world-historic role by ensuring the victory of socialism in the U.S.S.R. At the same time, in the process of the building of socialism it has undergone changes itself. In connection with the liquidation of the exploiting classes, the function of suppressing their resistance withered away. The chief functions of the socialist state—economic-organizational and cultural-educational—have developed comprehensively. The socialist state has entered a new period of its development. The process of the state's evolution into an organization of all the working people of socialist society has begun. Proletarian democracy is becoming more and more a socialist democracy of the people as a whole.

The working class is the only class in history that does not aim to perpetuate its power.

Having brought about the complete and final victory of socialism—the first phase of communism—and the transition of society to the full-scale construction of communism, the dictatorship of the proletariat has accomplished its historical mission and has ceased to be essential in the U.S.S.R. from the point of view of the tasks of internal development. The state that arose as a state of the dictatorship of the proletariat has in the new, present stage turned into a state of the entire people, an agency expressing the interests and will of the people as a whole. Since the working class is the most advanced and the best organized force of Soviet society, it performs its leading role in the period of full-scale construction of communism as well.

The working class will have completed its function of leader of society when communism is built and classes disappear.

The Party proceeds from the principle that the dictatorship of the working class will cease to be necessary before the state withers away. The state as an organization embracing the entire people will survive until the total victory of communism. Expressing the will of the people, it is called upon to organize the creation of the material and technical base of communism and the transformation of socialist relations into communist relations, to exercise control over the measure of work and the measure of consumption, to ensure a rise in the well-being of the people, to safeguard the rights and freedoms of Soviet citizens, socialist law and order and socialist property, to instill in the masses of the people conscious discipline and a communist attitude to labor, reliably to ensure the defense and security of the country, to develop fraternal cooperation with the socialist countries, to champion the cause of universal peace and to maintain normal relations with all countries.

Comprehensive extension and perfection of socialist democracy, active participation by all citizens in the administration of the state and in the management of economic and cultural construction, improvement of the work of the state apparatus and intensification of control over its activity by the people—such is the main direction of the development of the socialist state system in the period of the building of communism. As socialist democracy develops further, the agencies of state power will gradually be transformed into agencies of public self-government. The Leninist principle of democratic centralism—which ensures the proper combination of centralized leadership with maximum development of the initiative of local agencies, the extension of the rights of the Union republics and greater creative activity of the masses—will be still further developed. It is necessary to strengthen discipline, to exercise day-to-day control over the activities of all links in the administrative apparatus, to check up on the execution of decisions and laws of the Soviet state and to heighten the responsibility of every official for their strict and prompt implementation.

The Soviets and the Development of Democratic Principles of State Administration

The role of the Soviets, which have become all-inclusive organizations of the people embodying their unity, will grow in the course of communist construction. The Soviets, which combine the features of state and public organizations, operate more and more like public organizations, with the masses participating extensively and directly in their work.

The Party considers it necessary to perfect the forms of popular representation and to develop the democratic principles of the Soviet electoral system.

In nominating candidates for Deputies to Soviets, it is necessary to guarantee the widest and fullest discussion of the personal qualities and qualifications of the candidates at meetings and in the press in order to elect those who are most worthy and who enjoy the highest authority.

To improve the work of the Soviets and bring fresh forces into them, it is desirable that at least one-third of the members of a Soviet be replaced by new Deputies at each election so that *more millions of working people may go through the school of administering the state.*

The Party considers *systematic renewal of the executive agencies* necessary to bring a wider range of able persons into them and to rule out the possibility of abuses of authority by individual state officials. It is advisable to establish the principle that the leading officials of Union, republic and local agencies may as a rule be elected to their offices for not more than three consecutive terms. In cases where it is the general opinion that the personal talents of an official make his further activity in an executive agency useful and necessary, his re-election may be permitted; the election in such cases shall be considered valid only if at least three-fourths of the votes, and not a simple majority of them, are cast in his favor.

The Party regards the improvement of the principles of socialist democracy and their rigid observance as a most important task. It is necessary to employ to the full: regular accounting by the Soviets and Deputies to their constituents; the right of the electorate to recall Deputies who have not justified the confidence placed in them; publicity about all important questions of state administration and of economic and cultural construction, and free and full discussion of these questions at sessions of the Soviets; regular accounting by executive agencies of authority at all levels to sessions of the Soviets; checkup on the work of these agencies and control over their activity; regular discussion by the Soviets of interpellations by Deputies; criticism of shortcomings in the work of Soviet, economic and other organizations. . . .

The transition to communism means the fullest development of personal freedom and the rights of Soviet citizens. Socialism has granted and guaranteed the working people the broadest rights and freedoms. Communism will bring the working people further great rights and opportunities.

The Party sets the task of ensuring the strict observance of socialist legality, the eradication of all violations of law and order, the abolition of crime and the removal of all the causes of crime.

Justice in the U.S.S.R. is exercised in full conformity with the law. It is based on truly democratic principles: electivity and accountability of the judges and people's assessors, the right to recall them, open hearing of court cases, and the participation of public accusers and defenders in court with strictest observance of legality and all the norms of trial procedure by the courts and by investigation and inquiry agencies. The democratic principles of justice will be developed and improved.

There should be no room for lawbreakers and crime in a society that is building communism. But as long as there are criminal offenses, it is necessary severely to punish those who commit crimes dangerous to society, violate the rules of the socialist community and do not wish to live by honest labor. Chief attention should be focused on preventing crime.

Higher standards of living and culture and greater social consciousness of the working people will create all the conditions for eradicating crime and for the ultimate replacement of measures of criminal punishment by measures of public influence and education. Under socialism anyone who has strayed from the path of a working man can return to useful activity. . . .

As the socialist state system develops, it will gradually become public *communist self-government,* in which will be united the Soviets, trade unions, cooperatives and other mass organizations of the working people. This process will signify a further development of democracy, ensuring the active participation of all members of society in the management of public affairs. Public functions similar to the present state functions of economic and cultural management will be preserved under communism, changing and being perfected in accordance with the development of society. But the character of the functions and the ways in which they are carried out will be different than under socialism. The agencies for planning, accounting, economic management and cultural development, now state bodies, will lose their political character and will become agencies of public self-government. Communist society will be a highly organized community of men of labor. A single body of universally recognized rules of communist community life will be established, and the observance of these rules will become an inner need and habit of all people.

Historical development inevitably leads to the withering away of the state. For the state to wither away completely, it is necessary to create both domestic conditions—the building of a developed communist society—and external conditions—the victory and consolidation of socialism in the international arena. . . .

The Establishment of Communist Morality

In the process of the transition to communism, moral principles become increasingly important in the life of society; the sphere of operation of the moral factor grows and the importance of the administrative regulation of human relationships diminishes accordingly. The Party will encourage all forms of conscious self-discipline of citizens leading to the establishment and development of the basic rules of the communist community.

In contrast to the distorted, egoistic views and mores of the old world, the Communists, rejecting the class morality of the exploiters, present communist morality, the most just and noble morality, expressing the interests and ideals of all working mankind. Communism makes the simple standards of morality and justice, which were distorted or shamelessly flouted under the rule of the exploiters, into inviolable rules for relations both between individuals and between peoples. Communist morality includes the basic universal moral norms evolved by the masses of the people in the course of millenniums in the struggle against social oppression and vices. The revolutionary morality of the working class is of particular importance to the moral development of society. In the course of building socialism and communism, communist morality becomes enriched with new principles and new content.

The Party holds that *the moral code of the builder of communism* includes such principles as:

—devotion to the cause of communism, love of the socialist homeland, of the socialist countries;

—conscientious labor for the good of society: He who does not work, neither shall he eat;

—concern on the part of each for the preservation and growth of public wealth;

—a high sense of public duty, intolerance of violations of the public interest;

—collectivism and comradely mutual assistance: One for all and all for one;

—humane relations and mutual respect among people: Man is to man a friend, comrade and brother;

—honesty and truthfulness, moral purity, guilelessness and modesty in public and private life;

—mutual respect in the family and concern for the upbringing of children;

—an uncompromising attitude to injustice, parasitism, dishonesty, careerism and money-grubbing;

—friendship and brotherhood of all peoples of the U.S.S.R., intolerance of national and racial animosity;

—an uncompromising attitude toward the enemies of communism, peace and the freedom of peoples;

—fraternal solidarity with the working people of all countries and with all peoples.

The Development of Proletarian Internationalism and Socialist Patriotism

The Party will untiringly rear Soviet people in the spirit of proletarian internationalism and will promote in every way the strengthening of the international solidarity of the working people. In developing the Soviet people's love of their fatherland, the Party proceeds from the fact that with the formation of the world socialist system, the patriotism of the citizens of socialist society is expressed in devotion and loyalty to their own homeland and to the entire commonwealth of socialist countries. Socialist patriotism and socialist internationalism organically embody proletarian solidarity with the working class and the working people of all countries. The Party will continue perseveringly to combat the reactionary ideology of bourgeois nationalism, racism and cosmopolitanism.

All-Round and Harmonious Development of the Individual

In the period of transition to communism the opportunities increase for *rearing a new man, in whom are harmoniously combined spiritual wealth, moral purity and physical perfection.*

The conditions for all-round development of the individual have been created by historic social gains—freedom from exploitation, unemployment and poverty, from discrimination on account of sex, origin, nationality or race. Every member of society is provided equal opportunities for creative work and education. Relations of dependence and inequality between people in public and family life disappear. The personal dignity of each citizen is protected by society. Each is guaranteed an equal and free choice of field of endeavor and specialty, with due regard to the interests of society. As the time spent on material production is reduced, ever greater opportunities are afforded to develop abilities, gifts and talents in the fields of production, science, technology, literature and the arts. People's leisure will be increasingly devoted to public activities, cultural intercourse, mental and physical development and artistic endeavor. Physical culture and sports will become a firm part of the everyday life of people. . . .

THE PARTY IN THE PERIOD OF THE FULL-SCALE BUILDING OF COMMUNISM

As a result of the victory of socialism in the U.S.S.R. and the consolidation of the unity of Soviet society, the Communist Party of the working class has become the vanguard of the Soviet people, a party of the whole people, and has extended its guiding influence to all aspects of the life of society. The Party is the wisdom, the honor and the conscience of our epoch, of the Soviet people, who are carrying out great revolutionary transformations. It looks keenly into the future and shows the people scientifically determined roads along which to advance, arouses titanic energy in the masses and leads them to the accomplishment of imposing tasks.

The period of the full-scale building of communism is characterized by a further *rise in the role and importance of the Communist Party* as the leading and guiding force of Soviet society.

Communist society, unlike all previous socio-economic formations, does not develop spontaneously but as a result of conscious and purposeful activity of the masses, led by the Marxist-Leninist party. The Communist Party—which unites in its ranks the most advanced representatives of the working class and all the working people, is closely linked with the masses, enjoys unbounded authority among the people and possesses knowledge of the laws of social development—ensures correct leadership in all the work of communist construction, giving it an organized, planned and scientific character.

The heightening of the role of the Party in the life of Soviet society in the new stage of its development is determined by:

—the growing scope and complexity of the tasks of communist construction, calling for a higher level of political and organizational leadership;

—the growth of the creative activity of the masses and the enlistment of new millions of working people in the administration of state affairs and of production;

—the further development of socialist democracy, the heightened role of public organizations, the expansion of the rights of the Union republics and of local organizations;

—the growing importance of the theory of scientific communism, of its creative development and propaganda; the necessity for intensifying the communist upbringing of the working people and for fighting to overcome survivals of the past in the minds of people.

There must be a new, higher stage in the development of the Party itself and of its political, ideological and organizational work that conforms with the full-scale building of communism. The Party will constantly improve the forms and methods of its work, so that the level of its leadership of the masses, through the building of the material and technical base of communism and the development of society's spiritual life, will keep pace with the growing requirements of the epoch of communist construction.

As the vanguard of the people building a communist society, the Party must also march forward in the organization of its inner-Party life, serving as an example and model in developing the most advanced forms of communist public self-government.

Undeviating observance of the Leninist norms of Party life and of the principle of collective leadership, heightening of the responsibility of Party agencies and their officials to the Party masses, the ensuring of a growth in the activeness and initiative of all Communists and of their participation in working out and carrying into effect the policy of the Party, and the development of criticism and self-criticism are laws of Party life. This is an imperative condition of the ideological and organizational strength of the Party itself, of the unity and solidarity of the Party ranks, of comprehensive development of inner-Party democracy and of activization on this basis of all Party forces, and of the strengthening of ties with the masses.

The cult of the individual and related violations of collective leadership, inner-Party democracy and socialist legality are incompatible with the Leninist principles of Party life. The cult of the individual leads to a belittling of the role of the Party and of the masses of the people and hampers the development of the ideological life of the Party and the creative activity of the working people.

In order to apply the Leninist principle of collective leadership consistently, to ensure a wider influx of fresh new Party forces into the executive Party bodies and to combine old and young cadres properly, and also to rule out the possibility of an excessive concentration of power in the hands of individual officials and to prevent instances of loss of control over them by the collective, the Party considers it necessary to carry out the following measures:

(a) To introduce in practice a systematic turnover of a certain proportion of the membership of all elected Party bodies, from the primary organizations to the Central Committee, at the same time ensuring continuity of leadership.

At all regular elections of the Central Committee of the C.P.S.U. and its Presidium, not less than one-quarter of the membership shall be newly elected. Presidium members may as a rule be elected for not more than three successive terms. Certain Party workers may, by virtue of their recognized authority and high political, organizational or other abilities, be successively elected to executive bodies for a longer period. In such cases, election requires a majority of at least three-quarters of the votes cast by secret ballot.

At least one-third of the members of the Central Committees of the Union-republic Communist Parties and of territory and province Party committees chosen at each regular election, and one-half of the members of region [okrug], city and district (borough) Party committees and the committees or bureaus of primary Party organizations shall be new members. Furthermore, members of these executive Party bodies may be elected for not more than three terms, and secretaries of the primary Party organizations for not more than two consecutive terms.

A Party organization may, in consideration of the political and work qualities of an individual, elect him to an executive body for a longer period. In such cases election requires that not less than three-quarters of the Communists participating in the voting cast their ballots for him.

Party members who are not re-elected to an executive Party body on the expiration of their terms may be re-elected at subsequent elections.

It is established that a decision to remove a member from the Party Central Committee or other executive body shall be adopted solely by secret ballot and is valid when not less than two-thirds of the members of the body in question vote in favor of the decision.

(b) To extend the application of the elective principle and that of accountability in Party organizations from top to bottom, including Party organizations working in special conditions (army, navy).

(c) To heighten the role of Party meetings, conferences, Congresses and plenary sessions of Party committees and other collective bodies. To ensure favorable conditions for free and businesslike discussion within the Party of questions of its policy and practical activities and for comradely discussions of controversial or insufficiently clear matters.

(d) To reduce steadily the paid Party apparatus, enlisting Communists more extensively to do nonsalaried volunteer work.

(e) To develop criticism and self-criticism in every way, as a tested method of work and a means of disclosing and rectifying errors and short-comings and of rearing cadres correctly.

In the period of full-scale communist construction the role and responsibility of the Party member will steadily increase. It is the duty of a Communist by his entire behavior in production, in public and in private life, to be a model in the struggle for the development and strengthening of communist relations and to observe the principles and norms of communist morality. . . .

The indestructible ideological and organizational unity of the Party is a most important source of its invincibility, a guarantee of the successful accomplishment of the great tasks of communist construction.

The people are the decisive force in the building of communism. *The Party exists for the people, and it is in serving the people that it sees the purpose of its activity.* A further extension and deepening of the ties between the Party and the people is a necessary condition for success in the struggle for communism. The Party considers it its duty always to consult the working people on major questions of domestic and foreign policy, to bring these questions before all the people for discussion, and to attract nonmembers more widely into participation in all its work. The further socialist democracy develops, the deeper and more comprehensive must be the work of the Party among the working people and the stronger will be its influence among the masses. . . .

The Communist Party of the Soviet Union will continue to strengthen the unity of the international Communist movement, to develop fraternal ties with all the Communist and Workers' Parties, and to coordinate its actions with the efforts of all the detachments of the world Communist movement for joint struggle against the danger of a new world war, for the interests of the working people, for peace, democracy and socialism.

Such is the program of work for the construction of communism that the Communist Party of the Soviet Union sets forth.

The construction of communism in the U.S.S.R. will be the greatest victory mankind has won throughout its age-long history. Each new step made toward the shining peaks of communism inspires the working masses in all countries, renders tremendous moral support in the struggle for the liberation of all peoples from social and national oppression, and speeds the triumph of the ideas of Marxism-Leninism on a worldwide scale.

When the Soviet people enjoy the blessings of communism, new hundreds of millions of people on earth will say: "We are for communism!" It is not through war with other countries but by the example of a more perfect organization of society, by the flowering of productive forces, the creation of all the conditions for the happiness and well-being of man, that the ideas of communism are winning the minds and hearts of the masses.

The forces of social progress will inevitably grow in all countries, and this will give support to the builders of communism in the Soviet Union.

The Party proceeds from the Marxist-Leninist thesis that the people make history and that the establishment of communism is the work of the hands of the people, of their energy and intelligence. The victory of communism depends on people and communism is being built for people. Each Soviet man brings the triumph of communism nearer by his labor. The successes of communist construction spell abundance and a happy life for all and enhance the might, prestige and glory of the Soviet Union.

The Party is confident that Soviet people will accept the new Program of the C.P.S.U. as their own vital cause, as the greatest purpose of their life and as a banner of nationwide struggle for the building of communism. The Party calls on all Communists, on the entire Soviet people—men and women workers and collective farmers and workers of mental labor—to apply their energies to the successful fulfillment of the historic tasks set forth in the Program.

UNDER THE TESTED LEADERSHIP OF THE COMMUNIST PARTY, UNDER THE BANNER OF MARXISM-LENINISM, THE SOVIET PEOPLE HAVE BUILT SOCIALISM.

UNDER THE LEADERSHIP OF THE PARTY, UNDER THE BANNER OF MARXISM-LENINISM, THE SOVIET PEOPLE WILL BUILD COMMUNIST SOCIETY.

THE PARTY SOLEMNLY PROCLAIMS: THE PRESENT GENERATION OF SOVIET PEOPLE WILL LIVE UNDER COMMUNISM!

WHAT'S COMMUNISM? IS IT BEING ACHIEVED?

HARRY SCHWARTZ*

"The Congress of the Builders of Communism" is the name the Soviet press has given to the Twenty-second Congress of the Soviet Communist

* Economist, specializing on Soviet affairs, *New York Times*. Author of *Russia's Soviet Economy* and of *The Red Phoenix*. The article originally appeared in *The New York Times Magazine*, Oct. 15, 1961, and is reproduced with the permission of the author and the newspaper.

Party. No Communist party gathering anywhere has ever before been labeled as being of such high importance from the point of view of Communist ideology. The reason is simple: no previous Communist party conclave has ever met explicitly to consider and approve a program which promises specifically to build the ideal Communist society of tomorrow. The meeting had as the central item on its agenda the draft of a new party program promising exactly that, and ending with the words:

"The party solemnly proclaims: the present generation of Soviet people shall live under communism!"

The historic nature of that promise deserves to be underlined. For more than a century Marxists have used the concept of the Communist Utopia purely as a propaganda weapon to attack the capitalist system and to win converts. Now the party that rules one of the two richest and most powerful nations on earth has gone on record that it intends to deliver the goods—to realize ideal communism—within the lifetime of most present-day Soviet citizens.

All this presents an occasion to explore two key questions: What do the Russians mean by "communism"? How close are they to attaining that state?

At the very outset, one is struck by a curious fact: for all the many decades of discussion and propaganda about communism, nowhere is there any clear, simple and generally accepted blueprint explaining exactly what a Communist society would be like. And the more one searches the literature, the more one suspects that there has been a kind of unspoken agreement among Communist theoreticians through the generations to leave the idea as vague as possible.

Karl Marx never supplied any detailed scheme in the millions of words he wrote. In "The Communist Manifesto," for example, he began by asserting, "A specter is haunting Europe—the specter of communism," but he never bothered to define communism beyond the statement that the "theory of the Communists may be summed up in the single sentence: abolition of private property."

The nearest Marx ever came to a definition was in his "Critique of the Gotha Program," in which he talked of two stages of communism, the first immediately after a successful revolution, and the second or higher phase, which he described this way:

"In a higher phase of Communist society, after the enslaving subordination of individuals under division of labor, and therewith also the antithesis between mental and physical labor has vanished; after labor, from a mere means of life, has itself become the prime necessity of life; after the productive forces have also increased with the all-round development of the individual and all the springs of cooperative wealth flow more abundantly—only then can the narrow horizon of bourgeois rights be fully left behind and society inscribe on its banners: from each according to his ability, to each according to his needs!"

For almost a century that brief paragraph has dominated all discussion of communism—a system whose propaganda image has been presented as the final realization of abundance, equality, justice and freedom for all. Such vagueness had the advantage of permitting each individual to read into the idea of communism all that he personally hoped and wanted for a better future.

The first indication that this vagueness could not continue forever came three years ago from Communist China. In the summer and fall of 1958 some Chinese Communist writers began claiming that the People's Communes formed in that country then were making it possible for Communist China to reach ideal communism within a very short time, even ahead of the Soviet Union.

These grandiose claims by a nation the Russians looked down upon as backward and primitive infuriated Moscow, and soon the Chinese beat a hasty retreat from their ideological presumptuousness. Nevertheless, the challenge from China brought home to Premier Khrushchev and his ideologists the need for making clear what they meant by communism and for defining the means by which the Soviet Union would lead the march to the ideal society.

The new Communist party program in the Soviet Union is the answer to this challenge, but even its definition of communism and of the Communist man shares the vagueness shown by Marx. It states:

"Communism is a classless social system with one form of public ownership of the means of production and full social equality of all members of society; under it, the all-round development of people will be accompanied by the growth of productive forces through continuous progress in science and technology; all sources of public wealth will gush forth abundantly, and the great principle 'From each according to his ability, to each according to his needs' will be implemented. Communism is a highly organized society of free, socially conscious working people in which public self-government will be established, a society in which labor for the good of society will become the prime vital requirement of everyone, a necessity recognized by one and all, and the ability of each person will be employed to the greatest benefit of the people.

"A high degree of Communist consciousness, industry, discipline and devotion to the public interest are qualities typifying the man of Communist society."

But even that latest formula is obviously still vague, so the orders have gone out to Soviet theoreticians to come up with something more concrete. The result has been to make plain how cloudy the whole business is.

Some Soviet writers declare that personal property will continue to exist under communism—clothing, books and the like. Others deny that personal property of any kind is compatible with communism. The top Soviet theoretician, Academician S. G. Strumlin, has drawn a picture of Communist society as one in which people live together in communal dwellings of 2,000 to 3,000 people each, within ten-minute walks of where they work. Others have assailed this picture as obsolete, insisting that "communism" can be built without "communes." The debate goes on.

Yet even amid all the cloudiness of current Soviet thinking about the perfect Communist future, certain points are clear and can be used as a basis for trying to judge how close the Soviet Union now is to the ultimate Communist society. Let us look at four vital points in this matter:

(1) *Communist society will have to be one of great abundance so that all needs can be met.*

Soviet spokesmen have shown an awareness of the potential insatiability of human desires. They have stated bluntly that they do not envisage communism as a state in which everyone can have all the automobiles, houses, yachts and trips around the world he wants. Instead, they talk about the "reasonable needs" of people, implying that it is intended to set up a system of norms—so many pounds of meat, so many suits of clothes and the like—defining what people are entitled to.

But even on such limited terms, Soviet spokesmen have admitted that it would require more production than that of the United States at present to meet the requirements for Communist "abundance."

On this score it is evident that the Soviet Union is still far from the Communist ideal. By Premier Khrushchev's own admission, the Soviet Union still does not have anything like enough housing, enough food, enough clothing, enough durable consumer goods to meet its people's needs.

Moreover, the new Communist party program concedes that even if its ambitious economic plan for the next twenty years is fulfilled, full Communist abundance will not have been reached, although by 1980 the U.S.S.R. is planning to produce more than twice as much as the United States produces now. There is, of course, no assurance that these ambitious production plans will be achieved.

Just how far behind the United States—let alone a state of Communist abundance—the Soviet Union is may be seen from a few statistical comparisons. Last year [1960], for example, the United States produced three times as many eggs per person as did the Soviet Union, more than twice as much meat per person and 70 per cent more grain per person. Soviet production of automobiles last year was only equal to about one week's normal production of the United States passenger-car industry. Soviet production of cotton cloth—the basic clothing material in that country—was only about half that of the United States per person.

Putting all the available material together, it seems safe to say that the standard of living in the United States is on the average almost three times as high as that in the Soviet Union.

(2) Communist society will have to be inhabited by people moved by motives different from those the West knows.

Work in that society, the Soviet blueprint holds, will be "the prime vital requirement of everyone." Moreover, the amount and quality of work people will do in that society will apparently have no relationship to their income, so that apparently the citizens of the Communist society will not require incentives. Are the Soviet people anywhere near such a highly developed sense of social obligation and social responsibility as this requirement suggests?

For the moment, at least, the answer seems to be clearly in the negative. The Soviet wage system contains substantial inequalities of payment, aimed deliberately at rewarding those who work hard and have the most skill while giving the least payment to those who work poorly and have little or no skill. At the beginning of this year, Premier Khrushchev underlined the importance of the incentives in modern Soviet society by blaming the failures in agricultural production in part on the failure to reward the hardest-working peasants generously enough in comparison with their fellows who worked poorly.

Moreover, it is clear that the Soviet Union contains an appreciable number of persons whose main object in life seems to be to get along with as little work as possible, or at least as little honest work as possible. The tightening up of Soviet law this past year testifies to this. A campaign has been waged against "idlers" and "parasites" who disdain honest factory or farm labor but make their living in the black market. Such unsavory characters can now be exiled from their places of residence. Another recent revision of Soviet law makes it possible to apply the death sentence to counterfeiters, to persons who embezzle large amounts of state property, to speculators in foreign currency and the like. Several such death sentences have already been handed down.

All in all, the picture of the ordinary Soviet citizen that is recorded daily in the Soviet press is hardly one to suggest a population of near-paragons who have almost reached the level of selflessness that perfect communism seems to assume. Rather, the picture that emerges is one of human beings just as subject to the pull of self-interest, to laziness and to the desire for easy, sometimes illicit, gain as those of other lands.

(3) Communist society is one in which there will be "full social equality of all members of society."

How near to perfect equality is Soviet society today? Not very near at all, any candid inspection of the Soviet scene suggests. The real income of a top Soviet official, writer or scientist is on a level with that of an average resident of Westchester County; at the bottom of the Soviet economic system there are millions living at a poorer level than the American who receives unemployment insurance.

Inequality of power is even more marked than economic inequality.

There is no analogue in our society for the contrast between the political power of Premier Khrushchev and the complete political powerlessness of the average Soviet citizen. Further, it must be remembered that in each sphere of Soviet life—in each province, city, town and district—there tends also to be a hierarchy of power in which the man at the top makes the key decisions to which those below must submit.

These inequalities in contemporary Soviet life have led inevitably to sharp social inequality. A standard target for Soviet satire is the upperclass mother who is appalled when her son or daughter comes home and announces he or she plans to marry the offspring of an ordinary worker. Soviet college students, and their parents, tend to look down upon proletarians doomed to lives in the factory or on the farm, and upper-class Soviet families pull every string possible—and sometimes pay expensive bribes—to avert the awful calamity represented by the failure of a son or daughter to enter the university.

It is true that Premier Khrushchev has sought to combat some of the most extreme aspects of inequality. He has reduced some of the highest salary categories and raised minimum wages. He has introduced the requirement that most high school graduates work for two years before entering the university full time. He has denounced the wire-pulling and bribery that upper-class parents use to get their not-overly-bright children into the university.

But his own liking for the good things of life—for Italian-made clothes, American pens and foreign hunting equipment—has set an example that others in important positions have not ignored. And his obvious favoring of his son-in-law Alexei Adzhubei, who is now editor-in-chief of Izvestia, has given an example of the use of power that is much more vivid than are his words denouncing such practices.

(4) *The Communist society is to be composed of "free" people.*

How free are the Soviet people today? Not very free. The dictatorship of the Communist party not only is strong now, but is apparently envisaged as continuing indefinitely. The demand that the press, radio, schools, theatre and the like adhere to the party line is no less insistent than it was in Stalin's time. And the identification of political opposition with subversion continues unchanged.

It is true that there has been some parting of the Iron Curtain under Khrushchev. A small fraction of the Soviet people is allowed to go abroad these days, some even to the capitalist West. Jamming of foreign broadcasts is less frequent than it was in Stalin's day, and there is greater access to foreign writing. But all of these concessions are far from being what "free men" have a right to expect.

Soviet society today, one must conclude, is a long way from the Communist Utopia. It is still a poor civilization inhabited by people who are moved by self-interest rather than by idealistic concern for others. Soviet society is shot through with many different kinds of inequality and its citizens are far from free.

Undoubtedly, the Soviet Union is likely to make much material progress over the next two decades, so that by 1980—if World War III is avoided— the Soviet people should be able to live much better than they do now. But anything approaching the kind of abundance genuine communism assumes seems far out of reach.

Even more out of reach, it would appear, is the kind of selflessness that the official picture of communism calls for. Whether that ideal of selflessness is ever realizable in any society is doubtful indeed.

As for the inequality rife in the Soviet Union, it is based in part upon the dictatorial character of the regime and in part simply upon natural inequalities of talent.

Finally, the lack of freedom of Soviet people is a necessity of the Communist party dictatorship and could be ended only by removal of that dictatorship—something Khrushchev and his colleagues do not envisage at all.

The conclusion seems inevitable that whatever kind of society the Soviet Union will have in 1980 or later it will not be the ideal communism Marx had in mind but was careful never to spell out. But there is nothing to stop the Communist rulers of the Soviet Union—if they are still in power two decades from now—from calling whatever society they may have then "communism." After all, one of the powers a dictatorial regime enjoys is the power to decide what words mean, and that power has been exercised by the Soviet regime for many years.

THE C.P.S.U. PROGRAM: A CREDO OF CONSERVATISM

Robert C. Tucker*

The new Program of the Soviet Communist Party is far more than a program in the specific sense of the word. Covering past and present as well as the projected future, treating of capitalism as well as communism, of foreign as well as internal policy, it offers an apologia for the Soviet regime and its actions over the years, a blueprint of sorts indicating the future directions of Soviet policy, and a general redefinition of the articles of faith for a Soviet or Moscow-oriented Communist in the year 1961. . . .

Khrushchev's name goes unmentioned in the text of the new Program, as if to underscore the rather strong statement in the final section against the "cult of the individual" and in favor of the "Leninist principle of col-

* Professor of Government at Indiana University; author of *Philosophy and Myth in Karl Marx*. The selection is from *Problems of Communism*, Vol. X (Sept.-Oct. 1961), pp. 1-4. By permission.

lective leadership." Yet the imprint of Khrushchev's political orientation lies clearly upon it. His innovations in internal policy, such as the development of the virgin lands and the establishment of the regional economic councils and reorganizations of the MTS (Machine Tractor Stations), are duly approved. His ideas in regard to revitalizing the Soviet bureaucratic machine receive further elaboration. Even agrogorods are back in fashion, though under a new name ("agrarian-industrial complexes") and only as a distant goal. And Khrushchevian over-optimism as to the potentialities of economic progress under the existing system is evident in various places. A case in point is the assertion that the USSR will surpass the United States in per capita production (including agricultural production) by 1970. Another is the promise to raise the national income by nearly 250 percent in ten years and by 500 percent in twenty. . . .

Unlike the party programs of 1903 and 1919, which were primarily concerned with the immediate rather than the ultimate goals of the Communist movement, the new Program directly addresses itself to the task of achieving full communism in the USSR. Part Two, entitled "Tasks of the CPSU in the Construction of a Communist Society," starts with the declaration that the building of such a society has now become the "immediate practical task" of the Soviet people, and it ends with the solemn affirmation: "The present generation of Soviet people will live under communism!" The communism that they will live under is described as a "highly organized" classless society founded on public property and composed of socially equal people who work voluntarily according to their abilities and receive according to their needs. It might be mentioned in passing that no reference is made here to a point that Marx considered essential in the definition of ultimate communism, viz., the abolition of the division of labor in all its forms.

Although it gives solemn assurance that the present generation of Soviet people will enter the promised land of Communist society, the new Program does not specify a target date for the entry. Indeed, it is evidently predicated on the assumption that this will be a rather long-lived generation of Soviet people. For it projects the years 1961-1980 as the epoch of full-scale *construction* of communism, at the end of which only the foundations but not the edifice itself will have been built. Thus, by 1980 there will have been created "the material prerequisites for completing *in the subsequent period* the transition to the communist principle of distribution according to needs" (italics added). Communism itself, as distinguished from the building of it, lies beyond the horizon—an ever-receding utopia.

The new Program, then, is a prospectus, not for life under full communism, but rather for the coming two decades of "full-scale construction." What it envisages for this period is essentially a huge improvement of living standards, indeed the creation of a genuine Soviet welfare state with heavy accent on the provision of goods and services through the public sector. An abundance of variegated food products is to be available by the end of the period. Every family ("including newlyweds"!) is to be provided by then with a separate apartment of its own, and rent-free at that. Collective farmers will be receiving paid vacations as well as old-age pensions and sickness and disability benefits. Medicines will be issued free of charge. Free lunches will be served in schools and places of work. Electrical household appliances will be abundantly available to lighten the labor of women in the home, and so forth. In effect, communism as of 1980 is to mean the Soviet regime plus livings standards as high or higher than those now enjoyed in the most advanced Western welfare states.

Considering the chronic agricultural difficulties, the desperately overcrowded housing conditions of the great majority of citizens, the abysmal poverty of some, the ubiquitous shortages of essential consumer goods, and the growth of the Soviet population by three million or more each year, this goal is a highly ambitious one indeed. The question is whether it is a serious and realistic target, or merely one more set of grandiose promises destined to go unfulfilled like so many previous ones made by the Soviet government to the peoples of Russia. Unfortunately, there is ground to believe that it is rather the latter than the former. For some evidence on this score we have to look no farther than the text of the new Program itself.

One would have thought that a plan of all-out improvement of living standards would necessitate—at the very least—a shift in Soviet economic policy towards substantially greater emphasis on light industry and consumer goods production. But of this there is little sign in the new Program —notwithstanding Khrushchev's reported statement at the opening of the British trade exhibition in Moscow to the effect that from now on heavy and light industry in Russia will develop at the same tempo. The Program, echoing the formula in vogue in the latter Stalin period, says the chief economic task of the next twenty years is to create the "material-technical base" of communism. And in this connection it places very heavy emphasis on the need for "further development of heavy industry." As if to accentuate the point, it sets the colossal task of raising Soviet steel capacity to 250 million tons annually by 1980. It says at a later point that "efforts" will be made to ensure the rapid growth of consumer goods production, but the theme of the need for continued development of Soviet heavy industry and basic technology is the dominating one. Indeed, by comparison with the present blueprint of economic policy during the full-scale building of communism, Malenkov's speech of August 8, 1953, which called for a serious and systematic Soviet effort to raise living standards by developing light industry and consumer goods production, was a revolutionary document. There is no "new course" in the new Program.

Not only in economic policy, but in very many other areas as well, a fundamental conservatism is the leading characteristic of the Program. The section on agriculture states the party's intention to preserve the existing institutional structure of *kolkhozy* and *sovkhozy*, while gradually eliminating the differences between them and paving the way for the voluntary(!) abandonment by the collective farmers of their private garden plots. We see the conservative tendency, too, in the declaration that commodity-money relations must be preserved intact all through the epoch of the building of communism, and that prices must always allow "a certain profit for every normally operating enterprise" (in contrast to the 1919 Program, which called for the steady replacement of trade by state distribution of goods and for early preparatory measures leading to the "destruction of money.") Again, the pronouncement on future nationality policy suggests no significant changes, and the section on literature and art affirms the continued validity of the principles of "socialist realism." . . .

The sections of the Program dealing with the development of the Soviet state and the Communist Party in the coming period have been so drafted as to imply that exciting changes are in store or already in progress, but in point of fact they contain little, if anything, to contradict the interpretation of the Program as basically conservative in nature. For example, the "dictatorship of the proletariat" is said to have fulfilled its historic mission and to have undergone transformation into a "state of the whole people," but the state is not due to wither away pending the "complete victory of communism" in the still indefinite future. This is an adjustment in the ideological system that carries no apparent implications affecting the political system. The new formula ("state of the whole people") does, of course, contradict the Marxist view of the state as a strictly repressive mechanism that is *always* the agency of one class and that will vanish as soon as class division and antagonism have been brought to an end after world-wide Communist revolution. But this contradiction has long been implicit in the Soviet doctrine of the *Soviet* type of state as an institution that combines class-repressive with various non-repressive functions, such as those of economic administration and cultural construction. The new formula simply makes explicit and official a long-standing departure of Soviet political doctrine from Marxist theory.

Of greater interest and significance are the various provisions relating to the soviets, the so-called social organizations, and the Communist Party. They plainly merit the closest and most detailed analysis by students of Soviet political institutions, especially in the light of whatever information is forthcoming on the manner of their implementation. On the whole, however, they do not reveal any intent to introduce serious changes in the existing Soviet political system. The most novel and notable of the political provisions are those that establish the principle of regular rotation of membership in public bodies, including party committees from bottom to top, and the companion principle of a limitation (with appropriate exceptions of course) on the number of successive terms of office permitted. This will perhaps be a healthy development, if adhered to steadily over a lengthy period of years. But such circulation *within* the elite will in no way disturb the self-perpetuating character of the Soviet oligarchy.

Moreover, it is not at all apparent how it could have the effect—attributed to it in the Program—of reinforcing collective leadership and excluding the possibility of "excessive concentration of power in the hands of individual officials." As for the further provision that removal from the party Central Committee shall require a two-thirds vote of the Central Committee membership, conducted by secret ballot, the only novelty is the secrecy rule—and it is not at all clear just how effective this rule will be in practice. If a personal dictatorship similar to Stalin's is avoided in the coming period in Russia, it will not be because of safeguards established by the new Party Program and Rules.

Despite the impression of radicalism created by its use of revolutionary phraseology, the new Communist Manifesto is, in its underlying significance, a credo of Soviet conservatism. It is the political expression of a ruling and possessing class which wants to project an image of a Soviet Russia on the march—and towards full communism at that—but which, in actuality, is concerned most of all with the preservation, without radical change, of the existing institutional structure and its associated pattern of power, policy, and privilege.

Appendix

CONSTITUTION

OF THE UNION OF SOVIET SOCIALIST REPUBLICS

As Amended and Added to
at the Seventh Session
of the Supreme Soviet of the U.S.S.R.,
Fifth Convocation
(December 1961)

CHAPTER I. THE SOCIAL STRUCTURE

Article 1 —The Union of Soviet Socialist Republics is a socialist state of workers and peasants.

Article 2.—The political foundation of the U.S.S.R. is the Soviets of Working People's Deputies, which grew and became strong as a result of the overthrow of the power of the landlords and capitalists and the conquest of the dictatorship of the proletariat.

Article 3.—All power in the U.S.S.R. belongs to the working people of town and country as represented by the Soviets of Working People's Deputies.

Article 4.—The economic foundation of the U.S.S.R. is the socialist system of economy and the socialist ownership of the instruments and means of production, firmly established as a result of the liquidation of the capitalist system of economy, the abolition of private ownership of the instruments and means of production, and the elimination of the exploitation of man by man.

Article 5.—Socialist property in the U.S.S.R. exists either in the form of state property (belonging to the whole people) or in the form of co-operative and collective-farm property (property of collective farms, property of co-operative societies).

Article 6.—The land, its mineral wealth, waters, forests, mills, factories, mines, rail, water and air transport, banks, communications, large state-organized agricultural enterprises (state farms, machine and tractor stations and the like), as well as municipal enterprises and the bulk of the dwelling-houses in the cities and industrial localities, are state property, that is, belong to the whole people.

671

Article 7.—The common enterprises of collective farms and co-operative organizations, with their live-stock and implements, the products of the collective farms and co-operative organizations, as well as their common buildings, constitute the common, socialist property of the collective farms and co-operative organizations.

Every household in a collective farm, in addition to its basic income from the common collective-farm enterprise, has for its personal use a small plot of household land and, as its personal property, a subsidiary husbandry on the plot, a dwelling-house, live-stock, poultry and minor agricultural implements—in accordance with the rules of the agricultural artel.

Article 8.—The land occupied by collective farms is secured to them for their use free of charge and for an unlimited time, that is, in perpetuity.

Article 9.—Alongside the socialist system of economy, which is the predominant form of economy in the U.S.S.R., the law permits the small private economy of individual peasants and handicraftsmen based on their own labour and precluding the exploitation of the labour of others.

Article 10.—The personal property right of citizens in their incomes and savings from work, in their dwelling-houses and subsidiary husbandries, in articles of domestic economy and use and articles of personal use and convenience, as well as the right of citizens to inherit personal property, is protected by law.

Article 11.—The economic life of the U.S.S.R. is determined and directed by the state national-economic plan, with the aim of increasing the public wealth, of steadily raising the material and cultural standards of the working people, of consolidating the independence of the U.S.S.R. and strengthening its defensive capacity.

Article 12.—Work in the U.S.S.R. is a duty and a matter of honour for every able-bodied citizen, in accordance with the principle: "He who does not work, neither shall he eat."

The principle applied in the U.S.S.R. is that of socialism: "From each according to his ability, to each according to his work."

CHAPTER II. THE STATE STRUCTURE

Article 13.—The Union of Soviet Socialist Republics is a federal state, formed on the basis of a voluntary union of equal Soviet Socialist Republics, namely:

The Russian Soviet Federative Socialist Republic
The Ukrainian Soviet Socialist Republic
The Byelorussian Soviet Socialist Republic
The Uzbek Soviet Socialist Republic
The Kazakh Soviet Socialist Republic

The Georgian Soviet Socialist Republic
The Azerbaijan Soviet Socialist Republic
The Lithuanian Soviet Socialist Republic
The Moldavian Soviet Socialist Republic
The Latvian Soviet Socialist Republic
The Kirghiz Soviet Socialist Republic
The Tajik Soviet Socialist Republic
The Armenian Soviet Socialist Republic
The Turkmen Soviet Socialist Republic
The Estonian Soviet Socialist Republic

Article 14.—The jurisdiction of the Union of Soviet Socialist Republics, as represented by its higher organs of state power and organs of state administration, embraces:

a) Representation of the U.S.S.R. in international relations, conclusion, ratification and denunciation of treaties of the U.S.S.R. with other states, establishment of general procedure governing the relations of Union Republics with foreign states;

b) Questions of war and peace;

c) Admission of new republics into the U.S.S.R.;

d) Control over the observance of the Constitution of the U.S.S.R., and ensuring conformity of the Constitutions of the Union Republics with the Constitution of the U.S.S.R.;

e) Confirmation of alterations of boundaries between Union Republics;

f) Confirmation of the formation of new Autonomous Republics and Autonomous Regions within Union Republics;

g) Organization of the defence of the U.S.S.R., direction of all the Armed Forces of the U.S.S.R., determination of directing principles governing the organization of the military formations of the Union Republics;

h) Foreign trade on the basis of state monopoly;

i) Safeguarding the security of the state;

j) Determination of the national-economic plans of the U.S.S.R.;

k) Approval of the consolidated state budget of the U.S.S.R. and of the report on its fulfilment; determination of the taxes and revenues which go to the Union, the Republican and the local budgets;

l) Administration of the banks, industrial and agricultural institutions and enterprises and trading enterprises of all-Union importance; over-all direction of industry and construction under Union Republic jurisdiction.

m) Administration of transport and communications of all-Union importance;

n) Direction of the monetary and credit system;

o) Organization of state insurance;

p) Contracting and granting of loans;

q) Determination of the basic principles of land tenure and of the use of mineral wealth, forests and waters;

r) Determination of the basic principles in the spheres of education and public health;

s) Organization of a uniform system of national-economic statistics;

t) Determination of the principles of labour legislation;

u) Establishment of the principles of legislation concerning the judicial system and judicial procedure, and of the principles of the criminal and civil codes.

v) Legislation concerning Union citizenship; legislation concerning rights of foreigners;

w) Determination of the principles of legislation concerning marriage and the family;

x) Issuing of all-Union acts of amnesty.

Article 15.—The sovereignty of the Union Republics is limited only in the spheres defined in article 14 of the Constitution of the U.S.S.R. Outside of these spheres each Union Republic exercises state authority independently. The U.S.S.R. protects the sovereign rights of the Union Republics.

Article 16.—Each Union Republic has its own Constitution, which takes account of the specific feature of the Republic and is drawn up in full conformity with the Constitution of the U.S.S.R.

Article 17.—The right freely to secede from the U.S.S.R. is reserved to every Union Republic.

Article 18.—The territory of a Union Republic may not be altered without its consent.

Article 18-a.—Each Union Republic has the right to enter into direct relations with foreign states and to conclude agreements and exchange diplomatic and consular representatives with them.

Article 18-b.—Each Union Republic has its own Republican military formations.

Article 19.—The laws of the U.S.S.R. have the same force within the territory of every Union Republic.

Article 20.—In the event of divergence between a law of a Union Republic and a law of the Union, the Union law prevails.

Article 21.—Uniform Union citizenship is established for citizens of the U.S.S.R.
Every citizen of a Union Republic is a citizen of the U.S.S.R.

Article 22.—The Russian Soviet Federative Socialist Republic includes the Autonomous Soviet Socialist Republics: Bashkirian, Buryat, Daghestan, Kabardino-Balkarian, Kalmyk, Karelian, Komi, Mari, Mordovian, North Ossetian, Tartar, Udmurt, Chechen-Ingush, Chuvash, Yakut, and Tuva; Autonomous Regions: Adygei, Gorny, Altai, Jewish, Karachai-Cherkess, and Khakass.

Article 23.—Excluded.

Article 24.—The Azerbaiijan Soviet Socialist Republic includes the Nakhichevan Autonomous Soviet Socialist Republic and the Nagorny Karabakh Autonomous Region.

Article 25.—The Georgian Soviet Socialist Republic includes the Abkhazian Autonomous Soviet Socialist Republic, the Ajarian Autonomous Soviet Socialist Republic and the South Ossetian Autonomous Region.

Article 26.—The Uzbek Soviet Socialist Republic includes the Kara Kalpak Autonomous Soviet Socialist Republic.

Article 27.—The Tajik Soviet Socialist Republic includes the Gorny Badakhshan Autonomous Region.

Article 28.—The decision of questions relating to the Regional and Territorial Administrative Structure of Union Republics is left to the jurisdiction of Union Republics.

Article 29.—Excluded.

CHAPTER III. THE HIGHER ORGANS OF STATE POWER IN THE UNION OF SOVIET SOCIALIST REPUBLICS

Article 30.—The highest organ of state power in the U.S.S.R. is the Supreme Soviet of the U.S.S.R.

Article 31.—The Supreme Soviet of the U.S.S.R. exercises all rights vested in the Union of Soviet Socialist Republics in accordance with Article 14 of the Constitution, in so far as they do not, by virtue of the Constitution, come within the jurisdiction of organs of the U.S.S.R. that are accountable to the Supreme Soviet of the U.S.S.R., that is, the Presidium of the Supreme Soviet of the U.S.S.R., the Council of Ministers of the U.S.S.R., and the Ministries of the U.S.S.R.

Article 32.—The legislative power of the U.S.S.R. is exercised exclusively by the Supreme Soviet of the U.S.S.R.

Article 33.—The Supreme Soviet of the U.S.S.R. consists of two Chambers: the Soviet of the Union and the Soviet of Nationalities.

Article 34.—The Soviet of the Union is elected by the citizens of the U.S.S.R. voting by election districts on the basis of one deputy for every 300,000 of the population.

Article 35.—The Soviet of Nationalities is elected by the citizens of the U.S.S.R. voting by Union Republics, Autonomous Republics, Autonomous Regions, and National Areas on the basis of 25 deputies from each Union Republic, 11 deputies from each Autonomous Republic, 5 deputies from each Autonomous Region and one deputy from each National Area.

Article 36.—The Supreme Soviet of the U.S.S.R. is elected for a term of four years.

Article 37.—The two Chambers of the Supreme Soviet of the U.S.S.R., the Soviet of the Union and the Soviet of Nationalities, have equal rights.

Article 38.—The Soviet of the Union and the Soviet of Nationalities have equal powers to initiate legislation.

Article 39.—A law is considered adopted if passed by both Chambers of the Supreme Soviet of the U.S.S.R. by a simple majority vote in each.

Article 40.—Laws passed by the Supreme Soviet of the U.S.S.R. are published in the languages of the Union Republics over the signatures of the President and Secretary of the Presidium of the Supreme Soviet of the U.S.S.R.

Article 41.—Sessions of the Soviet of the Union and of the Soviet of Nationalities begin and terminate simultaneously.

Article 42.—The Soviet of the Union elects a Chairman of the Soviet of the Union and four Vice-Chairmen.

Article 43.—The Soviet of Nationalities elects a Chairman of the Soviet of Nationalities and four Vice-Chairmen.

Article 44.—The Chairmen of the Soviet of the Union and the Soviet of Nationalities preside at the sittings of the respective Chambers and have charge of the conduct of their business and proceedings.

Article 45.—Joint sittings of the two Chambers of the Supreme Soviet of the U.S.S.R. are presided over alternately by the Chairman of the Soviet of the Union and the Chairman of the Soviet of Nationalities.

Article 46.—Sessions of the Supreme Soviet of the U.S.S.R. are convened by the Presidium of the Supreme Soviet of the U.S.S.R. twice a year.

Extraordinary sessions are convened by the Presidium of the Supreme Soviet of the U.S.S.R. at its discretion or on the demand of one of the Union Republics.

Article 47.—In the event of disagreement between the Soviet of the Union and the Soviet of Nationalities, the question is referred for settlement to a conciliation commission formed by the Chambers on a parity basis. If the conciliation commission fails to arrive at an agreement or if its decision fails to satisfy one of the Chambers, the question is considered for a second time by the Chambers. Failing agreement between the two Chambers, the Presidium of the Supreme Soviet of the U.S.S.R. dissolves the Supreme Soviet of the U.S.S.R. and orders new elections.

Article 48.—The Supreme Soviet of the U.S.S.R. at a joint sitting of the two Chambers elects the Presidium of the Supreme Soviet of the U.S.S.R., consisting of a President of the Presidium of the Supreme Soviet of the U.S.S.R., fifteen Vice-Presidents—one from each Union Republic—a Secretary of the Presidium and sixteen members of the Presidium of the Supreme Soviet of the U.S.S.R.

The Presidium of the Supreme Soviet of the U.S.S.R. is accountable to the Supreme Soviet of the U.S.S.R. for all its activities.

Article 49.—The Presidium of the Supreme Soviet of the U.S.S.R.:

a) Convenes the sessions of the Supreme Soviet of the U.S.S.R.;

b) Issues decrees;

c) Gives interpretations of the laws of the U.S.S.R. in operation;

d) Dissolves the Supreme Soviet of the U.S.S.R. in conformity with Article 47 of the Constitution of the U.S.S.R. and orders new elections;

e) Conducts nation-wide polls (referendums) on its own initiative or on the demand of one of the Union Republics;

f) Annuls decisions and orders of the Council of Ministers of the U.S.S.R. and of the Councils of Ministers of the Union Republics if they do not conform to law;

g) In the intervals between sessions of the Supreme Soviet of the U.S.S.R., releases and appoints Ministers of the U.S.S.R. on the recommendation of the Chairman of the Council of Ministers of the U.S.S.R., subject to subsequent confirmation by the Supreme Soviet of the U.S.S.R.;

h) Institutes decorations (Orders and Medals) and titles of honour of the U.S.S.R.;

i) Awards Orders and Medals and confers titles of honour of the U.S.S.R.;

j) Exercises the right of pardon;

k) Institutes military titles, diplomatic ranks and other special titles;

l) Appoints and removes the high command of the Armed Forces of the U.S.S.R.;

m) In the intervals between sessions of the Supreme Soviet of the U.S.S.R., proclaims a state of war in the event of military attack on the U.S.S.R., or when necessary to fulfil international treaty obligations concerning mutual defence against aggression;

n) Orders general or partial mobilization;

o) Ratifies and denounces international treaties of the U.S.S.R.;

p) Appoints and recalls plenipotentiary representatives of the U.S.S.R. to foreign states;

q) Receives the letters of credence and recall of diplomatic representatives accredited to it by foreign states;

r) Proclaims martial law in separate localities or throughout the

U.S.S.R. in the interests of the defence of the U.S.S.R. or of the maintenance of public order and the security of the state.

Article 50.—The Soviet of the Union and the Soviet of Nationalities elect Credentials Committees to verify the credentials of the members of the respective Chambers.

On the report of the Credentials Committees, the Chambers decide whether to recognize the credentials of deputies or to annul their election.

Article 51.—The Supreme Soviet of the U.S.S.R., when it deems necessary, appoints commissions of investigation and audit on any matter.

It is the duty of all institutions and officials to comply with the demands of such commissions and to submit to them all necessary materials and documents.

Article 52.—A member of the Supreme Soviet of the U.S.S.R. may not be prosecuted or arrested without the consent of the Supreme Soviet of the U.S.S.R., or, when the Supreme Soviet of the U.S.S.R. is not in session, without the consent of the Presidium of the Supreme Soviet of the U.S.S.R.

Article 53.—On the expiration of the term of office of the Supreme Soviet of the U.S.S.R., or on its dissolution prior to the expiration of its term of office, the Presidium of the Supreme Soviet of the U.S.S.R. retains its powers until the newly-elected Supreme Soviet of the U.S.S.R. shall have formed a new Presidium of the Supreme Soviet of the U.S.S.R.

Article 54.—On the expiration of the term of office of the Supreme Soviet of the U.S.S.R., or in the event of its dissolution prior to the expiration of its term of office, the Presidium of the Supreme Soviet of the U.S.S.R. orders new elections to be held within a period not exceeding two months from the date of expiration of the term of office or dissolution of the Supreme Soviet of the U.S.S.R.

Article 55.—The newly-elected Supreme Soviet of the U.S.S.R. is convened by the outgoing Presidium of the Supreme Soviet of the U.S.S.R. not later than three months after the elections.

Article 56.—The Supreme Soviet of the U.S.S.R., at a joint sitting of the two Chambers, appoints the Government of the U.S.S.R., namely the Council of Ministers of the U.S.S.R.

CHAPTER IV. THE HIGHER ORGANS OF STATE POWER IN THE UNION REPUBLICS

Article 57.—The highest organ of state power in a Union Republic is the Supreme Soviet of the Union Republic.

Article 58.—The Supreme Soviet of a Union Republic is elected by the citizens of the Republic for a term of four years.

The basis of representation is established by the Constitution of the Union Republic.

Article 59.—The Supreme Soviet of a Union Republic is the sole legislative organ of the Republic.

Article 60.—The Supreme Soviet of a Union Republic:

a) Adopts the Constitution of the Republic and amends it in conformity with Article 16 of the Constitution of the U.S.S.R.;

b) Confirms the Constitutions of the Autonomous Republics forming part of it and defines the boundaries of their territories;

c) Approves the national-economic plan and the budget of the Republic and forms the economic administrative Regions;

d) Exercises the right of amnesty and pardon of citizens sentenced by the judicial organs of the Union Republic;

e) Decides questions of representation of the Union Republic in its international relations;

f) Determines the manner of organizing the Republic's military formations.

Article 61.—The Supreme Soviet of a Union Republic elects the Presidium of the Supreme Soviet of the Union Republic, consisting of a President of the Presidium of the Supreme Soviet of the Union Republic, Vice-Presidents, a Secretary of the Presidium and members of the Presidium of the Supreme Soviet of the Union Republic.

The powers of the Presidium of the Supreme Soviet of a Union Republic are defined by the Constitution of the Union Republic.

Article 62.—The Supreme Soviet of a Union Republic elects a Chairman and Vice-Chairmen to conduct its sittings.

Article 63.—The Supreme Soviet of a Union Republic appoints the Government of the Union Republic, namely, the Council of Ministers of the Union Republic.

CHAPTER V. THE ORGANS OF STATE ADMINISTRATION OF THE UNION OF SOVIET SOCIALIST REPUBLICS

Article 64.—The highest executive and administrative organ of the state power of the Union of Soviet Socialist Republics is the Council of Ministers of the U.S.S.R.

Article 65.—The Council of Ministers of the U.S.S.R. is responsible and accountable to the Supreme Soviet of the U.S.S.R., or, in the intervals between sessions of the Supreme Soviet, to the Presidium of the Supreme Soviet of the U.S.S.R.

Article 66.—The Council of Ministers of the U.S.S.R. issues decisions and orders on the basis and in pursuance of the laws in operation, and verifies their execution.

Article 67.—Decisions and orders of the Council of Ministers of the U.S.S.R. are binding throughout the territory of the U.S.S.R.

Article 68.—The Council of Ministers of the U.S.S.R.:

a) Co-ordinates and directs the work of the all-Union and Union-Republican Ministries of the U.S.S.R. and of other institutions under its jurisdiction and exercises direction over Republic Economic Councils, and over the Economic Councils of the economic administrative Regions through the Union Republic Councils of Ministers.

b) Adopts measures to carry out the national-economic plan and the state budget, and to strengthen the credit and monetary system;

c) Adopts measures for the maintenance of public order, for the protection of the interests of the state, and for the safeguarding of the rights of citizens;

d) Exercises general guidance in the sphere of relations with foreign states;

e) Fixes the annual contingent of citizens to be called up for military service and directs the general organization of the Armed Forces of the country;

f) Sets up, whenever necessary, special Committees and Central Administrations under the Council of Ministers of the U.S.S.R. for economic and cultural affairs and defence.

Article 69.—The Council of Ministers of the U.S.S.R. has the right, in respect of those branches of administration and economy which come within the jurisdiction of the U.S.S.R., to suspend decisions and orders of the Councils of Ministers of the Union Republics, of Republic Economic Councils, and the Economic Councils of the economic administrative Regions and to annul orders and instructions of Ministers of the U.S.S.R.

Article 70.—The Council of Ministers of the U.S.S.R. is appointed by the Supreme Soviet of the U.S.S.R. and consists of: the chairman of the U.S.S.R. Council Ministers; the first vice-chairmen of the U.S.S.R. Council of Ministers; the vice-chairmen of the U.S.S.R. Council of Ministers; Ministers of the U.S.S.R.; the chairman of the U.S.S.R. Council of Ministers' State Planning Committee; the chairman of the U.S.S.R. Council of Ministers' Soviet Control Commission; the chairman of the U.S.S.R. Council of Ministers' State Committee on Labor and Wages; the chairman of the U.S.S.R. Council of Ministers' State Committee for Vocational and Technical Education; the chairman of the U.S.S.R. Council of Ministers' State Scientific and Technical Committee; the chairman of the U.S.S.R. Council of Ministers' State Automation and Machine-Building Committee; the chairman of the U.S.S.R. Council of Ministers' State Committee on Aviation Technology; the chairman of the U.S.S.R. Council of Ministers' State Committee on Defense Technology; the chairman of the U.S.S.R. Council of Ministers' State Committee on Radio Electronics; the chairman of the U.S.S.R. Council of Ministers' State Committee on Shipbuilding; the chairman of the U.S.S.R. Council of Ministers' State Chemistry Committee; the chairman of the U.S.S.R. Council of Ministers' State Committee on the Use of Atomic Energy; the chairman of the U.S.S.R. Council of Ministers' State Committee on Construction; the chairman of the U.S.S.R. Council of Ministers' State Committee on Cereal Products; the chairman of the U.S.S.R. Council of Ministers' State Committee on Foreign Economic Relations; the chairman of the U.S.S.R. Council of Ministers' State Committee for Cultural Ties with Foreign Countries; the chairman of the U.S.S.R. Council of Ministers' State Committee on State Security; the chairman of the Board of the U.S.S.R. State Bank; the director of the U.S.S.R. Council of Ministers' Central Statistical Administration; the chairman of the U.S.S.R. Council of Ministers' State Scientific and Economics Council.

The U.S.S.R. Council of Ministers includes the chairmen of the Union Republic Councils of Ministers, ex officio.

Article 71.—The Government of the U.S.S.R. or a Minister of the U.S.S.R. to whom a question of a member of the Supreme Soviet of the U.S.S.R. is addressed must give a verbal or written reply in the respective Chamber within a period not exceeding three days.

Article 72.—The Ministers of the U.S.S.R. direct the branches of state administration which come within the jurisdiction of the U.S.S.R.

Article 73.—The Ministers of the U.S.S.R., within the limits of the jurisdiction of their respective Ministries, issue orders and instructions on the basis and in pursuance of the laws in operation, and also of decisions and orders of the Council of Ministers of the U.S.S.R., and verify their execution.

Article 74.—The Ministries of the U.S.S.R. are either all-Union or Union-Republican Ministries.

Article 75.—Each all-Union Ministry directs the branch of state administration entrusted to it throughout the territory of the U.S.S.R. either directly or through bodies appointed by it.

Article 76.—The Union-Republican Ministries, as a rule, direct the branches of state administration entrusted to them through corresponding

Ministries of the Union Republics; they administer directly only a definite and limited number of enterprises according to a list confirmed by the Presidium of the Supreme Soviet of the U.S.S.R.

Article 77.—The following Ministries are all-Union Ministries: Foreign Trade; Merchant Marine; Transportation; Medium Machine Building; Transport Construction; Power Plants.

Article 78.—The following Ministries are Union Republic Ministries: Higher Education; Geology and Conservation of Mineral Resources; Public Health; Foreign Affairs; Culture; Defense; Communications; Agriculture; Finance.

CHAPTER VI. THE ORGANS OF STATE ADMINISTRATION OF THE UNION REPUBLICS

Article 79.—The highest executive and administrative organ of the state power of a Union Republic is the Council of Ministers of the Union Republic.

Article 80.—The Council of Ministers of a Union Republic is responsible and accountable to the Supreme Soviet of the Union Republic, or, in the intervals between sessions of the Supreme Soviet of the Union Republic, to the Presidium of the Supreme Soviet of the Union Republic.

Article 81.—The Council of Ministers of a Union Republic issues decisions and orders on the basis and in pursuance of the laws in operation of the U.S.S.R. and of the Union Republic, and of the decisions and orders of the Council of Ministers of the U.S.S.R., and verifies their execution.

Article 82.—The Council of Ministers of a Union Republic has the right to suspend decisions and orders of the Republic Economic Council and of the Councils of Ministers of its Autonomous Republics and to annul decisions and orders of the Executive Committees of the Soviets of Working People's Deputies of its Territories, Regions and Autonomous Regions and of the Economic Councils of the economic administrative Regions.

Article 83.—The Council of Ministers of a Union Republic is appointed by the Supreme Soviet of the Union Republic and consists of:
The Chairman of the Council of Ministers of the Union Republic;
The Vice-Chairmen of the Council of Ministers;
The Ministers;
The Chairmen of the State Committees, Commissions and heads of the other offices of the Council of Ministers appointed by the Supreme Soviet of the Union Republic in conformity with the Constitution of the Union Republic.

Article 84.—The Ministers of a Union Republic direct the branches of state administration which come within the jurisdiction of the Union Republic.

Article 85.—The Ministers of a Union Republic, within the limits of the jurisdiction of their respective Ministries, issue orders and instructions on the basis and in pursuance of the laws of the U.S.S.R. and of the Union Republic, of the decisions and orders of the Council of Ministers of the U.S.S.R. and the Council of Ministers of the Union Republic, and of the orders and instructions of the Union-Republican Ministries of the U.S.S.R.

Article 86.—The Ministries of a Union Republic are either Union-Republican or Republican Ministries.

Article 87.—Each Union-Republican Ministry directs the branch of state administration entrusted to it, and is subordinate both to the Council of Ministers of the Union Republic and to the corresponding Union-Republican Ministry of the U.S.S.R.

Article 88.—Each Republican Ministry directs the branch of state administration entrusted to it and is directly subordinate to the Council of Ministers of the Union Republic.

Article 88-a.—The Economic Councils of the economic administrative Regions direct the branches of economic activity entrusted to them and are directly subordinate to the Union Republic Council of Ministers.

In Union Republics where Republic Economic Councils are formed, the Economic Councils of economic administrative Regions are subordinate in their activities to both the Union Republic Council of Ministers and the Republic Economic Council.

The Economic Councils of the economic administrative Regions, within the bounds of their competence, make decisions and issue directives on the basis and in execution of the laws of the U.S.S.R. and the Union Republic and of the decrees and directives of the U.S.S.R. Council of Ministers and the Union Republic Council of Ministers.

Article 88-b.—The Republic Economic Council coordinates the economic activity of the Economic Councils of economic administrative Regions and is directly subordinate to the Union Republic Council of Ministers.

The Republic Economic Council, within the bounds of its competence, makes decisions and issues directives on the basis and in execution of the laws of the U.S.S.R. and the Union Republic and of the decrees and directives of the U.S.S.R. Council of Ministers and the Union Republic Council of Ministers.

The Republic Economic Council has the right to suspend the decrees and directives of the Economic Councils of economic administrative Regions.

CHAPTER VII. THE HIGHER ORGANS OF STATE POWER
IN THE AUTONOMOUS SOVIET SOCIALIST REPUBLICS

Article 89.—The highest organ of state power in an Autonomous Republic is the Supreme Soviet of the Autonomous Republic.

Article 90.—The Supreme Soviet of an Autonomous Republic is elected by the citizens of the Republic for a term of four years on a basis of representation established by the Constitution of the Autonomous Republic.

Article 91.—The Supreme Soviet of an Autonomous Republic is the sole legislative organ of the Autonomous Republic.

Article 92.—Each Autonomous Republic has its own Constitution, which takes account of the specific features of the Autonomous Republic and is drawn up in full conformity with the Constitution of the Union Republic.

Article 93.—The Supreme Soviet of an Autonomous Republic elects the Presidium of the Supreme Soviet of the Autonomous Republic and appoints the Council of Ministers of the Autonomous Republic, in accordance with its Constitution.

CHAPTER VIII. THE LOCAL ORGANS OF STATE POWER

Article 94.—The organs of state power in Territories, Regions, Autonomous Regions, Areas, Districts, cities and rural localities (stanitsas, villages, hamlets, kishlaks, auls) are the Soviets of Working People's Deputies.

Article 95.—The Soviets of Working People's Deputies of Territories, Regions, Autonomous Regions, Areas, Districts, cities and rural localities (stanitsas, villages, hamlets, kishlaks, auls) are elected by the working people of the respective Territories, Regions, Autonomous Regions, Areas, Districts, cities or rural localities for a term of two years.

Article 96.—The basis of representation for Soviets of Working People's Deputies is determined by the Constitutions of the Union Republics.

Article 97.—The Soviets of Working People's Deputies direct the work of the organs of administration subordinate to them, ensure the maintenance of public order, the observance of the laws and the protection of the rights of citizens, direct local economic and cultural affairs and draw up the local budgets.

Article 98.—The Soviets of Working People's Deputies adopt decisions and issue orders within the limits of the powers vested in them by the laws of the U.S.S.R. and of the Union Republic.

Article 99.—The executive and administrative organ of the Soviet of Working People's Deputies of a Territory, Region, Autonomous Region, Area, District, city or rural locality is the Executive Committee elected by it, consisting of a Chairman, Vice-Chairmen, a Secretary and members.

Article 100.—The executive and administrative organ of the Soviet of Working People's Deputies in a small locality, in accordance with the Constitution of the Union Republic, is the Chairman, the Vice-Chairman and the Secretary elected by the Soviet of Working People's Deputies.

Article 101.—The executive organs of the Soviets of Working People's Deputies are directly accountable both to the Soviets of Working People's Deputies which elected them and to the executive organ of the superior Soviet of Working People's Deputies.

CHAPTER IX. THE COURTS AND THE PROCURATOR'S OFFICE

Article 102.—In the U.S.S.R. justice in administered by the Supreme Court of the U.S.S.R., the Supreme Courts of the Union Republics, the Courts of the Territories, Regions, Autonomous Republics, Autonomous Regions and Areas, the Special Courts of the U.S.S.R. established by decision of the Supreme Soviet of the U.S.S.R., and the People's Courts.

Article 103.—In all Courts cases are tried with the participation of people's assessors except in cases specially provided for by law.

Article 104.—The Supreme Court of the U.S.S.R. is the highest judicial organ. The Supreme Court of the U.S.S.R. is charged with the supervision of the judicial activities of all the judicial organs of the U.S.S.R. and of the Union Republics within the limits established by law.

Article 105.—The Supreme Court of the U.S.S.R. is elected by the Supreme Soviet of the U.S.S.R. for a term of five years. The Supreme Court of the U.S.S.R. includes the Chief Justices of the Supreme Courts of the Union Republics, ex officio.

Article 106.—The Supreme Courts of the Union Republics are elected by the Supreme Soviets of the Union Republics for a term of five years.

Article 107.—The Supreme Courts of the Autonomous Republics are elected by the Supreme Soviets of the Autonomous Republics for a term of five years.

Article 108.—The Courts of Territories, Regions, Autonomous Regions and Areas are elected by the Soviets of Working People's Deputies of the respective Territories, Regions, Autonomous Regions or Areas for a term of five years.

Article 109.—The People's Judges of the district (or town) People's Courts are elected by the citizens of the district (or town) on the basis of universal, equal and direct suffrage by secret ballot for a term of five years.

The People's Assessors of the district (or town) People's Courts are elected by general meetings of workers, office employees and peasants at their places of work or residence, and of servicemen at military units, for a term of two years.

Article 110.—Judicial proceedings are conducted in the language of the Union Republic, Autonomous Republic or Autonomous Region, persons not knowing this language being guaranteed the opportunity of fully acquainting themselves with the material of the case through an interpreter and likewise the right to use their own language in court.

Article 111.—In all Courts of the U.S.S.R. cases are heard in public, unless otherwise provided for by law, and the accused is guaranteed the right to defence.

Article 112.—Judges are independent and subject only to the law.

Article 113.—Supreme supervisory power to ensure the strict observance of the law by all Ministries and institutions subordinated to them, as well as by officials and citizens of the U.S.S.R. generally, is vested in the Procurator-General of the U.S.S.R.

Article 114.—The Procurator-General of the U.S.S.R. is appointed by the Supreme Soviet of the U.S.S.R. for a term of seven years.

Article 115.—Procurators of Republics, Territories, Regions, Autonomous Republics and Autonomous Regions are appointed by the Procurator-General of the U.S.S.R. for a term of five years.

Article 116.—Area, district and city procurators are appointed by the Procurators of the Union Republics, subject to the approval of the Procurator-General of the U.S.S.R., for a term of five years.

Article 117.—The organs of the Procurator's Office perform their functions independently of any local organs whatsoever, being subordinate solely to the Procurator-General of the U.S.S.R.

CHAPTER X. FUNDAMENTAL RIGHTS AND DUTIES OF CITIZENS

Article 118.—Citizens of the U.S.S.R. have the right to work, that is, the right to guaranteed employment and payment for their work in accordance with its quantity and quality.

The right to work is ensured by the socialist organization of the national economy, the steady growth of the productive forces of Soviet society, the elimination of the possibility of economic crises, and the abolition of unemployment.

Article 119.—Citizens of the U.S.S.R. have the right to leisure.

The right to leisure is ensured by the establishment of a seven-hour working day for workers and employees and by the reduction of the working day to six hours for a number of trades with arduous conditions of work and to four hours in shops with especially arduous conditions of work; by the establishment of annual paid vacations for workers and employees; and by providing the working people with a broad network of sanatoriums, rest homes and clubs.

Article 120.—Citizens of the U.S.S.R. have the right to maintenance in old age and also in case of sickness or disability.

This right is ensured by the extensive development of social insurance of industrial, office, and professional workers at state expense, free medical service for the working people, and the provision of a wide network of health resorts for the use of the working people.

Article 121.—Citizens of the U.S.S.R. have the right to education.

This right is ensured by universal and compulsory eight-year education; by extensive development of general secondary polytechnical education, technical-trade education, specialized secondary and higher education on the basis of linking instruction with life, and with production; by the comprehensive development of evening-school and correspondence-course education; by free education in all types of schools; through a system of state stipends; by instruction in the schools in the native language; and by the organization in the factories, on state farms and collective farms of free vocational, technical and agronomic training for the working people.

Article 122.—Women in the U.S.S.R. are accorded equal rights with men in all spheres of economic, government, cultural, political and other public activity.

The possibility of exercising these rights is ensured by women being accorded an equal right with men to work, payment for work, rest and leisure, social insurance and education, and by state protection of the interest of mother and child, state aid to mothers of large families and unmarried mothers, maternity leave with full pay, and the provision of a wide network of maternity homes, nurseries and kindergartens.

Article 123.—Equality of rights of citizens of the U.S.S.R., irrespective of their nationality or race, in all spheres of economic, government, cultural, political and other public activity, is an indefeasible law.

Any direct or indirect restriction of the rights of, or conversely, the establishment of any direct or indirect privileges for, citizens on account of their race or nationality, as well as any advocacy of racial or national exclusiveness or hatred and contempt, are punishable by law.

Article 124.—In order to ensure to citizens freedom of conscience, the church in the U.S.S.R. is separated from the state, and the school from the church. Freedom of religious worship and freedom of anti-religious propaganda is recognized for all citizens.

Article 125.—In conformity with the interests of the working people, and in order to strengthen the socialist system, the citizens of the U.S.S.R. are guaranteed by law:

a) freedom of speech;
b) freedom of the press;
c) freedom of assembly; including the holding of mass meetings;
d) freedom of street processions and demonstrations.

These civil rights are ensured by placing at the disposal of the working people and their organizations printing presses, stocks of paper, public buildings, the streets, communications facilities, and other material requisites for the exercise of these rights.

Article 126.—In conformity with the interests of the working people, and in order to develop the organizational initiative and political activity of the masses of the people, citizens of the U.S.S.R. are guaranteed the right to unite in public organizations: trade unions, co-operative societies, youth organizations, sport and defence organizations, cultural, technical and scientific societies; and the most active and politically-conscious citizens in the ranks of the working class, working peasants and working intelligentsia voluntarily unite in the Communist Party of the Soviet Union, which is the vanguard of the working people in their struggle to build communist society and is the leading core of all organizations of the working people, both public and state.

Article 127.—Citizens of the U.S.S.R. are guaranteed inviolability of the person. No person may be placed under arrest except by decision of a court or with the sanction of a procurator.

Article 128.—The inviolability of the homes of citizens and privacy of correspondence are protected by law.

Article 129.—The U.S.S.R. affords the right of asylum to foreign citizens persecuted for defending the interests of the working people, or for scientific activities, or for struggling for national liberation.

Article 130.—It is the duty of every citizen of the U.S.S.R. to abide by the Constitution of the Union of Soviet Socialist Republics, to observe the laws, to maintain labour discipline, honestly to perform public duties, and to respect the rules of socialist intercourse.

Article 131.—It is the duty of every citizen of the U.S.S.R. to safeguard and fortify public, socialist property as the sacred and inviolable foundation of the Soviet system, as the source of the wealth and might of the country, as the source of the prosperity and culture of all the working people.

Persons committing offences against public, socialist property are enemies of the people.

Article 132.—Universal military service is law.

Military service in the Armed Forces of the U.S.S.R. is an honourable duty of the citizens of the U.S.S.R.

Article 133.—To defend the country is the sacred duty of every citizen of the U.S.S.R. Treason to the Motherland—violation of the oath of allegiance, desertion to the enemy, impairing the military power of the state, espionage—is punishable with all the severity of the law as the most heinous of crimes.

CHAPTER XI. THE ELECTORAL SYSTEM

Article 134.—Members of all Soviets of Working People's Deputies—of the Supreme Soviet of the U.S.S.R., the Supreme Soviets of the Union Republics, the Soviets of Working People's Deputies of the Territories and Regions, the Supreme Soviets of the Autonomous Republics, the Soviets of Working People's Deputies of the Autonomous Regions, and the Area, District, City and rural (stanitsa, village, hamlet, kishlak, aul) Soviets of Working People's Deputies—are chosen by the electors on the basis of universal, equal and direct suffrage by secret ballot.

Article 135.—Elections of deputies are universal: all citizens of the U.S.S.R. who have reached the age of eighteen, irrespective of race or nationality, sex, religion, education, domicile, social origin, property status or past activities, have the right to vote in the election of deputies, with the exception of persons who have been declared insane in the manner prescribed by law.

Every citizen of the U.S.S.R. who has reached the age of twenty-three is eligible for election to the Supreme Soviet of the U.S.S.R., irrespective of race or nationality, sex, religion, education, domicile, social origin, property status or past activities.

Article 136.—Elections of deputies are equal: each citizen has one vote; all citizens participate in elections on an equal footing.

Article 137.—Women have the right to elect and be elected on equal terms with men.

Article 138.—Citizens serving in the Armed Forces of the U.S.S.R. have the right to elect and be elected on equal terms with all other citizens.

Article 139.—Elections of deputies are direct: all Soviets of Working People's Deputies, from rural and city Soviets of Working People's Deputies to the Supreme Soviet of the U.S.S.R., are elected by the citizens by direct vote.

Article 140.—Voting at elections of deputies is secret.

Article 141.—Candidates are nominated by election districts.

The right to nominate candidates is secured to public organizations and societies of the working people: Communist Party organizations, trade unions, co-operatives, youth organizations and cultural societies.

Article 142.—It is the duty of every deputy to report to his electors on his work and on the work of his Soviet of Working People's Deputies, and he may be recalled at any time upon decision of a majority of the electors in the manner established by law.

CHAPTER XII. ARMS, FLAG, CAPITAL

Article 143.—The arms of the Union of Soviet Socialist Republics are a sickle and hammer against a globe depicted in the rays of the sun and surrounded by ears of grain, with the inscription "Workers of All Countries, Unite!" in the languages of the Union Republics. At the top of the arms is a five-pointed star.

Article 144.—The state flag of the Union of Soviet Socialist Republics is of red cloth with the sickle and hammer depicted in gold in the upper corner near the staff and above them a five-pointed red star bordered in gold. The ratio of the width to the length is 1:2.

Article 145.—The Capital of the Union of Soviet Socialist Republics is the City of Moscow.

CHAPTER XIII. PROCEDURE FOR AMENDING THE CONSTITUTION

Article 146.—The Constitution of the U.S.S.R. may be amended only by decision of the Supreme Soviet of the U.S.S.R. adopted by a majority of not less than two-thirds of the votes in each of its Chambers.

Selected Bibliography

ARMSTRONG, JOHN A. *The Politics of Totalitarianism: The Communist Party of the Soviet Union from 1934 to the Present.* Random House, New York, 1961.

ARMSTRONG, JOHN A. *The Soviet Bureaucratic Elite.* Praeger, New York, 1959.

BALZAK, S. S.; VASYUTIN, V. F.; and FEIGIN, YA. G., eds. *Economic Geography of the U.S.S.R.* Macmillan, New York, 1949.

BARANSKY, N. N. *Economic Geography of the U.S.S.R.* Foreign Languages Publishing House, Moscow, 1956.

BARGHOORN, FREDERICK C. *The Soviet Image of the United States.* Harcourt, Brace, New York, 1950.

BARGHOORN, FREDERICK C. *Soviet Russian Nationalism.* Oxford University Press, New York, 1956.

BAUER, RAYMOND A. *The New Man in Soviet Psychology.* Harvard University Press, Cambridge, 1952.

BAUER, RAYMOND A.; INKELES, ALEX; and KLUCKHOHN, CLYDE. *How the Soviet System Works.* Harvard University Press, Cambridge, 1956.

BAUER, RAYMOND A., and WASIOLEK, EDWARD. *Nine Soviet Portraits.* John Wiley and Sons, New York, 1955.

BAYKOV, ALEXANDER. *The Development of the Soviet Economic System.* Harvard University Press, Cambridge, 1946.

BELOV, FEDOR. *The History of a Soviet Collective Farm.* Praeger, New York, 1955.

BERDYAEV, NICOLAS. *The Origin of Russian Communism.* Geoffrey Bles, London, 1948.

BEREDAY, GEORGE Z. F.; BRICKMAN, W. W.; and READ, G. *The Changing Soviet School.* Houghton Mifflin, Boston, 1960.

BEREDAY, GEORGE Z. F., and PENNAR, JAAN, eds. *The Politics of Soviet Education.* Praeger, New York, 1960.

BERGSON, ABRAM. *The Real National Income of Soviet Russia Since 1928.* Harvard University Press, Cambridge, 1961.

BERGSON, ABRAM, ed. *Soviet Economic Growth.* Row, Peterson, Evanston, 1953.

BERGSON, ABRAM. *The Structure of Soviet Wages.* Harvard University Press, Cambridge, 1944.

BERGSON, ABRAM, and HEYMANN, HANS, JR. *Soviet National Income and Product, 1940-1948.* Columbia University Press, New York, 1954.

BERLIN, ISAIAH. *Karl Marx.* Oxford University Press, New York, 1959.

BERLINER, JOSEPH S. *Factory and Manager in the U.S.S.R.* Harvard University Press, Cambridge, 1957.

BERMAN, HAROLD J. *Justice in Russia.* Harvard University Press, Cambridge, 1950.

BERMAN, HAROLD J. *The Russians in Focus.* Little, Brown, Boston, 1953.

BECK, F., and GODIN, W. (pseuds.) *Russian Purge and the Extraction of Confession.* Viking Press, New York, 1951.

691

BIENSTOCK, GREGORY; SCHWARTZ, SOLOMON M.; and YUGOW, AARON. *Management in Russian Industry and Agriculture.* Cornell University Press, Ithaca, 1948.

BLACK, CYRIL E., ed. *Rewriting Russian History.* Praeger, New York, 1956.

BLACK, CYRIL E., ed. *The Transformation of Russian Society.* Harvard University Press, Cambridge, 1960.

BOBER, M. M. *Karl Marx's Interpretation of History.* Harvard University Press, Cambridge, 1948.

BOFFA, GIUSEPPE. *Inside the Khrushchev Era.* Marzani & Munsell, New York, 1959.

BROWDER, R. P., and KERENSKY, A. F., eds. *The Russian Provisional Government, 1917 Documents.* Stanford University Press, Stanford, 1961.

BRUMBERG, ABRAHAM, ed. *Russia Under Khrushchev.* Praeger, New York, 1961.

BRZEZINSKI, ZBIGNIEW K. *The Permanent Purge.* Harvard University Press, Cambridge, 1956.

BRZEZINSKI, ZBIGNIEW K., and FRIEDRICH, CARL J. *Totalitarian Dictatorship and Autocracy.* Harvard University Press, Cambridge, 1956.

BUKHARIN, NIKOLAI I. *Historical Materialism.* International, New York, 1928.

BUKHARIN, NIKOLAI I., et al. *Marxism and Modern Thought.* Harcourt, Brace, New York, 1935.

BUNYAN, JAMES. *Intervention, Civil War, and Communism in Russia, April-December, 1918.* Johns Hopkins Press, Baltimore, 1936.

BUNYAN, JAMES, and FISHER, H. H. *The Bolshevik Revolution: 1917-1918.* Stanford University Press, Stanford, 1961.

BURNS, EMILE, ed. *A Handbook of Marxism.* International, New York, 1935.

CAMPBELL, ROBERT W. *Soviet Economic Power.* Houghton Mifflin, Boston, 1960.

CARR, EDWARD HALLETT. *A History of Soviet Russia* (Vols. I-VI on the years 1917-1926). Macmillan, New York, 1951-1960.

CARR, EDWARD HALLETT. *Studies in Revolution.* Macmillan, London, 1950.

CHAMBERLIN, WILLIAM HENRY. *The Russian Enigma.* Charles Scribner's Sons, New York, 1943.

CHAMBERLIN, WILLIAM HENRY. *Russia's Iron Age.* Little, Brown, Boston, 1934.

CHAMBERLIN, WILLIAM HENRY. *The Russian Revolution, 1917-1921.* 2 vols. Macmillan, New York, 1935.

CLARKSON, JESSE D. *A History of Russia.* Random House, New York, 1961.

COLE, G. D. H. *What Marx Really Meant.* Knopf, New York, 1934.

COMMITTEE OF CENTRAL COMM. OF THE C.P.S.U. *History of the Communist Party of the Soviet Union, Short Course.* International, New York, 1939.

CONDOIDE, MIKHAIL V. *The Soviet Financial System.* Ohio State University, Columbus, 1951.

CONQUEST, ROBERT. *Power and Policy in the U.S.S.R.: The Study of Soviet Dynasties.* St. Martin's, New York, 1961.

COUNTS, GEORGE S. *The Challenge of Soviet Education.* McGraw-Hill, New York, 1957.

CRANKSHAW, EDWARD. *Khrushchev's Russia.* Penguin Books (Atheneum), Baltimore, 1960.

CRANKSHAW, EDWARD. *Russia and the Russians.* Viking, New York, 1948.

CRANKSHAW, EDWARD. *Russia Without Stalin.* Michael Joseph, London, 1956.

CRESSEY, GEORGE B. *Soviet Potentials: A Geographical Appraisal.* Syracuse University Press, Syracuse, 1961.

CURTISS, JOHN S. *Church and State in Russia, 1900-1917.* Columbia University Press, New York, 1940.

CURTISS, JOHN S. *The Russian Church and the Soviet State, 1917-1950.* Little, Brown, Boston, 1953.

CURTISS, JOHN S. *The Russian Revolutions of 1917*. D. Van Nostrand Company, Inc., Princeton, 1957.

DALLIN, DAVID J. *The Real Soviet Russia*. Yale University Press, New Haven, 1947.
DANIELS, ROBERT V. *The Conscience of the Revolution: Communist Opposition in Soviet Russia*. Harvard University Press, Cambridge, 1960.
DANIELS, ROBERT V. *A Documentary History of Communism*. Random House, New York, 1960.
DANIELS, ROBERT V. *The Nature of Communism*. Random House, New York, 1962.
DEUTSCHER, ISAAC. *The Great Debate*. Oxford University Press, New York, 1960.
DEUTSCHER, ISAAC. *The Prophet Armed*. Oxford University Press, New York, 1954.
DEUTSCHER, ISAAC. *The Prophet Unarmed: Trotsky, 1921-1929*. Oxford University Press, New York, 1959.
DEUTSCHER, ISAAC. *Russia in Transition, and Other Essays*. Coward-McCann, New York, 1957.
DEUTSCHER, ISAAC. *Russia: What Next?* Oxford University Press, New York, 1953.
DEUTSCHER, ISAAC. *Soviet Trade Unions*. Royal Institute of International Affairs, New York, 1950.
DEUTSCHER, ISAAC. *Stalin*. Oxford University Press, New York, 1949.
DEWITT, NICHOLAS. *Education and Professional Employment in the U.S.S.R.* National Science Foundation, Washington, D.C., 1961.
DEWITT, NICHOLAS. *Soviet Professional Manpower*. National Research Council, Washington, 1954.
DJILAS, MILOVAN. *Conversations with Stalin*. Harcourt, Brace & World, New York, 1962.
DJILAS, MILOVAN. *The New Class*. Praeger, New York, 1957.
DOBB, M. *Soviet Economic Development Since 1917*. Routledge and Kegan Paul, London, 1958.

ENGELS, FREDERICK. *Ludwig Feurbach*. International, New York, 1941.
ENGELS, FREDERICK. *The Origin of the Family, Private Property and the State*. International, New York, 1942.
ENGELS, FREDERICK. *Selected Works*. 2 vols. Co-operative Publishing Society of Foreign Workers in the U.S.S.R., Moscow, 1935.
ENGELS, FREDERICK. *Socialism, Utopian and Scientific*. International, New York, 1935.
ERLICH, ALEXANDER. *The Soviet Industrialization Debate, 1924-1928*. Harvard University Press, Cambridge, 1960.

FAINSOD, MERLE. *How Russia Is Ruled*. Harvard University Press, Cambridge, 1953.
FAINSOD, MERLE. *Smolensk Under Soviet Rule*. Harvard University Press, Cambridge, 1958.
FEUER, LEWIS S., ed. *Basic Writings on Politics and Philosophy by Karl Marx and Friedrich Engels*. Anchor (Doubleday), Garden City, 1960.
FIELD, MARK G. *Doctor and Patient in Soviet Russia*. Harvard University Press, Cambridge, 1957.
FISCHER, LOUIS. *Russia Revisited*. Doubleday, New York, 1957.
FISHER, RALPH T. *Pattern for Soviet Youth: A Study of the Congresses of the Komsomol, 1918-1954*. Columbia University Press, New York, 1959.
FLORINSKY, MICHAEL T. *The End of the Russian Empire*. Collier, New York, 1961.
FLORINSKY, MICHAEL T. *Russia: A History and an Interpretation*. 2 vols. Macmillan, New York, 1955.

FLORINSKY, MICHAEL T. *Towards an Understanding of the U.S.S.R.* Macmillan, New York, 1951.

FLORINSKY, MICHAEL T.; SCHWARTZ, HARRY; TURKEVICH, JOHN; SHABAD, THEODORE; and UBEL, EARL, eds. *Encyclopedia of Russia and the Soviet Union.* McGraw-Hill, New York, 1961.

GALENSON, WALTER. *Labor Productivity in Soviet and American Industry.* Columbia University Press, New York, 1955.

GOLDER, F. A. *Documents of Russian History 1914-1917.* Century, New York, 1927.

GORER, GEOFFREY and RICKMAN, JOHN. *The People of Great Russia.* Chanticleer, New York, 1950.

GORKY, M., *et al.*, eds. *The History of the Civil War in the U.S.S.R.* 2 vols. International, New York, 1938.

GRANICK, DAVID. *Management of the Industrial Firm in the U.S.S.R.* Columbia University Press, New York, 1954.

GRANICK, DAVID. *The Red Executive: A Study of the Organization Man in Russian Industry.* Anchor (Doubleday), Garden City, 1961.

GREGORY, JAMES S. *Land of the Soviets.* Penguin, London, 1946.

GRIERSON, PHILIP. *Books on Soviet Russia 1917-1942.* Methuen, London, 1943.

GROSSMAN, GREGORY. *Soviet Statistics of Physical Output of Industrial Commodities: Their Compilation and Quality.* Princeton University Press, Princeton, 1960.

GRULIOW, LEO, ed. *Current Soviet Policies: The Documentary Record of the Nineteenth Communist Party Congress and the Reorganization after Stalin's Death.* Praeger, New York, 1953.

GRULIOW, LEO, ed. *Current Soviet Policies: The Documentary Record of the Twentieth Communist Party Congress and Repercussions of De-Stalinization.* Praeger, New York, 1957.

GRUILOW, LEO, ed. *Current Soviet Policies III: The Documentary Record of the Extraordinary 21st Congress of the Communist Party of the Soviet Union.* Columbia University Press, New York, 1960.

GRUILOW, LEO, and SAIKOWSKI, CHARLOTTE, eds. *Current Soviet Policies IV: The Documentary Record of the 22nd Party Congress.* Columbia University Press, New York, 1962.

GSOVSKI, VLADIMIR. *Soviet Civil Law.* 2 vols. University of Michigan Law School, Ann Arbor, 1948-1949.

GUINS, GEORGE C. *Communism on the Decline.* Philosophical Library, New York, 1956.

GUNTHER, JOHN. *Inside Russia Today.* Harper, New York, 1962.

GURIAN, WALDEMAR. *Bolshevism: An Introduction to Soviet Communism.* University of Notre Dame Press, Notre Dame, 1952.

HAIMSON, LEOPOLD H. *The Russian Marxists and the Origins of Bolshevism.* Harvard University Press, Cambridge, 1955.

HARCAVE, SIDNEY S. *Russia: A History.* Lippincott, Philadelphia, 1959.

HARPER, SAMUEL N., and THOMPSON, RONALD. *The Government of the Soviet Union.* D. Van Nostrand Company, Inc., New York, 1949.

HAZARD, JOHN N. *Law and Social Change in the U.S.S.R.* Carswell, Toronto, 1953.

HAZARD, JOHN N. *The Soviet System of Government.* University of Chicago Press, Chicago, 1960.

HINDUS, MAURICE. *House Without a Roof.* Doubleday, New York, 1961.

HODGMAN, DONALD R. *Soviet Industrial Production, 1928-1951.* Harvard University Press, Cambridge, 1954.

HOLZMAN, FRANKLYN D., ed. *Readings on the Soviet Economy*. Rand McNally, Chicago, 1962.

HOLZMAN, FRANKLYN D. *Soviet Taxation*. Harvard University Press, Cambridge, 1955.

HOOK, SIDNEY. *Marx and the Marxists*. Anvil Books (D. Van Nostrand Company, Inc.), New York, 1955.

HOOK, SIDNEY. *Towards the Understanding of Karl Marx*. John Day, New York, 1933.

HUBBARD, LEONARD. *The Economics of Soviet Agriculture*. Macmillan, London, 1939.

HUNT, R. N. CAREW. *Marxism: Past and Present*. Macmillan, New York, 1955.

HUNT, R. N. CAREW. *The Theory and Practice of Communism*. Macmillan, New York, 1957.

INKELES, ALEX. *Public Opinion in Soviet Russia*. Harvard University Press, Cambridge, 1950.

INKELES, ALEX, and BAUER, RAYMOND A. *The Soviet Citizen*. Harvard University Press, Cambridge, 1959.

INKELES, ALEX, and GEIGER, KENT, eds. *Soviet Society: A Book of Readings*. Houghton Mifflin, Boston, 1961.

JASNY, NAUM. *Essays on the Soviet Economy*. Praeger, New York, 1962.

JASNY, NAUM. *The Socialized Agriculture of the U.S.S.R.* Stanford University Press, Stanford, 1949.

JASNY, NAUM. *Soviet Industrialization, 1928-1952*. University of Chicago Press, Chicago, 1960.

JORRE, GEORGES. *The Soviet Union, the Land and its People*. Longmans, Green, London, 1950.

KAMMARI, M. D. *Socialism and the Individual*. Foreign Languages Publishing House, Moscow, 1950.

KARPINSKY, V. *The Social and State Structure of the U.S.S.R.* Foreign Languages Publishing House, Moscow, 1950.

KARPOVICH, MICHAEL. *Imperial Russia 1801-1917*. Henry Holt, New York, 1932.

KELSEN, HANS. *The Political Theory of Bolshevism*. University of California Press, Berkeley, 1949.

KERENSKY, ALEXANDER. *The Catastrophe*. Appleton, New York, 1927.

KERENSKY, ALEXANDER. *The Crucifixion of Liberty*. John Day, New York, 1934.

KLINE, GEORGE L., ed. *Soviet Education*. Columbia University Press, New York, 1957.

KLUCHEVSKY, V. O. *A History of Russia*. Five vols. E. P. Dutton, New York, 1931.

KOHN, HANS. *Basic History of Modern Russia*. Anvil Books (D. Van Nostrand Company, Inc.), New York, 1957.

KOLARZ, WALTER. *The Peoples of the Soviet Far East*. Praeger, New York, 1954.

KOLARZ, WALTER. *Religion in the Soviet Union*. Macmillan, New York, 1961.

KOLARZ, WALTER. *Russia and Her Colonies*. Praeger, New York, 1952.

KOROL, ALEXANDER G. *Soviet Education for Science and Technology*. Massachusetts Institute of Technology Press, Cambridge, 1957.

KOVALEVSKY, MAXIME. *Russian Political Institutions*. University of Chicago Press, Chicago, 1902.

KROPOTKIN, PETER. *Fields, Factories and Workshops*. Putnam, New York, 1907.

KULSKI, WLADYSLAW W. *The Soviet Regime*. Syracuse University Press, Syracuse, 1959.

KURSKY, A. *The Planning of the National Economy of the U.S.S.R.* Foreign Languages Publishing House, Moscow, 1949.

LABEDZ, LEOPOLD, ed. *Revisionism.* Praeger, New York, 1962.

LAMONT, CORLISS. *The Peoples of the U.S.S.R.* Harcourt, Brace, New York, 1946.

LAMONT, CORLISS. *Soviet Civilization.* Philosophical Library, New York, 1952.

LANGE, OSCAR. *The Working Principles of the Soviet Economy.* Research Bureau for Post-War Economics, New York, 1944.

LAQUEUR, WALTER, and LABEDZ, LEOPOLD, eds. *The Future of Communist Society.* Praeger, New York, 1962.

LEITES, NATHAN C. *The Operational Code of the Politburo.* McGraw-Hill, New York, 1951.

LEITES, NATHAN C. *A Study of Bolshevism.* Free Press, Glencoe, 1953.

LEITES, NATHAN and BERNAUT, ELSA. *Ritual of Liquidation.* Free Press, Glencoe, 1954.

LENIN, V. I. *Selected Works.* Vols. I-XII. Co-operative Publishing Society of Foreign Workers in the U.S.S.R., Moscow, 1934.

LEROY-BEAULIEU, ANATOLE. *Empire of the Tsars.* 3 vols. Putnam, New York, 1896.

LIBERMAN, SIMON. *Building Lenin's Russia.* University of Chicago Press, Chicago, 1945.

McCLOSKY, HERBERT, and TURNER, JOHN E. *The Soviet Dictatorship.* McGraw-Hill, New York, 1960.

MARCUSE, HERBERT. *Soviet Marxism.* Columbia University Press, New York, 1958.

MARX, KARL. *Capital.* 3 vols. Kerr, Chicago, 1909.

MARX, KARL. *A Contribution to the Critique of Political Economy.* Kerr, Chicago, 1904.

MARX, KARL. *Critique of the Gotha Program.* International, New York, 1938.

MARX, KARL. *Selected Works.* 2 vols. International, New York, 1942.

MARX, KARL and ENGELS, FREDERICK. *Selected Correspondence.* International, New York, 1942.

MASARYK, THOMAS G. *The Spirit of Russia.* 2 vols. Macmillan, New York, 1919.

MAVOR, JAMES. *An Economic History of Russia.* 2 vols. Dutton, New York, 1925.

MAVOR, JAMES. *The Russian Revolution.* Macmillan, New York, 1929.

MAYNARD, SIR JOHN. *Russia in Flux.* Macmillan, New York, 1948.

MAYNARD, SIR JOHN. *The Russian Peasant and Other Studies.* Gollancz, London, 1942.

MAYO, HENRY B. *Introduction to Marxist Theory.* Oxford University Press, New York, 1960.

MAZOUR, ANATOLE G. *The Rise and Fall of the Romanovs.* Anvil Books (D. Van Nostrand Company, Inc.), Princeton, 1960.

MAZOUR, ANATOLE G. *Russia: Tsarist and Communist.* D. Van Nostrand Company, Inc., 1962.

MEAD, MARGARET. *Soviet Attitudes Toward Authority.* Tavistock, London, 1955.

MEDINSKY, Y. N. *Public Education in the U.S.S.R.* Foreign Languages Publishing House, Moscow, 1950.

MEHNERT, KLAUS. *Stalin Versus Marx.* Allen and Unwin, London, 1952.

MEISEL, JAMES and KOZERA, EDWARD. *Materials for the Study of the Soviet System.* George Wahr, Ann Arbor, 1953.

MEISSNER, BORIS. *The Communist Party of the Soviet Union.* Edited with a chapter on the Twentieth Party Congress by John S. Reshetar, Jr. Praeger, New York, 1956.

MEYER, ALFRED G. *Communism.* Random House, New York, 1960.

MEYER, ALFRED G. *Leninism*. Harvard University Press, Cambridge, 1957.

MEYER, ALFRED G. *Marxism*. Harvard University Press, Cambridge, 1954.

MILIUKOV, PAUL. *Outlines of Russian Culture*. 3 vols. University of Pennsylvania Press, Philadelphia, 1942.

MILLER, WRIGHT W. *Russians as People*. Dutton, New York, 1961.

MILLS, C. WRIGHT. *The Marxists*. Laurel (Dell), New York, 1962.

MITRANY, DAVID. *Marx Against the Peasant*. Collier, New York, 1961.

MOORE, BARRINGTON, JR. *Soviet Politics—The Dilemma of Power*. Harvard University Press, Cambridge, 1950.

MOORE, BARRINGTON, JR. *Terror and Progress, U.S.S.R.* Harvard University Press, Cambridge, 1954.

NOVE, ALEC. *The Soviet Economy*. Praeger, New York, 1961.

NUTTER, G. WARREN, et al. *The Growth of Industrial Production in the Soviet Union*. Princeton University Press, Princeton, 1962.

OLGIN, MOISSAYE J. *The Soul of the Russian Revolution*. Holt, New York, 1917.

PAGE, STANLEY W. *Lenin and World Revolution*. New York University Press, New York, 1959.

PARES, SIR BERNARD. *The Fall of the Russian Monarchy*. Knopf, New York, 1939.

PARES, SIR BERNARD. *A History of Russia*. Jonathan Cape, London, 1926.

PIPES, RICHARD. *The Formation of the Soviet Union: Communism and Nationalism 1917-1923*. Harvard University Press, Cambridge, 1954.

PIPES, RICHARD, ed. *The Russian Intelligentsia*. Columbia University Press, New York, 1961.

PISTRAK, LAZAR. *The Grand Tactician: Khrushchev's Rise to Power*. Praeger, New York, 1961.

PLAMENATZ, JOHN. *German Marxism and Russian Communism*. Longmans, Green, London, 1954.

PLEKHANOV, GEORGE. *Essays in Historical Materialism*. International, New York, 1940.

POKROVSKII, M. N. *History of Russia from the Earliest Times to the Rise of Commercial Capitalism*. International, New York, 1931.

PONOMARYOV, B. N., et al., eds. *History of the Communist Party of the Soviet Union*. Foreign Languages Publishing House, Moscow, 1960.

REED, JOHN. *Ten Days That Shook the World*. Modern Library, New York, 1935.

RESHETAR, JOHN S., JR. *A Concise History of the Communist Party of the Soviet Union*. Praeger, New York, 1960.

RESHETAR, JOHN S., and NIEMEYER, GERHART. *An Inquiry into Soviet Rationality*. Praeger, New York, 1956.

ROBINSON, GEROID T. *Rural Russia Under the Old Regime*. Macmillan, New York, 1949.

ROSENBERG, ARTHUR. *A History of Bolshevism*. Oxford University Press, New York, 1934.

ROSTOW, W. W., and LEVIN, ALFRED. *The Dynamics of Soviet Society*. Norton, New York, 1953.

RÜHLE, OTTO. *Karl Marx*. Viking, New York, 1929.

RUSH, MYRON. *The Rise of Khrushchev*. Public Affairs Press, Washington, D.C., 1958.

SALISBURY, HARRISON E. *To Moscow—and Beyond*. Harper, New York, 1960.

SALISBURY, HARRISON E. *Moscow Journal: The End of Stalin.* University of Chicago, 1961.

SCHAPIRO, LEONARD. *The Communist Party of the Soviet Union.* Random House, New York, 1960.

SCHAPIRO, LEONARD B. *The Origin of the Communist Autocracy.* Harvard University Press, Cambridge, 1955.

SCHUMAN, FREDERICK L. *Government in the Soviet Union.* Thomas Y. Crowell, New York, 1961.

SCHUMAN, FREDERICK L. *Russia Since 1917.* Knopf, New York, 1957.

SCHWARTZ, HARRY, ed. *The Many Faces of Communism.* Berkeley-Medallion, New York, 1962.

SCHWARTZ, HARRY. *The Red Phoenix: Russia Since World War II.* Praeger, New York, 1961.

SCHWARTZ, HARRY. *Russia's Soviet Economy.* Prentice-Hall, New York, 1954.

SCHWARTZ, HARRY. *The Soviet Economy: A Selected Bibliography of Materials in English.* Syracuse University Press, Syracuse, 1949.

SCHWARZ, SOLOMON. *Labor in the Soviet Union.* Praeger, New York, 1952.

SCOTT, DEREK J. R., *Russian Political Institutions.* Praeger, New York, 1961.

SETON-WATSON, HUGH. *The Decline of Imperial Russia.* Praeger, New York, 1956.

SETON-WATSON, HUGH. *From Lenin to Khrushchev.* Praeger, New York, 1960.

SHABAD, THEODORE. *Geography of the U.S.S.R.* Columbia University Press, New York, 1951.

SHTEPPA, KONSTANTIN F. *Russian Historians and the Soviet State.* Rutgers University Press, New Brunswick, 1962.

SHUB, DAVID. *Lenin.* Doubleday, New York, 1948.

SIMMONS, ERNEST J., ed. *Continuity and Change in Russian and Soviet Thought,* Harvard University Press, Cambridge, 1955.

SOMERVILLE, JOHN. *Soviet Philosophy.* Philosophical Library, New York, 1946.

SOUVARINE, BORIS. *Stalin.* Longmans, Green, New York, 1939.

SPECTOR, IVAR. *An Introduction to Russian History and Culture.* D. Van Nostrand Company, Inc., Princeton, 1961.

SPULBER, NICHOLAS. *The Soviet Economy.* Norton, New York, 1962.

STALIN, JOSEPH. *Economic Problems of Socialism in the U.S.S.R.* International, New York, 1952.

STALIN, JOSEPH. *Problems of Leninism.* Foreign Languages Publishing House, Moscow, 1953.

STEIN, SOL, ed. *Culture in the Soviet Union.* Praeger, New York, 1955.

STEINBERG, ISAAC N. *In the Workshop of the Revolution.* Rinehart, New York, 1953.

SUKHANOV, N. N. *The Russian Revolution, 1917: A Personal Record.* Oxford University Press, Oxford, 1955.

SWAYZE, HAROLD. *Political Controls of Literature in the U.S.S.R., 1946-1959.* Harvard University Press, Cambridge, 1962.

TIMASHEFF, NICHOLAS S. *The Great Retreat.* Dutton, New York, 1946.

TIMASHEFF, NICHOLAS S. *Religion in Soviet Russia: 1917-1942.* Sheed and Ward, New York, 1942.

TOWSTER, JULIAN. *Political Power in the U.S.S.R. 1917-1947.* Oxford University Press, New York, 1948.

TREADGOLD, DONALD G. *Twentieth Century Russia.* Rand, McNally, Chicago, 1959.

TRISKA, JAN F., ed. *Soviet Communism: Programs and Rules.* Chandler, San Francisco, 1962.

TROTSKY, LEON. *The History of the Russian Revolution*. The University of Michigan Press, Ann Arbor, 1955.

TROTSKY, LEON. *My Life*. Scribner, New York, 1930.

TROTSKY, LEON. *The Revolution Betrayed*. Doubleday, Doran, New York, 1937.

TROTSKY, LEON. *Stalin*. Harper, New York, 1941.

TUCKER, ROBERT. *Philosophy and Myth in Karl Marx*. Cambridge University Press, New York, 1961.

TURGEON, LYNN, and BERGSON, ABRAM. *Prices of Basic Industrial Goods in the U.S.S.R.* The Rand Corporation, Santa Monica, 1957.

ULAM, ADAM B. *The Unfinished Revolution*. Random House, New York, 1960.

U. S. DEPARTMENT of HEALTH, EDUCATION and WELFARE, OFFICE of EDUCATION. *Education in the U.S.S.R.* U. S. Government Printing Office, Washington, 1952.

VAKAR, NICHOLAS. *The Taproot of Soviet Society*. Harper, New York, 1961.

VERNADSKY, GEORGE. *A History of Russia*. Yale University Press, New Haven, 1961.

VERNADSKY, GEORGE and KARPOVICH, MICHAEL. *A History of Russia*. 3 vols. Yale University Press, New Haven, 1953.

VOLIN, LAZAR. *A Survey of Soviet Russian Agriculture*. U. S. Department of Agriculture, Washington, 1951.

VUCINICH, ALEXANDER. *Soviet Economic Institutions*. Stanford University Press, Stanford, 1952.

VYSHINSKY, ANDREI Y. *The Law of the Soviet State*. Macmillan, New York, 1948.

WALSH, WARREN B. *Readings in Russian History*. Syracuse University Press, Syracuse, 1959.

WEBB, SIDNEY and BEATRICE. *Soviet Communism: A New Civilization?* 2 vols. Scribner, New York, 1936.

WILSON, EDMUND. *To the Finland Station*. Doubleday, Garden City, 1955.

WOLFE, BERTRAM D. *Communist Totalitarianism*. Beacon Press, Boston, 1961.

WOLFE, BERTRAM D. *Khrushchev and Stalin's Ghost*. Praeger, New York, 1957.

WOLFE, BERTRAM D. *Three Who Made a Revolution*. Dial Press, New York, 1948.

WOLIN, SIMON, and SLUSSER, ROBERT M., eds. *The Soviet Secret Police*. Praeger, New York, 1957.

YUGOW, AARON. *Russia's Economic Front for War and Peace*. Harper, New York, 1942.

An Index to Persons

Abramovich, R., 232
Acton, H. B., 97n
Adenauer, Konrad, 572
Adzhubei, Alexei, 665
Agranov, I. S., 372
Aleksandrov, G. F., 306, 313; "The Pattern of Soviet Democracy," 313-316
Aleksei, son of Peter I, 21
Alekseyev, P., 121
Alexander II, 19, 26, 27, 29, 30, 32, 34, 116, 344, 613, 615
Alexander III, 30, 32, 33, 34, 35, 44, 344, 349, 611n
Alexandra Feodorovna, 33, 196, 199
Alexeev, General M. V., 211, 212
Andreev, Andrei, 244n
Andreyev, A. A., 413
Andreyev, Leonid N., 23, 409
Arendt, Hannah, 629
Aristov, Averky B., 431
Armstrong, John A., 436n, 437n, 438n
Aron, Raymond, 627, 635, 637, 639; "Soviet Society in Transition," 627-635
Augustulus, Romulus, 613
Augustus, Caesar, 613
Avtorkhanov, A., 431n, 432n
Axelrod, Paul, 116, 124, 125, 126, 127

Babeuf, F. N., 611
Bacon, Francis, 2
Bakunin, Michael, 24, 25, 121, 249n
Balitsky, V. A., 372
Balzac, Honoré de, 584
Baturina, 409
Bauer, Raymond A., 575, 576; "How the Soviet System Works," 576-582
Baykov, Alexander, 466n
Bazhonov, B., 273n, 275
Beck, F., 375, 378
Beliaev, Nikolai I., 431
Bell, Daniel, 437n
Benda, Julien, 90n
Béranger, P. J. de, 595
Bergson, Abram, 493n, 502n, 504n
Beria, Lavrenti, 353, 372, 375, 382, 383,

392, 399, 400n, 402, 408, 409, 420, 427, 428, 429, 430, 431n, 434n, 435, 438, 444, 593, 607, 620, 621, 622, 633
Berliner, Joseph, 565n
Berman, Harold J., 4; "The Devil and Soviet Russia," 4-8
Bernal, J. D., 91n
Bernstein, Eduard, 117, 147
Bialer, S., 429n, 430n, 435n
Bismark, Otto von, 82, 611n
Blackman, James H., 493n, 504n
Bloch, Joseph, 103
Bloss, Wilhelm, 385
Bober, M. M., 97n, 99, 101
Bociurkiw, Bohdan R., 424; "The Case of Khrushchev," 424-440
Boffa, Giuseppe, 429n, 430n
Bogdanov, Alexander A., 127, 128
Böhm-Bawerk, Eugen, 161n
Borisov, 396n
Borkenau, Franz, 96n
Borodin, Alexander P., 23
Brezhnev, Leonid I., 320
Bruhat, Jean, 97n
Brusilov, General A. A., 196
Budënny, Semen M., 371
Bukharin, Nikolai I., 158n, 161n, 162n, 164n, 243, 266, 270, 280, 282, 289, 294, 371, 454, 593
Bulganin, Nikolai A., 413, 420, 423, 428n, 430, 431, 432, 434n, 511, 610, 620
Burg, David, 574; "The Voice of a Dissenter: An Interview with a Graduate of Moscow University," 589-598
Burns, Robert, 341

Caesar, Julius, 600, 613
Campbell, Robert W., 492, 516, 523, 538; "The Special Case of Agriculture," 516-522; "The Soviet Economic Challenge," 538-546
Camus, Albert, 548
Carlyle, Thomas, 102
Carr, Edward Hallett, 47, 106, 109, 230n,

700